Praise for
Brain, Consciousness, and God

"This is an amazing book. It is both lucid and brilliant. Deeply informed by Bernard Lonergan's systematic treatment of human knowing as a composite of experience, understanding, and judgment, Daniel Helminiak masterfully places study of spirituality within the self-transcending dimension of the human mind and in so doing differentiates and interrelates neuroscience, psychology, spirituality, and theology."

— Ralph W. Hood, University of Tennessee at Chattanooga

"In this book, magnificently and comprehensively Helminiak struggles toward an integrated perspective on the unfolding of the universe. Focused on humanity, his topic is actually the origins and dynamics of human yearning. As best he can, he meets contemporary theorists on their own ground and repeatedly nudges their thinking toward a more coherent position. The result cuts both ways. It challenges students of Lonergan who underappreciate natural and social processes, and it challenges natural and social scientists who seek a science of mind while subtly sidestepping their inquiring selves. Yet Helminiak presents only a seedling. Its full bloom would be Lonergan's new, global, omnidisciplinary science, envisaged in *Method*. It does, indeed, qualify as Patricia Churchland's sought 'real humdinger of a solution.'"

— Philip McShane, author of *Randomness, Statistics and Emergence*

"Intense, yet lucidly clear, this work by Daniel Helminiak provides a sequel to Michael H. McCarthy's *The Crisis of Philosophy*. Helminiak turns a laser on the crisis and not only exposes significant counterpositions, but also offers a solution using the intellectual epistemology of Bernard Lonergan. Worth a read by anyone seeking real explanation rather than mere description, this work invites readers to be weaned from picture-thinking to claim the reality of their intelligence, whatever their field."

— Carla Mae Streeter, Aquinas Institute of Theology

BRAIN, CONSCIOUSNESS, AND GOD

Fearless in the Face of Wonder
by Fred Richards-Daishi (2013)

Acrylic on canvas with mixed media, 30" × 40"

Like everyone else I know, I've had my share of difficult times, times full of discontent, discouragement, and defeat—experiences that can break one's will to live or lead one deeper into his or her soul and what lies waiting below the so-called ordinary, familiar surface of things. I'm fortunate, however, to have been surprised by timely moments of wonder or joy or hope or grace, arriving when all seemed lost or in jeopardy.

The world can surely be, at times, a place of darkness and despair, but it is also a place of wonder. I have known this even when things appeared to be falling apart, or when I was falling painfully short of who I longed to be. The true heart in all religious traditions knows that healing and the possibility of waking up to life can emerge from the depths of our suffering if we are willing to open wide to the suffering of others and ourselves. And the lost will be found and the blind see only when that wretched ego, that tiny fortress of a self, lets go of its desperate, driven need to be in control and have its own way.

Spiritual teachers tell us one is wise to journey through life unafraid to see ordinary experiences as holy and full of wonder. We can come to know the world of things is full of radiance when we truly see and feel. They ask us: Why are you so afraid to discover that you are part of everything around you and it is all alive? Why do you think it is foolish to believe washing dishes or growing flowers can be spiritual experiences? Who is the wiser and more alive, St. Francis of Assisi or those who spend their lives driven to earn money and then die without knowing intimacy or their own true identity? Why are you afraid of freedom, of letting go, of being surprised by wonder?

The world is alive. It is full of meaning-making moments, flowing through us like a life-giving stream. Moments that can free us from the fear of loving, of opening our hearts and eyes to know how utterly amazing it is to have been born, to be here with one another, if only for a while.

—Fred Richards-Daishi

BRAIN, CONSCIOUSNESS, AND GOD

A Lonerganian Integration

DANIEL A. HELMINIAK

Cover painting (detail) entitled "Fearless in the Face of Wonder" by Fred Richards-Daishi (2013). Photo of artwork by Ricky Stilley.

Published by State University of New York Press, Albany

© 2015 State University of New York

All rights reserved

Printed in the United States of America

No part of this book may be used or reproduced in any manner whatsoever without written permission. No part of this book may be stored in a retrieval system or transmitted in any form or by any means including electronic, electrostatic, magnetic tape, mechanical, photocopying, recording, or otherwise without the prior permission in writing of the publisher.

For information, contact State University of New York Press, Albany, NY
www.sunypress.edu

Production, Diane Ganeles
Marketing, Kate R. Seburyamo

Library of Congress Cataloging-in-Publication Data

Helminiak, Daniel A.
  Brain, consciousness, and God : a Lonerganian integration / Daniel A. Helminiak.
    pages cm
  Includes bibliographical references and index.
  ISBN 978-1-4384-5715-4 (hardcover : alk. paper)
  ISBN 978-1-4384-5716-1 (e-book)
  1. Cognitive neuroscience. 2. Neuropsychology. 3. Spirituality—Physiological aspects. 4. Brain—Miscellanea. 5. Psychology, Religious. 6. Lonergan, Bernard J. F.—Criticism and interpretation. I. Title.

QP360.5.H45 2015
612.8'233—dc23   2014034273

10 9 8 7 6 5 4 3 2 1

To dear friends
who supported and sustained me
during my solitary toils in Atlanta:
John Adamski
Kerry Clark
Marcus Fleischhacker

And to
Jukebox
mi gran amor aun

Contents

Preface ... xi

Chapter 1
Introduction ... 1
- 1.1 Mystical, Religious—or Transcendent—Experiences ... 2
- 1.2 Consciousness of Consciousness, Not Experience of God ... 3
- 1.3 An Interdisciplinary Study ... 5
- 1.4 Reliance on a Coherent and Consistent Epistemology: Lonergan ... 6
- 1.5 Broader Issue of Interdisciplinary Studies ... 8
- 1.6 Attention to Major Thinkers in Neuroscience and Consciousness Studies ... 11
- 1.7 Attention to Intelligence, Not Merely to Logic ... 12
- 1.8 An Interrelated and Unfolding Presentation ... 13
- 1.9 The Centrality of Consciousness ... 14

Chapter 2
Epistemology: A Portentous Prolegomenon ... 17
- 2.1 Lonergan's Cognitive Theory and Epistemology ... 18
- 2.2 The Empirical Level of Knowing: Experience ... 27
- 2.3 The Intellectual Level of Knowing: Understanding ... 45
- 2.4 The Rational Level of Knowing: Judgment of Fact ... 61
- 2.5 The Scientific Affinity and Status of This Epistemology ... 66
- 2.6 The Accuracy of Human Knowing and the Transcendental Precepts ... 70
- 2.7 Transcendental Method ... 73
- 2.8 Different Kinds of Realities, Including the Spiritual ... 75
- 2.9 The Challenge of Lonergan's Breakthrough ... 79

Chapter 3
Neuroscience: The Biological Bases of Transcendent Experiences 81
- 3.1 Neurophysiological Bases of Transcendent Experiences 82
- 3.2 A Genetic Basis of Transcendent Experiences: Hamer 99
- 3.3 A Neurochemical Basis of Transcendent Experiences: "Entheogens" 101
- 3.4 An Electromagnetic Basis of Transcendent Experiences: Persinger 105
- 3.5 A Quantum-Physics Theory of Consciousness: Penrose and Hameroff 106
- 3.6 The Contribution of Neuroscience 107

Chapter 4
Psychology: The Problem of a Real Body and a Real Mind 109
- 4.1 The "Reality" of the "Parts" of the Human Being 110
- 4.2 Some Terminological Clarifications 115
- 4.3 The Actual Existence of Mental Realities 121
- 4.4 The Unity of the Human Being: Dualism 123
- 4.5 The Unity of the Human Being: Epiphenomenalism 124
- 4.6 An Excursus on Causality 125
- 4.7 The Unity of the Human Being: Epiphenomenalism Revisited 134
- 4.8 The Unity of the Human Being: Nonreductive Physicalism 137
- 4.9 Analogies for Mind as a Property of the Brain: Searle 143
- 4.10 The "Naturalness" of Consciousness 149
- 4.11 Multiple Realities in One Thing 153
- 4.12 The Priority of Intelligence Over Perception, Theory Over Common Sense 159
- 4.13 A Resolution of the Mind–Body Problem 169
- 4.14 The Relation of Mind to Body: Emergence 171
- 4.15 The Causality Across Levels of Emergence 178
- 4.16 The Impact of Gödel's Theorem on Formal Causality 186
- 4.17 The Coherence of a Dynamic Universe 192
- 4.18 The Proposed Distinction Between Weak and Strong Emergence 195
- 4.19 Filling in the Gap of Emergence: Dennett 206
- 4.20 Panpsychic Construals of Emergence: Griffin for Whitehead 214
- 4.21 Panpsychic Construals of Emergence: Chalmers 222
- 4.22 Summary on the Mind–Body Problem 235
- 4.23 Review and Preview 238

Chapter 5
Spiritualogy: Consciousness and Transcendent Experiences — 241
- 5.1 A Tripartite Model of the Human: Beyond "Body and Mind" — 243
- 5.2 The Mechanism of "Spiritual Growth" — 251
- 5.3 Consciousness as Both Conscious and Intentional — 254
- 5.4 The Limitation of Consciousness to Intentionality — 281
- 5.5 Still Seeing Red: Mere Givenness Versus *Qualia* — 289
- 5.6 What Is It Like to Be? — 302
- 5.7 The Priority of Non-Intentional or Conscious Consciousness — 312
- 5.8 Unbounded Human Consciousness and Transcendent Experiences — 317
- 5.9 The Coherence of Neuroscience and Naturalistic Spiritualogy — 326
- 5.10 Summary on Spiritualogy — 340

Chapter 6
Theology and Theotics: Union of Creator and Creature — 343
- 6.1 The Place of Theology in Scientific Explanation — 343
- 6.2 What is God? — 345
- 6.3 Four Perspectives on the Possibility of Experiencing God — 353
- 6.4 The Restricted Arena of Talk About God — 361

Chapter 7
Conclusion — 365
- 7.1 A Brief Summary of the Argument — 365
- 7.2 The Contributions of the Various Disciplines — 366
- 7.3 Summary About the Brain, Consciousness, and God — 369

References — 371

Name Index — 389

Subject Index — 395

Preface

This book has been long in the making. In 2005, I presented a paper to the American Psychological Association entitled " 'God' in the Brain: Untangling Neurology, Psychology, Spirituality, and Theology." The editor of a prestigious European psychological journal invited me to work up the presentation into a publishable article. I did so, but the paper was rejected. Of course, it was long. But the telling editorial judgment was the following: "the need to take out the long treatment of Lonergan and the pieces that to psychologists are too philosophical and/or theological."

Supposedly, treatment of this topic for psychologists must not be too philosophical, and questions about God are not to engage technical theology.

Mais au contraire, mes amis! My fundamental argument is precisely that philosophy is the problem. Ignored or muddled theories of knowledge (epistemology) and incoherent philosophy of science confound all discussion of psychology, consciousness, spirituality, and—why neuroscientists and psychologists ever believe it's in their bailiwick, I'll never know—theology. Only through application of a coherent and consistent epistemology and philosophy of science can today's bedeviling interdisciplinary questions of psychology, science, and religion be answered satisfactorily.

Yet how strange that psychologists and other social scientists would think the study of knowledge is not central to their subject matter! Knowing is a function of the human mind, and knowing is inextricably linked with consciousness. In its abstract forms, knowledge is the unique product of human beings. It distinguishes humans from all other species. How could a science of humanity not consider knowing essential to its concerns? Only the historical accident of an outdated and now clumsy division of academic disciplines has segregated philosophy and the human sciences. My presentation might be judged too philosophical and too theological for psychologists, neuroscientists, and other social scientists, but, I argue, our disciplines are languishing precisely because we ignore the philosophical issues that clandestinely control and distort our theorizing.

Unfortunately, however, academia is suffering through a dark age of agnosticism. There exists no consensus whatsoever on epistemology and philosophy of science. Some are even absolutely certain that one can be certain of nothing. Nonetheless, I rely optimistically on Bernard Lonergan to provide the needed philosophical grounding. I am betting that his position meets the contemporary challenges—surely, better than any other position I've seen.

So over nearly a decade, I worked that paper into a full-length book. A 2011 sabbatical allowed me to delve deeply into current consciousness studies and to clarify my fundamental argument with copious examples of misguided endeavors. The final result is what you now have before you, a consistent and coherent interdisciplinary integration, as best I can offer. I am deeply grateful to the State University of New York Press for deeming this project worthy of publication. I hope that interested folk of all stripes, including students and my professional colleagues, will also find this book worthy of serious consideration.

Over the course of this book's production, I have become indebted to many people. I thank Ellen Dodson, J. Patrick O'Brien, Anne Richards, and Carla Mae Streeter, who reviewed entire drafts at various stages and provided most helpful criticism. I thank Ralph Hood, Stanley Krippner, Philip McShane, and Carla Mae Streeter for generous blurbs for the back cover, and Fred Richards-Daishi for the artwork on the front cover. For substantive consultation and criticism regarding important topics and large sections of this book, I thank, above all, Philip McShane, who has so very generously become my Lonerganian mentor of late, and then also Eric Bussien, John Carter, Barnet Feingold, Richard Murphy, Terrance Quinn, and my departmental chair, Donadrian Rice. And for other criticism, comments, consultation, and support, I thank John Adamski, Ted Barnett, Kerry Clark, Dave Devitt, Marcus Fleischhacker, Allan Helminiak, Kevin Johnson, Paul Drew "Jukebox" Johnson, Francis Kennedy (R.I.P.), Cecilia McHirella, Thomas Meredith, Dan Rausi, Rembert Weakland, Calvin Williamson, and William Zanardi, along with still others of my ever-congenial and generous colleagues at the University of West Georgia: Dean N. Jane McCandless, Christopher Aanstoos, Muriel Cormican, Jeannette Diaz, James Dillon, Hannes Gerhardt, Paul J. Glenn, Tobin Hart, Perry Kirk, David Leach, Lisa Osbeck, Lisa Paciulli, Alan Pope, and Douglas A. Stuart; and my research assistants, Timothy David Carroll and Andy Drinkard.

Of course, only I am responsible for whatever errors, misrepresentations, or misunderstandings this book inevitably contains. I sincerely apologize for them all, and I hope they will not distract from my central offering. One can only do one's best, and we humans need one another to do better individually and collectively.

My hope is that my effort will at least open a new perspective. What with the globalization of our human society and the demise of once helpful but now conflicting traditional religions, our pluralistic times are certainly in need of some unifying vision. I hope this book might help the willing contribute mightily to a happy and wholesome human community—willing, that is, to pursue today's hard questions in profound openness, insightfulness, honesty, integrity, collaboration, patience, and good will. These personal qualities alone have ever been our species' hope because they express the epitome of our human uniqueness and point to the ultimate fulfillment of our existence.

Chapter 1

Introduction

> A little learning is a dang'rous Thing;
> Drink deep, or taste not the Pierian Spring:
> There shallow Draughts intoxicate the Brain,
> And drinking largely sobers us again.
>
> —Alexander Pope

Ever-expanding research in neuroscience now engages religious topics. As liberally as the popular press (Aaen-Stockdale, 2012; Hagerty, 2009), professional discussion links brain function to supposed experiences of God Almighty Himself—or Herself? Itself? Godself? The very uncertainty in even knowing how to accurately refer to God—and traditions that forbid naming G-d at all—should give one pause. Still, the complexity of the neurological findings and the subtlety of the philosophical issues open a space for the free run of popular religiosity, esoteric beliefs, impatient curiosity, creative imagination, and marketing opportunities and sales. Thus, whether well-conceived or not, talk of "the God gene" (Hamer, 2004), "The God Helmet" (Persinger, n.d.), the "God" part of the brain (Alper, 2001, 2006), the "God spot in the brain" (Crutcher, 2003), "neurotheology" (Ashbrook, 1984; Bekoff, 2002, p. xvii; d'Aquili & Newberg, 1999; Joseph, 2003), "entheogens" (Forte, 1997b; Richards, 2003, 2005), "theobiology" (Rayburn & Richard, 2002), "theistic psychology" (Helminiak, 2010, 2013a), and the like has become commonplace across academic disciplines. To bring some clarification to this discussion is my ambitious goal.

1.1. Mystical, Religious—or Transcendent—Experiences

The focus of this neuroscientific research is what is called mystical or religious experiences (Belzen & Geels, 2003; Carmody & Carmody, 1996). These terms refer to a range of personal occurrences of varying intensity. They include a pervasive sense of wonder and awe within everyday living: mysticism as a way of life ("enlightenment" in the East). And they refer to occasional moments of overwhelming intensity in which the epitome is the ineffable experience of the unity of all things and a loss of a sense of self: mysticism as an extraordinary experience. Fred Hanna (2000) provides an intimate account of such experiences, and, instructively, he does so apart from the more common context of religious belief and reference to God. To refer to such phenomena, I will speak of transcendent experience. I use *transcendent* as a loosely defined term to replace the also loosely defined terms *religious* and *mystical*. These latter terms, themselves often equated, can have importantly different meanings (e.g., Roy, 2003, pp. xix–xxi). Likewise, the term *transcendental* is also sometimes used to name meditative and psychedelic experiences (e.g., Aaen-Stockdale, 2012; Szalavitz, 2011) and carries similar ambiguities and vagueness, usually implying something other-worldly or, perhaps, mysterious. I would avoid prejudicing the discussion from the outset. Accordingly, with a neutral term, *transcendent*, and a lower-case *t*, I indicate a particular kind of experience without implying *a priori* any specific interpretation of it.

In the broadest sense, by *transcendent* I mean simply whatever is, or takes one, beyond one's present state in a positive, non-self-destructive way (Helminiak, 1987b, pp. 23–24). Simply to pose a question, for example, opens one to a broader perspective. Or to realize a new fact expands or even reconfigures one's way of thinking and acting. Or to love another person or to admire a thing of beauty or to marvel at the stars and the ocean moves one out of oneself and into a broader and shared universe. Any activity, even getting off to work in the morning, can be self-transcending—indeed, just waking up qualifies—insofar as it invites us to new experiences and the possibility for personal growth—that is, the expansion of our awareness, understandings, abilities, and commitments. Understood in this way, self-transcendence appears to be a built-in and defining facet of humanity; it is what contemporary movements of "personal growth" intend. In contrast, that this process entails, rather, a connection with some non-human entity, such as God or the "Sacred," or the work of some supernatural force (e.g., Beauregard & O'Leary, 2007; Engels, 2001; Hill et al., 2000, p, 64; Larson, Swyers, and McCullough, 1998; Pargament, 1997, p. 31; Pargament & Maloney, 2002; Reber, 2002, 2006b, p. 199; Richards & Bergin, 2005, pp. 101, 114; Richardson, 2006, p. 242, n. 12; Slife & Whoolery, 2006, pp. 225, 226)—this is a greater supposition than I am willing to make. It is the very supposition that is in question.

1.2. Consciousness of Consciousness, Not Experience of God

Of course, I do have my own interpretation and explanation of transcendent experience, as the previous paragraph betrays. I argue that we can account for transcendent experiences by appeal to a self-transcending dimension of the human mind—referred to variously as consciousness, Atman, Buddha Nature, nous, soul, higher self, and the like. In accord with long-standing aspects of the Western philosophical tradition, I prefer the term human *spirit* (Helminiak, 1996a, pp. 50–56; Lonergan, 1957/1992, pp. 372, 394, 538–543, 640–642, 670–671, 696–697, 711; 1968/2006, tracks 46, 48, 51; 1972, pp. 13, 210, 302, 352; Peters & Mace, 1967). I take all these terms to be roughly synonymous. This supposition is surely open to debate, but profitable debate would presume the very clarification toward which I aim. So I freely state my position at the outset, further suggesting, of course, that I believe I am on target: we can account for transcendent experiences through appeal to a self-transcending dimension of the human mind. If so, by application of Occam's razor or Morgan's canon, no added reference to God is needed, nor to the Hindu Brahman. These are experiences of the outward-oriented, open-ended, dynamic human spirit, namely, at its epitome, pure consciousness of consciousness. They pertain to human *spirit*uality, not to some direct or immediate (i.e., non-mediated) divine encounter or uncovered divine identity. In my understanding, although the divine is spiritual, not everything spiritual is therefore divine. And although, by definition in standard Western theology, God is somehow involved whenever anything exists or happens, immediate and unnuanced appeal to God to explain these instances is theologically and scientifically naïve (cf. Helminiak, 2010, 2013a; Helminiak, Hoffman, & Dodson, 2012). In the first instance, transcendent experience is a possibility or occurrence that is fully human. It expresses a marvelous capacity due to one dimension of the human mind. Questions about God's role in such experience are, indeed, appropriate. However, the theological questions are secondary. They are further questions, not to be confounded with the primary question. They are but possible, subsequent considerations when scientific explanation—not yet theology or, above all, not devotional rhetoric or controlling religious lore—is the prime concern (Helminiak, 1987b).

Abraham Maslow (1954/1970) made something of the same point when describing his "self-actualizers," those rare, highly developed specimens of humanity. With a blatant spiritual allusion, Maslow reports that these individuals view things "*sub specie aeternitatis* [in light of eternity]" (p. 160). Moreover, he says, they are particularly prone to mystical experience. But Maslow incisively adds, "It is quite important to dissociate this experience from any theological or supernatural reference, even though for thousands of years they have been linked. Because this experience is a natural experience, well within the jurisdiction of science, I call it the peak experience" (p. 164; see also Maslow, 1964/1970).

Similarly, Roberto Assagioli's (1965/1976) rich treatment of spiritual growth, under the name of psychosynthesis, is a completely psychological proposition. Granted, Assagioli does obscurely relate the human "higher Self," the focus of spiritual psychosynthesis, to the "Supreme Spirit" and the "universal Self" of Vedantic philosophy (the divine Brahman, which is supposedly identical to the human Atman: see 6.3.5, i.e, Chapter 6, section 3, subsection 5 of this book), but he has no real investment in this connection (pp. 20, 44–45, 194–195). He insists that psychosynthesis is a "scientific conception." It "does not aim nor attempt to give a metaphysical nor a theological explanation of the great Mystery—it leads to the door, but stops there" (pp. 6–7; see Helminiak, 1987b, pp. 12–19).

To extricate God from the scientific explanation of transcendent experiences focuses the true, contemporary, scientific question: the so-called "mind–body problem" or the "mind/brain" problem (Searle, 1998; Shafer, 1967). This problem entails the challenge of accounting for the nature of the human spirit and its relationship to the human "brain" (i.e., the human organism). To be sure, then, my proposed explanation of transcendent experience will address this challenge head-on. Indeed, its treatment fills the long, central chapters in this book—Chapter 4, on the mind, and Chapter 5, on consciousness. In contrast, actually, the theological questions are comparatively simple. Long-standing theological discussion about the relationship of the Creator to creation provides readily available answers. The empirically constrained puzzle of the mind–body problem remains the pivotal challenge in this discussion and demands its own clarification. The lack of this clarification is today's nemesis.

The supposed identification of the human spirit and Divinity is a pervasive bugaboo. By reverting to classical Greek usage, consonant with much Eastern philosophy (Helminiak, 2008a, pp. 167–168; Muesse, 2003), some theorists use the terms *God* or *divine* simply as alternative words for the spiritual dimension of the human mind. The unspoken assumption is that the human spirit and Divinity are somehow one and the same, as in the Hindu formula "Atman is Brahman." Thus, any extraordinary mental occurrences—except, inconsistently and tellingly, psychoses and temporal lobe epilepsy (Brown, 2002; Crutcher, 2002; Helminiak, 1984b; Persinger, 2001, 2002; but see 3.1.2)—might still be taken today to be encounters with God. This ambiguous usage might be unwitting, resulting from casual theological and philosophical thinking. Or it might be deliberate, expressing an attempt to reject distance between the human spirit and the divine. Albert Hofmann (2000), famous for the discovery of LSD, for example, uses the terms *spiritual* and *divine* seemingly interchangeably. He speaks of the need to transcend "the division between humankind and nature" or, phrased supposedly otherwise, to abolish "the separation of creator and creation" or "the duality of creator/creation" (p. 37). As is typical of this topic, it is difficult to know what such statements mean exactly, half technical in terminology and half popular. From a critical perspective, the problem of the meaning of *spiritual* and *divine* might be simple equivocation—different terms are applied to the same reality, or different realities are subsumed under the same term.

However, in the West there does exist a long-standing distinction between Creator and creature, the Uncreated and the created, necessary being and contingent being. In light of this distinction, whether one believes in God or not, the term *Creator-God* must be taken to denote a distinct reality or being that might actually exist (as some religions insist); and the Uncreated and the created must not be taken to be one and the same (as mere logic requires). Two different terms, *Uncreated* and *created* or *Creator* and *creature*, defined by a mutual negative relationship, imply that two different proposed entities are in question.

If so, to appeal to God to explain transcendent experiences would require an account of the nature of God in addition to the nature of the human mind (Delio, 2003). Under these conditions, God's role in transcendent experiences can, indeed, be explained—or, more exactly, as in all science, a credible hypothesis can, indeed, be proposed. But such explanation is theology, not psychology; and, as such, it exceeds the content matter and the competence of neuroscience and psychology. Once again, not God's role in human experience but rather the mind–body problem and the nature of consciousness emerge as the true psychological challenge: how does organic matter relate to mental and even spiritual—transcendent—experience?

1.3. An Interdisciplinary Study

I elaborate on my argument by treating, in turn, neuroscience, psychology, spiritualogy, and theology. In passing, with gratitude to Philip McShane, I propose a much-needed neologism: *spitualogy*. I take *spirituality* to mean a person's lived commitment to enhancement of his or her spiritual sensitivities (Helminiak, 1996a, Chapter 2). Most people, at least in the West, associate this particular process of growth with religion or some notion of God and describe it in religious terms. Currently, however—in English translation from the French in the mid-20th century, replacing the Roman Catholic terms *ascetic* or *mystical theology* (Principe, 1983; e.g., Tanquerey, 1930)—the term *spirituality* also names the study of that lived commitment. So confusion often results. I offer the term *spitualogy* to name the academic study or research discipline pertinent to the lived commitment (Helminiak, 1996a, pp. 31–39; 2009). Spiritualogy is the study of spirituality.

Now, in this book, chapter by chapter, I both differentiate and interrelate neuroscience, psychology, spiritualogy, and theology, and I specify their respective contributions to a comprehensive explanation of transcendent experiences. However, this central task requires a substantive prolegomenon to treat epistemology. Etymologically "the study of knowledge," epistemology is an account of the human ability to know; it is an explanation of what knowing means and what validity human knowledge can enjoy. Epistemology is the controlling yet ignored specter that haunts the discussion of "God in the brain" and current consciousness studies overall. Without an understanding of knowledge adequate to non-palpable realities—such as emotions, thoughts, the mind, consciousness, and God, not to mention quarks, leptons, black holes, and dark matter—the topic of this book cannot be treated coherently. Thus my first chapter treats epistemology.

1.4. Reliance on a Coherent and Consistent Epistemology: Lonergan

Echoing Bernard J. F. Lonergan (1957/1992, 1972, 1980/1990), I maintain that human knowledge is a composite of experience, understanding, and judgment; so accurate explanation must be attentive, intelligent, and reasonable. I consider my summary and application of Lonergan's epistemology to be the major contribution of this book. Amidst the jungle of theological, philosophical, spiritual, religious, devotional, evaluative, cognitive, emotional, psychological, neuroanatomical, neurophysiological, and neurochemical considerations that impinge on our topic, I propose a framework in which these relevant matters can be ordered and given their due. My purpose, though quite bold, is rather restricted. On a philosophically cluttered playing field, others have taken on whole swaths of religiosity and speculated about their relationships to brain function (e.g., Alper, 2001/2006; Beauregard & O'Leary, 2007; d'Aquili & Newberg, 1999; McNamara, 2009; Murphy, 2006). My humble yet daunting goal is merely to order the field.

My reliance on Bernard Lonergan offers a novel approach—novel in that Lonergan's is just becoming a mainline philosophical position and novel, too, in that his position actually promises a coherent treatment of the difficult questions before us. Lonergan took up the traditional philosophical question, dating from the pre-Socratics, about the possibility, nature, and limits of accurate human knowing and presented a core understanding of knowledge that applies to all fields of intellectual endeavor. As such, his position qualifies as a kind of "foundationalism" (Braman, 2008, pp. 80–81, 86–91), that is, the proposal of a common basis, the discovery of an Archimedean point, from which one could supposedly deal coherently with all matters of knowing. Among philosophers today, foundationalism is mostly a shattered dream. However, Lonergan's proposal appears unique. His foundation is the inherent and unavoidable processes of human consciousness itself. Overlooking insight and restricted merely to logic, most other foundationalist theories propose a set of basic beliefs, some suggested first principles, which via deduction and inference would ground all other beliefs (Poston, 2014)—an ultimately unworkable solution (4.16). Digging deeper, Lonergan claims to have elucidated the primordial engine that generates all beliefs, all knowledge. His analyses offer a strikingly new approach to foundationalism (2.7.1). Chapter 2 relates parts of that story of despair over ever explaining the essence of human knowing (2.2.6–7; see McCarthy, 1990). As Lawrence Cahoone (2010) reports, over the course of the 20th century, Western philosophy fragmented into basically three incompatible schools: continental phenomenology, Anglo-American linguistic analysis, and American pragmatism. These schools of philosophy

> rarely spoke across party lines. Rather than opposing each other like three different baseball teams—as in much of the history of philosophy, schools of thought opposed each other—they became more like a baseball, football, and a soccer team, each playing its own game, addressing its philosophical questions in its own particular language, to which the other teams had nothing to say because they were playing a different game. (p. 47)

That breakdown of intellectual consensus, even as to what are the important questions, underlies the discombobulating pluralism that more and more characterizes the postmodern world gone global. My bet is that

Lonergan offers a solution to this human dilemma of our times. Staying with the traditional question, he has proposed a new answer. Its heart is the trenchant and consistently applied distinction between sensate- or perception-modeled theories (knowing is like taking a good look and seeing what is actually there) and an intelligence-based theory (knowing is the achievement of correct understanding). The one theory of knowing implicitly assumes that reality is palpable stuff lying out there about us or imaginable stuff hidden down inside us. The other theory holds that the real is what correct judgment affirms. In light of the intellectual chaos that reigns in academic circles today, in the very least this answer deserves a hearing. So in this book I summarize Lonergan's position, foundational though it be, and I apply it, in a telling and most challenging case, to the mind–body problem, the relationship of the "hard" and "soft" sciences (Percy, 1989/1990), the nature of consciousness, and the notion of "God in the brain."

1.5. Broader Issues of Interdisciplinary Studies

My exemplification of Lonergan's thought in this book is sufficiently challenging in itself. Yet my effort is but a student's exposition of Lonergan's far-reaching theory, and I want to highlight this point, if only briefly. Pragmatically, I meet current thinkers somewhere close to where they already stand and nudge their thinking along as best I can, so in this book I list standard disciplines to be interrelated—neuroscience, psychology, and theology—and I could not avoid including yet another contrived discipline, spiritualogy. But, ultimately, this breakdown of disciplines is highly inadequate. It results from the rather haphazard emergence of ever-novel disciplines that fill out the list of arts, theology, law, and medicine in the medieval universities.

In fact, for example, neuroscience is the hottest thing going in psychology today. Are the two really distinct disciplines? What, then, of sociology, anthropology, criminology, history, economics, political science, philosophy, and literature? They all regard humanity and the human situation, and the overlap among them is extensive. My university recently divided the College of Arts and Sciences into the College of Arts and Humanities, the College of Social Sciences, and the College of Science and Mathematics. We colleagues within the Department of Psychology gave serious consideration to our future affiliation: does our humanistic and transpersonal orientation fit better with the lush human concerns of the humanities or with the mostly anemic statistics-controlled endeavors of the social sciences? We actually fit with neither alone, but practicality and politics have us now as a department in the College of Social Sciences. Yet don't physics, chemistry, and biology also have major contributions to make toward understanding humanity? Additionally, our campus also comprises a College of Education, a College of Nursing, and a College of Business. Again, the duplication among all these supposedly diverse colleges, disciplines, and sciences is enormous. Clearly, the division of labor at our current universities is chaotic, ineffective, even irrational. The problem shows most obviously in any treatment of the human, for in its polymorphic constitution our species entails everything from subatomic particles through consciousness to belief in God. What kind of a discipline would adequately treat of humanity? (See Henriques, 2003, 2004, for related discussion and references.)

In *Method in Theology*, Lonergan (1972) proposed a novel answer to that question. The answer is the suggestion, not of yet another new discipline, but of a new way of doing human science. Note at the outset that, although the book has "theology" in the title, it actually proposes a method for all the humanities and human sciences. Let this observation make the point: if a method can actually sort through the jungle of religious beliefs and teachings, that method can surely order the current disarray among the social sciences.

The brilliance of the method is to divide scholarly activities, not according to myriad topics or congenial objects of study, but according to the kinds of intellectual activities each involves. These intellectual activities parallel the structure of the process of human knowing, "the native spontaneities and inevitabilities of our consciousness" (p. 18)—about which, much more in Chapter 2. For example, if knowing depends on appeal to relevant data, one specialized function of scholarship would be Research—that preliminary digging up and assembling of relevant facts and tidbits, that explorer's fascination, which absolutely delights some curious people but absolutely weighs down others who are preoccupied with the bigger questions. So let the researchers do what they do best, and let them pass their results along to others for further processing. For example, again, then, if knowing also depends on proposing viable explanations, understandings, or hypotheses, another specialized function for creative intellects would be Interpretation of the collected evidence. And so on. Functional specializations, not contrived objects of study, would organize, differentiate, and interrelate scientific endeavors.

Uniquely, Lonergan's method also includes elaborated functions for assessing conclusions for accuracy or error and for wholesomeness or dysfunction—epistemology and ethics—the nemesis of postmodernism: normativity. The social sciences completely lack a systemic way of determining normativity, yet without a measure of it social science could never become prescriptive (cf. Helminiak, 2013a, p. 48; 2014, pp. 127–128), as is every full-fledged science. Namely, when science actually comes to understand how something works, it can prescribe what ought to be done if a project is to succeed. Medical science, for example, takes prescription for granted. Without apology physicians tell us how to live, what to eat, where to work, and so on, if we want to be healthy. Yet, confusing unbiased objectivity with value-neutrality, social science still often harbors the untenable notion of science as a "value-free" enterprise (e.g., Paloutzian & Park, 2005, p. 560). The rub, of course, is that matters of value are both unavoidable and highly contentious in human affairs, and, as noted at 1.4, the bottom has fallen out of philosophical consensus on such matters. As a result, unable to take a grounded stand on the quintessential human questions of epistemology and ethics, human science cannot become genuinely scientific. Lonergan offers a solution to this problem. The goal is that today's mere "academic disciplines" become genuine "sciences" (Lonergan, 1972, p. 3), methodically "yielding cumulative and progressive results" (p. 4).

Organized in this new fashion, the collective enterprise of human knowing—human science—would function in institutionalized patterns that actually parallel the pattern of knowing built into the human mind. The university would operate as one collective knowing agent, a juggernaut of collaborative human minds—investigating, inquiring, theorizing, checking, integrating, assessing, and finally proposing and popularizing conclusions ever to be refined, corrected, and updated. In a cycling process this collective knowing agent would pursue the open-ended human quest for correct understanding.

This overall project is far too elaborate to explicate here. Indeed, we can only wait to see how it might unfold. Philip McShane (1985, 2013a, 2013b; see also www.philipmcshane.org) has mounted a heroic campaign of advancing a Lonerganian reorganization of the academy. In fact, that vision is so far-reaching that even most Lonerganians shy away from its demands (McShane, 2013a, pp. 53–56), and only half tongue-in-cheek, McShane muses that Lonergan's system "will be as familiar as the periodic table in chemistry by 9011 A.D." (p. 67). Lonergan (1985) himself showed similar perspicacity about the methodological revolution he has proposed:

> Is my proposal utopian? It asks merely for creativity, for an interdisciplinary theory that at first will be denounced as absurd, then will be admitted to be true but obvious and insignificant, and perhaps, finally, be regarded as so important that its adversaries will claim that they themselves discovered it. (p. 108)

1.6. Attention to Major Thinkers in Neuroscience and Consciousness Studies

Throughout this work, in only today's slogging way, moving from neuroscience, to psychology, to spiritualogy, to theology, I clarify my argument by contrasting it with others. My references to other positions are selective because my goal is restricted. My intention is neither to summarize the field (see, e.g., Blackmore, 2012) nor, far less, to try and discern what the multitudinous confounded statements in this subtle discussion might actually mean in each case. Rather, my limited intention is to highlight and clarify the underlying theoretical issues, and they are pervasive, intricate, and recurrent. When I focus on individual positions, sometimes in considerable detail, my goal is not comprehensive exposition and criticism, but revealing exemplification. Mostly I want to illustrate how confusion in epistemology provokes many of the problems in these discussions and how the problems can be resolved if the epistemology is cleaned up.

This book is a bold, perhaps even a fatuous, attempt to address major methodological questions in relatively short compass. The presentation even presumes a way of thinking that is foreign to most people. Perhaps this application of Lonergan's thought even qualifies for what Patricia Churchland (1996) derisively called a "real humdinger of a solution" (p. 405) to the mind–body problem, "some fundamental new understanding," a "rethink of the nature of the universe" (Blackmore, 2012, pp. 29–30). Nonetheless, granted the novelty—I would call it a breakthrough—the relevant contributions of the various sciences and disciplines fall rather easily into place. Unfortunately, however, this place might not always be congenial. Given a coherent and consistent epistemology, the requirements of our own minds sometimes force us into positions we might prefer not to have to hold—especially when our topic has existential and even religious implications. But the chips must fall where they will. Despite the far-reaching implications of my position, I believe this book presents the necessary detail that, given careful reading, clinches my argument or, at least, credibly expounds it. The audacity of this presentation does have the advantage of offering a relatively brief overview of fundamental philosophical issues, which most people could not explore in tomes of hundreds of pages and on which there exists only an array of differing opinions; but, as far as I know after 35 years of comparison, no coherent position other than Lonergan's is available (cf. McCarthy, 1990, 1997; Webb, 1988; Willis, 2007, pp. 8–23). If I can convey only a main idea and open a potential new perspective, I will have achieved my purpose of pointing to a brighter horizon.

1.7. Attention to Intelligence, Not Merely to Logic

My argument is to be coherent and consistent from beginning to end. As a result, it cannot be grasped in part or by selective reading. It would, of course, be useful to read the Conclusion at the outset just to get some idea of where I am going, but one might read my Conclusion and state that Helminiak holds such and such and even affirm or dismiss a summary statement, all without understanding what I actually mean. In these matters the same terms mean different things to different people working within different philosophical perspectives, so, apart from their broad contexts, summary statements are easily misunderstood. The commonplace terms *mind, person, nature,* and *substance,* or in mathematics even the terms *point* and *line,* offer instructive examples because they mean different things to different people in different contexts. One needs to be sure one understands what an author means by this and that term before judging the statement.

Besides, in my case, the argument is not a matter of deductive logic, which produces a necessary conclusion on the basis of easily stated premises. Rather, as already intimated, the argument turns on explicit attention to intelligence, which demands prolonged effort to achieve understanding and to which we seldom attend explicitly. Not logic but understanding is at stake. The difference is that intelligence makes leaps, transcending or dismantling prior systems and setting up new ones in which, only then, logic again can make its demands (Lonergan, 1957/1992, pp. 301–302, 595–600).

Thus, the whole of my argument holds together only through a grasp of the parts, and the grasp of the parts depends on the meaning of the whole. Such is the case with any fully systematic statement such as a new mathematics or the equation that expresses a scientific breakthrough: the elements codefine one another; they lock one another together in a pattern of relationships that make one another be what they are. At stake is "implicit definition," as mathematician David Hilbert (1902/1971) named the matter in absolute generality (4.6.5). A rather concrete example would be the relationship $d = rt$ (distance = rate of speed x time traveled). This relationship fixes the value of the terms so that, given any one of them, the other two are already colimited in what they could be; and given two of them, the third is absolutely limited to only one possible value.

My presentation aims at such refined scientific articulation, which expresses its meaning through the interrelationship of terms—such as experience, understanding, and judgment—whose mutually defined meanings are grounded in an insight into what is being affirmed. Intended meaning depends on insight. The statements need to be understood, not merely noted, reported, and "parroted" back.

1.8. An Interrelated and Unfolding Presentation

Said otherwise, at stake is the proverbial hermeneutic circle—as when a sentence makes sense only given the meanings of the words, but the meanings of the words depend on the sense of the sentence. For example, consider the word *sense* in the previous sentence: the word does not regard sensations, vague impressions, a discerning awareness, or—if heard, not read—American coins of the smallest denomination. This situation does, indeed, constitute a vicious circle, but only logically. If logic were our only intellectual tool, we would be at an impasse. But we also have intelligence, and it breaks the vicious circle. Intelligence grapples back and forth with the meaning of the words and of the sentence and eventually transcends them both in a moment of insight, usually unnoticed (as in the simple case of *sense* just described), which provides an interpretation that determines the one, consistent, interlocking meaning of both the words and the sentence. Similarly, the parts of this book mutually clarify one another. For this reason, throughout the text I have included cross-references to chapter, section, and subsections within this book (e.g., 4.6.5 equals Chapter 4, section 6, subsection 5).

Moreover, as the book unfolds, I introduce only the epistemological ideas that seem necessary at each point along the way and later expand and clarify the exposition as further questions demand further elaboration. As we move from brain to mind to consciousness to God, the questions do become more subtle. Chapter 4, in particular, on the mind–body problem, offers telling examples of the difference between a sensate-modeled and an intellectual epistemology, important clarification about the notion of causality, specification of the unity of a "thing" in contrast to its constitutive "parts," and an account of emergence within cosmic and evolutionary process. Chapter 5, on spiritualogy, requires a difficult elaboration about the nature of consciousness or human spirit, not only intentional (that is, directed toward some object), as is commonly held, but also conscious (that is, unmediatedly "self-present"). These two chapters—Chapters 4 and 5—address the most difficult questions in this discussion and present what I think is a coherent resolution of them. From this point of view, this book could well have been entitled *The Nature of Consciousness* or *The Mind-Body Problem* or something similar. However, as the actual title of this book witnesses—for no good reason except the confusion in question over mind, consciousness, spirit, and Divinity—neuroscientists and psychologists have entangled God in this discussion. So, finally, Chapter 6, applying the same epistemology, presents an understanding of God—absolutely standard in the Western theological tradition—that far outstrips the pious notions controlling current discussion and that accounts for the role of God in human biological, mental, and conscious or spiritual functioning. So be forewarned: the argument is not complete until the book reaches its conclusion. Chapter 3, on neuroscience, turns out to be the least significant in this book—not because the topic is irrelevant to a comprehensive scientific account of the human, but because that field already enjoys a consensual methodology and elaborated technologies, and its current offerings, nonetheless, remain tentative, still highly speculative, and merely indicative of the robust understanding that will someday be achieved. Still, whatever the final understanding, the relationship between brain and mind can be clarified in principle.

Finally, the challenging subject matter of this book provides occasions to concretely apply and pointedly exemplify the breakthrough ideas summarized only generically in the critical chapter on epistemology—Chapter 2. To engage the multidimensionality of this book's subtle topic is to encounter a particularly fruitful opportunity. Can any epistemology deal consistently and coherently with that whole array of issues? I believe so, and I offer my exemplification. Then, my point here is, again, that the reader is unlikely to appreciate the argument without working through the unfolding topics along the way in order to understand both each different concrete issue in question and the one methodology guiding every resolution and projecting the coherence of them all.

1.9. The Centrality of Consciousness

Given that human consciousness or spirit is central to this discussion—for both its content and its method—the reflexivity I have been highlighting should not be unexpected (Helminiak, 1998, p. xii). After all, the essence of human consciousness is a peculiar self-consciousness, an unmediated self-presence, which is non-objectifying, which does not turn the subject into an object to her- or himself but is experienced as subjectivity *per se* (5.3.1). Because of self-consciousness, the very condition for the possibility of subsequent cognitive reflexivity, we have the ability to reflect back on ourselves and to turn even our insights into objects of awareness and thought. Thus, an adequate understanding of consciousness entails also an understanding of human knowing. Moreover, at its core, my argument is that transcendent experience is such consciousness of consciousness—or "awareness of awareness" (Lonergan 1957/1992, p. 346), as many would alternatively say, making little distinction between the English terms *consciousness* and *awareness*. Following the very helpful suggestion of Louis Roy (2003, pp. 27, 29), as best I can, I reserve the term *aware* to refer to intentionality, that is, a subject's relationship to some object; and I use the term *conscious* to refer to that uniquely human, non-objectified self-presence that constitutes subjectivity (5.1.2; 5.5.1). Yet even apart from these distinctions, consciousness and knowing easily appear as two academically distinguished sides of the same coin.

On many fronts, then, the subtle matter of consciousness is central to this study. I therefore beg the reader to bear these considerations in mind, to give this book a fair and repeated reading, and to reject its conclusions only if they prove incoherent on the basis of their own presuppositions. Chapter 2 begins this intellectual project by laying out these presuppositions.

Chapter 2

Epistemology

A Portentous Prolegomenon

They know who know how to learn.

—Henry Adams

Learn to teach yourself.

—Anonymous African-American proverb

What we call basic truths are simply the ones we discover after all the others.

—Albert Camus

Time advances; facts accumulate; doubts arise. Faint glimpses of truth begin to appear, and shine more and more unto the perfect day. The highest intellects, like the tops of mountains, are the first to catch and reflect the dawn. They are bright, while the level below is still in darkness. But soon the light, which at first illuminates only the loftiest eminences, descends on the plain and penetrates to the deepest valley. First come hints, then fragments of systems, then defective systems, then complete and harmonious systems. The sound opinion, held for a time by one bold speculator, becomes the opinion of a small minority, of a strong minority, of a majority—of mankind.

—Thomas Babington Macaulay

Relating transcendent experiences to biological processes, neuroscientific research has raised peculiar questions. What is the object of transcendent experience? Does it actually have an object? Is the object God? If so, is the brain structured to be sensitive to God just as the retina, for example, is sensitive to light (Fingelkurts & Fingelkurts, 2009)? What is "God," anyway, and especially if God could be the object of neurological function and even be elicited by its manipulation (Doblin, 1991)? Must a psychology of transcendent experience address questions of God? If so—that is, if implication of the supposedly ineffable God is essential to psychological explanation, as many psychologists insist (1.1)—and if, in contrast, psychology is to be an empirical science whose conclusions depend on the appeal to appropriate evidence, how is a psychology of transcendent experience even possible?

Such questions are more philosophical, or methodological, and theological than strictly psychological. For this reason, the proposed answers within psychology differ widely. Without an epistemology adequate to the subtlety of non-physical realities—emotions, ideas, thoughts, decisions—coherent answers to these questions cannot be forthcoming. Even worse, at this point in postmodern history, when, curiously, the very possibility of knowing anything is debated, it is unlikely that neuroscientists or psychologists would share consensus on epistemology. Hence, debate over "God in the brain" thrives.

2.1. Lonergan's Cognitive Theory and Epistemology

Remarkably, I approach this daunting matter with optimism—because I rely on the philosophical work of Bernard J. F. Lonergan, namely, his analysis of human consciousness and its correlative epistemology. Lonergan's starting point is the givens of the human mind—the data, from the Latin for "given," where *datum* is singular, and *data* is plural—namely, the very structures, processes, mechanisms, and inherent constraints of human mental functioning. We have access to these matters when the mind is our concern.

2.1.1. Evidence on the Mind

Within our own experience of our own mental functioning, we have evidence on how our minds work. Lonergan counts this experience of our inner mental life as valid evidence. He speaks of this evidence as "the data of consciousness" (1957/1992, p. 299; also pp. 95, 260, 358; 1972, pp. 8–9, 201–202) and insists that these data are as valid in the realm of the mind as are "the data of the senses," to which the natural sciences limit themselves, in the realm of physical realities. This insistence is hardly novel although its explanation is highly debated. The whole field of non-behaviorist psychology, especially in its psychotherapeutic application, rests upon it. Psychologists and counselors presume that people know something of what is going on in their hearts and minds. On the basis of personal experience, we all now presume we can know our own minds, at least to some extent, by attending to them. In striking contrast to the ancients, for example, we do not imagine thinking to be conversation with the gods or clever insights to be inspirations from the muses (Snell, 1960).

Thus, in its own way, in a manner appropriate to its object, Lonergan's theory of knowledge, like natural science, is empirical. It relies on evidence. It is a form of science: evidence-based explanation. It is not mere speculation. It depends on a phenomenology-like (Lonergan, 1980/1990, pp. 270–271) attentiveness to one's own mind. Lonergan calls this process "self-appropriation" (pp. 2–21)—popularly, "getting to know yourself" or, in terms that resonate with Eastern meditative theory, "realizing what you actually are." Accordingly, his theory is grounded in the evidence that is relevant to the mind and that is available, presumably, to anyone who cares to attend to the workings of her or his own mind.

Not all would agree about human access to data on consciousness. Some would resist broadening the legitimate evidence of science to include inner mental experience because it is not "available for public observation." Yet the appeal to supposed "objective" sense data can appear to be as subjective as the appeal to inner mental experience. Bishop George Berkeley, the quintessential idealist, made this very argument in response to John Locke's nascent empiricism at the birth of modern science. Idealism is the position that reality is only ideas in our mind. Berkeley argued that all "reality," as in *The Matrix*, is just subjective experience: even sense experience is an inner mental phenomenon, as private as the experience of anything else. Indeed, any perceptual experience—"I hear a gushing sound; I see a plume of white rising up into the sky"—is a report of an inner experience: "*I* see, *I* hear." Any appeal to "objective sense data" relies on personal awareness, so the sense data that support scientific theorizing depend on subjective experience and report (5.7.3). There is no avoiding this state of affairs. We have no reportable human experience free of subjective components. The basis of reports of inner conscious experience is no different from the basis of reports of outer sense experience: we have access to both the data of sense and the data of consciousness only through our own consciousness. In this sense, both are inner experiences. Nonetheless, a gratuitous, narrow requirement of science has limited legitimate evidence to sense experience and, in effect, limits reality to the material or physical.

This limitation on science becomes a key methodological problem when the topic is consciousness. The upshot of such limitation must be that consciousness simply could not be a valid topic for science. Many scientists would just leave it at that and beg off discussing consciousness. Whether respectfully or dismissively, they would let others pursue the topic however they wished, insisting simply, all the time, that such an enterprise is not science. I present examples of two conflicting positions on this matter: one from Sir Roger Penrose and David Chalmers, and the other from Daniel Dennett.

2.1.2. Argument for a Genuine Science of Consciousness: Penrose

The mathematician Penrose (1994b) takes a creative middle stand. He is rare among theorists of consciousness in that he makes a double assertion—both that consciousness is a kind of reality in itself, fully irreducible to brain function and in principle incapable of replication in computers, and that, nonetheless, in some way there can be a science of consciousness. This double assertion leads him to call for a new kind of science, and that is my point. He urges, "If science is yet incapable of saying much that is of significance concerning matters of the mind, then eventually science must enlarge its scope so as to accommodate such matters, and perhaps even modify its very procedures" (p. 12). "It may well be that . . . we shall need a broadening of what we presently mean by 'science' " (p. 50). Indeed!

Penrose approaches consciousness in the context of computer modeling. He argues powerfully—conclusively, I believe, by appeal to Gödel's theorem (4.16)—that insightful mental function is simply incommensurate with the algorithmic, computational processes of computers and the strictly mathematical procedures of contemporary physics. Yet he believes consciousness must somehow fall within scientific explanation as currently conceived because "our brains are completely controlled by physics of some kind" (Penrose, 1994a, p. 243). To support his argument, he proposes scientific examples relevant to consciousness. He scours physics for instances of phenomena that are non-computational yet still compatible with physics, still explicable on the basis of scientific laws. One striking example is gravity. In the Einsteinian universe, gravity turns out to be a phenomenon in its own right, unique among the forces of nature because it can bend light, but completely integrated into physics. But in the Newtonian universe, gravity was taken to be almost an epiphenomenon, a computational effect of mass (Penrose, 1994b, pp. 217–227)—an epiphenomenon, an insignificant side-effect, like the steam spouting from an engine, as consciousness is often said to be in relation to the brain (4.5, 4.7). So Penrose wonders if, like gravity, consciousness could likewise eventually be recognized in its own right as an aspect of the natural world, another fundamental force or principle of nature, explicable in some form of science similar to physics. I summarize his theory at 3.5.

But to my point: I welcome Penrose's (1994b) acknowledgement that consciousness is a distinctive reality in its own right, and I welcome his insistence that consciousness is amenable to some kind of scientific explanation, even possibly a broadened notion of science. However, I am not optimistic that a physics-based model of science could prove adequate to consciousness (p. 350). With Lonergan I would propose that the essence of science is simply evidence-based explanation, and this one and the same definition applies variably to various subject matters. With its appeal to the data of the senses and with its computational, mathematical, and even quantum methods, physics is only one of those applications. Consider, for example, Wilhelm Dilthey's well-known distinction between *Naturwissenshaften* and *Geisteswissenshaften*, natural sciences and social or human sciences. This distinction exemplifies a broadened and nuanced understanding of "science"—from the Latin *scientia*, which simply means "knowledge." The German term *Wissenschaft*—literally, "knowledge craft" or "enterprise of knowing," translated as *science*—actually applies to any researched, reasoned, critical, evidence-based scholarship, including but not exclusive to natural science. As *Wissenschaft*, "science" characterizes any methodically guided pursuit of accurate understanding about anything. In 19th-century Germany, modern historiography became a *Wissenschaft*, and Lonergan's *Method in Theology* proposes even a scientific theology. The study of consciousness need not be excluded from evidence-based understanding. Indeed, if Lonergan's appeal to "self-appropriation" is a legitimate empirical enterprise, he has already proposed a scientific or systematic account of consciousness in itself, and he has accounted for the relationship of consciousness to the brain as an instance of evolutionary emergence through a number of stages, not by a single leap from matter to consciousness (5.9.2). Yet his account hardly depends on measurement, mathematics, computation, quantum mechanics, and the methodologies appropriate to physics. Still, in its own way, as appropriate to its particular subject matter, Lonergan's account of consciousness does retain the evidence-based and implicitly defined explanation that characterizes physical science and its mathematical equations.

The last three sentences are long and dense. With unexplained technical terminology, they encapsulate Lonergan's position, in contrast to most others, yet it will come clear only as my exposition unfolds. The point to be made here is easier: Penrose's double assertion includes the possibility of some kind of a truly scientific account of consciousness. Such an account, Penrose insists, would somehow respect the essence of scientific thinking and, on the basis of relevant evidence, coherently relate consciousness to other natural realities, such as the workings of the human brain.

2.1.3. Argument for a Genuine Science of Consciousness: Chalmers

Preeminently, philosopher David Chalmers has also argued that consciousness is a kind of reality in its own right and that there can be a science of consciousness. His *The Conscious Mind* is a sustained argument of hundreds of pages to this effect. Having attempted "for a number of years" to find a theory that would virtually equate consciousness with brain function, he gave up that project "quite reluctantly." In honest self-revelation, he reports, "Temperamentally, I am strongly inclined toward materialist reductive explanation, and I have no strong spiritual or religious inclinations" (Chalmers, 1996, p. xiv). Yet, committed to taking both science and the undeniable experience of consciousness seriously, he now holds "consciousness to be a natural phenomenon, falling under the sway of natural laws" (p. xiii). It is true that "consciousness is not directly observable in experimental contexts," he writes, but "we each have access to a rich source of data in our own case. We know about our own detailed and specific conscious experiences" (pp. 215–216). "The main intuition at work is that *there is something to be explained*—some phenomenon associated with first-person experience that presents a problem not presented by observation of cognition from the third-person point of view" (p. 110).

Engaging considerable detail on these matters, Chalmers's presentation also opens itself to many points of criticism. These initial quotations already exhibit an entangled use of the terms *data, knowledge,* and *intuition* and evince a global, significantly undifferentiated conception of consciousness and knowing: what are data, knowledge, and intuition, and how do they relate to one another? Accordingly, periodically throughout this book, I will address Chalmers's arguments and suggest how Lonergan's starting point—so much at variance with contemporary philosophical thinking, as comparison with Chalmers's phenomenology-tinged mix of linguistic analysis and pragmatism, under the name of "functionalism," makes lucid (4.12.4)—allows a consistent and coherent philosophy of science, applicable in all fields, avoiding much of the tortured argumentation that burdens Chalmers's exposition. Still, with tremendous admiration for his herculean effort, I note that Chalmers, too, insists that, not reducible to physics or the biology of the brain, consciousness is a reality in its own right and is amenable to scientific explanation of some appropriate kind.

2.1.4. Argument Against a Genuine Science of Consciousness: Dennett

In contrast, the philosopher Daniel Dennett (1991), another leading theorist on consciousness, goes to an extreme in the opposite direction. Also intent on having a true science of consciousness, he would not expand the realm of true science. Rather, he would make narrow sensate empiricism definitive. He insists, "Since you can never 'see directly' into people's minds, but have to take their word for it, any such facts as there are about mental events are not among the data of science, since they can never be properly verified by objective methods" (p. 70). Dennett explicitly dismisses any appeal to internal experience: "Postulating special inner qualities that are not only private and intrinsically valuable, but also unconfirmable and uninvestigatable is just obscurantism" (p. 450). Dennett takes this emphasis to its logical conclusion and allows that only what is known through such narrowly defined science is actually real. Thus, he maintains, any explanation of consciousness "will have to be constructed from the third-person point of view, since all science is constructed from that perspective" (p. 71). Dennett stands by a "third-party perspective" (p. 70) and even a "third-party absolutism" (Chalmers, 1997, p. 384). It appears, then, as John Searle (1997, pp. 111–112) provocatively but effectively suggests, not only that Dennett does not provide an explanation for consciousness, but also that he actually needs none—because from the start he denies the existence of consciousness as a particular kind of reality to be explained in itself. Unavailable to public observation, consciousness could not be credited scientifically. It is, then, as if there really is no such thing as consciousness although science can supposedly explain *why we would think there is*, and for Dennett precisely such explanation would be the scientific account—actually, a dismissal—of consciousness. As Chalmers (1997a) construes this matter, Dennett " 'solves' the problem by ducking the question" (p. 16).

I have already noted that one could mount a powerful argument to the effect that even sense experience and its data are as private a mental affair as any other mental experience. That touted "third-party perspective" is only a comforting social fiction (5.7.3). So, on Dennett's strict definition of empirical science, even appeal to sense data could be discredited; even the claimed public availability of the data of physical science could be dismissed. Every claim ultimately rests on someone's personal inner experience. Faithfully applied, à la George Berkeley, that definition of science would rule out any science whatsoever—as was Berkeley's conclusion. After all, in *The Matrix* nobody knew their "objective experience" was just in their minds.

However, at this point, I do not want to engage the ideology of narrow scientism. At 4.19, I will suggest what I see as the valid intent in Dennett's thorough-going reductionist enterprise, and I will elucidate what I see as its epistemological errors. Summarily stated, I see no reason for apodictically restricting the range of human inquiry to the objects that natural science has deemed its legitimate concern. In fact, that concern has been redefined frequently since the time of Nicolaus Copernicus, Francis Bacon, Galileo Galilei, and their contemporaries (for a succinct overview, see Harrison, 2010). Indeed, the "objects" of contemporary physics—quarks and leptons, fields and space-time—are as fully imperceptible as is consciousness. Dependent on a fully intellectualist epistemology, these physical realities are the conclusions of evidence-based reasoning—meanings!—not the objects of crass sense experience. Accordingly, with Lonergan and many others today, I believe that we do have personal experience of inner mental events, and I submit that this experience constitutes valid data. Thus, Chalmers (1996): "There is certainly a sense in which all these arguments [for consciousness] are based on intuition [i.e., internal experiences], but I have tried to make clear just how natural and plain these intuitions are, and how forced it is to deny them" (p. 110).

2.1.5. *The Makings of a Science of Consciousness*

If there is something there to be explained, if data are available, inquiry can ensue, and hypothesis and verification (or falsification) could follow along with replacement or refinement of the hypothesis, and so on *da capo*, in an open-ended process of ever more accurate, evidence-based explanation: science. If many come to the same conclusion by following this same knowing process, then an accumulation of similar results in an array of independent subjects would seem to support the shared conclusion about inner mental events. Many noses would have been counted; the research results would have been replicated. To be sure, this replication would have occurred in different subjects and been reported by different investigators; but adjusted to match its particular subject matter, this procedure does not differ from standard scientific replication, which appeals to different representative instances on the part of different investigators. Such a rigorous process of evidence-based explanation is nothing other than science.

Thus, I proceed by accepting the presupposition of mental experience and go on to try and make sense of it. I presuppose that our experience of mind and consciousness expresses some kind of *sui generis* reality. The challenge is to accept the data as given and to explain them.

Disconcertingly but unavoidably, anyone who claims to have no such mental experience disqualifies him- or herself from productive discussion in this matter (Lonergan, 1972, pp. 16–17). The point is not, from a third-person perspective, to try and tell others what is going on in their minds. The point is simply an unavoidable question with a rather obvious answer: is someone worth hearing out who denies ever having had any mental experience? Who refuses to own such experience as significant in its own right? Who shirks the responsibility such experience seems to entail? Such a denial discredits any interlocutor.

Socrates argued in a similar way against the skeptics millennia ago. Skeptics argue knowingly that nothing can be known. Or, as regards consciousness, they presuppose and employ the functioning of aware, intelligent, and reasonable consciousness to construct creatively elaborated arguments to dismiss the reality of consciousness. They express their mind to argue that mind does not exist. Their doing belies their saying; their actions contradict their speech. To me, this threat of self-disqualification—Hegel's "procedural self-contradiction" (see Donceel, 1974)—is an insurmountable bulwark that makes Lonergan's starting point invulnerable, namely, the mental experience we all have and use.

2.1.6. Lonergan's Theory of Human Knowing

Thus, Lonergan (1957/1992) begins with an empirical question, "What is happening when we are knowing?" (p. 16) or, phrased otherwise, "What am I doing when I am knowing?" (p. 779, note f). This latter phrasing is more accurate because, in the nature of the matter, I can approach an answer only through my own experience. I cannot examine what transpires in other people's minds. The instances of human knowing to which I have access are uniquely my own. Moreover, if such is the case, it matters little what others speculate, argue, conclude, insist, or opine. I cannot deny my own experience without denying the denier, myself. *Cogito, ergo sum*: I think, therefore I must exist. In this peculiar matter, no one is asked, or could ever responsibly be able, to take someone else's word for it—as in that ludicrous, druggy party question, "Are we having fun yet?" Each must speak for her- or himself, and the stakes in this enterprise are high. Hanging in the balance is a personal belief about what I am—and you, too, dear reader—as a human being.

The general answer to that question is as follows. As a knower, in the pursuit of knowledge, I attempt to make sense of, to understand, the puzzling given that I encounter. Awareness that prompts wonder or awe is the starting point of every intellectual endeavor. When wonder turns to question and, after appropriate effort, insight occurs, I generate an idea, and I formulate it in an interpretation, a hypothesis, a theory, a proposed explanation. Naturally concerned that my understanding actually be correct, I check it against the given data. Then via another kind of insight whereby I grasp that my understanding does indeed account for all the data and that no further relevant questions remain, I am constrained by the very demands of my own mind to affirm my explanation: *Eureka!* I have correct understanding. I know. Or, no, I was mistaken. This process of knowing is supposedly built into the human mind. The process is spontaneous. It constitutes a dynamism that, in the healthy mind, is relentless, ongoing, ever self-correcting, ever further integrating, ever self-refining. It expresses "the detached, disinterested, and unrestricted" (p. 696), "the pure desire to know" (pp. 372–375). Its ultimate ideal goal is the understanding of everything about everything.

More technically and summarily formulated, human intellectual knowing entails three components:

- experience,
- understanding, and
- judgment.

This conclusion is the result of Lonergan's attending to human knowing, borrowing on, integrating, and advancing the thought of Socrates, Plato, Aristotle, Augustine, Thomas Aquinas, Immanuel Kant, Georg W. F. Hegel, John Henry Newman, David Hilbert, Albert Einstein, Edmund Husserl, Kurt Gödel, and others. Given the scope of his work, it is understandable that *Newsweek* (Anonymous, 1970) would have styled Lonergan as the Thomas Aquinas of the 20th century. With more terminological precision than I need to preserve in this book, Lonergan's (1957/1992, 1980/1990) conclusion includes three contents:

- it presents a *cognitive theory*, an account of the *de facto* human knowing-process, which the prior paragraph rehearsed;
- it grounds an *epistemology*, an account of the validity of the human knowing that results from this process; and
- it opens onto a *metaphysics*, an account of what is known through this knowing process—namely, being, what actually is, what there is to be known, what could (eventually) be correctly and comprehensively affirmed.

Lonergan portrays these three contents also in the form of questions:

- What do we do when we know?
- Why is this knowing?
- What do we know when we do it?

I will use the term *epistemology* less strictly and in it include both cognitional theory and epistemology as differentiated by Lonergan. As in the general usage, by *epistemology* I will mean more casually an account of human knowing.

In his standard terminology, Lonergan refers to experience, understanding, and judgment as cognitive operations on three successive "levels of consciousness." Given that consciousness is not a physical reality, the term *level* is obviously a metaphor. It implies no actual scaffolding or layering—and, ultimately, because of the interaction among the levels, not even a fixed sequence (Helminiak, 1996a, pp. 101–103; 2014)—but, rather, suggests distinct but interrelated facets, aspects, or functions of human conscious operation. Below I will invoke Lonergan's metaphor of "level" as a convenient way to name and refer to aspects of conscious functioning. I now elaborate each of the three in turn.

2.2. The Empirical Level of Knowing: Experience

All human knowing depends on experience. Contemporary psychology makes clear that we are born with reflexes and, most impressively, with a remarkable capacity for observing and making connections and with powerful skills in relating to caregivers, so it is not unqualifiedly true that an infant's mind is a *tabula rasa*, a blank slate only to be written on (Shaw, 1984). The "slate" itself is already shaped, structured, and receptive in a particular way. Nonetheless, John Locke's famous empiricist insistence on the *tabula rasa*, following Aristotle, remains valid as regards the personal acquisition of specific knowledge about the world around us. Human knowing does depend on experience.

2.2.1. Experience and the Initial Givens or Data

Thus far I have been using the term *experience* in a commonsensical way. For Lonergan, however, *experience* is a technical term. It applies only to the specific event of encountering data, of becoming aware of something to be understood. *Experience* no longer carries that more prevalent sense as a global term for the entire range of possible human engagements: "What an experience I had last night!" Use of the term *experience* in its global sense is standard not only in popular usage but also in philosophical and psychological discussion. Griffin's use of the term, representing Whitehead, provides a lucid example (4.20.5). Usage in existential philosophy, humanistic psychology, and phenomenology provides further examples. Whereas others speak of "experience" to name the whole product of human self-conscious subjectivity, Lonergan analyzes this supposedly global primordial phenomenon and actually goes on to propose the facets that constitute it—experience, understanding, judgment, and decision. Thus, Lonergan's technically defined "experience" is just a first component of the more commonly, globally, and undifferentiatedly named "experience." Narrowly and technically, Lonergan defines experience by its relationship to understanding. Namely, experience is that on which understanding works; experience provides the data that understanding attempts to explain. And in its turn, understanding is that which discerns intelligibility in, or explains, data. Via implicit definition, the coinage of perfected science (4.6.5), experience and understanding codefine each other. Both occur within consciousness, and they (partially) constitute and, thus, explicate consciousness. Evidence for this construal of the matter is found in the occurrence of an insight, wherein data and intelligence conspire to produce ideas about the experienced-understood. Insight is always into some data, and data precondition the occurrence of insight: if there is nothing there to be understood, insight would not occur.

Next, the term *data* applies on a sliding scale, as it were, to whatever is to be understood. The first perceptual input that an infant begins to integrate into some grasp of life; the meaning-filled gestures, coos, signs, and words that children appropriate within their growing understanding of the world into which they are being socialized; the selective facts of learning and personal happenings that teenagers weave into tentative and ever-changing philosophies of life; the array of numbers, diagrams, and computer printouts that a team of physicists struggles to explain; the text before your own eyes, which you ponder to understand—all these are examples of data. They are the substance of "experience" in Lonergan's restricted sense of the word. They are the input that prompts, shapes, and constrains the overall subjective occurrences that popularly we call "experience."

The data are the initial conscious input whose recognized presence prompts a complex process of "meaning making," that spontaneous human proclivity for organizing and finding sense in provocative givens. Accordingly, experience alone is not yet knowledge. Experience is a condition for knowing, and the data of experience determine or specify the known. Experience merely provokes but, more significantly, also constrains knowing. Without the initiating step of experience, that is, openness to a world of wonder and question, human knowing does not occur.

2.2.2. Knowledge Equated with Experience: Commonsense Realism: Wilber

For some, in contrast, the account of knowing stops at the point of experience, and they take the notion of experience in a broad and non-specific sense. Thus, supposedly, experience is knowledge. The result is what philosophers call naïve or commonsense realism. It is the epistemological claim that one does, indeed, know reality and quite simply so; one knows by immediate experience, encounter, engagement, confrontation. In this case, quite commonly if only implicitly, perception—not intelligent and reasonable mind, be it noted, but perception—is taken to be the criterion of reality: "Want to know what's real? Run into that wall, and you'll know what's real!" Supposedly, what one feels or sees, senses or perceives in some way, is what is real—hence, Samuel Johnson's notorious "refutation" of idealism by kicking his podium: "Thus I refute Berkeley!"

This same criterion of confrontation or immediate experience gets extended from external physical encounters to internal mental encounters. Then it usually goes by the name of *intuition*—or perhaps *inspiration* or *revelation*—so that an intense mental experience would *ipso facto* be deemed, for example, "spiritual knowledge" (Hart, Nelson, & Puhakka, 2000). In all these cases, what is real is what is experienced, and reality is supposedly known simply through direct experience.

To various degrees, the appeal to direct experience as the criterion of human knowing is widespread (e.g., d'Aquili & Newberg, 1999, p 191; Gorsuch, 2002; Richards & Bergin, 2005, pp. 101–102; Slife & Richards, 2001). Ken Wilber's (1996) theory provides a lucid example. It explains knowing by appeal to "three strands of knowledge." The first is the injunctive strand; it entails the directions to be followed to achieve knowledge in any particular realm. For example, "To know if it's raining, go and look" (p. 32). Evidently, the attainment of knowledge is to be a matter of immediate experience, in this case, taking a look. The second, the "illuminative or apprehensive strand," is one's actual following out the injunction. Compliance with the directions results in "illuminative *seeing*" by means of an "eye of knowledge." To know, you have to be willing to do what is required. In this case, one looks, and one knows. Finally, "a communal strand," namely, social consensus, results in "true seeing" (pp. 31–32). If others also look and come to the same conclusion, their agreement confirms the knowledge; it is correct. In this theory, the basis of knowledge is "intuitive apprehension" (p. 43). The actual knowing somehow occurs in the "black box" of "apprehension." That is, simply by encountering data according to a specified procedure—for example, by looking out the window—one knows. The knowing seems almost automatic. No attention is paid to what goes on in that black box of the mind, but what comes out is knowledge. Through illuminative seeing, knowing just happens.

Explaining all knowledge in this way, Wilber achieves a major goal. He sets science and spiritualogy on the same epistemological ground—in an endeavor similar to mine in this book. In this way, he intends to legitimize and integrate these two diverse fields of knowledge. Specifically, Wilber would credit meditative experience as actual knowledge because contemplative training (strand #1) allows "direct seeing into one's spiritual nature," "direct apprehension" (strand #2), about which spiritual adepts agree (strand #3) (p. 60; for criticism of Wilber, see Helminiak, 1998, pp. 213–292).

Note that instead of *meditation,* the classic Western spiritual tradition uses the term *contemplation,* although, as with Wilber here, so now with others who study meditation across religious traditions (e.g., Garrison et al., 2013; Vago & Silbersweig, 2012), the terms *meditation* and *contemplation* are being used as virtual synonyms.

For an account such as Wilber's, focused encounter is the means of knowing, and experience is already knowledge. To experience is to know. This theory of knowledge is consistently perceptual: it usually appeals to the metaphor of seeing; and knowledge is a matter of looking, either outside at physical reality or inside at spiritual reality. Knowledge of spiritual reality via immediate experience is the famed "noetic" characteristic of mystical experience as traditionally presented, that personal conviction that "I now know reality" (e.g., Hood, 2003). Moreover, this theory of knowing is confrontational: knowing is a matter of the subject's encountering the object. As discussed in the next section, the confrontational aspect of this theory raises its biggest problem, the so-called "problem of the bridge." Perception sets a subject opposite an object. Perception supposes two separate things out there, the one encountering the other. Any sensation-modeled theory of knowing must presume a gap between the subject and the object, but *ipso facto,* this self-debilitated theory has no way to bridge the gap. Thus, the theory can account only for knowledge of the external characteristics of a thing—what is seen, felt, or heard. It cannot explain how the subject could ever get beyond these external perceptions to know the thing in itself.

2.2.3. Another Example of Commonsense Realism: Searle

John Searle (1998, lecture 7) holds a similar position and offers another example. His insistence is that "we perceive the real world." That is, "In the normal perceptual situation, you just see the object directly. Your perception reaches right up to the object. . . . When you're looking at the object at point blank range in good light, you directly see the object." He rejects any need for making an "inference from the perceptual experience to the real world." Thus, he takes for granted, he overlooks, the intellectual component that is making the connections behind the scene in human knowing. Speaking here completely in terms of perception, he suggests that simply to see is to know, and he implies that the real is the perceived.

2.2.4. Yet Another Example of Commonsense Realism: Chalmers

These examples are important to cite because these theorists are major and representative figures in the current thinking about the mind and consciousness and they evince major deviations from the Lonerganian epistemology that I am explicating. Thus, I note that Chalmers (1996) also evinces this same sensate-modeled working theory of knowledge and reality. For him it is as if, for something to be real, it must be visible, perceptible in some way, or at least imaginable; reality has to have some intrinsic properties that one could almost get one's hands around. The contrasting understanding is telling, so I must digress briefly to make my point.

Twentieth-century modern science has broken through to a more subtle, a purely intellectual, mode of explanation. In terms of what, following David Hilbert, I called "implicit definition" (1.7; see 4.6.5), science explains things, not by saying what they truly look or feel like to us, that is, not by saying what their relationship is to us, but by relating them to one another to express what can be understood about them, what intelligibility they entail. "What they are" does not mean how they appear or how we could use them but, rather, what explains their functioning, what makes sense of our experience of them, what accounts for their being what they are, what natures they possess, what intelligibility is inherent in them. Thus, equations become the coinage of perfected science. They are statements of interrelationships such as $a^2 + b^2 = c^2$ in the case of a Euclidean right triangle expressed algebraically. Inquiry and insight make the breakthrough and finally determine the necessary and sufficient elements to account for things, and scientists express that breakthrough with absolute precision by formulating the relationship among these elements. More stunningly than

Pythagoras, for example, but exemplifying the very same intellectual "trick," Einstein proposed $E = mc^2$. In this usage, terms and relations mutually imply, constrain, specify—indeed, they define one another. The relations dictate what terms must be in question, and the terms in question require what the relations must be. If a, b, and c are the sides of a plane figure and $a^2 + b^2 = c^2$, this figure is and could only be a right triangle. The suggestion from Einstein is that the very natures of energy, mass, and light are precisely such that they lock together in the specific relationship, $E = mc^2$. It expresses what is there to be understood; it expresses the realities that are there. Energy, for example, is precisely that which exhibits certain characteristics, namely, these specific relations with mass and light. Science proposes an exact account of the intrinsic nature of things. Notice, however, that so conceived, the characteristics are not perceptual; they are nothing we can see. Rather, they are relational, purely intellectual, grasped by understanding. The equation $a^2 + b^2 = c^2$ looks nothing like a right triangle, yet the equation expresses the essence of a right triangle. Relationships constitute and express understanding.

Now, Chalmers (1996) is very uncomfortable with this scientific state of affairs—as is fully understandable: refined explanation often counters common sense and challenges assumptions in the everyday world. Famously, Galileo and early modern science confronted challenges repeatedly on this very matter. The sun is not moving, but the Earth. Metal and wood might be the same temperature, but the metal feels cooler than the wood. It is strange to think that the solid materials in our world would be mostly empty space, as physicists suggest. In computerese, Chalmers depicts the scientific account as a theory of "It from Bit": reality is "a world of pure information" (p. 303), a "pure causal flux." He accurately understands that "physical theory only characterizes its basic entities *relationally*. . . . The picture of the physical world that this yields is that of a giant causal flux" (p. 153). His discomfort is that he wants something more substantive.

> Many people still have great difficulty accepting that matter itself is ultimately insubstantial and that the world's appearance of solidity is more a reflection of how our sensory systems are constructed, and how brains do their work, than of anything else. (Donald, 2001, p. xi)

The sensate-modeled epistemology of common sense demands its satisfaction.

Thus, Chalmers (1996) thinks contemporary physics leads "to a strangely insubstantial view" (p. 153), "too lacking in substance to *be* a world" (p. 304). He misses "the very 'massiveness' of mass, for example" (p. 153). He wants something he could feel. A purely intellectual accounting of our world does not seem to treat reality. Supposedly, the real must be palpable in some way: reality is what is sensitively encountered, not what is correctly understood. Besides, also missing the point of implicit definition (2.2.4; 4.6.5)—as does, evidently, Bertrand Russell, whom Chalmers echoes on this point (pp. 153–154, 166, 305)—Chalmers believes this causal flux "tells us nothing about what all this causation *relates*. Reference to the proton is fixed as the thing that causes interactions of a certain kind, that combines in certain ways with other entities, and so on; but what is the thing that is doing the causing and combining?" (p. 153), he asks. Supposedly, "this view subtracted the world of all intrinsic qualities, leaving a world of causal relations, with nothing, it seems, to do the causing. . . . One might find this picture of the world without intrinsic nature not to be a picture of the world at all" (p. 304). However, when scientists propose the inherent qualities of things, they formulate the generalized intelligibility of things—which, of course, applies to this one and that one, to the one here and now or to the one there and then (4.18.3), so that "giant causal flux" does not lose the individuality of things (on the "empirical residue," see Lonergan, 1957/1992, pp. 50–55, 540). But when Chalmers asks about intrinsic qualities, he means perceptible characteristics. Chalmers's innocent but repeated use of the metaphor "picture" is itself revealing. It's as if he wants something he could see.

Chalmers wants the entities of physics to have some internal qualities, some intrinsic properties, and he objects that physicists "tell us nothing directly about what those properties might be" (p. 153). Puzzlingly, the elaborate specifications that physics gives about a proton, for example, are not enough. Seemingly relying on a sensate-modeled epistemology, searching underneath the explanations for something perceptible, he opines, "Intuitively, it is more reasonable to suppose that the basic entities that all this causation relates have some internal nature of their own, some *intrinsic* properties, so that the world has some substance to it" (p. 153). But by *intrinsic* or *substantial*, Chalmers means perceptually discerned, not reasonably concluded. He even ventures to suggest what those intrinsic properties might be: phenomenal properties (p. 154)—that is, properties that characterize our experience, for example, red or blue, firm or soft. In other words, said succinctly, the primordial properties of matter would be percepts. Or, if this claim is too much, "an alternative is that the relevant properties are protophenomenal properties" (p. 154). Namely, "every time a feature such as mass and charge is realized, there is an intrinsic property behind it: a phenomenal or protophenomenal property, or a *microphenomenal* property for short" (p. 305). These could in some way perhaps aggregate to explain how we experience, say, redness in the everyday world: "Microphenomenal properties add up to macrophenomenology" (p. 307). And yes, then, as somehow perceptual, as potential objects of awareness, supposedly all entities somehow also actually have consciousness, a necessary counterpart of awareness. (This claim is fatuous to me. I see no reason why every perceptible body must itself also be conscious.)

By positing these microphenomenal properties in the entities of physics, Chalmers now has bodies to relate in that causal flux, dots of matter that could be connected by causal lines, as it were—and all could be pictured. Moreover, by positing these microphenomenal properties in the entities of physics, he has also supposedly supplied a basis for our awareness of objects, namely, bits of perception that accumulate as we move up from subatomic particles to objects in our everyday world. We have perceptions because even quarks and lepton have diminutive percepts attached to them, and these microphenomenal qualities build up until we are able to experience them through sensation.

Chalmers is proposing a theory of consciousness under the name of ubiquitous percepts. His theory has turned theoretic science into a matter of sensations and perceptions; his theory reduces consciousness to perception. Or, more accurately, in the name of doing science, his theory has mixed science and common sense, theory and perception. Chalmers labors under a working notion of science that is at odds with itself, a science dependent on perception that vies against intelligence. He would reintroduce into theoretical physics the seeing and hearing, the touching and feeling, that characterize our living in the everyday world—where, at least, the world is "substantial," not mostly empty space. In the process, his science reverts to the outdated assumptions of early modern science: the hands-on enterprise of Galileo, the imaginable push-pull causality debunked by David Hume, the homogenous space and time in Isaac Newton's theory of planetary motion. But 20th-century relativity theory and quantum physics finally transcended the perceptual assumptions of early science, fixed contemporary science as an enterprise resting ultimately on intelligence, and proposes reasonable explanation as its account of reality.

Chalmers is using a sensate-modeled epistemology to determine the reality even of the invisible, imperceptible entities discovered by contemporary physics. He would insert perceptual contents back into the intellectual account of science. Routinely appealing to science and struggling to propose a "scientific" theory of consciousness, he would, nonetheless, make perception, not confirmed understanding, a criterion of reality. The insistence is that quarks and leptons and all those others must somehow be perceptible, "substantial," if they are to be real.

As intimated in the paragraph before last, this perception-driven view is closely linked to causality, and a particular understanding of causality is in question, namely, that of the perceptible tug-and-pull interaction of efficient causality in the everyday world. Whereas physicists are content—if they speculate about it at all—to understand causality as the relations of interdependence among the elements named in their equations (which is Aristotle's formal causality; 4.6.4), Chalmers wants causality to be more perceptible and to entail palpable bodies that encounter one another: causality is to be the push-pull among some kind of imaginable substantive properties, miniature lumps of stuff, microperceptibles, primordial bits of sensate contents, lying behind or within the physicists' equations. The problem is muddled epistemology. Two notions of knowing are vying for dominance.

These matters stretch far afield, and I address them in detail, especially in Chapters 4 and 5. Besides, although I present Chalmers's position to starkly make my point, in no way do I want to demean Chalmers or his work. His overall analysis is a brilliant and massive effort, an undeniable highpoint of today's thinking in the field of consciousness studies. I must note and regret, however, that his representative statements labor under a widespread confounded epistemology—or, more accurately, the confounding of two different epistemologies, namely, perceptual determinations in the realm of everyday living and intellectual determinations in the realm of theory. He is far from alone in the self-sabotaging intellectual struggle he engages. The point to be made at this stage is simply that, despite his rarified intellectual *tour de force* and his forthright insistence on the unique nature of consciousness in contrast to all things material, Chalmers also exemplifies an epistemology that identifies the real with the sensate: what is real is what is perceived, and consciousness is quintessentially the experience of percepts—redness, for example. Then, what is not perceptible could hardly be anything at all because one knows reality only through sensate encounter.

2.2.5. Two Kinds of Knowing: Sensate and Intellectual

To be sure, *sensate knowing* is a kind of "knowledge." The word can be used in that sense: I "know" the taste of an orange, I "know" the sound of a violin, I "know" the color *red*. Moreover, in its own right, such "knowledge" is correct. Animals live in a sensate, perceptual mode, and "animals are not mistaken; they survive beautifully. Insofar as men [and women] are guided by that attitude, the errors that arise are, on the whole, negligible" (Lonergan, 1980/1990, p. 107). Before learning language and entering the world mediated by meaning, infants live in a realm of sensate immediacy (Lonergan, 1972, p. 28). The infant's world is what lies before her or him in the nursery. The infant's world is determined as what can be seen, felt, heard, smelled, and chewed. The infant's world goes only that far, and it depends on immediate perception: out of sight, out of mind. For the infant, reality is the realm of immediate sensate experience. The striking story of Helen Keller offers an illuminative parallel case. It exemplifies the power of breaking out of the world of sensate immediacy and into an unlimited world of meaning (p. 70).

The human world mediated by meaning is most easily illustrated as the realm opened up by language, which can present the past and the future, the real and the imagined, the present and the absent. However, attention to language must be kept in perspective. The world we engage is mediated by meaning—not simply by language. Yet Ludwig Wittgenstein, Ferdinand de Saussure, Claude Levi-Strauss, the structuralists, and postmodern poststructuralists seem to be skating on the surface of words, never penetrating to the meaning that words embody and only intelligence grasps. These theorists hold that words find their meaning in their interrelationships within language, that the meaning of one word is another word, and so on in a circular tour through the dictionary. What they overlook is the intelligence that must be operative to grasp meaning, whether portrayed in language or, each in its own way, by other means such as art, ritual, gestures, shared feelings, or human interaction (pp. 57–99).

In fact, extraverted sense experience, taken as knowledge, works well enough for everyday living and for many technical problems, such as replacing the headlight in my car, baking a cake, building a simple bridge, or even designing that bridge. But such an account of knowledge is blatantly oversimplified. Preoccupied with the challenges of the physical world, that account takes for granted the human intelligence and meaning that are also involved in solving those everyday problems. The same applies to determining if it's raining by taking a look. The solutions in these cases are not just a matter of encountering and manipulating physical materials. To solve those problems, we need to understand what the things are, how they function, and what we must do to successfully manipulate them. We have to understand, for example, what the term *rain* means or understand the spring mechanism that holds the auto headlight bulb in place. But we usually overlook the intelligence behind our everyday activities. Taken up so much by the demands of living—and, unfortunately of late, schooled to parrot back information and to believe this ability to repeat constitutes knowing—we easily think we are operating on the basis of mere perception and physical engagement.

Even more to the point, such sensate knowing and its accompanying theory of knowledge are absolutely inadequate for the subtleties of psychology, philosophy, and theology because their objects are not perceptible. These topics must rely, not on sensate knowing, but on *intellectual knowing*, acknowledged and explicated as such. Indeed, even contemporary physicists are well aware that what they know about physical matter—such as quarks and leptons and four-dimensional space-time—is neither perceptible nor imaginable. It is completely beyond sensate experience. They do not encounter these physical realities, as such. Knowledge of them does not consist in revelatory contact via perception or intuition. Rather, this knowledge consists of reasonable (i.e., evidence-based) judgments regarding intelligent accounts of the available perceptual data. The object of this knowledge is conclusions that must be affirmed if one will reasonably account for the evidence; the reality in question is what can be thus affirmed. It is what Chalmers uncomfortably calls "a world of pure information" or a "pure causal flux."

Nonetheless, we humans are peculiarly polymorphous beings—material as well as organic, animal as well as human, sensate as well as intelligent. Moreover, we are already habitually functioning animals long before we develop disciplined critical rationality (Lonergan, 1972, pp. 28–29). No wonder that we are often hard pressed to give untrammeled reign to "the detached, disinterested, and unrestricted," "the pure desire to know" (2.1.6). We easily fall back into a less distinctively human way of knowing and of thinking about knowing. Thus, we confound our scholarship and debilitate our science; with picture-thinking we mistake the sensate immediacy of perception and imagination for human intelligence and knowledge.

Roughly summarized, Lonergan's core contribution in this regard is to sort out the difference between an epistemology based on sensate metaphors—knowing is like taking a good look—and an epistemology based on understanding and judgment. The task is

> to account for the confusion, so natural to man [and woman], between extroversion and objectivity. For man observes, understands, and judges, but he fancies that what he knows in judgment is not known in judgment and does not suppose an

> exercise of understanding but simply is attained by taking a good look at the "real" that is "already out there now." (Lonergan, 1957/1992, p. 437)

> Cartesian dualism had been a twofold realism, and both the realisms were correct; for the realism of the extraverted animal is no mistake, and the realism of rational affirmation is no mistake. The trouble was that, unless two distinct and disparate types of knowing were recognized, the two realisms were incompatible. . . . The attempt to fuse disparate forms of knowing into a single whole ended in the destruction of each by the other; and the destruction of both forms implied the rejection of both types of realism. (p. 439)

The history of philosophy can be sifted through a sieve of these two epistemological stances (pp. 388–398, 426–455), so what Lonergan has incisively explained is the reason for the current collapse of all certainty about the validity of human knowing.

2.2.6. A Brief History of Western Epistemology

The epistemological crisis in the West erupted with the Protestant Reformation in the 16th century. Until then, divine revelation and religious belief, buttressed by reason, were accepted as a reliable source of truth, but this source split into conflicting Catholic and Protestant versions. The concomitant emergence of modern science intensified the crisis by providing still another source of truth alongside the already fragmented religious source. The crisis became full-blown in the 17th and 18th centuries when philosophers formulated these inconsistencies explicitly and undeniably. However, at least science still provided a promise of valid knowledge.

For a couple of centuries, then, disregarding the religious differences and putting their faith in modern science, people believed we were on a path toward absolute and definitive knowledge. Yet, with the development of non-Euclidean geometry, symbolic logic, probability theory and statistical method, and evolutionary theory in the mid- to late 19th century and, in the beginning of the 20th century, with the shift from classical physics to relativity theory and quantum mechanics, the epistemological crisis surged anew and more intensely than ever. These scientific advances discredited the supposed absolutes of perceptual experience as a valid explanation of even physical matter. Whereas the stunning synthesis of Isaac Newton's explanation of gravity and planetary motion had assumed a homogenous space and time, Albert Einstein argued convincingly that the continuum of space–time is simply not so. Not even the distances of space or the intervals of time can be taken as absolutes. Is there no constancy anywhere?!

Today, with the emergence of instantaneous mass communication and the burgeoning global community, the crisis has become universal. We are relentlessly confronted, every woman and man on the street, with conflicting opinions. We cannot avoid the disorienting fact that we share no consensus whatever on what is true or false and right or wrong, and we know no way of achieving consensus.

An early key element in this crisis is the distinction between the so-called primary and secondary qualities of things. Galileo Galilei introduced this distinction, and others, such as John Locke and Isaac Newton, accepted it. This distinction supposed that certain perceptual qualities, such as extension in space and duration in time, are inherent in things themselves. Other qualities, secondary in status—such as color, taste, or smell—were recognized to be dependent on our sensation and were thought not to be inherent in the things themselves. The object of scientific explanation was those supposed primary qualities of things. But this distinction lives off of the sensate metaphor of knowledge as a kind of sight and the supposition that reality is the object of perception. As it turns out, even extension in space and duration in time are not inherent physical qualities.

2.2.7. Kant's Solution and its Problem

Toward the end of the 18th century, Immanuel Kant realized a mistake in that metaphor of knowing as seeing, but he was not able to fully correct it. He recognized that the knowing human subject has input into the knowledge of objects, and to account for that subjective input, he posited forms and categories in the human mind, such as space and time, and substance and causality. He argued that these unavoidably structure any experience, determining the specific form that any knowledge of objects can take. We are made to experience a world of things, "substances," that appear to us as "spatial" and "temporal" and as related via "causality." These characteristics are unavoidable; they are part of the built-in structures of human knowing and are not in reality itself. As human, supposedly, we can have nothing more. We inevitably and unavoidably "filter" and "configure" whatever we know. The result, for better or worse, is unapologetically and unavoidably the inherent limit of human knowing.

From those assumptions, Kant's necessary conclusion was that we cannot know things in themselves but only things as we experience them in conformity with the filtering structure of our minds. In Kant's terms, we cannot know the *noumena*, only the *phenomena*; we cannot know the *Ding an sich*, the thing in itself. We cannot know reality—or, to nuance the point: what we might call reality is only the ideas we have, and there is an unbridgeable disconnect between the ideas with which we live and reality in itself. This tack of Kant's obviously leads to another cul de sac: idealism. It locates reality in the human mind and its subjective ideas, not in an objective realm, the universe of being. It supposes that our human reality comprises the *ideas* with which we live, the world we make up for ourselves—hence, the name *idealism* (in this usage, the term has nothing to do with ideals: high standards or lofty goals). *The Matrix* movies have happily supplied us with a fully accessible portrayal of how true idealism would function. Of course, that to some extent we all live "in our own worlds" is an undeniable fact, but this fact provokes the question about the validity of the ideas that make up "our own world." They might well be only illusions. We might well be living in a fabricated fantasy. Indeed, to some extent we all do although science and all evidence-based critical thinking—indeed, also life experience itself—move us toward objective reality, being, and overturn our merely personal constructions.

Then, can we never know reality as it actually is in itself? Kant's well-reasoned and discomforting answer had to be No: we know only our experiences of things, not things in themselves. This notion, resting ultimately on a sensate-modeled notion of reality, grounds much contemporary philosophy of science, and it explains why Chalmers would want something "more substantial" underneath the equations of physics. Yet, in the face of conflict between science and religion, Kant and his era welcomed this outcome. Cogently, it granted the science of the day—Robert Boyle, Isaac Newton, Christian Huygens, Anton van Leeuwenhoek, Carl Linnaeus, Joseph Priestley, Antoine Lavoisier—a secure, though qualified, validity; and it left the realm of religious faith unassailable in the face of science. Science could explain our world of experience, but only religion could portray the truth about ultimate reality in itself, so both science and religion were content.

2.2.8. Idealism: Halfway From Materialism to Critical Realism

As history unfolded from that point, the only assurance we seem to have is consensual agreement about what is "real," so cultural preference, religious affiliation, and political hegemony have become the measures of claimed truth and falsehood and, similarly, of touted right and wrong in our day (see McCarthy, 1990). As philosopher Lawrence Cahoone (2010) reports, for example, "The most famous American contributor to postmodernist philosophy, [Richard] Rorty argued that . . . knowledge is simply whatever the verification procedures of a society say it is" (p. 85). The current prevalence of religious fundamentalism supplies the full-blown, blatant, popular example (Armstrong, 2000). We are left with the dizzying pluralism of the postmodern world of the 3rd millennium, and we share no agreed-upon way of determining which opinions are actually correct and which, mere illusion. Supposedly, we can only know our own ideas about reality, not the universe of being for what it is in itself—if such a thing even exists, if the notion of objective reality makes any sense at all.

To the good, idealism at least recognizes the role of the knower in all knowing. There is no doubt that we know via the ideas we have in our minds. To recognize and name this aspect of human knowing was a major achievement; it was millennia in coming. Moreover, pursuing Kant's "turn toward the subject," Hegel impressively elaborated far-reaching implications of the mind's processes and dynamism. But to its detriment, idealism retains the unspoken presupposition that actual reality is that array of stuff we perceive lying out there before us. Idealism maintains the unspoken assumption that things truly are the physical bodies that we encounter through sensate and perceptual experience, but idealism is explicitly aware that we can encounter them only through the particular structures of our human perception and reason. So idealism must hold that, because of our unavoidable subjectivity, we cannot ever really know reality in itself; we cannot get from our ideas about them to the bodies themselves out there.

Paradoxically, although it makes some advance in the understanding of human knowing, idealism still covertly bows to the perceptual model of knowing: its unspoken presupposition is that the real is the perceptible and that knowing is something like seeing or encountering or confronting. As such, idealism is a mixed bag. It is an incoherent theory. It is a halfway house between thorough-going materialism or sensible empiricism, on the one hand, and the goal to be achieved, a coherent critical realism, on the other. Husserl's and Heidegger's contribution of phenomenological method provided no better solution to the problem of knowledge because as its object it took "experience" (5.6.3), understood in the global, not Lonergan's technical, sense (2.2.1). Thus, despite its insistence that experience is always a subjective matter, phenomenology still approached this experience as a kind of encounter or confrontation: intentionality, a subject–object interaction. Scientific description in phenomenology still presumes that knowing is like looking; it is one undifferentiated operation that engages us in a world of personal experience.

2.2.9. Lonergan's Solution to Kant's Problem

Many believe that Lonergan solved the Kantian problem of knowing the thing in itself. One could say that he did so by moving beyond that halfway house of idealism and following Kant's emphasis on the human subject to its natural conclusion: critical realism. For Lonergan, the upshot is that knowledge is the product of human judgment—not of human understanding or creative conceptual interpretation alone nor, far less, of simple human sensate experience. The judgment assesses the understanding in light of the data of experience. As with idealism, then, it remains that knowing is massively and inextricably entwined with human subjectivity; knowing is the doing of our own minds. It is, indeed, a subjective process—not, however, in the sense of being necessarily biased, but in the sense that knowing is inescapably an activity of a human subject. But Lonergan's account of knowing retains realism. Lonergan avoids the relativism inherent in Kantian idealism because what we know is not simply ideas in our minds. Rather, we know reality *by means of* the ideas in our minds; and correct judgment, the affirmation of those ideas, bespeaks the reality as known in itself.

We know reality, and we know it as it is in itself because, in contrast to Kant's, in Lonergan's account no mental categories predetermine the ideas in the mind and force the data to conform to human mental patterns. Intelligence grasps what is there to be understood. If it did not, intelligence would not be very intelligent! Despite the wide range of our imaginative powers, when engaging the real world, our ideas are not free to be whatever we might like or however we would suppose. The data of experience provide the raw material for our insights; therefore, the data limit the possibilities of our understanding and constrain the interpretations we could generate. Additionally, judgment comes into play as the discerning arbiter. Judgment determines whether our proposed understanding actually squares with the data, whether our interpretation validly accounts for the experiential input, whether we have truly grasped the intelligibility inherent in the given, and whether our ideas express it. When judgment pronounces, we have knowledge: Yes, it is so; or No, it is not so. What judgment pronounces on is the understanding we have of the given; judgment confirms or disconfirms the validity of what we are proposing. Then we know what is there to be known; we know reality. This account is a critical realism—an explanation of how we actually can know reality in itself (realism), but only through a complex and nuanced process (critical).

As for the reality known by this process, it turns out *not* to be physical bodies, stuff lying "out there," waiting to be stumbled upon, or gripping feelings or images or intuitions lurking "in here," forcing themselves upon us, as we tend to think. Neither could reality be only a subjective construct of ideas in the mind because both the constraints of data and the assessment of judgment restrict which ideas could be valid. Rather, reality is being, that which actually exists, that which can be correctly affirmed. Being is the object of our knowledge; being is the natural and spontaneous goal of human knowing. Being is what we know when we actually achieve knowledge through intelligence and judgment, not simply through perception. Thus, being and knowing are correlates, opposite sides of the same coin. Accordingly, being, or reality, is inherently constituted by meaning—and not necessarily in every case by perceptible qualities. Some kinds of being are perceptible, but not all are. Body and mind offer the most salient examples. This emphasis once and for all rejects the pervasive, unspoken supposition that reality could only be material bodies and that they are lying out there waiting to be encountered. This emphasis also allows, with postmodern awareness, that human reality is constituted by meaning. However, this nuanced emphasis avoids the postmodern relativism and agnosticism that usually accompany that insistence on meaning. With this emphasis, reality is actually the object of reasonable judgments. The real is what is correctly affirmed, and we know by judging suppositions against the evidence—not by merely experiencing, encountering, perceiving, or intuiting.

Therefore, strikingly, peculiarly, astoundingly, most provocatively—it is hard to convey the impact of this realization against which even the brilliant David Chalmers struggles—the universe and its reality is a realm of meaning, not a landscape of physical bodies and "microphenomenal properties" (Chalmers, 1996, p. 305). Through and through, reality is meaningful: literally, intelligibility constitutes it in part. In some sense and to some extent, this account of knowing is, indeed, a theory of "It from Bit," and it does project "a world of pure information" (p. 303). The realities we know—including plains and mountains, plants and organisms, emotions, memories, images, minds, insights, thoughts, and values—are only sometimes perceptible bodies. Not all that can be correctly affirmed is material and palpable. On the self-same criterion of reasonable judgment about an understanding of experienced data, the mental can be deemed as real as the physical. Consciousness can be deemed as real as the brain. The spiritual can be deemed as real as the material. Indeed, overall, meaning—not materiality—is the distinctive characteristic of human reality and the universe we humans share. Ours is a world "mediated by meaning and motivated by value" (Lonergan, 1972, p. 265). Then, objectivity in knowing is not a matter of grappling with bodies lying "out there" in the material world or images and feelings encountered "in here" in the mental world. Neither is objectivity a matter *per impossibile* of somehow eliminating all subjective input from human knowledge. Rather, "objectivity is simply the consequence of authentic subjectivity, of genuine attention, genuine intelligence, genuine reasonableness, genuine responsibility" (p. 265).

At this point, Lonergan's epistemology validates something of the postmodern realization that human reality is a social construction. We have input into what we take to be the human world. To a large extent, we create our reality. Our knowledge includes insight and judgment in addition to data. Our knowledge is a human construction, which parallels the structure of being (4.17.2). However, Lonergan's epistemology represents a moderate postmodernism, not the radical brand that is caught up in inextricable cultural relativism and personal agnosticism and in religious and political hegemony. His epistemology includes criteria for sorting out reasonable social constructions from merely fanciful, preferred, power-mongering, entitling, inherited, or untenable ones. Knowledge is both constrained by the data and confirmed by a judgment. Knowledge is not free to be whatever one likes, feels, prefers, or has been taught to accept. Knowledge accords with being.

2.2.10. Summary About Experience

But I get ahead of myself. I anticipate the end of the story although this section focuses only on its first element: experience.

Some theories of knowledge stop at this first element. They bottle up the complex process of knowing in one undifferentiated operation: experience. They assume that we know simply by looking—or touching, hearing, smelling, tasting, feeling, or intuiting; and they assume that what we encounter and "know" in this way is actually objective reality. In such a theory of knowledge, reality is what is lying out there or in here, whole hog, ready-made, available to be observed, discovered, encountered, uncovered, tripped over; and in no way is human reality a construction. A narrative of looking and finding, a story of seeking and discovering, a legend of hunting down quarry in the woods unconfessedly controls the heart of this sensate model of knowing. But appeal to mere experience, whether external or internal, allows for no explanation of things. Indeed, sensate knowing needs no explanation; it wants none. For sensation and perception, there they are: things are just givens. What you see is what you see. This fact is clear in the case of non-human animals. They poke, sniff, taste, and chew to "know" the "realities" in their "world." Their world is a given; they take it as it is; they have no option. They subsist in a mere habitat. Something of the same also applies to human sensation–modeled theories of knowing. Their emphasis on perception overlooks the intelligence that is inevitably working "behind the scenes" when people think they know just by taking a good look or just by grappling with a thing. Intelligence is the "secret ingredient" in the recipe for human knowing, and most theorists are oblivious to it. Yet, as a way of knowing, appeal to mere experience is a scientific dead-end. It ignores the intelligence that so strikingly characterizes science and all human knowledge.

2.3. The Intellectual Level of Knowing: Understanding

According to Lonergan's theory, in addition to experience there is a second element in human knowledge: understanding. We gain insight into the given. To the data, understanding adds interpretation—hunches, suppositions, ideas, thoughts, hypotheses.

2.3.1. The Occurrence and Effect of Insight

Repeatedly and routinely we achieve acts of understanding—insights—but we seldom attend to them as such. We are too busy with the practicalities of life; these have an urgency that eclipses our ubiquitous acts of understanding. Still, sometimes we do recognize a particularly clever idea, and we congratulate ourselves on the insight. A conspicuous example is the puzzle or riddle with which one struggles for hours, days, perhaps months or even years. Then, suddenly insight occurs, and in one's mind all the pieces fall together, and the solution is lucidly obvious. How could one have ever missed it?!

Yet the result is more than what lay there prior to the insight. With understanding, all is changed. Intelligence has added insight to the potential intelligibility of the data. In the "light" of intelligence, these givens became intelligible and then were even actually understood. The understood now includes more than the mere perceptual data. Insight discerns patterns, order, coherence, interrelationship, systematization, explanation where earlier none was available. Intelligence grasps a new whole, an integrated unity, some one thing where earlier there lay only a random array of elements, clues, somehow-related parts. Understanding makes an addition to the data. This addition is coherence, interrelationship, unity, explanation, and it is the primordial referent of the axiom, "The whole is greater than the sum of its parts." When humans are involved, the whole is always an intelligible conglomerate.

With understanding, the knowing process has moved to a new level. Meaning now permeates the scene. And if the understood is something sensible, perceptual, merely physical, the process has moved one into a new realm. The world of meaning is not the world of palpability.

2.3.2. The Meaning of Meaning

Let me clarify my use of the term *meaning* and, in the process, help clarify the focus of this discussion. By *meaning* I mean intelligibility, the understanding or sense that one could find in a thing: what is there to be understood. In this usage, because of the epistemological emphasis in this book, I limit *meaning* to its cognitive sense, its first sense as listed in *Merriam-Webster's Collegiate Dictionary* (11th edition): "the thing one intends to convey esp. by language." I do not intend the more popular but alternative—and still, even philosophically, legitimate (Lonergan, 1957/1990, pp. 96–99; 1972, pp. 57–85)—meaning of *meaning*, namely, significance or import, wherein the "meaningful" is what matters to you, me, or someone else.

The popular usage dominates contemporary psychological circles—as if, pragmatically, psychology did not include objective research but meant only psychotherapy—and this fact evinces the confused and undifferentiated state of the field as an attempted human science. In psychology, talk of the human propensity for "meaning making" has become commonplace. It refers to the personal quest for purpose in life, so it mixes cognitive meaning with personal significance—that is, with relevance, interest, and individual or social concern (e.g., Park, 2005; see Helminiak, 2013a). This usage is inattentive to the differences among emotions, ideas, values, and decisions and lumps them all together. Even in supposedly technical psychology, then, *meaning* usually functions as an umbrella term.

The popular usage is built on the pragmatic relationship of things to ourselves: "What does it matter to me? What difference does it make [to us]? Well, then, what does this *mean*?" Plans within a short-term purview and concern to get things done cannot but include a swirl of practical considerations and existential preoccupations. This pragmatic attitude defines what Lonergan (1957/1992) calls "common sense"—in contrast to theory (pp. 196–269), whose long-term focus is eventual accurate explanation. In this usage—which I will invoke throughout this book—the term *common sense* does not carry its popular meaning: be smart, don't be dumb, have some basic intelligence, "use your common sense." Rather, in this usage, common sense is the kind of understanding appropriate for getting along in the everyday world. Accordingly, this one and the same generic kind of understanding, common sense, tends to express itself variably and then characterizes and even defines different cultures and subcultures. In those different instances, "common sense" names the shared understandings and values that various groups hold and that structure the consensual worlds in which these various groups live. When in Rome, to do as the Romans do is to follow the common sense of the Romans—that is, to function according to their mores and practices, to accept their worldview, to share their guiding concerns, to respect their ways of doing things, and, thus, to get along successfully in the world of everyday living. A shared common sense is a shared collective meaning about life and living. Its short-term purview is its impact on us, and its goal is to get things done. So in its popular or commonsense sense, *meaning* is of this kind, whether collective or individual; it refers to the global significance that things hold for us—what they "mean."

A similar understanding lies behind philosophical pragmatism, so I add this long paragraph simply to flag this issue. On my reading, pragmatism tends to presume a commonsensical or naïve realist epistemology. That is, it tacitly assumes that reality is material bodies lying about out there in the world; it focuses on a push-pull interaction among them; and it is concerned about getting things done effectively and efficiently. The controlling commitment of pragmatism is commonsensical, not theoretical, in Lonergan's sense of these terms. As noted at 2.2.5, such a commonsensical approach, such reliance on a sensate-modeled epistemology, works well enough for most matters of survival and living—checking for rain, replacing a headlamp, baking a cake, building a simple bridge. Because such an approach is sufficient insofar as (but only insofar as) our world is partially material, pragmatism emerged as the most promising philosophy by the end of the 20th century (Cahoone, 2010, lecture 34). Its criterion of effectiveness—as William James popularized and oversimplified it, "true means what works" (lecture 17, track 6)—is actually an expression of the reliance on data and the insistence on evidence that condition human knowing on its first level. So in its limited way, pragmatism embodies a viable epistemology; hence, its appeal. However, its attention to concrete results limits what genuine knowing means. Indeed, not knowing, but doing, is its controlling interest—even as Charles Peirce initially formulated the matter, canonizing that popular usage of *meaning:* " 'The meaning of a term is its role in the guidance of conduct' " (lecture 17, track 4). Yet the fact is that human doing cannot proceed effectively without human knowing, so the pragmatist attempt to avoid a foundational account of accurate human knowing (see 1.4) is but a stopgap measure. Ultimately, it is not realistically sufficient or, perforce, humanly satisfying. Incoherence is inevitable in the application of pragmatism because actually intelligence and understanding, not merely behavior in a material world, must also be involved to guide human activity. To allow a space probe to successfully reach far distant Jupiter and Saturn, for example, required the precision of Einstein's relativity theory. It surpasses Newtonian notions of homogenous space and time that apply well enough in the everyday world of perceptions. Fully abstract relativity theory expresses an understanding that is in no way even imaginable. Yet without its precision, the probes would never have reached their targets. Pure understanding, not mere practicality, was an imperative; and between the two, understanding held priority. Of course, since the probes did reach Jupiter and Saturn, one could insist that pragmatism's criterion of effectiveness still held firm, but the effectiveness was subordinate to the knowing. The effectiveness in this case required a kind of knowing that the principles of pragmatism cannot support *per se*. So to sustain its criterion of effectiveness, pragmatism must smuggle into its account a kind of knowing that its defining conception does not address. This case and many commonplace others—such as lasers, optical switches, electron beams on TV screens, medical assay tests, genetically modified plants, cloned animals—depend on highly nuanced physical, chemical, and biological science, whose guiding principle is theoretical understanding, not experienced activity in the everyday world. Of course, again, one could point out that knowing is a kind of doing; knowing is an activity geared toward assessable goals. Yet, when the doing of knowing is defined by intricate entanglement with practical outcomes in the spatiotemporal world, it appears that the distinctive nature of intellectual knowing is confounded with sensate-modeled knowing. Thus, in pragmatism two different kinds of knowing indiscriminately intermingle, and two notions of science are at silent war with each other. Unwittingly specifying the combatants and attempting to mediate the conflict, pragmatic philosopher Joseph Margolis (2010) proposed that the knowledge claims of true or false in mathematics and the natural sciences differ from knowledge claims in the human domain where intermediate categories such as apt, reasonable, appropriate, or valid often necessarily dilute the stark bifurcation between true and false (Cahoone, 2010, lecture 34, tracks 10, 11)—leaving us in a highly rationalized, "schizophrenic" postmodern world. In the human domain, the difference between the multiplicity of valid and complementary perspectives and the uniqueness of objective reality needs only to be sorted out so that *true* and *false* can pertain there, too (Lonergan, 1972, pp. 214–220). This same situation of science at war with itself also holds for the pragmatism-related functionalism that pervades current consciousness studies (4.12.4; 4.19.2; 4.21.6). However, in the case of functionalism in consciousness studies, when the topic is the non-material mind rather than the physical challenge of a space probe or the successful cloning of a sheep, the inadequacy of these commonsensical positions comes unavoidably to the fore.

This point about pragmatism can be made otherwise to fit the present context: the *meaning* at stake in pragmatism conflates and confounds the *meaning* of pure understanding or explanation and the *meaning* of significance or import in everyday living. I want to distinguish them. My use of the term *meaning* aims ultimately toward science-like clarity and precision, so the term must refer to one thing and only one thing within a complex of other interrelated terms. In focus is a cognitive matter—pure explanation, theoretical science and its rarified ideal of knowledge for knowledge's sake. My usage in this book is not that of applied science and everyday living wherein the personal significance and pragmatic urgency of common sense—the desire to get things done and to move on to other satisfying activities—tend to outweigh the long-term and ongoing theoretical commitment that characterizes theoretical science.

Hence, as I use the term in this book, *meaning* means intelligibility; it indicates solely a cognitive matter. Nothing is lost in thus limiting the meaning of *meaning* because other terms—such a significance, relevance, ego-investment, personal concern, purpose, evaluation—easily name those other aspects of "meaningfulness." Besides, my presentation gains precision when, for the purpose of my overall argument, I limit and specify meaning or intelligibility as the specific object of intellectual consciousness on its second level in contrast to conscious acts on the first, third, and fourth levels.

2.3.3. *The Unitive Nature of Insight*

Understanding names the functioning of consciousness on its second level. Understanding entails intellectual insight—having a hunch, getting an idea, sensing an intuition, proposing an explanation, suggesting a hypothesis, supposedly figuring something out. Understanding refers to the act of grasping some intelligibility in the data. To the data of experience, understanding adds meaning, intellectual content. To the *intelligibility*—the possibility of being understood—within the data, understanding adds intelligence. Then potentiality is actualized, the intelligible is understood.

However, like experience on the first level and even when added to experience, *understanding* is not yet knowing—because it might be wrong.

Still, attention to understanding moves us a step further along in our analysis of knowing.

Already it might be clear that human intellectual knowing entails identity, not confrontation, with the known. Insight is a unitive occurrence; intelligence grasps intelligibility and makes it one's own. The essence of insight on the second level of consciousness is to discern relationships—order, coherence, system—and the relationships that insight discerns are precisely those within the data. In no way, then, is understanding distant from what it understands. In insight, the understanding and the understood—namely, the intelligibility at stake—are one and the same.

In contrast—this point is pivotal—perception is confrontational. Its essence is to experience only sensible qualities provoked by physical energies: light, sound, heat, pressure, ambient particles. Although sensible qualities might describe a thing, they do not constitute it. The essence of a thing lies in the relationships that are inherent in it and that make it what it is. A heart is a heart, for example, not because of its "substantive" qualities (Chalmers, 1996, pp. 153, 304): darkish color, bulging arteries, and pulsating surface, but because of its intelligibility: its structure, its regularity, the nature of its muscle tissue, and its function within the circulatory system. A particular intelligibility, not perceptual qualities, makes a heart a heart. Hence, an artificial heart is a heart although it does not look or feel or sound like a natural heart.

With attention to insight—here's the payoff of that pivotal point—the "problem of the bridge" from subject to object is already overcome; it is averted. This problem depends on the metaphor of knowing as taking a look. Looking—or touching, hearing, tasting, smelling, imagining—insurmountably sets the subject against the object: I, here, see it, there. But knowing dependent on insight incurs no such distance or problem. In insight, the intelligence of the subject and the intelligibility of the data unite so that the understanding in the mind is nothing other than an understanding of the understood. In the technical terms of Aristotelian and Thomist philosophy, the intelligibility of the understood "informs"—or shares its "form" with (4.6.4)—the intelligence even as the intelligence "actualizes" the intelligibility of the understood. What intelligence grasps is the intelligibility within the data, so what the subject eventually knows is precisely that to which the data and their intelligibility pertain, namely, the known object.

Images and metaphors—such as "levels" of consciousness—help understanding. But in the present case, picturing or imagining two bodies coming together and eventually touching, "uniting," "becoming one," hardly models the identity inherent in the act of understanding. This intellectual event is, precisely, *not* sensate or perceptual. Ultimately, it cannot be pictured, graphed, or modeled. Rather, dear reader, you must grasp the nature of insight in your own experience of it: *understanding* understanding requires attention to an instance of the actual phenomenon of understanding—Lonergan's "self-appropriation" (2.1.1; 5.6.3). Alternatively, as a preliminary step, you could ponder these paragraphs and conclude, at least logically, that, if the intelligibility within the data and the intelligibility grasped by intelligence are one and the same, then an identity must have occurred. In this identity—unlike in perceptual experience—there is no this-against-that or subject-versus-object, but a unity of "understander" and understood.

Legitimately, however, you might wonder or even protest, "What mystification is operating here?! What is this proposed identity?" For a satisfying answer—there is no other, in the final analysis—you could notice your own questioning. You are, in fact, questioning, protesting, pondering this matter. You could own your spontaneous insistence that this and every other thing make sense. You could wonder about your own intelligence as you attend to its functioning. You might then catch yourself in a moment of insight (5.3.6) and consider what just happened. You could realize that the understanding in your mind is the very understanding that pertains to what you just understood. If not, did you really understand it? Thus, in your own experience you could recognize the identity in question.

In the most hoped-for example, dear reader, you could perhaps grasp what I am arguing here. You could understand the data I am laying out before your eyes. And if you did, the understanding in your mind would be the understanding I am expressing in my words. You would have understood me. Remarkably, then, the understanding in my words and in your mind would equally be the understanding I hold in my mind. On the basis of a concrete instance—empirically—we would be correct to say we transcended space and time and bridged personal, cultural, and perhaps even philosophical differences. We would now share one and the same understanding about the intellectual apparatus that, as fellow humans, we must, then, also share.

The intellect and the understood coincide in the understanding. In the words of the Scholastic axiom, *Intellectus in actu fit intellectum in actu*: In the moment of actual understanding, the intellect becomes the understood (Thomas Aquinas, 1961 version, 1a, q. 55, a. 1, ad 2 and q. 87, a. 1, ad 3. See also 1a, q. 14, a. 2, c and q. 85, a. 2, ad 1). The ambiguity in this statement is deliberate. Informed by its object, the intellect takes on, and into itself, the essential determinatives of the other that is to be understood. The intellect brings the other into the realm of intelligence, conforming itself to the other. In its peculiar intellectual mode, the intellect becomes the other that is to be understood. Then the intellect itself becomes the object of its own understanding. In being one with itself, fully present "to" itself (5.3), the intellect grasps in itself the intelligibility of the object that currently concerns it. By understanding itself precisely insofar as the very intelligibility of the object informs it, actuates it—that is, engages, "turns on," activates it—the intellect understands the object. Herein is a precise example of the "non-duality" (see also 5.8.3) that becomes the obfuscating topic of so much current "spiritual" discussion.

A suggestive sensate analogy would be the brightness of stage lights that takes on the color of the filters through which it passes to become itself red, blue, or green. The brightness of the light illuminates the darkness of the filter, and the color of both is one and the same because to be able to take on colored brightness is the nature of light. In a similar way, such is also the nature of radiant intelligence, informed by the intelligibility it grasps and, thus, illuminating that particular intelligibility in its own brightness of actual understanding. This process stands in stark contrast to the opposition of a material agent against a material object in an act of perception.

This notion of the identity of the understanding and the understood makes sense if one considers that what is understood in the understanding is precisely that which is understood, namely, the object of understanding. If such were not the case, the understanding would not be an understanding of the object understood. The point of identity is the intelligibility that is shared, the intelligibility that is, indeed, one and the same in the understood and in the understanding. This peculiarity cannot be further explained, I believe, except to note that it expresses the precise nature of the intellect. It is of a different kind in comparison with material and corporeal realities. It is not bounded by the limitations of spatial and temporal separations or contiguity. To appeal to such primordial peculiarity seems justified in that the appeal does seem to account for the functioning of the intellect whereas other accounts incur inherent inadequacies (4.20 & 4.21; 5.3.6).

Explicitly rejecting this account in an early formulation (Helminiak, 1984), Natsoulas (1986) reported my words but missed my point. He did not recognize that this position is originally Aristotle's, although Natsoulas (1983, p. 439) recounted Aristotle's position elsewhere without criticism, but not without perplexity. This account is a pure application of Aristotle's theory of potentiality and actuality (potency and act). By way of illustration, the point comes through rather easily in a consideration of sensation, which, more than intelligence, is imaginable. The senses are geared to specific input—for example, sight is geared to the visible or, for Aristotle, to color. But to call something visible already implies a relationship to sight, and in fact, in actuality, the one is not had without the other. Both are merely potential without each other. Only through a seeing does a color become actual, namely, seen. Of course, our current understanding could elaborate the matter in terms of electromagnetic waves and even detect them mechanically, so it could be said that the color—or, at least, the appropriate electromagnetic phenomenon—is there apart from any actual eye. But the question at hand regards human experience, and it was Aristotle's question, too. In this arena, his analysis does hold up. Actual color depends on actual seeing, and the one and the other coincide. The color is both the actually seen and the seeing of the color. Similarly, the feeling of hardness in a rock is in the hand that feels it. Apart from the feeling hand, the feeling of hardness is but potential. To be actually hard, the rock must be actually being felt. The hardness and the feeling of hardness, as far as a human experience is concerned, are one and the same. Appropriating this incisive Aristotelian understanding, the medievals could express it in a statement parallel to the above statement about the intellect: *Sensus in actu est sensum in actu*: In the moment of actual feeling, the sense is the sensed. The senses take on the character of what they sense, and in this way they sense the sensed, not something else.

Application of the theory of potency and act to the case of understanding requires only an apposite change in the object of experience and the experiencing "faculty." In this case, intellect and intelligibility are in question, and the suggestion is the following: the intelligibility's being actually grasped rests in the intellect's actually grasping it; the intelligibility is not actual until it is understood. The understanding in the object and in the intellect are sides of the same coin, as it were. But this metaphor, more appropriate to sensation, is risky because sides of a coin are actually different and separate, but the actually grasped intelligibility is only one, the same in both the understood and the understanding. The actuality of both depends on only one actuation, an act of understanding, which makes both the understood actually understood and the understanding actually understanding. And if not, the object is not actually understood; that is, that which is there in the object to be understood would not be actually grasped by the intellect. Accurately summarizing Aristotle's opinion with reference to consciousness, but calling it awareness (see 1.9), Natsoulas (1983) phrased it this way: "His key tactic seems to have been to identify the content of awareness with the awareness, and then to suggest that awareness of an awareness is the same as the awareness, namely, awareness of its content" (p. 439).

To grasp the nature of insight is the highest hurdle in understanding Lonergan's theory of knowledge. Why so? Because to grasp the nature of insight is to recognize a dimension of human experience beyond the merely perceptual. To experience insight is to quintessentially engage the consciousness or spiritual dimension of the mind, which becomes the subtle topics of Chapters 4 and 5. The challenge is to understand understanding—that is,

- to realize how one's mind grasps relationships and, thus, generates meaning and,
- granted that neither meaning nor relationships are perceptible, in the process to also recognize a conscious, a spiritual, mental activity.

Moreover, attention to the unitive nature of intelligence already suggests a non-theological understanding of the unitive or "non-dual" experience called "mysticism" (5.8.3).

2.3.4. *The Intelligible Nature of Being*

Attention to insight already suggests that human intellectual knowing entails identity, not confrontation, with the known. Next, attention to insight already also makes clear that the content of human knowing is beyond the merely material. Even granted that the data in question might pertain to a material thing, the addition of intelligence to sense data carries the knowing to a new level. The human known is not in the field of experiential data, some "already out there now" given (Lonergan, 1957/1992, p. 437, et passim), upon which one could stumble even while sleepwalking. The human known is meaningful reality; it includes something of intelligence. It is not a merely palpable *body* lying "out there." Ultimately, the known is what philosophers call *being*, namely, that which we could correctly determine to exist. Essentially, it lies in the realm of meaning, and specifically, in the realm of what is correctly understood, not *ipso facto* in the realm of what is perceived. Or, at least, this is what I am arguing with Lonergan. Human knowing and the human known entail a world of meaning. Knowing and known depend on insights, ideas, and their formulations over and above the sensible contents of perception. Human knowing regards actualities, not mere appearances; our knowing attains to the noumena, not merely the phenomena.

Grounded in this realization, Lonergan's theory of knowledge is postmodern. On the one hand, it fully acknowledges what has been styled "the social construction of reality" (Berger & Luckmann, 1967). Human knowledge is, indeed, a human production. So Lonergan's theory avoids the overly optimistic, naïve realist, and "objectivist" certainty that characterized antiquity, early modern science, and "modernism" (4.16.4). But on the other hand, insisting on the constraints of data and judgment, Lonergan's theory presents a moderate postmodernism. It avoids the anything-goes relativism—including the lack of consensus or even any means of consensus—that characterizes the radical and ultimately nihilist brand of postmodern thinking, epitomized in Jacques Derrida's deconstructionism (Cahoone, 2010, lectures 30, 31). Lonerganian nuance denies both that we can actually know nothing at all for sure and that human knowing is certain and foolproof. Rather, human knowing is an inherently normed and ongoing quest, and in the big picture its best proposals remain ever tentative.

Thus, Lonergan's theory, like other moderate postmodern thought (e.g., Willis, 2007), delineates the much desired middle ground between the nihilistic skepticism of radical postmodernism and the discredited absolutism of modernism (2.2.6; 4.16.4). Also like science as currently understood, this theory presents human knowing as an ongoing process, ever open to new data, ever facing new questions, ever correcting past mistakes, ever adding splinters of knowledge to a growing synthesis, and true to its inherent norms, ever moving asymptotically toward its elusive goal, knowledge of being, correct understanding of everything about everything.

The surety in this theory of knowledge lies in the norms inherent in the knowing process. Surety is not found in its ever-advancing product, human explanation. Human explanation grows and changes, but the normative process of rational inquiry remains ever the same. As explicated at 2.6, the identity of the process grounds the coherence of all knowing.

2.3.5. Tentative Explanation Versus Secure Matters of Fact

In this section we are considering understanding as an intellectual activity. It is a different activity from experience, the mere encounter of data. For this reason understanding represents an additional intellectual process that, as Lonergan expressed it, defines a second level of consciousness. Understanding entails the achievement of insight and the formulation of some hypothesis about the data. However, even when added to experience, understanding is not yet knowing. As everyday living makes all too clear, and as Lonergan (1972) was fond of saying, "Insights are a dime a dozen" (p. 13). Grand ideas rise and fall like the stock market. The desired achievement is not simply to have an insight and to suggest some idea, but to hit upon the correct insight and to know the truth of the matter.

Were the account of knowing to stop at understanding, the result would be idealism—which we already saw in mention of Berkeley and discussion of Kant (2.1.1, 2.1.4, 2.2.2, 2.2.7). Idealism is the epistemological claim that one knows by proposing a good idea, a coherent explanation. The notion is that reality is in the mind—or in some World of Ideas or Forms, as Plato literally believed. The notion is that we live in *The Matrix*. For idealism, creative suggestion and logical coherence are the criteria of reality. What's "only logical" is taken to be what's real.

In contrast, however, we've all encountered "a really great idea" that is totally impracticable; it's out of touch with the real world. Such ideas—utopian dreams—often occur in the seductive guises of religious beliefs or political ideologies. They "work" only by forcing the square pegs of real people into the round holes of wishful thinking. As a highly technical illustration of the same idealist phenomenon, fully coherent mathematical creations oftentimes bear no relationship to reality. Mathematicians know well that they are, as it were, spinning intricate webs of intellectual speculation—some of which, remarkably, do prove to relate to the real world.

Even more to the point, scientists, who do deal in real matters of this world, are notorious in their insistence that they do not offer sure knowledge. They never claim to *prove* their theories. They propose no final word on reality. They offer only "the best available opinion of the day": a good idea, a repeatedly supported hypothesis, an accepted theory, an increasingly probable explanation. Why so? Because scientific explanation is unlike matters of fact. Facts pertain to particular cases—Did Caesar cross the Rubicon? Am I sitting in this chair? Is traffic already backing up on a Friday-afternoon expressway? Does the measurement on this instrument read 5.697? Matters of fact are relatively easily and securely determined.

In contrast, science deals in a peculiar kind of cognitive pursuit: explanation. Science—and all theorizing—aims toward understanding that applies, not to just one case, but universally, to each and every similar case. However, such explanation rests on only limited representative instances. That is, science depends on induction to reason from a selection of known cases to proposed general principles—just as statistical analyses make inferences from samples to populations. The conclusion is never certain or absolute. Scientists today are well aware that any such explanation might need to be revised. New data might come into play; alternative explanations of data are frequently possible; numerous curves and their formulas could connect the sample of data points on a graph—so a better explanation might well emerge. The embarrassing lesson from logic courses makes the point. For decades the stock example of a universal statement was "All swans are white." But then black swans in Australia became known. Now logicians bet on "All crows are black." Scientists routinely hold a cautious interpretation of their craft. Today—unlike in the early, overly confident days of modern science or in religious true believers' insistence on their "revealed facts" (cf. Helminiak, 2001a, 2010, 2013a; Helminiak, Hoffman, & Dodson, 2012)—scientists explicitly nuance any claim about knowing for certain; they present only "the best available opinion of the day."

In terms of Lonergan's theory of knowledge, science is actually a specialization on the second level of consciousness, and explanation is a refined form of understanding. Explanation is not sure knowledge, not a matter of fact. Fact pertains to the third level of consciousness, yet to be considered. Of course, matters of fact—readings on a dial, observed differences, experimental results—support or undermine scientific theories: these do not float in midair. Yet even the most secure theories remain ever "mere" understandings, hypotheses, supported suppositions, the best available opinions of the day. Thus, Lonergan's differentiation of three interacting levels of consciousness grounds a philosophy of science, showing why science, a specialization on the second level of consciousness, is ever tenuous in its conclusions even while it relies on mounting and converging matters of indubitable factual evidence, products of the third level, and, thus, hopefully, moves asymptotically to fully reliable explanation.

The pertinent point here, illustrated by the nature of mathematics, inductive science, and any bright ideas we might have, is that ideas, interpretations, hypotheses, or theories are not facts. Mere ideas, however clever and coherent, are not *ipso facto* correct. Ideas must be checked out against the available data. Through and through, human knowing is an empirical enterprise. We can know only that on which we have data. Knowledge is a matter of the actual, not the imaginable, the possible, or the conceivable.

2.3.6. *The Flaw in the Conceivability Argument in Consciousness Studies*

This emphasis on empiricism, Lonergan's "generalized empirical method," bears mightily on contemporary thinking about consciousness, which constitutes the major question in Chapters 4 and 5. Basically, much contemporary thinking is idealist. It argues on the basis of logical coherence to propose what is actual, so the logical coherence of ideas becomes a supposed criterion of the real, and the need for grounding in data gets overlooked. This appeal to mere logical coherence is so widespread that it even has technical names: "conceivability argument" (Chalmers, 1996, p. 98) or "the modal argument (the argument from logical possibility)" (p. 145).

Of course, appeal to logic can definitively determine what could possibly be—but only negatively: the illogical cannot be real. In a stock case, for example, yes, it is true that God cannot make a square circle. This fact is no argument against divine omnipotence. The telling fact is that a square circle is nothing to be made. The "squareness" and the "circleness" logically cancel each other out. Nothing remains. And it is no failure to be unable to make what is nothing to be made. Logic does usefully eliminate mistaken possibilities.

However, on the positive front, logical possibility is no guarantee of actuality. The paradigmatic example is the creations of mathematicians. These mathematics, highly elaborated and totally coherent logical systems, are purely speculative; they presume no dependence on reality although they often find practical applications. Just because something is logically possible is no guarantee that it exists—or, even further, that it *might* exist. Our universe and its structures are *de facto*. It is not by necessity that they are as they are. In the technical philosophical term, they are contingent. They just happen to be so.

Logical coherence does not imply actuality. On this point consciousness theorists and even physicists routinely make a mistake. They speculate elaborately about other logically possible worlds. There, for example, water could be something other than H_2O but still be water (Chalmers, 1996, pp. 131–138). In this case, *water* is taken to be a commonsensical term meaning merely some kind of "watery stuff" (p. 57) as back and forth these theorists trade off the everyday word for the chemical formula for water. Recurrently, ambiguity reigns about whether popular linguistic usage or explanatory science determines reality and about how they relate to each other (see 4.9, 4.12). Similarly, the consciousness theorists rest some of their fundamental arguments on the notion of zombies, supposed creatures that externally perform in every way exactly as a human would although they are not human because they lack consciousness (see Blackmore, 2012). No doubt, phenomena such as zombies and chemically alternative "water" can be imagined and proposed. Moreover, granted the presuppositions of the argument, the reality of such phenomena or, at least, their possibility can be argued powerfully. On that matter of H_2O, for example, Chalmers's (1996) argument is fully coherent. His logic is impeccable. His grounding, however, is mere speculation.

The mistake is not in the logic of the arguments but in their presupposition—namely, that whatever is logically possible actually has a bearing on the real world. In fact, our reality is what it is. It could possibly have been otherwise. But it is not otherwise. There are, indeed, myriad possibilities, but even our imagination of these tends to be limited by our experience of the *de facto* world. Even in science fiction, despite every effort at novelty, extraterrestrials and robots bear obvious similarities to human beings and their physiognomy. Even argument from logical possibility derives from the requirements of the logic that is built into our minds—as they happen to be. The *de facto* world just happens to be what it is; there is nothing necessary about its being. Therefore, to understand it, we must attend to it in itself, not to ideas of other suppositions in our minds. Such is the enterprise of science: it depends on the availability of data to ground its insights and judgments. Such was the Renaissance breakthrough that gave birth to modern science. In our world as it happens to be, data constitute an inescapable requirement for any knowledge. The supposition that other universes could be structured other than our own—and, according to our thinking, in a logically coherent way—has no bearing whatsoever in determining what our actual world must be like and how it must function.

Yet scientists propose other supposedly logically coherent universes and, on the basis of appeal to them, proffer conclusions about the actual world. That appeal to the supposed possibility of zombies is standard fare in consciousness studies. Because, supposedly, such zombies could actually exist, there is no reason to believe that consciousness adds anything to the humanity we see about us in the real world, and there is every reason to believe consciousness is nothing more than the biological functioning of the organism that zombies have in common with humans (Dennett, 1991). Or turning this same speculation in the other direction, theorists conclude that the consciousness we do, indeed, experience must be a dimension of the entire universe and every facet of it. Supposedly, consciousness is fundamental and unique unto itself, and for us it is a bonus of purely internal experience with no actual external effects. According to this theory, consciousness could not be reduced to the materialism and biology of the organism because this consciousness is something over and above all the discernible, external functioning our zombie twins supposedly exhibit in common with us; and on the other hand, consciousness could not make real differences in our world because, it if did, zombies could not function in every regard exactly as we humans do (Chalmers, 1996). Arguments on both side, either denying or affirming the reality of consciousness, depend on the existence of zombies. In both cases consciousness supposedly makes no different whatsoever in the external world. Tellingly, however, we have no idea whatsoever what biology would actually operate in a zombie, behaviorally similar in every way to a human being but without consciousness. Without that much sought understanding of the relation of consciousness and the brain, we have no idea what effect consciousness might actually have on human biology, what "top-down" causality might actually be operating. Nonetheless, speculators attribute to consciousness-less zombies a biology identical to a human's in every last unknown detail. We have no idea whether such a being could actually even exist. Except for cinematic entertainment or for creative pastime, the idea seems ludicrous on its face. We have no idea whatsoever because we have no data whatsoever on zombies. We have no instance of them to which we could appeal to actually know what they might actually be like. Therefore, not knowing what zombies are actually like, we cannot reasonably appeal to them to make an argument.

If human knowledge depends on the availability of data, sheer speculation carries no weight in answering scientific questions. Idealism, like any creativity, is certainly free to construct its many projections, but that these supply grounds for determining what the world is actually like is a badly mistaken assumption. Our universe is contingent; there is no necessity in what it happens to be. Except for eliminating logical impossibilities, freewheeling conceivability tells us nothing about what our universe actually is. Whereas science has learned to limit its claims to what can be grounded in evidence, theorists intent on developing a science of consciousness continue to invoke armchair speculation to conclude what reality could, should, might, must, or ought to be. The trenchant lesson at the birth of modern science, in contrast to the then reigning Aristotelian speculation, was the requirement of evidence for any knowledge claims.

Lonergan (1957/1992) reflected on scientific method and equally on the structure of human knowing and noted a momentous congruence between them. Among "The Canons of Empirical Method," he formulated the requirement of evidence as "the canon of selection" and "the canon of parsimony" (pp. 93–97, 102–107): empirical science pertains only where there can be appeal to discernible consequences (evidence, data); and the empirical scientist cannot claim knowledge of what is not verified or claim to be able to know what is not verifiable. These principles of science and constraints on human knowing discredit much of the argumentation currently controlling thought about human consciousness; and the misunderstanding about human consciousness opens wide and easy paths for even farther-out speculation about "God in the brain." The *de facto* status of our universe and the limitation of our knowing as *de facto* are far-reaching realizations of modern science that have yet to be fully digested. When idealism still reigns, speculation mushrooms and irresolvable arguments abound. The problem is epistemology or, said otherwise in this case, methodology.

2.3.7. Summary About Understanding

All knowing begins with experience. It provides us something to be understood: data. Awareness of data provokes in us a desire to understand. Sometimes quite readily but oftentimes only with prolonged effort, inquiry results in insight. Insight is expressed internally in a concept or an idea and externally in formulations, usually verbal articulations, but not necessarily only verbal. This process of inquiry, insight, conception, and formulation is the process of understanding. It adds to initial experience a second component of knowing.

But as is true of experience alone, neither do ideas alone constitute knowledge. When the goal is to understand the world as it actually is, bright ideas are subservient to the relevant evidence. Scientific hypotheses, like everyday suppositions, remain ever vulnerable to further testing against the data. And confirmed theory and factual knowledge are two different expressions of human cognition. Ideas and facts are not necessarily the same thing. Knowledge is inevitably an idea, but every idea is not necessarily knowledge: the idea might be mistaken. And apart from evidence against which to test the idea, there is no way of knowing. Human knowing, as it happens to be, requires the data of experience, and it also requires the insight of understanding. Yet achieved knowledge, or fact, requires still another component—a confirmation of the idea, an assessment of the insight in light of the relevant evidence, a judgment of fact.

2.4. The Rational Level of Knowing: Judgment of Fact

2.4.1. The Absoluteness of a Judgment of Fact

Only with the *judgment* of fact does knowing come to term. In contrast to the act of understanding, judgment is another kind of insight, another kind of cognitive realization, another kind of intellectual act. A judgment is a response to a particular kind of question.

The question for understanding is of the type, "What is it? Why is it? How is it?" This question allows an array of possible answers in succinct or elaborate form: ideas, hypotheses, understandings, theories, interpretations, book-long explications. In contrast, the question for reflection leading to judgment asks simply, "Is it?" or "Is it so?" The possible answers are only "Yes" and "No" or, perhaps, "I don't know" and "Maybe." These two kinds of question are familiar from courses in communication skills. The first is the open-ended question, the staple of the therapist and of good friends. This kind of question leaves lots of room for, and actually invites, self-expression. The second is the closed question, the staple of lawyers and—as I have noticed—BBC interviewers. This kind of question leaves no room for explanation but tends to shut down self-expression, to pin down the interlocutor, to demand a Yes–No response, to prove a point. The one kind of question asks about explanation, the other about actuality. The one deals in suppositions, the other in facts.

Clearly, two different kinds of intelligibility are at stake in the thrust of these two different kinds of questions; two different matters are up for being understood. The second follows upon the first and requires a different kind of insight. It is a grasp of the fact that some idea, hypothesis, or understanding is, indeed, well grounded. The judgment tests the understanding against the data. That all the data are accounted for and no relevant questions remain—this is the content of this second kind of insight; this is the realization expressed in a judgment of fact: "Yes, it is so."

Thus understood, a judgment attains a kind of absolute. A judgment expresses an unconditioned—such that if x, y, and z, then P; but x, y, and z; therefore, P. This conclusion is firm. *Unconditioned* means that no restrictions remain; all requisites are met; nothing else is needed; "all systems are go." Via this second kind of intellectual act, judgment grasps the fact that the conditions for P are fulfilled: all the requirements for the idea's being correct are found in the data, so the idea expresses a *de facto* necessity. No more conditions remain to call P into question. P is unconditioned; all reservations are met; so P must be so. P is necessary—but not absolutely so, only *de facto*. P did have conditions, so P is not absolutely unconditioned. But P's conditions just happen to be fulfilled, so it is no longer conditioned. There might have been conditions, but they are, indeed, fulfilled—in fact, *de facto*. In a contingent universe nothing is, nothing exists, or is as it is by necessity. The conditions could just as well happen not to be fulfilled. Things could have been different. Fact is simply the statement of what does happen to be so, and no more. For this reason Lonergan (1957/1992) explains the judgment of fact as the achievement of a "virtually unconditioned" (pp. 305–306), namely, a conditioned whose conditions happen to be fulfilled. The contrast, the only contrast, is the absolutely unconditioned, necessary being, "God," according to standard Western theology. This idea of necessary being becomes central only in Chapter 6.

The status of *unconditioned* carries with it a surety, a firmness, an invulnerability. Through a judgment of fact, one transcends oneself—one's sensations, perceptions, imaginations, suppositions, expectations, hopes, preferences—and reaches what is so in itself. One achieves objectivity, fact, truth. One knows something of the real. To reach such achievement is what it means for humans *to know*.

2.4.2. *The Subjective and Objective Dimensions of Knowledge of Being*

Despite the double insightful input on the side of the subject—understanding and judgment—such knowledge is not "merely subjective" (in the sense of being biased or whimsical) because data constrain the possibilities of understanding and judgment. Similarly, despite its reliance on data on the side of the object, such knowledge is not "fully objective" (in the sense of being independent of a subject) because human knowledge includes understanding and judgment in addition to experience.

Some philosophers want more rigorous objectivity and would credit as true knowledge only a "God's eye view" of things. This popular metaphor—and, of course, it is a metaphor—brings us again to the difference between a sensate-modeled and an intellectual epistemology. The metaphor refers to absolutely objective knowledge, and the metaphor is conceived and even named according to a sensate model of knowing. Supposedly, to know objectively, humans would have *to see* things as God *sees* them. The conception is imaginal, not insightful. For it, reality is what is lying out there to be seen, not what is reasonably—that is, by appeal to appropriate evidence—affirmed to be so. Emphasizing *seeing*, I niggle to make a point. Still, the point has its validity otherwise.

Even if—legitimately enough—"view" and "see" are taken only metaphorically to refer to understanding, the proposed God's eye view is an inane fantasy: it demands that, to pass muster, human knowledge must exist apart from a human knower; humans must know as God knows. This is the implication, logically enough, of Hegel's idealism. But no such self-contradictory criterion could be met. In contrast, as a matter of fact—as attention to one's own knowing might suggest—human knowledge includes both objective and subjective elements; it is a composite of experience plus understanding and judgment. Human knowledge appears to be of this kind, not of some other imagined, required, expected, desired, or preferred kind. As discussed at 2.6, human knowledge is valid or objective, not to the extent that *per impossibile* the human subject is removed from the knowing, but to the extent that the subject in question respects the inherent norms of human knowing. Carefully, insightfully, and honestly pursued, such knowing grants to humanity some grasp of reality. Such a grasp of reality is what human knowing entails. Success in this process is what it means for humans to know.

That which correlates with human knowing is that which *is*. The object of the pure desire to know is *being*. We marvel, inquire, and assess because our very constitution inclines us to experience, understand, and judge and, thereby, to know. We are geared to the universe; our very being reaches out to reality; we want to know what is real. The outpouring of questions from the human mind bears witness to this state of affairs. Even to question whether this assertion is correct provides evidence to the same effect: why would one even question this assertion except for an irrepressible personal requirement to get the thing right? Our very nature is outreach, desire, *eros*, love. Our path is a quest. The goal of this dynamism is to comprehend what actually is. The pursuit of correct understanding is a repeatedly incremental increase in the knowledge of being. As contemporary science is well aware, our knowledge quest is open-ended and ongoing. Experience provokes questions, insights, understandings, and affirmations. The answer to one question provokes further questions, opening onto ever broader and deeper explanation, ever more intimate engagement with reality. The affirmations name what is; they delineate aspects of being. Thus understood, being correlates with intelligence—not with perception. Being is what is correctly affirmed; it is not the physical bodies lying about and encountered by sensate experience. This understanding of being echoes the distinction that runs through this whole exposition: the difference between sensate-modeled and intellectual epistemologies and, concomitantly, the difference between a human world of meaning and value and a physical habitat of sensations, perceptions, and biological survival.

To experience, understand, and judge is what humans do to know. Through this process we attain to the real, and the real is precisely what is known in this way. There is no other option when human knowing is in question. This is what human knowing *de facto* happens to be. By achieving the absolute of a virtually unconditioned, we know what *de facto* is.

2.4.3. *The Need for Reflexive Consistency in a Theory of Knowledge*

Lonergan's account of knowing would seem to represent the best available opinion of the day (McCarthy, 1997; Webb, 1988). Stunningly, his account embodies the reflexivity—namely, self-awareness—that is characteristic of human consciousness and that accords his account a unique status. The formulation of a three-level process of knowing rests on consistent application of this same three-level knowing process to knowing itself.

- Have you ever encountered something that appeared peculiar and struck your interest?
- Have you ever had an insight and thought you understood that peculiarity?
- Have you ever wondered whether your understanding was correct and gone back to check it against the available evidence?
- Do these experiences count as data, evidence, on the workings of your mind?
- Does Lonergan's three-level theory articulate these data in their interrelationship?
- Does that articulation stand up when judged against the data?

Attentiveness to the workings of one's mind suggests an account of the mind's workings that can be grounded in the very data of these self-same mental experiences. The result is an empirical, intellectual, and rational account of the empirical, intellectual, and rational process of human knowing. Empirically derived from the human mind, this theory is adequate to the human mind.

Other epistemologies do not pass the test of reflexive consistency. For example, "Hume thought the human mind to be a matter of impressions linked together by custom. But Hume's own mind was quite original. Therefore, Hume's own mind was not what Hume considered the human mind to be" (Lonergan, 1972, p. 21). Similarly, Kant claims that in knowledge we reach only phenomena, never the noumena, only our own experience, never the thing in itself. This claim is a judgment. But, on the basis of Kant's theory, this particular judgment could be true and fundamental only "if the truth of judgment is fundamental. But, for Kant, judgment is not fundamental" (Lonergan, 1980/1990, p. 179), but only regulatory: it "oversees" the application of the categories of the mind to its perceptual input. Likewise, in the arena of neuroscience, Eugene d'Aquili and Andrew Newberg (1999) claim that "the subjective vivid sense of reality" (p. 191) is the criterion of knowledge, but this claim is a judgment, not a vivid subjective sense. Besides, people suffering from psychosis have vivid subjective senses all the time, but nobody takes their claims to be true. Also highlighting the inconsistencies that result when consciousness is ignored, Percy (1989/1990) offered further examples:

> Neither [Darwin nor Freud] can account for his own activity by his own theory. For how does Darwin account for the "variation" which is his own species and its peculiar behavior, in his case, sitting in his study in Kent and writing the truth as he saw it about evolution? And if Freud's psyche is like ours, a dynamism of contending forces, how did it ever arrive at the truth about psyches, including his own? (p. 4)

All these theorists (must!) make judgments, yet none leaves explicit room for judgment in their accounts of knowing. In varying degrees they remain captivated by the perceptual analogy. Supposedly, knowing is like taking a good look or having an intense feeling, and reality is some physical body "already out there now" or some impression "already in here now," waiting whole-hog to be encountered and uncovered. Alternatively, reality is ideas in the mind, and the coherence of the ideas guarantees their correctness. The inconsistency—the positing of judgments about what is real despite the absence of judgment in the theory of what is real—disqualifies these epistemologies. In contrast, Lonergan's theory advances the ideal of reasonable appeal to evidence, deployed in science, into the very arena of philosophy and, thus, the human sciences and the humanities (Doran, 1981; Helminiak, 1998, 2006a, 2014; McCarthy, 1997). Built on attention to the workings of the human mind, his theory provides an empirically grounded epistemology adequate to the human mind.

Obviously, questions, blatant and subtle, surround this theory of knowledge. Most arise because of the persistent, pesky intrusion of a perceptual theory of knowing. Lonergan has dealt with the questions in exhaustive detail. Here below, I merely highlight some salient points.

2.5. The Scientific Affinity and Status of This Epistemology

Lonergan's account of knowledge is hardly arcane or esoteric. The textbook account of scientific method proposes a parallel three-stage process: observation, hypothesis, and verification. This correspondence is no accident, and such convergence of theory invites credibility. As empirical method stands in the case of modern science, Lonergan now also appears to be on to something important in the case of epistemology. This philosophical breakthrough, parallel to that in the sciences, was long in coming—so long, in fact, that many, most, have given up the search (1.4; 2.2.8).

Gradually the human history of trial-and-error efforts to know elucidates the subtle process of human knowing itself. An accumulation of successes exposes the standard of correct knowing that is inherent in the knowing process. As through the centuries humanity has struggled to understand correctly, proposing different ideals along the way, the normative process of human knowing, unavoidable in the human mind, ever more insistently expresses and clarifies itself so that human knowing can eventually be understood (Lonergan 1980/1990, pp. 6–13). It appears that Lonergan might well have made a definitive breakthrough by articulating this matter. Gradually, only gradually, we come to understand knowing, that pervasive but most elusive dimension of human experience. We realize what *de facto* knowing means. In sum, intelligent and reasonable appeal to evidence—empirical method—represents our best approximation to that in-born standard to date, and the stunning achievements of modern science offer the most vivid examples of that standard in application.

Science has restricted its method to the external data of the senses, yet the same method of intelligent and reasonable appeal to evidence can be broadened to apply also to one's own experience of the mind, the internal data of consciousness. William James (1902/1961, pp. 59–63) endorsed such an appeal to internal evidence and on that basis provided his encyclopedic classic, *The Principles of Psychology* (James, 1890/1950), free from the narrowness of the later behaviorism that misdirected the trajectory of academic psychology well into the 20th century (Koch, 1971, 1981). Lonergan called this extension of scientific method "generalized empirical method" (Lonergan, 1957/1992, pp. 95–96, 260–261, 268, 299–300, 358–359; 1972, pp. 72, 201–202) and, later, "transcendental method" (Lonergan, 1972, p. 17). The result, as we have seen, is an empirical, intellectual, and reasonable account of the empirical, intellectual, and reasonable process of human knowing. The result is a peculiarly scientific account of human knowing itself, a science of knowledge, an empirically grounded epistemology.

The scope of the human pursuit of understanding is unlimited. Intertwined with the scientific effort to explain the physical universe runs the philosophic effort to explain knowing itself. However, if the explanation of knowing is to be an empirical enterprise, it must look to actual instances of successful knowing to understand knowing. Yet only in the past four centuries has the breakthrough of modern science provided unambiguous examples. Naturally, then, the philosophic effort to understand knowing has lagged behind the impressive record of modern science. Whereas the natural sciences appear to have gotten "on track," achieving ever more cumulative and progressive results, philosophy as a field still languishes in disarray.

The breakthrough for science was Renaissance and Early Modern insistence on induction guided by reasonable appeal to evidence. A second breakthrough came with the explicit acceptance of the open-ended and tentative nature of scientific explanation, provoked by probability theory and evolutionary thinking in the late 19th century and relativity theory and quantum mechanics in the early 20th. These breakthroughs in scientific method challenged and finally discredited the Aristotelian ideal of deductive knowledge that reigned for millennia. The paradigmatic instance was the knowledge derived from a syllogism: "All humans are mortal; Socrates is a human; therefore, Socrates is mortal." Additionally, the mathematics of the day, that is, geometry, provided other examples of genuine knowledge, and it, too, depended on deductions from supposed universally valid first principles: axioms and corollaries. On these early bases, the supposition was that genuine knowledge must be (a) necessary, (b) universal, and (c) unchanging. In direct contrast, natural scientists now comfortably accept the facts that

(a) their knowledge is merely *de facto*: it enjoys no cosmic or logical necessity but represents only what in fact happens to be the case;

(b) their knowledge applies only restrictively, only with the qualification of "all things being equal," and they seldom exactly are; and

(c) their knowledge is not final: it is likely to be revised, hopefully not radically, but most certainly in nuance and detail.

Contemporary science explicitly recognizes human knowing as an ongoing and open-ended process. Nonetheless, in many circles the Aristotelian ideal still tenaciously holds sway. People still presume that human knowledge could be necessary, universal, and unchanging—that is, as lucid as the Ideas in Plato's World of Forms, as infallible as the conclusion of an Aristotelian deductive syllogism, as certain as the proofs in Euclidean geometry, as eternal and reliable as the "revealed word of God," as cogent as a universe of heavenly bodies moving in perfectly circular orbits around a stationary earth, as indubitable as Descartes's clear and distinct ideas, as fixed as the species that came directly from the hand of the Creator. In the face of the mix of current opinions, the complexity of the issues, the subtlety of the necessary arguments, and the temptation to rely on naked power politics, precious little consensus about knowing appears on the horizon, whether on university campuses, in the marketplace, or around the globe. It will certainly take decades or centuries, require vast and cooperative effort, and likely cost the weakest among us, as always, abusive oppression and immense suffering before a comfortable and sane consensus on the nature of knowing coalesces to match the trust granted to humanity's earlier mistaken ideas. A major challenge is that, in fact, we must live with much more uncertainty than we would like. Then mutual respect and goodwill become all the more important.

In the meantime, Lonergan appears to have provided a foundation for such consensus, seemingly as secure in the realm of philosophy as the natural sciences are in their realm. Examining those breakthroughs in scientific method, retrieving the self-insight of great thinkers of the past, and recognizing a congruent pattern in the workings of his own mind, Lonergan proposed what can only be called a scientific account of knowing. His theory is no mere speculation but rests on evidence that, supposedly, anyone could find in his or her own mind.

In disconcerting contrast, exploiting the ethical requirement to be sensitive to the religious beliefs of psychotherapeutic clients (American Counseling Association, 1995; American Psychological Association, 1992) and resonating with the uncertainty of our times, widespread regressive speculation would insinuate into a supposed scientific psychology "revelation," "inspiration," "intuition," "spiritual knowing," and personal religious conviction as sources of knowledge on a par with that of empirical research (Elkins, 1998; Gorsuch, 2002; Hart, Nelson, & Puhakka, 2003; Hill, et al., 2000; Jones, 1994; Larson, Swyers, & McCullough, 1998; Marquis, Holden, & Warren, 2001; Pargament & Maloney, 2002; Rayburn & Richard, 2002; Schudel, 2006; Tan, 2003; Watts, 2001). Indeed, insisting that extraordinary divine interventions (miracles) are so pervasive that their influence must be factored into any adequate scientific theory, a movement called "theistic psychology" would construct a psychological theory around belief in God and propose it as a parallel to other schools of psychology such as psychoanalytic, behaviorist, humanistic, or cognitive (Bartz, 2009, p. 69; Reber, 2006a, 2006b; Richards & Bergin, 2005, pp. 10–11, 18; Richardson, 2006; Slife & Melling, 2006; Slife & Whoolery, 2006; Slife & Richards, 2001). In disciplines other than psychology, the vagaries of postmodern thought replace traditional academic commitment to truth with a fascination for what are styled "interesting" ideas. And in society at large, appeals to fanciful sources of knowledge—esoteric ancient texts, exotic spiritual traditions, charismatic teachers, supposed cultural superiority, alphabetic patterns in sacred scriptures, half-truths from popularized contemporary science, libraries in the sky, crystals, mediums, palm-readers, and extraterrestrials—emerge in waves as people desperately grasp at any hope for security in the discombobulating swirl of the current culture shift. In the United States, a deliberate antiscience campaign in conservative religious and political circles threatens to actually undo the hard-won progress of modern science and medicine—and, indeed, to doom the very planet by denial of human-caused climate change (Otto, 2012; Stengor, 2013). On many fronts, regressive thinking threatens to undermine the very epitome of Western epistemic achievement (Summarizing the judgment, 2005). Hopefully, this book's application of Lonergan's epistemology to thorny questions in contemporary human science and religion will demonstrate the power of this epistemology and orient the human quest in a more promising direction.

2.6. The Accuracy of Human Knowing and the Transcendental Precepts

Lonergan has provided a coherent epistemology that matches the breakthrough in the natural sciences. To be sure, however, transcendental method, like scientific method, is not automatic or foolproof. Constituted by experience, understanding, and judgment, transcendental method presses for attentiveness, intelligence, and reasonableness; but in these matters, no one is perfect. People make mistakes. How, then, can one guarantee correctness in knowing? How can one ensure that a judgment of fact is definitive?

2.6.1. *The Precarious Nature of All Human Knowing*

There is no guarantee. We do the best we can. Such is the human condition. We are not purely spiritual entities inhabiting a Platonic World of Ideas or Forms. We do not know by Aristotelian deduction and its necessary, universal, and unchanging conclusions. We cannot claim a God's eye view through divine revelation or inspired and inerrant texts or religiously guaranteed infallible decrees. Nonetheless, honest and good-willed collaboration within the scientific, academic, and human communities welcomes multiple inputs. These, at least, lend some assurance of accuracy. We humans need one another to keep ourselves alert, thinking, and honest—that is, attentive, intelligent, and reasonable. Besides, far from discrediting human knowing, the honest recognition of a mistake and its humble correction confirm that, with dedicated pursuit of an asymptotic goal, correct human knowing is possible.

In addition to honest human mistakes, sad to say, there is also deliberate fraud; and there are the bias and distortion that come from unconscious forces and cultural and social embeddedness (Lonergan 1957/1992, pp. 214–127, 244–267). Again, there exists no guarantee against bias from whatever source. However, the pursuit of knowledge is an ongoing process that takes effort, dedication, and goodwill. These eventually unearth bias or fraud and reverse them. The self-correcting process of knowing itself invites such reversal.

2.6.2. The Inherent Subjective Requirements of Human Knowing

Knowing is not a random affair; it carries its own requirements. Accurate knowledge does not follow from any old way of thinking, but only from thinking that respects its three-level process. If the availability of data, the pursuit of insight, and the grounding of judgment are indeed the makings of knowledge, these components imply requisites for the correct outworking of the knowing process.

- To the experience of data, there corresponds the need for open-mindedness.
- To the inquiry that leads to insight, there corresponds the need to question and to apply one's intelligence.
- To the surety that judgment promises, there corresponds the need for honesty in the face of the evidence.

Lonergan (1972) calls these inherent requirements of human knowing "the transcendental precepts" (pp. 20, 53, 55, 231, 302). He formulates them technically as follows:

- Be attentive.
- Be intelligent.
- Be reasonable.

And completing the account of consciousness as it moves beyond knowing into doing, a fourth precept applies: Be responsible. This precept relates to judgments of value and pertains to ethics and exceeds the scope of this book.

These are precepts because they entail requirements for human knowing and becoming. They are transcendental because they apply across the board to any and every human endeavor; they apply wherever human consciousness is operating. More technically, they are transcendental because they are purely formal—that is, they are content-free and completely open-ended in their purview. The term *transcendental* derives from Kant's usage wherein it named the categories of the mind that, supposedly, constrain and structure all human knowing. Unlike Kant's transcendental categories, however, Lonergan's structure of consciousness imposes no *a priori* forms on the known—such as homogenous space and time or causality and substance—which, supposedly, "box in" human experience and fit it into inherent, unavoidable, and shared human configurations, preventing us from ever knowing things in themselves. The transcendental precepts articulate a human absolute, but they are not absolutist. They imply no preconceived content in any endeavor. They impose no predetermined outcome on any process. They merely require that every endeavor be undertaken attentively, intelligently, reasonably, and responsibly and let the chips fall where they may. The truth is what will be learned to be so when a reasonable judgment can be made; the good is what responsible discernment will show best needs to be done in any situation. The transcendental precepts are requirements that only "the devil" would oppose, obscuring attentiveness, dissuading inquiry, pooh-poohing insistence on evidence, and discouraging good will—and thereby illustrating and defining the very essence of evil, namely, that which not only lacks grounding in reality but also outright undermines reality, precluding any unfolding, long-term future. Metaphorically, Jesus spoke of this matter in terms of building a house on sand, and Buddha encouraged right faith, right resolve, right speech, right action, right living, right effort, right thought, and right concentration. Tellingly, Lonergan arrived at a similar conclusion, not by appeal to religious authority, but through empirical analysis of the very makeup of humanity.

2.6.3. *The Criteria of Genuine or Authentic Humanity*

Fidelity to the transcendental precepts defines human genuineness (Lonergan, 1957/1992), or *authenticity* (Lonergan, 1972). One is a genuine human being insofar as one lives by these precepts, whether implicitly or also explicitly. Said otherwise, these precepts elucidate the essential ideal nature of the human being; they anticipate the goal and present the guiding principles of authentic human development (Helminiak, 1987b). Inclusion of this dimension of humanity in a personality theory provides the holy grail of an empirically grounded, normative or prescriptive, not just a descriptive, psychology and social science—because any deviation from these precepts, deliberate or unconscious, entails some dehumanization: the shutting down of human potential, the curtailment of open-ended unfolding.

Thus, human knowing is correct, not to the extent that *per impossibile* the human subject is extracted from it, but to the extent that the human subject in question is authentic. In Lonergan's (1972) trenchant phrase, "Genuine objectivity is the fruit of authentic subjectivity" (p. 292). Accuracy in knowing cannot be absolutely guaranteed because the authenticity of its agents—you, me, and our human sisters and brothers—cannot be guaranteed. Said in popular language, only the honest person will come to affirm the truth. Human knowledge cannot be dissociated from human virtue. This requirement, however, does not suggest that correct knowledge is an impossibility. Rather, this requirement invites each of us to live up to our own human dignity and capacity.

2.7. Transcendental Method

2.7.1. The Inherent Workings of the Human Knowing Process

Lonergan (1972) applies the term "transcendental" also to the process of human knowing conceived as a method: "transcendental method" (pp. 13–20). If a method is "a normative pattern of recurrent and related operations yielding cumulative and progressive results" (p. 4), then this definition applies to the spontaneous functioning of human consciousness on its three interrelated levels. This functioning is a built-in method of knowing within us. Even before anyone pays attention to it, even before a philosopher ever wondered about the nature of knowing, it is the very method of knowing inherent in, and working through, the human mind: transcendental method, "the native spontaneities and inevitabilities of our consciousness" (p. 18). Transcendental method is the primordial or generic method that undergirds and finds specification in the particular methods of the sciences and the commonsense guidelines for everyday endeavors. Particular methods are applications and adaptations of the mind's innate attentiveness, intelligence, and reasonableness to this or that specific task, problem, project, or research program.

Awareness of this fact clarifies what Lonergan (1957/1992) is about. Ultimately, he is not invested in his theory of knowledge as formulated. The formulation is merely an attempt to capture in words the actual workings of the human mind. The formulation is merely an expression of the reality of concern. The theory is a proposed articulation of intentional consciousness, an objectification of agent subjectivity, an express knowledge of human knowing, or—to echo and use the terminology of much of modern philosophy's "turn toward the subject"—a *noêma* of *noêsis*, a *pensée pensée* of *pensée pensante*, an *intentio intenta* of *intentio intendens* (pp. 19–20). The inherent process is what matters. It is what is at stake. As in any scientific or commonsense endeavor, the formulation never perfectly and completely captures the reality being articulated. With clumsy human words this theory of knowing seeks to express primordial human reality. The formulation itself is certainly open to refinement and elaboration, and the reality in question might be expressed otherwise. But even whether acknowledged or not, even whether articulated or not, transcendental method, used well or poorly, is at work in the mind of anyone who experiences, questions, thinks, reflects, and claims to know.

2.7.2. *The Invulnerability of This Epistemology*

That set of circumstances leads to a striking realization. Essentially, Lonergan's theory of knowledge is not revisable (Lonergan, 1957/1992, pp. 12, 418–419, 591, 757–758; 1972, pp. 18–19). No one can refute this assertion without presupposing its validity for the argumentation. The reason is clear: the inherent workings of the human mind—adverted to or not, respected or distorted, well used or ineptly applied—are operative in the production of any argument. We have no option in this matter. We cannot but use our given minds when facing any novelty, question, judgment, or choice. The same human mind would be engaged even to reject this assertion.

As an empirically validated matter of fact—at least, as Lonergan has argued—the human mind functions in a particular way. Thus, someone committed to another epistemology, deliberately or unwittingly, will inevitably incur contradictions, whether in the logic of her or his argument or between what is said and what is done—because the human mind works in one way and the foreign epistemology, actually created and constrained by the mind, feigns that the mind works otherwise. I illustrated this point at 2.4.3 in the cases of Hume, Kant, d'Aquili and Newberg, Darwin, and Freud. The inconsistencies are inevitable, and the incoherence calls for correction. The very process built into the human mind prompts the reversal of mistaken accounts of it.

If Lonergan's theory captures at all the key operations in human knowing, any attempted revision of the theory, itself an intellectual enterprise, would need to employ the same operations that the theory seeks to articulate: appeal to the relevant evidence (experience), proposal of an alternative interpretation (understanding), and confirmation via the revisionist assessment that the alternative interpretation better accounts for the relevant evidence (judgment). Simply by mounting an argument, one would be doing in deed (following Lonergan's theory) what one denies in word (the accuracy of Lonergan's theory). Despite oneself, the activities of one's very attempt at revision of the theory would provide further procedural evidence for the validity of the theory (see also 6.4).

Of course, in radical postmodern conceit, one could whimsically dismiss these claims out of hand, opting for irrationality, incoherence, and ultimately nihilism—as in Oscar Wilde's quip, "Consistency is the last refuge of the unimaginative," or David Eddings's claim, "Consistency is the defense of a small mind." Of course, likewise, in nostalgic longing for simpler times, one is always free to insist on some speculative, *a priori* opinion about what human knowing could, would, should, might, or must be. Even so, one would be using the mind that Lonergan's theory intends to formulate. If this mind actually entails inherent structures and processes, these would perforce be operative in some way in every case. "The native spontaneities and inevitabilities of our consciousness" (Lonergan, 1972, p. 18) are unavoidable. Transcendental method pervades all human activity.

I see no avoiding this conclusion—except for the relativist nihilism of radical postmodernism. This recent craze would throw to the wind even the principle of non-contradiction as a small-minded concern of Western cultural bias. Such myopia must ignore the fact that scientists *cross-culturally* understand this principle and live by it in their collective and highly successful global enterprise. Thus there is good reason to believe that Lonergan has effected a definitive breakthrough toward an explanatory account of human distinctiveness. There is good reason to believe that his theory of knowledge grounds a secure epistemology.

2.8. Different Kinds of Realities, Including the Spiritual

Most pertinent to discussion of "God in the brain" is a final consideration—the existence of spiritual realities. By *spiritual* I mean simply non-physical, that is, not inherently conditioned by a spatiotemporal array (Lonergan, 1957/1992, pp. 541–543). I emphatically do not imply anything having to do with God or other purported supernatural entities; I do not identify the spiritual with the divine or with some "other-worldly" realm (5.8.2).

Completely down-to-earth, a paradigmatic example of the spiritual would be an insight: a grasp of meaning within a set of data. The insight produces an idea, which is in no way perceptible and whose potential range of relevance transcends the here and now, for example, $a^2 + b^2 = c^2$. Similarly, thought, meanings, and values are spiritual, as is consciousness itself. Indeed, as explicated and nuanced in Chapter 4, consciousness and human spirit are one and the same.

2.8.1. Equally Real Material and Spiritual Entities

The criterion of human knowledge is the reasonable judgment of fact. It determines fact, truth, actuality, reality. But the judgment regards an idea, a hypothesis, a formulation, which results from insight. And insight grasps intelligibility in data. Therefore, when intelligibilities differ—and, on the basis of reasonable judgment, really do so: one is not the other—different kinds of reality are at stake. When the meanings really differ, the realities are different. When what is there to be understood in each case really differ, the realities are different. Reasonable affirmation of diverse intelligibilities implicates different kinds of realities. As knowledge is a composite of data, understanding, and judgment, so reasonable judgment about an intelligibility grasped in some set of data specifies the reality itself that is in question. If the data set is physical and perceptible, the reality will be known as material: a real embodied entity of a particular kind or intelligibility. If the data set is not perceptible—the data of inner experience: emotions, memories, images, thoughts, insights, judgments, decisions—the reality will be known as non-physical: a real non-material entity of a particular kind or intelligibility.

When reality is determined by the reasonable affirmation of a distinct intelligibility within an experience—not through experience alone, not through palpability, visibility, perception, intuition, or subjective vivid sense—on the basis of this self-same criterion, affirmations of both material and spiritual realities are similarly conceived, similarly grounded, and equally valid. On this criterion, different kinds of realities can validly be known and affirmed. On this criterion, the spiritual can be known and affirmed as surely as can the material. Even as, for a range of reasons, few would deny that material realities are real; on the criterion of attentive, intelligent, and reasonable knowing, the spiritual is real, too. The reasonable affirmation (judgment) of distinct intelligibilities (understanding) within data (experience) determines and specifies realities. Under these circumstances, spiritual realities and material realities must be deemed equally real.

2.8.2. *The Meaningful—Spiritual—Dimension of Material Things*

The implications of this epistemology, consistently applied, cut also in the other direction. They call for rethinking even about the true nature of material reality. To take reasonable judgment, not palpability, as the criterion of the real is to recognize that even material reality is not what naïve or commonsense realism would suppose. The chair on which I sit (Gorsuch, 2002) is not the object of my extraverted sense experience—although feeling the chair on my bottom and seeing it with my eyes, I do have such sense experience. For my dog, in contrast, my "chair" is indeed such an object of mere perceptual experience, and my "couch" or "bed" would meet the criteria of Fido's organic need for sleep as well as my "chair" does. Fido does not know my "chair" as a chair; he has no idea of it. On the other hand, when I know the chair, I bring to my perceptual experience the consensual idea of *chair* plus the realization—the judgment—that the idea squares with the experience. I recognize this object to be a chair. This case is prosaic. It entails a learned instantaneity that obscures the true complexity of the process. The complexity remains obvious in infants who struggle to learn the correct *meaning* of words. But prosaically I say "chair," and what I name is not just an "already out there now" object of perceptual experience, not some configuration of material stuff taking up space, but the embodiment of a particular understanding that is part of the meaningful human world. A chair is a meaningful reality. Thus, even in the most mundane of instances, the world in which I live participates in the spiritual—a non-spatial, non-temporal, intellectual content: meaning. If so, the determinative "substance" of physical realities is not material stuff out there. That material stuff is merely an aspect of meaning-constituted beings.

The same point can be made otherwise. Consider this ***reductio ad absurdum***. Thorough-going materialism asserts that material is all there is; so materialism purports to explain things on the basis of lower-level material bodies—mind on brain, brain on cells, cells on molecules, molecules on atoms, and eventually atoms on quarks and leptons. However, according to the best available opinion of the day, at the base of this reductive process rest invisible, impalpable, and unimaginable entities, best characterized in one case as waves and in another as particles. Quarks and leptons are the objects of reasonable judgment. They are known and knowable, not at all through direct sense experience, but only through a reasoned conclusion about peculiar intelligibilities that make sense of disparate relevant evidence. Quarks and leptons are meanings that reasonable judgment is constrained to affirm to explain the relevant data. Viewed reductionistically—and, therefore, composed ultimately of invisible entities—physical reality itself must actually be invisible. What is composed of the invisible must itself be invisible. This is to say, followed to its logical conclusion, physical reductionism leads to absurdity. As quarks and leptons, which constitute material, are invisible, so, too, all material things must likewise be invisible. What?! Long anticipating Einstein's problem and far from Einstein's solution, Zeno proposed similar paradoxes and illustrated the incoherence of taking space to be a homogenous expanse lying out there (Lonergan, 1957/1992, pp. 50–56).

The logically necessary implications of materialistic reductionism are disconcerting. So some intended spiritual theorists incoherently adopt the opposite emphasis, which I call a "spiritualist reductionism": an idealism or spiritualism. They would insist, " 'The world is nothing but mind,' and 'All is Mind,' " " 'All the world is Brahman,' " (Wilber, 1996, p. 290); "all things, including subatomic particles, are ultimately made of God" (p. 165); "Perhaps . . . the only reality is God" (John Templeton and Robert Herrmann, cited in Richards & Bergin, 2005, p. 100). But materialistically they still image reality as sensible or imaginable; they continue to picture reality as if it were perceptible matter. They portray the sensible on a continuum of fuzziness so that physical matter is dense spirit and spiritual reality is a gossamer materiality, thus: "In the physical realm, space and time are the densest, the grossest, the most head-knockingly concrete [instances of spirit]. As we move up the spectrum of consciousness, space and time become subtler and subtler" (Wilber, 1996, p. 79). In this case, in contrast to materialism, supposedly and equally absurdly, only the spiritual is real and the material is illusory. Nonetheless, contradictorily, the verbiage of materiality controls the formulation of the spiritualist theory.

2.8.3. Ontological Pluralism: Different Kinds of Being

Those logically necessary conclusions about those creative speculations are patently absurd. Both extremes, both physical and spiritual reductionism, belie even our everyday world. Bodily creatures, we are well aware that our minds include a transcendent dimension. We are neither merely physical nor merely spiritual. And even our supposedly "merely physical world" is a realm of meaning and value; it includes a spiritual dimension; in its own way it embodies the spiritual. The spiritual is real, as real as the material. Lonergan's epistemology coherently allows these assertions.

2.9. The Challenge of Lonergan's Breakthrough

Only an epistemology consistently adequate to both physical and non-physical reality is adequate to the array of questions about the brain, the mind, the spiritual, the Divine, and their distinction and interrelationship. Lonergan has proposed such an epistemology, and I have attempted to summarize it briefly. Being realistic, however, I expect no easy agreement on these epistemological matters. Although allowing a relatively simple—because coherent—resolution of subtle philosophical questions, fidelity to transcendental method also leads to striking and disconcerting conclusions for many 21st-century audiences. For example,

- the human mind does entail a non-physical, a spiritual, dimension;
- the spiritual is as real, then, as the material;
- there exist, then, different kinds of realities;
- humans do not live in a mere habitat, the oft cited "material world," but literally in a universe of meaning and value;
- perforce, for humans the real is not perceptible bodies lying "out there," upon which one could stumble;
- nor is the real some imperceptible inkling or impression emerging "in here," which one could "feel" or "intuit" deeply;
- nor is the real simply a construct of ideas, a personal or cultural construal, *The Matrix* in which we live; a horizon of hermeneutic "meaningfulness" (Helminiak, 2013a);
- rather, for humans the real is a composite of data, intelligibility, and actuality;
- that is, reality is a confluence of the objective and the subjective and for humans subsists within the field of subjectivity and not, as such, independently of the knower;
- so the bane of Logical Positivism, "metaphysics," usually defined as the study of being (Lonergan, 1957/1990, chaps. 12–17), is absolutely unavoidable when questions of correct human explanation, science, are at stake—the concern of science is beings;

- and "non-dualism" (2.3.3; 5.8.3), a notion borrowed uncritically from Eastern thought and buttressed by opposition to Descartes, an insistence in some unspecified way that "all is one"—whether spiritual or material—is equally a red herring (see Helminiak, 1998, pp. 253–256).

John Searle (1997) highlighted the poignant challenge of Lonergan's thought as follows: "It seems that to accept dualism [namely, the position there exists a different kind of reality besides the material] is to give up the entire scientific worldview that we have spent nearly four centuries to attain" (p. xiii). Of course, such qualms ignore that 20th-century science already moved beyond naïve sensate materialism and the 4th century of science reconceived the suppositions of the first 3 regarding the nature of "matter." Searle elaborated, "The intensity of feelings [about dualism] borders on the religious and political" (p. 189). David Chalmers (1996), who does support dualism (esp. pp. 168–171), made a similar observation: "Motivation to avoid dualism, for many, has arisen from various spiritualistic, religious, supernatural, and other antiscientific overtones of the view." Insightfully and colorfully, he responds, "A naturalistic dualism expands our view of the world, but it does not invoke the forces of darkness" (p. 170). My own experience unequivocally confirms these attitudinal assessments. Indeed, for many contemporaries, the conclusions in the preceding paragraph come too close to religion and belief in God, with all their checkered history, including a fictitious, antiintellectualist medievalism (Harrison, 2010; Principe, 2006) and conservative religion's current hegemonic urgency. After all, first and foremost, Lonergan considered himself a theologian (1990/1980, p. 17), and his work in theological method (1972)—yet not theology *per se*, be it noted, but method, the interdisciplinary topic at stake in this book—capped his career.

Lonergan's account of human knowing and human reality challenges current thought on many fronts and prompts as many reasons, personal and theoretical, emotional and reasoned, for rejection. Nonetheless, I hope that my attempt at a coherent integration of neuroscience, psychology, spiritualogy, and theology would mollify emotional backlash and provide reasonable warrant for reconsideration. In the meantime, committed to transcendental method as Lonergan articulated it, I will engage the difficult questions before us. My approach in the chapters that follow is to attentively, intelligently, and reasonably differentiate and interrelate the pertinent disciplines relevant to current discussion on "God in the brain."

CHAPTER 3

NEUROSCIENCE

THE BIOLOGICAL BASES OF TRANSCENDENT EXPERIENCES

> The Brain—is wider than the Sky—
> For—put them side by side—
> The one the other will contain
> With ease—and You—beside—
>
> —Emily Dickinson

> Between my brain and me there is always a layer that I cannot penetrate.
>
> —Jules Renard

A range of neuroscientific research programs investigates transcendent experience: brain-imaging techniques to discern the neural mechanisms triggered by meditative practice; ingestion of hallucinogens or the application of magnetic fields to induce transcendent experiences; and the search for genetic differences in more and less spiritually sensitive subjects. An earlier generation of research used the electroencephalograph (EEG) to investigate neural functioning during meditation (Hood, Spilka, Hunsberger, & Gorsuch, 1996, pp. 193–198). Today, quantitative (or computerized) EEG and, more so, magnetoencephalography (MEG) hold renewed promise for such real-time neuroscientific research (Evans & Abarbanel, 1999; Muthukumaraswamy et al., 2013).

This chapter briefly summarizes some of the conclusions of such varied neuroscientific research. The result is probable accounts of aspects of the brain function that lies behind transcendent experiences. To be sure, though trends are coalescing, none of these conclusions is secure. The research is still new, and it is ongoing. While the data build up, we are still dealing in educated guesses. So, although the title of this book names the *Brain*, this chapter might be the least important in the book. The problematic of "God in the brain" is more philosophical or methodological than neuroscientific, and this book's focus is those presuppositional matters.

Nonetheless, usefully and unavoidably, this chapter stands to exemplify the kinds of neuroscientific research that seem to impinge on transcendent experience and are sometimes even said to relate to God. But given the still rudimentary stage of current neuroscience, the material this chapter summarizes is, as in all science, "merely" the "best available opinions of the day." To be sure, the summary here is far, far from comprehensive. This chapter serves only to illustrate the kind of firm conclusions that might possibly—nay, that surely will—be available one day: we will eventually understand how the brain relates to consciousness. At the same time, this chapter provides examples of the neuroscientific conclusions that philosophers and psychologists are invoking to ground their own, much broader claims. Additionally, parts of this chapter suggest how some neuroscientific opinion oversteps the bounds of its competence and indulges in quite loose philosophical speculation. In fact, these self-awarded liberties explain how reference to God ever entered neuroscience.

3.1. Neurophysiological Bases of Transcendent Experiences

3.1.1. *The Mystical Mind of d'Aquili and Newberg*

The research and speculation of the late Eugene d'Aquili and of Andrew Newberg (1999; Newberg, d'Aquili, & Rause, 2001) might have been the best popularly known of the new neuroscientific agenda. In the least, they are likely the most responsible (see also Newberg & Waldman, 2010) for the flurry of public interest in "God in the brain" (Aaen-Stockdale, 2012; Begley, 2001; Broadway, 2004; Heffern, 2001; Holmes, 2001; Kaufman, 2005; Kluger, 2004; Robb, 2004; Saylor, 2004). Using single photon emission computed tomography (SPECT), d'Aquili and Newberg (1999) observed

Buddhist monks and Catholic nuns at the high point of their meditation practice. The research results squared with already-known aspects of brain function, and on that basis d'Aquili and Newberg's suggested a possible explanation for transcendent experience.

In their model, meditation begins with a deliberate intention, determined by the type of meditation—whether to focus on some object or to clear the mind of all thought; either way, the neurological processes are largely the same. The intention stimulates the *right* attention association area (AAA: prefrontal lobe, seat of the "will") and, thus, begins a cascade of effects that eventually reverberate through the brain—*right* orientation association area (OAA: posterior superior parietal lobe), hippocampus, amygdala, hypothalamus, and peripheral autonomic nervous system—ever gaining in intensity. When this stimulation reaches an unsustainable maximum, a "spillover" effect results. This effect stimulates the corresponding *left* brain structures and, importantly, both the sympathetic and the parasympathetic nervous systems, producing a paradoxical state of simultaneous quiescence and arousal—as also occurs in sexual experience: to get excited and orgasm, one must relax and let go. The resultant experience is ecstasy. But the continued escalating neural activity also simultaneously results in the total deafferentation (cessation of all input) of the right and left OAAs. Ordinarily, the OAA receives and integrates input from all the senses and, thus—through sight, hearing, touch, and internal bodily feedback—orients the body in space and in relation to the external world. However, when all input is excluded, the experience must be one of totally empty space. Moreover, without any orienting spatial context in the external world, this experience of space would be "subjectively experienced as absolute unity or wholeness" (p. 112). Depending on the type of the meditation, on religious and cultural categories, and on the dominance of either activating or quiescent hypothalamic discharge, the experience might be reported positively, in the West, as union with God or negatively, in the East, as the emptiness of nirvana. Thus, in a creative neuroscientific tour de force, d'Aquili and Newberg (1999) proposed a plausible account of peak transcendent experience.

Puzzlingly (Delio, 2003), however, and obviously exceeding the competence of their neuroscientific training and, thus, necessitating the present discussion, d'Aquili and Newberg (1999) refer to this experience in conflicting ways: as "a state of altered consciousness," "the realm of God or ultimate reality" (p. 14), "God or pure consciousness" (p. 18), and "the higher being or state of being—mystical mind" (p. 19). They choose to name this experience or state or being—which is it?—"absolute unitary being" (AUB) (p. 14, et passim). Much ambiguity typifies these speculations, and echoes of incoherent Eastern philosophy (3.1.4; 5.8.3) reverberate through them.

D'Aquili and Newberg also propose neurological explanations for other kinds of religious concerns—specifically, the human propensity to create myths (ch. 4) and to use rituals to resolve existential crises (ch. 5). Despite the difficulty inherent in these issues, the ambitious discussion in these chapters suggests proposed neurological foundations—under the name of "cognitive operators"—for the most subtle of phenomena, such as synthetic and analytic thinking, causality, concept formation, and mathematics, and even for intelligence and, then, consciousness itself (ch. 3). Such informed speculation points to neuroscientific understanding that will someday be secure.

Clearly, d'Aquili and Newberg are treating matters of the mind, not merely those of the brain. Clearly, too, their theory provides no consistent or coherent understanding of the relationship between brain and mind—as the added italics in the following statements evince:

- "The mind and brain are simply two different ways of looking at *the same thing*" (pp. 21–22; see also p. 50);
- the brain is "the neurophysiological *substrate for* an individual mind" (p. 48);
- "the brain function *results in* . . . the function of the mind" (p. 51);
- "the most sophisticated mathematical, logical, or grammatical operation can ultimately be *reduced to* the simplest spatial and spatiotemporal analysis [in the brain]" (p. 80); and
- "no matter what degree of complexity the nervous system has attained, . . . this complexity *never implies in itself* the existence of subjective awareness" (p. 185).

Five different conceptualizations in five different statements of this relationship! Then, perhaps their extravagant summary of this relationship—unfortunately continuing to give mysticism a bad name—is this:

- "The brain and mind may be considered together in a '*mystical union*'" (p. 16).

Symptomatic of our age, the culprit responsible for this conceptual confusion is inadequate epistemology and even a resultant intellectual agnosticism. For d'Aquili and Newberg, "the word *real* . . . is used in the same sense as in the utterance, 'This rock and this table are real' " (p. 192). Here, apparently, the criterion of truth and reality is sense experience, which we have in common with Fido—the commonsensical or naïve realism discussed at 2.2.2–2.2.4. Nonetheless, they write, "if the traditional definition of truth as the *adaequatio intellectus ad rem* be taken at all seriously, then truth can be at best an approximation, perhaps a fairly weak one at that" (p. 186). So at this point, intellect is also allowed as a determinant of reality, and truth is *the approximation of the intellect to reality*—although the Latin *adaequatio* means, rather, equalization or equality, not approximation. Nonetheless, rather than something intelligible, reality still seems to be imagined as a body lying "out there," against which ideas are measured. But measured by what? Some meta-look at the looking, or meta-touch of the touching, of that rock or table? The controlling metaphor is, again, one of material bodies and sense perception.

But the theory shifts yet again. In the final analysis, as d'Aquili and Newberg elaborate, supposedly, "one cannot be certain whether or not . . . any . . . phenomena . . . are generated by the brain and mind, or experienced by them" (pp. 48–49). So "the wave-particle metaphor may be useful for understanding what is experienced during mystical states" (p. 50). Indeed, "opposites such as good and evil are . . . understood as being two different ways of looking at the same thing" (p. 50), as are "right and wrong, justice and injustice, . . . heaven and hell" (p. 55), and "life-death" (p. 85). Oh, really? And how do they know these things—or anything? And why should anyone take these assertions seriously when, supposedly, their being right or wrong has no inherent significance but is merely a matter of "different ways of looking" (that perceptual metaphor again)? Like many others today, these theorists make sweeping truth statements that ultimately rest on a professed inability to know the truth about anything (e.g., Richards & Bergin, 2005, p. 105).

For philosophical reasons I differ with d'Aquili and Newberg (1999; d'Aquili, Newberg, & Rause, 2001) on many points, but to dilate on them is not the purpose of this book. Many of the same criticisms also apply to Mario Beauregard and Denyse O'Leary's (2007) *The Spiritual Brain*. Most welcome is their outright rejection of materialism, their advocacy for a "nonmaterialist neuroscience" (p. xiv et passim), and their repeated insistence on "The Spiritual Nature of Humans" (p. 290). Also welcome is their report of the brain regions involved in the mystical experiences of the Carmelite nuns whom Beauregard studied: "no single 'God spot' in the brain located in the temporal lobe," but "a number of brain regions normally implicated in perception, cognition, emotion, body representation, and self-consciousness" (p. 272)—many of the same regions associated with meditative practice and psychedelic experiences as in the lists at 3.1.3 and 3.3. But their lack of theoretical alternatives leads them too easily to leap with uncritical traditional religiosity (e.g., pp. 6–8, 24–28, 293) from human spiritual experiences to the affirmation of non-human powers, spaces, and entities: "People who have such experiences have actually contacted a reality outside themselves" (p. xvi), "an objectively real force outside themselves (God)" (p. 38). Rather than to be celebrated, then, the fact that on this score they find d'Aquili and Newberg's "approach consistent with" their own (p. 259) is actually unfortunate. It demonstrates again how delicate and nuanced from every side a credible treatment of these matters must be. I trust that my analyses throughout this book provide sufficient clarification to make further dilation here unnecessary. Then, overlooking the unwarranted philosophical speculation, it suffices to acknowledge these researchers' contributions to an understanding of the neurological functions involved in transcendent experiences.

3.1.2. The "Religious Circuit" of Patrick McNamara

Like d'Aquili and Newberg, Patrick McNamara (2009) has also presented a grand synthesis of neuroscience and religion. It provides another detailed proposal about the brain structures involved in religious phenomena, so it merits consideration here. First, however, some contextualizing observations are in order.

Unlike d'Aquili and Newberg, and unlike Beauregard and O'Leary, McNamara refrains from philosophical speculation. Nonetheless, his psychologist's reliance on currently reigning psychological presuppositions—particularly the mechanistic constructs of cognitive psychology and computer modeling (e.g., pp. 48–49)—obscures his contribution, as well. Moreover, in all these cases, I believe, there is the attempt to make too much of too little. The research evidence simply does not sustain the broad applications that an explanation of all religious phenomena would entail. Indeed, we lack even consensus on what those phenomena are or how they should be defined (Cohn, 1962; Henman, 2013; Spilka & Ladd, 2013; Vago & Silbersweig, 2012).

Despite the title of the book, *The Neuroscience of Religious Experience*, McNamara's (2009) topic is not transcendent experience in particular, but religiosity, broadly conceived. The book addresses an array of phenomena associated with religion—such as religious ideation related to temporal lobe epilepsy, schizophrenia, frontotemporal dementia, scrupulosity and obsessive-compulsive disorder, and bipolar disorder (ch. 5); religious behaviors and practices (ch. 7); spirit possession and dissociative identity disorder or multiple personality disorder (ch. 8); God concepts (ch. 9); prayer and religious language (ch. 10); ritual (ch. 11); religiosity through the life span (ch. 12); and the evolution of religion throughout history (ch. 13). Transcendent experience (ch. 5), characterized as "ecstasy" (pp. 55–56), is also a topic.

The bulk of the book elaborates a theory of the Self and its transformation. McNamara's concern is really the question of how religion nurtures virtue in people. To me this concern seems to reflect the focus of Protestantism, more on morality than on spirituality (for a contrast, see Helminiak, 1996a, pp. 235–236), but spirituality is the focus here. Center stage in this transformation is a process McNamara (2009) calls "decentering." A pervasive, elusive, and shifting notion, decentering is in some way pertinent to all the cases listed in the prior paragraph. It entails "the reduction in Self and the enhancement of an alternative identity" such that "the individual sets aside his or her own identity to interact with or participate in the identity of the spirit or God" (p. 208). The goal of this process and of life is to achieve "a unified sense of Self, a unified consciousness" (pp. 257–258), by "aiming at an ideal self, ultimately God" (p. 43)—that is, to be exact, a Self *symbolized* by "God" (pp. 42, 55, 147, et passim): McNamara explicitly disavows any claims about "the metaphysical status of supernatural agents and forces" (p. 168) and laudably remains ever focused on psychology. Said simply, McNamara's thesis is that religion builds character and to do so is its purpose: "The divided Self is the problem religion addresses and solves" (p. 23); "Religion is required to help build a Self that is capable of consistently choosing the good and the appropriate over long periods of time" (p. 43); "Religiosity, in short, promotes development of an executive Self by promoting development of character strengths" (p. 31). What McNamara fails to consider (his topic is only religion) is that other social agencies are also dedicated to building character, and even brainwashing might qualify as an instance of decentering. So there is question as to why the social and mental mechanisms he discerns should be properly called "religious." An even bigger question, essential to religion but ignored in psychology of religion, also remains: what and who define "the good and the appropriate" that religion and those other agencies foster? (see 1.4; 2.6.2–2.6.3)

As in much psychological discussion of the self, it is unclear what Self actually means in McNamara's discussion. A chapter devoted to explication of the Self left me still wondering. Why, for example, a capital letter highlights Self, Will, and Mind throughout the book remains a mystery never addressed. At one point, McNamara speaks of "the strength of the ego or Self" (p. 238). In this case, the Self in question is closely related to, and seems to be, the *ego* of Jane Loevinger's (1976) classic work. There *ego* refers to a "structure," the very mental makeup of a person that can change over time, one would hope toward ever further harmonization. But McNamara (2009) also extensively treats Self in terms of identity. In this case, it seems, self-concept is in question. Yet one's self-concept, what one "thinks" of oneself whether explicitly or implicitly, does not necessarily square with the ego structure one might have developed to do the thinking or even to avoid it. Consistently, McNamara's focus on character formation emphasizes "a centralized executive Self" (p. 30), which seems to have more to do with ego structure than with identity or self-concept. At stake are "autonomy, abstractive powers, and freedom," and McNamara "call[s] this high conception of the agent the 'executive Self'" (p. 41). It is that, according to McNamara's thesis, that religion seeks to develop.

Weaved into McNamara's conception of the executive Self is an appeal to Aristotle's and Thomas Aquinas's *intellectus agens*. This referent relates, in fact, precisely to the *intellectus in actu* discussed at 2.3.3 and specifically indicates the actuation of the spiritual/intellectual capacity that one experiences when insights actually occur. So regarding spirituality this referent is right on target. However, apparently knowing it only in English translation as "the agent intellect" (p. 41)—"active or actuated intellect" would be a better translation, highlighting the intended contrast with *intellectus possibilis* or "potential intellect"—McNamara conflates *intellectus agens* with the executive Self, seeing the psychological construct *agency* in both cases, and then mixing intellect and will, confounding the *intellectus agens* with the capacity for deliberation, freedom, choice, and self-determination. Thus, supposedly, "Religion provides the individual with a range of practices and ideas to enhance the agent intellect and to strengthen the executive Self" (p. 40) or "to strengthen the agent intellect and/or the Self" (pp. 40–41). From one point of view, this conception makes utter nonsense of Aquinas and is akin to asserting today that religion increases people's IQ. But from another point of view, McNamara is engaging, unwittingly and ineffectively, to be sure, but engaging, nonetheless, the very heart and basis—the human spirit—of my naturalistic explanation of spirituality (5.8.2). For this reason, I make a point of this misrepresentation of Aristotle and Aquinas. McNamara does, at least, recognize some profound psychological understanding in the classical and medieval Western tradition. Would that others did, as well (5.5.3)! Yet the wealth of possible explanation in it is obscured and dissipated when casual contemporary psychological speculation misunderstands and misapplies that contribution. A similar misunderstanding pertains regarding the farther reaches of Buddhist teaching about meditation (3.1.3). These facts stand as more lamentable testimony to the conceptual confusion that reigns in the field of psychology (Cahoone, 2010; McCarthy, 1990, 1997) and that prompts the present methodological book.

At last, we come to the neuroscientific point of this chapter. Amidst that discussion of transformation of the Self, McNamara proposes a neural system he calls "the 'religious circuit'" (pp. 135–137). He believes that it is involved in that process of transformation via decentering and that it applies to religious phenomena. In one place, McNamara summarizes this circuit as follows:

> The most important regions of the brain for studies of religious expression appear to be a circuit linking up the orbital and dorsomedial prefrontal cortex, the right dorsolateral prefrontal cortex, the ascending serotonergic system, the mesocortical DA [dopamine] system, the amygdala/hippocampus, and the right anterior temporal lobes. (p. 127)

More succinctly, McNamara suggests "the Self and religion are associated with a distinct functional circuit involving the amygdala, the prefrontal lobes, and the anterior temporal region." Citing conflicting research results, McNamara freely admits "the theory remains controversial" (p. 257). Indeed, whereas other research specifically on meditation (discussed at 3.1.3) does focus on some of these same regions of the brain, the meditative research also emphasizes others regions as essential to meditative experience and transcendent experience.

In another treatment of religious experience, McNamara appeals to a long-standing theory that linked religious ideation quite directly with the temporal lobe. In many cases—the percentages are debated—people suffering from temporal lobe epilepsy report religious conversions, explicit calls from God, states of heavenly exaltation, angelic voices, or saintly visions. Tellingly, non-religious epileptics are more likely to make secular allusions: political conspiracies, radiation in space, all-controlling electronic brains, alien presences, and the like. Nonetheless, because of the religious reports, theorists linked religious experiences to the temporal lobe, initially the left. Later research involved the right temporal lobe more explicitly. Additionally, the prefrontal cortex, the amygdala, and the hippocampus were also implicated. McNamara concludes that "the right-sided temporal and prefrontal networks . . . attach religious concepts to the impulses originating in the amygdala" (p. 93), the hippocampus also being involved in some way (p. 94). Others have seriously questioned this whole line of argument, both religiously and neuroscientifically (Aaen-Stockdale, 2012; Beauregard & O'Leary, 2007, pp. 57–77; Helminiak, 1984b). Important here is also the realization that these emotion- and imagery-filled epilepsy-related experiences differ substantively from the unitive experience on which I am focusing. Besides, once again, no firm conclusions can be reported, as McNamara (2009) allows. Yet he has generously offered his obviously arduous attempt to make sense of a jungle of neuroscientific findings.

Hence, we have another account of the brain structures that play into religiosity, if not specifically into transcendent experience. The sweep of the structures in McNamara's account gives one pause. Because McNamara is concerned about human development and the mechanisms that foster ongoing human integration, the structures he names appear to be those involved in all higher human functioning—such as awareness, attention, habit formation, learning and unlearning, emotions, bias and clarity, and decision making. Why these structures should be named as a specifically "religious circuit" remains a valid question. However, a similar sweep of structures appeared in d'Aquili and Newberg's theory (3.1.1); and the same brain regions and even more elaborate networks or circuits appear in the research specifically on meditation, reviewed immediately below. I raise questions, not to deprecate the neuroscientific conclusions, but to highlight the challenge in neuroscientific research. Whereas we would like some simple account of neuronal processes; in fact, the brain is a highly intricate, long-evolved, and multiply interconnected collection of different functioning units, sometimes too interconnected to even qualify as separate units. No individual parts, but the brain's collective functioning supports our experience as human—and if as human, why not also as religious? After all, my recurrent insistence is that transcendent experience is a fully human affair, not one dependent *per se* on God or other religious powers and non-human entities. A valid neuroscientific account of the inherent capacities of human nature would provide a sure foundation for understanding the lofty cultural achievements of humanity as well as the subtle, specifically religious ones.

3.1.3. *The Networks of Recent Research on Meditative Practice*

Recent years have seen a flood of research on meditation and brain function. An increasing focus of the research is the extraordinary potential of meditation for addressing a range of prevalent mental-health concerns, including depression, anxiety, attention deficit/hyperactivity disorder, bipolar disorder, borderline personality disorder, eating disorders, Alzheimer's disease, and substance abuse (Brewer et al., 2011; Hölzel et al., 2011; Taylor et al., 2012; Vago & Silbersweig, 2012). Because of this focus on clinical applications, this research tends not to engage issues of religion, spirituality, or mystical—transcendent—experience explicitly. For the same reason, this research does not focus on the high point of meditative experience, the "mystical moment," which was d'Aquili and Newberg's (3.1.1) concern. Nonetheless, this research is highly revealing of the neuronal structures involved in meditative practice and its lasting effects on the brain.

Britta Hölzel and her colleagues (2011) provide a relatively accessible summary of the research results currently available. Their goal is to "integrate the existing literature into a comprehensive theoretical framework" (abstract). Sorting out the various mental activities involved in meditation, they propose a four-point overview: (a) attention regulation; (b) body awareness; (c) emotion regulation, including the reappraisal of, exposure to, and the extinction and reconsolidation of emotions; and (d) change in one's perspective on oneself. These four aspects of meditation could be taken to be a sequence, but, apart from the most adept meditators, during practice emphases shift back and forth among the four. To each of these aspects taken singly, a list of brain regions pertains, usually in highly interconnected networks (also called "systems"). Like other researchers noted below, these researchers also scoured the neuroscience literature for conclusions relevant to these various meditative activities. For example, outside the context of meditation, significant research has been done on the mechanisms of attention, of emotions, and of self-reference. All these data are relevant for a neuroscientific understanding of meditation. The proposed framework, then, is a construction of many pieces gleaned from different areas of research and correlated with the results of research specifically focused on meditation. The major areas of the brain involved in the four-stage process would be these: (a) anterior cingulate cortex; (b) insula and temporo-parietal junction; (c) dorsal prefrontal cortex, ventromedial prefrontal cortex, hippocampus, and amygdala; and (d) medial prefrontal cortex, insula, and temporo-parietal junction.

Even in this simplified list, overlaps are apparent as are repetitions of brain regions already indicated by d'Aquili, Newberg, and McNamara. These overlaps highlight the fact that sorting out brain function is no easy task. One reason is that the same neuronal regions are often involved in very different functions at different times and under different circumstances. Nonetheless, amidst this complexity strands of consensus promise to emerge.

One recent focus of promising research is the "default-mode network" (DMN) (Raichle et al., 2001). The DMN is thought to set a baseline of ongoing neuronal activity dedicated, in part, to self-referential experience. As such, this network is involved with one's sense of oneself. The two "hubs" of this network—that is, areas of extensive interconnectivity in the brain—are the medial prefrontal cortex (subdivided into dorsal, ventral, and orbital areas) and the posterior cingulate cortex. These hubs can be usefully pictured such that the first lies in the front, and the second to the back of the brain, both situated along the inner (medial) regions of the cortex, hidden in the longitudinal fissure, the split between the right and left cerebral hemispheres. One could imagine that the neuronal basis for the sense of self is sequestered safely in the inner folds of the cortex. This network also includes a number of other brain regions. They are connected among themselves as if in a loop or a continuous track, which includes and, thus, connects also the two hubs. These other regions are the dorsomedial and ventromedial prefrontal cortex, the precuneus (a medial area of the parietal lobe lying above the posterior cingulate cortex), the right and left inferolateral temporal cortices, the right and left inferoparietal lobules, and the right and left parahippocampal gyri. Together with the medial prefrontal cortex and the posterior cingulate cortex, these brain regions constitute the complete default-mode network (Taylor et al., 2012).

Evidence is accumulating to the effect that meditation affects the functioning of this network and eventually even induces lasting changes, namely, a reset of the default to "a more present-centered mode" (Brewer et al, 2011, p. 20255). Specifically, meditation decreases the activity in the two hubs of the network; and meditation also changes the levels of activity in the connectivity of this network, decreasing the connectivity in some cases and increasing it in others (Brewer et al., 2011; Garrison et al., 2013; Taylor et al., 2011, 2012). The overall result is twofold: a decrease in activity in brain regions related to preoccupation with oneself, self-referential thinking, worry about the past and future, and mind wandering; and an increase in regions related to facets of self-control such as conflict monitoring, cognitive management, and access of working memory. These neuronal results square with the kind of inner experience that meditators report—a more focused and "centered" state of mind: increasing ability to be in the present moment, free from distracting thoughts and emotions, and an increased ability to dismiss distractions and to restore calm to the mind. Thus, attention to the DMN provides "a basis for a new understanding of the neural bases of mindfulness meditation practice" (Brewer et al., 2011, p. 20258). Indeed, providing meditators real-time fMRI (functional magnetic resonance imaging) feedback on the level of activity in the posterior cingulate cortex, only one component of the DMN, allows them to efficiently learn to decrease that activity and, seemingly *ipso facto*, achieve the healthful effects of meditation as well as learn to meditate more effectively (Brewer & Garrison, 2014; Garrison et al., 2013).

To be sure, these results are new, and they await replication in additional experiments. All of the sources I cited note complications, inconsistencies, and limitations in the conclusions achieved thus far. Moreover, different research teams pursuing different hypothetical angles advance different theories.

David Vago and David Silbersweig (2012), for example, provide an integrative neuroscientific article on meditation that is virtually encyclopedic. This rich—although difficult and sometimes poorly edited—24-page paper lists 301 references! Although Vago and Silbersweig cover much the same neuronal territory to which I have already referred, they mention that proposed default-mode network only once parenthetically: "the brain's default network" (p. 7). Instead, they offer a different theoretical framework for understanding and managing "mindfulness," understood both as a technique (meditation) and as its result (a mindset, "mindful awareness" [p. 2]). Concerned to bring focus and consistency to neuroscientific research on meditation, they extensively discuss the confounding meanings that today's proliferating usage is giving to the term *mindfulness*, and they propose specifications for a number of aspects of meditation. Additionally, as is commonly done, they usefully distinguish three basic types of meditation. First, "focused attention (FA), a type of concentrative practice," is central to all meditation since some control over the flitting and meandering mind is the presupposition of any more specialized training. Second, a common next step is "insight or open monitoring (OM), a type of receptive practice," which allows one to observe, note, and eventually transcend the many shifting contents of the mind, including images, ideas, memories, and emotions. Third, some meditative techniques are specifically designed for the "cultivation of ethical qualities (e.g., loving-kindness, compassion, forgiveness)" (p. 3).

Additionally, Vago and Silbersweig summarize the major effects of meditation with their clever acronym, S-ART: self-awareness, self-regulation, and self-transcendence—to know oneself, to manage oneself, and, in personal and social growth, to move beyond oneself. It is useful to recognize that these three are basic to any stability of personality and mental health, so the relevance of meditation to concerns of mental health, not necessarily to religion or transcendent experience, comes clearly to the fore once again, echoing something of McNamara's (2009) project under the name "religious."

Vago and Silbersweig (2012) propose different mutually interdependent neuronal structures and networks pertinent to those different kinds of meditation and their specialized effects, all bearing on the experience of self. Namely, a network called the "experiential enactive self (EES)" regards the unconscious processes, given by inherited temperament or acquired through experience, that monitor and control the body's relationship with the external environment and with its own internal feedback and functioning (pp. 7–8). In addition to vision, hearing, the other senses (exteroception), and the sense of one's body in space (proprioception and kinesthesia), interoceptive processes such as heart rate, digestion, and respiration are also in question here—the body's self-regulation. The term *enactive* refers to the organism's *action* within its *en*vironment. Another network, similarly regarding bodily behaviors, but this time behaviors consciously experienced and personally controlled, is named "the experiential phenomenological self (EPS)"—"phenomenological" because it is available to awareness (pp. 8–10). This brain system underlies the personal sense of an embodied "I" who is acting. These two networks, EES and EPS, both variably regard the body–self. "At the core"—evidently, in different ways: the presentation is unclear—they involve what is called the (only one) "dorsal attentional system (DAS)" (pp. 6–7) of the brain and include a long list of different brain regions and their interconnections.

The matter is so complicated that it would be counterproductive to reproduce all the lists except for some exemplification below. Indeed, viewing them all, one could validly wonder what parts of the brain are *not* involved, and the answer would be mostly only those in the more "primitive" parts of the brain (hindbrain and midbrain) dedicated basically to biological survival and the cortices dedicated to the senses: visual, auditory, and sensorimotor—though even these are distantly involved.

The third network regards our personal sense of self, the "me" about which we can think and talk and to which we ascribe various characteristics. These constitute an innumerable and ever updated list of remembered qualities, from external looks and developed skills to internal feelings, propensities, beliefs, and values. Rather descriptively, this system is called "the evaluative narrative self (NS)." This sense of self depends on "the hippocampal-cortical memory system (HCMS)" (p. 7). It entails structures such as the ventral medial prefrontal cortex, the pre- and subgenual anterior cingulate cortex, the medial parietal cortex, the prefrontal cortex, and the retrosplenial cortex as well as important connections with the anterior thalamus, hippocampus, amygdala, and others (pp. 10–11).

In light of their specific concern to explain the self-awareness, self-regulation, and self-transcendence (S-ART) of meditative practice, Vago and Silbersweig invoke yet a fourth neural network. They propose that it integrates the functioning of the three already-mentioned networks, which specifically regard the self. This fourth network is the "frontoparietal control system (FPCS)" (pp. 11), parts of which are the repeated focus of meditative studies. The FPCS is supposed to be a major integrative network of the brain. This network entails the rostral frontopolar prefrontal cortex, the right ventrolateral prefrontal cortex, the dorsal medial and dorsal lateral prefrontal cortex, the dorsal anterior cingulate cortex, the anterior insular cortex, the lateral cerebellum, and the anterior inferior parietal lobe.

I dare to report these lists of brain regions only to underline the overwhelmingly interactive complexity at stake in these matters—such that, at least for lay folk, to speak simply of "brain function" might not be far from sufficiently accurate. For specialists, on the other hand, to speak simply of the prefrontal, temporal, or parietal cortex would be to speak very grossly, indeed. Neuroscientists have long differentiated many different functional regions of the major divisions of the brain, for example, the "cortical regionalization maps . . . generated by Korbinian Brodmann a century ago . . . although refinements and alternative interpretations abound" (Swanson, 2013, p. 35). Moreover, focus is increasingly on the interconnectivity among these regions, not simply, again, on gross or even refined divisions of the brain. And the repetitions—almost variations on a theme, which even lay folk can recognize—in the listed brain regions, incorporated differently into the different theories, serve again as a reminder that neuroscience is a young and ongoing enterprise. So we are left with many enticing, provocative, and sometimes seemingly compelling, but never definitive, accounts of the brain function that pertains to meditative experience.

As I have noted, this recent research is concerned about clinical applications rather than explicitly about religious or spiritual matters, so emphasis is on the process of meditation, not on its high point in "mystical" or transcendent experience. Nonetheless, building their neuroscientific accounts on theory and practice derived substantively from Buddhism, Hölzel and her colleagues and Vago and Silbersweig do broach that subtle experience at the high point of meditative practice. They speak of it as "meta-awareness" and describe it as "a form of . . . executive monitoring, in which one takes a nonconceptual perspective" (Hölzel et al., 2011, p. 547); or they speak of it as an acquired "skill" in which "awareness itself become the object of awareness" (Vago & Silbersweig, 2012, p. 11), "a highly developed form of executive monitor" (p. 13) by which "one may 'see and know' when they [sic] have lost the focus of attention on the object, or emotion has become reactive and ruminative" or by which one may "determine whether there is dullness or too much excitation during the practice" (p. 17).

In line with my argument throughout this book, I want to illustrate that these accounts have not yet touched the unitive experience, the high point of meditation, consciousness as conscious, consciousness as a fully non-objectified and non-reflecting self-presence—rather than consciousness as intentional, as directed toward some object (5.3; see already 1.9.) These theorists' phraseology—except perhaps for that illusive "nonconceptual"— evinces throughout a this-against-that-ness, a subject-object duality, despite verbal assertions to the contrary borrowed from Buddhist theory. Psychologically, "executive monitoring" is the subject's overseeing and managing contents of the mind or of experience—as is also the realization of a wandering mind or of excitation. In these theorists we have, once again, the modeling of consciousness as a kind of perception: this against that, light striking the retina, sound waves moving the tympanum, the subject encountering the object. Neuroscience might well be able to reveal the brain structures and functions that underlie our perceptual experience, even our experience of ourselves as objects to ourselves; but, I submit, neuroscience will never in itself account for the human experience of subjectivity *per se*. Why not? Without doubt, at some level, human consciousness depends on the functioning of the brain; but consciousness, emergent from the brain and psyche, is a different kind of reality in comparison to the spatial-temporal array of brain anatomy and physiology, complex as it might be (4.14).

At best, as the more fulsome statements of Vago and Silbersweig (2012) suggest, these theorists are highlighting the virtuous and ever-to-be-exercised skill of eschewing bias in one's experience: to be "free of the choosing, evaluating, and projecting that is sometimes described as 'grasping, aversion, and delusion'" (p. 23), to develop the "attentional capacity for encoding and recollecting experiences efficiently—without forgetfulness or distraction," to perceive things "'as they truly are,' without distortions or biases," to achieve "perception without interpretation" (p. 2). This unbiased experience, nothing more, is precisely the intent of Husserl's "epoche" (p. 17). Such impartial or dispassionate living—what Lonergan (1972) called "authenticity" (2.6.2–2.6.3)—pertains to *intentional* consciousness (5.1.2; 5.3) and regards a subject's engaging the universe of being in unbiased objectivity. Authenticity, laudable and desirable as it is, is not the pure, lucid, contentless, unbounded, non-reflective self-presence—the human spirit—that uniquely characterizes human consciousness and accounts for the unitive experience of "mysticism" (1.2; 5.8.2).

This same point can be made in another and simpler way. Even according to Buddhist teaching, the experience of Buddha nature is not a skill to be achieved. Our Buddha nature—consciousness (1.2)—is ever with us. It needs only to be "cultivated" or "revealed." It regards a dimension of the human mind that is ever available such that, in one version of the tradition, samsara is nirvana (Kalapahana, 1992). Neuroscience can let us eventually understand the reconfiguration of the brain that allows this already given dimension of the mind to emerge in fuller force as we increasingly integrate the spiritual dimension into the supporting organic and psychic structures of our being (Helminiak, 1987b; 5.9.4), but consciousness is there apart from meditative practice or any restructuring of the brain.

3.1.4. Regarding the Buddhist Notion of "No Self"

One further aspect of these theorists' appropriation of Buddhist theory needs comment because it turns fully on epistemology—that matter of "no self." Thus, "One of the advanced outcomes or aspects of insight, developed through mindfulness-based meditation practice is the realization of 'no self' " (Vago & Silbersweig, 2012, p. 23), the realization "that no self is to be found in the elements of our experience" (Hölzel et al., 2011, p. 547). The all-telling question is whether these statements are to be taken ontologically or merely psychologically. That is, do they mean that the subject absolutely does not exist, that "I" am nothing real at all? Or do they merely mean that what we take to be ourselves is often mistaken, biased, confused, deluded, and we need—in popular lingo—to "get real"? This crucial ambiguity pervades the statements of these neuroscientific theorists. For example, they say "there is no such thing as a permanent, unchanging self" (p. 547). Does this statement mean there exists no self, no person, no subject, no "I" at all? Or only that we are always changing? And if the latter, what wonder is there in it? Even a statement attributed to the Dalai Lama can be read with the same ambiguity: "This seemingly solid, concrete, independent, self-instituting I under its own power that appears actually does not exist at all" (p. 547). Or again, "there is no truly existing self (i.e., subject) that continues through life without change" (Vago & Silbersweig, 2012, p. 23).

Is it that there exists no unchanging self or, rather, no self whatsoever? The valid meaning is the former. It was at issue in the third-last paragraph above. It is the main thrust in Buddhist teaching, which regards clear thinking, unbiased living, mental health, a matter of good psychology. The ontological meaning is a later development, the result of speculation on the implications of Buddhist practice. The Buddha himself deflected any such speculation and offered no metaphysical teaching. Moreover, I submit, this accretion is mistaken. The literal suggestion, that there exist no persons, no selves, no "I," is ludicrous on its face. In this case, whether one's epistemology is the sensate-modeled or the intellectual (2.2.4–5), the same conclusion results. Even merely perceptually it is obvious that I exist—because I am physical, material, organic, as well as mental and conscious: anyone could bump into me to confirm my perceptual reality. Also via an intellectual epistemology, I can reasonably affirm my own being on the basis of indubitable evidence (2.1.1; 2.8.1). As René Descartes argued, *Cogito, ergo sum*: I think, therefore I must exist. Moreover, I can reasonably affirm my own being as a distinct being even in comparison to Brahman (6.2.4). No doubt, this "self" that I experience, namely, "me" as an object to my conscious subjectivity, the "self" that psychology treats, is, indeed, ever changing, coming and going in my experience, if only when, for example, I wake from dreamless sleep or anesthesia. "This perception [of a self] reoccurs very rapidly in the stream of mental events, leading to the impression that the self is a constant and unchanging entity" (Hölzel et al., 2011, p. 547). To be sure! Nonetheless, there must still be something, someone, an "I," there to get this impression of constancy by experience of a changing "me." After all, as I said, the conscious person that I am is more than just intentional, more than just aware of objects, including myself. My intentional awareness of myself as well as my conscious subjectivity might wax and wane, but I do not. I change, yes; but grammatically and ontologically there remains a constant subject of whom the changes are predicated. As argued at 5.8.3, Eastern philosophy is mistaken to base its claims about reality merely on inner conscious experience—as if such experience could occur without the brain! As if the brain and the world we inhabit is nothing real at all! As if everything in it is merely illusion—including those making this claim (in blatant self-contradictory assertion)!

Even in rarified Buddhism the problem is epistemology, the sensate-modeled version that is incapable of affirming the reality of both the material and the immaterial. That the "self can be experienced as an event," that via meditation "there emerges a tendency to identify with the phenomenon of 'experiencing' itself" (p. 547), that there can be the "non-dual" (2.3.3; 5.8.3) experience of "no distinction between knowing subject and perceived or known object" (Vago & Silbersweig, 2012, p. 13)—these statements, struggling for accuracy, are more on target. They point to the fact that what is experienced in meditation, eventually pure consciousness of consciousness, is nothing of the kind that we tend to deem real in our material-worldly experience and via a sensate-modeled epistemology; so we conclude that the "I" is not real, that it is nothing at all (5.6.2). Yes, consciousness itself is nothing of the material, sensate, perceptual kind; but this fact does not mean that it is nothing. The issue is merely that human consciousness is a different kind of reality, and sensate-modeled thinking is incapable of affirming the non-material as real.

3.1.5. A Critical Conclusion About the Neuroscience of Transcendent Experience

Current neuroscience, bolstered by new imaging techniques and computer-assisted analyses, offers promising explanations of the brain structures, interconnections, and processes underlying transcendent experience. Yet, facing the central and daunting question of consciousness, some neuroscientists too easily slip into speaking of "God in the brain." Others, concerned about the clinical application of meditation but beholden, nonetheless, to Eastern philosophy and religion, slip too easily into speaking about the ontological non-reality of human persons—who are the object of their science and who are actually doing the science! The conceptual confusion that pervades these studies allows neuroscientists to accept not only the uncritical, pious, popular lore of Western theism but also the mistaken notions of Eastern philosophy, and then to try and justify them on the basis of neuroscience. I present this criticism to highlight a main point once again: epistemology is the bugaboo of current scientific and scholarly discussion about "God in the brain."

3.2. A Genetic Basis of Transcendent Experiences: Hamer

Another approach to the biological basis of transcendent experiences involves the search for a genetic difference. Following a long-standing technique of comparing identical twins to non-identical twins, Katherine Kirk, Nicholas Martin, and Lindon Eaves (1999) engaged in that search. The supposition of such a study is that identical twins share the exact same DNA, so behavioral characteristics common between identical twins result from a genetic predisposition, not from environmental influences and upbringing. Using a measure of self-transcendence to assess all the twins, this study did find that the identical twins were twice as likely to get similar scores than were the non-identical twins. The implication is that genes play a discernible role in a person's experience of transcendence.

Dean Hamer (2004; see also Broadway, 2004; Kluger, 2004) used more recent technology and actually suggested a specific gene linked with spiritual sensitivity. He had a 1,000-subject database, collected for another purpose. Among the data were DNA samples and scores on a personality scale that included a self-report measure of self-transcendence. On this basis, Hamer ranked the subjects from low to high on self-transcendence, and in their DNA he examined nine genes known to be involved in the production of monoamines: dopamine, epinephrine, norepinephrine, and serotonin. These constitute an important class of neurotransmitters that are associated with mood and emotions. These neurotransmitters are the target of many mind-altering drugs such as antidepressants and antianxiety drugs, as well as cocaine, methamphetamine, and other "street drugs" that produce "highs." Hamer found a correlation between the subjects' scores on self-transcendence and variations in the gene VMAT2. "Those [subjects] with the nucleic acid cytosine in one particular spot on the gene ranked high. Those with the nucleic acid adenine in the same spot ranked lower" (Kluger, 2004, p. 66). The conclusion was that this gene might be a genetic basis of spiritual sensitivity.

Hamer is well aware that, standing alone, this conclusion is incomplete, to say the least: no one gene could explain complex human traits. More seriously, the discovered genetic difference explained less than 1% of the variance in the self-transcendence scores (Zimmer, 2004)—a result that was statistically significant (that is, mathematically reliable, not likely to be a fluke), but hardly substantive in practice. This outcome is similar to using a massive magnifying glass to discover an otherwise invisible nick in the paint of a car. The nick would really be there, but whether it would matter is another question. Hamer's results actually explain exceedingly little about differences in people's likelihood of having transcendent experiences. Nonetheless, the effect was discernible, so this research exemplifies another way in which biology could account for transcendent experience.

Assessing the implications of his research with appropriate professional reserve—despite the reckless title of his book: *The God Gene*—Hamer (2004) refrained from drawing conclusions about the existence of God: " 'My findings are agnostic on the existence of God,' he says. 'If there's a God, there's a God. Just knowing what brain chemicals are involved in acknowledging that is not going to change the fact' " (Kluger, 2004, p. 65). Well said! Besides, the uncritically invoked and all-too-common leap from transcendent experience to God is simplistic. Whether the existence of God is actually related to transcendent experiences is a question that requires far more nuance—a major point of this book, which I address head-on in Chapter 6.

3.3. A Neurochemical Basis of Transcendent Experiences: "Entheogens"

A third neurological approach to transcendent experience focuses on the neurotransmitters themselves—or, rather, on drug-induced shifts in neurotransmitter concentration and function. The use of mind-altering drugs is long-standing in sacred traditions. Credible speculation suggests that the Eleusinian Mysteries of ancient Greece and Rome involved the ingestion of a psychedelic, probably derived from ergot, a fungus that grows on grains and wild grass in the Mediterranean area and elsewhere. The psychoactive elements were probably "*lysergic acid amide* and *lysergic acid hydroxyethylamide*, near relatives of *lysergic acid diethylamide*, the chemical name for LSD, also a product of ergot" (Hofmann, 2000, p. 34). Similarly, the spiritual insights of the Vedas probably depended on the use of *soma* (Muesse, 2007, Lectures 2 & 3), the sacred plant discussed in the ninth mandala of the *Rig Veda*, which might have been the mushroom *Amanita muscaria* (Forte, 1997a), whose active ingredient is muscimol, a potent $GABA_A$ agonist. Gamma-aminobutyric acid (GABA) is the primary inhibitory neurotransmitter in the human brain, and $GABA_A$ receptors are widely distributed in the brain. The ingestion of muscimol affects the cerebral cortex, hippocampus, cerebellum, and other brain structures, producing most frequently what is described as a lucid dream state. Siberian shamanism likely employed this same substance, which is also the sacred mushroom of the Mayan tradition of South Mexico (Forte, 1997a). Catholic friars of the Spanish Conquest noted this latter practice in the early 1550s (Riedlinger, 1997). Similarly, by the 2nd century CE, the Huichol of North Central Mexico were using peyote, whose active ingredient is mescaline, in religious ceremonies. In 1994, the United States Congress passed legislation giving Native Americans the right to continue such use (Sterling, 1997). In 2006, the U.S. Supreme Court ruled that the *União de Vegetal* of New Mexico, a religious group based in Brazil (Metzner, 1999), could likewise legally use its hallucinogenic "sacrament," *ayahuasca* (Drinan, 2006). Western Christians today, like those early Spanish friars, might find these practices strange, yet the Communion wine of the Christian Eucharist, especially when consumed on an empty stomach, also has a mild tranquilizing, mind-altering effect, and Christians believe this ritual unites them with Christ, God's divine son.

In all these cases, sacred rituals are believed to open a spiritual realm, and the religions freely associate these drug-induced altered states of consciousness with the Sacred or Divine, however conceived. It is understandable that prescientific cultures would see the divine in extraordinary mental experiences and that the Western tradition would define mysticism as direct communion with God (6.3.5). As is obvious in the topic of this book, this same connection perdures in much contemporary thinking. Lamentably, current use of the neologism *entheogens*—sources of the divine within—continues the usage wherein *divine* or *godly* implies nothing about a Creator but merely indicates, as in classical Greek usage, for example, anything eternal and unchanging, such as Plato's perfect triangle (Muesse, 2003). Emphasizing the spiritual implications of psychedelics, Gordon Wasson insisted, "It is a shabby word, 'hallucination.' It is not a hallucination what you experience when you consume the mushrooms that produce visions and that speak" (Forte, 1997a, p. 69). Wasson explained,

> A committee of us headed by Professor Carl Ruck, a classical scholar at Boston University, devised that word [*entheogens*] and we all adopted it unanimously rather than "hallucinogen" for those plant substances revered by Early Man for their potency, for their ability to command respect. (p. 68)

Nonetheless, the exact nature of these experiences remains an open question; and uncritical, inspirational language—useful in religion, but not in the sciences—does not contribute to a coherent answer.

Although we do not yet know the exact and complete mechanisms by which psychedelics work, we do know that they are all chemically related. One point of consensus is that, as for LSD, the primary effect of psychedelics is on the brain's serotonergic neurons, specifically the 2A receptors (Carhart-Harris et al., 2012, p. 2141; Lee & Roth, 2012; Muthukumaraswamy et al., 2013, p. 15171). To some degree psychedelics probably also affect the dopaminergic neurons (Pellerin, 1998). More than others I know, McNamara (2009, pp. 134–135, 139–144; 3.1.2) emphasizes the role of dopamine in transcendent experiences—perhaps because of his focus on the "religious circuit," which is supposed to explain most religious phenomena, not just transcendent experiences, as I have noted at 3.1.2. The dopaminergic circuits of the brain are involved in the action of addictive drugs (e.g., alcohol, nicotine, and especially cocaine and amphetamines), which produce a very different kind of "high" (Pinel, 2014, pp. 368–391).

Ayahuasca provides an example of a psychedelic used explicitly for religious purposes (Callaway, 1999; McKenna, 1999). It is a tea brewed primarily from two plants: *Banisteriopsis caapi* and *Psychotria viridis*. The former contains harmala (β-carboline) alkaloids, which act as potent monoamine-oxidase (MAO) inhibitors. That is, in the brain they prevent the degradation, and weakly prevent the reuptake, of serotonin, so it accumulates to produce a major hallucinogenic effect. *P. viridis*, on the other hand, contains N,N-dimethyltryptamine (DMT), which fits certain serotonin-receptor sites and, above all, thereby produces other vivid psychedelic phenomena. Taken orally, DMT is generally ineffective because of rapid degradation via endogenous MAO, but in combination with ayahuasca's MAO-inhibitors, the DMT contributes to a sustained and powerful experience of altered consciousness.

Robin Carhart-Harris's recent research on psilocybin—the prodrug of psilocin (4-hydroxy-dimethltryptamine), the primary psychedelic ingredient in "magic mushrooms"—offers an even richer understanding of the effect of psychedelic drugs. Although the concern of his research team is not explicitly religious, Carhart-Harris (2013) explicitly acknowledges that the drug induces "spiritual-type experiences," for example, a breakdown in the perception of differentness and separation in a state described as "union" or "oneness." This research presents robust evidence regarding a number of facets of the drug action; and a focus on the default-mode network (DMN), already implicated regarding meditation at 3.1.3, suggests a fascinating convergence of results.

One of the findings in this research was surprising. It had long been thought that psychedelics function by "revving up" the brain. But no. In two important regards, deactivation and decoupling, the effect of psilocybin *inhibits* neuronal function (Carhart-Harris et al., 2012). First, activity in the posterior cingulate cortex (PCC) and medial prefrontal cortex (mPFC), the hubs of the DMN, shows remarkable decrease under the effect of psilocybin. As already noted, the PCC, mPFC, and the other facets of the DMN are involved in one's sense of self, in self-referential thinking, and in mind-wandering. The inhibited activity in these areas suggests that psilocybin decreases such preoccupation with self, opening one to broader mental experience, as subjective reports of the drug experience relate. Second, psilocybin decreases the positive coupling of the mPFC and PCC as well as the connectivity among the other components of the DMN. Desynchronization of the entire network results. It is as if a fundamental structure of overall experience relaxes and allows the human spirit to soar, unleashed from the normal constraints of perceptual input. That is, the psychedelic drug breaks down the normal patterning of experience, dissolves ego-boundaries between external and internal experience, and, thus, as it is said, expands one's consciousness.

Initially, functional magnetic resonance imaging (fMRI) showed these results (Carhart-Harris et al., 2012). Then other studies confirmed them. One used magnetoelectrograph (Muthukumaraswamy et al., 2013), and a second using fMRI compared the effects of psilocybin with those of 3–4 methylenedioxymethamphetamine or MDMA (Roseman et al., 2014). This popular club drug is called "ecstasy," "Molly," and "Mandy" on the street and has mixed effects, some described (non-technically) as psychedelic and others generally associated with amphetamines. Across all three experiments, the reported effects of psilocybin remain firm.

In addition to revealing the regions of the brain that psilocybin primarily affects, this research also explains some details of the drug's chemical mechanism (Carhart-Harris et al., 2012; Muthukumaraswamy et al., 2013). As noted, psychedelics function primarily by activating serotonin 2A receptors. These are in high concentrations in the cortical regions affected by psilocybin. The overall neurochemical mechanism is complicated. It is well known that serotonin excites neurons by inhibiting the outflow of potassium ions in them, thus increasing their positive electrical potential and making the cells more likely to fire. But the overall effect of psilocybin is inhibitory. Involved in particular are pyramidal cells and inhibitory interneurons (connector cells) in the cortex. In a way not yet completely understood, the interaction of these cells results in decreased activation overall by increasing the availability of GABA (Gamma-aminobutyric acid), the primary inhibitory neurotransmitter in the nervous system. In seemingly paradoxical processes that are actually commonplace in neuronal transmission, excitatory transmitters often provoke overall inhibitory effects. Here is a case in which such an overall result accounts for the deactivation and decoupling of the DMN and explains neuroscientifically how a psychedelic drug induces transcendent experiences by desynchronizing a major cortical network.

These research results raise an important theoretical question about the relationship of consciousness or human spirit to its neurological and perceptual underpinnings. The question arises because the research detects a disconnection, a freeing of pure consciousness from its normal perceptual base. But if consciousness emerges from these supportive substructures, how can it continue to function? I address this question at 5.9.

To be sure, once again, the standard caveat pertains: these results are new. Their report notes anomalies, conflicts with other research, and the need for methodologically consistent confirmatory studies. Nonetheless, these results are impressive in themselves. Besides, they square well with the recent neuroscientific findings regarding meditation, summarized at 3.1.3. Thus, again, we have a credible understanding of a neurological mechanism that accounts for transcendent experiences. In this case, they are the product of psychopharmacological intervention.

3.4. An Electromagnetic Basis of Transcendent Experiences: Persinger

A fourth approach to the neuroscience of transcendent experiences is the research of Michael Persinger (1999, 2001, 2002, 2003). By the application of low-level, complex magnetic fields to the temporoparietal regions of the brain, he has routinely induced paranormal experiences, similar to those associated with epileptic seizures, such as a sensed presence, fears, smells, and auditory phenomena (3.1.2). Application of the magnetic fields to the right hemisphere usually results in neutral or positive experiences, which subjects might relate to the presence of a dead relative or a spiritual or religious figure. Application to the left hemisphere usually induces presences that are experienced as negative or aversive. It has been suggested that a person's sense of him- or herself involves the linguistic processes of the left hemisphere. Persinger hypothesizes that his electromagnetic treatment stimulates analogous processes in the right hemisphere, causing those experiences of presences. Further, Persinger (2001) speculates, the sensed presence might be "the prototype for all the other experiences that include spirit visitations: alien 'abductions,' the Greek Muses, incubi and succubi, and perhaps even the god experience itself" (p. 517). Indeed, when the magnetic fields are applied around the head in a counterclockwise direction—a procedure hypothesized to counter the electrical patterns of the cortex that are associated with consciousness—the subjects describe their experiences in terms characteristic of religious experiences: darkness, inner peace, harmony, and contact with an eternal and infinite presence. Similarly, measurements of geomagnetic fluctuations suggest an explanation for the experience of transcendence that people might have when visiting sacred locations. In brief, the cerebral application of magnetic fields might not only be able to explain an array of transcendent experiences but also, like drugs, to actually cause them in the laboratory.

However, no published research has been able to report replication of Persinger's results. The magnetic fields he applies might be so low as to not even penetrate the cranium. And measures of suggestibility have correlated positively with the reports of experiencing a presence (see Aaen-Stockdale, 2012, for a scathing review with references).

Unfortunately, with the uninformed enthusiasm of neuroscientists who are experts in their field but know only popular religion and might have no formal philosophical or theological training, such as we have already seen, in his popular statements Persinger (n.d) does not hesitate to claim outright an explanation for belief in God. Persinger identifies the experiences that his "God Helmet" might induce with the experience of the God of theism of whatever stripe and suggests that the supposed existence of God is nothing more than a biologically induced solution to the anxiety of death. The conflation of the spiritual and the divine is ubiquitous in these discussions (1.2; 6.2.5) and, propagated by self-appointed experts, seriously distorts popular thinking about religion.

3.5. A Quantum-Physics Theory of Consciousness: Penrose and Hameroff

One other novel attempt to ground consciousness in the brain deserves attention because of my reliance on consciousness to explain transcendent experiences. This theory does not appeal to the commonly known structures, interconnections, and processes of the brain, but highly creatively appeals to the theory of quantum physics.

Collaborating with anesthesiologist and neuroscientist Stuart Hameroff, Roger Penrose specifies a locus and a mechanism by which moments of consciousness could be occurring amidst the most elementary structures of physical matter. These theorists advocate a position called "orchestrated objective reduction," or OrchOR. It applies quantum mechanics to explain the emergence of consciousness as a non-computational effect in the microtubules in the neurons of the brain. Microtubules are the microscopic structures that partially constitute the cytoskeleton, the internal "girders," of cells (Penrose, 1994a).

At stake is a phenomenon called "collapse of the wave function" or "quantum decoherence" (4.19.5), a situation in which a number of statistically possible outcomes in "superposition" eventually "collapse" and result in only one outcome (although some physicists claim that the other possibilities endure in alternate universes). The suggestion is that "consciousness depends on biologically 'orchestrated' quantum computations in collections of microtubules within brain neurons." This indeterminate or non-computational effect "is taken to result in a moment of conscious awareness and/or choice" (Penrose & Hameroff, 2011, abstract). That is, decoherence involves indeterminacy, random occurrence, which is taken to imply an act of choice. Additionally, quantum processes also include non-locality and communication without contact. All these characteristics also pertain to consciousness, so Penrose and Hameroff propose that a moment of "proto-consciousness" occurs at every instance of decoherence in the microtubules, and these micro events somehow ground or add up to the macro experience of consciousness or subjectivity that we humans have.

This theory qualifies as a kind of panpsychism, the notion that consciousness is operative throughout the universe, not just in humans (4.20; 4.21). And meeting Penrose's concern for a genuine science of consciousness (2.1), this theory suggests how consciousness could be something real in itself, irreducible to physical reality, yet also explicable on the basis of physical science.

This theory has also been the object of severe criticism and even harsh derision (Blackmore, 2012, pp. 282–285). Nonetheless, Penrose and Hameroff continue to refine and defend their theory resolutely as "the most rigorous, detailed, and successful theory of consciousness yet put forth" (Hameroff, 2014).

3.6. The Contribution of Neuroscience

From five different perspectives I have summarized some of the neuroscientific research and theory that bears on transcendent experiences. Clearly, we already understand a good deal about the brain anatomy and physiology that underlie these experiences as well as their genetic, neurochemical, and electrophysiological correlates. To be sure, in none of these areas is explanation complete or certain, yet it is only a matter of time before the neurological function will be understood. However, the exact and final details of the biological research are not necessary for the present discussion. Whatever the eventualities, all the research points to the same conclusion: biological factors constitute an essential aspect of transcendent experiences. Indeed, manipulation of these factors can actually cause such experiences. To better understand the valid implications of this research, the more pressing need is to turn to these human experiences themselves and to propose a coherent understanding of them and their relationship to neuronal function. Hence, in the next chapter discussion shifts from neurology to psychology.

Chapter 4

Psychology

The Problem of a Real Body and a Real Mind

> We are only at the beginning. I am only a beginner. I was successful in digging up buried monuments from the substrata of the mind. But where I have discovered a few temples, others may discover a continent.
>
> —Sigmund Freud

> What is matter? —Never mind.
> What is mind? —Never matter.
>
> —Anonymous

Neurological explanations of mental experience raise doubts about the mind's distinctive reality. Is the mind merely brain function? According to reports, transcendent experiences are so overwhelming that their peculiarity cannot be denied. Yet if the mind itself is thought not to be a distinctive reality but only a by-product of the brain similar to the stomach's production of digestion (Searle, 1997, p. xiii), what is the brain engaging in these awesome experiences? A standard answer is quick in coming: it must be some spiritual entity such as God; something about the brain must make it sensitive to Divinity.

That answer makes quite a leap. Surely, it would be useful to resolve the ontological status of the mind before positing encounters with an even less ontologically secured God. If the mind is, in fact, a non-physical reality of its own kind, transcendent experiences could well be just the mind's experience of itself. Then, without invoking God or other non-human entities, transcendence would be natural to the human picture. Appeal to God would be unnecessary for explaining these experiences.

The reality of the mind needs to be resolved before any coherent talk of "God in the brain" can proceed. Thus, this chapter addresses the mind. The thorny issue called "the mind–body problem" provides the focus. How does the mind relate to the brain? Is the mind a reality in its own right? Is it real or just a self-deception? Is it nothing more than a spin on matter? If not, what is the nature of the mind?

Questions such as these stand at the heart of the topic of this book, so this chapter is by far the longest. This is the pivotal issue—the mind–body problem. Resolution of it is essential to all the other issues, and treatment of it hones the intellectual tools needed to address the other issues. This chapter engages the mind–body problem by first unpacking the problem and clarifying terminology; then by building an argument for the genuine and distinct realities of both body and mind—including appeal to the major positions on consciousness and the elimination of false starts; and finally by elaborating the process called "emergence" as the link between body and mind. These analyses include important discussions of causality, implicit definition, and philosophy of science in general; and they conclude with extended criticisms of major theories of consciousness.

In this chapter I speak globally of "the mind," but in Chapter 5 I explicitly distinguish two different facets of the mind: (a) psyche and (b) consciousness, or spirit. These latter precisions go beyond usage—and awareness, it seems—in current consciousness studies in which the terms *mind* and *consciousness* are used virtually interchangeably; so insistence on full precision is not necessary at this point. Nonetheless, I flag this further issue because appeal to it for accuracy's sake becomes unavoidable now and again in this chapter. The point at stake is that within the mind even psyche and consciousness are distinct kinds of realities: humans share psyche with other animal species, but consciousness is uniquely human and spiritual.

4.1. The "Reality" of the "Parts" of the Human Being

How does the mind–body problem arise? At bottom, it is a matter of conceptual inconsistency. The problem is subtle and difficult. As much as physics, it requires carefully crafted theory. But pure theoretical thinking is hard to come by. Picture-thinking intrudes. It imagines the mind or anything at all to be somehow perceptible, palpable, imaginable stuff of one kind or another. At work is a sensate-modeled epistemology, and it is inadequate to treatment of the mind. How is the problem resolved? By consistent application of an intellectual epistemology, such as that presented in Chapter 2.

4.1.1. Inconsistencies in Thinking About Body and Mind

Standard psychological usage speaks of the human being as body and mind. In parallel fashion, not worth addressing explicitly, religious usage speaks of body and soul (see Helminiak, 1996a, pp. 7–11). The challenge is to specify the reality of these two components without turning the mind into a separate thing so that two separate things or independent "substances," body and mind, would appear to be in question—that dastardly Cartesian dualism again (2.9; 4.4)! Yet such reification is commonplace. For example, in contrast to a stereotype of demeaned religion, Teske (2006) would not understand the mental and spiritual "as separate entities or substances, somehow supernaturally injected into human beings" (p. 174). Similarly, Brown (2002) suggests that neuroscience raises questions about "the existence of an ontologically distinct soul" (p. 1815), and he wonders under what conditions soul or spirit could be considered "separate, distinct entities" (p. 1816). Notice that, despite the technical terms employed, the underlying conception appears to be that minds or souls are some kind of "separate entities," "substances," something "injected into human beings," "ontologically distinct" beings. As described, these appear to be free agents, existing somewhere out there on their own, seeking connection with bodies—imagined and pictured as ghosts of the horror-movie genre.

It is telling that the reality of human corporeality gets taken for granted whereas the reality of the mind comes into question. Seemingly, a commonsense realism rules the discussion: on the criterion of perceptible or imaginable encounter, the bodily is easily deemed real, but the mental can enjoy only a nebulous status, at best. If it is to be real, it must be some kind of independently existing stuff. Materialist suppositions seem to control the argument: unless the mental is as palpable as the bodily, it cannot be real; and *entity* and *substance* imply palpable or imaginable realities, separable—not merely distinct (4.2.1)—by nature.

But if the mind actually is independently existing stuff, how can it relate to the brain? How can mental stuff contact and influence material stuff, or vice versa? This is the problem of dualism. The easiest solution—indeed, the solution required by the controlling materialist presupposition—is that the mind is not real at all.

However, my prior discussion of epistemology raises caveats. Different epistemologies lead to different conclusions. On the one hand, on the criterion of palpability, the human body itself, composed ultimately of impalpable quarks and leptons, must likewise be impalpable; but patently, it is not. Consistent commonsense realism leads to absurdity (2.8.1). On the other hand, on the criteria of attentive experience, intelligent understanding, and reasonable judgment, once again the human body—or my chair (2.8.2)—is not some *per se* palpable thing "already out there now." Rather, it is the object of a reasonable and meaning-filled judgment that includes an affirmation of materiality on the basis of the sense data pertinent to what I call my *body*—or my *chair*. My "body" and my "chair" are not simply material; they are meaningful realities. Moreover, on the very same criteria applied to a different data set, which also pertains to me, I could as legitimately affirm another kind of reality, my mind, which happens not to include sense data as part of its intelligibility. My mind is certainly related to my body. Happy hour proves it every time! But clearly, too, my mind is different from my body. In both cases and equally so, ever attentive to the data, reasonable judgment affirms the actuality—but of different kinds—of the body and of the mind. But on the one hand and on the other, conclusions vary with epistemologies.

If being real depends on palpability and the concern is to avoid the multiplication of separable parts in the human being, why is there no preoccupation over the separable arm or stomach or femur? Why this multiplication of parts? Answer to this question requires a prior consideration of the parts that might make up a thing and the unity of the thing that is made up of its parts. And, as always, different epistemologies imply different understandings about the nature of a thing and propose different answers to this question about the constituents of a thing.

A perception-based epistemology imagines things to be made up of separable and palpable parts, which are also taken to be things in themselves: many things conglomerate to form a new thing. For example, the frame, motor, wheels, and so on make up an automobile, and the roots, trunk, and branches make up a tree. Such a perception-based epistemology lies behind the challenge of the mind–body problem. Questions must arise because this way of picture-thinking implies a logical inconsistency, namely, concern about a separable mind but not about a separable arm.

4.1.2. Thing, an Intelligible Whole

Lonergan (1957/1992) describes a *thing* as a "unity, identity, whole" that insight grasps and judgment affirms in a relevant data set (pp. 270–295).

The criterion is intelligibility that is reasonably affirmed. In this sense, a tree, a dog, a chair, an automobile—each would be a thing because a particular meaning or intelligibility is proper to each, and in each case that meaning takes in and unites all facets of the item. A fender removed from a car, for example, is not a car although the car, even missing a fender, is still a car because the meaning *car* still remains. The thing is the intelligible whole. The wholeness and "thing-ness" depend on insight, which discerns a "unity, identity, whole" pertinent to each of the different cases.

In contrast, a perception-modeled epistemology would appeal—whether deliberately or, more likely, unthinkingly—to palpability and visibility to discern an individual thing: "Well, all these parts are connected; looks like it's all one thing." So the trunk, branches, leafs, roots, and even the surrounding ground would all be the tree? An ICU patient and his life-sustaining feeding, drainage, and IV tubes would all be the person? Not at all. The roots, but not the ground, are the tree. The patient, but not the tubes, is the person. Intelligible unity, not contiguity or conglomeration of parts, determines a thing.

In common usage, we would be comfortable calling an automobile a thing and, perhaps, even calling a tree a thing. We might balk at calling a dog a thing, and we would certainly object to calling a person a thing. However, the term *thing* is used here in a technical sense. Its intent is the unity in question, not the animal, vegetable, mineral, or personal nature of the item. *Thing* is merely Lonergan's chosen alternative for the philosophical term *substance*. This traditional term, going back to Aristotle, is so misunderstood that it is useless (see 4.1.1, first paragraph). So, to speak of individual existents, Lonergan chose to speak of *things*—even as Immanuel Kant used an everyday German term *das Ding an sich*: the thing in itself (2.2.7). In this technical sense, a person is a *thing*, a single existent or entity, which includes all its aspects. It is this thing, the human person, that is the topic of our discussion. The present concern is to avoid a multiplicity of separable and independent parts in this thing, above all, the mind—but, inconsistently, not the arm or stomach.

4.1.3. Levels of Analysis

The pervasive complication is that one can consider things at different levels of analysis. One could focus on the "parts" as such—the arm, stomach, pituitary, femur, brain, mind—or one could focus on the whole, the person who includes all these "parts." Each focus does have its validity. Indeed, each focus determines different academic disciplines. Physics and chemistry would be interested in the femur; biology, in the stomach; neuroscience, in the brain; psychology, in the mind; and . . . what?—psychology, again? philosophy? anthropology (etymologically taken)?—would be interested in the whole person (see 1.5). However, on the basis of a sensate-modeled epistemology, this pervasive complication of levels of analysis tends to be oversimplified because any parts of the person are supposedly as palpable as the whole person—that is, the whole . . . what? The whole body? The thinking reader, unless a thorough-going materialist, should take pause at this implicit identification of the person with the body, and that pause is the point to be made: people really are more than bodies—and more on this point anon. Yet on these presuppositions, the arm or stomach might well be as much a separable part as a supposedly separable mind or soul. Then why no concern over the separable stomach?

The reason is easy to specify. Talk of a person as one thing (in Lonergan's sense) does not depend on a manual grasp or visual sight that holds together an arrangement of other things, physical parts, LEGO-block-like. Nor does talk of a person depend on the imaginative association of sensations and simple "ideas"—that is, images—mental parts, à la John Locke or David Hume. Rather, talk of a person as one thing depends on an insight that "grasps" and affirms the identifiable wholeness, the intelligible unity, of the thing in question in the totality of the data that pertain to it. When one conceives the whole, every single facet of the thing belongs to the thing.

On this basis, no facet of the intelligibility of a thing could also simultaneously constitute the intelligibility of, and therefore be, a different thing. The principle of non-contradiction precludes this option. It disallows that certain facets of the person could simultaneously be the person and also be a different thing, not the person. The person includes all that constitutes him or her; all of it is the person. In Lonergan's (1957/1992, pp. 283–284) provocative formulation, there are no "things within things." This is not to deny that a thing has its facets, aspects, properties, or "parts," which could even become the object of study at a lower level of analysis; but in Lonergan's technical sense, they are not other *things* so long as they belong to the whole. Of course, parts could be excised, separated, or severed from the whole, for example, limbs on a tree or a person and the fender on a car; but once separated, now dying or already dead, no longer integral to the whole, these limbs constitute things in themselves, wood or decomposing human flesh, or else a fender lying in the junk yard. These realizations all hold if one consistently relies on an intellectual epistemology, but not if one applies a sensate-modeled epistemology and distinguishes "things" by the ability to separate or picture them. The following discussion about things and their properties, their constitutive facets (or "conjugates," in Lonergan's technical term), explicates this matter of "parts."

4.1.4. *The Actuality of Mind and Body in Summary*

The encounter of a person is not like the encounter of a store-window manikin—or the completely physical amputation of an arm. In a person one encounters a multifaceted being with feelings, thoughts, memories, opinions, interests, skills, ambitions, and loves in addition to a physical and organic presence. All this constitutes the relevant data. Insight into these data unites them all. One recognizes that they all pertain to one entity. The whole, then, is the thing in question; it—that is, she or he—is this totality that insight "grasps" as a unity. One encounters a person. Within this human totality, but not separate from it—only thus, even the stomach is veritably a stomach. Cut out of the person, what was a stomach is just a piece of dead meat, like the gizzard of a chicken or the tripe of a cow, valuable sources of protein. Similarly, then, the mind is also veritably another aspect of this whole, neither separate nor separable from the whole. (I bracket out the further question of possible separability, the possible before-birth or after-death existence of the mind or soul or spirit apart from the body, as explained at 4.2.1.) The mind might be unique and wondrous, a reality of a different kind in comparison to the palpable stomach, but just as much as the stomach, the mind is an aspect of the whole and exists only as an aspect of the whole. Indeed, if truth be told, even the stomach is unique and wondrous, a different kind of reality in comparison to the chemical materials of an excised, dead piece of meat that once was a stomach. The stomach, as such, as much as the mind, exists only as an aspect of the whole person. But imagination and perceptual epistemology would *picture* the matter otherwise and would have no concern over seemingly separable "parts" of a "person"—unless they were invisible: non-pictorial, they could not be "real." So the mind becomes problematic, but not the arm or the stomach. Epistemology is the issue.

4.2. Some Terminological Clarifications

4.2.1. *Distinctions and Separations*

In the previous section, and in passing, I insinuated a difference between *distinct* and *separate*. This difference is not found in colloquial usage but is commonplace in some philosophical circles. It is instructive that Brown (2002), cited at 4.1.1, seemingly uses these terms interchangeably: "separate, distinct entities" (p. 1816). Yet when epistemologies differ, the meaning of terms can also differ, so I need to specify exactly what I take these terms to mean.

I use the term *distinct* to indicate intelligently discerned differences—the judgment that, on the basis of different intelligibilities, this is not that. And I use the terms *separable* or *separate* to indicate the possibility or actuality of spatial and/or temporal contiguity or distance. Things that are separate must also be distinct; what is physically distant and disconnected from some other thing cannot be that other thing. In contrast, realities that are distinct need not be separate, the mind and the brain, anxiety and bowel cramps, for example. Distinctions pertain to intelligence; separations pertain to physicality. Distinctions are grasped by insight; separations are experienced by sensation or perception.

Accordingly, I am arguing that the mind is distinct from the body—and actually, not just notionally, so: their intelligibilities differ, so the one could not be the other. But the mind is not separate from the body; it is not distant from it; it cannot be detached from it. I would not posit a mind apart from a brain. Other examples might be helpful. The wood is distinct from my desk, but they are not separate. Water is distinct from hydrogen and oxygen, but water is not separate from its constitutive elements. Life is distinct from the organic molecules that sustain it, but life is not separate from these biochemicals. A mental image is distinct from the elaborate pattern of neuronal firing that sustains it, but the image is not separate from the neuronal functioning. God is distinct from creation because logically the Creator could not be the created; but by definition, as the sustainer of all existence, God is not and cannot be separate or distant from anything that exits (1.2; 6.3.2).

It is a further question whether at some point, before or after death, the mind (or the soul) is also separable from the body as an independent thing. (The parenthetical implies no identity between mind and soul; these terms are notoriously fuzzy. See Helminiak, 1996a, pp. 26–27.) Arguably, this further question about afterlife merits an affirmative answer (Lonergan, 1957/1992, pp. 539–543). However, it would be best to ignore this further question and not allow concern for it to confuse and prejudice our current and circumscribed discussion about the flesh-and-blood persons that concern neuroscience and psychology. We must base our assertions on the evidence available to us, and thus far the evidence on life before birth or after death is disputable, to say the least. One might argue for personal existence after the "separation of body and soul," but this judgment has no easy data on which to stand. Ever consistently, on the basis of transcendental method or generalized empirical method (2.5), without relevant data there can be no human knowledge. Let us, then, not allow mere speculation, pious hope, religious belief, or human longing to obscure the scientific argument at stake in this book. I bracket the question of life after life and distance myself even further from the question of life before life.

4.2.2. Realities and Things

I also need to clarify my differential use of the terms *reality* and *thing*. In the hope of being more easily understood and only for this strategic reason, I am attempting to use the term *reality* in a sense different from Lonergan's. For him, and in standard English, the terms *reality* and *thing* are often interchangeable, especially when preceded by an article: a reality and a thing, or the reality and the thing. Yet, even in standard English, when the article is lacking, *reality* has a sense different from *thing*. Indeed, as far as I can discern, *thing* always takes an article or some defining demonstrative adjective. In this case, *thing* clearly indicates some individual, existing being, some particular existent. In contrast, *reality* often conveys the sense of a nature or a kind. We can ask, "What is the reality of the situation?" Then the answer explicates a nature: "It is of this or that kind"—an exuberant friendly encounter, merely male roughhousing, a veritable brawl. Or we can ask, "What is this black reality on the sole of my shoe?" Alternatively, we could ask, "What is this substance?" It is clear that the question is not about the existence of whatever is on the shoe, but about its kind—despite the fact that *substance*, like *reality*, could also be used, and in Aristotelian and Scholastic philosophy *was* used, to indicate an entity, a particular, existing thing: this reality, that substance.

    The usage in which *reality* indicates kind and *thing* indicates a particular existent is the one that I adopt here. Introduction of Lonergan's analyses makes my usage of these terms technical, and the technicality is far from merely suggestive or assertive. This difference between *reality* and *thing* is the difference between what is grasped on the second level of consciousness and on the third, respectively (2.1.6). These terms and their difference, as I am using them, pertain to specifiable facets of the very structure of human knowing. They correspond to two different kinds of questions (2.4.1). On the one hand, there is the question for understanding, What is it? or What kind is it? This question asks about realities, about the kinds of things involved. On the other hand, there is the question for reflection,

Is it? or Is it so? This question asks about individual existents, regardless of their kind. The meanings that result from these two different kinds of questions are the contents of two different kinds of insights. The first deals in intelligibility, understanding, or meaning, and the second, in factuality, actuality, or existence.

Thus, in the present case, body and mind are two realities, two different kinds of being, but they are not two things. Only one thing is in question: the human being. But a human being encompasses both body and mind, includes different realities, comprises different kinds of being. A human is both physical and mental. One marvel and bedeviling complexity of humanity is that a human person includes a swath of different realities in one being. The human being virtually encapsulates or recapitulates the unfolding of the universe: cosmogenesis (material body), biological evolution (organism and psyche), and cultural history (consciousness or spirit). This one thing, the human being, entails all these realities, all these kinds of being.

A further clarification is also called for because the three-level process of human knowing—experience, understanding, and judgment—is reiterative. Hence, concerned about the reality of a thing, one can wonder if the reality really is of such and such a kind as might have been suggested, and a judgment answers this question—not to confirm the existence of the reality (Is it? Does it exist?), but, in this case, to confirm that such and such a kind is actually at stake (Is it so? Is it of this kind?). Both the second and the third levels of consciousness are in play, but the focus is the second: one wonders what kind this reality *truly* is. So, for example, by tapping and listening, I can gather evidence to determine whether the bumper on my car is metal or plastic. One makes a judgment (third level) to confirm the accuracy of a hypothesis (second level): yes, it is plastic, or no, it is not. On this basis, I suggested that the body is one reality (one kind of being), the mind is a second (another kind of being), and the one is not the other (because they are of two different kinds). On the basis of different intelligibilities—said simply, that of the material and that of the immaterial—body and mind are two realities, and they are really distinct. Two different kinds are, indeed, at stake.

Then, moving further on in the analysis, one can shift the focus to the third level again and ask about the existence of these realities, just confirmed as truly distinct, and the wheel of knowing makes another turn. Then one concludes that *in the human being* these two kinds of reality do, indeed, exist. The body exists and the mind exists; and in the one human being, they constitute one thing, a person. Judgments, conscious acts on the third level of consciousness, come into play twice: once to determine that these two kinds of reality, physical and mental, *truly* are different and again to determine that these two different kinds of reality *truly* exist.

Given an existent person, but only granted this given, both body and mind do exist. They do not exist in themselves, on their own, independently: they are not things. They exist in the person, as aspects, facets, constituents, properties, or "conjugates" (4.12.1) of the person. They are different realities that constitute one thing, one unity, identity, whole: a person. The person is that which is. The person exists, and with the person exists all that constitutes her or him. Accordingly, this time, to the question for understanding, "What is it?" one would respond that it is a polymorphous being of both the physical and mental kind. Here the focus in on the second level of consciousness; concern is for the nature or kind of being that is in question. And to the question for reflection, "Is it?" one would respond that, yes, it is; this polymorphous, physical-mental being, this person, exists. Now the focus is on the third level of consciousness; concern is for the concrete being in question, the existent or actuality, the thing that exits.

Actual existence is a correlate of the third level; to it the person, the thing, pertains. The nature of the person is a correlate of the second level; to it the physical and mental kinds pertain. The person is one thing that entails distinct kinds of realities, which really do exist as aspects of this one thing.

When one affirms, "This is a person," of course, the big question still remains: "How could physical and mental reality constitute just one thing?" I address this question in detail at 4.1.3. However, the clarifications provided by the present analyses already provide the makings of a coherent answer to that further question. A person is a complex thing that entails different kinds of being. Intelligence grasps and judgment affirms the unity of this thing, and sound methodology leaves to further inquiry an explanation of this thing's integrated complexity. The unity is a given; the complexity of the given calls for further investigation and reasonable understanding. The challenge of explaining the thing does not impugn the actuality of the thing.

These assertions rest on the nature of human knowing. On the basis of available evidence, one concludes that the thing does exist. Then human understanding proposes the kind of reality that is in question and then confirms or disconfirms the accuracy of the proposal. Ever working reiteratively are experience, understanding, and judgment. An explicit epistemology guides the explanation along its way until we "get it right."

4.2.3. Concrete-Operational and Formal-Operational Thinking

As simple propositions, those assertions are easily made. The challenge, however, is to keep from trying to understand those assertions by picturing the matter. Picture two kinds of realities that together constitute one thing and you are picturing three things and wondering how they could be only one thing—and this is not trinitarian theology! At stake here, rather, is merely Jean Piaget's (1936/1963) formal operational thinking.

It is a kind of thinking that becomes possible only in adolescence. Until then, children think concretely. They are completely logical, and they can work out problems efficiently; but to do so, they have to have the stuff before their eyes and in their hands. Give them a balance and different-sized weights, and they will easily figure out how to position the weights so that the balance sits level across the fulcrum. With still other weights, they will be able to find the balance again and again. What they will not be able to do is formulate the rule that explains how to achieve such balance in every case without having to work it out in the concrete each time. Do you know the rule?

The rule is this: to achieve balance, the weight multiplied by its distance from the fulcrum on one side must equal the weight multiplied by its distance from the fulcrum on the other: weight x distance = weight x distance. But this rule is completely abstract. It is formal—hence, the name "formal operational thinking." That is, this rule is a general principle free from the specific contents of any particular cases—pure *form* without *matter*, to invoke the Aristotelian categories, which never occur in actual beings in isolation for Aristotle. This rule pertains to any balance, anytime, anywhere on earth. The number that results from the multiplication corresponds to nothing that can be seen, felt, or imagined, *per se*. It is a sheer—and cleverly conceived and very useful—calculation. It entails the equalization of two proportions, the equalization of weight-to-distance on one side with weight-to-distance on the other. They are understood; they are not seen. The calculation could be named "pressure" or "balance units" or whatever. But the naming does not make the product of two measures concrete or imaginable. It is a sheer calculation. The rule and its result are nothing that can be pictured—although images and examples help in grasping and understanding the rule. The rule itself is beyond the concrete operational thinking of childhood.

One study I remember from many years ago concluded that only about 17% of college graduates could think formal-operationally across all fields of study. Even worse, only about two thirds of college graduates could use formal operational thinking in their own field of specialization. For most of us, and for the most part, we think concretely. Moreover, for the most part we get by quite successfully by thinking only concretely. Most of what we deal with in everyday life is concrete, material, physical. We are intent on getting things done in the work-a-day world. We are natural-born pragmatists. The challenge in the present case, however, is to move beyond concrete operations and into the formal-operational realm of abstract thinking. It alone suffices for science, systems, and psychological, philosophical, and theological analyses. And granted full disclosure, it alone actually gives us the answers we need in the long run to solve any complex problems even in our work-a-day pragmatic efforts to get things done.

4.3. The Actual Existence of Mental Realities

Even common sense is uncomfortable denying the distinct reality of the mind (Bloom, 2006; Searle, 1997, p. 135). Even apart from the fearsome mind control of religious implications and beliefs, common experience suggests that, in comparison with the mere bodily, the impalpable dimensions of a person are real—indeed, oftentimes more real—and they are of a different kind: they are of a peculiar reality. Mental images, emotions, memories, thoughts—not to mention insights, opinions, knowledge, values—do not appear to be physical. Neuroscience points out that these mental experiences depend on brain function. But are they something more, something different? The attentive, intelligent, and reasonable answer must be yes. Following the epistemology I am applying—wherein intelligibility, not sensitive qualities, specifies kinds, and a judgment, not perceptual encounter, specifies actuality—the conclusion must be yes.

Emotions or thoughts are of different kinds in comparison to the biology of the brain. Regardless how complex the patterns, how many the involved brain areas, how exact a possible one-to-one correspondence, no interacting set of neurons is a thought or an emotion—nor is the pattern itself. As given to human experience, the intelligibilities of these phenomena are simply different. The fact that there is no human thought apart from a neurological substrate means neither that the thought is the substrate nor that the thought is merely a wispy by-product of the substrate yet something of the same kind or, alternatively, nothing real in itself. It is something of a different kind. To be sure, we are still far from achieving the much desired, fully scientific

(2.1.2), implicitly defined (4.6.5), explanatory (4.6.5) account of a thought or of a brain state. We cannot yet specify what they are in themselves. Still, it is clear that, on the basis of the experiential data, answer to the question, "What is it?" would have to be different in each case. The brain function is not the thought. The two might be inseparable, but they are indubitably distinct. Then reasonable judgment rightly concludes that the thought is one reality and the brain function is another and the two are not the same. If they were the same, why retain two different names, different concepts, for them, especially in scientific discourse? Why do English professors and philosophers, who deal in thoughts, not work with fMRIs wearing white lab coats and examining patterns of neuronal firing? Moreover, to the extent that the one is not intrinsically spatial or temporal and the other is intrinsically both spatial and temporal, they are appropriately called *spiritual* and *material*, respectively (Lonergan, 1957/1992, pp. 539–543). Of course, these firm conclusions presume an epistemology according to which knowing depends on intellectual acts, on understanding, not on imagination, perception, or sensation.

Aspects of human mental life clearly do transcend space and time. The universal category or concept is a commonplace example: Fido is a dog. The concept *dog* as such exists only in the mind and in no individual dog, yet the concept applies to any and all dogs. It transcends space and time.

More cogently, the trans-material (metaphysical) nature of Pythagoras's famous theorem controlled the thought of Plato. He was well aware that (expressed algebraically) $a^2 + b^2 = c^2$ perfectly matches no right triangle in the physical universe. Nothing in the physical world is that perfect. The power of Plato's realization and his overenthusiasm led him to postulate a World of Forms or Ideas existing apart from the physical world. Supposedly, in that ideal world the perfect forms of triangle, dog, and everything else existed as the really real, and the things in this transient and changing world were merely imperfect, embodied, illusory copies. Plato's realization of the metaphysical nature of the mind holds even beyond Euclidean space. Einstein's calculation, for example, of the relative time intervals in two different frames of reference $t' = t\sqrt{1 - v^2/c^2}$ applies to any and all frames of reference. Moreover, general relativity theory fully abstracts from all concrete space and time and, as such, is beyond all such particularity. It expresses pure intelligibility. It is the pure intelligibility of matter in motion. It is applicable to every individual, concrete, physical case.

In each instance, the trans-material—the inherent intelligibility—is as much an aspect of physical reality as is the palpable. For humans realities are meaningful. The human mind that can grasp this fact is obviously capable of transcending space and time and, perforce, in some way participates in the ubiquitous and timeless. Granted Einstein's theories, this realization should be a commonplace in the third millennium—but, curiously, it is not. On the basis of hard science, we know that space and time are not absolutes. When actually explained, physical reality is not what it *appears*—looks, sounds, feels—to *be*. In the act of understanding, insight transcends looks, sounds, and feels, and engages something of a different kind. Human mind entails a *sui generis* reality.

Although unfortunately only in passing, I must flag this other implication of the spiritual dimension of the mind: its transcendence of space and time provides a promising angle for a theory to explain parapsychological phenomena—distant viewing, clairvoyance, precognition, psychokinesis (Carpenter, 2012; Redgrove, 1987; Roll, 1972/2004). The fact that we live in a world of meaning, not limited by space and time, suggests that we humans are actually in communication with one another and, indeed, with the whole of our universe in ways that we hardly imagine. The base of our constitution is stardust; our entwinement with the environment is inextricable; our very nature is transpersonal (Hart, Nelson, & Puhakka, 2000; Helminiak, 1979; Walsh & Vaughan, 1980). The universe of being, toward whose fullness our spirits lead and in which we currently muddle along, might well include a material dimension amenable to sensation and perception; but more so, that universe exists as conterminous with a realm of unbounded consciousness. As even the 2014 documentary *Cosmos: A Spacetime Odyssey* makes clear in fully naturalistic terms, our existence is caught up in mystery that physical matter alone hardly begins to characterize. Acknowledgement of the spiritual nature of humanity opens an essential perspective on this all-embracing mystery.

4.4. The Unity of the Human Being: Dualism

Almost all would agree that the body is real. I have argued that the mind is also real. Except for the crassest materialists, most would agree, and most would also acknowledge that the mental is of a different kind in comparison to the brain. The problem is to explain how this duality of body and mind can be real and the person still be one. Of course, the unity is obvious; it is a given. When we encounter a person, we recognize that we are dealing with a single being. But when we explore more deeply, the polymorphous nature of a person makes the unity puzzling.

A number of common positions or theories try to account for the unity of the human being. Most prominent are *dualism* and *epiphenomenalism*—along with variations on them. I begin by discussing these two, and this discussion offers a useful overview—the "lay of the land"—of this labyrinthine philosophical territory. Then I focus on one important variation called *property dualism*. Consideration of it takes us into the heart of the territory and reveals a promising path to follow.

Dualism is the most common opinion, certainly among non-philosophers. For example, the standard religious belief, that we are body and soul, is a version of dualism. The notion is that the bodily and the mental are two different things. The problem is to explain their union in one person. If I am really body and soul and if my body goes into the grave and my soul goes to heaven, where do I go when I die? I am not just a soul—although that I am is precisely what many actually believe. Judaism deals with this problem by generally not affirming life after death. With similar reasoning—you can't be a human being without a body—Christianity insists on reconstitution of the human being through resurrection of the body. Hinduism avoids this problem altogether by suggesting from the beginning, at least in popular lore, that the physical is only illusion and our true being is only spiritual. Much Western spirituality eagerly accepts this same supposition—the belief about the soul's separating from the body to find its true nature and fulfillment. Acceptance of dualism and awareness of its problems are, in fact, commonplace.

Dualism relies on commonsense realism: it takes things just as they seem to appear. In the process, dualism tends to reify mental reality and *imagines* it as a thing in itself rather than as one real aspect of a complex thing, a person. Philosophical dualism tends to name the mental with a misunderstood scholastic term *substance,* roughly Kant's *ding an sich* and Lonergan's *thing* (4.1.2). Thus, dualism affirms a duplicity of things, two substances: body and mind (Descartes' reified *res extensa* and *res cogitans*, extended stuff and thinking stuff).

But then how do we explain their interaction? If the body is physical and the mental is spiritual, how can they affect each other?

In fact, consistent dualism loses the unity of the person. Most often, however, certainly in popular thinking, dualistic beliefs save the unity by sacrificing the physical in favor of the spiritual and suppose that people are really spirits temporarily inhabiting bodies: "a spiritual being having a physical experience," as the bumper sticker reads.

4.5. The Unity of the Human Being: Epiphenomenalism

Epiphenomenalism takes a different tack. Committed to the *intellectual* achievements of physical science, epiphenomenalism is—quite curiously—much more willing to sacrifice the mind in favor of the body. It imagines the mind to be some kind of projection of the body or brain, but still something of the same kind—an epiphenomenon, an incidental by-product of little importance, like the white plume spouting from a steam engine. Wanting to insist on the unity of the person but, more important, committed philosophically to the presupposed uniformity—a one kind of all reality: physical matter—epiphenomenalism refuses to go the dualistic way. It rejects any duplicity. It refuses to allow that body and mind could be two different kinds of reality. It implicitly holds that there is only one kind of reality, physical matter. However, also unable to deny some difference between mental experience and physical experience, epiphenomenalism *imagines* the mental to be some diffuse, fuzzy, and ephemeral—what, exactly? a precise answer is never forthcoming—expression, production, emanation, or aura of the brain, but certainly no distinct reality in itself.

Ambiguity is commonplace in these discussions of consciousness. The terms applied—such as *epiphenomenalism* here and *functionalism* below (e.g., 4.12.4; 4.19.2)—are not even used consistently (Dennett, 1991, p. 401–406; Searle, 1997, p. 141). What matters, then, is not the name a position claims but the argument it entails; and even figuring out what the argument could actually mean also often remains a challenge. In accord with my concern in this book, I focus on the arguments.

Expressing rejection of dualism, an essential facet of epiphenomenalism is denial of any independent causal power to the mind (Dennett, 1991, pp. 71, 401–406; Griffin, 1991, pp. 53–54; Searle, 1998, lecture 7). Supposedly, if the mind is actually able to do something, such as effect bodily behavior, such causal efficacy would imply that the mind enjoys some kind of independent existence. One thing, mind, would be affecting a second thing, body, and dualism would raise its head again. But, trying to preserve the unity of the human being, epiphenomenalism does not grant any independent reality to the mind, so it denies that the mind has any causal capacity. A practical implication would be that, although we might think we are leading our own lives, in fact, biological processes are the whole of it. One's life and self is nothing more than "a human body's journey through life" (Dennett, 1991, p. 431). Supposedly, the mind has no control over the body nor over anything else; the mind is nothing in itself.

4.6. An Excursus on Causality

4.6.1. The Focus of Early Modern Science on Aristotle's Efficient Causality

Epiphenomenalism stakes its position on an argument about causality. But like everything else in this discussion, notions of causality differ with different epistemologies. The epistemology at work in epiphenomenalism seems, ever and again, to be some version of sensate-modeled epistemology, that naïve realist assumption that knowing is like perceiving, so we know by taking a good look, and things are stuff lying out there or hidden inside ourselves waiting to be uncovered and seen. Following suit, the causality that troubles epiphenomenalism is a broadly conceived efficient causality, the *imagined* billiard-ball-like push or pull of one physical body upon another.

Aristotle proposed four basic causes: material, formal, efficient, and final. In one standard example, the shipbuilder (efficient cause) makes the ship from wood (material cause) on the basis of a blueprint (formal cause) for the purpose of sailing the seas (final cause). At the beginnings of modern science, Galileo focused on material and efficient causes to understand how things happen in the physical world, and he dropped attention to formal and final causes. Since then, most science regards real or imaginable material things and attends to the forces that make them do what they do, and an image of activity in the physical world is taken to define the realm of science. So science tends to be focused on efficient causality, and it is presumed that this easily imagined push-pull type of causality is what scientific explanation is about.

Treating consciousness, Griffin (1991), for example, reports Mortimer Taube's "cogently defined" efficient causality: " 'An event A causes event B, when B results partly from some activity or influence originating from A' " (pp. 57–58). But activity, influence, and origination seem to be corporeally, imaginatively, or spatiotemporally conceived criteria. On such criteria, causality is not about understanding but about physical encounter and its results. Lucidly exposing the perceptual grounding of this construal of causality, Lonergan (1957/1992) described it as "the image of the transmission of effort through contact" (p. 563). Notice that anthropomorphically these words derive cleanly from the perceived relationship of things to us and our senses—effort through contact—rather than to the understood relationship of things among themselves.

This matter of causation is central to the mind–body problem, and the matter is subtle, so I must expend a few pages dealing with it. Chalmers (1996), for example, speculates "that consciousness and causation have some deep metaphysical tie. Both are quite mysterious, after all, and two mysteries might be more neatly wrapped into one" (p. 152). Well, yes, the two are somehow related, but the suggested packaging makes quite a leap. Chalmers and all philosophers have problems with causality because of David Hume's trenchant criticism of it in the 18th century. Hume was lucid regarding the fact that causality cannot be seen. That is, narrow empiricism, the reliance only on sense data, invalidates any appeal to causality. All we see is one event following another. We do not see the causality. Then, of course, if we remain faithful to this narrow empiricism and its sensate-modeled epistemology, the immediate conclusion hits us in the face: If it cannot be seen, it must not be real. Then, what is causality? Said with more sophistication, "external evidence only gives us access to regularities of succession between events; it does not give us access to any further fact of causation" (Chalmers, 1996, pp. 74–75).

4.6.2. Reliance on Perception and Imagined Efficient Causes

What's the problem here? Only intelligence, not perception, grasps causation. If so, Chalmers's packaging of consciousness and causality together, because they are both "mysterious," does have some thin plausibility. However, this plausibility has little to do with consciousness and causality in themselves. Rather, an intervening variable links them, namely, human intelligence. When you overlook intelligence as an explicitly named factor, you also perforce ignore the genuine nature of consciousness, and you ignore all matters of understanding—such as causality—that go with it. This oversight is glaring. Even to Hume's valid criticism, it must be added that one could only note the "regularities of succession between events" by using one's intelligence. Perception alone would grant no such awareness of regularities. Perception alone is a cinema in which all the audience has fallen asleep; images continue to light up the screen one by one, but nobody is there to notice and link the passing images in an ongoing narrative (5.5.1). Bare perception includes no connections. The mystery of causality and the mystery of consciousness are linked only because both pertain to the realm of genuine explanation, and it must be intellectual. A sensate-modeled epistemology has no way at all to deal with these matters because it overlooks them from the outset—after all, they're not visible!

Theorists almost universally presume a sensation-based notion of causality and apply it to the mind–body problem. The major hurdle is still Descartes's problem—to explain how the mind, a non-physical thing, could have an effect on the body, a physical thing, and vice versa. The picture is of two things somehow tugging and pulling at each other. Supposed evidence that the mind does, indeed, affect the body is readily provided: I am able to lift my arm if I decide to do so (Griffin, 1991, p. 59; Searle, 1998, lecture 7). More dramatically, as illustrations of the power of mind over matter, Griffin (1991) points to "psychosomatic phenomena—both ordinary phenomena, such as ulcers and the placebo effect, and extraordinary phenomena, such as stigmata and sudden cancer cures—as well as to large-scale psychokinetic effects" (p. 59). Consistently, however, the assumption is that mind and matter are separate forces or stuff that act upon each other in some push-pull manner. Causality is supposed to provide explanation, a matter of intelligence; but theorists portray causality as pictorial and imaginable, a matter of sensation and perception. But irrefutably, Hume argued that causality is not something that can be seen. As explanatory, causality must be something that is understood.

4.6.3. The Sole Agent, the Person

Another pervasive oversight helps control this doomed discussion of efficient causality: the unity of the person. At 4.11 I again address this matter. I insist that the person, not some facet or aspect or part of the person, is the agent in every case. This is the same point implied in discerning the person as one thing, one unity-identity-whole, in Lonergan's suggestive usage.

Discussion of imagined efficient causality between body and mind violates the unity of the person. The standard arguments have the body doing this and the mind doing that, and at times the one supposedly works upon or against the other. This overall construal of the mind–body problem is mistaken. It is not the body or the mind that does this in one case and that in another; but the person, a unified whole, one thing, is the agent and uses his or her human capacities—namely, body and mind, muscles and nerves, perceptions and memories, hopes and fears, understandings and decisions—to effect whatever is done. To be sure, because of the polymorphism of the human makeup, people struggle with drives, urges, impulses, and ideals. Indeed, the challenge of humanity is to find some wholesome integration of these multiple inputs into one's experience and behavior (Helminiak, 1996a, chapters 16–18; 5.8.2). This challenge is commonly portrayed as the goal of the spiritual quest (McNamara, 2009; 3.1.2). It is also the goal of contemporary psychotherapy. Still, when all is said and done, except in cases of genuine pathology or somnambulation, it is the person who acts and who is responsible for his or her acts. One should not attribute acts to the person's spirit or emotions, drives or loins—as if one could validly protest, "The devil made me do it."

The human being is a remarkable thing with an array of abilities. None of them operates apart from the rest, for in every case it is the person who operates. Why, for example, suppose that my mind is what moves my arm when that movement is my doing through the intelligent and self-determining organism that I am? I move myself: I move. Why suppose that telekinesis demonstrates the power of mind over matter when, as seems likely, this remarkable phenomenon depends largely on processes that physicists can measure and that are grounded in the person's tripartite makeup (Carpenter, 2012; Redgrove, 1987; Roll, 1972/2004; see 4.3)? Only imagination posits body and mind as separate stuff tugging and pulling at each other. Such thinking about efficient causality is mistaken on many fronts.

4.6.4. Efficient Versus Formal Causality

Efficient causality is not even the coinage of scientific explanation. When explanation is the goal, formal causality is actually at stake, not efficient causality. Formal causality expresses the intelligibility within any given phenomenon that accounts for its being what it is and its functioning as it does. Beauregard and O'Leary (2007; 3.1.1) make something of the same argument when they object to a restricted "mechanistic" causality. Their proposed alternative, however, gets lost in a vague and misapplied appeal to quantum-level physics (compare 3.5) and non-human spiritual entities (p. 30–34).

Popularly conceived, the "form" expresses the particular kind of reality in question so that, in another stock example, given a block of marble, one and the same material, the imposition of different forms would result in, say, a statue or a pillar or a birdbath. Forms make things be the kinds that they are. However, it is intelligibility that specifies forms. It is not their looks or shapes that distinguish a statue from a pillar or a birdbath, but their meanings, the consensual concepts that apply to each. Statue, pillar, and birdbath are meaningful realities. Their meanings make them what they are. Indeed, given the possibilities for contemporary art, one might be hard pressed to recognize a statue merely from its shape. Given human ingenuity and need, a statue could be used for a pillar, or a birdbath, for a wash basin and, thus, actually be one. In contrast, given merely their perceptible characteristics and despite their different shapes, Fido would be content to pee on any of these vertical contrivances and not really know the difference.

In stark and instructive contrast, it must be recognized that most talk of Aristotle's causes—material, formal, efficient, and final—deals in palpability and imagination. The form of the statue is usually taken to be the imaginable shape that is imposed on the physical marble, and the impression given is that discussion is about stuff lying out there, able to be seen and felt, and that matter and form describe material objects that are real because they are palpable. A sensation-based epistemology controls the discussion.

Through long years of philosophical, theological, and psychological study, I had never heard this commonplace topic presented otherwise until

Lonergan. Under the tutelage of Aquinas, Lonergan recognized that Aristotle's concern was intelligible beings, the objects one knows via reasonable judgments—not, as is commonly thought, simply material bodies lying out there, composed of palpable building material and imaginable shapes, which one could encounter by approaching. Fundamentally, implicitly defined, matter and form refer to data and intelligibility, respectively. As the essential determinants of things, matter and form are correlates of the first and second levels of consciousness (2.3), through whose composite processes we know realities. Form expresses the intelligibility that insight discerns in the data. Form is the essence of a thing, the nature or kind of a thing; form represents the necessary and sufficient conditions to make something what it is.

Formal causality, therefore—not efficient causality—is the object of the scientific quest to explain things. When science pursues the "laws of nature," it attempts to understand the forms, the essences, the individual natures that in intelligible interaction make "nature" what it is. Explanation concerns intelligibility; it entails forms.

4.6.5. Formal Cause and Implicit Definition

Within the scientific ideal of long, arduous, and oftentimes adjusted and refined advance toward pure explanation, formal causality expresses intelligibility via the insightful interrelationship of the telling factors. Let the example be the familiar equation $a^2 + b^2 = c^2$ in the case of the Euclidean right triangle. This equation defines a right triangle. With absolute precision the equation expresses the form of a right triangle.

We could, of course, also say, as we more commonly do, that the 90-degree angle is what determines a triangle as right; so talking of right triangles, I obviously mean triangles that include a right angle. But wanting ultimately to treat of the mind, consciousness, and God, I need a more abstract line of thought to be able to make my point, a line of thought that does not depend on actually measuring the angle in a concrete, given triangle. I want something that applies to any conceivable triangle and would insure that it is or is not right. So I attend to the algebraic equation that fits and, in a valid sense, actually defines a right triangle. When I invoke this example, I am also presuming that I am talking about a plane figure, some hypothetical polygon in two-dimensional Euclidian space. I insert this qualification because the relationship $a^2 + b^2 = c^2$ also pertains in the abstract to any set of integers (whole numbers) that fit this particular relationship. Mathematicians call them Pythagorean triples, and there exists an unending number of them, the most commonly known being (3,

4, 5): $3^2 + 4^2 = 5^2$. There are also (5, 12, 13), (6, 8, 10), (7, 24, 25), (9, 40, 41), (11, 60, 61), and so on. However, whenever any of these triads is applied to the case of a plane figure, this particular relationship of *a*, *b*, and *c* produces a right triangle. It produces a right triangle and nothing else. A right triangle entails this particular relationship, and this particular relationship entails a right triangle. It is in this sense that I mean that this equation $a^2 + b^2 = c^2$ defines a right triangle. It captures the essence, the form, the nature, of a right triangle.

Think about it. At stake is pure understanding abstracted from any particular concrete instance yet applicable to them all. The equation precisely and brilliantly expresses the striking particularity of a right triangle, a formulation of its essential intelligibility, an articulation of the inherent interrelationship of the telling facets of a right triangle. The equation expresses the meaning that makes a right triangle what it is. As already noted (1.7), I am calling this way of expressing meaning *implicit definition* (see Helminiak, 1996a, Chapter 5; Lonergan, 1957/1992, p. 37). The term is David Hilbert's (1902/1971), and, as he proposed it, it is actually much more abstract than even my application to the right triangle. To speak of a triangle, even in general, one is already quite concrete. One limits oneself to a plane figure, and in the process one presupposes such notions as plane, line, point, and distance, and one works with images of them. Hilbert's usage moved beyond any such concreteness and expressed what I want to call pure intelligibility, the sheer defining meaning that is at stake within or behind this or that concrete phenomenon. The term *implicit definition* works well for what I mean because, with Hilbert, Lonergan, and contemporary mathematicians and physicists, I am not in the least averse to projecting that absolute generalization—it is the anticipated goal and driving force in all human questioning and knowing: to understand everything about everything (see Lonergan, 1957/1992, pp. 36–37, 417, 460–461, 515). "Using other terminology to express [implicit definition], contemporary science might speak of 'rigorous' definition or 'formal' argument, and mathematics might speak of an interlocking set of terms and relations as an 'algebra'" (Helminiak, 1996a, p. 77, n. 5). This matter is commonplace in the hard sciences, and many terms exist to refer to it in different contexts. "Explanatory definition" would be another synonym, and this same meaning is what I intend when, following Lonergan (1957/1992, pp. 37, 61–62, 538–543), I use the terms *explain, explanatory,* and *explanation* and often contrast them with *describe, descriptive,* and *description* (4.12.3). Referring to his example of the roundness of a circle and the philosophers' long-sought understanding of "primitive terms," Lonergan related this matter as follows:

> For every basic insight there is a circle [or nest] of terms and relations, such that the terms fix the relations, the relations fix the terms, and the insight fixes both. If one grasps the necessary and sufficient conditions for the perfect roundness of this imagined plane curve [a circle], then one grasps not only the circle but also the point, the line, the circumference, the radii, the plane, and equality. All the concepts tumble out together, because all are needed to express adequately a single insight [namely, that a circle must be round if all the radii are equal]. All are coherent, for coherence basically means that all hang together from a single insight. (p. 36)

4.6.6. Causality as "An Intelligible Relation of Dependence"

Via such implicit definition, terms and relations define one another to express "an intelligible relation of dependence" (Lonergan, 1957/1992, p. 563; see also pp. 100–102). This relation of dependence is what Aristotle meant by formal cause—the *insightfully* discerned, inherent necessary and sufficient conditions that make a thing what it is. In this case, genuine dependence is indeed at stake, but no push-pull of *imagined* efficient causality.

Given those clarifications, let me elaborate my example of the right triangle. In it, c is what it is because of its particular relationship to a and b, and the same is so respectively for a and b in relation to c and to each other. Change in the value or magnitude of any of the elements results in proportional change in the others even while the overall relationship remains unchanged. Chronology is irrelevant; no element precedes any other. It makes no sense to ask whether the right triangle is prior to the hypotenuse or vice versa. The elements codetermine one another. They all *depend on* one another, and in this sense they *cause* one another. But any change in the relationship specified by the equation would actually change the reality in question. In Euclidean space, $a^2 + b^2 = c^2$ expresses right-triangle-ness and nothing else; it expresses the essence of right-triangle-ness, the pure intelligibility of any and every right triangle, that peculiar relationship between the sides and hypotenuse that makes a right triangle a right triangle. Yet $a^2 + b^2 = c^2$ looks nothing like a triangle. Implicit definition expresses pure relationality; it specifies realities in terms of relations; it formulates a "relational ontology" (for related discussion see Kaypayil, 2003; Oliver, 1981; Polkinghorne, 2010; Stetsenko, 2012).

Implicit definition is the goal and coinage of perfected science, and this fact explains why science has a penchant for mathematical equations.

They express relationships, the essence of explanation. In specifying intelligibility, relationships specify ontology: they say what is there, they determine what exists, they explicate some facet of being. Whenever we come to finally understand and explain something—and we seldom do so, and our most successful attempts remain ever only "the best available opinion of the day"—we do so by positing the precise relationships among the elements discerned as essential to that something. Moreover, when explanation is precise, the elements and their relationships mutually specify one another; they make one another be what they are. This fact is what I mean to exemplify by appeal to Pythagoras's theorem and the nature of a two-dimensional right triangle in light of its three sides and the mathematical relationship among them. The right triangle presents a relatively simple instance of what scientists achieve in other fields in much more sophisticated ways. It is not necessary to understand all science in order to understand what is at stake in doing science, in achieving precise explanation. Consideration of the right triangle offers a cogent and lucid instance of the goal of explanation: to specify things via the interrelationships of their constitutive elements, to define things by insightful determination of the constitutive relationships among their essential factors.

Paramount is the fact that relationships are intelligible, not perceptible; they depend on insights, not on seeing or touching or imaging. As Hume made clear, one does not experience the efficient causality between an approaching cue ball and the ensuing movement of another pool ball. One sees a succession of perceptual changes, and, if at all, via insight one concludes to a relationship of dependence between the two moving balls. Perhaps not explicitly aware of its own achievement, contemporary science does, indeed, operate on the premise that intelligence, not perception, determines the real. Perfected science produces coherent explanations, not perceptual mock-ups or mere "models" of the phenomena in question (compare Barbour, 1974).

Thus, implicit definition provides scientists with an utterly unambiguous linguistic tool for precise explanation and communication. This usage belies the too often touted claim that we are incapable of expressing anything in absolutely exact formulation (e.g., Jones, 1994), and it laments the turn in linguistic analysis to ordinary language and grieves the narrow emphases in structuralism and postmodern deconstructionism, as if the precise usage of implicit definition were not available or not more relevant to science and philosophy. In their respective specializations—and other technicians, in theirs—scientists across cultures around the globe share exact formulations all the time. They understand precisely what each other mean.

Moreover, this usage, implicit definition, also makes clear that causality means the interrelation or interdependence of the essential—the necessary and sufficient—elements, which hard-earned insight must discern. At stake in science and all mature explanation is Aristotle's formal causality—not the push-pull by which imagination usually pictures causality and which, in the physical world, pertains to efficient causality.

4.7. The Unity of the Human Being: Epiphenomenalism Revisited

Epiphenomenalism would solve the mind–body problem by portraying the mind as an epiphenomenon, an incidental by-product of the brain, but nothing essential in itself. For fear of making the mind appear to be some independent reality, epiphenomenalism is concerned to avoid attributing causality to the mind because, if the mind can make things happen, it must be independently real in some way. However, when the meaning of causality is explained and different kinds are posited, the epiphenomenalist preoccupation turns out to be misguided. An intellectual, rather than a perceptualist, understanding of causality allows that, like a, b, and c in a right triangle, within a person mind and brain could also be causally dependent on each other without requiring that they be two independent chunks of stuff that push and pull on each other. Within the triangle neither a, nor b, nor c is controlling the others; they function as a unity in mutual interdependence. Their relationship is what makes them what they are and what makes the triangle what it is. Their interactive unity determines all three, thereby constituting nothing other than the whole, the right triangle.

Similarly, body and mind are not two elements vying for control. There is no validity to the question about which has the upper hand: Does the brain cause the mind, or does the mind change the brain? They are interactive factors within one whole. Given the whole and applying intelligence with an intent to understand, it makes sense to posit constitutive factors, so then talk of brain and mind arise. Yes, then, too, it is true that the mind cannot operate apart from the brain. Mind depends on neuronal processes. Yet, similarly, the brain is not independent of the mind. The brain functions so as to sustain the mind in its operations, and because the mind is operating, the brain is entrained to function in a compatible way (5.9.2.3).

In a cell, for example, the pattern of biochemical functions is such as it is precisely because this overall interactive functioning constitutes life. Because the cell is alive, not just a conglomerate of complex molecules, the molecular functions in the cell are of a particular kind; they are constrained in a particular pattern. Otherwise, they do not support life; the cell is not alive. Simply said, the cell is a functioning unity, and for it to be alive is precisely what it means for it to be the self-sustaining unity that it is.

Brain and mind are likewise aspects of one functioning unity, the human being. They do what they do in interrelationship within each other. The kinds of neuronal processes and patterns of operation that go on in the brain are such precisely because they support mental processes. So the mental processes and the neuronal processes are mutually determinative. Each is what it is because of its relationship with the other. There is no push-pull between them, no vying for priority or control. They function as a unity. To be sure, the unity is dynamic; it is shifting, developing, advancing. But every advance entails the cooperative interaction of the varied processes. Apart from pathology and eventual death, no one process can run off on its own, domineering the others, neither in active nor in passive aggression, as it were. There exists only a slim margin of give and take in maintenance of the unity that all the processes constitute. The effect of cyanide through disruption of the chemical processes in the body is an easy example of what happens when that margin is breached. Brain and mind are partners in a three-legged race; they run together or not at all; and as they run, they accommodate each other to their mutual advantage. The accurate understanding is not body over mind or mind over body but the harmonious interactive functioning of body and mind as a person. The seat of efficient causality is not in one or the other; it lies in the human unit.

Of course, the question remains how the brain and mind, two different realities, two different kinds of being, can influence each other. I already intimated the answer in the prior paragraph, and I can say a bit more here. Further elaboration will also follow as this chapter unfolds and especially when I treat emergence at 4.14. So, if one pushes the question and asks what is controlling the whole, what gives direction to these interactive processes, what is working throughout the whole system to make it one, the answer must be the intellectual consciousness that characterizes the whole, the peculiar mentality that determines the human being as a person—just as in the cell, life characterizes the whole and determines the cell as alive. Intelligence is the constant between brain and mind, intelligibility in the one case and full-blown intelligence in the other (4.20.4). The brain functions such as it does to sustain intelligent mental functioning. But apart from a human mind, there is no intelligence or intelligent functioning to sustain. I know I speak loosely here of mind, intelligence, mentality, and only in Chapter 5 do I specify the human uniqueness that I intend. Yet in the broadest of terms, surely, there is a human mental distinctiveness, and it is this that I invoke. The intelligent, then, is the constant between brain and mind. The one dynamism that functions in both, the dynamism that flows from brain to mind, is the one that expresses intelligence. Otherwise, there would be no whole of this particular kind: a person, a human being. Stupidity, irrationality, incoherence, and randomness do not conduce to unity or advance. What links the brain and mind in a human unity must be the intelligence that characterizes the human as an emerged species. Intelligence in the human corresponds to intelligibility in the brain. That is, the brain is structured and functions—it entails a discernible ordering—so that it conduces to full-blown intelligence in the human being. Therein lies the link. In the human, it is, as it were, that the universe—as in all of cosmogenesis and evolution—is drawing up lower processes, brain function in this case, to subserve higher and more far-reaching processes, mentality in this case. In this sense, the mind is certainly dependent on the brain, but the function of the brain is also dependent on the nature of the mind, which the brain subserves. The link through it all is the intelligibility—the order, coherence, lawfulness—that runs through the unfolding cosmos and gets understood through human intelligence.

I add a caveat. As treated in Chapter 6, I intend nothing whatsoever to do with God when I point out a dynamism that acts within the universe as we have come to understand it since the mid-19th century. This dynamism is evidently a dimension of the universe as it exists (Lonergan, 1957/1992, pp. 470–476). The movement from the Big Bang to quarks and leptons, to particles, nuclei, and atoms, to molecules and, then, organic molecules and life, to sensation, perception, intelligence, and consciousness—this movement is not a theological postulate. It is a scientific theory. Indeed, much religion still rejects this well-documented scenario (Summarizing the judgment, 2005) or, at best, would claim—in some undifferentiated way, correctly, yes, but still in absolutely untutored and simplistic belief—that God is actually making all this happen, as if an engineer (ever and again portrayed in picture-thinking) were turning valves and pulling levers to effect various adjustments and changes. In contrast, as in Chapter 6, a critical theology would hold that God did create this universe and does sustain it in its every function and operation, but as created this universe or any of its processes could not be the Creator. The dynamism of the universe is an inherent dimension of the (created) universe itself. This dynamism is no ghostly, metaphysical, or mythical being acting behind the scenes. Like physicists, chemists, geologists, astronomers, and biologists, I am in no way invoking here or even alluding to God when I speak of an unfolding cosmos.

The current account presupposes the idea of emergence within cosmic process (for detail see 4.14). Under the common-enough names of cosmogenesis and evolution, I invoked the idea of emergence, and I hope that some intuitive understanding of my solution to the epiphenomenalist problem of causality came across.

At this point, however, the topic is merely epiphenomenalism as a prevalent way of construing mind–body unity. Epiphenomenalism is preoccupied not to attribute causality to the mind for fear of projecting some separate, independently existing entity that could affect the body. Still controlling the discussion is the problem of dualism that Descartes provoked, and a sensate-modeled epistemology with a push-pull notion of efficient causality sustains this epiphenomenalist preoccupation. In contrast, I suggest that a more appropriate understanding of the relevant causality is formal—not efficient—causality, formulated via implicit definition, as an expression of the mutually determinative, interactive factors—simply said, body and mind—that explain a single thing, the person.

4.8. The Unity of the Human Being: Nonreductive Physicalism

Another approach to relating mind and brain is *nonreductive physicalism* (Brown, 2002; Murphy, 2006; Teske, 2006; see also Searle, 1997, pp. 143–144, on David Chalmers's "nonreductive functionalism"). The very name of this approach suggests the struggle philosophers have trying to grant the mind some kind of reality of its own while avoiding any hint of two different kinds of realities. Murphy (2006) considers whether " 'nonreductive physicalism' is an oxymoron" (p. 109). I say, "Verbally? Yes, indeed."

4.8.1. Reductionism: Explanatory and Eliminative

In philosophical usage, reduction is generally considered a false approach. It suggests that one thing is really just something else—for example, a combination of simpler things. The telltale phrases of all-out reductionism are "nothing but" and "only." For example, "Life is only complex chemistry." "Thought is nothing but the firing of neurons." In such usage, reduction explains a thing away. However, philosophers also commonly allow another notion of reduction that does not explain a thing away. For example, "The problem is this pin here. It's bent, and it's blocking the action." This account reduces the problem to its explanatory elements; it explains the problem but does not explain the problem away. Philosopher John Searle (1997) calls the first kind of reduction, "*eliminative* reduction" (pp. 210–212), and Lawrence Cahoone (2008) calls it "ontological reduction" (p. 43). Searle calls the second kind of reduction "*causal* reduction" (pp. 210–212), and theologian Wayne Proudfoot (1985) calls it "explanatory reduction" (ch. 6). This complexity over reductionism arises because some people, usually out of deep personal commitment, reject any explanation; they see any explanation at all as a rejection of their "facts." For example, "I saw a flying saucer, and nothing you say will make me think otherwise." The fear is that explanation cancels out a belief—and in the example of the flying saucer, it might well do so. But genuine explanation always does account for one thing in terms of others. To do so is what explanation means. So philosophers insist on the validity of some kind of "reductionism." Unfortunately, the terms *causal reduction* and *explanatory reduction* are easily misleading because no real reduction of one thing to another is intended, but only the explanation of one thing in terms of others. Still, usage is what it is, and the distinction, however named, is valid.

It is difficult to understand from the term itself, *nonreductive physicalism*, what sense of reduction is in question. The intent is clearly double, and it is as follows. On the one hand, as total "physicalism," nonreductive physicalism would avoid dualism. It would deny the existence of mentality as a reality of a different kind in comparison with the physical brain. On the other hand, as "nonreductive," not wanting to suggest that mentality really is only physical, not wanting to reduce mind to nothing but the brain, this position admits the mind's causal efficacy and, thus, in some vague way, its reality and, thereby, hopes to avoid epiphenomenalism, as well. In some way this position wants to let the mind actually be real, so nonreductive physicalism might be a middle way between dualism and epiphenomenalism. Allowing some causal efficacy to mental phenomena, this approach introduces a new twist. As we shall see, this new twist will actually open onto some very useful thinking.

Nonetheless, if the physicalism in *nonreductive physicalism* is total, how can it be non-reductive? In this case, mental phenomena must actually be physical. If the physicalism is not total, why use this term, and why not just admit that mentality is something other than physical? We seem to be back to either a covert dualism or a standard epiphenomenalism. Most likely, however, we are just struggling with ambiguous terms again. Most likely, the intent of this position is inadequately conceptualized, and the term *nonreductive physicalism* does not suggest what it is intended to mean.

Nancey Murphy's (2006) argument for nonreductive physicalism supports that assessment of this unhappily named theory. She offers superb historical surveys about the notions "mind" and "soul," even presenting parallels between Thomas Aquinas's analyses and neuroscientific research. Yet her nonreductive physicalism is incoherent. On the one hand, she rejects any dualism. "We are bodies," she insists; "there is no additional metaphysical element such as a mind or soul or spirit" (p. iv), no other "entity" (p. 12), no "immaterial mind or soul in addition to the body" (p. 69). Note how these statements are loaded with reified, perceptually conceived notions, which, as such, are, of course, rightly rejected (4.15.2; 5.3.2–3.3). On the other hand, Murphy forcefully affirms "the high-level capacities that our bodies enable: consciousness, memory, moral character, interpersonal relationships, and, especially, our relationship with God" (p. 6). Supposedly, these capacities are not immaterial because they "are all the province of brain studies" (p. 69). That is, because neuroscience contributes to our understanding of all aspects of human experience, Murphy suggests that they are all merely neuronal productions. Are they, then, just epiphenomena—but, in this case, somehow significant? Not epiphenomena at all for Murphy! Verbally she outright denies any eliminative reductionism. In no way is she involved in "nothing-buttery" (p. 5)—because she does allow these high-level capacities. Well, then, must they not be more than just physical or material? Must not some other kind of reality be affirmed? Surely, as I suggested, nonreductive reductionism is inadequately conceptualized.

Also worthy of mention is another consideration that burdens Murphy's presentation. From Fuller Theological Seminary in the Evangelical tradition, she writes to address not only neuroscience and philosophy but also "Christian theology" (p. ix). Thus, that notion of "relationship with God" (e.g., pp. 6, 118, 132) recurs to jar the scientific discussion. One wonders how relationship with God would not be a spiritual matter. Yet Murphy finds that "biblical studies and neuroscience are both pointing in the same direction: toward a *physicalist* account of the person" (p. 69, emphasis added). Now, the Bible clearly holds a wholistic understanding of the person. Unlike the Greek, the Hebrew mind would make no sense of a soul or spirit inhering, or even imprisoned, in a body. To the Hebrew mind the person is one, single entity. Hence, the Hebrew Bible struggles with the notion of life after bodily death, and the Christian Testament insists on restoration of the body via resurrection. However, the point of that biblical unicity was not mere physicality or an emphasis on it—as even the term in Murphy's book title *Spirited Bodies* could mistakenly suggest.

Murphy bends the biblical understanding too far in making it match current scientific materialism. Her masterful scholarship falters in trying to unify the undifferentiated consciousness of commonsensical statements in the Bible with the theoretically differentiated consciousness of the intellectually sophisticated statements in science (see Lonergan, 1972, pp. 85–96; 4.9; Helminiak, 1986b, pp. 47–64; 1998, pp. 195–205; 2013a). She is aware of some difference. She writes, "It is hard to find any clear *teaching* on the metaphysical make-up of the person—this is simply not a question in which the biblical authors were interested" (p. 37). Yet she persists in this methodologically confounded endeavor.

Ever and again, this self-defeating outcome seems to result from acquiescence to an ideology that imposes required terminology: an understanding of science as merely materialist precludes any hint of dualism, so terms that endorse only materialism are *de rigueur* even if they misrepresent the genuine insight of the position. This unfortunate situation parallels that of Searle's (1991) "biological naturalism" and other similar positions, which I discuss at 4.10. The punch line there is this: probably physicalism and biologism really mean naturalism. That is, the concern is to avoid seeming appeal to other-worldly, ghostly, supernatural entities; the concern is to insist that the mind is part of the natural world. Then, well, yes, of course. But actually crediting the mind with such naturalism in the face of the materialistic hegemony in current science can be challenging. Something has to give.

4.8.2. Properties of the Brain

Unlike epiphenomenalism, in a new twist, nonreductive physicalism does attribute causal capacities to the mind—in terms of "emergent *properties*" such as human subjectivity, awareness, planning, choice, and even relationship with God, properties that are not inherent in the brain itself. This shift to properties (in contrast to different "substances" or "entities") with their own causal capacities is new.

Again, however, does talk of properties suffice? Despite itself, such talk appears to be just another version of dualism. Instead of naming two separate substances, mind and brain, that somehow combine to make up a person, the position names one substance and its "properties," and mind is considered a property of the brain. So philosophers speak of "substance dualism," which implies two separate substances, namely brain and mind; and they speak of "property dualism," which implies one substance, the brain, and its properties, the mind. By putting the name "properties" on the matter, it might seem that the problem is solved because there is no insistence on two separate substances. But there still remain two different realities in question: the physical brain and its mental properties—hence, the name "property *dualism*." Moreover, brain and mind are still usually portrayed as pushing and pulling on each other. This proposed solution does not avoid the doubleness that dualism entails, and it hardly explains how brain and mind are related. Calling the mind a "property" of the brain helps little—unless, as at 4.11.3, the whole matter can be reconceived in terms of persons, not just brains, and the properties would be properties of persons, not properties of brains.

More likely, however, nonreductive physicalism supposedly avoids dualism because, despite its name, it is reductive, after all. It reduces mind to brain, mentality to physicality. Insistence on properties, rather than substances, is supposed to preserve the unity of the human being. But does it? The telling question now becomes, "What does *property* mean?" Additionally, which is the one substance that has the properties? Is it the brain or the mind? In light of the name "physicalism," the answer would have to be the brain. Supposedly, it is the brain that has properties, and mind is one of them. How, then, could the mind not be physical? Physical things have physical properties; that is, physical things have the kind of properties that characterize the things as physical. And what of the person, who "has" both the brain and the mind? Is nonreductive physicalism really different from epiphenomenalism and the physical reductionism that epiphenomenalism implies? Nonreductive physicalism does attribute causal capacities to the mind, but if the mind is not really some reality of its own kind, how can it have causal capacities proper to it rather than what is proper only to the brain? Again, appealing to *properties*, we have another solution for the mind–body problem, but it raises as many problems as it tries to solve. We are still left with the question about how the mind relates to the brain.

4.8.3. Properties via Emergence

Nonreductive physicalism offers a second new twist and with it addresses that question of how the brain and mind relate. Nonreductive physicalism speaks of mental properties as *emergent*. The suggestion is that somehow the mind is a product or emanation of the brain. Once again, this suggestion opens onto some very useful thinking, as we shall see at 4.14.

However, to simply assert that the mind emanates from the brain is not to explain how this emanation could occur or what kind of reality, if any, this emergent mind is. The question remains whether standard talk of emergent properties does, in fact, adequately acknowledge and account for a real, an ontological, difference of the human mind in contrast to its biological base. Is this emergent property a new kind of reality? Or is it somehow still only some kind of an imagined wisp of physicality, an epiphenomenon like the screams of a roller-coaster ride? If the epistemology is sensate-modeled, the only emergent properties must be imagined wisps.

4.8.4. *The Ideology of Physicalism in Defense of Science*

The recurrent insistence on physicalism in this discussion is disturbing. This bending over backward to avoid any hint of so-called dualism, this concerted effort to deny the possibility that there exist different kinds of reality, backs people into awkward corners. Repeating Searle's (1997) observations: there is fear of losing "the entire scientific worldview that we have spent nearly four centuries to attain" (p. xiii), so "the intensity of feelings borders on the religious and political" (p. 189). Yet how reasonable is it to insist that strikingly novel mental capacities are nothing more than what is proper to the physicality of a biological organ *per se*? The fully non-scientific need to reduce consciousness to material reality and biology is ever in control. A restrictive ideology, not an open-ended rationality based on evidence and characteristic of genuine science, has taken over the field. If mentality is just a property of biology, is grass also conscious? Grass is biological, after all. Or must the biology in question be more complex? Then how complex? Are all mammals conscious? Or only humans? (Criticizing Griffin, 1991, and Chalmers, 1996, at 4.20 & 4.21, I directly address and reject panpsychism, the supposition that consciousness adheres in all levels of reality.) In whatever case, how is it that biological complexity at some point turns into mind and not just into more of the same: life, robust life, complex life, exquisitely refined life? Are being alive and being conscious one and the same thing? For functioning humans they usually are, but surely not for thriving grass. Then, consciousness and life are not only distinct but actually also separable. Not only is life not consciousness, but also in grass or a comatose human, for example, the one exists without the other. Current insistence on physicalism is a theoretical black hole, and a dark obscurantism reigns.

To be fair, however, nonreductive physicalism does make valid contributions. The mind is dependent on the brain. The mind is no independent, free-floating entity, the proverbial "ghost in the machine." The mind is a "property" of the brain, it emerges from the brain; perforce, the mind is somehow different from the brain. These suggestions show some validity. But there remains the critical need to explain the meaning of *property* and to explain *emergence*, the proposed relationship between the brain and the mind. Besides, this approach continues to attribute the mind too simply to the brain, instead of to the person.

4.9. Analogies for Mind as a Property of the Brain: Searle

4.9.1. Analogies, Properties, and Features

Attempts have been made to explain that relationship between the brain and the mind in terms of "properties of the brain." Searle (1997, 1998) provides an outstanding example of such attempts. Rightly famous for his insistence that consciousness is both related to the brain but also not reducible to the brain, Searle offers a number of analogies—for example, the mind is to the brain as digestion is to the stomach—to make his point. Frankly, Searle's analogies are not valid; they do not make his point—which, I believe, is nonetheless absolutely valid. The root problem, again, is the epistemological confusion that fails to distinguish and mixes together sensate and intellectual knowing. To exemplify and clarify this matter, I will consider Searle's analogical argumentation. My intent is to show why the analogies fail and to suggest what would be needed for a cogent argument. Bit by bit I forge the elements to make that argument. Focus on the notion of *properties* is most useful. Indeed, a coherent account of things and their properties could provide a coherent solution to the mind–body problem. Thus, in extensive detail I consider Searle's talk of properties of the brain.

Already, however, I must acknowledge a complication. This field is a jungle. In a "Conclusion," which appears to be an attempted advance or refinement over earlier statements, peculiarly, Searle (1997) backs away from talk of properties (pp. 194–195). He would insist that, if property language is to be allowed at all, then "there are lots of real properties in the world," not just the bodily and mental (p. 211). Yes, indeed! And what if this realization were taken literally and its implications followed through?! Searle does allow the term *property* (pp. 13, 18) although he does not like it. He thinks it still carries dualistic baggage (pp. 194–195), so he prefers an even less defined term and speaks of consciousness as "a *feature* of the brain" (p. 18; also xiv, 8, 17). That both terms, *property* and *feature,* are fuzzy is significant. This ambiguity leaves wiggle room for formulating a difficult matter only suggestively, and it emphasizes that we are far from understanding what consciousness is and, perforce, how it should be articulated precisely. This situation highlights my recurrent point that clarity on these matters is impossible without an epistemology adequate to non-physical phenomena, but current positions probably universally rely to some extent on sensation-based, perceptual models of knowing. So talk of properties usually does imply covert dualism. In this regard, only Lonergan's epistemology comes clean.

4.9.2. Liquidity in Water and H_2O

Despite his reservations, Searle (1998, 1997) proposes a number of analogies to argue that the mind is irreducible to the brain, but none of them holds up to scrutiny. Here is one dominant analogy about consciousness as a property of the brain: liquidity is to water as the mind is to the brain (1997, pp. 18, 211). The liquidity in this analogy is the flow that eyes see, the slick that hands feel, and the gurgle that ears hear. It is a commonsensical notion. But scientific explanation implicates multiple other considerations. The suggestion that liquidity is a systemic property of water falls into question. True, no single water molecule is wet or fluid, so in accord with some systems theory, one could say the liquidity is a new "property" that pertains to the whole "system" and is not reducible to the individual molecules as such—just as the mind is supposedly a property that emerges from a system, the brain.

However, the supposed system of water is no such thing. It is just a collection of more and more of the same H_2O molecules. Besides, the liquidity of this collection is inherent in H_2O molecules within a certain range of physical conditions. Given water, there is nothing new or emergent in the slide of weakly bonded H_2O molecules against one another, which we experience as liquidity or wetness. Moreover, Searle's liquidity is a perceptual characteristic, but *liquidity* is also a chemical term with technical meaning. Searle's commonsense analogy—legitimately—presupposes the ambient conditions in most places near the surface of the Earth, so it ignores the interactive effect of pressure and temperature, and it ignores the resultant different states of matter. Under these same ambient conditions, carbon dioxide, CO_2, passes directly from its solid state ("dry ice") to its vapor state; it has no liquid state. For chemists liquidity is a state of matter. In no way is liquidity a taken-for-granted property, not of water or of anything else. Even to propose an analogy that begins "liquidity is to water" is chemically puzzling.

What is the error in Searle's analogy? It mixes common sense with scientific theory. It contrasts the perceptually experienced liquidity of water with the scientifically known individuality of an H_2O molecule and a supposed system of many such molecules. It mixes sensate-based epistemology with intellectual epistemology. The analogy depends on an argument about water molecules, which contemporary science knows but which human perception has never experienced as such; yet the liquidity in the analogy is the everyday experience of human perception. As Searle presents it, liquidity is a sensible property. It parallels other sensible characteristics of water such as weight and transparency. As commonly accessible, these, too, depend on human perception, not on scientific explanation. However, when they are actually explained, when science pronounces, in themselves these characteristics are inherently related to the chemical structure of water under specifiable conditions. Thus, it becomes clear that the experienced liquidity of water includes nothing beyond the inherent nature of water under certain conditions. The proposed analogy confounds perceptual experience and scientific explanation. The first speaks in terms of felt wetness, and the second, in terms of explained molecular structure, temperature, pressure, and states of matter. Yet both address the same thing: flowing water. Thus, Searle's analogy illustrates no emergent property at all. Rather, it confounds two kinds of knowing. It proposes what is known by sense experience as something different and additional to what is known scientifically by intelligence. In no way does this analogy serve to illustrate how, as a supposed emergent property, like liquidity to water, consciousness is a human phenomenon that is irreducible to the brain.

4.9.3. Digestion in the Stomach and in the Organism

For similar reasons, Searle's (1997, pp. xiii, 6, 14, 163) other prime analogy—consciousness is to the brain as digestion is to the stomach—also proves unsatisfactory. Digestion is, in fact, the very process that determines the "stomach" as such. Digestion is no added-on feature of the stomach. Indeed, not even the stomach, one isolated organ, is in question here. Rather, if digestion is what specifies the stomach as such, *stomach* is being used as a shorthand symbol for the entire digestive system plus multiple other systems—circulatory, respiratory, glandular, muscular, nervous—that support and sustain the biological function of digestion. If digestion is to be called a property of anything, it must be a property of the organism, not of the isolated stomach. Then, to finally get the matter correct, digestion is simply one of the inherent processes of organisms. Far from being a property, and far from being irreducible to the organism, then, as consciousness is supposed to be to the brain, digestion and its related processes are precisely what constitute the organism as an organism. They are essential to the organism; they are not some emergent properties, added-on extras, as it were. Without them there would be no living organism of which digestion might appear as a supposed property at a purported higher level of analysis.

The consistent error in these analogies is the mixing of science and common sense. This is the same kind of error that I highlighted at 2.2.5 (see also 4.8.1). There I called it the confusion between a sensate-based or perceptualist (commonsense, naïve realist) epistemology and an intellectual (scientific) epistemology. I noted that Lonergan's key contribution to epistemology was to sort out and interrelate these two basic kinds of knowing. Through exemplification, I am elaborating Lonergan's breakthrough. I show how the sensate-based epistemology of common sense understands things in relation to ourselves, that is, to our senses; and the intellectual epistemology, which 20th-century science has so successfully deployed, explains things by using intelligence to relate things to one another. In Lonergan's (1957/1992) usage, these two approaches are named *description* and *explanation*, respectively (pp. 107–109, 201–203, 316–317, 320–321). I merely introduce this distinction here and elaborate at 4.12.1.

Searle urges that he is relating different levels of explanation and, thus, non-reductively accounting for irreducible properties *at different levels*—an H_2O molecule and felt liquidity, the isolated stomach and the process of digestion. In fact, he is mixing *different kinds of understanding*—on the one hand, the implicitly defined explanatory account of science, which explains things in terms of one another, and on the other, the descriptive account of perceptual experience, which describes things as they relate to our senses—that is, on the one hand, science, and on the other, common sense. Besides, when the explanation is consistently scientific, the purported emergent properties fall out. Liquidity is nothing proper to H_2O molecules, and digestion is not a property of the stomach.

4.9.4. Felt Solidity and Spacious Molecular Structure

The point of criticism easily comes clear in the parallel case of another of Searle's (1998, lecture 7; 1997, p. 161) analogies. Supposedly, the molecular structure of metal explains and causes the solidity of an engine's piston. Supposedly—like liquidity in the case of H_2O molecules—solidity is an emergent property of molecules of metal. Supposedly, the *individual molecules* at one level of analysis produce the felt solidity in a *system of molecules* at a higher level. The suggestion, of course, is that consciousness is similarly an emergent property of the brain, a property that becomes salient at a higher level of analysis.

However, solidity is an everyday perceptual characteristic of metal, dependent on touch. In contrast, molecular structure is a scientific theory, dependent on verified insight into relevant data. So, whereas solidity depends on sensate experience, molecular structure depends on insightful and reasonable intelligence. Accordingly, unlike solidity, molecular structure is fully imperceptible to the unaided human senses. This proposed analogy entangles two different epistemologies. To combine solidity and molecular structure in a single argument—or liquidity and H_2O or "digestion" and "stomachs"—is to confound perception with intelligence, sense experience with reasonable judgment, common sense with science.

The point comes home undeniably in a comparison of Searle's analogy with Sir Arthur Stanley Eddington's (1928) famous advertence to his desk. Understanding both the perceptual experience and the scientific account, Eddington commented on what were, as if, two very different tables before him: "One of them was visible, palpable, brown, solid, and heavy; the other was mostly empty space with here and there an unimaginable wavicle" (Lonergan, 1972, p. 274). If one goes with the scientist, the solidity of metal, like that of the desk, disappears into mostly empty space. Consistently apply only one kind of knowing, in this case the intellectual or scientific, and solidity falls out of consideration—simply because solidity is a perceptual, not a scientific, property. Precisely that was Eddington's point.

Searle's analogies demonstrate no properties at all, let alone irreducible properties. By the same token, the analogies provide no parallel for the irreducibility of consciousness to the brain. We are still far from any coherent account of *properties* that would do justice to the mind, the brain, and their relationship.

4.9.5. The Analogy of the Chinese Room

To give credit where credit is surely due, those analogies might work for another of Searle's (1997, pp. 11–14; 1998, lecture 4) purposes. In addition to insisting that consciousness is irreducible to the brain, he also wants to insist—as he is rightly famous for doing with his Chinese Room Argument—that a computer simulation of human behavior does not demonstrate consciousness in the computer (1997, p. 59). That a computer, for example, could be successfully programmed to follow an algorithm and thus generate correct responses to questions submitted in symbols corresponding to a catalogue of Chinese characters does not mean that the computer actually understands Chinese—any more than a human being performing the same rote operations would. Similarly, that a computer could be programmed with the rules of chess and could quickly run through all possible moves, five, six, even eight moves out, and select the most likely successful move at this point in the game does not mean that the computer understands chess or can think—any more so than an abacus, adding machine, or today's hand-held calculators can think simply because they execute a preprogrammed, mechanical, arithmetic process or any more so than a computer is intelligent because it can win a game of *Jeopardy*.

These analogies do indeed show that a computer has no mind, but they do not show how the human mind is related to the brain. Successful in one instance, Searle has pushed his analogies beyond their usefulness. They work in the case of the Chinese Room Argument because they unfold consistently within a commonsense mode of thinking. Everything about the analogies could be pictured, graphed, or imagined as mere mechanistic functions—everything, that is, except the mind; and this exception makes the valid point of the analogical argument: the mind is of a different kind in comparison to the programmed functioning of the computer. But Searle's use of the analogies to demonstrate emergent properties depends on mixing commonsense understanding with scientific understanding; hence, in that case they offer no coherent illustration or valid argument.

I have considered a number of analogies that purport to illustrate how the mind is irreducible to the brain. None of the analogies is valid, and the flaw is always epistemological. We are still left with the conundrum of the mind–body problem. To the good, we have the double assertion that the mind is somehow inherently related to the brain and that the mind is irreducible to brain function, is something more than the brain. But problematically—because of the supposed need to avoid that bugaboo, dualism, because of aversion to the suggestion that something non-material might actually be real, and because there exists no clarity about what "real" means, in any case—the insistence has been that the mind is not some reality different from the brain but merely a property or feature of the brain. Attention to properties provides a helpful clue, and I will follow up on it at 4.12.1 and 4.13. I will clarify what *properties* means, and I will continue to insist that the properties in question must be properties of the person, not of the brain. This emphasis will bring us to our goal, a coherent explanation of the mind–body problem.

Thus far, I have been chipping away at counterarguments. I have optimistically been applying Lonergan's distinction between sensate knowing and intellectual knowing. We have at least seen that this distinction pinpoints the flaws in invalid arguments. The ultimate goal is to apply the distinction to propose a coherent and consistent argument.

In passing, I submit a similar criticism of Albright and Ashbrook's (2001) *Where God Lives in the Human Brain*. This book would also fall to the same mistake of trying to combine science and common sense—if the book were a scientific endeavor. In fact, the book is an extended homily, a sermon, sometimes an apologia, a discourse intended to bolster faith in God. The book "presents evidence of how the brain works to make sense of religion and God" (p. xxix). As the Psalmist (19:1) exclaimed, "The heavens declare the glory of God," Albright and Ashbrook would propose that the brain—the epitome of God's creation, the most complex reality we know—likewise declares the glory of God. Accordingly, examining aspects of brain function, in each case Albright and Ashbrook discern characteristics of God: "ever present, nurturing, meaningful, and purposeful" (p. xx).

This book is a clever contemporary but standard project of defending beliefs by appeal to some latest cultural concern. The watchmaker analogy served that purpose in the 18th and 19th centuries. The inconsistency in this project is that it pairs the findings of scientific research with traditional faith and personal piety, taken uncritically. Such a project is the perennial work of a good preacher who, for better or worse, keeps faith alive; but this project itself lives off of an epistemological incoherence as common sense, especially religious, ever struggles to deal with the sophisticated conclusions of theoretical thinking (see Lonergan, 1972, pp. 97–99; also Helminiak, 2013a).

4.10. The "Naturalness" of Consciousness

4.10.1. Seemingly Reductive Insistence on Biology

I digress briefly in this section to suggest a friendly interpretation of the arguments I criticize relentlessly. As the poor unfortunate, Searle (1997) has been standing in as the poster child for them all at this point. He is intent on linking consciousness with the brain; yet he wants to insist that the mind is irreducible to the brain but, simultaneously, to avoid any hint that consciousness is "a separate entity" (p. 8). Does he mean *thing* or *reality*? (Recall that, as explained at 4.2.2, I am using *thing* to refer to an individual actual existent, and I am using *reality* to refer to the kind or kinds of being of an actual existent—so the mind could be a distinct kind of reality in comparison to the physical brain but still not be an entity independent of the person, including her or his body.) The pervasive insistence is to reject the notion that the human mind is some separate "reality somehow supernaturally injected into human beings"—thus, Teske (2006, p. 174). But, again, does *reality* in this case mean *thing*?

Recurrently, we see the preoccupation to reject dualism, the idea that mind and brain are actually different realities. Thus, Searle (1991) speaks of consciousness as a "natural biological phenomenon" (p. xiii) and "an ordinary biological phenomenon" (p. 6), and he holds what he calls "biological naturalism" (p. xiv) and refers to consciousness, not only as biological, but even as "a part of the ordinary physical world" (p. 7, see also 147, 214).

I resonate wholeheartedly with what I believe to be Searle's intent, but as his position stands, I can see in it only biological reductionism. If Searle had spoken of consciousness as "a natural phenomenon" or as "part of the ordinary world"—omitting the terms *biological* and *physical*—I would concur. However, I would understand *world* to mean, not the totality of palpable physical or biological matter out there, but the universe of *being*, that is, "the objective of the pure desire to know" (Lonergan, 1957/1992, p. 372), "what is to be known by the totality of true judgments" (p. 374). I would also concur that consciousness is inherently related to human biology and, perforce, to physical and chemical realities. However, I would not categorize consciousness *among* biological and physical realities. Rather, I would insist that consciousness—attentively, intelligently, and reasonably conceived—is of a different kind in comparison to them, a different reality.

Searle's language, despite his best commonsensical intentions, appears undeniably reductionist. Indeed, if consciousness is a "biological phenomenon" and biology is merely biochemical, which is merely molecular, which is merely atomic, and so on down the line, then Searle's position—and not his alone—consistently applied, is ultimately pure materialism: consciousness is really—fully imaginable!—matter in motion. The only escape from this imagined reductionist spiral is to admit the existence of different kinds of realities at each level, as I elaborate at 4.11. The only escape is to admit that there are different kinds of reality in our world; animal and mental are only two among them. Ah, but the ideological crusade against a simplistically conceived dualism will have none of it!

Consider again the brain and the arguments about its supposed properties. The properties of the brain that exactly parallel the wetness of water would be the wetness, grayness, and squishiness of the brain, but mentality is not among them, and it is not of the same order—even as Searle (1997), invoking a technical philosophical term, wants to insist: "consciousness has a first-person or subjective ontology" (p. 212; see also 98–99, 112, 120).

Consider further that the brain also controls vital functions: respiration, circulation, and also digestion. Without a functioning brain, they cease. If we apply Searle's analogical argument, these must also constitute properties of the brain. Granted, attention to them moves our focus beyond the mere sensible properties—the wetness, grayness, and squishiness—of the brain; yet, unambiguously, respiration, circulation, and digestion remain fully and merely organic; they are quintessential biological processes. Consciousness is of a still different order. Respiration, circulation, and digestion are also of a different order compared to the brain's wetness, grayness, and squishiness. Obviously, Searle's analogy collapses significantly different realities into one. At best and despite himself, his argument never gets beyond biology—which, I think, is exactly where he wants it. But why so?

4.10.2. Biological Means Non-Supernatural

My sense is that Searle (1997) does want to preserve the unique quality of consciousness, and for this reason he relentlessly insists on its irreducibility. Yet, conflictingly, he also unbudgingly insists on its biological nature—indeed, sometimes to the extreme: "consciousness is as much a biological process as digestion or photosynthesis" (p. 163) and "is as restricted in its biology as the secretion of bile" (p. 161). These protestations bespeak an outright biological reductionism, but Searle explicitly rejects biological reductionism. Apart from the trivial truism that the mind has something to do with the brain, what can one make of these conflicting emphases?

My optimistic reading is that in his commonsensical style Searle is unwittingly using *biology* as a symbol, not a literal reference. My sense is this: Searle's point is that consciousness is part of the natural world; *biological* stands for natural, non-supernatural, this-worldly, non-other-worldly. I wonder if Dennett (1991) isn't trying to make the same point by taking the matter to the extreme and denying any unique quality whatsoever to consciousness. With loaded rhetoric he contrasts heaven and Earth as he refers to human intelligence with these words: "our brains are responsible on their own, without miraculous assistance, for our understanding" (p. 438)—as if anyone could reasonably believe that insights are miraculous interventions, strictly taken (but cf. Helminiak, 2010, p. 63–65). Similarly, it strikes me that, to address a 21st-century audience, James Cameron's blockbuster movie *Avatar* also used biology—the Tree of Souls, *Vitraya Ramunong*—to suggest and elaborate its blatant concern for a spiritual dimension that is natural in persons, whether Na'vi or human. And no wonder. The metaphor *life* has been a staple of spirituality and religion: the spiritual "life," eternal "life," divine "life." For Searle, Dennett, and Cameron, the biological symbols suggest that consciousness is not a supernatural entity; it is not some otherworldly infusion into a living body; it is not some non-human or, perhaps, even divine or other-worldly phenomenon.

Chalmers (1995/1997) is explicitly non-reductionist; he suggests that in our universe consciousness is a fundamental entity of its own kind, and he even allows that his position is "a variety of dualism." But once again, to make clear that "there is nothing particularly spiritual or mystical about this theory," he would call it "*naturalistic dualism*" (p. 20). He explains, "There need be nothing especially transcendental about consciousness; it is just another natural phenomenon" (Chalmers, 1996, p. 128; see also xiii–xiv).

On all fronts, despite obvious risks of exaggeration, there seems to be a need to outright reject any "supernaturalism" and to emphasize the natural nature of consciousness. Thus, I believe that Searle's, Dennett's, and Cameron's insistence on biology, agreeing even with Chalmers on this point, serves as insistence on naturalism. I applaud and fully agree with this insistence—although at 5.8, with no other-worldly intent whatsoever, I will characterize consciousness as spiritual and relate it to mysticism.

I read that same symbolic usage of the term *biological* in David Hay's (2006/2007) *Something There*. Its subtitle *The Biology of the Human Spirit* badly describes this superb book. Only one chapter squarely treats the biological bases of consciousness. The rest, from beginning to end, exemplifies and insists on the naturalness of the human sense for the spiritual—even in a research population that is, at best, only loosely affiliated with religion or committed to belief in God. Trying to make his point, Hay writes, "The European cultural value [of interest or self-interest, in both the fiscal and personal senses] has closed off the full story of our *biological* makeup," namely, "the plausibility of more communally minded metaphors" and "the empirically supported claim that spiritual awareness is a *biological* reality and not just a socially constructed fantasy" (p. 239, emphasis added). He elaborates: our secularist social conditioning obscures "the recognition of the role of our *physiology* in opening up awareness of transcendence" (p. 214, emphasis added).

With Hay as with Searle, Dennett, Cameron, and Chalmers, appeal to biology and physiology seems to be insistence on naturalism. I wonder if Brown (2002), Murphy (2006), and Teske (2006) are not trying to make the same point by proposing that puzzling *nonreductive physicalism*, discussed at 4.8. If so, the point is well taken, but in every case the formulations beg for much needed precision. While, indeed, related to the organism, could the mind be inherently non-physical and non-biological and still be part of the natural world? Could spirituality be a phenomenon natural to humans, not some divine or other-worldly connection? I believe so. Others, however, would preemptively answer these questions by restricting the possible meaning of *natural* to *material* or, at best, *biological*; and with confused epistemology they would *imagine* mind and spirit, if they are to be natural, as somehow necessarily sensate or perceptual realities, somehow to be identified with biological brain processes. Nevertheless, could insights and concepts be non-physical but also be part of the natural world? Beyond doubt, they are. The quote from Dennett immediately above makes this very point emphatically. The challenge is to recognize the immaterial nature of insights and to integrate this recognition into a coherent understanding of humanity.

4.11. Multiple Realities in One Thing

4.11.1. *The Automobile: One Thing Composed of Many Realities*

We are still faced with the conundrum of the human being. We know the person to have both physical and mental properties. We want to be able to credit them all without suggesting that the bodily and the mental are two separate entities or substances that somehow get cobbled together to form a person. After all, despite a polymorphous nature, a person is a unity, one thing.

Lonergan's technical usage of the term *thing* fits this very situation. The thing is a unity-identity-whole, which insight can grasp in an array of data (4.1.2). Said otherwise, a single entity can encompass a number of different realities. That is, different kinds of being can cohere to constitute one entity. Throughout this analysis, it is presumed that our knowing depends on insight, concepts, and judgments. We are not picturing or imagining different chunks of matter somehow pieced or glued together to form a composite body. We are making our assertions on the basis of reasonable judgments, not perceptual experience.

I know, dear reader, that these ideas might still remain enigmatic. I am painfully aware of this probability, and I struggle to explain myself intelligibly. In the next subsection I offer one detailed, specific, precise, and rather simple example to illustrate my point. My insistence is that many realities can constitute one thing. Remember that I am using *reality* to refer to the different kinds that make beings what they are, as specified by the respective intelligibilities of these realties; and I am using *thing* to refer to the existent that is of this or that kind or perhaps of many kinds, as specified by an insight that grasps the unity-identity-whole of the single actuality in question (2.3.1; 4.2.2). Understood in this sense, one thing could encompass many realities; one existent could embody a number of different kinds of being. The insistence is that a human being includes a material body, organic physiology, emotional responsiveness, intellectual potential, and capacity for self-determination. Different kinds of realities cohere to form one polymorphous being, one thing, a human.

As a preliminary exercise, consider this crass, imaginable, yet usefully suggestive example. An automobile comprises a metal frame, engine, and steering system, plastic paneling, rubber wheels, glass windows, upholstered seats, and a silicon-based electronic entertainment system. Despite these different materials, on the basis of a consensual concept, a shared understanding, an automobile is one intelligible whole—one thing. Similarly, the human being comprises organism, psyche, and spirit yet is one thing. These analyses hold if intelligence is the criterion; they do not hold if perception is. Now let me move on to a technically precise example.

4.11.2. Water From Hydrogen and Oxygen

The case in point is water. Searle's suggestion (4.9.2) that liquidity is an emergent property of water (just as the mind is supposed to be an emergent property of the brain) does not hold up—because this analogy mixes the hard-won intellectual account of water as H_2O with the perceptual experience of water as wet and, further, because from the scientific perspective liquidity is a state of matter, not a property, and it is inherent in the very makeup of H_2O molecules under specifiable conditions.

However, had Searle's analogy remained consistently within the realm of chemistry and had it compared the elements, hydrogen and oxygen, with the molecule, water, the intended point could have been made—because, tellingly, new reality would have been posited, water, not just a supposed new property of hydrogen and oxygen. Water truly is a distinct reality, a new thing, emergent from the bonding of hydrogen and oxygen, just as human consciousness is also a distinct reality, a new kind of being, emergent as a higher integration within a human organism and psyche. (I treat emergence at 4.14.) Thus, more accurately to the point, Searle's analogy should have been this: water is to hydrogen and oxygen as consciousness is to the brain.

Let me elaborate. In no way is water a property of hydrogen and oxygen or of either, neither emergent nor otherwise. In comparison to them, water is a different reality. Both chemically and experientially, water has its own properties, and they are strikingly unlike those of its two constituents. In comparison to them, then, water is something new. It involves different interrelationships with other elements and compounds and implies different chemical laws—that is, it entails a different intelligibility. Therefore, it presents a different reality.

One illustration regards the everyday fact that ice floats. It does so because cooling water reaches its greatest density at about 4° C. As cooling continues below this temperature, water molecules begin to be ordered; they crystallize. As a result, the liquid begins to expand—because the bond angles between the atoms of hydrogen and oxygen result in a "misshapen" molecule and molecules of this shape crystallize as a "spacious" hexagonal structure. This structure explains the six-pointed shape of snowflakes. Reaching its solid state, ice is lighter than liquid water, so ice floats. This phenomenon is a chemical anomaly. It differs from the expected relationship of temperature and density in which the solid state "should" be denser than the liquid.

More to the point, this anomaly could not have been known by deduction from an understanding of the synthesis of water from hydrogen and oxygen; it could not be known bottom up. And it could not have been known by analogy with other known molecules. Once known, however, this anomaly can be understood. It is completely *consistent* with what is known about hydrogen, oxygen, their bonding, the resultant H_2O molecule, and other molecular processes. That ice floats is intelligible. We know why it floats. But intelligence is not simply logic; *de facto* understanding is not explained necessity; *consistency* is not deduction.

Some might loosely insist, "Yes, this phenomenon is totally explicable. It's no mystery that water and ice behave as they do. The whole chemical picture fits perfectly." But this insistence is inexact. Yes, we can explain this anomaly, but only because we have water to work with. From the top down, yes, chemists are able to specify the intelligible consistency between water, with all its peculiarities, and the synthesis from which it emerges. Given water, we can explain how it fits with what we know of its constituents, their chemical bonding, the shape of the resultant molecule, and the crystalline structure of the solid state. But bottom up, given only hydrogen and oxygen and even the realization that they easily and strongly bond, from known chemical principles we could not predict, we could not *deduce* this peculiar property of H_2O. Water is its own kind; it behaves in its own way; it is something in itself; it is a *sui generis* reality; it can be known only once it exists.

Being a physical reality, water also presents a different perceptual experience in comparison to hydrogen and oxygen. For example, water feels wet;

gaseous hydrogen and oxygen do not, and liquid hydrogen or oxygen would destroy the very possibility of a person's feeling anything. Besides, water does not look like liquid hydrogen or oxygen. These differences in both physicality and intelligibility should not obscure the point being made here. This argument does not appeal to the perceptual qualities of water in contrast to those of hydrogen and oxygen. Indeed, misleadingly, it would be much easier to imagine, to picture, and even to see the differences than to actually understand and explain them. It took millennia before we could actually explain the nature of water. Initially, with earth, air, and fire, water was thought to be one of the fundamental elements. Because of its flow, Plato suggested water was composed of miniature balls. Aristotle classified water among the sublunar elements; its proper place was between Earth and air. Varying explanations were proposed for this one and the same thing, water, known to common sense since prehistory. Relying on empirical method, modern chemistry finally proposed the most coherent explanation to date, and the thing turned out not to be what it was so long thought to be. It is hardly a fundamental element. We had finally explained the water we'd known all along, and the effort took millennia.

My argument appeals to this hard-won, inherent intelligibility in the cases of H_2, O_2, and H_2O: what there is to be understood in each case is different. On the basis of an intellectual (or, in this case, a chemical scientific) account, hydrogen, oxygen, and water differ; their intelligibilities, their forms, their essences, their natures, their governing laws are not the same. Part of the explanation of water is, indeed, its component elements, hydrogen and oxygen. But when these combine to form water, the end product requires a different accounting if explanation is to be had. What is there to be understood in water is not what is there to be understood simply in hydrogen and oxygen and their chemical bonding. The properties of these elements do not explain the properties of water—nor does the bonding of these elements. *There is no bottom-up predictability.*

In fact, it is difficult to predict the exact properties of any chemical compound unless it can be examined in itself, already synthesized, or be compared to similar existing compounds. This fact explains why pharmaceutical companies expend so much money and energy testing novel compounds. To be sure, these days computer modeling helps mightily to predict the eventual shape of novel compounds, but we are able to effect the computer modeling only because we already know a good bit about complex molecules, and we know about them only because we have them, already existing, to study. Then, applying this knowledge back down to the novel complex molecules, we can predict to a large extent the eventual structures of the molecules. Still, this prediction is not *per se* a bottom-up process; rather, it depends fully on knowledge about complex molecules gained from already formed molecules. Once again, *de facto* understanding is not explained necessity; *consistency* with the known laws of chemistry is not deduction on the basis of these laws. In the end, one is never sure beforehand exactly how a molecule will configure, what interactions it will allow, and, perforce, how it will affect a patient. One must synthesize the compound and test it for what it is in itself.

Similarly, the intelligibilities of hydrogen, oxygen, and water differ; therefore, their realities differ. They are not the same kinds of being. Indeed, by way of further example, the same must be said about atoms and their constituent subatomic particles. The laws that govern leptons and quarks are not the same as the laws that govern the emergent atoms. The intelligibilities in both cases differ, so the realities in both cases differ. Atoms are not just varied combinations of subatomic particles, all just more of the same, all just one category—matter—all the way up and down. Different intelligibilities imply different kinds of being.

On the epistemology operative in this book, if the intelligibility is different, the reality is different, so water is a distinct reality in comparison to either hydrogen or oxygen. Thus, commonplace water presents a clear example of how new reality can emerge from lower-level things, can be truly different from them, genuinely distinct, can incorporate their realities to constitute a new thing, yet need not be separate from them. Water is hardly separate from the hydrogen and oxygen that constitute it, but water is a distinct reality in comparison to them. This analysis works if intelligibilities determine realities. This analysis does not work if realities are pictured and imagined such that, for example, two hydrogen atoms and an oxygen atom are pieced together, LEGO-block-like, to form a "different kind" of "stuff" that "uninformed common sense" takes to be "water," whereas it is "really" "just" a combination of "hydrogen and oxygen." (Yes, this caricature is satirical.)

4.11.3. Mind From Organism

The same analysis can be applied to the brain. The so-called "mental properties of the brain," that "subjective ontology," must imply a different reality, the mind, in comparison with the organic brain. Then, experience, understanding, judgment, and decision, which Lonergan discerned, are actually properties of the mind (and specifically, as elaborated at 2.1.6, properties of intentional consciousness; see 5.1.2; 5.3), not properties of the brain.

Besides, thus spelled out in detail, these conscious properties are correctly predicated of the human being, not separately of the brain, of the mind, or of intentional consciousness. They are the four properties that, interrelated in Lonergan's analysis, implicitly define awareness, and because they pertain to awareness, they are predicated of the person, whom intentional consciousness partially constitutes.

If one would begin with the initial data set that is to be understood, namely, the presentation of what we call a human being or person—and not begin with imagined "parts," which would somehow have to be cobbled together or could be splintered apart—one would have to acknowledge a range of properties in the single individual: material bodiliness and chemical composition, manipulable members and locomotion, sensation and environmental engagement, perception and internal imagery, and insight, self-aware thinking, and decision making. Intelligent accounting—that is, an accounting based on the intelligibilities discernible in the data in each case—would have to posit a series of kinds of functions and, then, relate them to a series of kinds of capacities and, perforce, implicate a series of kinds of realities (see Lonergan, 1957/1992, on the Aristotelian notions of act, form, and potency). These might be named material body, living organism, sensate animal, perceptual psyche, and distinctively human consciousness. Strikingly, independent academic disciplines would parallel this series: physics and chemistry, biology, animal psychology, and human psychology (cf. Cahoone, 2010, lecture 35, track 5). The distinction of disciplines arises because each attends to different sets of data pertinent to different properties that determine different kinds of objects of study. In an array of non-human specimens, these different kinds of objects of study are sometimes actually separate while in humans they all cohere in one remarkable being. The multiplicity of disciplines is required because the different kinds of objects of study and their different properties pose different questions in each case, require specialized methodologies, and result in different—and ultimately, it is hoped, interrelated—answers (4.18.6). Coherent and reasonable accounting for the polymorphous human being requires the interrelationship of this series of realities and the corresponding disciplines. What coherently interrelates and unifies them is intelligence and its consistently applied transcendental method (2.5). Said otherwise, these disciplines are all instances of human knowing. Thus, they ultimately rely on the human knowing process. It runs through them all and links them together to provide one, coherent understanding of the human being.

On this analysis, consciousness must be said to be a property of the human being. It is hardly a property of the brain. To conceive this human newness as a property of the brain neither truly credits its real novelty and distinct kind of reality nor, then, refrains from reducing it to biology and even materiality nor, additionally, avoids positing the brain as that which thinks in place of the person—the speculative "brain in a vat," imagined to survive and experience apart from underlying layers of sustaining physical, chemical, and biological processes. In fact, it is the person who not only has the brain, similar in its biochemical processes to the brains of other animals, but also has intellectual consciousness, which other animals do not have. Thus, with Lonergan, I argue that the human being is a polymorphous being; in it, as in the simpler case of water, many realities, different kinds of being, cohere and constitute one multifaceted thing. One existent enjoys an array of different properties or "conjugates." A consistent intellectual epistemology—but not a perceptual epistemology—coherently distinguishes, defines, names, and interrelates all the facets of the matter. The human being comprises organism, psyche, and spirit yet is one thing. Epistemology is the crux of the matter.

4.12. The Priority of Intelligence Over Perception, Theory Over Common Sense

4.12.1. Descriptive Properties Versus Explanatory Properties

At the heart of the complications in the current analyses lies the fact that *property* is a highly ambiguous term. Most commonly, presuming a perceptual epistemology, *property* refers to the descriptive, perceptual characteristics of things, to the qualities of things as related to us and our senses: water feels wet, metal feels hard, fire burns. Lonergan (1957/1992) technically names these characteristics *conjugates*. The term highlights their fundamentally relational nature—from the Latin *cum + jugare*, to link or join together: they pertain to a thing. Thus, the brain is wet, gray, and squishy. That is, the brain appears this way *to us*. The conjugates in this case—wetness, grayness, squishiness—are *descriptive*; they express the characteristics of things as we experience them through our sensate and perceptual capacities.

But with an intellectual epistemology, we could take *property* in another sense and with Lonergan name properties *explanatory* (no longer merely descriptive) conjugates. Formulated in terms of laws and frequencies, explanatory conjugates express the relations of things to one another, which only intelligence, not perception, could grasp (pp. 102–105, 271, 273, 274, 510, 521, 563). I illustrated this point under the excursus on causality at 4.6 when I noted David Hume's devastating critique of sensate empiricism. Namely, when one billiard ball strikes another, what is seen is merely the movement of one ball, then that of the other; what our senses experience is only a sequence. The causality at stake in this sequence is not seen. Causality must be understood, and such understanding entails explanation in terms of the relationship of the one moving ball to the other, a relationship that can be specified in terms of weights, velocity, friction, angle of incidence, and the like. What is specified by sense experience and what is specified by intelligence are very different. A thermometer specifies temperature (an explanatory conjugate) by relating a column of mercury in a graduated cylinder to the thermal energy in a room, independently of how warm or cold (descriptive conjugates) a particular individual might feel in that room. A piece of wood and a piece of metal might both be the same temperature (an explanatory conjugate), but the one would feel warm and the other, cold to the touch (descriptive conjugates).

Even more precisely, the physical concept *mass* exemplifies this same peculiarity. Popular science characterizes mass as a version of sensible bulk, weight, or size (experiential conjugates), the "massiveness" that Chalmers (1996, p. 153; 2.2.4) misses in the physicists' equations. Popular science appeals to experiential characteristics to try and explain technical science because most people think only perceptually, only with images, only concrete-operationally. Physicists, however, think formal-operationally (4.2.3); they understand mass and implicitly define it within a nest of terms and relations that, as in $a^2 + b^2 = c^2$, mutually codetermine one another and, via their interrelationships formulated in equations, express those aspects of things that truly make them what they are in themselves (explanatory conjugates), as best we currently know. Thus, for example, mass relates to force and acceleration and is defined by this interrelationship: $F = ma$; and mass relates to energy and the speed of light and is defined by this interrelationship: $E = mc^2$. The very same mass is at stake in each case, and in each case a measurement of mass is precisely what would result if the equations were solved for m. Precisely mass and nothing else consistently fits in these equations as m, and what does fit as m in these equations is mass and nothing else in the universe. However, these results would be no more perceptible or imaginable than the result of the multiplication of *weight* x *distance*, which we considered in the case of a balance on its fulcrum (4.2.3). These results would be as imperceptible or unimaginable as the sum of squared deviations from the mean (*SS*), which is central to the statistical technique of analysis of variance (ANOVA)—a fact I attempt to convey to my concrete-operational students as they stare blankly at me, wanting something to picture. Yet in all these cases, the results would be as equally useful and explanatory as the Pythagorean theorem. Mass as such is not perceptible; it is grasped and affirmed by intelligence; it is what evidence-based judgment knows, not what is seen or felt. Indeed, confounding popular conceptions, mass is still a critical consideration even in weightless space, and mass hardly correlates with size or bulk.

Coherent resolution of the mind–body problem depends on the consistent application of an intellectual epistemology. The person is the thing in question, and body and mind are conjugates that together constitute and explain the person. In the case of an automobile, the conjugates or parts can be seen, held, pictured, and imagined, and by hand taken apart or put together. Without obvious negative consequences, they can be conceived merely as descriptive conjugates: they are hard, heavy, shaped in this or that way, structured to fit one another. In the case of the person, the conjugates must be understood as explanatory. Obviously, for example, the mind cannot be seen, held, pictured, or imagined; and by hand the mind cannot be taken apart from the body or put back together. But the reality of mind and of body can be understood, conceptualized, verified, and reasonably related to the person. Then an affirmation—if not a picture—can elucidate precisely what a person is in his or her complexity of mind and body.

4.12.2. The Oxymoron, Knower-Independent Knowledge

Searle actually approaches that crucial distinction between descriptive and explanatory conjugates, and he seems to approach the precision needed to answer our question. He uses terms that are common enough among philosophers as he notes the difference between the "observer-relative" or "observer-dependent," and the "observer-independent" features of things (1998, lectures 5, 6). These terms would seem to parallel Lonergan's distinction between knowing things via their relationship to ourselves (observer-dependent) and knowing things by relating them to one another (observer-independent). Or, at least, these terms point in that direction.

Searle's analyses, however, remain muddled. Why so? He does not differentiate perceiving and understanding within the human "observer," who, tellingly, is conceived in terms of taking a look, of observing. Moreover, he forgets that human knowing is never observer- (that is, knower-) independent. There is no human knowledge apart from a human knower. For humans there is no God's eye view of things. Knower-independent knowledge is an oxymoron, and to this extent the notion *observer-independent* is, as well. Behind Searle's usage and confounding it, a usage commonplace among theorists, is the perceptual metaphor for knowing and the assumption that reality is stuff imagined to be lying out there waiting to be seen, observed, or stumbled upon.

What is the point of these seemingly distant and technical considerations? Ultimately, that a coherent explanation of the mind–body problem is possible; but to formulate it, we must remain true to intellectual thinking and refrain from falling ever back into perceptual thinking. The scientific concepts of temperature, force, and mass exemplify the kind of thinking that philosophers and psychologists must eventually also employ to speak coherently and accurately about the mind–body problem. Examples of such thinking are virtually non-existent in fields other than the "hard sciences." If the social sciences still wish to pursue the ideal of becoming "hard," they will, indeed, have to follow the example of physics—not, however, by limiting focus to the same kinds of material objects of study as physics, and not by confounding scientific method with the lingering hands-on thinking of early modern science, but by understanding, adapting, and implementing the same kind of purely intellectual thinking that emerged in force in early 20th-century physics. Talk of properties—and just about everything else regarding the mind–body problem—tends to mix perceptual knowing and intellectual knowing together. No wonder the result is incoherent! No wonder the multifaceted nature of the human being cannot be coherently expressed!

4.12.3. *The Explanation of Description*

Apply these analyses to the brain. Its grayness offers an easy example—because for color, unlike for most else in this discussion, science already provides a highly refined explanation. What appears as gray to us—or to most of us, and this discrepancy is telling—can be explained in terms of electromagnetic waves of particular lengths and the reflectivity of neural tissue in good light. On this analysis, given the attempt to say what is actually there to be understood and not merely to be seen or felt, the grayness falls out as a property of the brain because the human perception of grayness is not inherent in the "grayness" itself. Appeal to electromagnetic waves provides a precise accounting for the "grayness" and remains valid regardless of who might be looking at the brain with what acuity of eyesight or through what colored eyeglasses. So, the genuine property in question is reflectivity to particular light waves, a reality specified by the relation of things among themselves, not by the relation of things to our senses.

This "falling out" of descriptive characteristics or properties results from the attempt to explain data on the basis of insightful hypothesis and reasonable judgment, rather than on the basis of sense perception and picture-thinking. This falling out results from the application of scientific method, whose implicit definition (4.6.5) tends to reconceptualize the accounts that commonsensical, perception-centered thinking offers about everyday experience. Whereas, for example, an explanatory account would say that the Earth rotates once per day; everyday experience, relying on valid enough perceptions, would say that the sun rises and sets. The point of my appeal to intelligently conceived and reasonably affirmed explanation is not to disqualify commonsense understandings and to insist—in the manner, for example, of the logical positivists and my satire about water at 4.11.1—that only science knows reality and other opinions are mere myth and inspiration. While ever supposing that reality is stuff lying out there, this all-too-common either-or approach opts for one kind of knowing to the exclusion of another or, usually, for an incoherent mixture of the two. Lonergan's analysis differentially admits both kinds of knowing—and, more important, it differentially legitimates both and coherently interrelates them.

On the basis of reasonable understanding and as a peculiar case of the relationship of things among themselves, Lonergan's epistemology is able to validate commonsensical, perception-based, descriptive knowing in addition to theoretical, intelligence-based, explanatory knowing. Simply said, we can have a scientific explanation of perception. *From an explanatory perspective* perception can be construed as a relationship of things among themselves, namely, the relations of the things to the human senses. This set of perceptual relations can itself become the object of intellectual inquiry and explanation. Then the question becomes, "How is it that the eye determines what we see?" Although commonsensical knowing *per se* characterizes things as we experience them through our senses, such knowing does, indeed, entail relationships—of the object to the eye, for example. So, *from a third-party perspective*, perception can be understood as a particular and important instance of things related to one another, namely, the things as related to the human senses. That is, we could make human perception itself the object of scientific study. Then we would discern all the factors and their interrelationships that explain perception: energy input, sensory receptors, transduction of energy, neuronal transmission, brain processing. We would account for perception in terms of how all those factors relate to one another. In these terms (explanation), we would account for things as related to us through our senses (description). We would give an explanation of description.

Thus, we understand that the sun appears to rise and set—because of our position on a revolving Earth; so the human perception of a rising and setting sun is not false. Thus, we can explain why the human brain looks gray—because of the light waves involved and the calibration of human color vision; so the human perception of gray matter is not mistaken. Thus, we know that pieces of metal and wood of the same temperature feel cold and warm, respectively—because of the varying conductivity of different materials; so our sense of hot and cold is not mistaken.

Lonergan's epistemology loses nothing. To appreciate science, this epistemology need not disparage commonsense understandings. On the contrary, it specifies and delimits the validity of commonsense understandings. Moreover, it adds clarity and precision to the human enterprise of understanding. But—note this well—the reverse approach is unworkable. An explanatory account can validate the conclusions of a descriptive account; science can explain why we experience things as we do and, thus, validate our everyday experiences. Science can tell us why we experience the sun to rise and set. But a descriptive account cannot ground an explanatory account; common sense cannot *per se* generate or adjudicate science; a perceptual model of "knowing" cannot explain intellectual knowing; a sensate-based epistemology can never ground an intellectual epistemology. "Explaining and explained do not lie within the field of the imaginable, but imaginable and imagining lie within the field of explaining and explained." "The relations of thing to our senses and imaginations are included within the far broader sweep of the relations of things to one another; but they are not included as sensed nor as imagined nor as described but as explained" (Lonergan, 1957/1990, p. 536).

4.12.4. *The Inadequacy of Commonsensical, or Functionalist, Thinking*

Chalmers (1996) provides a striking example of the pervasive trend in contemporary philosophy to reverse that priority of intelligence over perception, to revert from theoretical commitments to commonsensical speculation. This reversal is related to the rejection of all foundationalism, mentioned at 1.4, and to that long paragraph on pragmatism at 2.3.2. Contemporary philosophy has despaired of ever being able to give a coherent account of human knowing (1.4; 2.2.6–2.2.7), to provide a cognitive foundation on which all knowledge would rest, such as Aristotle, Aquinas, Descartes, Kant, and Hegel sought and Lonergan again proposes. Current thinking is truncated. It settles for attention to "public action" in the everyday world (American Pragmatism) or else focuses on clarifying ordinary language usage (Linguistic Analysis) or else attends to commonplace intra-subjective experiences (Phenomenology) (Cahoone, 2010, p. 47). Under the name of functionalism, Chalmers employs an uneven mix of all three. Accordingly, functionalism focuses on what things do, how they interact, and what behaviors result, and the arena of this activity is the everyday world, available to human perception (and to some unspecified human intelligence). So, for example, the external behaviors of a consciousness-less zombie are all that matter, bafflingly presumed to behave in every way indistinguishably from a conscious human (2.3.6). Supposedly, science is to attend to such external, perceptible behaviors, and an account of their functioning constitutes the genuine contribution of science. Said otherwise, explanation is a matter of causal roles, a matter of how these things make those things happen, and the causality in question is the push-pull of imagined efficient causality (4.6).

Thus, for example, according to Chalmers (1996) heat "is the kind of thing that expands metals, is caused by fire, and leads to a particular sort of sensation" (pp. 44–45; I ignore the mixture of science and common sense in this list). That is, the most important thing about heat, what is primary, is how we experience it "in the actual world" (p. 45), the world of everyday interactions. In this work-a-day world of commonplace experiences, what heat means is what it does or could be used for. Its meaning is its significance, importance, practical implication—for us, personally, practically (2.3.2). Of course, modern science has gone to the heart of the matter and actually explained heat in itself and, on this basis, explains why heat does what it does and affects us as it does: the "motion of molecules is what plays the relevant causal role in the actual world" (p. 45). That is, we now know that the motion of molecules is what results from fire, makes metals expand, and makes skin hurt. But for Chalmers this scientific explanation is not the primary meaning of heat, not what defines *heat*. The scientific explanation is secondary. What defines *heat* is its significance for us, what heat does to us and around us, not what heat is in itself. "*Explaining* heat involves explaining the fulfillment of the causal role. . . . Once we discover how that causal role is played, we have an explanation of the phenomenon. As a bonus, we know what heat *is*" (p. 45). That is, in a mixture of science and common sense, for Chalmers *to explain* means to understand our encounters with heat in the everyday, spatial-temporal, material world of physical and perceptual push-pull interactions—"the actual world," the one we perceive around us. So the real is what we bump into, and science is a bonus.

Similar considerations apply to water. For Chalmers, primarily, first and foremost, water is "the dominant clear drinkable liquid in the oceans and lakes"; it is "the *watery stuff* in a world" (p. 57). Only secondarily and as another extra, water is H_2O. It might as well be XYZ. This fact would not matter as long of it *functions* as "'the dominant clear, drinkable liquid in the environment'" (p. 57). Realities are defined by the everyday, human experience and use of them. Science is neutralized—yet, ultimately incoherently: Chalmers freely borrows that scientific "bonus" to set up the contrast between H_2O and XYZ that allows him to argue for the priority of commonsensical thinking.

Philosophical discussion of these matters—the everyday meaning of words and the reality they perhaps intend—goes on interminably, as Chalmers's treatment of water-versus-H_2O or H_2O-versus-XYZ evinces (pp. 56–65). The debate has a long history. Echoed by the medievals, Aristotle had already distinguished between the *ordo inventionis* and the *ordo doctrinae* or *disciplinae*, that is, the sequence in the process of discovery and the sequence in the process of teaching or explaining the discovered (Lonergan, 1980/1990, p. 9 & n. e; 1967c, p. 127–128). They are the inverse of each other. The sequence of discovery would start with watery stuff in the everyday world and end with H_2O. The sequence of explanation—science—would start with the discovered essential, H_2O, and draw out everyday implications from there. Chalmers's understanding of science reverses these priorities, focusing the task of explanation on the watery stuff in the everyday world and relegating hard science to a secondary enterprise. Said otherwise, Chalmers opted for the priority of doing over being; he opts for the priority of interaction over understanding; and by implication, epistemologically he opts for the priority of perception over intelligence. To this extent, he sides with the existentialists, who insist we make ourselves by our choices because our being, our ongoing becoming, results from our doing. In contrast, the scholastic axiom is *agere sequitur esse*: doing follows being. It insists on the reverse: a being acts in accord with its kind—and the reason humans "make themselves" is because their nature is of a unique kind that allows such an enterprise: conscious, intelligent, self-responsible self-determination. Resolution of this debate is unlikely because from the beginning we have no consensus on what *being* means, in any case. *What is* could mean what we see, what happens out there in the "actual world." Or *what is* could mean what is intelligently understood and reasonably affirmed, visible or not. The choice of priority in this matter depends on the choice of one's theory of knowing. However, because contemporary philosophy has despaired of justifying human knowing, theorists make the best of a bad situation and opt for a supposedly obvious commonsensical approach—despite the fact that from its earliest beginnings modern science repeatedly called that "obvious" into question. So we go 'round and 'round the same circle of confounded epistemologies again.

However, the point to be made here is simple enough. The notion of science in much of contemporary consciousness studies seems to be at war with itself. Consciousness studies is committed to being as scientific as today's science stunningly is, yet in effect consciousness studies rejects the contemporary understanding of science. Current studies of consciousness in philosophy, psychology, and computer science aim toward some scientific account; yet the presuppositions of this enterprise run counter to contemporary science in its defining 20th-century forms—physics and chemistry. The inconsistency is palpable (pun intended). Whereas the "hard sciences" opt for an intellectual explanation of things, functionalism prioritizes a commonsensical, perceptualist understanding. Whereas the hard sciences are well aware that what they can reasonably affirm is hardly palpable, functionalism sets up palpable interactions "in the actual world" as a controlling criterion. Whereas the hard sciences see H_2O and molecular motion as the primary explanations of water and heat from which all other explanations can follow, functionalism focuses primarily on the "watery stuff" we drink and the "no-no" that causes burns, and functionalism relegates the intellectual achievements of science to the secondary status of a bonus. Whereas the hard sciences understand mass within a causal web of relationships with other fundamental realities, functionalism would suppose as "intuitively . . . more reasonable . . . that the basic entities that all this causation relates have some internal nature of their own, some *intrinsic* properties. . . . [such as] the very 'massiveness' of mass" (p. 153; see 2.2.4). Whereas science relies on intelligence reasonably grounded in evidence and with Einstein even transcends the perceptual particularities of space and time, functionalism still relies on perception and attends to personal experiences of push-pull encounters in the spatial, temporal world. In brief, whereas science opts for an intellectual epistemology, to a large extent functionalism is controlled by a sensate-modeled epistemology.

An intellectual epistemology can acknowledge and delimit a sensate-modeled epistemology; science can explain everyday living; theory can account for the observations of common sense; neuroscience can elucidate the mechanisms of vision; explanation can legitimate description. However, these happy outcomes cannot result the other way around. Nonetheless, despairing of actually knowing correctly yet incoherently committed in practice to a perceptual model of knowing, consciousness studies has entangled itself in a Gordian knot. There is no salvaging this rope; it needs to be severed. It is a weave of fundamental errors in thinking. Simultaneously, consciousness studies both celebrates and abandons the epochal breakthrough of modern science, and when these studies compare science with common sense, they get the priority wrong.

This realization bears decisively on the present discussion. Without an intellectual epistemology, alone adequate to non-perceptible reality, questions about the mind, consciousness, and "God in the brain" cannot be coherently addressed. Indeed, without an intellectual epistemology even a coherent philosophy of physical science and an adequate human psychology are impossible. Our homespun, commonsensical, sensate-modeled thinking in the everyday world is simply not up to these subtle, highly refined, culturally advanced, theoretical tasks.

4.12.5. Hopeful Trends Toward Explanatory Science

I see a plodding and groping but encouraging trend toward genuine explanation via intellectual epistemology in much contemporary discussion. As evidence of it, I note the proliferation of notions such as process, structures, information, systems, complexes. These replace earlier crass talk of bodies, things, or objects (Goldman, 2007). The insistence might be, for instance, that all "things" are actually "processes" (Griffin, 1991). Or one might suggest that things are constituted by relationships within a comprehensive ordering (Buchler, 1990; Cahoone, 2008, 2009), so "relational metaphysics" emerges as a current topic (Kaypayil, 2003; Oliver, 1981; Polkinghorne, 2010). Or again, notions of development and evolution are already commonplace among women and men on the street. We no longer imagine realities in our everyday world as static, fixed bodies, fully themselves in what we see before us. We expect change, interaction, complexity. The result is the diminution of picture thinking and the crediting of explanation via interrelationships grasped by intelligence. The implication—certainly not envisaged as clearly as here but nonetheless on the horizon—is that the real is the reasonably affirmed intelligible, not the perceptible, palpable, or imaginable. In these cases, theory begins to approach the requisites of transcendental method and Lonergan's epistemology as well as those of contemporary science.

I believe that, on the heels of evolutionary theory, the attempt to deal with the conclusions of contemporary physics is driving this trend toward more purely intellectualist ways of thinking. Howard Stein (1989) made this same suggestion, summarized by Cahoone (2008): "Advances in 20th century physics, precisely in the microphysical arena that might seem the natural realm of atomism, exhibit a 'deepening' of our knowledge of structures, not material components" (p. 59, n. 5). Although scientists themselves are not philosophers and are usually quite willing today to leave it to philosophers to debate the philosophy of science, scientists are well aware that they cannot see the realities they explain. The objects of their science are not perceptible, and their explanations consist in explicating relationships among relevant factors, usually by means of mathematical equations. When talk of fields and clouds replaces talk of particles and atomic bits of matter, thinking must adjust its mode. So theorists in all arenas begin to propose vaguer and broader concepts—systems, processes, structures. To be sure, these are still graphically modeled and continue to be imagined. Moreover, for lack of an adequate epistemology, this trend tends to bog down in an idealist worldview that—like Kant in his halfway house between materialism and critical realism (2.2.8)—still harbors the notion that reality is perceptible stuff lying about "out there." So Chalmers (1996) continues to look behind the physicists' equations for "the very 'massiveness' of mass, for example" (p. 153; 2.2.4). How difficult for us to grok that the human world is literally, ontologically, a realm of meaning, not *per se* an arena of sensations and perceptions! And how hard to recognize that our meaningful world is not any fancy we might imagine it to be! How hard to accept that the evidence of data and the judgment of fact constrain our knowledge of the actual! Nonetheless, a thrust toward pure explanation via the interrelationship of the telling factors—implicit definition (4.6.5)—appears to be at work. My hope is that Lonergan's contribution, especially his pivotal emphasis on the judgment of fact, which breaks the back of idealism, might push this trend to the turning point and onto an explicitly intellectual epistemology and critical realism.

4.13. A Resolution of the Mind–Body Problem

Possessed of its peculiar intelligibility, the mind is a distinct kind of reality; it is immaterial (it is spiritual, but only in part, only insofar as it includes consciousness: 5.1.1). Inhering in the human being, the mind exists, not as an independent thing (or substance), but as one constitutive facet or property or conjugate of a polymorphous thing, the human person. Indeed, determinative of a person is self-conscious mentality; it is the conjugate that makes a person a person in contrast to other animals. Thus, I affirm the non-material nature of the mind in contrast to the body: like the body, the mind is real, and it is a particular kind of *reality*, a specific kind of being. But I deny dualism: the mind is not a *thing* because it exists only as a facet of the human being, one intelligible whole, which is the one existent, the thing in question, despite the complexity of its make-up.

A polymorphous reality, the person is the one agent, the thing that acts, in any activity attributed to that human being. Although, using personification, for simplicity's sake I sometimes speak about the intellect's doing this and judgment's doing that, such usage is technically wrong and should now be recognized as such. It is the person who does whatever is done—by means of acts of locomotion, digestion, perception, imagination, understanding, judgment, and the rest. In part, the person is, indeed, spiritual and is thus capable of spiritual acts, such as insight, which transcend space and time (4.3). The mind is real and is really distinct from the brain, different in kind or intelligibility from "bodiliness," yet the mind is not separate from the brain, does not reside in its own space, and does not act apart from the organism. In every case, it is the person—body and mind—who acts.

In some ways, this account cuts a middle path through mind–body speculation. This account does preserve the unity of the person and, thus, avoids substance dualism. Body and mind are not separate things, somehow cobbled together. The one thing in question is the person. In addition, this account preserves the irreducibility of mind; it is a distinct kind of reality, different from the body, and, as discussed below, emergent from the body. On the other hand, this approach cuts its middle path via "property dualism"; it insists on a plurality of distinct kinds of realities, different facets of the one person (different conjugates or, to use other related terminology, different features or properties). However, this insistence on different realities is not a crass positing of different kinds of imaginable stuff out there, which talk of dualism based on perception-modeled knowing seems ever to entail, as Searle (1997)—not alone—needlessly presumes and then laments (pp. 210–211). The escape from this entangled speculation is through the distinction between sensate-modeled and intelligence-based knowing. Granted this distinction, the positing of different kinds of realities is hardly in accord with the offensive Cartesian usage, indebted to Galileo's and then Locke's misguided, perception-based distinction between primary and secondary qualities (2.2.6), which continues to appear in talk of "observer-independent" and "observer-dependent" features (4.12.2). Einstein definitively discredited this distinction: space and time, the "extensions" of physical material, are not absolute; like all else that is finally explained, they entail relationships—and these are intelligible, not perceptible. The empirical account of emergent properties within an explanatory purview, as "conjugates implicitly defined by verified laws" (Lonergan, 1957/1992, p. 563), offers a radically alternative and stunningly coherent understanding.

The decisive challenge, of course, is to distinguish and interrelate sensate and intellectual kinds of knowing and to consistently apply the one that alone is adequate to the difficult questions at hand—and "to bite the bullet and accept dualism" (Searle, 1997, p. xiii) or, more accurately, "property pluralism" (p. 211): constrained by one's own attentive, intelligent, and reasonable mind, to acknowledge that perceptual capacities and consciousness, if they are to be called properties or conjugates of the human being, must be affirmed to be different kinds of realities in comparison to the organic body, another property of the human being. Then, fully consistently, dependent again on intelligence and not perception, the unity of the person is to be found in the insight that grasps this unity-identity-whole, this one thing, the human person, in the entire array of the data pertinent to it, that is, to her or him. The unity is not to be found in graphically collapsing one set of data, those pertinent to perception and consciousness, into another set, those pertinent to the body, the brain or its biology, and then calling the mind a loosely defined "property of the brain"—as if it were a tint rubbed in on a coloring-book picture of human anatomy. If the properties in question, body and mind, are explanatory (not descriptive), they represent different sets of intelligibilities (not palpable or imaginable bodies) that cohere within one intelligently grasped and reasonably affirmed thing (not a palpable conglomerate lying out there). As intelligibilities, the conjugates of the human being—accurately formulated as organism, psyche, and spirit—in interrelationship explain what the thing, the person, is, just as a, b, and c in a singular relationship do for the right triangle (2.2.4; 4.6.5; 5.1.3). And all assertions remain equally within the field of the intelligent and reasonable accounting for data.

4.14. The Relation of Mind to Body: Emergence

One further question remains regarding the mind–body problem. As different kinds of realities, how do the mind and brain relate within one thing, the person? As suggested at 4.8.3 and specified here, the summary answer is "by emergence."

4.14.1. *The Basic Notion of Emergence*

Emergence is a process of continued unfolding whereby—given long times, large numbers, and the regularity of schemes of recurrence—a higher order systematizes what on a lower order was merely a coincidental aggregate. Aspects of our universe build on one another. The persistence of atoms and the laws that govern them allows for their interaction in higher syntheses called molecules, governed by their own laws. The regularity of function and the continued availability of certain complex molecules sustain higher syntheses called cells, which, again, exhibit proprietary laws and functions. The endurance and processes of various kinds of cells, in tissues and organs, allow higher syntheses called organisms. And so on.

In the higher order, the laws and probabilities that pertain to realities in the new syntheses are different from the laws and probabilities that govern the realities, the events, the functions, and the schemes of recurrence in the lower orders. If sensibility, palpability, and imagination are taken to be the criteria of realities, these higher systems appear simply as more complex conglomerates or aggregates of the same lower-level realities; they entail nothing qualitatively new; thorough-going eliminative reductionism holds sway. If, however, intelligibility is the criterion of distinct realities, then these higher systems are new realities in comparison to the lower systems; they are new and different kinds of being. Thus, personal behavior is not neuronal function; thought is not brain activity. In each case, different laws pertain to the interactions of different interrelated elements. That is to say, verifiably different intelligibilities pertain; varying discernible sets of interrelationships apply. In each case, differences pertain in what is there to be experienced, to be understood, and to be affirmed. Perforce, different realities are at stake.

Emergence is that process of nature whereby something new comes into being through a higher ordering of prior existing things, which then function as constitutive facets or conjugates of the new thing. The functioning of cells within organisms, of complex molecules within the cells, of atoms within the molecules, of probabilistic subatomic processes within the atoms—all are examples. Similarly, water is a new reality in relation to its chemical constituents, hydrogen and oxygen (4.11.2). Water is not merely an imagined "two parts hydrogen to one part oxygen"—none of which is actually visible, in any case—because water has physical properties and entails an intelligibility that neither hydrogen nor oxygen nor even the predictable synthesis of the two does. In each case, higher-order things incorporate, and present a new synthesis of, lower-order realities. Granted that the criterion of the real is a judgment that a grasped intelligibility is indeed grounded in the data, at stake is the emergence of truly new realities determinative of truly new kinds of things. With the emergence of life, a specimen is no longer simply an aggregate of chemicals and their reactions, but a cell, a plant, or an animal; with the emergence of consciousness, an organism is no longer simply an animal of extreme biological complexity, but a person.

4.14.2. A Brief History of Emergence Theory

Emergence is hardly a novel or esoteric notion, although its theory is young, circuitous, multifaceted, and controversial (Corning, 2002). It arose along with evolutionary theory in the latter decades of the 19th century and was associated with figures such as Samuel Alexander, C. D. Broad, John Elof Boodin, C. Lloyd Morgan, and Jan Christian Smuts. Through the early 20th century, when it seemed that quantum physics could explain chemistry, and chemistry explain biology, and so on, up the line, and when, perforce, physical reductionism reigned, emergence theory fell out of favor. Subsequent advances, however, especially in biology, uncovered phenomena that resisted explanation by mere appeal to chemistry and paved the way toward a resurgence of emergence theory in the late 20th century (Clayton & Davies, 2006). Evolutionary biologist and philosopher Ernst Mayr (1965; see also Pittendrigh, 1958), for example, insisted on the reintroduction of a kind of final cause—*teleonomic*, in contrast to *teleologic*—in order to explain certain biological phenomena. Thus,

> the evolutionary biologist does not merely say the following: "The wood thrush flies south and thereby escapes the winter." Now that statement's true. . . . But . . . what the biologist really wants to say is that the wood thrush flies south *in order to* escape the winter. The "in order to" is not mental or personal. . . . It's that the wood thrush has a genetic program, which it has acquired from evolution. It's acquired it *in order to* survive the winter. So there is a biological "in order to," which is a kind of final causation, teleonomy, that, Mayr would say, biologists can't get rid of. Now it appears that the science of more complex phenomena could not so easily be reduced to physics. (Cahoone, 2010, lecture 29, track 5)

So the basic insight of emergence theory accords with the reigning paradigm in contemporary science. As Karl Popper noted, "Science suggests to us—tentatively, of course—a picture of a universe that is inventive or even creative, of a universe in which new things emerge" (quoted in Cahoone, 2010, lecture 35, track 6).

Gone, finally, is the static universe of Aristotle's deductive explanation via necessary, universal, and unchanging knowledge within one logically coherent and closed system (2.5). Gone, too, is the mistaken cosmogony of the ancient cultures that—all too simplistically from today's perspective but understandably from theirs—posited fixed species coming directly from the hand of God. Similarly, gone, too, ought to be appeal to "intelligent design," that is, ongoing and unmediated intervention by God, which confuses the inherently dynamic nature of the created universe (5.9.2.4) with the uncreated Creator (e.g., Beauregard & O'Leary, 2007; cf. 6.2.4). Today, a well-known series of increasing complexification and differentiation of realities—in cosmogenesis, biological evolution, and cultural history—presents incontrovertibly documented instances of emergences. Despite Qoheleth's commonsensical wisdom, valid enough from one point of view: "Nothing is new under the sun" (Ecclesiastes 1:9), in fact, from other points of view, novelties do occur, and they need to be explained.

Understood in various ways, the process of emergence is related to contemporary theories of emergence, systems, self-organization, complexity, synergetics, and chaos (Bertalanffy, 1968, 1981; Blitz, 1992; Gleick, 1988; Holland, 1998; Prigogine & Stengers, 1984; Strogatz, 2002; Waldrop, 1992). Cahoone (2008) presents a sobering overview of this theoretical jungle (pp. 43–46). Relating emergence to its counterposition, reductionism, he begins his catalogue of relevant notions as follows:

> The debate between reductionists and anti-reductionists [i.e., emergentists] appears almost hopelessly complex. For it hangs first of all on multiple linguistic analyses of what should count as a reduction, not only ontological versus explanatory reductionism, but whether reduction "derives" or "deduces" or "constructs" or "explains" or "predicts" composite from simpler phenomena, whether it does so for tokens or types or phenomena, and whether merely "novel" properties or "top-down" causality is the hallmark of irreducibility—all these alternatives have distinctive implications for deciding the issue. (p. 43)

Under the name "emergent probability," Lonergan (1957/1992, pp. 138–151, 284–287, 506) presented his own theory of emergence, completely consistent with the intellectual epistemology within his overall position. To the common idea of emergence, his conception adds explicit insistence on the probabilistic nature of this process. Noting how current attention to statistical processes adds a new dimension of understanding to the closed systems of static, classical science (e.g., Aristotelian cosmology or Newtonian physics), Lonergan (1972) explained his position succinctly as follows: "A universe in which both classical and statistical laws are verified will be characterized by a process of emergent probability" (p. 288). The idea is simply that, with large numbers and over long times, there exists a probability that novel systematizations in nature will occur. These constitute new emergences, new things, which integrate manifolds of theretofore random lower-level realities. Momentously, by insisting on the judgment of fact as the criterion of the real—not perception or imagination and not current prevalent but ultimately idealist emphasis on speculative webs of relationships—Lonergan offers an incisive corrective. To understand that things are intelligently grasped wholes—not palpable bodies lying out there—allows for the literal affirmation of the emergence of truly new things with their distinctive intelligibilities rather than merely larger and larger conglomerations of the same old imaginable stuff. The precision of Lonergan's epistemology linked with the notion of a statistically unfolding universe could clarify much of the confusion and resolve many of the problems surrounding the topic of emergence.

4.14.3. Portrayals of Emergence

Speaking of emergent "properties" instead of emergent realities—speaking, unfortunately, ambiguously, and with a debt to reductionism—Brown (2002) nonetheless usefully describes this natural phenomenon: an emergent reality

> comes into being on the basis of the most complex interactive operations of multiple less complex subsystems. It is not just that the emergent [reality] is more than the sum of its parts. Rather, [it] create[s] new determinative . . . top-down influences. . . . the configurational regularities of the complex system affect the interactions of the more micro-level elements. So my conscious thinking . . . creates determinative influences on my behavior that cannot be accounted for solely on the basis of the underlying micro-level operations of my brain. (pp. 1817–1818)

An easy example is Fido. Who would insist that he is a mere packet of cells? (But see discussion at 4.18.4 about Chalmers's, 1996, elephant.) In Fido, cells are organized into tissues, tissues into organs, organs into systems, and systems into a new organism of the canine type. He sleeps, eats, barks, and runs. Fido does things that no cell or tissue or organ or system does—although Fido would do none of them apart from the ongoing functioning of his systems, organs, tissues, and cells. Indeed, Fido is nothing separate from his systems, organs, tissues, and cells. Yet Fido presents a different reality not only in contrast to his systems, organs, tissues, and cells but also in contrast to the molecules that make up the cells, and so on, down the line. Moreover, if we would speak in terms of Brown's "top-down influences," we must say, but only pictographically, that Fido "gets" his cells, organs, and systems "to do" what "they" would not "do on their own." More accurately said, in response to a call, Fido, the sole agent in question, engages muscles and legs and runs across the field. Fido runs—but not apart from the ions, atoms, molecules, cells, tissues, organs, and mentality that constitute him. Recall the metaphor of the three-legged race and the account of top-down causality (4.7).

Already, even in Fido, a number of different kinds of reality coalesce. Beyond the chemical molecules, remarkable in themselves (Nowicki, 2004), there is life. Echoing Gottfried Wilhelm Leibniz, philosophers marvel at the fundamental ontological question, "Why is there something rather than nothing?" Just so, biologists are also at a loss to explain the emergence of life (Hazen, 2003). The mystery is as great. Why is there no perplexity over the reality of life? Is it because we can see living things in the world about us or picture them in our minds and, then, suppose that, as pictorial, they are nothing different from physical matter?

Humble Fido provokes a further quandary. He is not only alive as is the stationary grass on which he runs; he is also sensate. He smells, hears, sees, feels, responds, and has a mind capable of perception and internal images, memories, and emotions, and he has a personality. The mind of Fido already transcends his organic body. Why is there no perplexity over the reality of Fido's mind? (Interest grows: e.g., Bekoff, Allen, & Burghardt, 2002; Goodenough, McGuire, & Jakob, 2010; Griffin, 2001; Menzel & Fischer, 2011; Wynne & Udell, 2013). A similar perceptual mental reality—called *psyche* in Chapter 5—also exists in human beings.

Could the ontology be avoided or would the reality be changed if reference were made, not to a "mind," but only to the mental characteristics evinced by an organism? Not at all. Still, some would prefer if the noun *mind* were not used and, instead, a verbal form such as "mind-ing" were employed. Supposedly, this more "process-oriented" emphasis avoids reifying the mind because a process or an activity does not easily appear to be a reality, something of its own kind. Yet I wonder if this "process" is not just another fuzzy image—like the entangled flying hands and feet in a fast-moving judo fight: it's all process. And I wonder, then, if sensate-modeled thinking doesn't still control the theorizing. To be sure, the image of a process is less fixed or imaginable than an image of a specific thing—Fido, for example, or a tree or a "soul," that gossamer-like substance that resides in the human heart—but isn't the process imagined, nonetheless? The grammatical game of replacing nouns with verbs might point in the right direction, but it does not yet nail the problem. It doesn't respect the intellectual epistemology and the judgment of fact that concludes with the unavoidable binary of either "Yes, it is" or "No, it is not." This ontological inevitability cannot be avoided. So calling whatever exists by this or that name, a noun or a verb, makes no ontological difference. More appropriate images and descriptions, better metaphors are certainly welcome, but they all still move within a perceptually imagined realm. In fact, any process of mental characteristics implies a mind. If the varied and shifting characteristics are there, something must account for them. *Mind* is simply the name we put on the intelligibility that unifies and makes sense of the mental characteristics. The term *mind* does not imply reification unless one is imagining the matter. This is the epistemological point that makes strikingly good sense of William James's insistence on speaking metaphorically of a "stream of thought," not a "train" or a "chain" (5.3.2).

Of course, in the human mind a still more novel reality emerges, and self-conscious humans are capable of marveling, questioning, theorizing, understanding, explaining, planning, deciding, and acting. In these functions they far surpass Fido and even transcend the limitations of space and time. Fido might be clever enough to solve some basic problems—how to solicit food or water, how to escape from his containment—but he hardly recognizes his insights as such, formulates and categorizes them, or theorizes about problem solving. He lacks what Donald (2001) calls "symbolic representation," which entails the ability to turn internal experiences into objects of attention in themselves, to "bracket [one's] own experiences or re-present them in memory" (p. 120). Even granted that Fido has insights, they reside ever in his behaviors, never, as far as anyone can discern, in abstractive thought about thought (Helminiak, 1996a, pp. 152–158). The human mind goes that much further.

Noting this latter marvel, d'Aquili and Newberg (1999) speculate,

> There are fundamentally two great discontinuities in the universe. The first . . . is the big bang. . . . The second . . . is the existence of subjective awareness. It simply represents an unexplainable jump from material organization to a level of

reality of another order, analogous to the jump from nothing to something. (p. 186)

The point is well taken, but this assessment oversimplifies the . . . matter—pun intended!—and, ironically, thereby exaggerates the mind–body problem. The jump is simply not from matter to spirit or consciousness in a single bound. Such thinking exemplifies what Cahoone (2010) calls "the dominant bipolar disorder of modern metaphysics, [namely,] thinking that matter or mind or both exhaust reality" (lecture 35, track 2). David Chalmers (2006) succumbs to this "bipolar disorder," insisting that consciousness alone exemplifies a genuine emergence. Then he posits retroactively two natural principles, matter and consciousness, that supposedly pervade the universe (1996; 4.21). In contrast, if we are to speak about matter attentively, intelligently, and reasonably, from the Big Bang on, matter already entails meaning: matter is a meaningful reality; intelligibility is inherent in it. Indeed, in different forms, matter actually entails different intelligibilities—bosons and fermions, atoms and molecules, for example. Should they even all be lumped together under one category, "physical matter"? Physicists recognized the seriousness of this question at least a century ago (Goldman, 2007).

Besides, if matter is real, in addition to its non-material intelligibility, matter also entails actuality. Thus matter itself already presumes intelligibility and actuality. These are meanings, correlates of acts of consciousness on its second and third levels. The meaningful, the spiritual is no late-comer on the cosmic scene as known to us (4.3).

Moreover, beyond the formation of particles from quarks, our world exhibits a range of emergent realities: particles to atoms to molecules to life to sensation to perception to intellectual consciousness. Each of these is novel in relation to their antecedents, and all constitute new realities. Surely, life is as mysterious as emotionality, imagination, or consciousness. Indeed, in the unfolding of the universe as current science routinely understands it dynamically, multiple realities lie on either side of blurry lines at major crossover points of emergence, and a new wonder looms on the leading edge of each crossover.

4.15. The Causality Across Levels of Emergence

4.15.1. *The Peculiarity of Causality in Emergences*

The concern of this chapter is to understand the human mind in relation to the human organism (the "body" or, more myopically, the brain). I argued that body and mind are both real; that as intelligible unities, they are distinct realities but not separate or separable; and that both truly exist, not in their own right as independent existents, but only as conjugates of the one thing, the one existent in question, the human being. The current suggestion is that the mind relates to the brain via emergence. Human mind emerges on the basis of the human organism and psyche. The task at this point is to suggest how.

Searle (1997) provides a useful lead by his repeated insistence that "brains cause consciousness" (p. 158; also pp. 55, 59, 110, 147, 150, 151, 159, 191, 192, 197, 201). The task becomes that of explaining what causation means in this case. In general, *cause* refers to some "intelligible relation of dependence" (Lonergan, 1957/1992, p. 563; see also pp. 100–102). In this sense, *causality* would indicate intelligibility or explanation, not imagination or the picture of one thing's somehow, as it were, giving birth to another. As we have seen at 4.9, Searle attempts to explain this process of causality via a number of analogies, but far from giving any insight into emergence, they failed even to demonstrate that the mind would be truly distinct from the brain. What, then, can we say about causality in the case of emergence?

I already treated efficient versus formal causality (4.6.4) and descriptive versus explanatory forms (4.12.1). I argued that perfected science entails formal (not efficient) causality and explanatory (not descriptive) forms—because to explain means to say what sense there is in a thing, what it is, how it works; to explain is to delineate the intelligibility, the constitutive or defining relations of a thing or, said in traditional terminology, to determine the thing's nature, essence, or form. However, causality in the case of emergence requires even further nuance—because emergence regards a new, logically coherent systematization that transcends and integrates a number of lower-level logically coherent systems. An emergence is a system of systems, but thus far I have presented formal causality only within individual closed systems.

4.15.2. Causality Within Closed Systems

In the case of emergence, not even the rigorously formulated interrelationship of the elements of formal causality—as in $a^2 + b^2 = c^2$—applies (4.6.5). Classical science pertains within logically coherent systems—as in Newton's universe and *par excellence* as seen in Marquis Pierre-Simon Laplace's fully deterministic portrayal of it (4.16.4). To treat emergence, we need to supplement classical science and its methods. We have learned that our universe also entails statistical processes and evolutionary novelties, for which a closed, logical system cannot account. The emergence of consciousness from neural function, like the emergence of water from hydrogen and oxygen (4.11.2), does not entail a logically coherent, completely computable, deductively predictable, or implicitly definable relationship—such as, say, that of a hypotenuse to the sides of a right triangle or the prediction of the next solar eclipse. Emergence entails some new reality, and a new reality entails a new system. Although the novelty builds upon lower-level realities and integrates them, systematizes them, to produce the novelty, the new systematization cannot be deduced from the lower-level realities. Their self-contained, individual defining systems are not the new, overarching system; they are not the novelty. Genuine novelty implies a new or different, a broader integrating system; genuine novelty implies a new or different intelligibility with its own coherent and lawfully interrelated properties and functions. But logical coherence, deducibility, does not pertain across different systems or among different intelligibilities: that is why they are different. Then, what does causality mean in this case?

Emergence within reality corresponds to a leap of insight within intelligence. Intelligence grasps the genuine novelty of the emergent reality, in comparison to its substrate constituents, even as its genuinely novel intelligibility determines the emergent reality as something truly new. As with insight, emergence establishes a new systematization of what was but a non-systematic manifold prior to the emergence. Recall the example of the puzzle or riddle at 2.3.1. Once the solution is found, what was puzzling appears coherent; the non-systematic has been systematized. Insight intelligently results in new systematizations. Similarly, emergence ontologically results in new systematizations. Intelligence and ontology are correlates.

> The prototype of emergence is the insight that arises with respect to an appropriate image: without the insight, the image is a coincidental manifold; by the insight the elements of the image become intelligibly united and related; moreover, accumulations of insight unify and relate ever greater and more diversified ranges of images, and what remains merely coincidental from a lower viewpoint becomes systematic from the accumulation of insight in a higher viewpoint. If the meaning of emergence is thus determinate, so also the fact is unmistakable. There are routine processes, and throughout them one can verify the same classical and statistical laws. There are changes of state, and during them statistical laws are modified but classical laws remain the same. But there also are emergent processes, and the classical laws that can be verified at their inception are not the

classical laws that can be verified at their end. There are correlations that can be verified in the adult organism. There are correlations that can be verified in the fertilized ovum. But the two sets of correlations are not identical. [Recognize the implication for debate over personhood and abortion.] In determinate materials, there has occurred a change in what can be grasped by insight, formulated as law, and affirmed as verified. One set of conjugate forms has given place to another. The process from one set to the other is regular. But this regular process is not in accord with classical law, for there are no classical laws about changes of classical laws; nor is it in accord with statistical law, for it is not an indifferent choice between a set of alternative processes; and so one is forced to recognize the fact of a third type of process [namely, emergence] to be investigated by a third [type of method, namely], genetic method. (Lonergan, 1957/1992, p. 506)

Suggestively to the point, when a jigsaw puzzle finally reveals its picture, the picture itself is now available for examination, marvel, and enjoyment. The "lower substrate" of the puzzle's pieces, constraints, and demands have been transcended. It might not even matter that the picture required tedious assembly. The picture is now a reality in its own right. More literally to the point, but not imaginable as is the jigsaw puzzle, recall the discussion of water and its constituents, hydrogen and oxygen (4.11.2). When they unite, a new thing emerges, water. It enjoys, and now behaves according to, its specific nature. It expresses a new systematization. Non-predictable from the bonding of hydrogen and oxygen, non-deducible from the lower-level systems, the new systematization entails new intelligibility, new laws, new reality. The water is a reality in its own right.

Another more striking, but far less understood, example is life, and it deserves some elaboration. Life presupposes, requires, and integrates an array of recurrent cycles of absolutely standard chemical processes and somehow unites and coordinates them all such that a new self-sustaining "unity-identity-whole," an organism, results. Or, more exactly, life does not effect all these operations as if it were an independent, reified, intervening agent with intelligence, planning, and determination of its own—an anthropomorphization or, perhaps, even a deification—but "life" is the name we give to this phenomenon, which is an integral dimension of our dynamic universe. Life is that very self-sustaining and self-replicating systematization of an otherwise random manifold of independent cycles of recurrence. Thus, life constitutes a reality in its own right.

Perhaps some people would be more comfortable speaking of "living things" rather than of "life" itself. They would admit that living things exist but question the reality of life as a phenomenon distinct in itself. After all, one can see and picture living things, but one cannot see life. How could it be real? Yet *life* merely names the conjugate or property—that intelligible set of interrelated characteristics—that pertain to organisms as living. Life does have an intelligibility of its own, the self-sustaining interrelationship of disparate cycles of chemical processes. This intelligibility is distinct, peculiar in itself. No one of the disparate chemical subprocesses, nor even the whole array of them, accounts for the overall integration of these processes, which constitutes life. Moreover, via a judgment of fact that grounds this intelligibility in the data of numerous documented instances, it—life—can be reasonably affirmed as actually existing. On the basis of an intellectual epistemology, life is, indeed, something in itself; it is a legitimate object of intelligent conceptualization and reasonable affirmation. To be sure, life does not exist in itself, floating about, as it were, as if waiting to attach itself to other things and make them live. Rather, it exists as a property or conjugate of a particular kind of things, organisms. But organisms do function in ways that non-living things do not, so organisms must possess something that non-living things lack. Similarly, "consciousness" merely names the conjugate that pertains specifically to humans, who are self-conscious, insightful, and self-determining. In every case, if explanation would be coherent, the behavioral characteristics, "self-determining," "insightful," "self-conscious," and "alive," evince real qualities that are lacking in rocks.

If the nouns, *life* and *consciousness,* are problematic, this is likely so only because picture-thinking tends to reify these realities, yet, in themselves, they are actually invisible. Then, on the ever bedeviling sensate-modeled criterion that reality is perceptible matter, life and consciousness do not qualify as real; or else, and equally mistakenly, they are pictured as supposed independently existing stuff, "substances" floating about "out there," able to be hooked up with other such stuff, other "substances" "out there." The problem is in the thinking, not in the realities: being will be what it is. Despite the inadequacy of sensate-modeled thinking, plants and animals continue to live, and with self-consciousness humans continue to think. And an attentive, intelligent, and reasonable epistemology is fully able to affirm that these behaviors evince distinctive qualities, which must entail distinctive properties, which must be real. Whether phrased in terms of things that are "alive" and "conscious" or things that "have life" and "have consciousness," the bottom line remains unchanged. Life is a reality, and consciousness is a reality. On the basis of relevant evidence, both are reasonably affirmed particular facets of our universe—and are, therefore, real; and both entail novel, non-deducible systematizations of lower-level random manifolds.

4.15.3. Causality Across the Gap of Emergence

Water from hydrogen and oxygen, life from complex organic molecules, sensation and perception from organic functioning, consciousness from perception—these are instances of the genuine emergence of new things from lower-level realities. Within each new systematization, logic reigns and implicit definition (4.6.5) holds. Classical and statistical methods apply within each of the individual systems. Logical consistency and statistical probabilities pertain within the newly emerged integrative system, as also within each of the individual lower-level systems. But what kind of causality pertains across the gaps of emergence? What kind of causality pertains between the manifold of lower-level systems and the overarching, integrative, higher-level system? Only a leap of intelligence—not logical deduction—accounts for coherence across the gap of emergence, which produces the new system. Therefore, within closed systems and across the gaps of emergence, causality cannot mean the same thing.

In these two cases, to be sure, causality is ever "an intelligible relation of dependence" (Lonergan, 1957/1992, p. 563), but in these different cases causality must be of different kinds. The "intelligible relations of dependence" differ. Simply said, the contrast is between the logical and the intelligible, between what can be deduced and what can be understood, between what is logically coherent and what is consistent overall but not necessarily deducible. The puzzle can, indeed, be solved. The question can be answered. The properties of water can be understood. But in many cases, not deduction within a logically coherent system, but only creative insight provides the solution. Intelligence entails more than logic. Deduction is only one expression of intelligence. Not all "intelligible relations" are strictly logical; some are insightful. These imply a cognitive leap and sometimes also an ontological emergence.

An instructive example is the shift from arithmetic to algebra (Lonergan, 1957/1992, pp. 37–42). The higher discipline expresses a broader system. With its own consistent rules or "logic," the higher system not only includes the lower but can also deal with puzzling issues—such as negative numbers in arithmetic—that the lower system cannot treat. But the higher system, algebra, cannot be logically deduced from the lower, arithmetic. In this sense, it could not be said that the lower "causes" the higher in the generally understood meaning of the term—efficient causality—nor even in the refined understanding of explanation—formal causality (4.6). Rather, a leap of intelligence, not a deduction of logic, proposes the higher system and accounts for its subsequent consistency with the lower. To move from arithmetic to algebra, intelligence must discern and name within the arithmetical operations patterns that are implicit and operative but not abstracted and formulated as such. The patterns are not deductions from arithmetic; they are principles grasped insightfully. Algebra "contains" arithmetic but not vice versa. Given algebra, arithmetic is a valid limit case. But given only arithmetic, there is no algebra. The consistency between algebra and arithmetic pertains, then, only top-down. Consistency results because the lower system constrains the higher; the higher could not emerge unless it is consistent with the lower, which supports it, on which it builds.

Another example, although looser, is the advance from Newtonian to Einsteinian physics. For the most part, within the limits of ordinary human experience, Newton's equations function perfectly well: we can predict the next solar eclipse. Einstein's theory adds refinement that becomes necessary only when gravitational fields are strong, or speeds approach that of light, or distances or times are extensive—as they do in cases of particle physics, astronomical observations, and deep-space probes. Einstein's equations pertain universally but, within restricted limits, will generate virtually the same solutions to problems as Newton's equations do. In this sense, Einstein's theory represents an advance over Newton, not a rejection. Einstein's theory does not disqualify Newton's theory but, rather, integrates it as a limit case within a broader perspective. Thus, from an Einsteinian perspective, physics is fully consistent; but the same does not apply from a Newtonian perspective because it does not include relativity theory.

The point is that emergence is a parallel to insight. Both result in new systematizations based on lower-levels systems—the one, ontologically, the other, intellectually. An understanding of the systematizing function of insight in the face of data is our best clue to an understanding of the emergence of new things from lower-level realities. As with insights and "higher viewpoints" (Helminiak, 1996b, 1998, 2011; Lonergan, 1957/1992, pp. 37–43)—Einsteinian physics over Newtonian, algebra over arithmetic, biology over chemistry, chemistry over physics—the lower-level realities constrain the possibilities for the emergence of the higher-level things. Precisely because of these constraints, however, the higher-level things evince consistency with the lower-level realities. Unlike in the case of water synthesized from hydrogen and oxygen, in most other cases we are still far from discerning the consistency across gaps of emergence. Specification of this "causality" is still beyond us. Yet the parallel with the achievement of an insight richly suggests the meaning of this other kind of causality.

4.15.4. Intelligibility and Ontology, Insight and Emergence

Emergence is to reality what insight is to understanding. Each is a process whereby something new arises. Moreover, given that both entail intelligibility—as, indeed, they do if intelligibility, not perceptibility, determines the reality or kind of a being—the parallel and coherence of this summary statement are ontological and should not seem surprising. Insight grasps intelligibility in data. When insight grasps completely new intelligibility that differs from what was otherwise grasped, something new must be in question. If nothing new were in question, new insight would not be needed. Intelligence and ontology are correlates.

Additionally, insight does not occur according to preprogrammed and logically consistent regularities. Insight is always novel. It discerns a new order with its own logic where previously none was acknowledged: the essence of insight is to grasp relationships; the meaning of explanation, knowledge, science, is to explicate relationships—as contemporary physics is forcing us to recognize. Like insight, the emergence of a new reality does not occur according to a preprogrammed and logically consistent regularity. What is new integrates the unsystematic and presents an organization that was previously not available. The new reality presents a new order, a new systematization, a system of systems, even as insight discerns new intelligibility, a new set of relationships, in what otherwise was a coincidental manifold of unordered elements, unrelated independent systems.

A key point for an understanding of emergence is that it is not automatic; it is not predictable; it is not a logical deduction or implication; it does not derive in any systematic way from the lower-level elements. If it did so derive, it would not represent something inherently new but only an extension, elaboration, aggregation, or clarification of what was already given—Chalmers's (1996) "logical supervenience" (pp. 34–38). A completely new intelligibility is indicative of a new reality, and the nonsystematic nature of the insight and of the emergence is essential to the novelty. Rather than deductive or necessary, emergences, like insights, are probabilistic. They presuppose large numbers and long times, and, as the history of evolution easily makes clear, they entail considerable waste—and in the case of humans, considerable heartache: how much does it cost to produce and support one genius, and how many human beings, demeaned in the status of worker ants, pass their existence in the mere struggle to survive and to support some social system's strain to advance? The unrealized possibilities of quantum-level processes, that is, the so-called "collapse" of the wave function (3.5); the formation and demise of stars, planets, and galaxies; the reversals and dead-ends of evolution; the tragic loss of human potential because of physical accidents, biological aberrations, or mental disorders—all provide lucid examples of the probabilistic and "wasteful" nature of cosmic unfolding. Nor have I mentioned here the pervasive irresponsibility, cruelty, and downright evil of humans. Once we humans are on the scene and in control of world process, on balance the blame for most human heartache and waste of nature's potential surely falls to our feeble consciences.

If the connection between the lower and higher systems were systematic, logical, deductive, no new order would be at stake—and no new reality, and no need for new insight. The higher-level *thing* cannot be predicted or deduced from its lower-level constitutive *realities* or *conjugates*. The relationship between the two is not logical. The novelty cannot be deduced; it cannot be computed. Nonetheless, once achieved, it is understandable, it is intelligible. The anomaly of floating ice is fully consistent with chemical theory, but that anomalous characteristic of frozen water is not deducible or predictable from the lower-level, constitutive molecules or their bonding (4.11.2). The emergence of a novelty is like an insight, and far from resulting deductively within a logical order, insight reconfigures data to propose a new order, which then has its own logic, its own laws, its own truths, its own facts.

4.16. The Impact of Gödel's Theorem on Formal Causality

4.16.1. Gödel's Theorem and Its Implications

The non-systematic phenomenon of emergence that I am describing might appear abstruse or fanciful, but in one form it actually occurs as a highly elaborated mathematical commonplace. I have in mind Kurt Gödel's incompleteness theorem—that is, his mathematical proof that certain conclusions cannot be proved in mathematics, that some inevitably go beyond any computational or logical system. In particular, I have in mind Roger Penrose's (1994b) appeal to Gödel's theorem to argue that mind is incommensurate with any mechanical, computational system.

The context of Penrose's argument is computer modeling of the mind, and his focus is the supposition that computers could actually have minds.

His argument against this supposition is that mind entails a dimension of insight or understanding that goes beyond the logically coherent system of computation, which characterizes a computer. Gödel proved that no logical or mathematical system can ever be comprehensive; it can never include all eventualities. It is "not possible to list all possible 'obvious' steps of reasoning once and for all, so that from then on everything could be reduced to computation—i.e., the mere mechanical manipulation of these obvious steps" (Penrose, 1994b, p. 56). "No formal system of sound mathematical rules of proof can ever suffice, even in principle, to establish all the true propositions of ordinary arithmetic" (pp. 64–65). "For every set of mathematical definitions and axioms there is also a set of further questions that arise, but cannot be answered, on the basis of the definitions and axioms" (Lonergan, 1957/1992, pp. 596–597; see also pp. 17–20). "For any sufficiently powerful logical system, statements can be formulated that can neither be proved nor disproved within that system. This assertion is known as the 'Incompleteness Theorem' because it shows that all sufficiently powerful axiomatic systems are necessarily incomplete" (Blackmore, 2012, pp. 281–282). "The project of finding an axiomatic system that will contain everything else is not a feasible business" (Lonergan, 1957/2001, p. 54).

All this is to say, no coherent system, mathematical or logical, can completely account for itself as a system; within any propositional system there will always be propositions that cannot be proved to be true or false within the system and potential questions that cannot be answered within the system. This is the brunt of Gödel's mathematically proven and indisputable theorem. Every system presupposes something from beyond itself—strikingly, for example, the very consistency of the system: we must "go beyond any given set of computational rules that we believe to be sound, and obtain a further rule, not contained in those rules, that we must believe to be sound also, namely the rule asserting the *consistency* of the original rules" (Penrose, 1994b, p. 94).

Penrose's point regarding computers is that in principle they could never replicate the human mind because "human understanding and insight cannot be reduced to any set of computational rules" (p. 65). "Insights that are available to human mathematicians—indeed, to anyone who can think logically with understanding and imagination—lie beyond anything that can be formalized as a set of rules" (p. 72). Any systematization or coherent explanation that the mind could propose depends on something that goes beyond the system or the explanation, namely, the insightful and unrestricted capacity of the mind itself. This is to say, the human mind is not merely logical; it is also intelligent. It does not deal only in computations and deductions; it also deals in insights. But computers are limited to the logical, the computational, the programmable, the deductive. Thus limited, devoid of insight and understanding, computers cannot be minds; they cannot have consciousness. This is Penrose's point, supported by Gödel's theorem.

4.16.2. *Gödel's Theorem Applied to the Emergence of Mind*

I want to suggest that this same argument applies to the relationship of the mind to the brain and to any other process of emergence. I am not aware of Penrose's making this explicit application. Lonergan (1957/1992, pp. 18–20, 596–597) does.

Despite Penrose's (1994b) involvement with highly intellectual mathematical matters, like most others he still seems to retain some notion of knowing as a perception-like affair. Given that Penrose is one of the very few major theorists who allow that consciousness is actually a kind of reality in itself, I find it important to highlight the remnants of sensate-modeled epistemology that lurk in his position.

Penrose does, of course, speak forcefully of "understanding" (pp. 51, 52, 55, 56) and "insights" (p. 56), and when he uses visual arrays to make a point (e.g., 3 x 5 – 5 x 3), he is precise in stating that the "'visualizations'" he means "are more concerned with the general issue of 'awareness' than with . . . the visual [perceptual] system," and by "awareness" he means "our understanding" (p. 59). Still, it is peculiar that he relates understanding to "the use of one's awareness" (p. 54), not one's intelligence or insight; that by *awareness* he seems to mean something perceptual, something stimulus-response-like, namely, the "passive" dimension of consciousness (p. 39; see 5.4.1); that he uses the perceptual term *visualization* in quotation marks to mean awareness/understanding (p. 59); and that he construes the steps in a chain of reasoning as "*perceived* as obvious" (p. 56, emphasis added). Moreover, laudably but ineffectively struggling to understand understanding but influenced by early emergentist thinking (Cahoone, 2008, lecture 21, track 5), Penrose literally links understanding to some kind of human access to already conceived ideas existing in Plato's World of Forms or Ideas (Penrose, 1994b, pp. 50–51, 54).

Admittedly, I am nit-picking. Still, the confrontational nature, the "this-against-that-ness" of a perception-modeled theory of knowing seems to color parts of Penrose's presentation (see 5.4.1). As in the cases of Chalmers (1996) and Searle (1997), who also affirm that consciousness is a reality *sui generis,* there remains a need to apply Lonergan's trenchant distinction between perceptual and intellectual "knowing" even to Penrose's theory.

To be fair, however, Penrose's sustained concern is the connection between computers and the mind, whereas my concern at this point is the connection between the brain and the mind. Penrose is satisfied to demonstrate that computers cannot have minds. He does not make a point of the mind–brain connection. Indeed, he might treat mind and brain collectively, thus: "the human faculty of being able to 'understand' is something that must be achieved by some non-computational activity of the *brain or mind*" (p. 48, emphasis added).

Nonetheless, I want to apply Penrose's argument about the computer and the human mind to the case of the brain and the human mind. I want to suggest that, like the computer, the brain is also a self-contained system; and just as the computational system of a computer could never account for understanding, insight, or mind, so, too, the biological system of the brain in itself cannot account for the human mind. The mind must be a new reality in relation to the brain.

The brain can legitimately be called a system: it is an organization of elements that form a coherent whole and entails processes governed by laws proper to it. The biological functioning of the brain—the neurons, glial cells, ionic potentials, transmitters—has a "logic" of its own. Computer-modeled theories of consciousness freely compare the brain to a computer.

Therefore, granted Gödel's theorem, there is no logically coherent path from the brain to the mind. The insightful capacity of the mind transcends even the most comprehensive system. That the human brain is incomprehensibly complex does not absolve it from the limitations of a self-contained system. Complex or simple, no system *per se* can account for the insightful, the non-systematic, functioning of the mind. The human mind is beyond the logical system of the brain or of any computer. The higher-level reality of the mind cannot derive seamlessly from the lower-level system of the brain, however complex. In this sense, it cannot be true that brains cause minds, or consciousness, in the standard way that Searle (1997) seems to suggest (4.15.1). The relationship between the brain and the mind is not logical or deductive. More accurately, and more provocatively, this relationship must be called creative. The emergence of the mind parallels the leap of insight. Both result in something new—a new reality, in the one case, and a correlative new understanding, in the other. Moreover, granted that intelligibilities specify and differentiate realities, the parallel is ontological. It pertains to the very nature of being. And we are back to epistemology again.

4.16.3. Nuances of Causality in the Case of Emergence

In cases of emergence, then, the notion of "causality" is highly ambiguous. I noted how implicit definition (4.6.5)—wherein terms define the relations and the relations define the terms as, for example, in $a^2 + b^2 = c^2$ in the case of a Euclidian right triangle—is an expression of formal causality (4.6.5). It names the essential factors, the necessary and sufficient conditions, and their peculiar relationships that make a thing what it is—the "form" or "essence" or "nature" of the thing. In this case, one could understandably and obviously speak of causality because the factors do express "an intelligible relation of dependence" (Lonergan, 1957/1992, p. 563; see also pp. 100–102; see 4.6.6); the factors all depend on one another and, in a sense specified by their relationships, make one another what they are. At stake is formal causality, not efficient causality.

But in cases of emergence, different kinds of reality are at stake. No single system, no single form, essence, or nature is at stake. In such cases, a number of different closed systems, each defining a different reality, are involved, and the emergence somehow interrelates these systemically disparate phenomena. Their interrelationship might, indeed, be able to be specified—but only from the top down. That is, only given the higher synthesis, which includes and expands on the lower system, can full coherence be specified. Only from the perspective of the higher can the integration of higher and lower be explained. The nature of water, compared to hydrogen and oxygen, provided an example at 4.11.2. So Searle's (1997) appeal to "causal reduction," wherein the lower system determines the higher, has the matter upside-down.

This inversion is another example of the recurrent lapse into perception-modeled thinking with its push-pull efficient causality in the physical world. Such perception-modeled thinking pictures the higher system as a mere rearrangement of the manipulable parts in the lower system and sees the new conglomeration somehow rising up out of the old with less novelty than that of a Phoenix rising up from ashes. Perception-modeled thinking completely overlooks insight's leap into new understanding or emergence's leap into new reality.

On the basis of the higher, yes, the lower can be accounted for; but the higher cannot be accounted for on the basis of the lower. The lower cannot explain the higher. In this sense, the lower cannot be said to "cause" the higher. To invoke Gödel again: any logico-mathematical system is incomplete in itself even to account for what in some way might be included in it and emergent from it. Only granted a higher-level system does the consistency of the whole—lower and higher—hold.

4.16.4. Only Top-Down Coherence Within Emergence

In classical scientific method, implicit definition pertains—as, for example, in Newton's theory of planetary motion, which entails a closed, logically coherent system. Indeed, Laplace took Newton's theory to imply strict determinism as the law of the universe. According to Laplace, given sufficient information on every particle in the current universe, the future could be infallibility predicted; it could be deduced. Wowed by Newton's genius, Laplace and many of his contemporaries thought the universe was completely deterministic, an absolutely logically coherent and closed system.

But classical method has been supplemented with statistical method wherein probabilities pertain, not the rules of logic or the inevitabilities of computation. The consistencies of logical method do not hold in the case of emergence. In this case, classical method is no longer explanatory because the probabilistic insightful leap from a lower system to a higher one is not logical. According to Gödel's theorem, the higher system cannot be computed on the basis of the lower.

From the perspective of the higher system and in the ideal, of course—most often, only in the ideal—the coherence of emergent levels might be able to be specified. In the simple case of arithmetic and algebra (4.15.3) or in the case of water known to be H_2O (4.11.2) or even in the case of Newtonian and Einsteinian physics (4.15.3), we already understand enough to actually be able to propose a comprehensive and reasonable coherence from the top down. Given the emerged higher syntheses, to an impressive extent we can explain their relationship to the lower-level systems. We can accommodate Newtonian computations in Einsteinian physics. However, had the higher syntheses not already occurred, we would not have been able to deduce them on the merely logical or computational bases of the lower systems. Apart from the givenness of the higher emerged system, we would not even be inquiring about it and trying to explain it. There would be nothing to ponder and explain.

4.16.5. The Challenge of Explaining the Higher-Level Emergences

We are nowhere near such comprehensive coherence in the more challenging sciences. As this discussion suggests, our standard approaches have hardly yet adequately conceptualized the questions. For the biological and human sciences, any comprehensive account still has to note gaps where the emergences of new realities intervene. The best we might do is to project the statistical probabilities of the emergences. We are far from developing the genetic method needed to explain them.

The new realities could, indeed, be grasped as new and even be named—cell, organism, plant, animal, human—but no actual explanation for their emergence might thus far be proposed. An obvious example is the emergence of life out of chemistry (4.15.2). We listen for confirmation—and thus far, ever in vain—whenever we hear claims that some laboratory has synthesized life. Despite exaggerated assertions (e.g., in Chalmers, 1996, pp. 25, 42; Dennett, 1991, p. 455; Searle, 1997, p. 201), we have no idea what life is *per se*. Its systematizing unity remains part of the given to be explained, although we are far along, yes, in understanding the biochemistry that supports life and that, for its part, life systematizes in a self-sustaining whole (Ricardo & Szostak, 2009). But biochemistry is not life; rather, biochemistry presupposes and expresses life. The question remains: how do the biochemical processes begin in concert and continue to sustain themselves in their complex patterns of closely modulated interrelationship? To explain the unifying system would be to explain life. Biochemistry merely explains the elements interacting in the system. The higher system with its own intelligibility and laws sublates the biochemistry. The biochemistry serves life; it does not explain it.

Gödel's theorem confirms that no emergence is logically deducible from its lower-level elements. The emergent is a new thing in relation to its constituent realities. The pressing example in our present discussion is the emergence of consciousness out of biology, sensation, and perception. When will we account for this emergence?

4.17. The Coherence of a Dynamic Universe

I take the mind and consciousness to be realities in their own right—distinctively intelligible kinds of being, not imaginable types of vaporous material stuff out there—and I propose to account for them by appeal to emergence. What coherence might this proposal eventually enjoy?

4.17.1. Supplements to Classical Science: Statistical and Genetic Methods

In cases of emergence, comprehensive explanation requires more than the logical systems that formal causality, implicit definition, and classical method provide. In these cases, also statistical method and genetic (or evolutionary or developmental) method must now also pertain. Statistical method would explain the likelihood of the emergence; and genetic method, the continuity of the realities across the gaps of the emergence

(Lonergan, 1957/1992, pp. 126–162, 484–507). Statistical method is well developed and widely known. Genetic method, hardly at all; but allusions to it are not completely unknown. C. D. Broad (1925) foresaw the discovery of "emergent laws" or "trans-ordinal laws," that is, explanations of the emergence of a higher reality from lower ones. Their only peculiarity, he noted—consonant with what I wrote above about bottom-up and top-down causality—is that

> we must wait till we meet with an actual instance of an object of the higher order before we can discover such a law; and we . . . cannot possibly deduce it beforehand from any combination of laws which we have discovered by observing aggregates of a lower order. (p. 79, as cited in Clayton & Davies, 2006, p. 9)

Similarly, David Chalmers (2006) also expects the discovery of "a further basic law or laws" "that express the connection between physical processes and consciousness," "fundamental psychophysical laws" (p. 247) or "supervenience laws" (1996, p. 127). He explains,

> Physics postulates a number of *fundamental* features of the world: space-time, mass-energy, change, spin, and so on. It also posits a number of fundamental laws in virtue of which these fundamental features are related. Fundamental features . . . and fundamental laws . . . must simply be taken as primitive. . . . To bring consciousness within the scope of a fundamental theory, we need to introduce *new* fundamental properties and laws. (p. 126)

The psychophysical laws specify "how phenomenal [conscious] . . . properties depend on physical properties," "how experience arises from physical processes" (p. 127).

4.17.2. The Projection of a Comprehensive Science

Lonergan (1957/1992) has offered considerable detail about the methods that would lead to those further naturalistic laws that others also deem necessary for accounting for consciousness and for all emergences. As in all attempts to understand, these more recently developed scientific methods—statistical and genetic—are specialized expressions of transcendental method, that consistent process for knowing built into the human mind, grounding the ultimate coherence of all explanation (2.5–2.7). In his own way, envisaging the addition of a theory of consciousness to ever-expanding science, Chalmers (1996) described the situation as follows:

> The world still consists of a network of fundamental properties related by basic laws, and everything is to be ultimately explained in these terms. All that has happened is that the inventory of properties and laws has been expanded, as happened with Maxwell [who added electromagnetic laws to the then known mechanical principles of physics]. Further, nothing about this new view [regarding consciousness] contradicts anything in physical theory; rather, it supplements it. (pp. 127–128).

For Lonergan, such a comprehensive scientific understanding is a matter of metaphysics—which regards being, that is, that which we know when we actually know. Completely and cleanly, Lonergan elaborated that comprehensive understanding as a heuristic framework or anticipatory projection on the basis of the structures, requirements, and implications of intellectual knowing, summarized in Chapter 2. To wit, if we know being by experience, understanding, and judgment, most fundamentally every being must entail correlates of this threefold knowing process: something to experience, something to understand, and something to affirm, and these must constitute being. This implied heuristic framework would function as a metaphysical blueprint that outlines any specimen while ongoingly we fill in the concrete specifics. Filling them in, we would come to know the specimen, to determine its nature, via verified instances of its functioning—much as particle physicists intellectually specify imperceptible entities. Bit by bit, further exploration, theorizing, and verification would provide the needed detail for the desired comprehensive scientific account. It would both classically explain the specimen in itself and statistically and genetically specify its relations with the rest of the universe of being.

To recognize emergence and envisage comprehensive science is to rethink the meaning of "causality." In general, causality becomes another name for explanation (Lonergan, 1957/1992, p. 674) and in different ways expresses "an intelligible relation of dependence" (p. 563). With the deployment of statistical and genetic methods, in addition to the logically coherent systems of classical method, the different ways of expressing intelligible coherence have multiplied, and scientific explanation has become subtle and difficult. Thus, we have seen a clarification and then a multiplication of the "fundamentals" of the universe (Chalmers, 1996, p.

126): space–time, mass–energy, gravity, the light constant, electromagnetism—and I would add life, perception, consciousness. Such pivotal matters about our universe must be taken as they are, novelties that themselves set the demarcation lines of explanation, realities of particular kinds and, given as such, brute facts of nature, allowing no eliminative reductive explanation. In the simple case of water, as we have seen, the standard laws of chemical bonding explain its synthesis; but to explain water in all its properties—as we can do—we must invoke the further laws that pertain to molecules, their shapes, their weak bondings with one another, their possible changes in state, and the like.

Our universe is complex and fascinating. Its full explanation will entail a wide net of interrelated insights. I do not pretend that the sketch I presented here is sufficient to fully elucidate the matter. If I have succeeded in projecting an intuitive understanding and have whetted an appetite for more, I have achieved some success. If appeal to Gödel's theorem has lent credibility to my argument, I am content. My more modest yet all-important point is to suggest that an intellectual epistemology opens seamlessly onto a comprehensive and coherent science—an intelligible whole—and Lonergan has explicated this process to a remarkable degree. In contrast, a perception-modeled epistemology can only imagine or picture higher-level realities and comprehensive syntheses as LEGO-block-like constructions from palpable pieces of lower-level things, aggregates of aggregates of aggregates of all the same stuff.

My boldness in the face of these daunting matters derives from Lonergan's epistemological theory. Just as Einstein's theory, once worked out, allows one to discern a limited legitimacy in Newton's physics, so, too, Lonergan's methodological breakthrough allows one to find in other theorists, read with generosity and good will, hints of similar methodological considerations, which I have attempted to point out. It might be apparent to those who know them that I quote other theorists highly selectively. This is so because I find the theories in consciousness studies to be jungles of shadowy, entangled speculation giving way only now and then to bursts of insightful light. I am trying to collect the light and pass by the shadows. In Lonergan, I have found, as it were, a light detector. Its sensitivity is so keen that it easily sorts out perceptualist from intellectualist epistemology and imagination from understanding. It illuminates the validly positive contributions that various theorists offer and focuses the unsuccessful offerings and their causes. In the end, however, nowhere in others' discussion of the mind–body problem and of "God in the brain" do I discern Lonergan's explicit and incisive clarifications. He makes invaluable philosophical contributions to the present discussion.

4.18. The Proposed Distinction Between Weak and Strong Emergence

4.18.1. *The Usefulness of Comparison With Other Elaborated Positions*

Before bringing this long chapter to a close, I devote this and the following three sections to detailed criticism of major lines of thought in current consciousness studies. I have already spelled out my own understanding and could forgo treating the positions of other theorists, but only further clarity could result from these comparative analyses. Besides, I am well aware that I am far out of sync with contemporary philosophical preferences. The likelihood of my being misunderstood is great. My starting point and presuppositions—Lonergan's analysis of intentional consciousness (5.1.2; 5.3) and its concomitant epistemology—are so foreign to the field that I do not want to leave it to others to make these applications or fail to engage them at all. I pursue this dialogue with four desires in mind: to understand the positions of these theorists; to highlight whatever positive contributions I discover; to pinpoint errors and their sources as I see them; and to suggest what corrections might lead to a coherent consensual position.

4.18.2. *Emergence as Weak or Strong*

Discussion of emergence routinely distinguishes between weak and strong emergence. David Chalmers (2006) defines the weak as imbued of features that are *unexpected* but, once known, are explicable on the basis of lower-level laws, are fully reducible to them, and, thus, are not genuinely emergent. Strong emergence, in contrast, pertains to realities that could in no way be accounted for on the basis of lower-level laws. Products of strong emergence "are not deducible even in principle from truths in the low-level domain" (p. 244). Chalmers believes that only consciousness qualifies as a clear case of strong emergence.

Puzzling to me, Chalmers also allows that some emergences, not deducible on the basis of lower-level laws or truths, might nonetheless be "deducible (or nearly so) from the low-level facts" (p. 248). In this case, the emergence would only be weak, not genuinely emergent. I believe my appeal to H_2O as a genuine instance of strong emergence (4.11.2) fits the description only of this debased category of Chalmers's because, although the properties of water cannot be deduced from the laws governing the synthesis of hydrogen and oxygen, given the synthesis of water and a study of the compound, its unexpected properties—e.g., ice floats—are consistent with all else that chemistry knows about atoms and molecules. Seemingly, for Chalmers such a situation would not qualify as a genuine emergence because the initially unexpected would eventually be explained. Thus, no truly new reality would be acknowledged.

4.18.3. Of Laws, Truths, and "Facts": Chalmers and Nagel

I am puzzled because I fail to understand Chalmers's difference between laws or truths, and those possible supplementary "facts." In this proposed distinction I detect a lapse from intellectual to perceptual epistemology and their confounding. "Facts" in this case seem to mean what one could encounter, bump into, see, or in some way discern out there in some lower-level of a material world; and by implication the real is taken to be what could be perceived. Let me justify this sweeping assessment.

The ambiguous terminological usage of *facts* is widespread. Chalmers (1996) states outright that "knowledge of what red is like is factual knowledge" (p. 104). That is, the percept is supposedly a fact, and experience of the percept is supposedly already knowledge. Similarly, when Mary, raised in a black-and-white room (Jackson, 1982), "sees red for the first time, . . . the knowledge she is gaining is knowledge of a fact" (Chalmers, 1996, p. 104). Chalmers's long discussion of Mary's case offers a striking exhibit on the pervasive confounding—not just for Chalmers—of perceptual experience with factual knowledge (pp. 140–146). Seemingly, "facts" are preconstituted givens to be encountered; they are not understood to be the products of intellectual achievement on a third level of consciousness. The epistemology at stake at this point is blatantly perceptual; it is naïve realism (2.2.2–2.2.4). Whereas truths and laws are products of intelligence, *facts*, as used in this case, appears to name products of perception: beyond the truths and laws of the case, "facts" might still be encountered. So *facts* for Chalmers means *data* in Lonergan's terminology, namely, that which could be observed or encountered and that, then, on the basis of which one could generate understanding or explanation: knowledge or facts. Chalmers's usage confounds acts on the first level of consciousness (experience) with those on the second or third (understanding and judgment).

Perhaps I appear perverse in insisting on these terminological distinctions when common usage shifts the terms routinely (2.1.3)—and even more perverse or even arrogant to impose Lonergan's usage again and again. But precision is precisely what is needed in these subtle discussions, and, as I hope to be demonstrating, it is widely lacking. In turn, in my experience, Lonergan alone has provided it. So, applying consistent terminology, I "perversely" deconstruct these theorists' positions in the hope of approaching some consensual understanding grounded in evidence and sound reason.

Such same ambiguous usage occurs in Thomas Nagel's (1974) acclaimed article about what it's like to be a bat. As if there could be human knowledge (or even non-human knowledge but somehow still known to us apart from a human knower), Nagel speaks of "facts beyond the reach of human concepts," "facts which *could* not ever be represented or comprehended by human beings" (p. 441), "the facts of experience—facts about what it is like *for* the experiencing organism" (p. 442). By "facts," Nagel is not referring to the end-products of intellectually processed data, namely, accurate accounts of what actually is the case, the determined facts of the matter. Rather, by "facts" Nagel, too, means some sort of "knowledge" that is supposedly lying out there on its own and could be stumbled upon. This observation is well confirmed.

- Nagel outright declares that "there are *facts* that do not consist in the truth of propositions expressible in a human language" (p. 441). This dissociation of facts from truth is curious, to say the least.

- He emphatically contrasts these "facts" in question with supposed other kinds of facts, the "*more* objective" facts (p. 443), "objective facts *par excellence*" (p. 442). By *objective* here—but not always elsewhere—he means *scientific*, that is, determined intellectually by appeal to relevant evidence even apart from "differing perceptual systems." In this vein, he speaks of "the acquisition of knowledge about bat neurophysiology by human scientists" (p. 442) and of sound as a "wave phenomenon" (p. 445). Indeed, paralleling Lonergan's distinction between sense-related "description" and intelligence-related "explanation," he refers to science as "a move in the direction of greater objectivity, toward a more accurate view of the real nature of things" (p. 444). This contrast makes clear that the "facts" in question are not scientific facts, not the product of correct understanding or the concern of science.

- Nagel explicitly contrasts such scientific knowledge with a supposed other kind that he calls "experience," that is, internal organismic, sensate, and perceptual feelings (pp. 442–445); and his point is that none except the perceiving organism itself could actually "know" how such feelings feel. Here, then, Nagel's "experience" is Lonergan's experience. However, its cash-out is supposedly "knowledge," not mere data. Moreover, with Lonergan I allowed at 2.2.5 that the term *knowledge* is used in this loose sense: I "know" the taste of an orange. In its own right, this experience constitutes a kind of "knowing." To some extent, then, Nagel has distinguished sensate-modeled and intellectual epistemologies, but he also continues to confound them as if both cases were somehow one and the same, as if "knowledge" were knowledge.

In sum, like Chalmers, Nagel also uses the term *facts* ambiguously. This lack of precision is widespread. *Facts* does not always refer to an intellectual achievement; it is also used to refer to the raw data of sensations and perceptions. By distinguishing three levels of consciousness, Lonergan has provided the basis for incisively clarifying this ambiguous usage and for fixing the terminology.

Nagel's overall point is valid, of course. There are matters within human experience and within the animal realm at large that science simply cannot explicate, namely, the specificity of those internal feelings proper to the organisms themselves, the particularities of experience. Chalmers (1996) grapples with a similar—but seldom associated—concern under the name of "indexicality" (pp. 84–85) and ponders the significance of someone's or something's being here rather than there, being now rather than then, being this one rather than that one of the same kind. Lonergan (1957/1992) treats this subtle matter in detail under the name *empirical residue* (q.v.), those data that are purely *de facto* givens and contribute nothing to an understanding of the matter—for example, one Euclidean circle rather than another, or space and time in Einstein's more subtle analyses. (See 2.2.4). Compounding such ambiguous terminological usage, Nagel (1974) suggests that subjects—genuinely conscious beings, as clarified at 5.3–5.4—are everywhere and equally in question when organisms experience their proprietary feelings. He uses the ambiguous and misleading term *subjective* to describe these feelings even in cases of non-human organisms: "the subjective character of experience" (p. 444).

Despite these ambiguities, which confound and confuse his point, Nagel's overall insistence is valid: internal feelings *per se* and certain dimensions of "experience" are irreducible to the organismic and neuronal processes that might underlie and support them. Chalmers (1996) sustains this insistence for chapters. Nagel and Chalmers argue convincingly that experience or "consciousness" is a phenomenon that is not amenable to current physicalist or materialist theories of mind. Consciousness cannot be reduced to brain function; consciousness is something of its own kind.

I surely welcome this conclusion and appreciate Nagel's and Chalmers's arguments to support it. Nonetheless, I need to point out that, like Chalmers's, Nagel's argument confounds perceptualist feelings with intellectual facts. In the process, Nagel seemingly limits human conscious experience to internal feelings or perceptions; and he confounds distinctively human experience with the putative internal feelings of non-human organisms—all "subjective" in some sense, all "conscious" in some sense, all "facts" in some sense, all "experience" in some sense (see discussion of Griffin's appeal to "experience" and "subjectivity" and Chalmers's to "information" at 4.20.2 and 4.21.2). Worst of all, because the topic is consciousness, Nagel overlooks the distinctively human dimensions of consciousness, the possible consciousness also of consciousness itself (5.3). Indeed, in glaringly minimalist insistence, Nagel (1974) asserts that the internal "feel" that organisms have "is the essence of the internal world" (p. 445)—whereas Lonergan (1957/1992, 1972) goes on for hundreds of pages explicating the richness of "interiority" (1972, q.v.), its different kinds, varied facets, and multiple activities (Helminiak, 2014). So Nagel's, Chalmers's, and virtually all treatments of consciousness (cf. Blackmore, 2012) focus on perceptual experience as the supposed paradigmatic instances of human consciousness (5.4.1). With obfuscating results, the problem of confounding perceptual and intellectual epistemologies extends into the deepest levels of consciousness studies.

In Lonergan's terminology, those additional "facts" to which Chalmers and Nagel appeal are actually data, that is, the observed or experienced that is to be understood. With the achieved addition of understanding and judgment, data contribute to facts, but in themselves data are not facts. Given this clarification, it is apparent that *facts*, *truths*, and *laws* are roughly synonymous; they are different words that apply to the same cognitive achievement: the articulation of what is actually the case, as best we currently know. They are forms of scientific explanation, the verified correlates of the second level of consciousness, or they are simple matters of fact, correlates of the third level of consciousness: they are what is known when ideas are confirmed as adequately grounded in data. If so, Chalmers's appeal to the truths and laws of a lower level and his appeal to its supposedly further facts are appeal to the identical criteria. His argument is fallacious. Its epistemology is muddled. His ground for distinguishing weak and strong emergence collapses.

4.18.4. Different But Not Further "Facts" About Elephants

I confirm the accuracy of my interpretation, and I further illustrate the devastating consequences of incoherent epistemology, by citing another example of misuse of the term *facts*. Chalmers (1996) explicates pure materialism as an instance of what he calls "logical supervenience" (pp. 32–89; on supervenience, see Davidson, 1970/2001). Materialism is the supposition that nothing but matter is real so that, given an accounting of it, by simple logical deduction, by logical supervenience, an accounting of all other things would follow (except, for Chalmers, consciousness). At stake is Laplacean determinism, pure and simple (4.16.4). Precluded is any possibility of emergence, any plurality of realities besides matter. Ignored, too, are the implications of Gödel's Theorem (4.16.1).

Given such materialistic, reductionistic presuppositions, Chalmers compares facts about elephants with microphysical facts—the facts of physics. Supposedly, the facts of physics completely account for the facts about elephants by mere logical deduction, yet the facts in question are not all the same. With emphasis, Chalmers insists, "They may be *different* facts, . . . but they are not *further* facts" (p. 41). Now, if the facts are different, one wonders what "not further" could mean, especially because "facts" are in question in both cases.

Of course, what Chalmers does mean by "further facts" is whatever would need more explanation. Supposedly, although attending to an elephant might provide more information about physical matter, the elephant requires no explanation beyond physics. Supposedly, an elephant is merely a highly elaborated instance of matter, and characteristics specific to elephants merely describe this instance of physical being, rather than a different instance. To anticipate my conclusion: Chalmers is using *facts* to mean *data*. For him, for example, conscious experience is a further fact and does need further explanation beyond all physical and biological understanding of a person: Chalmers holds that consciousness is something more than mere physics, chemistry, and biology. But, supposedly, no such further considerations pertain in the case of an elephant. Given the "microphysical facts" of physics, an elephant's chemistry, biology, and animal psychology present nothing more to be explained. An elephant entails no further facts beyond physics, but only an enhancement of one consistent physical explanation. A living elephant and an inert rock ultimately evince no significant differences.

That assertion about different but not further facts is perplexing. In the consistent realm of understanding and explanation, in the realm of facts, how can what is different not be something further? The different is the additional, which is the further. To say the fact is different but not additional or further is to say that the different fact is not different. Chalmers's argument obviously violates the principle of non-contradiction: "A thing cannot both be and not be at the same time under the same respect." Of course, this principle only holds for propositions within the realm of intellectual discourse, whereas Chalmers, as I suspect, is mixing in perceptions—sensations, looks, and feelings, which are hardly governed by logic.

Consider, by way of analogy, that mathematicians simplify equations. When they finish their task, the end product looks surprisingly different from the initial equation, but the simplified equation expresses no more intelligibility than the initial equation. What is there to be understood is one and the same. That is the point of simplification: the elimination of extraneous considerations, the expression of what alone matters, a statement of the barest essence of the matter. Only the appearances of the equations differ. The initial equation is more complicated and to this extent includes different elements in comparison to the simplified equation; but when all is said and done, the intelligibility is identical. The equations are equal. In this case, the perceptual difference truly adds nothing further intellectually. The facts are the facts.

Similarly, on Chalmers's analysis, the elephant might look different—a complex expression of matter—but, supposedly, the elephant is essentially nothing more than matter governed by microphysical processes. Between the two—matter and elephant—there is, supposedly, nothing further to be affirmed. The facts about these two, that which could be understood and known, the accounting for what is actually there, must be one and the same. In what, then, do those different but not further "facts" consist? They could only consist in illusory or insignificant differences—size, shape, movement: the elephant might well look like something different from primordial matter, but essentially, ontologically, factually, there is nothing further. The elephant is merely a non-simplified equation. Simplified, the elephant is obviously nothing but matter. The facts of the matter are the facts of matter, period.

Then, what are those "different facts"? Obviously, in this case again, Chalmers is using the term "facts" in two senses. For him, facts about microphysics are intellectual, explanatory, scientific. But "facts" about elephants are only apparent, illusionary, ostensible; they are not genuinely relevant to accurate explanation, not pertinent to ontology.

If this assessment is correct, what are those further but not different, those illusionary factual "facts"? I suspect they are the product of a perceptual, commonsense epistemology intermingled with an intellectual, scientific epistemology. Of course, Chalmers's usage—and Nagel's, as well—could simply be taken as a commonplace loose use of terms. But in these matters, as I am taking pains to demonstrate, such looseness can be catastrophic. Of course, again, Chalmers's distinction could be taken to indicate other genuine facts, that is, actual knowledge about elephants—where they live, what they eat, why they grow, how they mate, how they relate to other organisms in evolutionary history—but these different facts must not be what Chalmers means because they are extraneous to the philosophical topic, materialism. Granted that elephants are, supposedly, nothing but matter and that this determination is the point of interest—facts about elephantine existence are incidental. Besides, Chalmers is quite explicit: the different facts are merely different forms of the same facts; for this reason they are not further facts: "The B-facts [about elephants] merely redescribe what is described by the A-facts [about physics]" (p. 41). These two sets of facts are, as it were, just two different versions of the same equation, so the only difference is in the look of things.

4.18.5. Sensate-Modeled Versus Intellectual Epistemologies

Thus, the look of things and the genuine understanding of things are both posing as "facts." Conflicting epistemologies are at work. One relies on looks; the other relies on understanding. If so, those "different facts" pertaining to elephants are actually percepts. That is to say, in Lonergan's terminology, they are data. However, as additional data, they provide an opening toward something more to be understood. They entail the possibility of genuine facts, further facts, beyond the facts of microphysics. Perforce, they raise interesting questions. Are living things, such as elephants, in fact something different from mere matter? Is emergence a real possibility? Does the term "emergence" have any real meaning? Confounded epistemologies and loosely applied terminology do not facilitate answers. For the present, however, suffice it to say that Chalmers's appeal to *facts* confounds two different epistemologies.

"Facts" that actually add nothing further cannot be different facts. And alongside laws and truths, "facts" offer no supplement. Chalmers's appeal to "facts"—like Nagel's—confounds the intellectual with the perceptual in epistemological inconsistency. So Chalmers's argument about weak emergence is specious. Not even to mention the elephant in the room, when the epistemology remains consistently intellectual, even mere water evinces an instance of genuine emergence. The lower-level laws of chemistry cannot predict the nature of water; its properties cannot be deduced from them. In Chalmers's terminology, water exhibits no logical supervenience with regard to hydrogen and oxygen. Then, consciousness is not the only case of "strong emergence." Confounded epistemologies obscure the other cases.

4.18.6. Bottom-Up Non-Deducibility Versus Unexpectedness

Applying Chalmers's definitions, my focus throughout this discussion is only strong emergence. Only it is genuine emergence; only it is ultimately of interest. My argument is not only cognitive—regarding what we might expect or could explain—but also, concomitantly, ontological. Maintaining with Lonergan (1957/1992; 1980/1990) that knowledge and being are correlates (2.2.9), I reject the commonly proposed distinction between ontological and explanatory reductionism—the assertion, namely, that ontologically all things are nothing more than matter but explanatorily, because of their complexity, we are not able to demonstrate this supposed ontological identity and must settle for a multiplicity of scientific disciplines. On my understanding, what can be deduced from or within a given system is nothing specifically new. Its intelligibility is not different, so it is merely an elaboration, extension, or more intricate aggregation of the given. But what *cannot* be deduced from lower-level systems, what constitutes a new systematization of them—this is new reality.

Of course, most tellingly, the ability ultimately to explain is not the same as the ability to deduce. What we know of water is consistent with our full understanding of chemistry; we understand water. Yet this understanding could not be deduced from the lower-level chemical laws. We need actual instances of water to examine before we can understand its properties and explain its anomaly (4.11.2). Bottom-up deduction does not suffice. Thus, within an intellectual epistemology, bottom-up *non-deducibility* is the criterion of emergence. *Unexpectedness* ultimately matters little. When the unexpected is finally understood, unexpectedness falls out of the picture and, as in the case of water, might be categorized as a fully explicable anomaly. Encounter of the unexpected is but a passing stage in the history of science, an aspect of the ongoing human quest for understanding, but unexpectedness is not pertinent to the ontology of what is to be understood.

Because we can eventually understand the nature and properties of water, it might be tempting to see the synthesis of water from hydrogen and oxygen, at best, as only a "weak emergence," which is to say, actually no genuine emergence at all. This conclusion would be mistaken. In fact, we understand water only top down, only because we have water to examine in the first place. As a bottom-up non-deducible outcome, the emergence of water is genuine; it is "strong." Yet many succumb to the temptation.

In contrast to the example of water, the shift from chemistry to life might more likely suggest a strong emergence, and even more so, the shift from life to perception and especially—as evinced in Chalmers's allowance of only this one case—the shift from perception to consciousness. But why so? Why these inconsistent assessments? Only, I suspect, because we are not yet capable of profound explanation in the more difficult cases, and their unexpectedness, their novelty, and their current opaqueness incline us to recognize them as potential cases of emergence, if only, at this point in time, cases of "weak emergence," that is, only seeming emergence. If someday we could actually account, top down, for these novelties—if we could understand the consistency of consciousness with perception and brain function and the consistency of brain function, biology, and life with chemistry, even as we already understand the consistency of anomalous water and other compounds with synthesis from their atomic components—would we then demote these currently "weak" emergences to the status of no real emergences at all, as we tend to do with water and elephants? For we will, I believe, given a coherent epistemology, eventually be able to project coherence throughout the whole of nature (4.17.2). At that point, will all emergence—now weak, but then demoted to none—fall out of the scientific picture? Will materialist reductionism then appear correct to insist that life, mind, consciousness, and all else are just complex chemistry even as water is merely a molecule—all, supposedly, nothing more than physical matter? In the extreme, as "non-dualist" faddists seem to imagine (e.g., Hong, 1995; Wilber, 1996, pp. 75–77; see 2.3.3; 2.9; 5.8.3), is the ultimate goal of unified science the confirmation that all is one, that the universe is a single, homogenous, undifferentiated . . . mush?

I think not. Neither is such an imaginative, fanciful outcome the goal of physical science in search of a unified field theory. Instructively, unified physical science would be differentiated, multiply explicated, and richly interactively conceived—not a simplistic assertion that all is one. In conclusion, given attention to the preeminence of intelligence in these and all scientific matters, two observations seem apropos.

4.18.7. Conclusions About Weak and Strong Emergence

First, the distinction between weak and strong emergence is not robust. It appears to be an *ad hoc* solution to a problem yet to be resolved. I am arguing that consistent application of an intellectual epistemology points to a genuine resolution of the problem wherein the notion of weak emergence falls out. It is not ultimately helpful.

Second, then, if realities are determined by their intelligibilities—not by perception or imagination—water from hydrogen and oxygen, life from complex organic molecules, and consciousness from perception stand in principle as exactly parallel instances of emergence. None is less or more genuinely emergent—weakly or strongly—than the others. Of course, water and life appear to be very different kinds of reality, and they are. Water is perceptible, so water is more readily said to be real. Life is not perceptible *per se*; so, on the basis of a sensation-based epistemology—which seems ever to haunt these discussions—life would seem not to be real. And this same kind of reasoning would be applied all the more in the case of mental realities such as perception, imagination, emotions, and consciousness. The bugaboo is epistemology.

Chalmers's allowing genuine emergence only in the case of consciousness, but not in these other cases, makes one wonder what kind of epistemology ultimately supports his defense of consciousness, and wonder reciprocally, then, what understanding of consciousness, the "engine" of knowledge, sustains this epistemology. Already at 4.18.5, I have indicated the telling inconsistency—namely, the misidentification of consciousness with perceptual experience—and this matter resurfaces in extensive detail in Chapter 5. On the basis of an intellectual epistemology, water, life, perception, and consciousness equally exhibit reasonably affirmed, distinct intelligibilities. Each evinces a distinctive system specified by its own internal order and, perforce, governed by proprietary laws, consistent, yes, with its sustaining subsystems but, no, not deducible from them. Each, therefore, equally constitutes a distinct and emergent reality.

The widely invoked difference between weak and strong emergence is moot. It does appear that Chalmers (2006) has correctly specified the intellectual criterion of emergence: bottom-up non-deducibility. Further speculation is just obfuscating. Moreover, granted this criterion, application of a consistent intellectual epistemology recognizes emergence throughout the expanse of our dynamic universe, not only in the most fascinating case, that of consciousness.

4.19. Filling in the Gap of Emergence: Dennett

4.19.1. *The Bold Denial of Consciousness*

Daniel Dennett (1991) is notorious for his adamant denial that consciousness is anything in itself, anything apart from the firing of neurons in the brain. I certainly reject this position, but I struggle to understand why Dennett would adopt it, and I discern some positive contribution in his philosophical speculation.

On my reading, Dennett (1991) is actually attempting to bridge the gap between brain and mind; he would spell out the intricacies of the neuronal function that underlies and supports the emergence of consciousness—a worthy scientific project. Dennett, of course, understands this matter in no such way. He acknowledges no emergence and denies that consciousness is any new reality at all. Unabashedly, he is reductionist. In his customarily elusive literary style, he phrases the matter broadly and generically—for example, in terms of "what if?" and with provocative quotation marks around the quintessential reductionist marker *just*, meaning *nothing but*: "if all the phenomena of human consciousness are explicable as 'just' the activities of a virtual machine realized in the astronomically adjustable connections of the human brain . . ." (p. 431). But his point, of course, is that the phenomena of consciousness are, indeed, nothing but those activities of a virtual machine. Moreover, again in elusive circumlocution, Dennett is an outright materialist: "if, on the other hand, we are materialists who are convinced that one way or another our brains are responsible on their own . . . for our understanding . . ." (p. 438). And, curiously, especially in light of the explicitly non-perceptual, theoretical nature of the objects of contemporary physical science—quarks, leptons, and mass (2.2.4; 4.12.1), for example—Dennett opines that "the campaign that used to be waged against materialism has already succumbed to embarrassment" (p. 454).

4.19.2. Another Version of a "Functionalist" Interpretation of the Mind

Dennett (1991) is rightly known for his denial that consciousness is anything other than the activities of the brain. For him, consciousness is something like a program in a computer. Consciousness is a particular pattern of activity in a machine capable of multiple uses. Dennett's position is a version of *functionalism* (pp. 31, 460; Searle, 1997, p. 143)—which means, in this case, that states or patterns of activity in the brain actually have some effect; that is, they perform a function, they do a particular job. (This emphasis attempts to avoid epiphenomenalism. See 2.2.4; 4.12.1.) These states of the brain "show" in varied behaviors, and at the same time these brain states constitute the inner experiences related to those behaviors, such as our beliefs and desires. The experience of having a belief is just the feeling of a particular brain state, just as indigestion, for example, is the feeling of a particular situation in the stomach. These statements would seem commonplace enough if all Dennett meant is that our beliefs, desires, and inner experiences correlate with various states of the brain. But this is not what he means. For Dennett, beliefs, desires, and inner experiences *are* brain states, period; they are nothing other than brain states. Consciousness, like indigestion, is nothing in itself; it's just a particular set of biological circumstances. These circumstances are the makeup of external behaviors and the "subjective" "feel" that accompanies the behaviors. To constitute behaviors and their correlative experiences is the function of brain states.

It is helpful to realize that strict behaviorism provided the model for functionalism. As in behaviorism, one is to deny the reality of inner mentality and attend only to external productions. Supposedly, these are the sum and substance of brain states, and it makes no sense to keep looking inside for some further reality. These states of the brain are completely and merely these states of the brain. There is nothing else. These states are what is called conscious experience. Consciousness and its accompanying behavior is the function of brain states; it's what brains do. The reality of conscious experience is merely the particular state of the brain in question in each case, so the only thing worth attending to are the external behaviors that occur in the everyday, commonsensical world because of the brain states.

Now, I humbly admit, dear reader, that these sentences of mine about functionalism are in part perplexing even to me, yet I have done my best to present a fair and coherent summary statement of this theory. I believe that the conceits controlling functionalism are the behaviorist reduction of mind to behavior—as does philosopher Patrick Grim (2008): "Although philosophers have abandoned the letter of Behaviorism, its spirit lives on in Functionalism" (p. 31). On functionalist grounds, the Turing test is valid—namely, if a machine performs an operation indistinguishable from the performance of a human, the machine must be accorded the same degree of mentality as the human. Within a computer-modeling approach to the mind, functionalism is a theory of how a computer could be said to actually have mind. If a computer performs a certain function, it must have a mind equal to that function. If a calculator can solve arithmetical problems, it must have arithmetical intelligence. To have a mind is simply to behave in a particular way. Searle (1980; 1997, pp. 11–14, 59) proposed his Chinese Room Argument specifically to discredit these ideas (4.9.5).

Knowledge of this historical background makes functionalism somewhat understandable although its argument, stated outright, leaves one wondering. How could states of the brain *be* conscious experiences? Does this mean, rather, that what we experience when we are conscious is actually the state of our brains, just as the experience when we have indigestion is just the state of our stomachs? But the stomach has interoceptive receptors and a system for feedback about its current state; the brain is not equipped with any interoceptive receptors. This is why no anesthetization of the brain is needed during brain surgery. So how could one experience the current state of one's brain? Besides, a physiological experience such as indigestion is quite different from a conscious experience. I am baffled. This line of reasoning makes no sense to me. So if my attempted summary statement does not make sense to you, it is because I can find no way to make a fully sensible statement about functionalism—and I am not alone in lamenting this inadequacy (Blackmore, 2012, pp. 45–46). As for so much else written on the mind–body problem, coherence is often not to be had because, I believe, the arguments are simply not coherent. Rather, circumlocution, double-speak, and imaginative—that is, imaginable—suggestion reign.

4.19.3. Imagining the Brain as a Complex Computer

According to Dennett (1991), "a complicated slew of electrochemical interactions between billions of neurons" . . . "amounts to conscious experience" (p. 433). Expressed otherwise, "Multiple Drafts" of experiential input, "memes" (functioning for "nurture" as genes do for "nature") of enculturated and learned patterns of experience, work together "in the brain's larger economy of controlling a human body's journey through life" (p. 431).

It might be hard, Dennett suggests, to imagine that consciousness could be of this kind, hard to imagine that a computer or a robot could have a mind (p. 432) or that a zombie could actually be conscious—or, more exactly, that we ourselves are actually as unconscious as a zombie (pp. 76, 311, 406). But, Dennett explains, "The way to imagine this is to think of the brain as a computer of sorts. The concepts of computer science provide the crutches of imagination we need if we are to stumble across the *terra incognita* between our phenomenology as we know it by 'introspection' and our brains as science reveals them to us" (p. 433). This is to say, the concepts of computer science provide categories for thinking that could help us imagine how complex patterns of neuronal activity could actually add up to the experience of consciousness.

Dennett is absolutely correct to speak in terms of imagination. The overall style of his presentation, replete with anecdotes and crafted fables, appeals to imagination. He ends his book defending picture-thinking: "metaphors are the tools of thought" (p. 455). Compare what I wrote about implicit definition and the "hard" sciences (4.6.5). Dennett is not even beyond appealing to the fiction of homunculi, miniature imagined humanlike beings who could actually understand (in some unspecified way) and who could subsist in neural networks and in computer programs. "Is it 'cheating,'" he asks (again using elusive quotation marks), "to think of the software as composed of homunculi who quasi-understand . . . ?" (p. 439). Dennett is trying to provoke thought; he is using what he calls "intuition pumps" (pp. 282, 440). Then, let there be no doubt about it: what he is writing is science fiction. His is an imaginative presentation—and this can be to the good.

However, in the serious philosophical and scientific sense of my remarks in this book, Dennett's is also an *imagined* account of consciousness. Although it expresses understanding, its currency is images. It is more a function of psyche than of spirit or intelligence (5.1.1; 5.9.3). It rests on a sensate-modeled epistemology and depends on picture-thinking.

Easily it pictures a conglomeration of miniature bits of quasi-understanding coalesce to form human consciousness and full-blown understanding. Every "little bit of brain activity" (p 439) adds to the heap that mounts to an overall conscious experience. But how so? Dennett insists "it is hard to imagine how 'just more of the same' could add up to understanding" (p. 439). Yes, the supposition does boggle the inquisitive mind. But in another sense, to imagine this scenario is easy. One just posits it. After all, this is fiction. One just suspends disbelief. One curtails critical thinking. *The Matrix* movies and, as adaptations of a 1978 series, the third-millennium TV series *Battlestar Galactic* and *Caprica* have featured conscious computers for decades. Science fiction is replete with stories of robots who achieve mind, such as Hal of *2001: A Space Odyssey*. To imagine such an outcome is easy, and it is easy even to *imagine* how it could occur. What is difficult is to *explain* it, to propose a coherent account, one free from infinite regress and concepts pieced together like available parts already lying about. Like Griffin (1991) with "experience" and Chalmers (1996) with "information" (4.20 & 4.21), Dennett smuggles into his lower-levels the elements of consciousness—"quasi-understanding"—that in themselves are unreal but that, nonetheless, supposedly subsist in microlevel amounts, which, when combined, somehow produce full-blown consciousness, which is also not supposed to be real. It is easy to picture such a creation. Children playing with dolls and toys achieve something of the same all the time; they join together pieces and parts until, in their play world, they produce their own living, breathing, and speaking creations.

However, moving from science fiction to actual scientific explanation, how does one elude the constraints of Gödel's theorem (4.16)? How does one coherently arrive at the human experience of consciousness on the computational basis of a slew of electrochemical interactions? One can easily fantasize the shift, but one cannot so easily explain it.

Of course, Dennett (1991) does not claim to explain it. He denies the distinct reality of consciousness from the start. Although he labors to explain how such a set of experiential data could emerge—"our phenomenology as we know it by 'introspection'" (p. 433)—he denies that the data pertain to any new reality. He does not have to make any incoherent leaps of assertion. On his understanding, there is nothing to which to leap, nothing to assert. I continue to wonder, however, why anyone would even begin such an account as Dennett's when, supposedly, there is nothing real in experience to prompt one to inquire about it. And I wonder about the nature of that very urge to inquire, which drives Dennett as much as it drives all other humans and which Dennett uses so very intelligently and creatively.

4.19.4. Speculation as a Stepping Stone to Science

No doubt, Dennett's overall position is epistemologically flawed in many ways. It is not a genuine account of human consciousness. As even he admits, it's "more art than science" (p. 440). Indeed, it's literature, science fiction, fanciful and erudite speculation about the unreal.

Nonetheless, what I see in Dennett's speculation is an attempt to elaborate the lower-level neural realities, the non-systematic manifold of recurrent processes, which a higher order systematizes as consciousness (4.14.1). He is trying to fill in "the huge gap between phenomenology and physiology" (p. 434). He does so, of course, by denying any reality proper to the phenomenology and thereby eliminating an ontological gap. I, on the other hand, understand his efforts as a contribution to the task of filling in a genuine gap, of specifying the substratum needed to support the emergence of consciousness. Just as a hard-won explanation of atomic structure allows us to understand water as H_2O although water, dependent on hydrogen and oxygen, is neither hydrogen nor oxygen nor a property of either, but a new reality with its own laws and properties; so the effort to understand neurological function might allow us, someday, to credibly explicate the substratum of sensation, perception, and imagination out of which consciousness emerges although it itself is neither sensation nor perception nor imagination, and even less the biochemical processes of the brain, but a new reality specified by the intelligibility inherent in the experiential data it provides.

To be sure, the leap from atoms to molecules, $2 H_2 + O_2 \rightarrow 2 H_2O$, all within the material realm, seems incommensurate with the leap from physiology, sensation, perception, and mental imagery to human consciousness. In the latter case, the leap seems to be from matter to mind, whereas chemical elements and their resultant molecules seem to present merely, consistently, unequivocally "only physical matter" (especially when they are conceived as pictured or imagined). Nonetheless, the same process of intellectual knowing (dependent, rather, on intelligibility) applies consistently in both cases, so the one conclusion should be as legitimate and robust as the other. Water is a new reality in relation to hydrogen and oxygen, and consciousness is a new reality in relation to neuronal function, sensation, perception, and imagination.

4.19.5. Multiple Kinds of Matter

More radically, these considerations ought to suggest that, in speaking of "physical matter," we tend ever and again to fall back onto sensation-modeled thinking. Only thus could we so glibly contend that it's all "just physical matter." Contemporary awareness of the significantly different intelligibilities—scientific explanations—of quarks, leptons, other particles, atoms, and molecules, each implicating different implicitly defined systems with proprietary laws, should suggest we have oversimplified "matter" by subsuming these all under one and the same category. This is the conclusion that follows from application of Lonergan's intellectual epistemology. Strikingly, evidence from contemporary physics supports it (Goldman 2007).

Cahoone (2008) usefully reminds us that "the physical is not just matter; indeed, matter constitutes a minority interest in a universe that, given recent estimates, is mostly 'dark matter'" (p. 48). Today, the field of physics concerns itself with radiation in addition to matter. Radiation and matter have different properties, exhibit different intelligibilities, and demand different explanations; and they exercise "asymmetric roles in cosmogenesis" (p. 49). As best we currently know on the basis of an intellectual epistemology, radiation and matter are not one and the same. So the physical, the object of study in physics, includes more than matter. Intense quantum-physical debate surrounds this issue. Such debate focuses on "the decoherence of the wave function" (3.5) as the very point of crossover from microlevel wave functions to macrolevel particles. This crossover is the point of emergence of the realm of classical physics from that of quantum physics (Joos, 2006). Some argue that the decoherence is a genuine "collapse" so that the multiple possibilities in the quantum realm cease to have relevance; others insist that no collapse happens and the multiple possibilities of reality remain as alternate universes. The prior opinion seems more reasonable because it is based on available data about the *de facto* human world rather than on ungrounded speculation and imagination about possible parallel universes. I recall that ontological emergence or emergent probability is a probabilistic process, and it entails the waste of the multiple possibilities inherent in it (4.15.4). Our understanding of the universe that we do experience gives us no reason to believe that every possibility must be actualized, no reason to posit universes that we do not experience. To posit such alternative universes violates the canons of empirical method (Lonergan, 1957/1992, pp. 93–125) by relying on idealist speculation rather than appeal to empirical evidence (2.3.6). Whatever the case, however, the decoherence of quantum physics might document an instance of emergence as tightly explained as the chemical synthesis of H_2O.

Is it not, therefore, time to nuance talk about a supposed homogenous stuff out there, "physical matter"? Atoms

> are not the irreducible particles the Ancients expected. Rather, they are elaborate little universes in themselves, made up of even more microscopic, or subatomic, particles, some of which at the end of the day don't look at all material. In fact, the line between matter and energy gets blurry at this level, leading to another counterintuitive conclusion: that matter and energy are interchangeable. (Donald, 2001, p. xi)

Blatantly, this category *matter* is a leftover of commonsensical opinion dating from long before modern physics and chemistry developed. Such a primitive notion should hardly continue to control current thinking.

More promisingly, we might speak of kinds of matter. But, I fear, we would likely continue to categorize matter on the basis of perception and imagination—not scientific explanation. We have long outgrown the simple commonsense categories of the Twenty Questions game: animal, vegetable, or mineral. To be sure, when concern turns to biochemicals, cells, tissues, organs, and sensate organisms, a completely new category of "matter," so-called "living matter," is in question (4.18.4). All the more forcefully the phenomenon of life begs for greater precision in our thinking and speaking about matter. Moreover, beyond all sensate and perceptual organisms, there is the intellectually conscious human being, still a sensate and perceptual organism and still composed of atoms and molecules, but, again, a significantly new and different kind of matter, a "conscious living matter."

By discerning and sorting out conjugates within things, an intellectually coherent account can make sense of these differences and on the same epistemological basis explain them as the different kinds of realities they are (4.13; 4.22). In contrast, now more than ever, the materialist reductionism of Dennett and others appears to be gross, unscientific oversimplification.

4.19.6 In Search of Bold Hypotheses

Nonetheless, given a framework in which all the pieces could coherently fit together, Dennett's (1991) projection of possible neural bases of consciousness might be a useful contribution. After all, "literary theorists do valuable, honest intellectual work describing fictional entities" (p. 95). In the least, as Dennett intends, his fiction opens up speculation that might trigger a viable hypothesis and eventually contribute to genuine explanation. His efforts might legitimately help fill in the explanatory gap of emergence from the brain to consciousness. Undoubtedly, human science will eventually specify this emergence—perhaps even as coherently as the emergence of water from hydrogen and oxygen or of composite particles from quarks and leptons. For the present, however, we grope in darkness—and we fantasize: we perform thought-experiments and propose "intuition pumps." Granted also an adequate epistemology, we might also gain scientific benefit from the pumped intuitions.

4.20. Panpsychic Construal of Emergence: Griffin for Whitehead

4.20.1. Emergence as the Aggregation of Lower-Level Bits of a Reality

I have explained emergence as a higher-level integration of lower-level patterns of recurrence. In this Lonerganian sense, newly emergent things ("unities-identities-wholes" grasped by intelligence as single entities) represent a higher systematization of lower-level things, which, no longer as independent existents or things in their own right, now subserve the new thing merely as its conjugates (properties, features, aspects). An emergent is a system of underlying systems of systems. Its unity and actuality depend, not on its being visible or palpable as a coherent conglomerate, but on its entailing a new intelligibility. An emergence presents a new synthesis. Thus, for example, humans commonly engage in abstract thinking, but, as far as we know, cows do not. This realization allows that distinctively human consciousness (5.1.2) is truly a kind of reality in itself, that it truly exists as a conjugate of a complex thing, the person (4.13; 4.22), and that it appears as a new kind of reality only at a certain point in evolution.

Other theorists propose different accounts of emergence. Not uncommonly, philosophers have suggested that in varying degrees consciousness or a propensity toward it—the difference is critical but is insufficiently considered—inheres in all things. If this claim about "low-level consciousness" is accurate, the emergence of full-blown consciousness in humans would no longer seem remarkable. High-level human consciousness would be just the accumulation or aggregation of all that low-level consciousness. Noted repeatedly but never addressed at the international conference *Toward a Science of Consciousness 2014* in Tucson, Arizona, the major challenge to these theories of accumulative consciousness is to explain the compounding that would add up to the human experience of consciousness. I think there is no explanation because the very presuppositions of the problem are mistaken. We have just seen such an emphasis in Dennett's (1991) positing "quasi-understanding" in computer programs and brain processes, which supposedly accumulates to become full-blown consciousness in the human mind. By way of further example, I focus on the positions of David Griffin (1991) and then David Chalmers (1996).

4.20.2. Ubiquitous Experience

To make his case, Griffin (1991) appeals to the thought of Alfred North Whitehead (1929/1978) and the tradition of process and emergence theorists. In a word, Griffin's position is "panexperientialism" (p. 57), for which the older term is *panpsychism* (from the Greek *pan* + *psyche* = everything [is] mind). The summary notion is that experience is built into all levels of reality, so the emergence of experience as also conscious in humans is nothing completely novel. This position is a version of epiphenomenalism (4.5; 4.7) in that it allows for bottom-up causality, but not top-down. It also includes a version of emergence in that it attempts to explain how, through evolution, consciousness eventually becomes full-blown in humans. As is determinative of epiphenomenalism, the goal is to disallow any causality (top-down) to the mind and, thus, to deny that " 'consciousness' refers either to some full-fledged actuality or to the 'stuff' of some full-fledged actuality (namely, the mind)" (p. 53).

Griffin summarizes his position as follows: "Consciousness in itself *is* virtually epiphenomenal, being a nearly nonefficacious by-product of nonconscious experience" (p. 60). At stake again—although, this time, under the name of "full-fledged actualities" or their "stuff"—is that need of a sensate-modeled epistemology to reject its pictured dualism even while inconsistently affirming that consciousness is somehow, nonetheless, not reducible to physical reality. Ever and again, the desire to avoid the misconceived dualism of a sensate-modeled epistemology controls the argument (2.2.8; 4.8.4; 4.10.2; 4.12.4). Under this same constraint, also wanting to preserve the coherence of a naturalistic, a scientific, worldview, American pragmatist Charles Sanders Peirce also endorsed a form of panpsychism (cf. Cahoone, 2008, pp. 55–56).

According to Griffin (1991), realities at all levels have experiences. That Fido and other animals have experiences is, supposedly, a commonplace (p. 54). More controversial but nonetheless real, according to Griffin, would be experiences of, say, the chemical activity of macromolecules in brain cells. This biochemical example instantiates Griffin's analogy for a proposed resolution of the mind–body problem—namely, the fact that chemical reactions can play into cellular processes provides an example of bottom-up causality, the effect of lower-level experiences on higher-level experiences. This analogy supposedly suggests how, in the form of conscious experience, the mind could likewise emerge from the brain (p. 55). What exactly Griffin means by "experience" is difficult to know. Central to his meaning, however, is the insistence that even the physical world is filled with "spontaneities, in the sense of the capacity for self-determination" (p. 58). What can we make of this proposal?

4.20.3. Something of Consciousness Compounding Through All Levels of Reality

I believe that, by the composite notion of experience and spontaneity, Griffin means to refer to all the inherent and systematic processes that contemporary science has discerned from the formation of quarks after the Big Bang to the emergence of particles, then atoms, molecules, life, and so on up the line. He wants to attribute experience to these natural processes at every level—hence, to my mind, the absolute appropriateness of the term *panpsychism*. Clearly, Griffin is affirming the same compounding processes of emergence that I have invoked in my argument for emergence in cosmogenesis, evolution, and social history (4.2.2; 4.7; 4.14.2). Herein, then, lies an important similarity in our positions. However, I would never think, because of their "spontaneities," to call those processes *experiences*. Moreover, I would steer clear of the highly ambiguous description of these natural spontaneities as "self-determining." This term could suggest that, like persons, these natural spontaneities actually have a "self" that can both determine things and develop and, for this reason, they could have experiences. Still, in affirming some version of emergence, at least we have one point of similarity in our positions. There is a potential second.

Griffin's reason for suggesting that these physical, chemical, and biological processes are actually experiences is to have something of consciousness already afoot at those lower levels. Then the eventual emergence of full-blown consciousness at the top does not seem so novel. The parallel in my argument lies in my insistence that all realities entail intelligibilities, that is, cognitive meaning to be discerned, something to be understood—for example, attribution of the consensual concept "chair" to appropriate perceptual experience (2.8.2), specification of a particular relationship among the legs and hypotenuse of the right triangle in Euclid (4.6.5), or the explanation of the anomalous properties of H_2O (4.11.2). Insisting on intelligibilities as literally constitutive of realities and speaking in Lonergan's technical terms of explanation, not mere description (4.6.4; 4.12), I could fully agree with Griffin's (1991) "assertion that *no* things or processes in the world can be adequately [explained] in physicalistic terms" (p. 55). In a loose sense, then, one could say that I also posit something of consciousness in realities at every level.

4.20.4. Intelligibilities, Not Experiences, and Neither Without Intelligence

However, intelligibilities are not experiences. Intelligibilities are not solo agents, rogue vigilantes, already out there acting on their own and, via supposedly self-aware interrelationships among the discernible factors at stake in each case, precipitating experiences. Only imagination would seem to suggest such an account, picturing some deliberate tug-and-pull interaction on the part of these intelligibly discerned then reified explanatory factors. Intelligence-based knowing would not—because intelligence is needed to discern the interactions of the telling factors that intelligibilities entail, and there is no reason to believe that non-human realities possess the requisite reflective intelligence. The relationship and difference between intelligibility and intelligence need to be maintained (Lonergan, 1957/1992, p. 347).

It makes no sense to speak of intelligibilities apart from intellectual consciousness. Intelligibility is potential, a possibility of being understood. Only the "light" of human intelligence first reveals that possibility and then turns it into actual explanation (2.3.1; 2.3.3). The interacting elements, whose interrelationship intelligence specifies to produce explanation, do not themselves understand their interrelationship. They are not intelligent, so their intelligibility cannot be actualized in and of itself. It's not as if they know what they are—and, then, could be having experiences, self-aware interactions.

There are, indeed, discernible lawful interactions among the explanatory factors in lower-level realities. There are intelligibilities there to be discerned. Discerning and explicating them is what science is about. But without intelligence these realities could not experience, conceptualize, and know their own interacting factors. How could these interactions genuinely be experiences? Should we say that *a*, *b*, and *c* are having a satisfying, harmonious experience because they enjoy a precisely definable and mutually constraining interrelationship that determines a Euclidean right triangle? A literal assertion would be sheer anthropomorphism, material for an animated cartoon. At best, use of the term *experience* in such situations is metaphor.

A major new emergence is at stake when the intelligibility in question at the highest level is intelligence itself—that is, the distinctive quality of a person—when that which is there to be understood is understanding itself, when that which explains the uniqueness of humanity is the very capacity for explanation, when "in the limiting case of man [and woman], the intelligible yields to the intelligent" (Lonergan, 1957/1992, p. 294). This new emergence regards human consciousness and the abstractive intelligence it entails. Only through such human intelligence are the intelligibilities that pertain in all realities and at every level grasped and known. To posit intelligibilities at every level, discerning intelligence—and consciousness—must already be presupposed. But apart from human accounts of them, I do not hear any macromolecules in the brain narrating their experiences. Those brain processes do have intelligibilities, they can be understood, but the processes have no intelligence by which to understand themselves.

To posit "experiences" at every level provides no illuminating substitute or synonym for the intelligibilities that intelligence could grasp. But Griffin's proposal seems to suggest that it does. His proposal certainly insists that something that already in some sense participates in consciousness, namely, experience, occurs at every level; and the reason for his insistence is, indeed, to already have something consciousness-like at every level so that the eventual emergence of full-blown human consciousness would appear to be nothing novel. Stated outright, Griffin smuggles consciousness, disguised as experience, into all processes in the universe. His insistence on the imaginative oxymoron "nonconscious experience" (p. 55) enables the disguise. Obviously, the weak point in Griffin's argument is the nebulous notion of experience. Nonetheless, by suggesting it, Griffin does posit in realities at all levels something consciousness-like as a parallel to intelligibility—namely, experience—something inherently related to consciousness. So, in fuzzy formulation, we agree that "something of consciousness" pertains at all levels.

I have pointed out two instances in which Griffin's proposal parallels mine and in some way highlights important and valid considerations—namely, (a) systemic processes constitutive of realities compounding, complexifying, and emerging at ever higher levels and (b) "something of consciousness" already afoot in each of those levels. I now turn to criticism of Griffin's key concept, experience.

4.20.5. *The Oxymoronic Anthropomorphism of Unconscious Experience*

Roger Sperry hit the nail on the head and succinctly stated the error in panpsychism: "subjective qualities are . . . of very different quality from the neural, molecular, and other material components of which they are built" (cited in Griffin, 1991, p. 57). That is, even to attribute experience to lower-level realities still does not explain the particular subjective quality of consciousness when it arises in humans. Alternatively, to project some consciousness-like quality into lower level realities, namely, experience, is to attribute to them peculiar qualities for which they evince no evidence. In a word, to posit experience, a subjective category, in non-conscious processes is sheer anthropomorphism.

Of course, the heart of Griffin's argument is precisely his supposition, borrowed from Whitehead, that experience need not be conscious. I categorically reject this supposition, and I suggest its error. It seems to depend on a taint of picture-thinking that imagines some deliberate push-pull interaction among the "parts" of physical, chemical, and biological processes; and because there is intelligibility to be discerned in those processes and because intelligent humans can, perforce, know of them, this picture-thinking attributes "experience" to the processes themselves: anthropomorphism. The error is to confound and combine sensate knowing and intellectual knowing. The error is to reify the interrelationships of intelligently discernible explanatory factors in lower-level realities and then to picture the factors as interacting like gremlins in a machine, happily engaging one another and making merry on their own: they are having experiences!

To clarify the point, consider what constitutes experience. I do not consider *experience* to be a synonym for *interaction*, nor an appropriate metaphor or alternative term for interaction. As I am arguing here, experience is a distinctively human category. It names a particular human occurrence. In the common usage of the term (but not Lonergan's technical usage wherein *experience* names conscious function only on a first level: 2.2.1; 5.7.2), experience entails interaction that is reflexively conscious—such that I could speak of "my experience last night." Experience presupposes the capacity to be present "to" (5.3.1) one's own engagements with other things and then to reflect on those engagements as such, not simply to interact with the things engaged. That presupposed self-presence is the essential dimension of consciousness, which I find almost universally overlooked (5.4.1). Misconceiving consciousness, theorists are free to make what they want of it and, then, find it—rather, find what they've made of it—wherever they want. Thus, if experience is thought to be simply the encounter of one thing with another, then experience is everywhere in the natural world. But if experience depends on the self-conscious capacity to make that encounter itself the very object of one's explicit awareness and possible report, then experience pertains only where this peculiar kind of self-consciousness is operative. As far as we have evidence to determine, this latter set of circumstances pertains only in the case of human beings.

Does a tree limb that falls into a pond share an experience with the water, just as people can experience jumping into a pool? We already have assigned names and concepts—which entail sophisticated and verified intelligibilities—for the inanimate processes of falling and impact, which are in question. In the case of inanimate objects, what justifies the addition of another name and concept, "experience," to these others? Should we call the falling limb's "experience" *gravity*? And the water's "experience," *impact* at level $F = ma$? That we humans can discern and even specify the intelligibility in those physical interactions does not mean that the elements involved—the tree limb, the water—also discern the intelligibility and, thus, have an experience of those processes. There is no reason to project into those processes what only humans have, namely, self-conscious intelligence. There is no sense, apart from idiosyncratic terminological usage, in the Whiteheadian notion that at those lower levels an "occasion of experience" is "a subject" (Griffin, 1991, pp. 59–60), in whatever sense. Our physical explanations of the interactions already provide the necessary and sufficient explanation. By Occam's razor, there is no need to add the quality of "experience." Besides, as an actual phenomenon, experience has its own intelligibility; it entails reflexive awareness and, perforce, usually some possibility of being conceptualized and articulated. The intelligibility specific to experience does not pertain to falling limbs in themselves or to the ponds they hit—nor, despite prevalent ambiguous usage to the contrary, to unattended human occurrences, such as myriad perceptual inputs that never rise to the level of awareness, even as William James (1890/1950) put it: "My experience is what I agree to attend to" (vol. I, p. 402).

The same criticism, with further complexity, also holds in the case of Fido. Although most people would allow that animals have experiences, we say so, again, only anthropomorphically, only by projecting onto other animals what we humans experience in similar cases. The data on these two instances, human and non-human, are considerably different. Accordingly, the intelligibilities must also differ, so they cannot pertain to one and the same reality. This is not to deny that sensate and perceptual animals actively engage other things in the world and respond appropriately or to deny that they have sensations, memories, perceptual mental constructions, and physiological reactions, including pleasure and pain (Donald, 2001). It is to deny that they have reflexive awareness of these instances (data) and, far more, that they conceptualize them intelligently (understanding), verify their conceptualizations (judgment) (2.1.6), and could, in the general case, narrate them as "personal experiences": animals are not persons. To attribute experiences unqualifiedly to animals is to confound the sensate/perceptual and the intellectual natures of two different kinds of engagement and two different kinds of "knowing" (2.2.5; 5.1.2; 5.5.5). The fact that we humans can have purely sensate experience (for example, pain) as well as conscious experience ("It really hurt") makes it easy for us to attribute to other sensate creatures the same experiences that we have. But they are not the same.

4.20.6. The Subjective Form of an Intellectual . . . Feeling?

A similar confounding of sensate/perceptual experience and knowing, with intellectual experience and knowing, reins at the heart of Whitehead's definition of consciousness and controls the accompanying explanation of how it eventually emerges atop a series of "occasions of experience." Supposedly, lower-level processes are "experiences" for the "individuals" involved, and these experiences entail "feelings (or prehensions)," which accumulate and compound from the bottom up, level by level (Griffin, 1991, p. 54). At stake, supposedly, is "a process of creative synthesis," which "involves several phases [level by level], in which the received feelings are integrated into a more-or-less sophisticated prehensive unity. Consciousness arises, if at all, only in a late, derivative phase of the most sophisticated occasions of experience" (p. 54). And consciousness itself "*is the subjective form of an intellectual feeling*" (p. 52, italics original).

I am hard pressed to imagine what these prehensions, feelings, and consciousness as an intellectual feeling could be. I do not know what data would ground these concepts. Like the imaginative speculation of Baruch Spinoza, to which they hark back, or the logically coherent but empirically irrelevant creations of mathematicians, these concepts seem devoid of empirical reference. At best, they refer to the intelligently discernible relationships inherent in and among those non-human realities; but these can be specified with much more precision—as I just exemplified in the case of the limb's falling into the pond—than by predications such as "prehensions" and "feelings." Feelings are one thing, and consciousness is another: their intelligibilities differ (4.2.2; 4.14.1; 5.1.1). So, in my mind, the notion of "an intellectual feeling" is an oxymoron. I also wonder whether the ambiguous term *feelings* refers to something physical or emotional or even to intelligently discerned relationships, but I know that in current understanding feeling depends on the functioning of particular biological organs, which we are capable of specifying in elaborate detail and which are utterly lacking in non-sensate beings, so I have no idea what *feelings* could mean for them; and I have no idea what a "subjective form of an intellectual feeling" might be, either. Obviously, within the intricate system of Whiteheadian thought, these terms are used with non-standard meanings, so the face meaning of the proposed account appears rather opaque. I allow that an expert in Whitehead might make sense of them, and I confess that I am no such expert. To me, this much seems likely: this creative theory indiscriminately mixes the material, biological, emotional, and intellectual and loses their distinctiveness and interrelationships in the process. The apparent attempt to project some unification among these disparate aspects of humanity is welcome. As for the rest, I must leave it to others to sort out.

Nonetheless, my point: Griffin attempts to explain consciousness via emergence from an unfolding series of lower-level processes. As I interpret it, this attempt entails three assertions: a plurality of ever more complex realities builds up level by level; a cosmic dynamism operates throughout the overall process level to level; and consciousness is the final result, dependent on this complexifying series of lower-level realities. This triple assertion lends support to the hypothesis of emergence as an explanation for consciousness. On the other hand, this Whiteheadian attempt to explain consciousness confounds different ways of knowing—and explicitly so under the aegis of "experience." This set of affairs provides another reminder of the central challenge of the mind–body problem, namely, to have an epistemology adequate to it.

4.21. Panpsychic Construals of Emergence: Chalmers

4.21.1. *Consciousness and Matter as Primordial Realities of Nature*

David Chalmers (1996) offers another, and highly elaborated, theory of consciousness. It also contains a dimension that could qualify as emergence. Accepting the name dualist, Chalmers posits two mutually irreducible, natural realities in the universe: matter and consciousness. He nuances his assertion regarding consciousness: "I would bet fairly confidently that experience [or consciousness] is fundamental, and weakly that experience is ubiquitous" (p. 357). Granted these odds, supposedly consciousness may exist alongside matter even at the quantum level. Instances of consciousness, "protophenomenal" or "microphenomenal properties" (pp. 154, 304–305) at those lowest levels, somehow in compounding accretion add up to full-blown conscious or phenomenal experience at the human level. As also in the cases of Dennett's (1991), Griffin's (1991) and Penrose and Hameroff's (2011; 3.5), so, too, in the case of Chalmers's, it might not be fully accurate to call these theories "emergentism" because these theories hold consciousness to already exist at all levels of reality. That is, these theories do not hold that consciousness actually emerged as a new kind of reality on the basis of the complexification and higher integrations of lower-level realities, as genuine emergentism would hold. Nonetheless, insofar as these theories imagine consciousness to grow and expand to human form across the unfolding universe from the Big Bang onward, I treat these theories under the category "emergence." They do propose theories of how *human* consciousness is real and comes to be.

4.21.2. Ubiquitous Information

Despite important different twists, Chalmers's theory is susceptible to the same line of criticism as is Griffin's: Chalmers's theory also appeals to an anthropomorphic metaphor that allows the theory to insinuate primordial facets of consciousness everywhere. The metaphor for Griffin was experience; for Chalmers it is information. Widespread usage in the computer age unthinkingly appropriates the metaphor "information" and, as technically defined in computer science, rightly posits it at every level of reality. But like *experience,* the term *information* also finds its original meaning in the context of human intelligence and knowledge, so, despite its technical definition, the very term *information* likewise imports connotations of consciousness wherever it goes and likewise suggests the presence of intelligibility (4.20.3). Thus, residing in all things, information also supposedly entrains in all of them varying degrees of consciousness.

This problem of imported anthropomorphic insinuations is a common one. Donald (2001) exposes it well in regard to use of the term *algorithm,* which in some cases could almost serve as an alternative to *information*:

> Algorithms . . . are notations that capture the solution to a mathematical problem. Strictly speaking, there are no algorithms in nature. They exist only in our descriptions of nature. . . . Causal chains in the natural world are commonly referred to as

algorithms, but this can be a misleading use of language. It confounds the symbols with what they represent. (pp. 153–154)

Risking such confounding, the notion of information serves as the linchpin of Chalmers's (1996) theory of consciousness. Claude Shannon (Shannon & Weaver, 1998/1948) is noted for specifying *information* as a formally defined construct in information theory. Bateson (1972) provided an easily accessible formulation of the technical construct as "a *difference that makes a difference*" (Chalmers, 1996, p. 281; italics in original). So, for example, the difference between a light switch's being up or down determines whether the light goes on or off; this pattern, built into the switch, is information. In contrast, the switch's being only halfway up might not yet matter, so no effect would result, and the position of halfway up would carry no information. Similarly, the alternations in reflectivity on a CD or DVD carry information in the pattern of their placement, and when passed by an optical laser reader, the pattern of alternations on the disk produces a correlative stream of shifting electrical impulses that are ultimately converted into sounds or visual images. Understood in this way, it is clear, information is everywhere. The sharing of electrons in a chemical bond, the transportation of molecules across a cell membrane, the firing of neurons in the brain, the clicks of the cogs on the gears in a machine, the settings on a thermostat, the patterned array in a visual display—all are instantiations or realizations of information.

It is important to note that the stream of electrical impulses or the actual gears in the machine are not themselves the information; rather, the pattern of the variations is. Information is a theoretical notion; it is an abstraction. Information as such is not identical to the material itself; rather, the physical world can "realize" information, that is, instantiate or carry information. In common technical usage, information is said to constitute or reside in an "information space." Alternatively and more accurately conceived, even in information-theory usage, information can also be called, and is, data, that which could be understood and, as understood, has meaning. Use of the term *data* in a Lonerganian context highlights the all-telling connection to human intelligence, for which alone, I argue, there are data or information, that is, something to be known (2.2.1).

4.21.3. *Information as the Bridge Between Brain and Mind*

Applying that notion of information, Chalmers (1996) posits a link between the processes of the brain and the experiences of phenomenal consciousness: in two different formats, brain and mind carry one and the same information. Thus, "Whenever we find an information space realized phenomenally [i.e., consciously, in the mind], we find the same information space realized physically [in the brain]. And when an experience realizes an information state, the same information state is realized in the experience's physical substrate" (p. 284).

So far, so good—if intelligibility were in question; but Chalmers is speaking of a perceptible patterned array, not of intelligence or understanding. Note that, if à la Lonergan *information* were taken to mean *intelligibility* or *meaning*, the same in the understanding mind as in the understood data, then a unity would, indeed, be accounted for. The unity would be the identity of understanding and understood that pertains to the unitive moment of insight: "*intellectus in actu fit intellectum in actu*" (2.3.3). But Chalmers's usage is doubly different. First, not mind and world, but mind and brain, are in question. Chalmers is not referring to intelligence's encountering data in the universe of being; rather, he is referring to the mind's corresponding in some way with the neuronal firing patterns in the brain. Second, his analysis is completely perceptual. At issue are patterns that instantiate information—not data, insight, and concepts. There is nothing of intelligence at work in his analysis at this point.

Chalmers expresses that same theory in other terms. In his terminology, the "awareness" that results in a perceptual system—the sheer registration of, the response to, input stimuli—is an exact parallel to the experience that results in one's phenomenal *consciousness* of the percept. Note that for Chalmers *awareness* refers to a mechanical perceptual process, and *consciousness*, to a subjective one. The "patterns of similarity and difference" or the "similarity and difference relations" (p. 284) in a conscious experience carry the same information that the perceptual system carries. Think about seeing a panorama: visual experience is the paradigmatic example here. Of course, to imagine a visual panorama as similar in layout to the image on the retina and in the visual cortex is to think of information perceptually, as visible or imaginable patterns in physical space and time. Technically, however, information is an abstraction in an information space. In fact, information consists of intelligently grasped patterns, the intelligibility instantiated in this or that medium or format. As such, information only exists as a theoretical construct, and its very existence depends on its being grasped by intelligence. Yet explicit attention to intelligence plays no part in Chalmers's theory of consciousness. Perception rules all. Information *is* perceptual patterns. For this reason, his application of "information" is seriously problematic. This slippage back and forth from concrete perceptions to abstract theory pervades Chalmers's appeal to information.

So, in summary thus far, for whatever it means, Chalmers uses *information* as the bridge between brain and mind. Because the information in both is supposedly one and the same, this approach seems to account for a unity of body and mind.

However, to make his explanation work and to have it for further application, Chalmers needs to tighten up his understanding of awareness, so he does. For him the term "awareness" applies to any input we take in—any perceptual response, for example, is an instance of awareness (pp. 28–29). However, some of it remains subliminal; it has no correlate in consciousness (p. 233). James (1890/1950) offered a classic statement about this very selectivity, summarizing as follows: "We see that the mind is at every stage a theatre of simultaneous possibilities. Consciousness consists in the comparison of these with each other, the selection of some, and the suppression of the rest by the reinforcing and inhibiting agency of attention" (vol. I, p. 288). In Chalmers's (1996) terminology, the exact opposite of mine (1.9), we can be *aware* of things of which we are not *conscious*. This situation applies at the fringes of our visual field (pp. 27, 229). Memories offer another example (p. 221): they can be stored in the brain without being active in the mind, yet the fact that they could come up shows that they are there, shows that they are in my "awareness." So there exists a disconnection between awareness and consciousness, and it challenges Chalmers's theory of the unity of brain and mind.

Chalmers chooses to put these considerations aside. He opines, "It is more satisfying to put restrictions on the notion of awareness so that it is more truly parallel to consciousness" (p. 222). His theory needs awareness and consciousness to correspond, so he makes it so. After all, there is a difference between what is present to mind actively and what is not. "Perhaps the most salient difference is that in cases of awareness with consciousness, there is a kind of *direct* access that cases of awareness without consciousness lack." This direct access would make "a difference in the deliberate control of behavior." Such "functional differences" count heavily in Chalmers's theory. After all, it is "a dualistic version of functionalism" (p. 245), a matter of behavior in the external world. Chalmers argues that he "can therefore build this directness of access into a revised notion of awareness" (p. 222). He will make awareness and consciousness always correspond.

Confusingly, as I understand Chalmers's functionalism defined by his emphasis on external behaviors, the processes of the brain already account for all functions or behaviors, so it remains unclear what those functional differences because of consciousness might be. It is unclear why direct access to input, rather than merely subliminal, makes any behavioral or functional difference because, supposedly, all behaviors result from the cognitive processes in the brain, not from consciousness, in any case. At this point Chalmers is one with Dennett (1991). Quite logically, Dennett is willing to draw the natural conclusion: if brain processes explain all behaviors, if consciousness makes no difference, consciousness must be nothing at all; it does not exist; we only think it does (2.1.4; 4.19). But constrained by his personal experience of consciousness, Chalmers cannot take that logical path, so he posits consciousness as a fundamental principle of the universe, which, however, makes no real difference at all. Chalmers's zombie twin, for example, which has no consciousness, supposedly behaves externally in all discernible ways exactly as does the conscious Chalmers (1996, pp. 94–95, 120–121, 156, 158–160). Consciousness doesn't matter for explaining what goes on in our world. Therefore, the directness of access to the contents of awareness seems irrelevant. Why does Chalmers make a point of it? . . . Ah, but let's get on with exposition of the theory.

Declaring a correlation between awareness and experience, Chalmers formulates a principle: "consciousness is always accompanied by awareness, and vice versa. . . . this relationship provides a useful focal point in understanding the coherence between consciousness and cognition" (p. 222), that is, between mind and brain. Reformulated in terms of information, this coherence becomes "the double-aspect principle": "When a system is aware of some information, in the sense that the information is directly available for global control [of behavior], the information is conscious" (p. 237); "the space of relevant possible [information] states here [in the visual cortex] is isomorphic to the space of possible experiences; so we can see the same information state realized both physically and phenomenally" (p. 285), that is, both in the brain and in the mind.

4.21.4. Generalizing From the Uniquely Human Experience of Consciousness

It is clear that Chalmers derived this principle of informational isomorphism between consciousness and brain processes from the human case. It is the only case of consciousness to which we have access, so "the basic evidence comes from the correlations in familiar cases: ultimately, from me, in my own case" (p. 243). The unavoidable question, of course, is this: How legitimately may one generalize from the peculiar and restricted human experience to every other facet of the universe?

Chalmers's theory avoids or circumvents this question by invoking the notion of ubiquitous "information." Then, building a theory of consciousness on the basis of what is "natural to suppose," Chalmers generalizes from humans to "any system":

If consciousness is always accompanied by awareness, and vice versa, in my own case and in the case of all humans, one is led to suspect that something systematic is going on. There is certainly a lawlike correlation in the familiar cases. We can therefore put forward the hypothesis that this coherence is a law of nature: in any system, consciousness will be accompanied by awareness, and vice versa. . . . for any system, anywhere in space-time, the structure of consciousness will mirror and be mirrored by the structure of awareness. (pp. 242–243)

Indeed, "not only does consciousness arise from awareness, but the structure of consciousness is determined by the structure of awareness" (p. 243). Even further, then, "as a basic principle," Chalmers suggests, "information (in the actual world) has two aspects, a physical and a phenomenal [i.e., conscious] aspect" (p. 286). Note, again, that, clearly in this discussion, the structure itself is the information; that is, the information's instantiation is identified with the instantiated information. Data are confounded with understanding, and in the process intelligence is overlooked.

Chalmers's assertion is this: because we humans are conscious of some of the perceptual input through our senses and brain, anywhere in the universe where the activity of a patterned structure produces related "behavioral" results, there, too, is consciousness. Information instantiated physically entails information instantiated phenomenally. Information is the link between physical structures and experiences. Wherever there is information, there is consciousness.

That last sentence seems prosaic enough when understood in the everyday sense of the words that presume we are talking about conscious, aware, and intelligent human beings. In everyday usage, *information* implies understanding and knowledge, so it also implies consciousness as we humans experience it. But Chalmers's meaning of *information* is the usage of informational theory as defined at 4.21.2, and it is not restricted to humans. In its technical sense, information is everywhere; the term applies anywhere there is some arrangement that plays into any interactivity in our universe. So, because information in the information-technological sense is everywhere, also consciousness is supposedly everywhere.

4.21.5. Information, Therefore, Consciousness Everywhere

When Chalmers speaks of "any system, anywhere in space-time," he speaks literally. His assertion applies throughout the universe, so wherever there is any patterned structure that carries information that directs any response, there is awareness (capacity to respond) and concomitantly there is consciousness (subjective experience [i.e., consciousness], phenomenal presence). He is lucid in this claim: "As I have spelled out the notion [of information], we find information everywhere we find causation. We find causation everywhere, so we find information everywhere." If we "bite the bullet and accept that all information is associated with experience [i.e., consciousness] . . . then it is not just information that is ubiquitous. Experience is ubiquitous too" (p. 293).

So, for example, regarding that famous case (Nagel, 1974), "Using these methods [the principle of double-aspect, the coherence of awareness and consciousness], we might even get some insight into what it is like to be a bat" (Chalmers, 1996, p. 236). We assume from the beginning that the bat does have conscious experience, and on the basis of our knowledge of the perceptual physiology of a bat, we can conclude to an understanding of what bat experience must be like. Similarly, assuming consciousness in a dog, we could project the canine experience of a fire hydrant. "The same is also true for mice and even for flies" (p. 246; also p. 294). And these same principles apply to CD players, automobile engines, thermostats (p. 293), and computers (p. 275). Of course, this is not to say that their experience is just like ours: their processing systems are not as complex as our brains are. As we move "further down the information-processing scale" (p. 246), experience becomes less and less. But even thermostats enjoy a level of experience appropriate to the information they carry (pp. 293–297).

I do not hesitate to say that I think such speculation is pure science fiction sustained by ambiguous use of the terms *information* and *experience* [= consciousness]. The reasoning reminds me of the "pseudo-symbolic speculation" of ancient Gnostic religion, which insightfully found new meaning in available notions by creatively interrelating them with one another and with recently developed ideas (cf. Lonergan, 1976, p. 29; also pp. 8, 21, 134–137). My crafted presentation of Chalmers's theory intimated the obvious glitches in it, namely, the calculated limitation of awareness to what is also conscious and, via the identification of awareness and information, the imputation of somehow human-like conscious experience to the whole of the universe. But Chalmers finds such argument "the natural hypothesis," "the most natural way to think": "it seems reasonable enough" (p. 294). Certainly regarding our pets, we want to believe that they are conscious in some way and enjoy experiences. We anthropomorphize. Without doubt, Fido has perceptual and emotional responsiveness: he exhibits alertness, he reacts to stimuli, he interacts differentially with his environment—as does a thermostat in its way. But that Fido is, therefore, conscious, having internal experiences in any sense in which this word applies to humans: self-aware, reflective, scrutable, articulate? Hardly! And the thermostat?! Or the falling limb (4.20.5)?!

Chalmers believes that denial of experience to Fido, other animals, and mechanisms in our world "is often due to a conflation of phenomenal consciousness and self-consciousness" (p. 294). "Perhaps they [dogs and mice] are not self-aware, but that is a different matter" (p. 246). "A thermostat will not be *self*-conscious; it will not be in the least intelligent; and [he] would not claim that a thermostat can *think*" (p. 295). But one must wonder, then, what that "different matter" of "self-awareness" or "self-consciousness" means for Chalmers. Its nature is the pressing issue. It sets the critical difference between generic *mentality* and distinctively human *consciousness* (5.1.2). Chalmers mentions self-consciousness only in passing. As far as I can determine, his book offers only one six-line paragraph about it (p. 27; for other passing allusions see also pp. 4, 196, 204, 196–197), which restricts it to objectifications of a person, "self" as an object, completely ignoring the matter of a person's being a subject and self-present, self-conscious, as such.

Namely, in addition to the "me," the object, about which I can speak, there is also "I," the subject, who is conscious, who conceptualizes, who has the experiences, and who does the speaking. We do not have the one mode of self-consciousness without the other. Surely, to be self-conscious, to have experiences, to be self-aware, to be intelligent, and to think are all of a kind. These aspects of human experience are what talk of consciousness regards. But Chalmers's virtual limitation of experience to perceptual instances—the experience of seeing the color red, the readily construed parallel between patterns in the neural visual system and in an experienced visual array, the responses of a thermostat to changes in temperature—easily allows conflation of the human case of experience with lesser cases of perceptual responsiveness and, in the confounded process, both demeans the human experience and exalts the non-human. To ignore these different aspects of human experience is to ignore the essence of consciousness (5.3; 5.7.4).

What is left over when that distinctiveness is gone? Chalmers himself is hard-pressed to suggest what a non-human experience could possibly be. I myself also repeatedly ponder the mentality of non-human animals—which, in fact, is the topic at stake here. What could their mental life be like? The closest analogy I find is human somnambulation—complex behaviors such as, sometimes, even driving an automobile but without any consciousness, awareness, or subsequent memory: mental processing absent self-consciousness or possible reflective thought with, perforce, a significant limitation on the possible intricacy of the mental processing. Struggling with the same puzzle but insisting on calling it experience, despite its lack of consciousness, Chalmers ventures, "We need imagine only something like an unarticulated 'flash' of experience, without any concepts, any thought, or any complex processing in the vicinity" (pp. 295–296). But stripped of these determinative specifications—concepts, thought, complex processing—what could a "flash" of "experience" be? To ignore the defining subjective aspects of human conscious experience is to eliminate it, to reduce it to perceptual responsiveness and behaviors in the external world (4.20.4; 5.1.2).

Strikingly, for Chalmers, phenomenal conscious experience, supposedly, is even "*explanatorily irrelevant*" (p. 177, emphasis original) to these behaviors. The brain, not consciousness, explains them. In light of this thorough-going functionalism, which controls Chalmers's speculation—that is, truncated concern for external behaviors and interactions in the perceptible comings and goings of the everyday world—why would Chalmers even want to focus on phenomenal experience, consciousness, take the argument to such lengths, and make consciousness ubiquitous? Within Chalmers's functionalism, consciousness makes no discernible difference. I say again, the functionalist Chalmers might as well be the functionalist Dennett (1991), denying the reality of consciousness outright—except that Chalmers has an undeniable experience of his own consciousness, and he is committed to defending it.

4.21.6. Saving Functionally Irrelevant Consciousness by Positing It Everywhere

Ironically, that commitment to *his own* experience of *human* consciousness is what prods Chalmers to find consciousness in the entire universe. Because of that same commitment on my part, I was determined to understand what Chalmers is about: he, like me, insists that consciousness is a reality in its own right, not reducible to physical and biological processes in the brain. Now, massively disappointed, I think I understand.

Effectively and unwittingly, Chalmers (1996) has, in fact, separated consciousness from the brain. Chalmers's functionalism makes consciousness explanatorily irrelevant to any behaviors we perform or functions we execute. His zombie twin, supposedly, can function in all regards as well as he: in uttering sentences, writing books, and even verbally claiming to experience consciousness, the zombie presumably can also analyze theories, argue logically, generate scenarios, and speculate brilliantly. On functionalist presuppositions, the brain alone is sufficient to explain it all: after all, we already have a rather sophisticated understanding of how the brain effects perceptible behaviors. Moreover, on these same presuppositions, although consciousness is said to be a product of the brain in some way, consciousness itself could just as well not exist, and externally, observably, nothing would be different. However, internally Chalmers experiences consciousness, and he cannot deny the fact, so he holds that consciousness is something real and peculiar in itself, and he must find some way to fit it in despite his otherwise functionalist ontology.

His solution is to posit consciousness as a fundamental given, a component natural in the universe and coterminous with the universe, supposedly the sole other kind of reality alongside physical matter. Because consciousness makes no discernible difference according to this hypothesis, to posit it everywhere—or nowhere! (Dennett, 1991)—would leave things just as they are. Chalmers's (1996) theory would square with the known universe, and Chalmers would have preserved consciousness. Of course, this victory is empty. It champions an admittedly fully irrelevant factor. Whether it is real or not makes no difference; one is equally free to affirm or deny it. It rests on sheer speculation; it boasts no reasonable support, that is, no evidence-based argument. Even in the human case, where alone Chalmers has evidence for consciousness, he cannot say what difference consciousness makes because he virtually limits consciousness to the mere experience of percepts. Thus, consciousness appears to be an ornamental extra, which the cosmos gratuitously grants. Supposedly, nothing would change if consciousness did not exist. We might all be zombies, and no one would be the wiser.

Chalmers (1996) has boxed himself in. He cannot allow that consciousness—so fundamental an aspect of *his human* reality—could have just "winked in" (p. 244) for evolutionary purposes at some point in history because then consciousness would have to make some difference. (Is it not ludicrous to think that consciousness made no difference in our world? Was it only the opposable thumb that got us to the moon?) So Chalmers posits a meaningless consciousness everywhere and always. He protests, "Why should the world be set up so that awareness gives rise to consciousness only in beings with a particular biology?" (p. 244).

Well, why shouldn't it be so set up? We are not free to make the world whatever we think it should be (2.3.6). Human knowledge is constrained by evidence. Can valid explanation ignore the merely *de facto* status of human knowing? Do opinions find their credibility in the plausibility of arm-chair speculation? Has our understanding of science reverted to the standard or ideal of Aristotle's universal, necessary, and unchanging logical deduction?

But Chalmers elaborates, "There is something odd about the idea that a system with n elements could not be conscious but a system with $n + 1$ elements could be" (p. 297). Yes, that scenario would be odd. But this oddity holds only if one imagines that the complexification of nature from the Big Bang onward is merely the addition of more and more of the same: a refinement of one more LEGO block added to the toddler's humanoid does not produce a conscious human being, nor do two more or three more blocks, nor does the ever-refined humanoid shape. The oddity holds only because Chalmers does not allow for genuine emergence within the universe (4.21.1). He cannot allow genuine emergence because then consciousness would appear as a genuine novelty, and it would have to make some difference. (One blatant observable difference, of course, is that we—all putatively mere zombies—are here discussing consciousness relentlessly: Chalmers's "Paradox of Phenomenal Judgments," p. 172; 5.3.5.) But Chalmers's functionalism disallows that consciousness could make any detectable difference. So the only way Chalmers can defend the reality of consciousness, which he cannot deny in his own experience, is to posit consciousness as a fundamental element throughout the universe. In his struggle with the "bipolar disorder of modern metaphysics" (Cahoone, 2010, lecture 35, track 2), Chalmers (1996) acknowledges only two kinds of realities as absolutely natural and fundamental: matter and consciousness; and to have them without genuine emergence, he must posit them as co-existent, coterminous, from the beginning. So much is this the case that, consistent with his sensate-modeled epistemology entangled with functionalism and again evincing two notions of science at silent war with each other (2.3.2; 4.12.4; 4.19.2), he posits protophenomenal or microphenomenal properties (pp. 154, 304–305)—bits of imaginable, perhaps even perceptible and palpable stuff—lying behind the theoretical equations that, relying on an intellectual epistemology, physicists use to express their assertions about the real world (2.2.4). In this way,

- Chalmers can have "something of consciousness," namely, hypothesized phenomenal or experiential properties associated with information at the lowest levels of matter, to satisfy his commitment to consciousness; and

- simultaneously he can have something "substantial," something imaginable, to satisfy the sensate-modeled epistemology that is at work in his functionalism (2.2.4)

- —which precipitated these conceptual problems from the start.

4.21.7. Confounding Technological Information with Human Information

Application of the notion *information* allows Chalmers to declare consciousness a universal and ubiquitous kind of reality. Undoubtedly, in its information-technological sense information is everywhere; and understood as data, which intelligence could discern, information does correlate with human consciousness (4.21.3). However, *information* in this sense is originally a metaphor. Misleadingly the term carries connotations of human experience, intelligence, consciousness. *Data* better names what is actually at stake: everywhere in the universe there is something to be understood. When bit by laborious bit we accumulate a growing understanding of the data, we can stipulate the explanatory elements, their patterned relationships, their interactions, the causal connections, the guiding principles: we can spell out the inherent arrangements that information theory would call "information." Literally stated, then, available everywhere are intelligibilities, but not human information. Only when human intelligence is applied to the intelligible data do actual understanding and specifications result. Then we humans have knowledge; then we have information on the topic. But like the experiences that Griffin (1991) posits (4.20.2), this human information is not lying about out there on its own. It cannot be posited apart from the human intelligence that grasps it. It is not something actually intelligent on its own, actually knowingly orchestrating its interactions, actually having or constituting phenomenal experiences, actually enjoying and exhibiting consciousness. Technically defined, yes, information is everywhere. But only the uniquely human connotation of the metaphor "information" or Chalmers's functionalism-*cum*-perceptualism-induced speculation suggests that consciousness is everywhere: there is no evidence to support such a claim. Consciousness is a phenomenon that emerges in natural history only with the human species.

This same line of criticism applies to structuralism and poststructuralism (or postmodernism). Structuralism opines that meaning is located in patterns or relations within some reality—aspects of a culture, words in a language. In language, for example, meaning supposedly lies in the interrelationship of the words, and the meaning of one word is another word. But in this account, attention to intelligence is conspicuously absent. Supposedly, these interrelationships must somehow know themselves and, thus, generate an imagined kind of meaning that lies out there among them waiting to be stumbled upon—for there is no meaning apart from the intelligence that grasps it. There might be intelligibilities in all realities—interrelationships, patterns, technically defined "information"—but apart from active intelligence, no understanding or meaning or grasp of these relations pertains. Supposedly, we are to have meaning without mind. Ever and again, the richly insightful and highly elaborated theories of contemporary philosophy are oblivious to the intelligence that generates them, the intelligence that, if only acknowledged as an undeniably operative factor, could alone impart some coherence to the assertions they advance.

Chalmers's and Griffin's panpsychism both entail some kind of emergence of consciousness—emergence, namely, conceived as the compounding of a primordial given. Both theories arrive at the bottom-up emergence of human consciousness by positing "something of consciousness" afoot in all the universe, "experience" in Griffin's case and "information" in Chalmers's.

My parallel, something at least potentially "of consciousness" throughout the universe, something inherently related to consciousness, is intelligibility. Thus, in ways that are incompatible in detail but nonetheless real in purview, these three theories point in the same conceptual direction. I hope to have focused that direction and, challenging the oversight of insight in Griffin's and Chalmers's theories, to have elucidated the coherent conceptual goal. Consistent with my argument throughout this book, I have posed substantively identical criticisms to Griffin's and Chalmers's theories and to other treatments of consciousness. Underlying them all are epistemological confounds, the picture-thinking of a sensate epistemology entangled with the pure theory of intellectual epistemology. Consistent reliance on the intellectual could support a coherent resolution of the mind–body problem.

4.22. Summary on the Mind–Body Problem

The fact that people—including you, dear reader, who ponder what I write here—question the emergence of the human mind or question anything at all and seek understanding is itself evidence that, over and above quarks, particles, atoms, molecules, cells, tissues, organs, organisms, sensations, and perceptions, in humanity something new has emerged in the universe. Operating in sober yet awestruck attentiveness, intelligence, and reasonableness, an adequate epistemology can coherently affirm the actuality of this newly emerged reality, intellectual consciousness, as distinct but not separate from those other aspects of humanity, all of which cohere in and constitute one multifaceted thing, the human person. The person alone is the true subject of whatever is predicated of the person and his or her body, mind, faculties, capacities, or "parts."

In comparison with the others, the human being is a new entity of a peculiar kind, specified by intellectual consciousness. As a particular thing, the person is the genuine and proper object of the human sciences—especially of psychology, which focuses on the human being as such. Only misdirected inquiry looks to the brain to understand consciousness and then wonders how consciousness could ever arise or be real. When, instead, one starts with the person—not some of its "parts"—consciousness is already among the given. It does not have to be justified; its existence does not have to be proved; it is among the data to be explained. If it shows as something peculiar in comparison to whatever else we think we know, the scientific need is to acknowledge the peculiarity, not to deny it or explain it away by refusing to accept the given. Humans are intellectually conscious animals, and the meaning and implication of this fact will come clear through study of the person as such. As I have suggested periodically in this book, denial of this assertion disqualifies the denier because the scientific enterprise is patently intellectual (2.1.5; 2.7.2).

William James (1890/1950) advanced the same methodological tack, lamenting departures from it and speaking almost directly to the consciousness studies of our day. He rejected the thesis of the "Associationists"—John Locke, David Hume, James and John Stuart Mills—that simple impressions, sensations, or "ideas" get cobbled together to form complex ideas and that, therefore, the simple ideas should be the initial focus of explanatory attention. James would insist that ideas are wholes in themselves, inherently connected with their antecedents in an ongoing stream of consciousness. We experience consciousness in this way; only in this way, then, can we begin to analyze it. He argues,

> No one ever had a simple sensation by itself. Consciousness, from our natal day, is of a teeming multiplicity of objects and relations, and what we call simple sensations are results of discriminative attention, pushed often to a very high degree. It is astonishing what havoc is wrought in psychology by admitting at the outset apparently innocent suppositions, that nevertheless contain a flaw. The bad consequences develop themselves later on, and are irremediable, being woven through the whole texture of the work. The notion that sensations, being the simplest things, are the first things to take up in psychology is one of these suppositions. The only thing which psychology has a right to postulate at the outset is the fact of thinking itself, and that must first be taken up and analyzed. (vol. I, p. 224)

We may and should, of course, wonder about the relationship of the brain and consciousness, given that these are constitutive conjugates of the human being and, perforce, must have some specifiable interrelationship and interaction. We are now able to explain water on the basis of the bonding of hydrogen and oxygen; and given water and its peculiar properties, we are now able to understand this uniqueness within an array of chemical principles. Surely, someday we will likewise be able to explain how consciousness relates to, and interacts within, a sensate and perceptual organism to constitute an entity of the human kind. Surely, someday we will be able to formulate those "emergent laws" or "trans-ordinal laws," (Broad,1925, p. 79) or "fundamental psychophysical laws" (Chalmers, 2006, p. 247) that express coherent explanation across the gap of emergence between organism and consciousness. Surely, someday we will be able to explain consciousness. But just as it would be mistaken for hydrology to focus on hydrogen and oxygen and not on its subject matter, water, so too it is mistaken for the study of humanity and its distinctive feature, intellectual consciousness, to focus on neurons, transmitters, nuclei, tracts, brain networks, and their computer modeling and not first and foremost on the person as a functioning whole. Such an approach ignores the data on consciousness and then finds itself unable to account for consciousness.

I am not begging the question and saying that, if only we would grant the existence of consciousness from the start, we would have no problem admitting its existence. Rather, I spoke proleptically in the last three paragraphs. I propose no naive realism, but a critical one (2.2.9). I was appealing to the data of consciousness, not *ipso facto* to consciousness itself. I insist on attending to the data, on proposing some understanding of them, and on judging the adequacy of the understanding to the data. The end result, yes, then, I believe, would be affirmation of what we generally mean when we speak of "consciousness." But this conclusion depends on a specific process of human knowing (2.1.6), not on an *a priori* insistence on the intended conclusion.

At the root of the mind–body problem is an epistemology that would determine reality on the basis of palpability—emphasis is on sensations, the experience of seeing red, for example. But the human being is not simply something palpable, so on the basis of that truncated epistemology, human distinctiveness cannot be acknowledged as real. An appropriate epistemology resolves the problem. Given the data, a series of insights and careful judgments propose a coherent resolution. Its challenge is to acknowledge that there do exist many kinds of realities in our universe. Its greater challenge is to consistently differentiate realities on the basis of intelligibility, not palpability, visibility, or imaginableness, and to affirm their actuality on the basis of reasonable judgment, not sensate, perceptible, or imaginable encounter.

This proposed resolution of the mind–body problem is the pivot point in this discussion of "God in the brain." The mind–body problem is the great hang-up in this discussion—because the matter is more philosophical than anything else, because our world shares no consensus on epistemology, and because the conclusions of the epistemology that would allow coherent resolution are often unappealing to the contemporary critical thinker immersed in perceptualism.

Now, I say "this proposed resolution," but as I reread this chapter, open-minded and fair reader, I am indeed pleased with my work, but I feel for you. I must confess that even I wish I could make the resolution more obvious, stunning, imposing. I wish I could make my point more accessible and present it more graphically. But my very point is that these matters are not graphic; my resolution cannot be pictured any more than energy, quarks, mass, gamma rays, life, or emotions can be pictured. Curious that people accept that they cannot understand physics without extensive intellectual preparation yet they expect to understand the far more complicated issues about humanity on the basis of commonsensical discussion (1.5). Unfortunately, I cannot make my point by way of some clever, sensate analogy—because my topic is quintessentially non-sensate. So mine must be an intellectual solution, not a perceptible, imaginable, metaphorical, or graphic one. Herein lies its challenge, and the challenge of the topic before us. Nonetheless, with the epistemological intricacies sorted out, I have laid out the whole argument. Eight sections above, at 4.13, I had already summarized as briefly as possible the resolution I am suggesting. At this point, the warning in my Introduction comes to bear with a vengeance: "The argument turns on explicit attention to intelligence, which demands prolonged effort to achieve understanding" (1.7).

Be that as it may, I believe that, following Lonergan, I have proposed a coherent resolution of the mind–body problem. This resolution provides a perspective that allows similar clarification of the other aspects of the discussion on "God in the brain."

4.23. Review and Preview

Chapter 3's summary of neuroscientific findings stands as an example of what might someday be known with precision and breadth about brain function, so the accuracy and comprehensiveness of that summary are not ultimately telling. Moreover, from a methodological perspective, neuroscience comes to its conclusions relatively easily. After all, neuroscience deals with a physical object, the brain, so in its case epistemological issues are not as pivotal as in discussion of the non-material mind—except when neuroscientists verge off into philosophical speculation and theological assertion, but these excesses are easily recognized and contained. Besides, neuroscience has ready-made research methods from the physical, chemical, biological, and medical sciences, which it can apply. Furthermore, there is no question that processes in the brain somehow relate to the human experience of mind. So treatment of the neuroscientific aspect of this discussion is relatively straightforward, if incredibly complicated. What neuroscience provides is an ever more accurate accounting of the schemes of recurrence—the interactive functions of cells, neurotransmitters, neurological pathways and networks, and patterns of neuronal activity—out of which a higher synthesis, the mind, emerges. In contrast, the overwhelming challenge is to explain the relationship between these neurological processes and the mind. The present chapter has presented a theoretically coherent schematic explanation. It demanded close attention to the pervasive, subtle, and difficult epistemological issues in this discussion. It must leave to other specialists and to ongoing research the task of filling in the details.

The questions that remain about "God in the brain" regard spiritual matters. These, too, are daunting, but granted this chapter's clarification of the subtlety of mind and granted the contribution of long-standing theological opinion, treatment of the spiritual can follow relatively easily. As I see it, those spiritual matters fall into two significantly different categories, those that pertain to spirituality as a human phenomenon and those that pertain to theology and supposed divine involvement in this human phenomenon. The need is to tease apart human spirituality and theism. Not all agree with my delineation of these issues. Indeed, the prevalent opinion in psychology-of-religion circles in the USA tends to collapse the spiritual into the divine. Eastern philosophies—each in its own way but blatantly in Hindu thought: Atman is Brahman—tend to identify the two, as well. I submit that this identification is not only mistaken but, perforce, also makes resolution of the questions before us impossible (Helminiak, 2001, 2005a, 2006a, 2008a, 2008c, 2010, 2011, 2013a). But the proof is in the pudding. So Chapter 5 will take that next step and address spirituality so that, having put in place the neuroscience, psychology, and spiritualogy, Chapter 6 can finally consider "God in the brain" head-on.

Chapter 5

Spritualogy

Consciousness and Transcendent Experiences

> The human mind is part of the infinite intellect of God.
>
> —Baruch Spinoza

> Let a man not resist the law of his own mind, and he will be filled with the divinity which flows through all things.
>
> —Ralph Waldo Emerson

In the previous chapter I proposed a resolution of the mind–body problem. This resolution leaves us facing a hard fact about us human beings, and it also opens onto a ready explanation for transcendent experiences. The hard fact is that human nature encompasses a range of different realities. The mind is real, as real as the body, and the two are not one and the same. And even within the human mind, further precision requires a distinction between different realities. Imagery and emotions are one kind of reality, but insights are another. That is, the perceptual is one reality, and consciousness is another. Most significant for our discussion of spirituality, consciousness fully transcends space and time. We have an adjective for such reality: consciousness is *spiritual*. Therefore, the spiritual is real, too, and we humans are in part spiritual. When distinct intelligibilities—not sensations, perceptions, or images—determine realities, these are the conclusions that follow, difficult as they might be to accept literally in the face of the material, organic, and perceptual realities that impinge so forcefully upon us. But given these conclusions and a consistent intellectual epistemology, an explanation of transcendent experiences follows easily.

If we are in part spiritual, why could we not experience the spiritual in ourselves? We can experience our arms and legs, our rumbling stomachs, our emotions, and our daydreams. The routine functioning of our consciousness regards such objects that are parts of ourselves. In fact, however, within this conscious functioning we also simultaneously and concomitantly experience our own awareness, wonder, insights, and judgments. That is, we also experience our consciousness in operation, our subjectivity. To be able to have such experience of oneself is precisely what it means to be a subject. We do, then, have data on consciousness as a specific phenomenon. For this reason—how could we, otherwise?—we can go back and recall our awareness, elaborate on our wonder, formulate our insights, and own our judgments. This very exercise, self-appropriation (2.1.1; 5.6.3), is at the heart of Lonergan's contribution. The whole of Chapter 2 is built on it. We do experience the spiritual facet of ourselves.

Why might we not, then, through extraordinary occurrence—whether via cultivated skill, manipulation of our nervous system, or some quirk of neurological functioning—experience the pure, contentless reality of our consciousness? Why might we not experience an intense consciousness "of" consciousness itself? Inherently capable of transcending space and time (5.1.1), consciousness is not spatial or temporal in its intrinsic reality (Lonergan, 1957/1992, pp. 539–543). Why could it not, then, be present "to" itself—not as if seeing itself as an object of sight or feeling itself as an object of touch or introspecting itself as an object of internal exploration—that is, not in the mode of the material presence of sensation and perception, but simply by being what it is, subjectivity, the mode of the spiritual (Helminiak, 1984a, 1996a, pp. 45–47)? Why could we not experience a reality, our own subjectivity, that is geared to the universe of all that exists? If such an experience were to occur, it would be unbounded, infinite, universally unitive, veritably transcendent. The neurological mechanisms underpinning this experience might well be those described and summarized in Chapter 3, but the experience would not be an experience of the neurological substrate and its mechanisms, but of the reality emergent from them, consciousness or human spirit.

Granted the spiritual reality of the human mind, without needing to implicate God or some other spiritual entity, we can speak coherently of genuine transcendent experiences. Allowing that the mind is real and that, perforce, in humanity psychology has a distinct object of study, we can begin to construct an empirically grounded treatment of spirituality (Doran, 1981; Helminiak, 1996a, 1998, 2005a, 2006, 2008a, 2008b, 2008c; Roy, 2003). Once psychology explicitly broadens its purview to acknowledge human consciousness as a reality distinct (but not separate) from brain processes (4.2.1), spiritualogy appears to be, not an aspect of theology or religious studies, but in the first instance a natural and necessary aspect of human psychology. This is the argument that I elaborate as this chapter shifts from neuroscience and psychology to spiritualogy.

5.1. A Tripartite Model of the Human: Beyond "Body and Mind"

5.1.1. Mind as Both Psyche and Consciousness

The standard psychological model of the human being is "body and mind." Within the mind Lonergan's analyses differentiate and explicate a dimension that "makes meaning," that grasps universals, that abstracts from time and space (4.3): consciousness. In the treatment of epistemology in Chapter 2, we already have an exposition of the major facets or structure of consciousness, namely, four interactive levels or aspects or dimensions: experience, understanding, judgment, and decision (the latter having been mentioned in this book only in passing). Once consciousness is thus set off in relief, contrasting dimensions of the human mind also readily come into focus: sensitivity, imagery, memories, emotions, conations (i.e., innate purposeful inclinations, drives, urges), and structures of personality (Lonergan, 1957/1992, p. 206). In contrast to the spiritual nature of consciousness, these others indicate another kind of reality subsumed within the human mind. An insight, for example, might not occur apart from a suggestive image, but simply to conjure up the image is not, *ipso facto*, to understand. Similarly, the insight will not likely occur without some surge of emotion: Archimedes's "*Eureka!*" But simply to have experienced an emotion is, again, not necessarily to have understood and, more surely, not necessarily to have understood correctly. The two sets of phenomena entail different intelligibilities, so they are of different kinds, they evince different natures, they pertain to different realities. Though usually concomitant and interactive, insight, judgment, and decision, on the one hand, are not, on the other, sensations or perceptions or emotions or conations or images or memories.

Nonetheless, current fluid terminology includes those latter, too, under the topic "consciousness," and *consciousness* is taken to apply undifferentiatedly to all internal or mental experience. In a zero-sum game, mentality of any kind is exalted to consciousness, or consciousness is reduced to mentality (4.21.5). The distinction between the two is overlooked.

The journal *Imagination, Cognition and Personality* offers an example. It carries the subtitle *Consciousness in Theory, Research, Clinical Practice* and "explores the relationship of consciousness and the flow of life events to a variety of human processes and experiences." Evidently, current usage allows that any mental process or experience, any form of mentality, could pass as consciousness. Trying to credit the genuine mentality of non-human animals while also acknowledging the distinctive capacities of humans, Donald (2001) opines, "Humans have more of everything. We might be called superconscious. But other species share many component features of our conscious capacity" (p. 130). Thus, the elusive name *consciousness* functions as an umbrella term.

Not the pivotal concern of this book—namely, specifically human, intellectual consciousness or human spirit—but, rather, simple sensate reflexivity or mere perceptual responsiveness might only be in question: unthinkingly, I scratch an itch; automatically, I brake as the traffic signal goes red; while asleep, unconscious, I pull up a cover to protect against the cold. This ambiguity mixes environmental responsiveness of different kinds, on the one hand, and self-aware thought and activity, on the other, and thus confounds the discussion.

5.1.2. Consciousness and Other Kinds of Responsiveness

It is commonly said that humans enjoy (some form of) consciousness in common with Fido and other non-human animals. We, as they, through varying degrees of internal processing (Donald, 2001, pp. 106–113, 137–148)—what I will refer to generically as *mentality*—respond flexibly and appropriately to environmental and internal stimuli. Expressing their natural and spontaneous functions within the organism, the animal responses are systematic, not random, and not automatic or mechanical, either. They evince genuine mentality, internal processing that results in differential responses. The term *conscious* could apply. In fact, it is used widely in these cases. One could avoid ambiguity by adding an adjective to qualify the consciousness in question. Exemplifying this strategy, Lonergan (1957/1992) uses terms such as "extroverted consciousness" (p. 277), "extroverted biological anticipation and attention" (p. 279), or "sensitive consciousness" (p. 276), and he offers the example of a kitten approaching a saucer of milk (p. 276). Bekoff (2002) offers the term "perceptual consciousness" (p. 92).

Yet this further complication remains: humans not only respond to sensate stimuli but can also become explicitly aware of them, focus attention on them, and name, interrelate, and expound on them. So, in humans, the contents of sensitive consciousness can be subsumed within intellectual consciousness and also become present to humans via it: we not only respond to sensate stimuli as do other animals, but we can also be explicitly aware of, and are able to reflect upon, many of those stimuli and even to manage our responses to them thoughtfully, discursively, analytically, deliberately, purposefully.

The point to be highlighted is this: these two kinds of responses are not one and the same. I can unconsciously scratch that itch, but if I say to myself, "This itches," if in the least I reflect on the itch or speak of it, using a concept and the consensual, meaning-filled term *itch*—because the term and its meaning fit—I am already operating in a world of meaning, in the human realm of a distinctive kind of self-conscious experience. As humanly conscious, I bring meaning and terminology to a sensation, which I may now objectify and ponder *per se*. That is, I can experience the sensate itch or the red or the cold also as data within consciousness; and easily enough in these cases, I can name the experiences and treat them as explicit objects of my subjective (i.e., personal) awareness and wonder, and not merely react to them as organic, sensate feelings or "felt senses." Much of the content of which I am aware on the first level of consciousness (2.2.1) is such sensate and perceptual input: the data of the senses processed through perception and imagination (i.e., internal imaging).

Thus, there is extraverted sensitive consciousness, which humans share with other animals. Additionally, there is intellectual consciousness, by which sensate matters (and others) become possible objects of self-conscious human awareness, question, and thought. In this case, as well as entailing a self-presence, consciousness is also intentional, even as sensation is: both regard some object. In earlier chapters I dropped the term *intentional consciousness* with hardly a suggestive definition (e.g., 2.7.1; 3.1.3; 4.11.3; 4.18.1), but in the present chapter this term and the distinction it carries become critical, so I make a point of them. As applied to consciousness, the term *intentional* does not carry the popular and psychotherapeutic meaning of deliberate or planned: therapists instruct us to act intentionally. Rather, in this case the term carries the root Latinate meaning—*in* + *tendere* = to stretch or extend toward—and signifies directedness. It implies a subject–object duality and emphasizes the objective pole of subjectivity: the subject is directed *toward*, concerned *about*, reflecting *on* some object; the subject intends the object.

For the sake of clarity in the present discussion, when I use the term *consciousness,* I restrict its reference to that distinctively human dimension of the mind, intentional consciousness, that double consciousness by which humans, present "to" themselves, can also become present to, aware of, other contents of attention as the subject engages some object. This is the distinctively human consciousness that Lonergan (1972) explicated and implicitly defined by appeal to two modes and four levels (5.3.1). It is the consciousness that, with him (1.2), I am freely also calling *human spirit.* I want to avoid any hint of panpsychism (3.5; 4.84), and I want to highlight intentional consciousness as a uniquely human property. Not even to mention the response of thermostats to their environments (4.21.5), if others would call an appropriate organismic behavioral response to sensate stimuli an expression of consciousness, I would not. I prefer a term such as *sensate reflexivity* or *perceptual responsiveness,* which more accurately names what is at stake in non-human animals: they are responding to stimuli. For the sake of clarity, I choose to limit the term *consciousness* to distinctively human intentional consciousness, unless otherwise specified.

Indeed, this matter of animate responsiveness—i.e., the responsiveness inherent in living organisms—requires even further differentiation, and I struggle to propose terminology to highlight it. Even single-celled animals respond to stimuli, enjoy simple innate reactions, and are capable of conditioned learning. The *Stentor,* for example, a horn-shaped protozoan, reacts to offensive stimuli but habituates (stops reacting after several exposures) to a non-toxic stimulus, such as a jet of water, demonstrating what could be called simple memory (Jennings, 1906, reported in Wynne & Udell, 2013, pp. 232–233). Similarly, the primitive marine snail *Aplysia* has been classically conditioned to respond to a touch on its mantle as if it were about to be shocked on its tail (Carew, Hawkins, & Kandel, 1983, reported in Wynne & Udell, 2013, pp. 92–93). Such responsiveness is primitive, basic, fundamental; it is what would be called "reflex" in an animal with a developed nervous system. Yet such reflexivity hardly qualifies as evidence for mentality. The responses in question are rote, innate, inflexible. The same must be said of the much more complicated "fixed action patterns" in animal mating rituals, male aggression during mating seasons, and, famously, the egg-retrieval mechanism in the Graylag Goose (Tinbergen, 1951). A stimulus (the "releaser") activates an "innate releasing mechanism," a neural network, which sets in operation an indivisible series of behaviors that, once begun, runs to completion. For example, in response to seeing an egg fallen from its nest (or, if tricked, a golf ball or some similar object), the goose will initiate a sweeping-like maneuver, pushing the egg back into the nest with its bill (and will complete this innate behavior, an instance of genuine instinct, even if an experimenter perversely removes the egg from the goose's ministrations). Such reflexivity, in greater or lesser degrees of complexity, appears to be a characteristic of living beings, a very marker of life. Tropisms in plants and chemical communication between plants, insects, bacteria, and fungi exemplify other mechanisms related to animate reflexivity. Yet the automaticity and inflexibility of these responses precludes attributing any mental capacity to them.

I would call this responsiveness *animate reflexivity*. One notch up would be *sensate reflexivity*: the responsiveness of animals who have something of specialized sense organs (slugs, ticks, worms) but who respond only to isolated stimuli (warmth, humidity, light). On the one hand, however, the reflexivity in animate beings is clearly different from the physical and chemical reactions of, say, a thermostat or a bullet, which I would call *mechanical* and *chemical reactivity*, respectively. On the other hand, sensate reflexivity is also different from the responsiveness of Fido and other more developed animals because Fido's responses depend on intricate, complex, and flexible processing, genuine mentality, built on the inner perceptual systems related to specialized external organs and on memory, emotions, imagery, and conations, all bound together and working toward purposeful behaviors. In this case I apply the term *perceptual responsiveness*. Of course, I insist that human *intentional consciousness* is still another kind of responsiveness. Tellingly, it is not geared to the spatiotemporal world lying about us, but to the universe of being, namely, all that there is to be known and loved in the proprietary sense in which humans know and love, as elaborated, for example, by Lonergan. Thus, I differentiate an array of kinds of responsiveness and, by the same token, kinds of "intentionality"—agent–object interactions—and I plead for more precision in talk of "consciousness."

In proposing the term *perceptual responsiveness* and in denying consciousness to Fido, I do not mean to minimize or discount the processing that undoubtedly occurs in the minds of non-human species. I do not, with Descartes, think animals are merely complex machines. The mental processing of animals is a far cry from the merely programmed mechanical reactions of computers and thermostats—although these, too, already entail complex interactive processes of their own kind. That mental processing in Fido is also far advanced beyond the mere animate and sensate reflexivity of living beings. Moreover, mechanical and chemical reactivities also pertain on the even lower levels of *physical* and *chemical processes*, where terminology is already available from these mature sciences. Some examples would be the expansion or contraction of metal in the presence of changing thermal energy in a thermometer or thermostat, the electromagnetic processes that sustain computer operations, and the electrochemical processes operative in neuronal conduction. These physicochemical processes also deserve to be called by their own names, and they need to be distinguished from the emergent animate, sensate, and mental processes that occur in organisms on the basis of these lower-level physicochemical processes. Giving all these diverse processes the name "experience" is hardly helpful (4.20.2). Finally, on the far side of this continuum, the perceptual responsiveness of the animal mind should also be distinguished from human intentional consciousness, a further emergent reality.

To be sure, a continuity runs from the physicochemical processes through all the emergent levels of nature. After all, electrochemical neuronal processes sustain sensation and perception even as, in conjunction with these higher levels of integration, somehow they also sustain human conscious experience. So it is easy to understand how theorists would rightly insist on a similarity from physical and chemical processes through thermostats and computers to animate reflexivity to sensate reflexivity to perceptual responsiveness to human intentional consciousness. Moreover, given the prevalent neuroscientific and, perforce, materialistic (and, I say, downright reductionist) emphasis in consciousness studies, it is easy to understand how theorists could tend to construe as "all of a kind" distinctively human consciousness, animal responsiveness, animate reflexivity, sensate reflexivity, mechanical reactivity, and chemical and physical processes.

However, only an intellectual epistemology discerns even the physicochemical processes in the first place. At this point in history, physics and chemistry hardly depend on "taking a good look" at the relevant phenomena, which, in fact, are invisible and imperceptible in themselves. Therefore, if, thereafter, one consistently applies an intellectual epistemology, one must also acknowledge differences in kind among physical process, chemical interaction, animate reflexivity, sensate reflexivity, perceptual responsiveness, and intentional consciousness. Despite the fact that all rely in some way on the grounding physiochemical processes, different and additional intelligibilities are at stake in each case. Perforce, different realities are at stake (2.8.1). Beyond animate reflexivity, sensate reflexivity, and animal perceptual responsiveness, consciousness in humans is another kind of reality. With some consistent terminology and without denying animal mentality, I want to highlight this fact.

Undoubtedly, the possibility of appropriate response to environmental conditions is common to animate reflexivity, sensate reflexivity, perceptual responsiveness, and intentional consciousness, but in different ways—and herein lies the ambiguity that I want to highlight and avoid. Surely, intentional responsiveness does have intimate evolutionary connections with perceptual consciousness and sensate reflexivity. And undeniably, as in all emergences, the lines between the three are fuzzy, rather than fine (Helminiak, 1996a, pp. 152–158). Isolated examples of seeming incipient animal rationality are documented: Sheba's and another chimp's success with the "trap tube" problem; the chimpanzee Sarah's success with analogical reasoning, and, to a lesser extent, a pigeon's success with the box-stacking problem (Wynne & Udell, 2013, pp. 122–124); Scrub jays' retrieval of peanuts rather than (preferred but not after 4 hours when "known" to be decaying) dead wax worms (pp. 132–133); and the dolphin Akeakamai's correct responses to syntactically different visual commands (pp. 172–173). The gifted bonobo Kanzi might be demonstrating what is called "a theory of mind," the realization that the other has (or lacks) knowledge, when Kanzi seems to realize that his bonobo mates haven't a clue and helps them do what their caretakers want (Donald, 2001, p. 130). Besides, in organism, psyche, and spirit in humans, sensate reflexivity, perceptual responsiveness, and intentional consciousness are integrated in one polymorphous being, so one can distinguish but only with difficulty, perhaps, separate them in experience. Touch, because it is quite primitive, seems to provide the easiest case, both felt and, only with gross conceptualization, named. Yet the two, touch as felt and touch as named, entail strikingly different intelligibilities. The difference also applies to somnambulation and walking about in awake consciousness. The more I appreciate this difference, the less I am able to speak of mere perceptual responsiveness, let alone sensate reflexivity, as instances of consciousness.

I know I am countering a usage commonplace in the field of consciousness studies, in psychology overall, in general parlance, and even in Lonergan (1957/1992; Doran, 1996). This fact gives me even more reason to stand my ground because, as I see it, that usage is also the source of much ambiguity, misunderstanding, and even downright nonsense. Besides, my proposed differential terminology merely synthesizes well-documented facets of nature as we currently understand it. So I choose to reserve the term *consciousness* to the exclusively human capacity for self-conscious experience, and I elaborate this pivotal matter in what follows.

5.1.3. *The Human as Organism, Psyche, and Spirit*

The levels of consciousness, as elaborated in Chapter 2, enjoy an inherent interrelationship and cohere as facets of one reality, intentional consciousness. Similarly, those other dimensions of the animal mind also cohere: sensitivity, emotion, imagery, memory, conation, and personality. Emotion-filled imagery, for example, carries sensation-dependent and conation-powered memories, which together tend to determine habitual patterns of response, which constitute what psychologists call "personality." Sensitivity, emotions, conation, imagery, memory, and personality are of a kind. They pertain to perception; they constitute the integrated internal workings of externally oriented sensation; they are the makings of our inherited animal minds. Collectively, Lonergan (1957/1992) calls these dimensions of the mind *psyche* (pp. 229–230, 481–484; see also Doran, 1981; Helminiak, 1996a, Part 3).

Thus, Lonergan provides a possible name for this kind of reality, emergent from the biological processes of the organism, including animate and sensate reflexivity, and subservient to the higher emergent conscious capacities of the person. However, different theorists use the term *psyche* in many different senses. Indeed, all terminology in these subtle discussions tends to depend on the usage of each particular theorist. The field sorely needs terminological coherence if discussion is to be profitable. I adopt Lonergan's terminology (4.18.3), so the adjective *psychic* will not refer to precognition, telekinesis, clairvoyance, and other parapsychological phenomena, but, rather, simply to the dimension of mind that includes the phenomena that pertain to perceptual responsiveness.

Given the extensive elaboration that Lonergan has brought to consciousness, psyche remains the least understood aspect of the human mind and is what constitutes animal mind. As I understand it thus far, animal mind is more closely related to neurological processes—the organism—than is consciousness. Discussed in more detail at 5.9.2 to 5.9.3, psyche appears to mediate, to be the missing theoretical link, between neurological processes and consciousness in humans. Consciousness emerges from the psyche, not directly from the brain.

In psychology, the standard model of the human is "body and mind"— and in religion, "body and soul" (4.1.1). Given Lonergan's analyses, this bipartite model can be refined. A differentiation within mind results in a well-defined tripartite model, "organism, psyche, and consciousness." Given further that Lonergan regularly refers to consciousness also as spirit or spiritual (1.2), this tripartite model can also be formulated popularly as "body, psyche, and spirit" (for discussion of other terminology and proposed aspects of the mind, see Helminiak, 2005b, pp. 16–19). Animate and sensate reflexivity and sensation pertain to the human as organism; perceptual responsiveness, as psyche; and intentional consciousness, as spirit. This tripartite understanding opens obviously onto a naturalistic treatment of spirituality.

5.2. The Mechanism of "Spiritual Growth"

5.2.1. The Interaction of Psyche and Spirit

The differentiation of psyche and spirit within the human mind sheds light on the possible enhancement of human spiritual sensitivity. According to Aristotle's important contribution, retained and elaborated in medieval philosophy and refurbished by Lonergan (1967d, 1957/1992), one has insight into phantasm, that is, into images. Said otherwise, inquiry, which seeks insight on a second level of consciousness, presumes data to be understood, which are provided on a first level of consciousness: understanding regards data; and this entire process goes on within consciousness, not via confrontation with stuff lying "out there" in a spatiotemporal array (2.3). Aristotle's formulation can be broadened so that the term *images* represents more than visual presentations and includes all the perceptual data of the mind. In this sense, we could speak of auditory, tactile, gustatory, olfactory, and kinesthetic "images" and their perceptual integration in addition to visual images. The common psychological term "representations" provides a suggestive alternative (e.g., Kosslyn & Pomerantz, 1977; Pylyshyn, 1973; Shepard, 1978). Inquiry engages phantasms; one has insight into data.

It is the human psyche that presents within consciousness much of the data for understanding. Psyche is the substrate for intentional consciousness, and psyche presents data on which consciousness subsequently operates. Thus, on a first level of consciousness, we have experience, and much of this experience is the presentation of perceptual data into which inquiry seeks insight and out of which insight emerges on a second level of consciousness (2.2.9). The telling point is that psyche both supports and constrains the possibility of human insight. Psyche supports insight insofar as psyche presents the data that are to be understood; psyche constrains insight insofar as the understanding that is available to be grasped is that which is inherent in the data.

However, insight is a spiritual act, an actualization of intentional consciousness or human spirit (2.3.3; 2.8; 4.3). This basic realization about the spiritual nature of insight highlights an incisive fact about the interaction of psyche and spirit within the human mind. This clarification has implications for spirituality.

5.2.2. *The Naturalistic Process of Increasing Spiritual Sensitivity*

Most fundamentally, I understand spirituality to be a person's deliberate commitment to the enhancement of his or her spiritual capacity (see Helminiak, 1996a, Chapter 2, for definitions of spirituality). Accordingly, from a psychological perspective I understand the spiritual or religious practices that people undertake to be essentially means of releasing and intensifying the experience of the human spirit itself. Admittedly, in contrast, most popular piety—Buddhism offers a powerful exception—would understand these practices religiously in terms of "supernatural" intervention and a relationship with God or with some other non-human entity (see Helminiak, 2010, 2013a). However, to my mind, we can now offer a naturalistic explanation of spirituality.

The psyche is the substrate of the emergent human spirit; so just as in the paradigmatic case of phantasms and insight, the psyche both supports and constrains the unfolding of the spirit overall. This interaction between psyche and spirit is critical for human development. Yet, for the most part, contemporary psychology is unaware of it (5.9.2). Psychology overlooks the human spirit *per se* and collapses it into an undifferentiated notion of mind. Psychology tends to take the spiritual for granted and certainly does not name it as such even when dealing with blatantly spiritual aspects of human functioning such as intelligence, reasonableness, and the responsibility appropriate to self-determination and interpersonal and societal involvement. These matters are unavoidable aspects of psychological theory and, especially, practice, but they are not usually sorted out explicitly, and they are hardly recognized as *spiritual*. Rather, especially in psychotherapy, psychology tends to set its explicit focus on matters of the psyche.

Psychotherapy is my immediate concern because attention to it is illustrative. Multiple "theories" portray the goal and process of psychotherapy, but an overall conception might formulate its task well in terms of human integration—the harmonization of all facets of one's mental life in light of a hoped-for increase in inner peace and outer effectiveness in all aspects of living. This process is, I believe, what McNamara (2009; 3.1.2) intends by his varied, multiply modeled, and sometimes overly complicated discussions of "transformation of the Self" (e.g., p. 152). I believe this process is actually also behind Griffin's (1991; 4.20) reference to "the degree of attunement between consciousness and the unconscious portion of the mind" (p. 61). The common mechanism of such an integrative psychotherapeutic process is the restructuring of the psyche: to unearth and diffuse or redirect disruptive emotions, to recognize "unconscious" but controlling images of oneself and others, to free memories of the hurt and trauma that prevent the spontaneous engagement of life, to enhance interpersonal relationships and foster broader horizons, to gain deliberate control over defense mechanisms, and, in general, to refashion the personality, insofar as might be possible, so that it better serves satisfying and wholesome living. Of course, I have deliberately formulated this matter so that psyche comes to the fore. Still, I believe I have fairly represented the basic thrust of much psychotherapeutic practice.

5.2.3. Restructuring Psyche to Release Spirit

Insofar as the restructuring of psyche is the mechanism of human integration, attention to psyche is required for the enhancement of spiritual sensitivity. This suggestion is my point. Attention to the human spirit is, indeed, the *theoretical* key to explaining spirituality, but attention to the psyche is the *practical* key to enhancing spiritual sensitivity.

Understood from this perspective, much psychotherapeutic and even psychiatric practice is, in its own way, an instrument of the spiritual quest. To a large degree, what traditionally was spiritual consultation of the "spiritual director" or guru (Culligan, 1983; Kelleman, 2004; Stairs, 2000) has today become fully secularly conceived clinical consultation of the psychotherapist. Although spiritual directors and clergy tend to be somewhat (too often, frighteningly little) aware of the psychological dimensions of their ministry, secular psychotherapists tend to be even less aware of the spiritual implications of their profession (see Helminiak, 2001a, 2001b). By fostering the harmony of a client's inner life, psychotherapy facilitates the release of the human spirit. The standard practices of the spiritual quest—prayer, meditation, fasting, sleep deprivation, song and ritual, communal celebration, repentance, good works—similarly effect a softening and restructuring of the psyche and the natural unfolding inherent in the human constitution (Helminiak, 2005b, 2008b). Abraham Maslow (1968/1999) spoke of this process of human integration in terms of a shift from deficiency motivation (neurotic, self-serving, self-centered concerns) to growth motivation (healthy, mature, out-going, problem-centered concerns) or, again, in terms of a shift from D-love (deficiency love provoked by need) to B-love ("love for the Being of another person, unneeding love, unselfish love") (p. 47).

This release of the human spirit and unfolding of human potential is the leading edge of the dynamism that drives the universe (4.2.2; 4.7; 4.14.2; 4.20.2). This dynamism moves in cosmogenesis and evolution from matter to life to psyche and onto and through spirit. When free from psychodynamic entanglements, the human spirit is free to soar, to ever increasingly set the agenda for life, to open a person to an experience of transcendent living (Helminiak, 1987b, 2007/2013b)—and through the agency of authentic humanity, to orient the cosmos toward its ultimate fulfillment.

5.2.4. *The Possibility of a Non-Religious and Non-Theist Spiritualogy*

The point, once again, is simply this: Lonergan's differentiation of psyche and spirit within the human mind, when added to contemporary psychological attention to the shifting interaction of body, psyche, and spirit within the person, reveals spiritual enhancement to be a natural dimension of possible human cultivation and growth. Although most frequently this natural process is associated with religious belief and relationship with God, the process itself is first and foremost fully human. Only for this reason, I believe, attention to spirituality is ubiquitous in religions across time and cultures.

Recognition of spirit as an aspect of the human mind suggests a basis on which psychology can treat spirituality as constitutively human without needing to immediately involve appeal to God. Then, spiritualogy becomes first and foremost a specialization in psychology, not in theology—and still less in neuroscience. Elaboration on the human spirit in the sections that follow suggests how the human spirit undergirds and can even explain much of what the religions bespeak as mysticism, religious experience, or enlightenment, that is, transcendent experience.

5.3. Consciousness as Both Conscious and Intentional

The topic of Chapter 4 was the body–mind problem. There, my purpose was to establish the distinct reality of the human mind in contrast to the brain, so I treated the mind globally. Only now and again was there the need to suggest a difference between psyche and spirit within the mind. The topic of this 5th chapter, however, is spirituality. Its basis is the human spirit, so here it becomes imperative that I focus attention on the distinction between psyche and spirit. Moreover, I also need to further elaborate the nature of the human spirit or—what is the same in my usage—human consciousness (5.1.2).

5.3.1. *The Simultaneously and Concomitantly Dual Nature of Human Consciousness*

Chapter 2 elaborated the "levels"—emphases, facets, aspects—on which human consciousness or spirit functions: experience, understanding, judgment, and decision. This functioning implicates two complementary "modes" (Lonergan's, 1957/1992, pp. 299–300). I only intimated this matter in Chapter 2, I presumed it in the introduction of this chapter, and now I make an explicit point of it.

In Lonergan's (pp. 344–346; 1972, pp. 6–9) terminology, consciousness is *conscious* as well as *intentional*. As intentional, consciousness is directed toward some object; intentionality is consciousness *of* something. By consciousness in this sense, the subject tends toward, attends to, regards, is aware of an object. I repeat (5.1.2) that in this case *intentional* is used in its Latinate root meaning of "having external reference" or "tending toward," not in the more common English sense, which is part of psychotherapeutic jargon, that implies deliberation, choice, planning, or design. Yet even as the subject is intending some object, paying attention to it; simultaneously and concomitantly, in another mode the intending subject is also conscious "of" him- or herself as the intending subject. This latter consciousness is not that of a subject's regarding an object; that is, through this consciousness the subject does not become an object of concern or reflection to him- or herself in the same way that any other thing could become an object of interest to the subject. Hence, my quotation marks indicate a peculiar usage of the preposition. Grammatically, a preposition must take an object, but I need the preposition to reference a psychological subject. The subject is present "to" him- or herself precisely as the aware subject, experiencing him- or herself as aware of an object (Helminiak, 1984a; 1996a, pp. 43–59; Lonergan, 1957/1992, pp. 344–346). This presence "to" oneself is the more fundamental to the nature of human consciousness. It is because of this presence "to" oneself that the subject is present to the object being experienced. The subject attains to an object within an experience "of" him- or herself as the "experiencer"—namely, the experiencer of that particular object.

Thus, by way of example, even as I am regarding the density of expressway traffic outside my window, my attention wholly taken up by my detailed observation, I am also simultaneously *conscious* of my subjective act of seeing. Thus, if asked, I could easily *shift my attention* to my activity and reply, "Why, *I was looking* at the early traffic build-up." Within human sight are both the seen and the seeing. It is precisely because of the seeing, present "to" the subject in a non-objectified mode, that the seen can be present to the subject in an objective mode. The seen is experienced in the seeing, which is present "to" the seer.

This expressway example is merely perceptual; it regards the experience of simple visual input. Yet the duality of consciousness pertains also in intellectual experience. When I have a needed insight and finally resolve a problem, for example, I am aware of the solution and concomitantly also conscious of my finding it. Indeed, I tend to be more conscious in this intellectual realm than in the merely perceptual because I up the ante, as it were, as I ascend the levels of consciousness, performing on each higher level acts with more personal investment. Hence, having had an insight, having resolved my problem, I can go on to articulate the answer, *my* answer, the answer *I realize* I have achieved. I am aware of the answer, to be sure: it was my object of concern. But I am also conscious "of" my subjective act of achieving it, and I can easily—spontaneously, unthinkingly, prosaically—promote the conscious act to intentional awareness and state outright, "*I found* the answer."

Through consciousness I am present in two different modes—one presence is directed toward an object; and the other regards myself as the acting subject. Within my presence "to" myself as the acting subject, I experience the intended object.

I have also called these two kinds of consciousness *reflecting* and *non-reflecting* (Helminiak, 1996a, p. 45. See Roy, 2003, for useful criticism.). Reflecting consciousness is intentional. By reflection, one is aware of some object; one reflects upon it; reflection entails a this-against-that, a subject engaging an object. On the other hand, non-reflecting consciousness is conscious. By non-reflecting consciousness one is present "to" oneself, not as an object of reflection, but as the reflecting subject. This non-reflecting mode of subjective experience—experience "of" one's subjectivity as such—is inherent in consciousness; it determines the peculiar nature of consciousness; it is fundamental.

Even while experiencing some object in one mode, in this other mode one experiences oneself, one is present "to" oneself, one has a "sense" of oneself—apart from all objectification, conceptualization, or deliberate advertence—as the "experiencer" of the object. As I note at 5.3.5, Chalmers (1996, p. 197) seems to allude to this same subtle dimension of consciousness and offers the usefully suggestive term, *acquaintance*. As a result of this "sense" of oneself, one could later promote one's non-reflecting consciousness to reflecting consciousness: one could attend to the data of experience, make intentional what was previously only conscious, and then perhaps articulate the past experience. One could say what one was doing: "*I was looking* at the early traffic build-up" or "*I found* the answer." Yet even as one was now speaking of one's past experience, having become an object to oneself, another backdrop of non-reflecting consciousness would always already be operative, ever constituting the subjectivity of the subject, ever ready itself to become an object of further explicit awareness: "*I said* I was looking," "*I exclaimed* I found the answer."

The subject is always more than what can be articulated. I am always more than what I can say about me. The reported "me" never exhausts the agent "I" because the subject "I" is ever acting anew, ever generating further potential content for subsequent reflection about "me," even while the subject might be articulating the prior subjective experience and the self involved in it.

This peculiar bimodal phenomenon is the essence of human subjectivity (Helminiak, 1996a, pp. 43–59). Because of it, we are present "to" ourselves, and we can come to know what we experience within this presence. We can know other objects. More important in the present case, we can also come to know ourselves. This presence "to" oneself constitutes data not only on any intentional object of interest but also on oneself, the subject who is intending the object. This presence "to" oneself constitutes (a) the data of consciousness into which (b) inquiry can provoke insight and interpretation and (c) against which judgment can test the interpretation (2.1.6). Thus, as in Lonergan's analysis, in the three-step process of human intellectual knowing, we can even know our knowing: we experience the process; we have data on it (2.1.5). Consciousness provides not only the data of sense, perceptual content (5.2.1), but also the data of consciousness. Hence, we can experience ourselves as knowers and, thereby, come to know our knowing. Similarly, because of presence "to" oneself, we also have the experience of ongoing identity, the consistent experience "of" the one who is having the experience, the experience of an "I." This is Chalmers's (1996) "sense of self" (p. 10) in a lonely reference to this quintessential aspect of consciousness.

5.3.2. William James on Consciousness as Conscious

Without such presence "to" oneself, how would one ever be able to known oneself or one's own experiences, as such? They would pass by as a disconnected series of evermore-lost, un-self-conscious perceptions (4.6.2).

It was precisely such a fragmented understanding of consciousness that William James (1890/1950, vol. 1, ch. 9) rejected by proposing his metaphor of a stream of consciousness or stream of thought. This metaphor highlights a continuity among the diverse contents of consciousness—the contents are all connected—namely, the continuity of the one who is experiencing the contents. Of course, James hesitates and even refuses to speak of anything like "the one who is experiencing the contents." His reifying or hypostasizing epistemology is not up to this subtlety, as I will explain presently, but at least as I make sense of him, he is clearly attentive to the matter in his own way in his own time.

For example, he titles this pivotal section of his chapter "*The Sense of Personal Identity*," which begins to address "that pure principle of personal identity," "a distinct principle of selfhood" (p. 330). Again, specifying the physiological reactions that one might experience in the body while thinking—although offering a needed appreciation of the human body, James makes too much of these sensed physiological "adjustments" to characterize consciousness (pp. 333, 341)—he also allows "an obscurer feeling of something more; . . . of nothing objective at all but rather of subjectivity as such, of thought become 'its own object' " (p. 305). Or again, maintaining his phenomenological focus on the moment of mental experience, he speaks of the "Thought" as personified; it is also the "Thinker" (p. 342). Thus, in different ways James does acknowledge subjectivity and the human subject, a constant that perdures throughout the stream of thought.

I understand James to be speaking metaphorically of the conscious mode of consciousness in addition to the intentional mode, speaking of the subject's consciousness "of" him- or herself concomitant to the experience of awareness of any objective contents of the mind. To be sure, James's attention remains on intentional consciousness, the awareness of the mental contents, but he also *intimates* a subject who, though not explicitly or objectively *known* except by later reflection on the experience, is experiencing those contents and, thus, constituting them as contents of experience. James knows he must insist that both the content and the subject of the experience are somehow concomitant. His metaphor represents the subject as the very river in which the flow occurs. James (1890/1950, vol. 1) argues,

> Consciousness, then, does not appear to itself chopped up in bits. Such words as "chain" or "train" do not describe it fitly as it presents itself in the first instance. It is nothing jointed; it flows. A "river" or a "stream" are the metaphors by which it is most naturally described. (p. 239)

As "the river"—I would say, "as the conscious subject"—and only so, one can recognize a veritable flow and not, with each passing moment, produce merely a disconnected series of programmed responses to a series of disconnected stimuli.

With his insistence on a stream of thought, James opposed the Associationists, who would build up human experience from the simplest parts, individual percepts, bit upon bit, and thereby miss the perduring whole and the given continuity, the very essence of conscious experience. By the same token, James also opposes the behaviorists of the 20th century (e.g., Natsoulas, 1983, 1986, p. 202; 5.3.6) and the functionalists of our day, whom I see as neo-behaviorists (4.19.2). The functionalists focus on external behaviors, on observable differences, on only perceptual evidence. They would suppose that zombies without consciousness could function indistinguishably from humans with consciousness, thereby arguing against any true reality of consciousness (Dennett, 1991). Alternatively, they would grant consciousness to mechanistic thermostats and computers because some of their external outputs mimic those of human minds (Chalmers, 1996). In contrast, James's point is that attention to the mind offers evidence about a peculiar kind of human experience. It entails a sense of personal identity. It allows for subsequent self-knowledge. Such self-knowledge is precisely what makes humans unique. But such knowledge of oneself, objectified self-consciousness, objectification of oneself—evinced by one's ability to speak of oneself as the object "me" and of one's experiences as experiences of a subject "I"—depends on a more primordial, non-objectifying consciousness. It is "the indispensable subjective condition of their [the objective contents of the mind] being experienced at all" (James, 1890/1950, vol. 1, p. 304). With his metaphors, at least as I read them, James addresses this subtlety.

The closest James comes to specifying it is as a certain "act of appropriation," an agency depicted as inherent in thought itself. It functions via a "warmth and intimacy" (p. 333), a familiarity by which the self—or, rather, in the present moment, the Thought—recognizes its own. The Thought makes these "appropriations, or repudiations, of its 'own.' . . . it is the actual focus of accretion, the hook from which the chain of past selves dangles" (p. 340).

> The present moment of consciousness is . . . the darkest in the whole series. It may feel its own immediate existence—we have all along admitted the possibility of this, hard as it is by direct introspection to ascertain the fact—but nothing can be known about it till it be dead and gone. (p. 341)

James is talking about non-reflecting consciousness, and he attributes it to the Thought. He is anthropomorphizing. But, of course, in this case the anthropomorphization is completely appropriate. His very effort is to express that elusive experience of consciousness that distinctively characterizes a person, and he speaks, rather, of the Thought because he is trying to remain as close as possible to the very experience of the mind's activity and because the content of the mind is its most salient feature. James believes that the term "Thought" is most appropriate because "it immediately suggests the omnipresence of cognition"—although, again with excessive emphasis on intentionality, despite his own statements elsewhere, as I am arguing, he understands *cognition* as the contents and even the essence of thinking: "cognition (or reference to an object other than the mental state itself), which we shall soon see to be the mental life's essence" (p. 186). Nonetheless, James is, indeed, speaking of a person who is thinking; he is elucidating the experience of human consciousness. Perhaps, in place of the objectified metaphor "Thought," to speak, rather, of a more agential "Thinking" would better suggest the active point of "focus" and the "hook" among James's metaphors. I do believe James means "Thought" in the active, vivid sense of "the thinking."

Clearly, James does not intend some objective, physical, mechanical process such that the objects of consciousness would be "objects in the hands of something else. A thing [objective, material, perceptible] cannot appropriate itself; it *is* itself" (p. 340). "No material agent could thus turn round and grasp itself—material activities always grasp something else than the agent" (p. 343). In *De Trinitate* (ix, iii, 3), Augustine made the same point as follows:

> For whence does the mind know any mind, if it does not know itself? For it is not like the eye of the body that sees other eyes and does not see itself. . . . As the mind itself gathers information about bodily things through the senses of the body, so it does about incorporeal things through its own self. Therefore it knows itself through itself. (cited in Lonergan, 1967d, p. xii; translation mine)

Despite himself, then, and despite his explicit rejection of such a "metaphysical" option for a psychologist, James, like Augustine, is talking about the spiritual. Unlike material or sensate realities, "it ['the moment of consciousness'] may feel its own immediate existence" (p. 341). As experienced immediately, that is, without mediation, it is not known; it is no object of explicit cognition. But something of it is afoot, namely, the fact of knowing, the fact of the stream, as James niggardly elaborated as follows: Above and beyond the objects of consciousness, namely, the objectified "Self" and the "not-Self,"

> there *is* nothing save the fact that they are known, the fact of the stream of thought being there as the indispensable subjective

condition of their being experienced at all. But this *condition* of the experience is not one of the *things experienced* at the moment; this knowing is not immediately *known*. (p. 304)

"Nothing can be known about it till it be dead and gone" (p. 341).

Reading these lines through the lens of Lonergan's analysis, I make lucid and congenial sense of them. Something of consciousness itself is given in the moment of consciousness, in the Thought/Thinking: immediate experience—a "feel [of] its immediate existence." It is, indeed, hard to ascertain by "direct introspection," which would be appropriate if one were searching internally for some object. Nonetheless, this input, this immediate experience, could later be processed cognitively and then be named a fact—"the fact that they are known," "the fact of the stream." But as only a given, this "fact" is not a known (4.18.4–4.18.5). No merely given is yet known. Rather, the given constitutes data, something that is merely experienced and, as such, open to being questioned, understood, and eventually known. As such, it is, indeed, experienced; but it would not be correctly catalogued among the "*things experienced*" because *things* is taken to be the objects of consciousness. Given this restriction, we cannot allow that what is experienced of consciousness is itself a thing, and denying a thing, one might also mistakenly be inclined to deny the experience altogether. But if one credits the experience, another option opens: one might attend to, question, and eventually understand and know what was experienced. Accordingly, the knowing is "not immediately known"—because knowledge entails a process that mediates the known to the knower. The experienced data only provide material for possible inquiry, and insight and conceptualization might follow; further, the conceptualization could then be tested against the data (2.1.6). Then, only then, genuine knowledge would finally result—but only after the original experience as such was "dead and gone."

James's (1890/1950, vol. 1) phenomenological analyses of consciousness square impressively with the position I have been advocating in this book, but he cannot easily acknowledge their implication. An inadequate epistemology hobbles him. His understanding of "metaphysics" seems to be tied to a sensate-modeled theory of knowledge at this point. To affirm the actuality of what is understood and verified in appropriate data would mean for James to affirm the near unthinkable, namely, that consciousness, empirically approached—not, then, via some other-worldly metaphysics, but via this-worldly psychology—is something in itself. The experience of which James speaks provides the data to ground a correctly affirmed understanding of what could be named consciousness. Thus, as experienced, understood, and affirmed as correctly understood, consciousness is real. It is something that exists. It exists in its own right as a dimension of humanity, and it is a peculiar kind of reality, immaterial, incorporeal, or spiritual by nature. Logically, then, the spiritual must also be real. But James's pragmatism cannot accept such a conclusion, which pertains to the Spiritualists.

On James's understanding, beyond the phenomenal self the Spiritualists project some meta-self to whom experiences are attributed (as if it were *looking* at them: perceptualism all the way! 2.2.2). For the Spiritualists, this meta-self is to be the center of personal identity and continuity. James understands this meta-self to be "an invisible active soul-substance" (p. 305; also pp. 319, 330) or a "transcendental principle of unity" (p. 330). It is supposedly a substantial, immaterial, simple, immortal, individual, self-existent being (pp. 343–344). In fact, James's portrayal of the soul is an accurate summary of the Scholastic opinion of the times. However, by then that opinion had devolved far from the subtlety of Aquinas's opinions (Lonergan, 1967d; 1980/1990, p. 177), so it labored under "a confusing of sensible and intellectual knowledge" (Lambert & McShane, 2010, p. 50; 2.2.5), "a conceptualism inspired by scholasticism that had best be thought of as a nominalism, an exclusion of active thinking" (p. 37), "a transmission of concepts cut off from their source" (p. 38). So, as a reified concept, the imagined soul was "substantial" "stuff" existing somewhere "out there" on its own as an individual "being," that is, an imaginable, ghostly, gossamer-like, material "substance," a thing (4.1.2). This supposition, James could not endorse, and rightly so. Eugene Webb (1988) summarized this matter as follows:

> James was arguing against what he believed to be a mistaken tendency, especially in German philosophy since Kant, to speak of consciousness as though it were a sort of substance in the metaphysical sense or the stuff of which a 'transcendental ego' is constituted. He did not mean to deny on the other hand, that we have experience and perform intentional operations. (p. 7)

James (1890/1950, vol. 1) found that, as far as this-worldly living and thinking go, he could already account for all the functions that the Spiritualists attribute to the imagined soul-substance, so positing a "soul" (as James's Spiritualists understood it) was superfluous. I agree. However, James took exception on one point. According to James's understanding and that of decadent Scholasticism, "the Soul-Substance is supposed to be a fixed unchanging thing"—whereas thoughts come and go, people's minds develop (p. 345). However, immutability, a consciousness-relevant characteristic of the soul, is erroneously posited. That the soul was supposed to be outside of earthly time did not imply that the soul does not change. This mistaken supposition depends, ever again, on a misconceived sensate-modeled epistemology—in this way.

If knowing, perception-like, via confrontation with its object, is taking a good look, then the soul could view all things while it itself remained the same. But if knowing is via identity with the known (2.3.3), knowing entails in the "soul" increasing perfection, ongoing fulfillment, never-ending expansion toward all being.

> Then you might say that the more knowing there is in the subject that comes from himself [or herself] the better off he [or she] is. . . . The fellow who knows something is better off than a fellow who is ignorant. . . . Knowing is a perfection of the subject that knows. (Lonergan, 1980/1990, p. 159; see also 72–75, 87–88, 179–180)

Knowing, "the process of experiencing, understanding, and judging is a process of self-transcendence" (Lonergan, 1972, p. 239), a matter of what we today call "personal growth" (1.1; 5.2.2). In this chapter I am appealing to this very self-transcendence, built into the human mind with its bimodal consciousness, to ground a non-theological understanding of spirituality and "spiritual *growth*." Lonergan (1967d) found this notion of knowledge as perfection, development, growth, or self-transcendence of the individual in Aristotle's theory of knowledge and, then again, much more explicitly in Thomas Aquinas (1961 version, e.g., 2–2, q. 9, a. 1, ad 1; 3, q. 11, a. 2, ad 3). To be noted is this: Aquinas (1, q. 57, a. 4) allows that even angels continue to grow in knowledge although they are pure spirits (souls). Pure spirits or souls are not immutable.

Granted this correction about the supposed immutability of the soul, James would find nothing at all to reject in the notion of a soul. Indeed, apart from that reifying epistemology in James and the Spiritualists alike—"By the Soul is always meant something *behind* the present Thought, another kind of substance, existing on a non-phenomenal plane" (James, 1890/1950, vol. 1, p. 345)—James could say they were talking of the same reality:

> *It* [the Soul] *is at all events needless for expressing the actual subjective phenomena of consciousness as they appear.* We have formulated them all without its aid, by the supposition of a stream of thoughts, each substantially different from the rest, but cognitive of the rest and "appropriative" of each other's

content.... The unity, the identity, the individuality, and the immateriality [spirtualness?] that appear in the psychic life are thus accounted for as phenomenal and temporal facts exclusively, and with no need of reference to any more simple or substantial agent than the present Thought or "section" of the stream. We have seen it to be single and unique in the sense of having no separable parts . . .—perhaps that is the only kind of simplicity meant to be predicated of the soul. The present Thought also has being,—at least all believers in the Soul believe so—and if there be no other Being in which it "inheres," it ought itself to be a "substance." If *this* kind of simplicity and substantiality were all that is predicated of the Soul, then it might appear that we had been talking of the soul all along, without knowing it, when we treated the present Thought as an agent, an owner, and the like. (pp. 344–345).

I say, yes, indeed; they were talking of the same thing all along, without knowing it.

James and the Spiritualists were both aware of data, the "phenomenal and temporal facts" (see 4.18.4 about "facts"), which called for explanation. Both proposed conceptions to account for the data and, simplifying their supposition, they gave names to their understandings. The Spiritualists called it "soul," and James called it "Thought." Neither name is very helpful or happy, but the intended meanings are what counts. Meaning the same but, at this later date, using more nuanced and technically defined terms, I would suggest we call it "consciousness" or "subjectivity" and characterize it as bimodal, both conscious and intentional, both non-reflecting and reflecting. I find that James rather cleverly expressed this very notion.

5.3.3. Consensus Over Time and Across Opinions

Eschew the sensate-modeled epistemology, which pictures substance, being, soul, mind, and spirit to be globs of fuzzy stuff floating on their own somewhere out there separated from the rest of the person and the phenomenal world, and the pieces of the puzzle all fall easily into place. Then consciousness is what James was brilliantly describing in his commonsensical way; it is what Aristotle and Aquinas portrayed in their Aristotelian metaphysical terms; it is what the Spiritualists intended as reified "substance" and "soul" in their decadent Scholastic usage; it is even what the Associationist D. G. Thompson was intimating to James's (1890/1950, pp. 354–355) near satisfaction; and it is what Lonergan explicated by applying generalized empirical method to the data of internal experience. What was described, portrayed, intended, intimated, and explicated on shifting epistemological presuppositions finds grounding in the consistent experiential evidence on which the differing conceptualizations rest. Given Lonergan's three-stage epistemology, the description, the portrayal, the intension, the intimation, and the explication—these varied hypotheses—seek their verification in the data. The varying conceptualizations are not equally adequate to the data. Nonetheless, in that the engendering experience cannot but be reasonably affirmed under some conceptualization, there exists "something there" (Hay, 2007). After all, even fire was once a basic element, then the release of phlogiston, and now a process of oxidation, but through the centuries that object of commonsense encounter named "fire" has not changed in itself or moved in and out of reality. Similarly, consciousness is also an aspect of reality and can be reasonably affirmed as such. It's being real—no less than oxidation—does not depend on its being able to be seen, felt, or imagined. Unfortunately, we corporeally oriented humans are hard-pressed to rely only on a "detached, disinterested, and unrestricted desire to know" (Lonergan, 1957/1992, p. 696) in order to affirm this factuality. But we could. Indeed, we ought.

Moreover, even when affirming it, we are probably still left to wonder "what it is in itself"—even as when considering gravity, mass, leptons, and quarks—which are equally invisible, impalpable, and unimaginable but about which we can attentively list precise characteristics down to the 12th decimal point and insightfully and reasonably interrelate them in astoundingly coherent theories, explaining as much as perhaps could possibly ever be humanly known—we are still also left wondering "what they are in themselves" (e.g., Chalmers, 1996, p. 153). We still wonder because in these situations we come face to face with the deepest mystery, existence itself. We come face to face with being; we engage what is purely, simply, undeniably affirmed: it is. Gravity is. Mass is. Consciousness is. And we have no *palpable* sense of "what it is in itself." The most we can say, the best to be said, is that we are engaging aspects of being and we are able to list their disparate and interactive characteristics as we come to know being.

If so, being must be of different kinds. Beyond the most familiar entities, the material ones—my chair, the expressway, Fido, my body: they do exist, I cannot not affirm their facticity—my inherent requisite to affirm the reasonable has me affirming consciousness, as well, although it is not material. Evidently, the kinds of being in our universe include the spiritual—the Thought, the Soul. It may "feel its own immediate existence" (James, 1890/1950, vol. 1, p. 341). It is the essence of "subjectivity" (p. 305).

This non-objectified, non-reflecting consciousness "of" oneself is also the essence of the spiritual. Free from the this-upon-that-ness, over-against-ness, this-next-to-that-ness, agent-versus-object-ness that characterizes materiality, subjectivity and spirit constitute a reality *sui generis*. Its defining characteristic is presence "to" itself, a peculiar self-consciousness. James described it as warmth and intimacy resulting in ongoing appropriation of ever additional mental contents as in a river or a stream. He recognized that he was speaking of something strikingly similar to the "Soul," and I recognize that he was speaking of something strikingly similar to non-reflecting consciousness. Despite himself, he was speaking about the real, being, ontology, even his dismissed metaphysics, if you will. Indeed, how can one be a psychologist, how can one do any science at all, how can one intend to treat of the actual, without *ipso facto* engaging ontology? What else does the term *ontology* mean? Only muddled epistemology obscures and evades these conclusions.

Clean up the epistemology and William James provides substantive support for the argument I am making: consciousness is conscious as well as intentional. For James, there flows a stream that connects our thoughts. In addition to whatever mental contents might be involved in the individual thoughts, consciousness also entails a perduring subjectivity, a non-objectified presence of the subject "to" him- or herself as the "experiencer" of those contents.

5.3.4. An Argument Based on Common Experience

Is there really, as James suggests in opposition to the Associationists, a second mode of consciousness, concomitant and simultaneous with the intentional experience of any particular object? This is *the* question about consciousness. Are we also conscious of our seeing even while we give our deliberate attention to what we see? If not, how is it that I am now talking about such a phenomenon as seeing, can talk about things *I* have seen, and, I presume, you understand what I mean? Surely, at some point in your life, totally oblivious to yourself and your surroundings, someone called you out of a reverie, daydream, or deep thought and asked, "Where are you? What's going on with you? You seem to have drifted away." And without hesitation, you were able to say, "Oh, forgive me. I was thinking about such and such." Embarrassingly oblivious to yourself and your surroundings, in some mode you were, nonetheless, conscious of your activity, your daydreaming, your thinking, not merely aware of the object of your supposedly "all-consuming" distraction. If not, how were you then able to talk about yourself as thinking?

Of course, this consciousness "of" consciousness itself is not something to which we usually attend—and that's the problem here. And attending to it is difficult because we are used to attending to objects, but at this point the "object" of concern is our own subjectivity, and we do not experience it in the same way as we experience objects. Subjectivity is present "to" us in a different mode. So we tend just to take this consciousness for granted. It is, in fact, the presupposition for the possibility of our conscious awareness of, and later objectification of, anything we experience. Yet it is the proverbial water that the fish does not notice. We tend not ever to attend to it, not even in consciousness studies. But it is real.

Its reality can be argued by comparing two different sense modalities. I spoke of being conscious of our seeing even as our explicit attention was on the seen. A similar statement can be made about hearing. But then one can also compare seeing and hearing, and one must wonder what they have in common—certainly not the contents or the distinctive qualities of these different experiences. Lonergan (1957/1992) makes the point lucidly:

> Seeing is not merely a response to the stimulus of color and shape; it is a response that consists in becoming aware of color and shape. Hearing is not merely a response to the stimulus of sound; it is a response that consists in becoming aware of sound. As color differs from sound, so seeing differs from hearing. Still, seeing and hearing have a common feature, for in both occurrences there is not merely content but also conscious act. . . .
>
> . . . there are those that would define "seeing" as "awareness of color" and then proceed to argue that in seeing one was aware of color but of nothing else whatever, that "awareness of color" occurs but that a concomitant "awareness of awareness" is a fiction. This, I think, does not accurately reflect the facts. If seeing is an awareness of nothing but color and hearing is an awareness of nothing but sound, why are both named "awareness"? Is it because there is a similarity between color and sound? Or is it that color and sound are disparate, yet with respect to both there are acts that are similar? In the latter case, what is the similarity? Is it that both acts are occurrences, as metabolism is an occurrence? Or it is that both acts are conscious? One may quarrel with the phrase "awareness of awareness," particularly if one imagines awareness to be a looking and finds it preposterous to talk about looking at a look. But one cannot deny that, within the cognitional act as it occurs, there is a factor

or element or component over and above its content, and this factor is what differentiates cognitional acts from unconscious occurrences. (pp. 345–346)

The basic argument is that within human experience there is a dimension that perdures across the experiences of different mental contents and of different sense modalities. So, in addition to the seen, there is also the experience of the seeing; but in addition to seeing, there is also hearing, and across these acts of seeing and hearing, there is also a constancy: *I* see, *I* hear. Without such a constancy, statements of this kind could not be made. Some lasting center of experience is the presupposition of such statements. That perduring quality of human experience is consciousness—not as an intentionality specified by the content of its object, but as the very experience of having access to that and every content. Human intentionality is conscious; it is self-conscious. It offers data on its own functioning. Evidently, it functions in two modes. In addition to the more easily noted intentionality, there operates also a non-objectified, an immediate consciousness of the intending.

5.3.5. An Argument From the "Paradox of Phenomenal Judgments": Chalmers

Besides appealing to authority such as William James or appealing to the evidence of one's own experience, one can also mount a logical argument for the bimodal nature of consciousness. Chalmers (1996) provides the material for such an argument. In some intuitive sense he actually seems to be approaching the same argument as Lonergan. However, I say only "seems to be" because, as I will indicate, Chalmers's contribution is tightly entangled with distracting and even disqualifying elements, and it is not integrated into Chalmers's more elaborate and summary statements about consciousness (pp. 3–11).

The specific issue is what Chalmers calls "The Paradox of Phenomenal Judgments" (p. 172). The paradox is this: when one makes a statement—what Chalmers calls "second-order phenomenal judgments"—such as "I am having a red sensation" (p. 176) (that is, "I see redness"), it is difficult to account for the "I am having" part of the statement. Perceptual experience and standard brain function easily account for the "red sensation" part of the statement. But what input grounds the "I see" and the "I am having" parts of the statement?

The easy answer, in Lonergan's terminology, would be that, in addition to the intentional experience of the percept, the redness, there is the concomitant and simultaneous conscious experience of the experiencing, which *per se* entails an "experiencer." Along with the seen, there is the seeing, and both are present in consciousness, the seen pertaining to the objective pole of the experience, and the seeing pertaining to the subjective pole. To account for the experience as reported, there must be given within consciousness some other kind of data in addition to the perceptual data of redness. Only some such other kind of data, also constitutive of the experience, could ground the claim, "*I am having* a sensation." Two sources of data—the data of the sense and the data of consciousness—constitute the experience. Thus, the one experience provides a complex of data, which only a number of concepts could express, namely, the experiencer of the experience, I; the kind of experience, sight; the object of the experience, redness; all linked by an insightful grasp of the relationship among them to produce the reflective statement, "I see redness." This is not to say that these distinctions and relationships are explicit in the experience. Their ground is there, but their explication is not. Data are merely given. Their conceptualization and interrelationship require a further intellectual processing, namely, inquiry, insight, conceptualization, and formulation, which characterize a further dimension of conscious function called its "second level" (2.3). Of course, the present example, "I see red," is so very simple and routine that achievement of the statement is virtually instantaneous, taken for granted, and its complexity is easily overlooked. More challenging examples, which call for serious effort to achieve understanding, make these complexities more easily recognized.

Chalmers (1996) approaches that same argument and answer. However, as he and current consciousness studies have set it up, his problem becomes even more complicated; and the skeptic's question is whether such a complex experience ever happens at all. In the first place, against strong opposition Chalmers wants to argue that consciousness actually is something of its own kind over and above any physical and biological mechanisms in the brain. These, supposedly, easily enough already account for the experience of the redness, and Chalmers buys into this biological reductionism in the case of perceptions. The sticking point, then, is his zombie twin.

Supposedly, in every discernible way the zombie twin behaves indistinguishably from the conscious Chalmers although it differs in only this one way: it is not conscious (pp. 94–95, 120–121, 156, 158–160). On these presuppositions, the zombie could also make the statement "I see something red" because this statement is a mere external behavior, a verbal utterance, and like all behaviors, this statement is, supposedly, completely explained by the biological processes of the brain. We know how the neural system controls breathing and muscular contraction to produce audible speech, for example. But on what basis could the zombie make a statement about seeing when making it implies the experience of seeing, a conscious event, which by definition the zombie does not enjoy. Easily enough through vision and brain processes; the perceptual content, the redness, gets into the zombie's statement. But how could that content reporting conscious experience—I am seeing—ever get into the zombie's statement? From where would that content come? Certainly not from sense perception.

That the zombie could make such statements about consciousness while not having consciousness is the pressing instance of Chalmers's paradox: "It seems consciousness is *explanatorily irrelevant* to our claims and judgments about consciousness" (p. 177). "It is one thing to accept that consciousness is irrelevant to explaining how I walk around the room [mere external behavior possible even in sleepwalking]; it is another to accept that it is irrelevant to explaining why I talk about consciousness" (p. 182). 'Tis a puzzlement.

Of course, I believe this argument on the basis of the zombie twin is ludicrous; it is mere science fiction; it ignores the *de facto*, evidence-dependent status of human knowing (2.3.6). Only incoherent epistemology generates this curious paradox and sustains a struggle with it. Nonetheless, run with the argument and see where Chalmers's attempt to meet it leads him. And I give away the ending: Chalmers must believe there is a mechanism for knowledge of consciousness that is different from perception, which is the mechanism for knowledge of other things.

In the first place, Chalmers argues that some causal link to something other than consciousness cannot explain our access to consciousness—as, for example, the input of some stimulus on a receptor can explain a perception. Such an explanation applies only "when there is a gap between our core epistemic situation and the phenomena in question." Such an explanation would make our access to consciousness "*mediated*, in the way our access to objects in the environment is mediated, by some causal chain or reliable mechanism" (p. 196). He persists, "Knowledge of conscious experience is in many important respects quite different from knowledge in other domains. Our knowledge of experience does not consist in a causal relationship to experience, but in another sort of relationship entirely" (p. 193).

Then, taking the next fateful step, Chalmers characterizes that other sort of relationship. Although his argument is entangled in neurological functionalist reductionism, behaviorist emphasis on observables, mechanistic processes of this-against-that, and the picture-thinking that goes with it, he is forced to posit some non-materialistic explanation when he attempts to take consciousness seriously. He begins to speak of consciousness in ways that resonate with my non-reflecting presence "to" oneself, Lonergan's conscious (as well as intentional), Aquinas's identity of intellectual act and content (that matter of *intellectus in actu* at 2.3.3), and James's warm and intimate *appropriation*, which contrasts with cognition (5.3.2). Chalmers (1996) insists, "Intuitively, our access to consciousness is not mediated at all. Conscious experience lies at the center of our epistemic universe; we have access to it *directly*" (p. 196). "Consciousness is not an ordinary referent: our relation to it is unmediated, and it is the center of our mental life" (p. 204). "I *know* I am conscious, and the knowledge is based solely on my immediate experience" (p. 198).

In contrast to his more consistent usage wherein the experience of consciousness is identified with the particular and varied contents of consciousness, i.e., the percepts and their distinctive characteristics, their *qualia* (5.4.2; 5.5.1 & 4), the terminology in the present case is telling: not mediated, accessed directly, unmediated relation, immediate experience. Chalmers even proposes a term for this peculiar dimension of consciousness: "To have an experience is automatically to stand in some sort of intimate epistemic relation to the experience—a relation that we might call 'acquaintance'" (pp. 196–197). The denotative vagueness of the term *acquaintance* is usefully suggestive. Talk of this dimension of consciousness is not easy. At 5.3.1, I had to struggle to characterize non-reflecting consciousness as not-objectified, as a peculiar presence "to." Chalmers's term similarly suggests just some kind of primordial, not yet conceptualized, perhaps only "intuited" or "sensed" access to data. Natsoulas (1986) calls it "self-intimational." It is difficult to find words to name this experience, but the suggestive meanings of the proffered terms converge on a peculiar experience proper to what we call consciousness.

When all is said and done, I am not sure how Chalmers deals with the paradox of his twin zombie. It can supposedly make statements about consciousness, which it does not possess. For me, argument by appeal to zombies is a bust (2.3.6).

When Chalmers attends to his own experience, however, he ends up formulating it in terms similar to Lonergan's and James's. In human sight there are both the seeing and the seen. Perception easily accounts for the intentional object, the seen; but to account for the further undeniable data, the seeing and the ability subsequently to claim sight, requires positing another dimension to consciousness in addition to intentionality. So, to articulate the difference, Lonergan speaks of consciousness as *conscious* as well as *intentional*. I have coined the terms *non-reflecting* and *reflecting* to name these same modes of consciousness. Louis Roy (2003, pp. 27, 29) offers a very useful clarification (which I have been trying to follow: 1.9) by suggesting a distinction between *conscious* and *aware* and restricting the term *awareness* to intentional experience. James (1890/1950) speaks of *appropriation* via "warmth and intimacy" and contrasts it with *cognition* (vol. I, p. 186). In parallel fashion, Franz Brentano (1874/1973) distinguished between *Wahrnehmung* and *Beobachtung*: inner "perception" and inner "observation" (pp. 29–30; see Helminiak, 1996a, pp. 54). Chalmers proposes *acquaintance* and relates it to *experience*. This lineup of theorists presents parallel accounts of the two modes of human consciousness, and Chalmers's account matches the others.

Nonetheless, I must flag an indeterminacy in Chalmers's position. When I force Chalmers's terminology into that lineup, his term *experience* becomes ambiguous. Generally he uses it as an outright synonym for consciousness overall, and he takes consciousness to be virtually identical to intentional phenomenal experiences or *qualia*, such as redness, blueness, sweetness, or sourness; and his concern throughout this whole present discussion is mere perception, such as seeing redness. His overall treatment tilts overwhelmingly toward perceptions. However, in that lineup, the conscious dimension of conscious *experience* (acquaintance) stands in contrast to the perceptual dimension of conscious *experience* (experience), so the term *experience* is ambiguous. Usually it means consciousness overall, but in that lineup it denotes only one mode of consciousness, namely, consciousness as conscious. Additionally, Chalmers uses the terms *judgment* and *knowledge* more casually than I would. Moreover, the epistemological confusion of Chalmers's panpsychism, highlighted at 4.21, ever haunts this discussion. So to catch Chalmers's exact intent is sometimes a challenge. His account of consciousness remains rather undifferentiated (see Helminiak, 2014). Nonetheless, within his presentation, even at the level of mere perceptual experience and in terms of "the paradox of phenomenal judgments," I discern another argument for consciousness as conscious. Namely, human consciousness entails a non-reflecting mode—an immediate presence "to" what is experienced. This non-mediated experience constitutes potential data on consciousness itself and, thus, justifies statements about it—"second order judgments" such as "*I am having* a red sensation." Otherwise, as is Chalmers's point, how could such statements occur?

5.3.6. An Argument Against a Behaviorist Explanation: Natsoulas for Skinner

Thomas Natsoulas (1986) proposed a competing answer to that question and, apparently judging it plausible, attributed it to B. F. Skinner (pp.

202–203). This alternative answer seems to depend on memory. Supposedly, I have no unmediated consciousness of my experiences, but only memories of the experiences that had happened, and I know them by remembering them in another occurrence of intentional awareness. Thus, I see red; then almost instantaneously, I attend to the now past seeing of red; and on the basis of this latter, the later experience, I can say, "I had a red sensation." This kind of analysis is another instance of that which leads Buddhist theorists to conclude that there exists "no self," but only the rapidly alternating appearance of a self in intentional consciousness (3.1.4). Instead of allowing that two modes, the intentional and the conscious, simultaneously and inextricably constitute the one act of human consciousness, the one pertaining to the object and the other, to the subject who is experiencing the object; this competing answer would appeal to two successive acts of only intentional awareness, one regarding the seen red and the other regarding the memory of the red's having been seen. This alternative answer purportedly explains statements about self-awareness on the basis only of intentionality: by attending to the memory of the seen red, even as one had attended to the red itself, one knows that the red was seen. This answer limits human consciousness to its intentional mode; in step with prevalent theory, it models consciousness on perception via stimulus and receptor (5.4). True to behaviorist theory and today's functionalism (4.19.2; 5.3.2), this answer tends to explain "consciousness" as only an external behavior; it minimizes any claim for inner experience, mind, or non-corporeal reality. My point is that such a construal of human consciousness is incoherent.

I do not deny that one becomes intentionally aware of oneself by reflecting back on, by remembering, the initial conscious experience "of" oneself as subject. The initial experience is a conscious, not an intentional act, so in itself it is in no way objectified, reflected on, noted, categorized, or understood. It is a pure and mere given, something that *could be* reflected on (2.2.1). It is experienced in another mode, non-reflectingly. I sometimes use the phrase "to catch oneself in the act" to talk of becoming aware of an insight, but always with quotation marks. This phrase is inaccurate in that it suggests intentional experience of what can be only conscious experience. But it is accurate in that we do "catch ourselves," but only after the fact, only after some experience is already underway and, at least to this extent, already passed. As James (1890/1950, vol. 1) phrased the matter, "nothing can be known about it till it be dead and gone" (p. 342; 5.3.2). This accurate interpretation is what I mean at this point as I grant some validity to the behaviorist account of self-awareness. But the behaviorist account somehow posits self-awareness without self-consciousness. The problem is that, in the supposed remembering, the behaviorist account includes no basis for accounting for the subject, for I, who had the experience of seeing the red. This account explicitly denies a mental experience "of" a self who is having the experience and claims such inner experience is irrelevant or non-existent, so behaviorism allows for no data to support any subject's subsequent remembrance of him- or herself as a subject.

The behaviorist account allows for only two contents of awareness. The first regards the color red, and the second regards the red's having been seen. The first is the object of sense perception, and the second is an object of memory. However, percept and memory are of a kind. Processed in the brain and experienced within the mind, the one object and the other are of equivalent makeup, dependent, in fact, on the actuation of substantially the same neuronal systems. Accordingly, the experience in question might just as well have been that of seeing red and then, almost instantaneously, of seeing blue. There is no reason that the second intentional act of awareness of blue should give evidence of a subject in the first intentional act of seeing red. As objects of awareness, the memory of the first intentional act of seen red is no different from a second intentional act of now seeing blue. Both color and memory are objects of awareness. If somehow, additionally, the hypothetical organism in question could get access to its memory bank, this organism could have a memory of seen red and a memory of seen blue. One after the other, all intentional targets, these different experiences would come in a row, a continuous string of registered objects: red, blue, memory of red, memory of blue—like the train or chain that William James rejected as an inadequate metaphor for consciousness (5.3.2). But none of the objects in this train of experiences is the subject who had the experiences. None is James's "river" or "flow." There is no accounting for the "experiencer." This inadequacy is the problem.

The behaviorist theory provides no basis, no data, to ground a statement that "*I* saw red, *I* saw blue, *I* have a memory of seeing red and then of seeing blue." The only content available to attention is a string of objects of experience: red, blue, red remembered, blue remembered. This inadequacy applies to the memories as much as to the initial sightings. There is no content available to specify the subject of these sightings. If the experience of the red would need a memory to specify the subject who had the experience, then the experience of the memory of the experience of the red would equally need another memory to specify the subject of the memory, and so, ad infinitum. On the basis of such a string of merely intentional acts, access to the experiencing subject would never be available. No affirmation of a self could arise.

Appeal to merely intentional experiences cannot explain the experience of human subjectivity. Subjectivity is immanent in the experience because the very nature of an experience is to belong to someone (4.20.2). There is no experience without an experiencer, so data on the subject must be part of the data of the experience. If these data are not in the initial experience, neither will they be in the memory of the experience—and so on, ad infinitum.

In that alternative answer, it must be assumed that it was I who had the experiences. In the behaviorist analysis, there is no subject and, therefore, no genuine experience, as in the case of a tree limb falling into a pond (4.20.5). That the subject would be I must be an assumption, supposed and inserted into the analysis. Common sense would certainly suggest that it was I who had the experiences and have memories of them—but only because we are talking of human beings, and, in accord with our everyday experience and grounded in it, we have reason to take for granted, assume, suppose, understand, a consistent subject of our perceptions and memories and to affirm this subject, I, in our narratives. Making it explicit that this assumption is merely an assumption, Natsoulas (1986) states that a mental act "includes . . . normally . . . a reference to oneself as the one who" had it (p. 202). In the case of humans, yes, of course; it's only common sense; it's what is normal. But as a coherent argument about the nature of human consciousness, this answer has a hole in it, namely, an assumption without grounds.

After all, the organism in question could have been Fido, who certainly demonstrates perception of colors and can learn, can remember, to respond differentially to them. Yet Fido, perhaps responding as trained to the experience, does not, nonetheless, go around explicating his responsiveness, saying, "*I* just saw the color blue." Even more remotely, the mechanism in question could have been a computer, programmed to respond differentially to red and blue light, to retain in accessible memory the event of having detected red or blue, and even to print out or announce now in human language, "I just saw the color red." That perforce the computer is conscious, has a sense of identity, is a someone—well, I have addressed this science-fiction scenario (4.9.5, 4.16.1–4.16.2; 5.1.2). The computer can be said to be "conscious" only because consciousness is defined as the impoverished, solely intentional notion I am challenging.

Moreover, appeal to a merely intentional consciousness might seem to provide a plausible answer when only perceptual experiences are in question: I saw red. But what about having an insight? What would be the remembered report? Would it be something like this: problem encountered; insight had? The mere reportable memory of having had a problem and an insight into it provides precious little substance about the experience of the insight. Not only is the "I" not accounted for, as already argued, but the understanding, the resolution of the problem constitutive of the insight, is also not accounted for. An explanation of the experience of an insight must provide a basis for the subject who had the experience as well as for the understanding generated via the insight (2.3.3). Clearly, human mental experiences contain an array of data. In the case of an insight, something more than remembered encounter with some object obviously pertains, but the alternative answer provides no way to account for the added content of this peculiar experience, namely, the reported personal resolution of the problem. Attention to only perceptual experience easily overlooks the essential difference between human and other kinds of responsiveness to encounters with stimuli.

Human mental acts do, indeed, normally include a reference to oneself, as Natsoulas suggests. However, the present question is, How so? On the basis of the behaviorist answer, hard-nosed logical analysis could not sustain the imported assumption of reference to oneself. It rests on no evidence in the presented scenario—except, again, the extraneous appeal to the commonsensical experience that we all have but that this alternative answer is, in fact, trying to explain away. This alternative answer might, indeed, seem to successfully explain it away because this answer smuggles into its argument the unavoidable content it needs but is trying to discredit, and only so is it able to account for statements such as "*I* saw the red." In contrast, the claim, that conscious experience in humans entails two simultaneous and inextricable modes, here called "intentional" and "conscious," does provide a coherent account of such everyday statements. This peculiarity of dual modes constitutes the essence of human consciousness.

Some argument is needed to legitimate the attribution of an experience to the subject, I. The attribution cannot simply be assumed as "normal." Engaging the matter further, even Natsoulas (1983, pp. 435–436; 1986, pp. 202–203) admits as much. Echoing the behaviorists again, he proposes an argument. Succinctly said, the self-attribution is learned. Caregivers tell toddlers about the apparent experiences that the toddlers are exhibiting, and the toddlers learn names for these observed experiences and can then report them: "I saw the bunny." This learning, supposedly, becomes automatic and is then also generalized to all kinds of experiences. Eventually, without thinking, the child learns, after observing his or her behaviors, to name the experiences as his or her own and takes this result to suggest the presence of an experiencing subject, the child her- or himself. Thus, taught so as children, supposedly, we come to believe that we have unmediated experience of our own experiences whereas, according to this theory, this experience is second-hand, mediated to us via internalized and generalized learning.

A number of considerations indicate the inadequacy of this learning theory. First, there is the well-known difficulty of explaining vocabulary acquisition merely ostensively, and this difficulty applies directly in this case. The caregiver might point to an object and provide its name, but how does the child realize what exactly is being named? Say "ball" and show it to the child. What does the child experience? Numerous possible candidates apply: the object itself, its bouncing, its color or its shape, an invitation to play, a smile, excitement, and so on. Philosophical discussion about the nonsense word *Gavagai!* has elaborated this problem of ostensive learning (Cahoone, 2010, lecture 27, tracks 2–3; 28, 9–10). Primatologist David Premack (1986) emphasizes that there is "an important class of words" (p. 82) that can only be taught by multiple examples. "The word 'idea' is a good example of this class" (p. 83). *Self* and *I* would be others. Yet learning even the term *ball* would require multiple exposures for a child—and the lesson would come to conclusion only through the child's own insight, which would have to grasp the pertinent configuration within the child's global experience and come eventually to correctly attach the name *ball* to that particular item within the overall world of meaningful human encounter. Even while learning to name simple objects in the environment, the child would need to employ internal mental events, insights, to get the terminology right. The behaviorist explanation has no way, claims no need, to account for these internal mental events. To be sure, the required learning does occur, but neither classical nor operant conditioning alone can account for it. The challenge of teaching *ball*, let alone *I*, to the child gets entangled in the unavoidable need for internal events, on which behaviorism has foundered.

Second, the learning to name internal experiences entails even more complications than the learning of names for objects in the environment—because the intended "objects" are not out there to be pointed to, experienced at will, recognized as particulars, and named according to custom. Even after multiple examples and granted the needed internal insight, a child cannot learn to name things without some personal experience of them. Easily enough the caregivers can provide experiences of a ball, but how do they provide experiences of the child's "I," which is to be differentiated and learned? The external naming of various behaviors of the child and their attribution to the child—"Oh, Brooke is tired and needs to go beddy-bye,"

"Brady likes to be held standing up"—must have some experience to connect with. In this case, the experience cannot be given by the naming alone; there must be something to name. There must be some experiential set of data to be sorted out from all others and to be recognized through repeated examples as pertaining to this or that term. To be sure, as in the case of the external ball, so in the case of the internal feelings, sets of relevant data are available and purportedly could be learned to be named. However, the best that could be achieved through only external instruction is to relate the named feelings to the palpable organisms of Brooke and Brady. But the matter in question is not palpable organisms, but internal feelings and, ultimately, a sense of "I." The behaviorist suggestion, that the feelings have no relevant internal reality but are best understood as merely supposed internal events whose actual reality are particular kinds of external behavior, merits little credibility today. How could inner feelings come to be known without relevant data to be grasped and named? We must conclude that even to learn to recognize and name internal experiences via external verbal instruction, the child must have internal experience that accords with the names.

This requisite experience cannot be provided by the naming, and the learning cannot be explained on the basis solely of instruction and socialization. Donald (2001) makes this very point regarding the learning of Duane Rumbaugh and Sue Savage-Rumbaugh's star bonobo, Kanzi:

> We know that Kanzi can recognize himself in a mirror or a photograph. In that sense he has some self-awareness or self-recognition of his body. But self-referential language requires an awareness of inner states, and this apparently is absent or insufficient to enable Kanzi to use language in this way. (p. 122)

"The mere possession of symbols will not alter [or substitute for] basic ability" (p. 121).

Third, private learning sometimes occurs and supersedes anything formerly known. In addition to being socialized and learning conventional usage, people sometimes make breakthroughs and begin to speak of novelties. The notion of oxidation, the theory of evolution, the discovery of the unconscious, the delineation of DNA—all represent instances of claimed personal achievements that could not have been learned through the appropriation of existing language. No terms existed to name the novelties, yet they emerged, were named, and have become part of standard usage. Even children often come up with amazingly creative statements, attending to matters caregivers overlook, sensitive through innocence or by genetic endowment to matters opaque to others. On what experiential ground does such articulated creativity stand? What are the data from which novel concepts and words arise? As both novel and often abstract, the novelties are not available to be pointed to. The experiential data could not be external. Unique inner mental experience provides the only alternative explanation.

Fourth, behaviorist theory might try and explain these creative events by appeal to the proposed internalization and generalization of early learning. However, the creativity involved in these novelties is sometimes so stunning that, even granting the behaviorist hypothesis, one could only marvel at a generalization that so transcends anything from which it supposedly derived. The behaviorist explanation fails.

Fifth, phylogenetically, there recurs the question of infinite regress, which is inevitable when consciousness is characterized as only intentionality. If children learn to name themselves as "I"s because of the linguistic usage of their caregivers, from where did the caregivers get the notion of a self that they teach? From their own caregivers; and they, from theirs; and so on. But the buck must stop somewhere. In the first instance, the language usage that claims a unique "I" must have emerged apart from any conditioned learning. In its emergence, talk of "I" would not have had a prior linguistic system to explain its generation. The behaviorist hypothesis does not explain the peculiarity of *Homo sapiens*. Our emergence represents something new, something *sui generis*, in evolutionary history (4.14).

These criticisms are not to minimize the importance of social interaction for the development and deployment of mental capacities in human beings (Donald, 2001). Surely, without society humans fail to achieve any refined use of intelligence or developed sense of self. Usually they die. Humans are social beings, and from its earliest beginnings our development is an interactive process. Still, without placing the emphasis one-sidedly on one factor or the other, we must acknowledge that the social process requires a human givenness so that the interactive development might occur. "Either human mind or human interaction" are equally unviable explanations, both beholden to a sensate-modeled understanding of causality (4.6). This challenge to behaviorism's virtual denial of human mind is not a claim that mind alone explains human development and culture. It is merely a claim that, without human mind, behaviorism's explanations have nothing to work with. A lesson from animal studies is apropos: "The mere possession of symbols will not alter basic ability. The capacity to take a perspective on one's own mental states cannot be changed simply by one's possessing a lexicon or vocabulary. This is true of [the bonobo] Kanzi and well as of humans" (Donald, 2001, p. 121). Subjectivity must be real if language, learning, self-awareness, and culture are also to be real. Consciousness "is the evolutionary requirement for both constructing and navigating human culture. It remains the basis, the cognitive sine qua non, for all complex human interactions" (p. 87).

Sixth and finally, then, is that pervasive question regarding the sense of "I." What grounds this specific experience and insistence if only external language usage is on the scene? External language might well name for the child the experienced object, name the experiencing subject, and even name the connective between the subject and the object, but what experiential data grounds this compound teaching such that all elements could be appropriated? At best, as an extraverted observation, the learner could grasp that "they are telling me I am tired." How does this instruction account for the "I am tired" part of the observation and convert to a pure subjective assertion, "I am tired"? How, indeed, unless there are experienced an "I," a tiredness, and an attribution of the one to the other, and all are grounded in some available experience, and all are able to be sorted out somehow—via insightful intelligence?—and interrelated so that they square with the language usage?

The very empiricism that behaviorism champions, that defines science, and that characterizes human knowing rests on the availability of data. The behaviorist explanation might impute an "I" to the learning child, but the imputation does not provide the requisite data for the reality of an "I." In contrast, experience of consciousness as conscious would provide the requisite evidence and coherently explain first-person statements.

5.3.7. *An Appeal to the Experience of Consciousness*

With discussion of James, Chalmers, and Natsoulas and Skinner, I have presented arguments for the bimodal nature of consciousness. More immediately, to know the nature of consciousness, we can also experience it—if we are willing to attend to the functioning of our own consciousness. That very exercise lies behind Lonergan's analysis of intentional consciousness; it is the presupposition of the exposition in Chapter 2. The exposition there might have followed relatively easily enough. After all, who is not aware of ever having a provocative encounter, of ever wondering about it and having an insight into it, of ever assessing an idea as a potential explanation, of ever deliberating over the appropriate response via decision and action? Or who would ever publically deny these matters? And why not? Yes, the experience is there for anyone to attend to, and any denial of the experience discredits the denier. What was presupposed and, perhaps, accepted relatively easily enough in Chapter 2 returns in full force here to raise even more challenging issues.

Whether as experienced or as argued or both, it is hard to deny that consciousness does have this dual nature: it is intentional, yes, but also simultaneously and concomitantly conscious. Contrary to prevailing opinion, the intentional contents of consciousness do not exhaust the nature of human consciousness. They are not what characterize consciousness—because mere sensation is also intentional in its own way: sensation entails an agent's engaging some object. The presence "to" self, consciousness as conscious, is ultimately what is at stake in "the turn toward the subject" since Kant and his interlocutors: consciousness is self-consciousness: *Bewusstsein ist Selbstbewusstsein.*

5.4. The Limitation of Consciousness to Intentionality

5.4.1. That Consciousness Is Always Awareness of Something

I cannot stress enough—and in this section and the next three, I engage a sustained critique of standard theory about consciousness to make the point—I cannot stress enough that the "self-consciousness" at stake is not the everyday experience of one's becoming to oneself an object of awareness or concern; it is not about adverting *to* oneself or thinking *about* oneself; it is not about reflecting *on* oneself; it is not about becoming the object *of* one's own awareness. Nonetheless, this perceptualist interpretation is the understanding that theorists most commonly give to consciousness: awareness of an object. I see that old sensate-modeled theory of knowing operative again here. As if consciousness were another version of sensation wherein a physical receptor encounters a physical stimulus, consciousness is also imagined to be the confrontation of the subject and some object. Then the novelty of human consciousness that emerged in natural history, over and above the responsiveness of animal sensation and perception, tends to go unnoticed. The slogan says that "consciousness is always consciousness of something." All too simply, consciousness is defined only as intentionality. Natsoulas (1978) emphatically makes this point, saying, "It is arguably our most basic concept of consciousness. One's being conscious, whatever more it might mean, must include one's being aware of something" (p. 910). Even after considering an early version of my position here, Natsoulas (1986) insisted that, "understood *in the usual way*," consciousness or awareness entails "potentially or actually referring to and characterizing something beyond the awareness" (p. 203, emphasis added). I am advancing a different understanding of consciousness because I find "the usual way" inadequate.

Griffin (1991) seems to labor under that same, usual conception. Metaphorically he speaks of "primitive experience . . . not lit up by the searchlight of consciousness" (p. 68; also p. 54). Presumably, consciousness is taken to be only intentional awareness, a searchlight over here turned on some object over there. So Griffin also invokes—to me, mysterious—"nonsensory prehensions" to intimate some peculiarly defined experience that is neither sensory nor intentional. I suspect that, with Whitehead, he is struggling to express the notion of non-reflecting consciousness, of consciousness as conscious—although elsewhere (pp. 65–66, 68–69) and more consistently, these "prehensions" refer to other more clearly explained phenomena (see 4.20.6).

Penrose (1994b), too, despite his emphasis on highly abstract mathematical argumentation and the leap of understanding beyond any possible computation à la Gödel's Theorem—Penrose, too, seems to labor to some extent under a sensate model of consciousness. He describes two aspects in consciousness: the passive aspect is "awareness" and pertains to experiences such as "the perception of the color of red" and "the sensation of pain or the appreciation of a melody"; the active aspect is "the feeling of free will" and pertains, for example, "in the willful action to get up from one's bed" (p. 39). The passive has to do "with sensation ('qualia') and the active with the issues of 'free will' " (p. 40). Besides mixing in evaluative concerns about choice and free will with the epistemological concern about consciousness and cognition—although widely varied usage does allow that *conscious* could mean *deliberate* (Chalmers, 1996, p. 26)—this conception characterizes consciousness as a form of perception, presumes the confrontational image of object against subject, and entrains all the standard baggage: a basic notion of causality as the push-pull action of efficient causality in the physical world (Penrose, 1994b, p. 36; see 4.6) and a notion of consciousness as only intentional directedness toward some object.

Even Chalmers (1996), a nearly lone philosophical voice willing to wear the label "dualist"—even Chalmers, despite his paradox of phenomenal judgments (5.3.5), overwhelmingly characterizes consciousness as intentional. In my mind, he overlooks the essence of the uniqueness he would defend. To be sure, the matter is not black and white—or, at least, it is not easily determinable. Chalmers does speak repeatedly of "conscious experience" in the singular. Referring to the biological processes that neuroscience can specify, he writes, "When we perceive, think, and act, there is a whir of causation and information processing, but this processing does not usually go on in the dark. There is also an internal aspect; there is something it feels like to be a cognitive agent. This internal aspect is conscious experience" (p. 4). By "conscious experience" Chalmers might be alluding to non-reflecting consciousness, his *acquaintance* that I contrasted with his *experience* (5.3.5), the unitary experience of consciousness as conscious, that constant that pertains across the diverse experiences of different contents of consciousness and different sense modalities. If so, however, the allusion is quickly obscured. Perhaps it is not directly intended. Probably it would be noticed only by someone who already explicitly and consistently distinguishes the intentional from the conscious. It does not seem that Chalmers does.

Chalmers's singular *conscious experience* drifts into a plural, a multiplicity of conscious experiences, and they and their respective particularities become the actual focus of his concern about consciousness (pp. 4, 6). This drift appears deliberate. Chalmers asserts, "The subject matter [consciousness or conscious experience] is perhaps best characterized as 'the subjective quality of experience'" (p. 4). This phrase is a perfect parallel to Nagel's (1974) supposed "subjective character of experience" in bats and other creatures (p. 444; see 4.18.3). When Chalmers (1996) elaborates this experience, he shows that he does, indeed, take it to be multiple: "Conscious experiences [plural] range from vivid color sensations to . . . aromas; from . . . pains to . . . thoughts on the tip of the tongue; from sounds and smells to . . . musical experience. . . . All these have a distinct experienced quality" (p. 4). Clearly, now, the experienced quality in question, that "subjective quality of experience," is that quality proper respectively to each of the specific contents of awareness, not the quality of consciousness *per se*, regardless of its changing contents. Moreover, Chalmers makes this focus central to his theory of consciousness. In addition to the very existence of consciousness as his first theoretical concern, Chalmers's second target of theoretical concern is "the specific *character* of conscious experiences" (p. 5)—in the plural. That character is red, rather than blue (p. 5), book, rather than dagger (p. 220); and this singular "specific character" of the plural "conscious experiences" unfolds into a catalog of many different experiences with specific characteristics: touch, smell, taste, temperature, pain, bodily sensations, mental imagery, thoughts, emotions (pp. 7–10). For Chalmers, a conscious experience is structured; it has "a definite geometry to it." In a visual field, for example, "there is a large red patch here, with a small yellow patch in close proximity, with some white in between; there are patterns of stripes, squares, and triangles, and so on" (p. 223).

Clearly, Chalmers's attention is not on the experience of the presence of these contents "to" the experiencing subject, not on the consistent experience "of" experience itself. Rather, his attention is on the intentional dimension of consciousness, namely, the particular and diverse characteristics, and even the whole, of whatever object is being experienced. He notes that an alternative term for the experience in question is "*qualia*." It is a Latin neuter plural adjective used substantively to mean "such-ness-es" (*quale* is the singular); it is the term that virtually defines consciousness in contemporary consciousness studies. Thus, fully representing the field, for Chalmers *qualia* actually constitute consciousness: "We can say that a mental state is conscious if it has a *qualitative feel*—an associated quality of experience. These qualitative feels are also known as phenomenal qualities, or *qualia* for short" (p. 4).

Renowned for faulting theorists for avoiding the hard problem of consciousness, Chalmers is lucid: "The problem of explaining these phenomenal qualities is just the problem of explaining consciousness. This is the really hard part of the mind–body problem" (p. 4). While Chalmers is correct that accounting for the experienced qualities of any particular experience is a hard problem of consciousness—the very experience of *qualia* is, indeed, something different, if inseparable, from the underlying brain processes—Chalmers (1996) overlooks the even harder problem of accounting for the perduring subjective experience *per se* of any specific objective experience whatsoever, regardless of its particular *qualia*. He acknowledges this problem in passing: "One sometimes feels that there is something to conscious experience that transcends all these specific elements: a kind of background hum, for instance, that is fundamental to consciousness. . . . the phenomenology of the self . . . very hard to pin down" (p. 10; see also p. 246). What Chalmers calls "acquaintance" (p. 197) would seem to fit here (5.3.5).

Indeed! This is the very matter that constitutes the distinctiveness of human consciousness! It is what inclines me to reserve the term *consciousness* for only human consciousness and even to eschew accurately suggestive terms such as *sensate* or *extroverted* or *sensitive consciousness* and to use in their stead *perceptual responsiveness* (5.1.2). The really hard problem, non-reflecting consciousness, is hardly on the radar screen. The experiences of perceptual qualities has replaced the experience of consciousness itself, consciousness as conscious. Consciousness has been reduced to intentionality, and intentionality has become the topic of consciousness studies.

5.4.2. Those Unspecifiable Qualia of Red in Itself

Chalmers (1996) identifies consciousness with the diverse experiences of *qualia*. He characterizes the experience of consciousness, not in itself, but by the characteristics of the multiple contents that consciousness might have. His understanding of consciousness is merely intentional and, what is more, almost uniquely perceptual. Why?

A controlling concern in consciousness studies is to link consciousness with brain processes: the mind–body problem. We already know a good bit about some of them, visual perception, for example, although knowledge even of this best understood of mental phenomena quickly breaks down as neuroscience moves through the stages of visual processing in the brain. But understanding of wonder, question, insight, judgment, decision—all the distinctively human mental acts—is still pure mystery to neuroscience, still virtually the proverbial ghost in the machine (but see Kounios & Beeman, 2009, 2014). So, attempting to parallel neuroscientific findings and even to identify consciousness with them, consciousness studies focuses on "conscious experience" in terms of its contents, and percepts offer a ready and—well, relatively—easy topic. My attention to Chalmers's position offers a paradigmatic example; his construal of the question is far from unique. Evinced even in the few direct quotations I have included in this discussion (5.4), the emphasis on *qualia* is pervasive in consciousness studies. But this emphasis on subjective or qualitative "feels" is a distraction. It diverts attention from consciousness itself to the many objects of consciousness and their particular experienced qualities.

Supposedly, every experience has its own *qualia*. The experienced redness of the color red is the stock example. I must confess that I am extremely hard pressed to say what the experience of redness is *per se*. I have no such experience as far as I can determine. To be sure, redness does carry connotations for me: alertness, vividness, intensity, and the threat of an accident or fine at a traffic signal; and I am aware of these cultural and personal meanings. For me, a male in the United States, to wear red is often to make some kind of statement. But these feels are collateral, not inherent in the redness itself. Does the qualitative feel of *qualia* refer to these biographically and culturally conditioned, emotion- and meaning-filled, disparate experiences? Are these personal responses supposed to be what characterize the experience of redness *per se*? I do not think so. And given this alternate interpretation of *qualia*, I do not think other theorists think so, either. The experience of redness is supposed to be a particular and discrete experience, the particular characteristic of experienced redness, common to all who experience redness or, at least, consistent across all one's own experiences of redness. But the experienced connotations of red differ from person to person, and they differ for the same person on different occasions; they depend on personal and cultural contingencies. Not experiences of redness *per se*, a supposed quality of consciousness, but biographical particularities are in question. Then what is this touted qualitative feel of the experience of red?

Artists, decorators, designers, and even some researchers insist that different colors have different effects on us. Supposedly, the experience of "hot" red elicits a subliminal response that differs from that of "cool" blue. Does the experience of redness and its *quale* refer to these psychophysical effects, supposedly inherent in the human experience of these colors themselves? If so, aren't these effects, then, subliminal, but not actually conscious? Or have we another oxymoron: subliminal consciousness?

Of course, current theory would easily allow that these color effects are "experienced" (4.20.2) simply because they do have differentially specifiable psychophysical effects. Such theory would also readily call such effects "awareness," the possession of "information" (4.21.2) that could affect behavioral response, such as that found even in the settings of a thermostat, so the idea of oxymoronic "unconscious awareness" might seem perfectly natural. Chalmers (1996, pp. 219–222, 225–229) actually struggles with this precipitated anomaly. Such theory might further opine that experience so defined is synonymous with consciousness, and strange assertions would follow. The falling limb or the interactive macromolecules in brain cells (Griffin, 1991, p. 55) would supposedly be conscious because they were "having an experience." But as I made clear at 4.20.2 and 4.21.2, I reject such speculation and for the same reasons I am elaborating here: it overlooks the conscious mode of human consciousness and treats only the intentional, and then it uncritically, gratuitously, imputes to non-human organisms and even to machines—any device that exhibits some interactive response—the consciousness and, perforce, experience that is distinctive of humans.

I remain baffled as to the *quale* of redness in itself. Biographical associations might well be the only thing theorists can mean by appeal to *qualia*—and if so, the argument about *qualia* is specious. It does not pertain to consciousness *per se*, but merely to individual experiential differences. Talking about the paucity of our vocabulary in these matters, Chalmers (1996) makes something of the same point. He writes,

> Although greenness is [opined to have] a distinct sort of sensation with a rich intrinsic character, there is very little that one

can say about it other than that it is green. In talking about phenomenal qualities, we generally have to specify the qualities in question in terms of associated external properties, or in terms of associated causal roles. (p. 22)

Taking Chalmers's comment even further, I emphasize that even to put the name "green" on this sensation is to exceed the sensation itself. To say "green" is to add conceptual content. If *green* does have qualia *per se*, what could they possibly be apart from specifications that can only be made by adding to the experience *post hoc* conceptual clarifications?

Similarly, Chalmers (1996) stumbles when trying to describe the *quale* of conscious thought. He writes, "Some of the things we think and believe do not have any particular qualitative feel associated with them, but many do. This applies particularly to explicit, occurrent thoughts [i.e., conscious (p. 20) or "active" thoughts, in contrast to those stored in memory, for example (p. 221)]. . . . There is *something* it is like to be having such thoughts" (p. 10). To support the thesis that *qualia* characterize consciousness, Chalmers makes recourse to thoughts that do have a feel, and I suspect he means the emotional reaction that a particular thought, depending on its content, might evoke: anxiety, oppression, expectation, longing, joy, loss. But these feels are the collateral effects of specific and differing thoughts, not some supposed qualitative feel inherent in conscious thought *per se*. I believe Chalmers is more on target to allow that thought *per se* has no particular qualitative feel, and I believe the thoughts that evoke such qualitative feels do so because they entrain biographical connotations. Chalmers's appreciation of depth vision with new eyeglasses at age 10 (p. 7) seems likewise to depend on biographical particularities, not on the inherent *quale* of depth vision *per se*.

Perhaps, then, thoughts *per se* and redness or greenness *per se* and all the rest have no *qualia per se*. The feel that any of these might have is biographically embedded, not constitutive of their consciousness. Although, admittedly, it is hard to untangle the two, the contents, not the consciousness of them, provide the feels, and emphasizing the feels distracts from the truly hard problem of consciousness.

5.4.3. *The Qualia of the Activity of Thinking*

I digress from redness for the moment to attend to the experience of thought, which Chalmers raised (5.4.2). It does make sense to believe that, apart from its content, no particular thought *per se* has a distinctive *quale*. After all, thoughts are specified by their contents. The thought *per se*, the mere "givenness" of a thought, seems uncharacterizable (cf. Lonergan, 1957/1992, pp. 405–407).

In contrast, however, I would suggest that thinking does have *qualia*. The process, the engagement, the activation of consciousness does supply evidence—a particular kind of experiential data, perhaps the "background hum" (p. 10) or the "acquaintance" (p. 196–197) that Chalmers (1996) attributed to the experience of self—on the basis of which we can and do speak of thinking and other distinctively conscious processes. To this extent, I find valid meaning in what Chalmers disparaged as Descartes's "notorious doctrine that the mind is transparent to itself" (p. 12), and especially given Descartes's specification that he meant "the mind *qua* thinking thing" (p. 13). Taken with reference to non-reflecting consciousness (5.3.1), which I am explicating here, this specification justifies Descartes's supposed error of "assimilation of the psychological to the phenomenal" (p. 15).

Lonergan's far-reaching appeal to the experience of insight *per se* (regardless of what it's about) is the telling case in point, the point about non-reflecting consciousness, which I am developing. The experience of insight opens a panoramic window on consciousness. To have an insight is to experience a particular and distinctively conscious event. It frequently entails emotions, but they are neither the insight nor the inherent characteristics of the insight nor the feel of having an insight *per se*. They accompany the insight.

How, then, does one characterize the specific feel of an insight *per se*? I am hard pressed to say. Moreover, I am convinced that talk of a feel may be misleading since the term *feelings* pertains most directly to emotions and physical sensations whereas my goal is to discredit sensation and perception as distinctive of consciousness. Use of the very metaphor *feel* seems essentially misleading. To insist on feel and *qualia* as determinative of intellectual consciousness is to risk reducing it to perception, to model it on perception, and to conceive it as a version of perception.

How could one characterize the experience of consciousness itself? Its very nature, as I am arguing, is openness to any contents whatsoever. How does one characterize pure openness, unlimited receptivity? The best option our culture offers would appeal to the spiritual. In this book and especially in this chapter, I am specifying this term. I am insisting that in the human case *conscious* and *spiritual* are nearly synonyms, so I could accurately say that the experience of consciousness *per se* is spiritual. It is not a sensate, not a perceptual, not an emotional, but a spiritual experience.

However, given the controversy and confusion surrounding the term *spiritual* in common parlance, I doubt its use brings much specification to the discussion. Usually *spiritual* bears reference to God or some other purported spiritual being (1.1–1.2), but as I have insisted repeatedly and explicate at 6.2.5, by *spiritual* I mean nothing of the kind. Nonetheless, use of this term validly suggests another category of commonly cited experience that applies to consciousness more surely than any other. Admittedly, of course, this very suggestion might raise hackles on some of my secularist readers, whose reaction might further compound the challenge of explaining consciousness by discrediting *a priori* a potentially coherent explanation. On the other hand, this suggestion might distract my spiritualist readers, who would tend to invoke notions of God, celestial beings, and other supposed non-corporeal and non-falsifiable entities. Yet my only concern is to understand the human mind. In general, we lack any common vocabulary to express conscious experience *per se* although Tibetan Buddhism has a term: *kun-gzhi* (Tarthang Tulka, 1979). So the concept tends, in fact, to fall out of even technical discussion—as Chalmers insists by his emphasis on "the hard problem" even while the focus on *qualia* distracts from the really hard problem. If we had the shared vocabulary—as in Eastern philosophies, for example (Helminiak, 1996a, pp. 50–51)—I would not now be struggling to make a case for the distinctive experience of consciousness in itself. Yet anyone who has had an insight must be aware of this experience, must know that essentially it is not identical to the feel of any accompanying emotion or perception, and must be able to credit it, nonetheless, as data needing to be understood.

5.5. Still Seeing Red: Mere Givenness Versus *Qualia*

From the experience of thinking, I return to the experience of mere percepts. I have been insisting that attention to *qualia* does not define or specify consciousness. Now I must clarify, however, that *qualia* do implicate consciousness—but, be it noted, only because talk of *qualia* comes from *human* experience. So consciousness is presupposed; it has been smuggled in; and it remains hidden. The focus on *qualia* confounds important, distinguishable aspects of human consciousness. The *qualia* of experiences are not the key to the puzzle of consciousness.

5.5.1. No Qualia in the Merely Given

So back to the paradigmatic example, the experience of red: to me, red is just a given. It is, and it is what it is. It is a given just as every other pure experience, any perceptual input, is only a given. The supposed feel of such givenness *as given* would be the same in the case of every given. Then, what is the experience of givenness? What is its feel—apart from the additional, particular, supposed feels, the *qualia*, specific to different givens and different for different people (5.4.2)? What is the pure and exclusive "feel" of red? It has none, as far as I can determine. Givens are, well, just given, period. Such is what *given* means (cf. Lonergan, 1957/1992, pp. 405–407). The givens, the data, are the unspecified with which one begins before making relevant determinations (2.2.1).

When I see standard red next to fluorescent red, for example, I certainly notice the difference: I recognize the radiance of the fluorescent color—but I am already conceptualizing! I do notice a difference. I discern a contrast in perceptual input. I encounter two different givens. However, the difference and the contrast are not in the givens as given, but in their processing in my mind, in their being compared. In saying so, my mind harks back to David Hume's criticism of causality—it is not seen; it must be understood.

If, for example, I am just gazing absent-mindedly at some panorama, I notice no differences at all. I don't notice anything. I am conscious of the panorama, but I am not attending to it or to elements in it. "We can be phenomenally conscious of something without attending to it, as witnessed by the fringes of a visual field" (Chalmers, 1996, p. 27). In a technical usage (Roy, 2003, pp. 26–27), I could say I am *conscious* but not *aware* of the panorama (1.9; 5.3.5): I have not directed my attention to it. *Conscious* in this case refers explicitly to the non-reflecting consciousness that I am highlighting. The perception of the panorama is already within consciousness—I am not comatose—but I am not attending to the perception, so I am not aware of it. It is present "to" me only non-reflectingly. (Note that my use of *aware* à la Roy, 2003 (4.21.3), is absolutely opposite that of Chalmers, 1996, pp. 28–29. For Chalmers awareness, machine-like, refers to the mere registration of perceptual input that could affect behaviors—whether or not that input ever enters into conscious experience or phenomenal consciousness.) For me at this point, then, there are no particularities and differences in my absent-minded gaze at a panorama. All is merely given.

My years of meditative practice make the possibility of such occurrences commonplace for me. I am easily able to rest in the mere presence of mental inputs apart from any further mental processing, a pure "being with" whatever, unattended-to and unconceptualized, is occurring. Only granted mental activity above and beyond the experience of the givens themselves, only then do I discern the specifics and the differences. Apart from such further processing, I experience only givens as given, and as merely given—they have no particular qualities. So I have no idea what the "feel" of these givens in themselves—e.g., red—merely as givens, could possibly be.

To what does that metaphor "feel" actually apply, in any case? What is it that has a particular "feel"? I did articulate a contrast between standard red and fluorescent red, but, I insisted, the difference between them is not in the givens as given. Oh, of course, I can discern the difference there and posit it there and be correct in so positing it there and, on this basis, be right to say the difference is really there. I am a realist, after all. By the same token, the stimuli of the two reds and their effects within a perceptual system are also different. We can specify the mixed wavelengths of colored light, differentiate levels of stimulation in retinal cones, and plot visual pathways into and through the brain. These perceptual processes certainly differ in the case of the two different reds. They differ objectively; they differ in themselves. Undoubtedly, therefore, the two reds and their effects in perceptual organisms are not the same. The reds really do differ.

Ah, then, what of our animal friends? They "know" (2.2.5) differences in color. These differences are critical to their survival, and the animals can detect them. The differences are real. Then how can I insist that animals have no consciousness (5.1.2) and experience no *qualia*? Because the animal and the human mental occurrences are not the same. For animals, the differences mean only different responses. The detection of the difference shows only in different behaviors. Of course, if I were a behaviorist or functionalist (4.12.4; 4.19.2), such behavioral differences in the external world, available to sensation and perception, would count as my criterion of knowledge, and only what is detectable in the spatiotemporal world would count as real. Then, externalized differentiated behaviors would equal conscious capacities, not only in the animals but even in a computer or thermostat. The behaviorist-functionalist (4.19.2) criterion itself already precludes recognition of mentality beyond what the animals have—and they do have it; it is real. How can I say they do not experience *qualia*?

It is a matter of different epistemologies (3.2.5). Yes, I am a realist, but I am a *critical* realist. For me the criterion of knowledge is the reasonable judgment grounded in relevant evidence. The real is not some material stuff lying about out there, not physical movements, behaviors, seen out there, all accessible via mere sensate encounter and perception. The real is what is correctly affirmed to be so (2.2; 2.4.2), and it makes no sense to speak of the correctly affirmed apart from human affirmation, however implicit or yet unarticulated it might be. The difference between colors is real, and the real difference can have behavioral effects, but this real difference is *recognized* and *known* only when a contrast is made. To affirm a difference requires something more than simply to encounter two sets of data and even to act differentially on the basis of them. Comparison adds something to perception and behavior. For the somnambulant human—as for the non-human animal—a night in the woods has no *qualia*; the night's activities pass in irretrievable oblivion. There are no *qualia* to be reported. Color in itself, as merely a given, apart from some conceptualization, has no *qualia*. Standard red and fluorescent red, as mere givens, include no *qualia per se* and no comparison. The *qualia* and comparison only enter the discussion when a human with consciousness experiences them and at some level recognizes them for what they are. Only then does the *meaning-filled* term *red* apply.

Ah, but again, the animals do have emotions, and different colors will arouse different emotions. The sight of a predator will arouse attention and fear and then engage reactions in the body resulting in flight. These reactions will have their own accompanying emotions. Or at the sight of a potential mate, other reactions will occur. However, if these are what are meant by *qualia*, they are not proper to the colors themselves but are natural or learned concomitants of the colors (see 5.6.2 for a human example). And if these are what is meant, we already have perfectly good ways of specifying these physiological and mental responses, as just demonstrated, and the term *qualia* is superfluous (see 4.20.5 for an inanimate example). Besides, as with the colors themselves, so with these other internal responses, the animal will not be able to discern them as discrete aspects of its living, will not be able to compare and contrast them, will not be able to name and report them. They, too, will pass into irretrievable oblivion. There is no self-conscious being at home there, so there are no experiences of a self-conscious subject, no conscious data to be questioned, no characteristics of the data to be distinguished, no *qualia* to be reported. The animal does not have the consciousness within which biological, emotional, and perceptual processes could even become givens as the potential focus of wonder, question, and characterization. Mere givens have no *qualia*. The positing of *qualia* presupposes consciousness that is both conscious (to provide the givens) and intentional (to characterize them).

5.5.2. Chalmers's First-Order Phenomenal States and Lonergan's Data

Through his analyses of conscious experience at one point, Chalmers (1996) seems to support that assertion, as does the quotation from Chalmers (p. 27) in the sixth last paragraph. He acknowledges that "one might have an experience without conceptualizing the experience in any way" (p. 197). I would say he is speaking of pure data on Lonergan's first level of consciousness (2.2.1), the experience of what is already within consciousness and is not attended to but *could be* attended to and then even conceptualized although, in itself, it is merely given. As merely given—this is my insistence—it is in no way categorized or characterized; it has no *qualia*. With some painstaking analysis, I discern this very conclusion in another aspect of Chalmers's work, as follows.

At 5.3.5, I discussed Chalmers's paradox regarding what he called "second-order judgments," namely, statements specifically about a conscious experience, such as, "I'm having a red sensation now" (p. 176). Clearly, such a statement entails reflection on experience and is rightly called a second-order statement. Regarding a more primordial level of experience, Chalmers also speaks of what he calls "first-order judgments." This first order regards the raw and mere input of some experience, the "contents" of what is "*consciously experienced*" and "*cognitively represented* [i.e., registered in the perceptual system]" (p. 175). Chalmers ventures to illustrate this primordial experience with the statement, a judgment, "That's red!" (p. 176).

However, he is not comfortable with the name "first-order judgment" because what he means is not really a personal judgment, not any kind of processed, conceptualized, and propositionally articulated experience—and not even necessarily an attended-to experience: "If I am having an experience . . . I may not be paying attention to it, but I at least have the ability to focus on it and talk about it, if I choose" (p. 28). For example, there can be within experience "the contents of the fringes of my visual field," available to me but unattended-to "at least until I pay attention to them" (p. 232). These contents of consciousness are just givens. They do stand in the visual field, so they are phenomenal; they are within what Chalmers calls phenomenal consciousness; but they are not the objects of concern. In my terminology (1.9; 5.3.5), I would say I am conscious, but not aware, of them; they are within consciousness but are not intentional. They are not even reflectingly noticed although they certainly could be noticed, attended to, and then categorized and even questioned, discussed, and disputed. But as mere givens, as yet unattended-to, they possess no particular characterizations for me. So at this point, even the phrase "That's red" is misleading; it is too conceptually elaborated for what it's supposed to mean.

Then how could one ever explicitly formulate an experience at this primordial level? One could not—because by its very nature every formulation already imports meaning and adds it to the given; but at stake here is experience that is "nonconceptual" (p. 233). Perhaps a mere grunt such as "Red object there" (p. 290) or even more simply "Red" would be more accurate. But even these pared-down phrases embody conceptualizations.

Red, after all, is a consensually meaningful concept; the term imputes particular qualities to the relevant experiential input and, perforce, already adds something to the pure perception.

So, "to avoid confusion," Chalmers posits distinctions within this first order. He introduces "a broader term for representational states that are not necessarily judgments. [He] will use the term 'registrations'" (p. 232). He acknowledges that "there will be some first-order registrations that fall outside the contents of awareness, as with states of subliminal perception for example" (p. 233). Surely, we are constantly picking up vast swaths of perceptual input; but because it is irrelevant to our current concerns, most of it is not even noticed and probably not even processed in the brain. But constructing a theory about how brain and consciousness correlate, Chalmers is more concerned about those registrations that do enter consciousness and are experienced, however primordially—namely, "first-order *phenomenal* registrations." Within this focus, "so defined, the contents of awareness [perceptual inputs] correspond directly to the contents of consciousness [phenomenal experiences]" (p. 233). Chalmers offers further elaboration: "a first-order registration need not be a state that is endorsed by the subject" (p. 232). This registration is "the immediate product of perceptual . . . processes, before they are rationally integrated into a coherent whole." "The representational content of a first-order registration is probably best taken to be *nonconceptual*" (p. 233; also p. 383, n. 10). And, making the point succinctly: <u>"One might have an experience without conceptualizing the experience in any way"</u> (p. 197).

A terminological clarification: meaning the same thing, Chalmers says both "first-order phenomenal registrations" and "first-order phenomenal states." He seems to prefer *states* as his presentation develops. To avoid unnecessary complication, henceforth I will use only the term *first-order phenomenal states*. As evident in the quotation in the previous paragraph, the term *state* better expresses the personal nature of the experience at stake whereas *registration* suggests a more merely mechanical event: the stimulus did strike the receptor, and sensation occurred, but no attention accrued to it.

Clearly, Chalmers is intimating experiential input that has not yet entered into a person's active intentional processing. Indeed, at this point Chalmers's talk of *experience* approaches Lonergan's technically delimited use of this term. For Lonergan, on a first level of consciousness, experience provides data (2.2.1); these constitute the fundamental input for knowing. As data, they are within consciousness, but they are not necessarily yet attended to or, far less, conceptualized; they are merely given as that which could be attended to, questioned, conceptualized, and known. Just having data is not yet to know (2.2.2). Attending to the data and engaging intelligence, one needs to generate some understanding of the data; and then, moving toward a judgment, one needs to check out one's understanding against the data. Only then does one know.

Now compare Chalmers:

> I do not say that to have an experience is automatically to *know* about it, in the sense in which knowledge requires belief. . . . it [experience] provides *evidence* for our beliefs, but it does not in itself constitute belief. [By *belief*, I think Chalmers means the product of Lonergan's judgment, namely, a propositional conviction or assertion.]
>
> . . . Because beliefs about experiences lie at a distance from experiences, they can be formed for all sorts of reasons, and sometimes unjustified beliefs will be formed. . . . The claim is not that having an experience is the *only* factor that may be relevant to the justification or lack of justification of a belief about experience. The claim is simply that it is *a* factor—perhaps the primary factor—and provides a potential source of justification that is not present when the experience is absent. (p. 197)

Directly pertinent to the *qualia* of experiences and the potential lack thereof—the focus of my argument at this point—within his first order, Chalmers posited a distinction between first-order registrations and first-order phenomenal states, the registrations being mere input to the perceptual system and the phenomenal states being the input as also personally experienced. Moreover—this point is ambiguous in Chalmers's presentation, lying on the outer limits of his analyses, mentioned only in an endnote—in addition to the first-order phenomenal state, Chalmers allows that a first-order judgment could also follow (p. 383, n. 9). So in sum, we have first-order registrations, first-order phenomenal states, and first-order judgments. I take these "judgments" to refer to the actual categorizations or conceptualizations, in some form, of what was experienced. The judgment is the realization "Red object there" or "That's red" or "I'm having a red sensation now," the barest acknowledgment of some primordial perceptual input. On this interpretation, of course, I would say Chalmers's "judgment" is actually a concept, the product of intelligence and insight on Lonergan's second level of consciousness, not necessarily a judgment in propositional form (Chalmers's *belief*), as Lonergan would define *judgment* associated with the third level of consciousness (2.1.6). Alternatively and most likely, Chalmers's "first-order judgment" has collapsed Lonergan's distinction between understanding and judgment. In any case and despite the terminological complexity, the parallel with Lonergan's analyses seems solid. Chalmers is struggling, beyond mere sensate registrations, with the difference between pure data within consciousness (first-order phenomenal states) and conceptualization or categorization of this input (first-order judgments).

Now I make my point regarding Chalmers; then I add an observation. First, Chalmers recognizes the occurrence of consciousness "of" experiential input apart from any conceptualization: first-order phenomenal states. These are not yet first-order "judgments," but they are more than the mere sensate stimulation of first-order registrations. That is, he seems to discern the possible presence of input actually within consciousness but apart from the input's being attended to: conscious but not yet intentional and, perforce, not yet conceptualized. This line of analysis supports my claim that there exist mere experiential contents within consciousness and that in the first instance consciousness is experiential (in Lonergan's delimited technical sense), not yet cognitive or conceptual.

However, as non-conceptual—here is my present point—they do not have *qualia*. They have no specific experienced character, no qualitative feel. Mere data—first-order phenomenal states—have no *qualia*. *Qualia* pertain only to first-order "judgments." *Qualia* pertain only when data are actively processed within human consciousness, that is, attended-to, questioned, and understood. *Qualia* pertain only when insight—however spontaneous, instantaneous, habitual, routine, unnoticed, taken for granted—is added to data.

Chalmers's struggling analyses—at least as I have interpreted them here in all good faith—support the point I am making about *qualia*. So I say again—and, it seems, at this point with Chalmers, despite his incompatible supposition that *qualia*, qualitative feels, constitute consciousness (pp. 3–11, et passim)—I have no idea what the *quale* of the pure experience of red could possibly be. I say there is no such thing. To speak of *qualia* in any cases apart from already active human intentional consciousness is to seriously misrepresent consciousness. It is to overlook the difference between phenomenal experience as merely given within consciousness and phenomenal experience as attended-to and then, and only then, perforce, categorized or characterized, however primordially. Percepts and *qualia* do not necessarily go together—and they do not go together at all in the case of merely perceptual animals that lack human conscious intelligence, another point toward which I am working, as announced formally at 5.5.5. *Qualia* are characteristic of consciousness only in the human case.

5.5.3. Reinventing the Wheel of Consciousness

Then, second, my observation: Chalmers's (1996, pp. 233, 382–385, nn. 9 & 10) effort to distinguish first-order registrations, first-order phenomenal states, and first-order "judgments" resonates with Lonergan's differentiated analysis of consciousness. Perforce, Chalmers's list significantly parallels the findings in the classical and medieval sources. The "ancients" also portray three relevant notions regarding experiential input: potentially intelligible, actually intelligible, and actually understood. On the analogy of vision, these three would parallel color in darkness, color in light, and color actually seen. The color in darkness is potentially visible but not actually visible because no light is available. Given a source of light, the color is actually vis*ible*, that is, *able* to be seen. Finally, the color in light presented to an eye becomes actually seen. The medieval notion of *illuminatio*, "illumination" by the "light" of intelligence, links the visual analogy to an understanding of conscious functioning (Lonergan, 1967d, pp. 168–176). Thus, in themselves all phenomena are intelligible; in principle, what is there to be understood *could be* understood—yet apart from an intelligence, still without this *sine qua non*, the intelligibility is only potential, only a distant possibility. However, given intelligence and the presence of the phenomenon to intellectual consciousness, the phenomenon is actually intelligible; now there actually exists the possibility of its being understood. But it is not yet understood. To achieve understanding might take considerable effort and considerable time (or in prosaic cases, such as seeing red, insight and conceptualization could occur without ever being noticed). Only after inquiry, when insight occurs, only then is the phenomenon actually understood.

Thus, the two lists, Chalmers's and the medievals', correspond. First, perceptual input *per se*, first-order registrations, could become available to conscious experience: the input is *potentially intelligible*. Second, when this input actually enters consciousness and constitutes a phenomenal state, it is *actually intelligible* because it now actually stands within the realm (or "light") of intelligence. Finally, when—via the actuation of consciousness, namely in this case, via inquiry and insight—the input is categorized, characterized, or "qualified" (i.e., attributed some *qualia*), it is *actually understood*.

The parallel is quite close. As I read the texts, then, the contemporary efforts strikingly resemble the painstaking, long-sustained, and gradually fruitful analyses of former times. It is unfortunate that today's theorists virtually ignore those dusty, library-shelved medieval treasures of human contribution to humanity's perennial questions.

Another demonstration of this situation regards the notion *person*. Presumptuously, I have been freely making reference to the person in contrast to the brain. If mind is a property of anything, I suggested, it is a property of the person, not of the brain (4.8.2; 4.11.3; 4.13). By *person* I referred to the whole being, the one agent, the entity in question, the "thing" (4.1.2), that which actually exists and entails, is constituted by, or "has" a body and a mind. The person was the topic of extensive and prolonged analysis in late classical and medieval thought. To be sure, the motivation for that analysis was the attempt to clarify Christian doctrine about Christ as one person (the Eternal Son) in two natures (divinity and humanity) and about a Trinity of three persons (Father, Son, and Holy Spirit) in one nature (divinity) (Lonergan, 2002/1956, 2009/1964). As Saint Augustine defined *person* heuristically, it is that of which there is one in Christ and three in God, and *nature* is that of which there are two in Christ and one in God. Theological analysis forced attention to a distinction between *what* one is and *who* one is. Significantly, this analysis required and advanced the refinement of a purely intellectual epistemology (Lonergan, 1976), which modern science now employs and which I have been contrasting with perception-modeled epistemology (2.2.5). Regardless of its provenance, the distinction between *who* and *what* is useful. It parallels Lonergan's understanding of the "thing" (4.2.2) in contrast to its conjugates or properties (4.12.1); and well grounded in cognitional theory, it accords with the difference between the third and the second levels of consciousness (2.1.6). The accepted definition of *person* was *rationalis naturae individua substantia*: a subsistent with a rational nature; so what we are calling "consciousness" (5.1.2) was determinative (Thomas Aquinas, 1961 version, I, q. 29, a. 1). In contrast, seemingly, the notion of *person* is officially non-existent in modern psychology: the term does not even appear in major reference works of the field (e.g., Craighead & Nemeroff, 2004; Colman, A. M., 2006; Corsini, 1984, 1999; Kazdin, 2000; Matsumoto, 2009; Nadel, 2003; VandenBos, 2007; Weiner, 2003). Happily, however, theoretical psychologists have recently asked, "What is a person?" (e.g., Bickhard, 2012; Guignon, 2012; Martin, 2012; Smythe, 1998; Stetsenko, 2012). However, except for the classicist Robinson (2012), the contemporary *Zeitgeist*—interactional, mechanistic, pragmatic, functionalist, epistemologically perception-modeled—constrains the analyses to avoid any offense of "essentialism." Far be it from contemporary scholarship to presume that one could ever know what something is! So "the person" still languishes in obscurity in contemporary psychological theory.

Especially as today's scientific analysis turns to consciousness, an unavoidably phenomenological or introspective endeavor not requiring contemporary neuroscience or psychology or their sophisticated technology, the conclusions of premodern thinkers become abundantly relevant. My struggle through Chalmers's work, including his exchanges with colleagues, suggests to me that consciousness theorists are reinventing the wheel and, distracted by mechanistic thinking, have a ways to go before they get it round.

5.5.4. Qualia via Acts of Human Consciousness

The discerned contrast between standard red and fluorescent red presupposes some distancing from the experiences of the givens themselves (5.5.1). To discern a contrast requires some kind of reflexivity, a commandeering of attention, and a processing of the result—intentional consciousness of two givens that have discernibly different characteristics. The discernment inevitably moves beyond the merely given. To be able in any way to characterize those experienced differences, those different red *qualia*, one needs to begin processing the givens. Some other capacity beyond the mere reception of givens must come into play. To me, this distancing, processing, reflecting are signs of consciousness *at work*. In Lonergan's terms, the process has moved from a first level of mere availability of data to a second level of wonder, inquiry, and insight about the data—however spontaneous, primordial, fundamental, unarticulated, or taken for granted. This cognitive processing indicates the addition of something beyond the merely given.

So fluorescent red is, indeed, brighter than standard red, and I can experience this fact as a fact—a correct, humanly determinable insistence—because in some sense I reflect on their difference, but only for this reason. At a primordial, prosaic level, I bring to the givens my capacity to analyze, objectify, think.

Only when I introduce actuated human consciousness into the process can I maintain that these colors have their particular *qualia*. The *qualia* are not in the conscious perception itself as merely experienced. An act of consciousness, an insight, is the condition for the possibility of any assigned "feel." David Hume's argument about causality—that the efficient causality of one billiard ball's moving another and the necessity of that communicated movement are not perceived, are not in the perception *per se*, are not empirically given as such, but à la Lonergan are understood, are in the insightful mind—is a case analogous to what I am arguing about supposed *qualia*. They are not of the given as merely given.

"But of course," might come a standard reply. It would appear that my analysis of the givenness of redness supports the standard assertion: "We can say that a mental state is conscious if it has a *qualitative feel*—an associated quality of experience. . . . *qualia* for short" (Chalmers, 1996, p. 4). To speak of *qualia*, then, is to implicate consciousness. Yes, of course.

Explaining how red could actually have its particular *qualia* required me, beyond appeal to mere stimuli as givens, to introduce consciousness into the analysis on at least two of Lonergan's levels: experience and understanding. In Chalmers's formulation, beyond the mere first-order registrations there were also corresponding first-order *phenomenal* states and, then, also first-order "judgments." So, yes, no doubt, I was speaking of consciousness.

However, note this well: I was speaking of *human* consciousness. And, of course, all the other theorists in this discussion likewise *presuppose* human consciousness even when they presume to speak about supposed consciousness in general or in other species or in mechanical contrivances and natural processes—because, as Nagel (1974) made clear, we have no access to the supposed mental experience of other species, and as Chalmers made clear, Chalmers was basing his theory on his personal experience of consciousness. Ever and again, human consciousness is smuggled into the discussion, taken for granted, and overlooked. Indeed, what intellectual discussion or analysis proceeds apart from human consciousness?

Therefore, I insist that only in human experience do those givens take on *qualia* and that the attribution of *qualia* presupposes human consciousness. It is true, then—for humans—that the experience of *qualia* is a concomitant of consciousness. However, if one carefully attends to the givens, as I have just attempted to demonstrate with support by appeal even to Chalmers's first-order phenomenal states, in themselves the givens have no particular *qualia*. As givens, they are merely given. Of course, the givens are not all the same. They do differ in themselves, and for this reason they can entrain different *qualia*, and for the same reason analytic human intelligence can specify what those given differences are—differences in wavelengths of light, for example. But the experience of *qualia*, experience of the differences as different, presupposes further conscious processing whereas the givens, as given, are merely non-descript givens.

5.5.5. Human Consciousness versus Animal Responsiveness

I now state outright the other point that focuses my argument and toward which I have been working: animals other than humans do not experience *qualia* (5.5.1). *Qualia* are human constructs and apply, as far as I can determine, only in human experience. Collapsing consciousness into *qualia* opens a convenient but misleading path toward positing consciousness in animals where, otherwise, there is no evidence for its existence. I find the contrast between animal and human mind provides a useful perspective on the uniqueness of human consciousness.

Animals do respond to stimuli. They enjoy sensation and varying degrees of perception and memory. Some kind of processing is going on in their minds; they are not automatons. Independent evidence in their identifiable biological structures and in their responsive behaviors supports these statements. Animals show generally rote responses to a stock of species-specific sensitivities. In some species their responsiveness is amenable to shaping: they can learn. In fact, many of their responses to colors, scents, sounds, and other physical energies, even in the wild, are learned. Even the higher species, mammals and especially primates, which exhibit remarkable animal intelligence and, via clever problem solving, evince a form of insight, exhibit little capacity for grammatical language or abstract thinking: self-conscious cognition (Helminiak, 1996a, pp. 152–158). The most highly trained among the other primates offers no comparison with the average human child. "Whatever amount of conscious capacity we may concede to animals, there is no question that during the course of our evolution, our species crossed a great divide, a cognitive Rubicon that no other species on this planet has crossed" (Donald, 2001, p. 149). There exists a qualitative difference between the species. There is no documented evidence to justify imputing consciousness—in the refined way I am using this term (5.1.2)—to non-human specimens. Only anthropomorphism and ambiguous terminology allow this imputation.

Almost inevitably, the examples of *qualia* in consciousness studies are perceptual, for example, the experience of seeing red. Then, because animals exhibit sensation, they supposedly experience *qualia*. Then, because humans actually do experience *qualia* in percepts and because the human experience of *qualia* is correctly linked with consciousness, animals are said to have consciousness, too.

This line of reasoning begs the question. It ignores human distinctiveness. It overlooks the fact that humans know *qualia* only because humans are conscious. The logical priority is this: consciousness explains *qualia*; *qualia* do not explain consciousness. Why so? The explanatory consciousness in question is not merely intentional. To be consciously intentional, the consciousness in question must also, and with a logical priority, be conscious. But occurring in different kinds, intentionality—agent–object interaction—does pertain both to animal sensation and to human consciousness. Both involve an agent's directedness toward some object: the cat approaches the saucer of milk, and the human observes, "The cat is going for the milk." Accordingly, when consciousness is identified with intentionality, the intentionality of sensation is easily conflated with the intentionality of consciousness—and, especially, easily so when even the stock human examples are limited to the perceptual (but see Kounios & Beeman, 2009,

2014). Two kinds of intentionality are confounded. The biological and perceptual response of the cat is equated to the intellectual response of the person. Yet intentional consciousness, awareness, must first and foremost entail non-reflecting consciousness, which the cat in no way evinces.

Whatever is reflected on must first be in consciousness as conscious, as content available to the reflective capacity itself, before that content can be reflected on and, thereby, become an object of intentional awareness. Consciousness as conscious is the condition for the possibility of consciousness as intentional; non-reflecting consciousness is the presupposition of objectifying human awareness. I repeat the same formulation from William James (1890/1950, vol. 1): "the indispensable subjective condition of their [objects'] being experienced at all" (p. 304: 5.3.2). Only that unique kind of self-presence "to" ourselves as humans allows data within consciousness to be reflected upon as such, as data within consciousness. Only the potential self-presence of consciousness, consciousness "of" itself, allows us humans to step back from experiential input, from primordial experience, from sheer givens as given, from that of which we are conscious but not yet aware, and by stepping back, discern differences—*qualia*—within the input. The muddled identification of consciousness with the intentional experience of *qualia* allows for oversight of the genuine uniqueness of human consciousness as primordially non-intentional, namely, conscious.

5.6. What Is It Like to Be?

5.6.1. *The Uniqueness of the Human Experience to Be*

With the cat out of the bag, as it were, I address one more angle on *qualia* that also pertains to non-human species—the supposed feel of a being's being specifically what it is. For example, "What is it like to be a bat?" (Nagel, 1974). My insistence is that also this touted feel is a red herring. Like attention to merely perceptual input, it distracts from consciousness *per se*. Trying to define consciousness but missing the experience of consciousness *per se* because of focus on the experience of its contents, Chalmers says, "When I talk about consciousness, I am talking only about the subjective quality of experience: what it is like to be a cognitive agent" (p. 6). Likewise, as so many others do (Blackmore, 2012), echoing "a phrase made famous by Thomas Nagel," Chalmers (1996) holds that "a being is conscious if there is *something it is like* to be that being" (p. 4). I will not dispute this description, but I will insist that it pertains only in the case of humans.

I have no reason to believe that other species have any sense whatsoever of what it is like for them to be themselves. Oh, yes, they do exhibit sensate and even highly processed responsiveness to stimuli, but there is no reason to believe they actually experience their responsiveness and mental processing as an object, potential or actual, of their own responsiveness. Their sense organs are geared to responding to environmental stimuli, not to sensing their own sensing. Even what proprioceptive and interoceptive receptors they might have are geared to the efficient functioning of organic processes, not to their sensing their own sensing.

To say that animals actually have experiences, self-aware internal feedback, is a fallacious use of the term "experience" (4.20.2). Likewise, to say that animals experience "something it is like to be" is fallacious. To posit *experience* or *something it is like to be* inherently entails some kind of reflexivity, a potential distancing from the input itself and a characterization of it as experience—just as in the case of the *quale* "red." (5.5.1). That humans have such experience because their consciousness is conscious as well as intentional supplies no reason to presume that animals have such experience merely because their senses are intentional. Only because humans have non-reflecting consciousness are they able to experience and express the qualities, the *qualia*, of their intentionality. Only because humans have primordially non-objectified data on themselves are they able to become objects to themselves—and, thus, to experience something it is like for them to be themselves. I do not believe non-human organisms can do so; therefore, I do not believe they are conscious. They cannot realize something it is like for them to be; to them it is not like something for them to be; their being is not like anything subjectively; they are not subjects, not characterized by subjectivity. They just are. They have no consciousness of their being.

Absent non-reflecting consciousness, there can be no experience, no characterization, no inner experienced "like-ness." Non-human animals are, they respond, they interact, sometimes quite cleverly; but they have no *idea* that they are doing so. They do not reflect on their own inner experiences. What they are is in their doing, not in any awareness—reflecting consciousness—of this doing. They exist in their behavior; they have no self-consciousness of their being. The human experience of sleepwalking provides an analogous case—effective engagement of the environment, sometimes involving rather highly sophisticated behavior, but unconscious, amnesiac, irretrievable, unreportable.

> Animals lack detailed declarative knowledge about the world. Whatever knowledge they do have remains implicit because they cannot express, or declare, their knowledge in any form of symbolic representation. They cannot bracket their own experiences or re-present them in memory. This leaves animals immersed in a stream of raw episodic experience, from which they cannot gain any distance. Their mode of awareness is enormously restricted. (Donald, 2001, pp. 119–120)

On the basis of research on primates that recognize their body parts in a mirror, Gallup (1977, 1979, 1985) argues that they do have self-awareness. But his interpretation employs the very notions of consciousness that I criticize here and fails to take into account the further considerations I offer. His interpretation confounds perception with consciousness, and all too easily this interpretation identifies the physical body with the subjective self. As Wynne and Udell (2013) point out, human prosopagnosics cannot recognize themselves in a mirror but do have an intact self-concept. On the other hand, autistic children recognize themselves in a mirror but have an impaired self-concept (pp. 176–177). Evidently, the connection between self-recognition in a mirror and self-consciousness is not one-to-one. Besides, tool-use is commonplace among many species (pp. 117–121). Some animals can use a tool, a mirror, to perceptually recognize parts of their bodies. This achievement, remarkable in itself, hardly evinces an inner mental experience, consciousness, like that of humans—namely, a non-reflecting presence "to" that recognition, which would allow subsequent reflection on it as an object of awareness in itself. This was Donald's (2001) point in the prior paragraph. The feat of the mirror-savvy chimpanzees, orangutans, and possibly dolphins, elephants, a gorilla (Wynne & Udell, 2013, pp. 172–172), and even pigeons (p. 175) is only a bit more sophisticated than the routine ability of animals to recognize their toes as their own and lick them or to scratch behind their ears. Wynne and Udell suggest that, rather than self-concept, such an animal evinces an "'own-body' concept," the ability "to differentiate between itself and the rest of the world," "something that most animals surely must have" (p. 177). This explanation sufficiently accounts for the own-body-recognition in the animals' use of mirrors. However, I submit, the term *own-body concept* confuses the matter. I would reserve the term *concept* to name the product of self-conscious insights in humans (2.3.7; 4.18.3; see Lonergan, 1967d). As for the animals' body-recognition, proprioception and perception of one's own body with the use of a tool completely explain the capacity in question. Loosely attributing "concepts" to animals not only garbles the scientific terminology but also begs the empirical question. Additionally, of course, I freely acknowledge that the evolutionary line between perception and consciousness is fuzzy, not clean, so inchoate consciousness might evince seeming self-awareness.

Similarly, animal behavior evinces intelligent problem solving, so attribution of some kind of insight is not unwarranted. But the insight of non-human animals subsists in their behaviors; it does not generate concepts that are subject to examination. As with infants in Piaget's (1963) sensorimotor stage of cognitive development, intelligence shows in the learned ability to manipulate the body and navigate the physical environment; self-conscious concepts, facilitated later in infants by language, are nowhere yet on the scene. Animal insight is not a self-conscious event that animals experience as something they could reflect on. They do not have self-conscious ideas; they do not conceptualize, think, theorize, plan, and expostulate on their insights. On the basis of the evidence, insight in other animals is significantly different from insight in humans although the former might well lie along the evolutionary path to the latter.

In the final analysis, of course, the question about supposed animal self-consciousness is empirical (Bekoff, 2002, pp. 93–96), and the sole evidence that would settle the empirical question is the animals' actually communicating in some way to us about their conscious experience. Thus far, such evidence is not forthcoming. The well-trained bonobo

> Kanzi has never tried to describe his own experiences or feelings, using symbols. He cannot construct the kinds of memories that we call autobiographical, even though he has been given a set of symbols that could in theory enable him to do this. Human children use language in this way very early in their development, even before they can form grammatical sentences, but Kanzi has never tried this kind of self-description, despite his considerable symbolic and grammatical skills. (Donald, 2001, p. 121)

Besides, the question about animal consciousness cannot be answered unless the nature of consciousness is first clarified because self-consciousness and self-awareness (1.8) are of a kind. Moreover, the stark intellectual contrast between any primate and a human child still stands.

5.6.2. The "Something" It Is Like to Be

That frequently cited indicator of consciousness, "something it is like to be," comes from human experience. What does it mean? I know of no explicit exposition of this *something it is like* beyond the words themselves, so I offer some suggestions. As a parallel to perceptual *qualia,* which differ from conscious content to content and from subject to subject, the phrase *something it is like* most likely refers to the particular inner experience of every individual person, and in each case the report would be different. Let me explain.

I have been struck by a line of Madonna, "Do you know how it feels for a girl in this world?" One evening at a disco, I realized soberingly that, no, I do not. Nor do I know how it feels for anyone else in this world. Moreover, the organic and psychotropic effects of recently needed medications exposed me to a different experience of being Daniel. Suddenly I had to vigilantly monitor my moods and emotions and to discipline my lifestyle to ensure adequate rest and proper nutrition because my spontaneous inclinations, which had served me quite well over the years, were no longer what they were. The what-it-is-like-to-be-me was simply not what it had been. My "subjective feel" of myself had changed. At the same time, the challenges of a deeply intimate and honest relationship also exposed me to the existential profundity of that theretofore glib psychological term *individual differences.* I have come to realize grippingly that the internal lived experience of people—moods, energy levels, sensitivity, emotional intensity, tolerance for change, impulsivity, anxiety, in sum, what psychologists call temperament (Keirsey & Bates, 1978; Thomas, Chess & Birch, 1963) and what contributes, along with learning, to personality—can differ considerably from person to person. It is no wonder that structuring coherent and efficiently functioning relationships, organizations, communities, or societies is such an ongoing challenge. How does one build when the available stones are so differently formed?

Now, if such individual differences are the intent of the phrase "something it is like" to be, then this phrase speaks to me. However, I do not believe this phrase nails down the nature of consciousness. Once again, the theory focuses on different contents of individual experience, not on the nature of conscious experience itself. Yet this latter experience is also real. Although the internal feel of myself is not what it used to be, for example, I am still myself. I experience no discontinuity of identity. The awareness I hold of myself as a person, the experienced presence that makes me *me,* perdures. This subjective experience of myself as simply being myself is beyond the organic and psychological contents that also, from other perspectives, supply me with my very own internal experience. As I sit in my office studying, thinking, and writing, for example—despite the occasional wave of anxiety over a currently sick friend, the surges of frustration, disbelief, despair, elation, and weariness provoked in turn by my task, the distracting and urgent necessities of my aging biological organism—I inhabit the same intellectual space that I have always known. In this regard I recognize that same "subjective feel" of what Lonergan (1957/1992) would call the "intellectual pattern of experience" (pp. 209–210), namely, personal activity directed by, and aimed toward, the pure and unrestricted desire to know. At times this experience approximates the transcendent experiences of my meditative moments and certainly moves in the same cultivated mental space.

During intellectual work and, more so, meditative practice, I have a sense of open-ended, unconstrained, sometimes contentless being, my being what I am in my most self-transcending state. I experience myself precisely in my personhood, in that dimension of my being determined by consciousness and its concomitant intellectual acts.

The gurus of the East intimate a similar experience. When they repeatedly push the question, "Who is having this experience?" they intimate an achieved mental state, enlightenment, an abiding presence "to" oneself, that, without obliterating them, transcends physical feelings, emotions, moods, and discursive thinking. They speak of this state at its occasional epitome as an experience of pure consciousness, consciousness "of" consciousness, apart from any specific conscious content. Given this experience but still constrained by a sensation-modeled epistemology—that same bugaboo again—they unfortunately conclude that there actually is no experiencer who is having the experience (3.1.4). What they rightly note in this experience is unlike the categorical realities, the objects and the mental contents, we experience otherwise in our world. This peculiar experience is nothing of the kind that fills the world of everyday, usually material, experiences. So, meaning "nothing of the kind" and adhering to a sensate epistemology, they insist that subjectivity is nothing at all, that the subject is not. Well aware of the experience but unable to coherently articulate it, unfortunately and self-contradictorily, they insist that the "insister" does not exist.

The experience of oneself simply as a person, the consciousness of one's subjectivity beyond any specific contents, does occur, and not only for meditators (Greeley, 1975; Hay, 2007). It is akin to Lonergan's self-appropriation (2.1.1; 5.6.3). But it is not a matter of being *like* anything. It is simply a matter of being, of being conscious both intentionally and consciously, and especially of being conscious "of" one's own consciousness, that "quality" that makes one a person. It is what it means for a person to be. It is the kind of existence that characterizes personhood. It is the essence of subjectivity.

This experience of oneself does occur. I and others know it, and I am writing about it. Yet, I am hard pressed to say outright "what it is like" to be in this way. To experience consciousness *per se* is not like anything in particular because the experience is not "colored" by any content. The experience just is. It is an openness to all experiences. And in saying so, I guess I actually am, then, saying what it's like—not by comparing it to something else in a metaphor or a simile, which exercise is explicitly not the point (Nagel, 1974, p. 440, n. 6), but by acknowledging a distinctive kind of recognizable experience and characterizing it in itself. I recall that the most appropriate adjectives are *conscious* and *spiritual* (5.1.3; 5.4.3). This experience is a given, just as the experience of redness, before conceptualization, is just a given. Conscious experience is not like anything in itself or like anything other than itself. (For what it's worth, as I reread these words, it occurs to me that they sound like the Buddhist Heart Sutra.) Such "likeness" only pertains when I step beyond the pure experience and begin registering input, making associations, feeling moods and emotions, realizing connotations, having insights strikingly or hardly noticeably, discerning interrelationships, "making meaning."

5.6.3. Attempts to Articulate Consciousness

I fear the whole discussion of consciousness as "something it is like to be" is misguided. It is distracted by the experience of dimensions of humanity other than consciousness—simply summarized: perception, temperament, biography, culture, and history (5.6.2)—and entangled in epistemological theory grounded in sensation and perception (2.2.5) and encumbered by the mechanistic thinking of early modern science and contemporary computer science (2.9; 4.9.3; 4.9.5).

In humans this phrase *something it is like* must include reference to the pure experience of being conscious—not of being conscious of this or that, but of being conscious purely and simply, regardless of the content of consciousness at any one time or another. Of course, this situation could pertain in the case of meditators, who claim to experience moments of pure consciousness itself, consciousness "of" consciousness, apart from any specific content or object of consciousness; but my argument does not depend on such a cultivated and refined experience of consciousness. The far more common—indeed, the ubiquitous—experience of consciousness as conscious, concomitant to consciousness as intentional, provides cases enough, and I addressed this simultaneity and concomitance of the dual modes of consciousness (5.3.1).

Alternatively, this experience also appears to be the topic that Martin Heidegger (1927/1962, pp. 171 & n. 2, 214, 401–402, 460) set for himself when he asked what it is like to be human, *Dasein*. Incisively enough, he answered in terms of a uniquely human *Lichtung*, an opening or clearing, a lighted up space in which experience occurs. However, he never completely addressed his topic. He settled for analyzing particular experiences in the everyday world within that *Lichtung*, and phenomenologists continue providing accounts of what it's like to have this or that particular experience (e.g., Aanstoos, 1983; Pope, 2006). Accordingly, the term *phenomenal dimension of the mind* refers to much the same as does the feel or *qualia* of experience (Chalmers, 1996, pp. 6, 11–12) and stops equally short of attaining to the essence of human consciousness *per se*, apart from any particular contents.

Lonergan (1957/1992) went further. Attending to specific experiences, that is, to the different contents of consciousness, phenomenology never provided a phenomenology of consciousness *per se*. Lonergan's analysis does. Lonergan (1980/1990) deliberately called his phenomenology-like analysis "self-appropriation" (2.1.1) only to avoid entangled complications among the different schools of phenomenology (pp. 270–271). His work entails a kind of phenomenology, an attentiveness to one's own inner experience. Uniquely, his analyses attended to the conscious dimension of conscious experience even as the experience also entails its intentional, content-specific dimension.

Far better than speaking merely suggestively of "subjective feels," *qualia*, and *something it is like*, Lonergan's differentiation of human consciousness as both intentional and conscious allows a coherent theory. It differentiates two dimensions, two *modes* (Lonergan, 1957/1992, p. 299), within one experience and interrelates them in a mutually clarifying way, implicitly defines them by relationship to each other (4.6.5), much as the legs and hypotenuse of a right triangle mutually specify one another. The result is a kind of scientific account that would be appropriate to its topic. Its challenge, of course, is to recognize the conscious dimension of consciousness in addition to the more salient intentional dimension, to "catch oneself," as it were—if such were possible (5.3.6)—in a moment of insight, for example, to realize that one is conscious "of" one's own consciousness as well as "of" its content, to attend to this experience and credit it as valid evidence regarding consciousness, and to articulate the experience intelligently and reasonably, that is, to distinguish oneself as the "experiencer" from the experienced content with its particular qualities. In brief, the challenge is to grasp the nature of consciousness on the basis of the evidence available within our own minds—that which has been our task in this book all along. This challenge is the really hard problem of consciousness, and it appears that Lonergan, if he has not met it, has at least addressed it.

5.6.4. *The Projection of Human Experience Onto Non-Human Entities*

Tellingly, however, this emphasis would leave Nagel's (1974) bat and all other non-human organisms out of the discussion of consciousness and experience—and, all the more so, leave out their constitutive, lower-level, interacting biological, chemical, and physical systems. The shift from attention to the *qualia*, to attention to consciousness "of" them—the shift from emphasis on reflecting consciousness or intentional awareness to emphasis on non-reflecting consciousness as conscious—limits discussion of consciousness to the case of human beings. Humans alone experience consciousness.

Truth be told, human experience has ever been the paradigmatic example of consciousness studies anyway. It is the only case about which we have immediate evidence. This fact gets overlooked, so I am highlighting this unspoken presupposition of *human* consciousness. In the process—because I believe that human knowing depends on evidence, that human knowing is always merely *de facto*, that our universe could well have been other than what it is, that human knowing could well have had to produce knowledge other than what it has produced, that human knowing enjoys no logical necessity, that logical coherence alone does not determine what is or would be real—I am faulting the ubiquitous speculation in contemporary consciousness studies (2.3.6). Ungrounded speculation regards supposed zombies, parallel worlds, logically possible entities, behavioral specifications styled as "information," capacity to respond deemed "awareness," "consciousness" in all responding mechanisms such as thermostats or chemical processes, micro-bits of "consciousness" buried in all matter and lying behind the physicists' equations, and the like. Such speculation inevitably rests on a sensate model of epistemology and needs bodies, perceptible or imaginable, as determinates of the real. Such speculation clutters analyses and distracts from the *de facto* nature of human knowing and the unique actuality of human consciousness. Ironically, unfortunately, dismayingly, these speculations evince the striking creativity and the exquisite intelligence of the abstractive, trans-spatial, trans-temporal consciousness of the very speculators who, so attentive to the content of their speculations, miss in their own cases the workings of the human mind in the existential moment.

Because we humans have reflective intelligence, minds that can explore and theorize, we can specify the interactive functioning of animals, which enjoy sensate and perceptual responsiveness. Then, because we are similar to those other species in so many ways, we project our own experience onto them. We presume they also have some inner experience of themselves, experience that they somehow recognize as being of some kind, *something it is like to be.* We assume that they are conscious. In coherent explanation, however, we humans could recognize the *qualia* of our own experience only if our intentionality is not only intentional but also conscious. In contingent fact, only as conscious, not merely intentional, we have access to our experience as a potential object of experience itself, experience "of" experience; only thus does genuine experience occur. Without this same consciousness, the intentional events of the bat's biography—that is, the bat's sensations, perceptions, and responsive behaviors—must just pass as a sequence of one isolated engagement after another, a succession of one stimulus and response upon another, "a stream of raw episodic experience" (Donald, 2001, pp. 119–120), and in no way constitute genuine experience or *something it is like*. If there were "something that it's like to be" for bats and other such creatures, we would have to say that it is the very same for every one of them, namely, just an unaware succession of responses, and they themselves have no capacity to experience that succession even as a succession; they have no point of cognitive continuity—what Chalmers (1996), struggling to specify consciousness, refers to as "our core epistemic situation," "the center of our epistemic universe," (p. 196), "intimate epistemic relation" (p. 197), "the center of our mental life" (p. 204), what James (1890/1950, vol. 1) portrayed as the "river" or the "stream" (p. 239) in which all episodes flow, and what I name as subjectivity. The other species have no non-reflecting consciousness that perdures throughout all occasions of responsiveness, no "I" who is experiencing and is the subject of that succession of events. There is nothing particular, specific, individual, subjective, or personal that it is like to be a bat or any other non-human organism. They all lack the self-conscious experience that is unique to humans.

Despite the cute and cuddly name of a veterinarian clinic near my home, "Pets Are People, Too," and despite academic assertions to this effect (Bekoff, 2002, pp. 14–15), animals are not persons. They are not subjects. Yes, having *something it is like to be* does presume consciousness, and this experience could be said to be an indicator of consciousness. However, there is no evidence that every primate, every mammal, every living creature, or every interacting mechanism has experiences, something it is like to be, and, therefore, consciousness. The view that consciousness is so widely distributed is only an unfounded assumption. It rests on missing the essential and distinctive *conscious* nature of consciousness through a series of interrelated misunderstandings:

- to model human knowing on an analogy of sensate responsiveness, this against that: knowing is like taking a good look;

- to characterize consciousness solely as intentional, as awareness *of* some object;
- to recognize a kind of intentionality also in sensate and perceptual responsiveness—response to stimulus, agent against object, an eye registering light;
- to confound the responsive intentionality of sensation with the conscious intentionality of human awareness; accordingly, then,
- to attribute to non-human animals and even any "responsive" mechanisms the consciousness that humans alone enjoy—a bimodal consciousness, both conscious and intentional; and credulously
- to call those non-human interactions "experiences," the "subjective" "feel" of "something it is like," "consciousness."

5.7. The Priority of Non-Intentional or Conscious Consciousness

5.7.1. *Consciousness of a Range of Kinds of Data*

Emphasis on intentionality skews the account of human consciousness. Not the intentional, but the non-intentional dimension is the distinctive and the essential characteristic of human consciousness (Helminiak, 1996a, pp. 61–72). Sensation and consciousness both entail intentionality; they both entail what could be called a "subject"–object duality or, less specifically and more correctly, an agent–object duality. What sensation lacks and what human consciousness uniquely enjoys is precisely the non-reflecting dimension, consciousness as conscious. It is what makes human consciousness consciousness. A commonplace in Eastern thought, a concern also in the religious West, and both commonly associated with Brahman, God, and other supernatural suppositions, the conscious dimension of consciousness is routinely overlooked in consciousness studies (pp. 50–56). The regrettable result of this truncated notion of consciousness is to ignore the self-presence that accompanies human awareness of other things and even of oneself as an object. The concomitant result is to easily fall into thinking of consciousness as a kind of sensation—physical encounter, stuff out there impacting other stuff in here, this nudging against that, stimulus impinging upon receptor, eyes taking a deliberate good look at objects, distinct and vivid perceptual impressions impersonating knowledge, environmental interaction masquerading as information, thermostats and computers enjoying consciousness. Intelligence and the unitive moment of insight—*Intellectus in actu est intellectum in actu* (2.3.3)—get completely overlooked (pun intended!).

Consciousness is the root, the condition for the possibility, of Lonergan's self-appropriation (2.1.1; 5.6.3), and it is also the very content of self-appropriation. In self-appropriation, consciousness allows for the experience and subsequent objectification of consciousness itself. One can attend to the non-reflecting data of consciousness, and by reflecting on these data via intentional consciousness, one can process them—question them, understand them, formulate them, and know them. Such objectification, as for any insight, will require specification of a number of concepts and their relationship. Thus understood, consciousness is of a peculiar kind; it enjoys a self-presence. Unlike the senses, which cannot sense their own sensing, consciousness is conscious "of" itself as well as "of" the content of its intentionality. Consciousness can experience and, perforce, eventually know itself for what it is. This peculiar nature of consciousness is one meaning of the term *spiritual* (5.1.3). The spiritual is not restricted to an intentional presence of this against that, which characterizes material realities and sensate experience. The spiritual is present "to" itself in a peculiar non-reflecting mode. This peculiarity allows for self-appropriation.

But this exercise of Lonergan's, which can ground an epistemology (2.1.6; 2.2.9), addresses only one aspect of the contents of consciousness, for humans are not just conscious beings but also material, organic, sensate, and perceptual. In varying degrees, consciousness makes all these dimensions of the human constitution available for explicit experience and analysis. Thus, through consciousness one has the experience of the data even of non-reflecting consciousness itself, on the basis of which—attended to, questioned, conceptualized, formulated, and confirmed—one can know consciousness in its levels and its modes. But one also has the experience of psychic data, whereby one can make into objects of explicit concern and then come to know one's own images, memories, and emotions with the particular color and dynamics of one's personality. And one also has the experience of sense data, whereby one can come to attend to provoked sensations and thereby come to know physical realities in the world, including one's own body. All these different kinds of data are available to human experience within consciousness.

5.7.2. Consciousness "of" the Data of Consciousness

Conscious "of" the givenness of the varied kinds of data just noted, one can formulate the broad notion of "experience," namely, the presence of givens to be understood. This first level of consciousness—"experience" (2.2.1)—is the one on which current consciousness studies tend solely to focus. They tend to identity consciousness with the content of experience—that is, awareness, attentiveness to diverse givens—and leave it at that. Hence, in a further restriction, perceptual examples tend to dominate the field since they present obvious instances of awareness of some given. Moreover, intentionality alone then tends to characterize consciousness since the experienced content is the most salient aspect of perceptual experience, and consciousness gets defined and characterized in terms of its objects. Then, consciousness is said, above all, to be consciousness of something; and the "something" becomes controlling: hot, cold, green, blue, tough, soft. But once consciousness itself, not simply its most salient contents, becomes the topic, other data within consciousness can be noted. Thus, conscious "of" one's own wonder, inquiry, insight, conceptualization, and articulation, one can formulate the notion of "understanding." And conscious "of" one's reflection, one's checking out an idea, one's marshalling and weighing the evidence, one's need to test a hypothesis against the data, one can formulate the notion of "judgment." As conscious, as present "to" itself, consciousness provides data on itself, and one can attend to these data, examine and articulate one's findings, and check them out against the data available for each of the levels of conscious operation. In short, one can know one's knowing as a three-level process (2.1.1)

Said otherwise, beyond the experience of perceptual data—*qualia*, percepts—there are also within consciousness the experience of understanding and the experience of judging (and, not treated in this book, the experience of deciding). As surely as the experience of perceptions provides data, the experiences of understanding, judging, and deciding also provide further data. These further data constitute evidence that consciousness *per se* is much broader than only the experience of perceptions. Attention to these further data allows a conceptualization of these further aspects of consciousness, and the articulated conceptualization allows the verification of the conceptualization against the appropriate data. Such, again, is Lonergan's analysis. Thus, he derives the levels of consciousness empirically, by appeal to relevant evidence, by attending to the full range of the data of consciousness. As a result, his treatment of consciousness far outstrips current discussion, virtually limited to the experience of percepts and their *qualia* (Helminiak, 2014).

The point most relevant here is that the articulation of the levels of consciousness is grounded in data—not the so-called (2.1.4) "publicly accessible" data of the senses, to which natural science limits its evidence, but the data of consciousness, which pertain when subjectivity is the topic. Both kinds of data are available to human experience, both constitute legitimate evidence (5.3.6), and both can ground science—evidence-based explanation—in its various applications (2.1.5). But all too often, the primordial data of consciousness—that is, consciousness as conscious or as non-reflecting—gets ignored, and consciousness is taken to be only intentionality and, as such, is easily conflated with animal sensation and perception and mechanistic interactions.

5.7.3. Consciousness "of" the Data of the Senses

In fact, we are able to reflect even on sense data only because we are initially non-reflectingly present "to" our experience of them. We humans have sense data to question only because we are conscious (2.1.4). In this sense, all human data are subjective; that is, they inextricably involve a human subject (which fact does not necessarily imply that the data and their analysis are biased: 2.6.2–2.6.3). Other species have sense input, but they do not become aware of it as such, do not question and reflect upon it, do not analyze and think about it, do not theorize about it, do not confirm their theories. They have no self-awareness precisely because they are not conscious. They are incapable of abstract thought precisely because they are not conscious. All these matters—consciousness, subjectivity, experience, awareness, self, insight, meaning, thinking, theorizing—hang together and are of one kind. The animals' responsiveness to perceptual input is not "experience" in any sense like that distinctive to humans. For this reason I restrict the term *experience* to human situations and, to make my point, reject its attribution to animals (4.20.4). We humans manage our sensations and perceptions because, in addition to sensing and perceiving stimuli and, thus, responding to things other than ourselves, as other animals do, within consciousness we also experience the products of sensation and perception as such and can attend to them as such. Therefore, we can mediate them to ourselves via meaning, and as a result, we live in another realm not limited to that of external sensate encounter, namely, a world of meanings and values. Like other animals we humans not only respond to stimuli, but unlike them, via consciousness we can also know the stimuli as such and monitor our responses, increasing our adaptability by an evolutionary bound.

Physical science may legitimately limit its concern to sense data, but philosophers badly misrepresent the case when they insist that appeal to sense data constitutes the sole valid scientific agenda (2.1.4) or that perceptual examples typify the experience of consciousness (cf. Blackmore, 2012) or that the intentionality of consciousness, similar to that of perception, essentially characterizes consciousness (5.4.1). In fact, the condition for the possibility of human analysis even of sense data is conscious experience. It provides the cognitive material about which, on subsequent levels of conscious operation, intelligence proposes scientific explanations subject to confirmation or falsification.

5.7.4. Inverted Priorities Regarding the Modes of Consciousness

The restriction of science to sense data along with the subsequent dismissal of the possibility of a scientific treatment of consciousness has the matter precisely upside-down. It has taken for granted and ignored the condition for the possibility of attention to sense data as such. By appeal to the more obvious, this purportedly scientific stance overlooks the absolutely fundamental. In the case of the human capacity for explanation, this fundamental is consciousness—precisely as conscious, not as intentional; it is the necessarily presupposed factor in contrast to an intentionality common also to sensation and perception. Overawed by physical science and slavishly imitating its early modern version by addressing human realities via material, spatial, and perceptual modeling (2.2.4), philosophy and psychology have not yet taken the turn toward the subject seriously enough. Passing the time analyzing language and concepts and the particularities of this or that experience and computer models and speculation about all possible worlds, they camp out with Kant at that idealist halfway house between materialism and a coherent critical realism (2.2.8). Insistence on mere sense data without concomitant acknowledgement of the human experience of non-reflecting consciousness is a methodological oxymoron: unconscious data, unavailable givens. Yet the oxymoron reigns.

Without turning ourselves into objects to ourselves, we humans are conscious "of" our own consciousness and its functioning. Such presence "to" oneself is the essence of human consciousness or spirit. It entails evidence on itself. It is not the encounter of some object, stuff, or thing—in this case, oneself—given whole hog to intentional awareness as if consciousness were but another version of sensation (2.2); it is, rather, experience, the availability of data, access to what *could be* "lifted up," attended to, inquired about, understood, verified as understood, and talked about, as here. Thus objectifying our consciousness "of" consciousness, objectifying subjectivity as such, turning subjectivity into the "object" of our explicit concern, we can know consciousness—by applying the three-level process of human knowing: attending to the evidence; inquiring into it, generating an insight, and formulating a hypothesis; and confirming the accuracy of the hypothesis against the evidence. The result of this process, knowledge of consciousness, shows consciousness to be both conscious and intentional and to unfold on four levels. Not the intentional, but the conscious mode is the *sine qua non*; it constitutes the primordial given; its treatment poses the really hard problem of consciousness. Although, perforce, this non-reflecting consciousness is usually completely ignored, it is the more determinative, the constitutive, the essential quality of consciousness, a phenomenon unique to human beings.

5.8. Unbounded Human Consciousness and Transcendent Experiences

5.8.1. Heightened Experience of Consciousness

For the most part, we—via our consciousness—are concerned about other things. We attend to living, to objects in the world, to familial, professional, cultural, societal, and recreational pursuits. Seldom do we attend to our attending itself. For this reason, talk of consciousness might seem strange. Consciousness is not like those other phenomena that usually fill our attention. It is like the health we take for granted until an illness strikes. It is that in which, through which, by which we are human, so it goes unnoticed.

However, we are able to heighten our consciousness "of" consciousness—not by adverting to it, not by attempting to look at it, not by treating it as an object and chasing after it, not like Fido trying to catch his tail, but by being present "to" ourselves more intensely, by heightening our subjectivity. We are far more aware of our own conscious operations, for example, when faced with a difficult judgment of fact or, even worse, a personal choice with serious repercussions than when simply using our eyes to make out a distant object. In the latter case, the object of visual concern dominates our meager awareness; in the former cases, the existential implications force self-consciousness upon us. Lonergan (1967a) makes this same point as follows:

> To heighten one's presence to oneself, one does not introspect; one raises the level of one's activity. If one sleeps and dreams, one is present to oneself as the frightened dreamer. If one awakes, one becomes present to oneself, not as moved but as moving, not as felt but as feeling, not as seen but as seeing. If one is

puzzled and wonders and inquires, the empirical subject becomes an intellectual subject as well. If one reflects and considers the evidence, the empirical and intellectual subject becomes a rational subject, an incarnate reasonableness. If one deliberates and chooses, one has moved to the level of the rationally conscious, free, responsible subject that by his [or her] choices makes himself what he is to be and his world what it is to be. (p. 227)

Meditation and other "spiritual practices" have the deliberate effect of heightening our consciousness "of" consciousness. By changing the processes in our brain, meditation allows different mental experiences. Through spiritual practices one learns to be attentive "to" one's attentiveness, conscious "of" consciousness, aware "of" the experience in the living of it, indeed, in being it. Then, far from being concerned about other objects or even about ourselves as objects to ourselves, the "content" of our concern is consciousness itself, the very possibility of consciousness of any object—consciousness without any objective content, consciousness "of" pure subjectivity, consciousness purely as conscious apart from any intentionality. In this peculiar case the "content" of our experience would be open-ended, dynamic consciousness itself, which is geared to all that there is to be known and loved, geared to the entire universe of being—*capax infiniti*: open to the infinite, as the medievals phrased the matter.

I believe that we also become aware of contentless consciousness in rather familiar experiences of everyday "contemplation," such as peacefully enjoying the beauty of nature, gazing at the ocean, watching children at play, peering into the night heavens, making love. Then, if only for fleeting moments, the mind might be perfectly still, no questions might arise, no quest for understanding or fact or decision might distract. The mental operation would rest fully on the first level of consciousness, and the "content" of consciousness would be one's consciousness itself, not at all the objects provoking the wonder. The experience is one of simply being there, with no concern but to rest in the moment, conscious of beauty, marvel, and wonder, conscious of the immensity of one's own openness and of the concomitant immensity of the universe about which, if one wished at a more pragmatic time, one could begin to fill in the details, specifying the then intentional object of that openness.

5.8.2. A Naturalistic Explanation of Transcendent Experiences

I suggest that psychologically such experience of consciousness is the core of transcendent experience. Experienced in fullness, it would be a full-blown mystical experience. Human consciousness is the explanation of mysticism. Consciousness becomes both the "object" "of" the experience and the subject "of" the experience. Mystical experience is the intensified or even full experience "of" one's own being, which is capable of experiencing itself in its open-ended expanse.

Human consciousness or human spirit is dynamic, self-transcendent, open-ended, trans-spatial and trans-temporal, unitive, ineffable or mysterious, and experienced as gift or "grace"—

- dynamic in that it entails a self-regulated and relentless movement toward an inherently defined fulfillment: questions, for example, never cease;
- self-transcendent in that, as conscious, it is an opening to what already always lies beyond our objectified self: the agent "I" is always more than what can be noted in the "me";
- open-ended in that the terminus of its fulfillment is being, all that there is to be known: it is geared to the universe as it pursues that endless stream of questions;
- trans-spatial and trans-temporal in that its object is meaning, pure intelligibility, which, as universal concepts exemplify and Einstein's equations demonstrate (4.3), transcends the here and now and, all things being equal, applies everywhere and always;
- unitive in that its goal, as the scientific enterprise exemplifies, is coherent interrelationship of all that there is to be understood and affirmed, namely, the universe of being;
- ineffable or mysterious in that, being non-material, it is unlike the spatiotemporal, the sensate and perceptual, realities that fill our familiar world and dominate our everyday concerns; and
- experienced as gift or "grace" in that it correlates with being itself and in that its actuation in an insight, for example, is beyond our deliberate control.

Dynamic, self-transcendent, open-ended, trans-spatial and trans-temporal, unitive, ineffable, and graced—these are also the characteristics commonly attributed to mystical experiences (Belzen & Geels, 2003; Carmody & Carmody, 1996). It would appear, then, that an intense experience of consciousness "of" consciousness itself would account for overwhelming, open-ended, unitive, and transcendent experience—mysticism as an extraordinary experience. Likewise, as exemplified in the third-last paragraph, experienced only to some degree as an abiding dimension of life, consciousness "of" consciousness would result in spiritually sensitive living—mysticism as a way of life: the contemplative attitude, enlightened living (1.1). With a heightened sensitivity to consciousness, ordinary activities, events, and things in this world would include a sense of broader connectedness and wider implication. Concomitantly, the "meaningful" component, the significance (2.3.2), of everyday living would be enhanced, and the thrust of human life toward some bigger and ultimate reality would be manifest. At stake would be nothing other than spiritual or transcendent experience.

The neuroscientific research and theory summarized in Chapter 3 suggest the biological bases and neurological mechanisms of such transcendent experience, but, of course, these bases or their processes are not the experience itself. It depends on the emergence of the human spirit, a distinct reality (4.14.1). Appeal to it can explain the peculiarity of transcendent experience. Accordingly, apart from all implication of God or other supposed non-human, other-worldly entities, such experience is spiritual experience, experience of spirit, in its own right. Recognition of the human spirit as a genuine dimension of the human mind already allows for a fully psychological accounting for transcendent experiences.

5.8.3. The One and the Many in Transcendent Experiences

Cultivated transcendent experience is specialization on the first level of consciousness (2.1.6). It is the development of consciousness as conscious; the enhancement of experience itself; the heightening of consciousness "of" the very source of human wonder, awe, and question. The development of this enhancement requires that dynamic intentional consciousness be still and not raise the question, "What is it?" Such question—thinking—removes one from the moment of pure experience and advances intentional consciousness to its second level. Thinking entails distancing from the experiencing, shifts attention to the experienced, and eventually results in differentiated knowledge of multiple realities. All the while, of course, the function of the first level is still operative in that, aware of the object of thought, one is also simultaneously and concomitantly conscious "of" one's thinking (5.3.1). One does not lose consciousness "of" one's consciousness just because one is thinking, responding to the spontaneous questions of dynamic consciousness, and attending to its objects. A heightened consciousness "of" consciousness amidst engagement with life is the meaning of enlightened living.

Said otherwise, by way of example, meditative practice curtails the unfolding of intentional consciousness and its spontaneous movement from experience to understanding to judgment (2.1.6). That is, meditation "quiets the mind." The techniques of meditation enforce this curtailment: one is to gently dismiss from the mind any sensations, perceptions, images, emotions, thoughts, questions, judgments, or desires that arise, and each time one is to return to pure "mindfulness" (3.1.3). One repeatedly dismisses all mental content and activity and eventually learns to sit in pure, attentive, non-reflecting presence. At that point and for this reason, the unitive transcendent experience includes no this and that, no subject–object distinction, no differentiations of any kind. Meditative practice systematically excludes such matters, and I believe other transcendent experiences share the same characteristic. This learned ability to be genuinely present in the moment overflows into everyday living.

No wonder, then, that those who would base their account of reality on the transcendent moment aver that the really real includes no distinctions, no differentiations, no dualism, or no principle of non-contradiction, because all is one (e.g., Wilber, 1996, pp. 75–77; also Brown, 2002; d'Aquili & Newberg, 1999; Delio, 2003; Dennett, 1991; Searle, 1997; Teske, 2006). Because of the potential intensity of the transcendent experience, this philosophical position easily confounds mere experience with achieved knowledge; it accepts unprocessed data for the "really real"—although reality is known *de facto* only through intellectual acts on further levels of consciousness (2.3.6). At work is a notion of knowing as revelatory encounter, a version of the metaphor of knowing as taking a look. To gain this experience, one is only to peer deeply within. I reject this sensate epistemology. It is a version of naïve realism (2.2.2–2.2.4).

And no wonder that this same philosophy would claim that human consciousness itself is the ontological source of all things, that they "arise" out of consciousness, that everything is mind. Yet one is inclined to ask, "Out of what 'consciousness' do they arise? Human consciousness? Divine consciousness? Are these to be taken as one and the same?" From a Western theist perspective, the difference is all telling (6.2.4). Yet no differences are noted in mere experience (5.5.4). All questioning is irrelevant to the actual moment of transcendent experience. No distinctions are drawn because rationality does not pertain at the first level of consciousness. Herein lies an insurmountable problem with the claim that consciousness is the source of all reality, a claim typical of traditional Eastern philosophy and prevalent in many Western spiritual circles today—as, for example, in appeal to some vaguely defined, all-encompassing, undifferentiated "vital force" that would unite all experiences as "spiritual" (Ellens, 2009; Whitehead & Whitehead, 2009). This claim entails a regression to non-critical, pre-theoretical, undifferentiated thinking—as, for example, in the Bible (Helminiak, 1998, pp. 30–50; Lonergan, 1976; see 4.8.1). This claim is related to non-dualism (2.3.3; 2.9; 3.1.4, 4.18.6), the bugaboo we have encountered repeatedly in this book (2.3.3; 2.9; 3.1.4; 4.18.6). Supposedly, all is one, so the positing of distinctions—or is it separations? (4.2.1)—entails a misguided and even vile portrayal of the "really real."

Another ambiguity complicates that "non-dualist" claim: from another perspective it could be correct. From the point of view of epistemology, the point of view of the human knower, consciousness could, indeed, be called the source of all entities—of all entities as *known*. For knowing humans there is nothing apart from consciousness. For us "realities" do "arise" within consciousness—that is, according to the Eastern perceptual construal of the matter, our images, feelings, and thoughts arise in the human mind to "disturb" the quiet of pure consciousness—which is precipitously identified with Ultimate Reality itself. Indeed, even apart from that perceptual model of knowing, even on Lonergan's epistemology, two of the three components of human knowledge lie on the side of the subject: understanding and judgment (2.3.4); so anything that is known is known within consciousness. Furthermore, when the content of experience is consciousness itself, all three components lie there: in this unique case even the data with which one deals are the data of consciousness. Thus, presuming the case of the human knower, there is an acceptable interpretation of the claim that "all things arise out of consciousness." However, from the ontological perspective regarding the actual existence of things in themselves, this claim is untenable unless human consciousness were itself the Creator (6.2.2).

These considerations—the lack of distinctions in mere experience, the human dependence on consciousness for knowledge of any realities, and the distinction between human and Divine consciousness—discredit the ambiguous claim that all beings arise out of consciousness. Indeed, they not only discredit the claim, but they also explain wherein the mistakes lie, and they propose a coherent alternative explanation that, rather than simply sweep the data away, does account for the multiple phenomena involved.

From an ontological point of view, it is completely misguided to identify the objective existence of things with human access to, and knowledge of, them. To insist that beings emerge out of human consciousness is wrong. If one wants to reasonably account for the existence of things, the distinction between Creator and creature begs entry into this discussion (6.2.1) as does, then, the concomitant distinction between the divine and the spiritual (Helminiak, 2005a, 2006a, 2008a, 2008b, 2008c, 2010, 2011). But distinctions do not arise on the level of mere experience. Neither, moreover, do assertions—judgments. Yet the non-dualist claims are assertions, namely, that all is one without distinction and that the seemingly distinct beings arise only out of undisciplined consciousness. Articulated in the realm of discourse, where inquiry, insight, propositions, and judgments pertain, these claims discredit the realm of inquiry, insight, propositions, and judgments. This philosophical position uses judgments to assert that judgments are ultimately irrelevant. The inevitable self-contradiction inherent in a mistaken epistemology eventually shows (2.4.3).

Buddhist philosophy is well aware of this very "tension" within its core doctrine and attempts to resolve it by insistence on "two truths": the conventional or merely relative pertains to ordinary living, and the ultimate pertains to enlightenment (Eckel, 2001; Kalupahana, 1992, p. 168). Wanting to insist that the undifferentiated unitive experience of enlightenment regards the Ultimate yet undeniably unfolds in the world of space and time, Buddhism must propose two different ontologies and two correlative truths. At the root of this incoherence works a perception-based epistemology. In evidence, recall that commonsense analogies support some of Buddhism's most subtle philosophical teachings: the inability to find the innermost kernel of a seed pealed down layer by layer, the discovery by daylight that a snake in the night was merely a piece of rope, the discernment of an east and west side on "partless particles." Constrained by a perceptual epistemology, Buddhism has no way out of its dilemma except through insistence on two truths. Generously, this resolution is said to be "paradoxical." Analyzed with a coherent epistemology, it appears, rather, to be self-contradictory (Helminiak, 1998, pp. 249–264).

Following Lonergan's articulation of transcendental method, one is able to account both for undifferentiated, distinction-less transcendent experience as a specialization on the first level of consciousness and for attentive, intelligent, and reasonable knowing of multiple realities via acts of consciousness on subsequent levels. Recall, besides, that intelligently posited distinctions are not perceptually imagined separations. Distinctions can pertain within given wholes such that the distinctions specify the elements necessary and sufficient to explain the wholes, but explanation does not fragment the explained. Thus, a series of ever more complex wholes reasonably distinguished and related via emergence retain their interrelationship even as they constitute one intelligently grasped whole: being. On this understanding, being is, indeed, one. It is the goal of the human desire to understand everything about everything. In that projected ideal, the positing of intelligently discerned distinctions and interrelations within being constitutes an understanding of being. Only a perception-modeled epistemology, imagining the spatiotemporal separation of pictorial parts that had somehow combined to form larger wholes, encounters a problem in accounting for the unity of being—because this kind of thinking begins with a perceptual array, which *per se* is a spread of different times and places, a composite of spatiotemporally separate pieces. Perception does not grasp unities; it sees or hears or feels patterned arrays. Beginning with such patterned arrays and self-restricted to a tool chest of them, this kind of thinking can never avoid imagined separations and spatiotemporally defined pieces like LEGO blocks (4.1.3; 4.11.2; 4.17.2; 4.21.6). In contrast, without fragmenting the whole, intelligence discerns intelligibility within the whole and formulates it to express what the whole, still one, is (4.2.1). Nothing is lost in this intellectual approach, and theoretical coherence is gained. The much acclaimed unity of transcendent experience is explained, and the multiplicity of distinct entities is also explained, and reliance on intelligence and appeal to human consciousness, as it functions on different levels, hold this differentiated account together. Lonergan's epistemology recommends itself. It appears to reconcile and integrate the emphases of East and West—the monism of meditative experience and the unity of being, on the one hand, and the explanations of science via intelligently posited distinctions, concepts, interrelations, propositions, and reasoned conclusions, on the other.

Elsewhere I have treated these matters in more detail (e.g., Helminiak, 1987b, 1996a, 1998). I do not pretend that the present brief account addresses all the pressing questions. I merely suggest that transcendent experiences can be explained, and coherently so, on the basis of the human spirit, which is a real and distinct dimension of the human mind, which itself depends on a substrate of perceptual, sensate, and neural anatomy and physiology. Noteworthy is the observation that discussion of God or the Ultimate need play no role in the explanation of transcendent experience.

5.8.4. *The Supposed Religious Uniqueness of "Mystical" Experiences*

The religionists object that the proposed naturalistic account of transcendent experience does not apply to true mysticism. On the word of the mystics themselves, mysticism entails experience of God, not peculiar neurological occurrences and experience of one's own self. Witness R. C. Zaehner's

(1957) famous response to Aldous Huxley's reports of mescaline-induced transcendent experiences and, outrageously in contemporary psychology, the insistence that the testimony of religious believers must be respected as explanatory fact (Rayburn & Richard, 2002, p. 1793; Reber, 2006b, p. 200; Richards & Bergin, 2005, p. 137). Granted, Chapter 6 explains how God can, and for theists must, be implicated in these—as in all!—experiences, but I draw a line at any easy claim to the direct experience of God in Godself. After all, I have already accounted for the experiences in question. What further need is there to implicate extraordinary—miraculous—divine interventions (Helminiak, 2010, 2013a)? Besides, even when explicitly associated with religion, transcendent experiences have long been recognized to be of different kinds—cultivated, ritually induced, or spontaneous (Tanquerey, 1930). Religion might have traditionally explained them all by appeal to God's grace but today could hardly deny the contribution of individual differences in neurology, personality, and neuropathology (Helminiak, 1984b, 2005b). Similarly, Chapter 3 presented an array of probable neurological mechanisms, which would also be expected to correlate with phenomenologically variant experiences. However, to draw a line between those caused by God and the others makes no theological sense whatever: as Creator, God is the first cause of all things (6.2.2–6.2.3).

Current neurological and psychological understanding sheds new light on these matters, as the urgency of the present discussion evinces. Understandably, a prescientific era would attribute unusual experiences *ipso facto* to other-worldly spiritual powers and entities. Still, apart from its mystifying two truths, relative and absolute (5.8.3), the many strains of Buddhism do not. Moreover, contemporary neurological research, even among religiously committed people, less and less insists on a substantive difference between "religious" and other transcendent experiences (Carhart-Harris, 2013; Doblin, 1991; Griffiths, Richards, & Johnson, 2008; Griffiths, Richards, McCann, & Jesse, 2006; Maclean, Johnson, & Griffiths, 2011; Pahnke, 1966; Richards, 2005; Sterling, 1997). Many indigenous religions never did (3.3). Most likely, an outdated, uncritical popular religiosity leads current theologically untrained theorists to feel a need to implicate God in their neuropsychological conclusions (Helminiak, 2013a). Even in the case of sophisticated believers, a lifelong and costly commitment to religious beliefs, now not to be questioned, could have the same effect (Helminiak, 2006b, 2011; Kuhn, 1962/1970). Although research methodology in the sciences enjoys widespread consensus, no consensus exists on the philosophical and theological methodology relevant to this question, so almost any opinion could pass, and especially one that squares with prevalent piety. Firmly believing that religion and religious studies have entered a new era (Helminiak, 2008b, 2013a)—"It's a new ball game," as they say—I see no need to defend scientific explanations in the face of the religious reservations of the true believers. They fear eliminative reduction, but only explanatory reduction is at stake (4.8.1). Piety and science are different enterprises; but attentively, intelligently, and reasonably engaged, they are fully compatible.

5.9. Coherence of Neuroscience and Naturalistic Spiritualogy

5.9.1. The Sketchy Beginnings of an Elaborated Coherence

How do spiritualogy and neuroscience cohere? What are we to make of the relationship between my psychospiritual explanation of transcendent experiences based on a phenomenology-like account of consciousness and the neurophysiological explanations based on electromagnetic, serotonergic, or genetically conditioned systemic processes in the brain?

The account of emergence (4.14) in treatment of the mind–body problem already responded to this question in broad outline. However, the elaboration of mind in this chapter—especially the firm distinction between psyche and spirit within mind—suggests how sketchy that appeal to emergence was and how much research and theory are still needed. This section addresses this need and makes some suggestions to help bridge the theoretical gap between the brain, and human consciousness or spirit.

Regarding that coherence between neuroscience and naturalistic spirituality, before all else I admit I would not yet expect strict correspondence, and I hope that no one else would, either. The scientific status of both approaches is tentative, so only broad lines of explanation can be proposed. What both have in common is to account for the phenomenology of transcendent experiences, and in their own ways both do, the one from the low end and the other from the high end, as it were. These initial achievements make a good beginning, but as in digging a tunnel, the efforts from either end need to meet and the structure be joined, and the movements from two different levels of analysis pose the greatest challenge. For me, more important at this point than any definitive, comprehensive, coherent explanation is an overall philosophical framework that could eventually integrate firm research conclusions from either end, whatever they turn out to be. I believe that Lonergan provided such a framework, and I continue elaborating it.

5.9.2. The Need to Differentiate and Attend to Psyche

I suggested that psyche, sensate "consciousness" or perceptual responsiveness (5.1.2), is a kind of reality intermediate between brain function and the transcendent experience of self-consciousness. This suggestion introduces another kind of being into the purview of emergence and its many levels of realities. Troublingly, neither neuroscience nor psychology attends to psyche *per se*; for the most part, both continue to speak of the mind as one undifferentiated whole. At first blush, the neuroscientific explanations even appear sufficient without attention to the psyche. Alterations in neuronal functioning seem *ipso facto* to correlate with transcendent experience. Yet the leap from brain to transcendence is too long. Deeper probing belies the simplicity of this one-to-one correspondence. A number of considerations reveal the need for more intricate explanation.

First, the distinction between psyche and spirit, between sensate and intellectual consciousness, between animal and human mind, is a staple of ancient and medieval philosophy (Adler, 1985), but the distinction is virtually non-existent in the contemporary sciences. The ubiquity of the oversimplified—and so much berated—Cartesian model of humanity as "body and mind" (or, in religious circles, "body and soul") bears witness to this fact. Although in disparate studies psychology does differentially treat imagery, memory, emotions, concept formation, and other facets of mentality, differentiations tend not to be posited when discussion is of "the mind." The hegemony of this oversimplification would naturally preclude any attention to psyche as such, or to spirit as such, so none occurs. Further evidence to this effect is the uncertain usage of supposedly technical terms in many psychological presentations. For *cognition* and *cognitive*, for example, a precise definition is available and "official" (VandenBos, 2007). Yet, in his exceedingly helpful treatment of love, Robert Sternberg (1986) calls "decision/commitment" the "cognitive component" although it is obviously related to choice and is a matter of evaluation involving emotions and values (Lonergan's fourth level of consciousness), not simply knowledge or cognition (Lonergan's first three levels). Similarly, in a classic debate that entangles emotions, cognitions, and evaluations, Robert Lazarus speaks of cognitive appraisals. These include a swath of disparate elements: "values, goals, commitments, beliefs, and expectations" (Halonen & Santrock, 1996, p. 473). In contradictory contrast, I was struck that books on animal mind and animal cognition contain precious little treatment of animal emotions and bonding (e.g., Bekoff, Allen, & Burghardt, 2002; Griffin, 2001; Menzel & Fischer, 2011; Wynne & Udell, 2013) whereas a specific search under "animal emotion" easily provided specialized treatments of this dimension of animal minds (Bekoff, 2002, 2007). Evidently, animal psychology is more apt to distinguish cognition and emotion than is the human psychology I know.

Moreover, it is telling that, in the field of psychology, "Motivation and Emotion" routinely names a course and a textbook chapter (e.g., Halonen & Santrock, 1996; Weiten, 2007)—perhaps because "the terms *motivation* and *emotion* both come from the Latin *movere*, which means 'to move.' Both motivation and emotion spur us into action" (Halonen & Santrock, 1996, p. 468); or, perhaps more prosaically, as the tail wags the dog, because space is always short and topics need to be crammed in. But other more important factors besides emotions also move us to act—conspicuously, our values—and contemporary psychology also affirms as much: "For many decades, the study of motivation was dominated by a focus on biological *drives*. . . . But drive theories cannot account for the full complexity of human motivation" (Wade & Tavris, 2008, p. 440). Indeed! Yet, amidst items such as "Valium," "Variables, experimental," and "Viagra," *Values* occurs in the index of none of the psychology textbooks I've cited. Clearly, once psychology moves beyond *body* and into *mind*, the field is in considerable disarray. No wonder psyche is overlooked!

Second, reports of "religious experience" induced by psychedelic drugs do reveal stages along the way to transcendent experience. After relaxation and wondrous "spacey-ness," rich visual imagery, geometrical patterns, and other sensory-perceptual experiences are reported. Much low-dose "street use" of psychedelics never gets beyond this point, and users indulge in fascinating experiences of altered perception. But in clinical or religious contexts, higher doses coupled with professional facilitation release layers of powerful psychodynamic material and alter affect-laden programming of the personality, and many users later report spontaneous psychological integration (Doblin, 1991; Griffiths et al., 2008; Griffiths, Richards, McCann, & Jesse, 2006; MacLean, Johnson, & Griffiths, 2011; Pahnke, 1966; Richards, 2005; Sterling, 1997). Hence, psychoactive drugs can provide a powerful psychotherapeutic tool (Grof, 1976, 1987; Roseman et al., 2014). But during psychedelic experiences, only eventually does the full-blown transcendent experience arise, the experience of union with the universe, beyond all thought, feeling, and imagery. Even under the influence of psychedelic drugs, the road to the pure experience of consciousness passes through the psyche.

Third, d'Aquili and Newberg's (1999) hypothesis about transcendent experience posits as the trigger the deafferentation of the orientation association areas of the cortex (3.1.1). This is to say, I am speculating, that transcendent experience depends both on the quieting of other more palpable—that is, biological, sensate, perceptual, and self-referential—experience and on the entrainment of related neuronal systems into a configuration that supports the experience of transcendence. (I am not yet ready to broach the possibility of a human consciousness or spirit completely free of a human organism [Green, 1968; Monroe, 1971; see 4.2.1].) A kind of temporary reorientation and harmonization of neuronal functioning occurs, a change that can be ever more easily induced, that is, learned, as one experiences these temporary effects more frequently—perhaps via "neural reentrance, which holds that the same brain circuits can be reused for a variety of purposes" (Donald, 2001, p. 163) or else "'attractors,' that is, patterns of activity into which the brain tends to gravitate for short periods of time" (Roseman et al., 2014, p. 8). At stake in this alignment of brain function with pure consciousness is the restructuring, even the healing, and the integration of the psyche, but not the bypassing of the psyche. Likewise, implicating somewhat different neurological mechanisms, if under different names, but pointing in the same direction, the conclusions of Carhart-Harris et al. (2012; 3.3) also imply a disconnection between the normal cortical functioning for everyday living and the experience of pure consciousness at the height of psychedelic experience.

My supposition—neural "reentrance" or "attractors"—addresses this situation well enough, yet a further theoretical comment seems in order. The presupposition is that the standard functioning of human consciousness occurs in an integrated person: organism, psyche, and spirit. Specifically, for example, according to Aristotle, Aquinas, Lonergan, and empirical science, one has insight into data or, in Aristotle's terminology, into "phantasms," images in the mind (5.2.1). That is, the psyche, the perceptual system, provides the content on which intelligence works and out of which intellectual consciousness emerges. On a first level, consciousness functions as experience; it provides data, something to be understood. On a second level, consciousness seeks understanding and generates a concept via insight. The moment of insight exemplifies the full actuation of consciousness. It presents the nondual occurrence wherein the intelligibility in the data and the intelligibility in the intellect become one and the same in an experience of pure, trans-spatial, trans-temporal consciousness or spirit (2.3.3). Now, if the experience of insight is the full actuation of consciousness, what is the content of experience in transcendent experience? What is consciousness experiencing? The answer is that it experiences itself. Its non-reflecting presence "to" itself is the condition for the possibility of reflecting presence to anything else (5.3.1).

The same non-objectifying, non-reflexive self-presence—subjectivity—is ever operative in a person; such is the essence of human consciousness. So consciousness "of" consciousness is a possibility, and—on my understanding—it is the explanation of mystical or transcendent experience.

But transcendent experience is unusual; it is extraordinary. Chapter 3 reviewed neuroscientifically researched ways of inducing it. Moreover, sometimes it occurs spontaneously, and one must wonder whether the occurrence is healthy or pathological (Helminiak, 1984b). Certainly it is positively correlated with some pathological conditions (3.1.2). But the occurrence can also have a healing effect on the brain, movement toward healthy reintegration, the possible reconfiguration of functions as, for example, after the jolt of electroconvulsive therapy (ECT): "the psychedelic state rests on a particularly profound disturbance of brain function" (Roseman et al., 2014, p. 9). Still, transcendent moments, however achieved, can be healing. Roseman and her colleagues even envisage the use of research on psychedelic drugs to help "researchers to determine [neural] connectivity 'fingerprints' for characterizing different states of consciousness, . . . even pathological states" (p. 6) and, thus, be better able to heal those states. Hopefully, in every case the long-term result would be a more valid, a more wholesome, a richer life—in this world, not in one's mind.

Transcendent experiences would fall under that category of mysticism as an extraordinary experience. Yet it would seem that the more wholesome experience is mysticism as a way of life (1.1). It is the experience of harmoniously integrated humanity wherein the organic and psychic structures support the dynamism of consciousness and allow it to take the lead (Helminiak, 1987b). The result would be a life of openness and wonder, unbiased experience and learning, awe and gratitude, joy and compassion—"enlightenment," as I understand it. Its focus would be, not one's consciousness alone in fully contentless, open-ended wonder, but the universe of being, all that there is to be experienced, understood, known, and loved (2.1.6; 5.8.1; 5.8.3). Thus, the goal of living and of spiritual pursuit is not to achieve altered states of consciousness and live as if in a drug-induced high day after day. (At this point, we can freely make the connection between drugs and religious-based highs. See 3.3.) The emphasis on altered states represents a passé notion of spirituality that would, by drugs or abusive austerities, artificially dissociate the spiritual dimension from the rest of a person (Helminiak, 1987b, 2005b). On this score I fault the claims of Eastern philosophies that would judge the real against the moment of transcendent experience (5.8.3). I likewise fault the Western ascetic and mystical tradition that would see holiness in visions, voices, and ecstasies (Helminiak, 2006b). Neither Buddha nor Jesus stood with those other-worldly ideals.

In every case, the goal is human integration. My point here, then, is that integration includes attention to the psyche. The attempt to jump over psyche from brain to consciousness is misguided. The underlying structures that sustain consciousness—including especially neural reentrance—can be reconfigured, temporarily or even permanently to some extent, but they are not obliterated. Even the neuroscientific research on transcendent experiences supports this insistence.

Fourth, and finally, like the psychedelic, the meditative experience also passes through stages of relaxation, internal perception, and the gradual release over time of psychodynamic material, and only finally attains moments of pure presence (Helminiak, 2005b, pp. 89–106). Indeed, the basic technique of meditation is deliberately but gently to dismiss from mind any feelings, images, or thoughts and ever to return to some chosen point of attention until simple presence "to" presence, consciousness "of" consciousness, is easily experienced.

In all those cases, it is clear that psyche is indeed involved but is transcended—or, more accurately, integrated. Attention to the process discredits the notion of some single leap from brain function to transcendent experience and suggests, rather, a long and varied preliminary process. It entails the dismantling and realignment of the psyche—namely, suggestively phrased, the task of psychotherapy (5.2.2)—so that the psyche and the even lower levels of biology unobtrusively sustain transcendent experience (3.1.3; Helminiak, 1996a, Part Four; 2008b, pp. 121–137).

In the broad picture, transcendent experience—mysticism as a way of living—would then appear to be the ongoing experience of the common dynamism, the "finality" (Lonergan, 1957/1992, pp. 470–476) or "teleonomy" (Mayr, 1965; 4.14.2), that runs through the successive levels of cosmogenesis and evolution toward the integration of all things in consciousness or, what would be the same, that runs along an idealized line of intelligible unfolding, freed from the distractions of detours and dead ends. An analogy would be some line of unfolding through branching evolution that eventually leads to the human species and the emergence of consciousness. When in humans what is intelligible becomes intelligence itself (4.20.4), it can experience, explicate, and know itself and, then, more deliberately and more surely—that is, attentively, intelligently, and reasonably, and responsibly (it can only be hoped)—guide its own subsequent unfolding: to a large and sometimes frightening extent, the future of the universe lies in human hands. Accordingly, when transcendent experience is understood to be nothing other than wholistic, integrated, healthy human living, spirituality—apart from all entanglement with conflicting religions, beliefs in other-worldly entities, or appeal to divine interventions (e.g., Beauregard & O'Leary, 2007)—becomes essential to human life, culture, society, and the budding global community (Helminiak, 2008b). Such is the full, sweeping vision of Lonergan's analysis of human intentional consciousness.

On this hypothesis, the emergence of consciousness would presuppose the emergence of psyche, so any explanation of consciousness would require the prior explanation of psyche. Just as psyche emerges as a higher integration of a manifold of *per se* unsystematic cycles of recurrence of sensitive and perceptual neuronal processes, so consciousness emerges as a higher integration of the *per se* unsystematic cycles of psychic processes (pp. 110, 143–148). The guiding summary principle is that, as per Aristotle, insight is into phantasm; that is, understanding regards data, consciousness builds on internal mental experience. Now, for the most part, the data in question are the products of sensation and perception, subsumed into psyche. In perceptual data intelligence discerns intelligibility, an intelligible coherence, as consciousness shifts from its first, to its second, level of functioning. In general, if these processes could be so easily untangled, this shift is the crossover from psyche to spirit, from animal to human mind, from responsiveness to an external environment to explicit attention to inner contents of the mind. If so, the path to explanation of consciousness would seem to include a prior explanation of psyche. The practical conclusion is this: neuroscience might make better progress by focusing, not immediately on transcendent experiences, but first—or better, explicitly—on the neuronal processes that constitute the substrate of psyche. In fact, to a large extent, limited by a pervasive sensate-modeled epistemology, neuroscience is already only dealing with psyche, but confusedly because of the confounding of psyche and spirit (e.g., 3.1.4; but see Kounios & Beeman, 2009, 2014).

5.9.3. Research Approaches to Psyche

Still, the matter is complex. How would one ever research the psyche in itself? Phenomenologically, in humans the psyche is fully interactive with the human spirit, and in practice (if I could be allowed a material metaphor), the two could be said to interpenetrate. Distinction, not separation, determines the difference between psyche and spirit, even as distinction determines the difference between mind (psyche and spirit) and body. None is separate from the others—or separable—prescinding here, of course, from discussion about possible human life after death, personal continuity apart from a human body (4.2.1). The matter is daunting.

From an evolutionary perspective, Paul MacLean (1970) proposed a seductive "triune model of the brain." Its parts roughly parallel Lonergan's tripartite model of the human: organism, psyche, and spirit. The reptilian brain stem would control basic physiological functions: organism. The paleomammalian brain, comprising the limbic system, would relate to emotions, memory, imagery, and personality: psyche. And the neomammalian brain, the neocortex, developed most fully in humans, would account for the higher intellectual and volitional functions of human experience: spirit. This triune model would make neuroscientific research on psyche a rather straightforward affair—a consummation devoutly to be wished! But contemporary neuroscience is well aware that no such partitioning of brain function is sustainable, and MacLean's model is often no longer even mentioned in the historical narrative of standard neurophysiological textbooks (but see Albright & Ashbrook, 2001, pp. xxii–xxiii). We might still know relatively little about the brain, but we are sure that its many parts and systems are fully interactive. All the more so as we consider higher and higher human functions, we are hard pressed to locate any one, complete function in any single, precise place (recall the humbling lesson of 3.1.3). Evidently, the experienced "interpenetration" of psyche and spirit parallels the organic interpenetration of processing within the human brain. No easy path for the neuroscientific research of psyche emerges.

Relying on updated neuroscience, however, Merlin Donald (2001) usefully provides a current evolutionary sketch of mental functioning, and it offers some hope of specifying psyche within a comparative-psychological approach. The telling presupposition is that in the higher animals, especially mammals, we have instances of psyche's functioning apart from the further integrative complication of human consciousness. Animal psychology might provide the needed focus for specifying the psyche.

Donald's concern is the evolution of consciousness, but that purpose requires contrasts with animal minds. His summary, like MacLean's, also proposes three stages in brain development that suggest some parallel with the distinctions between organism, psyche, and spirit, but Donald's three stages all pertain to evolutionary changes in the cortex of primates in the sweep from monkeys to apes to humans (pp. 164–168). These three cortical areas are the primary, secondary, and tertiary (or association) areas for sensory processing and integration. They can be thought of as kind of a channel or as segments of a journey through cortical processing. As input and subsequent output move up from one to the other, complexity mounts and integration advances. The primary area, say, the occipital lobe for vision, receives and processes input from the retina via the thalamus and, simply put, detects various features of seen objects: lines, orientations, contours. The secondary visual cortex receives input from the primary cortex via two different pathways, dorsal and ventral, to adjacent parts of the brain in the occipital and temporal lobes. Suggestively said again, the secondary cortex combines those features and detects whole patterns or objects. A similar structure pertains to all the senses. Then, the tertiary areas receive input from a number of secondary areas and combine the inputs—they are *association* areas—to present what we would experience as whole objects and arrays of objects, enriched with visual, auditory, tactile, and other input, including pertinent emotions and memories. Recall that d'Aquili and Newberg appealed to deafferentation of the tertiary or association areas to explain transcendent experience as the result of loss of contact with an external world (3.1.1)

The important evolutionary point is that among the primates there has been no change in this basic structure of the brain; however, different areas within this basic structure have expanded in a consistent pattern.

> The relative balance of power within the cortex shifted over the course of primate brain evolution. Primary cortical areas remained unchanged in relative size. Secondary and tertiary areas became relatively larger in the brains of apes, as they evolved from a common monkey ancestor. Tertiary areas became especially large in humans. They are the largest structures in the human brain. (Donald, 2001, p. 165)

Additionally, in conjunction with the tertiary areas, parallel changes in size occurred in the cerebellum and hippocampus. These are some of the very cortical areas and brain structures, massively interconnected, that sustain the "higher" mental functions, such as awareness of different kinds of stimuli; independent, differential response to sensate input; perception of complex objects; memory for different lengths of time, complexity, and variability; delayed response or selective attention; ability to maintain a mental model of the world; updating of memory and adaptability of behavior in the face of changing situations; social intelligence to allow successful functioning within a structured and shifting group (pp. 122–130); and other different and related capacities that pertain to deliberate, or executive, control over, and use of, environmental input and that Donald calls "the executive suite" (pp. 137–146).

Donald's purpose is to plot the steps of "conscious" ability leading up to human consciousness, but in the process he provides highly useful lists of specific and researchable behavioral capacities, well correlated with neuronal function, in non-human animals. Inspired by Donald, my suggestion is that research into animal mind offers a rich approach to the study of psyche *per se*, perceptual responsiveness, once it is distinguished from mere sensate reflexivity, on the one hand, and human consciousness, on the other (5.1.2).

Other approaches to understanding psyche also come to mind. One regards the specializations that people achieve because of their particular gifts and professions. People develop different "patterns of experience" (Lonergan, 1957/1992, pp. 204–231) and achieve "differentiations of consciousness" (Lonergan, 1972, pp. 81–99, 276–281). That is, we are able to focus our conscious capacities on, say, commonsensical or theoretical or aesthetic or athletic or religious or interpersonal concerns. Research on meditators at their peak experience would seem to reveal physiological correlates predominantly of the human spirit (3.1.1–3.1.3). Perhaps, then, similar neuroscientific research on graphic artists, for example, would reveal brain function mostly related to visual imagery—and likewise, regarding musicians and auditory imagery (Sacks, 2007). Similar research with psychotherapists, who must be highly attuned to affective processes, might reveal another kind of result (Goleman, 1995). Research on memory is already well underway (cf. Baars & Gage, 2007; Carlson, 2010; Pinel, 2014). Perhaps, bit by bit we could come to understand how, not different areas of the brain, but different uses of the human brain, resultant from learned, specialized differentiations of consciousness, engage the interrelated capacities of the brain and steer them in different directions. My sense, however, is that within this mix the attempt to sort out the biological correlates of psyche from those of spirit individually will prove very difficult, perhaps futile: the human is one integrated being, for the most part functioning ever as a unity-identity-whole (4.6.3; 4.11.1).

If psyche is truly a reality of its own kind that emerges from neuronal functioning, psyche will have to be studied as a *sui generis* reality. It will have proprietary structures, mechanisms, and laws, which explain its functioning. Methodology appropriate specifically to psyche will need to be developed. Apart from attention to animal mind, so limited because it allows no feedback from the research "subjects," I struggle to suggest what this methodology might be.

One illuminative analogy is Lonergan's own study of human intentional consciousness via the method he called self-appropriation (2.1.1; 5.6.3). Similar attention to the imagery, memories, and affects of psyche might produce a delineation of the psyche. In this regard, Buddhism, with its centuries-old tradition of attention to mental process, might provide a rich resource. Its meditative attention to the arising and ceasing of phenomena in the mind appears to deal to a large extent with the structure and functioning of psyche. To be sure, the ultimate focus of Buddhist teaching could be said (in my terminology) to be consciousness or spirit, not psyche; but its analyses are heavily inclined toward psychic matters, its notion of this-worldly reality is largely determined by sensation, and its speculation is highly controlled by perceptual imagery (3.1.4; 5.8.3). To sort out in this resource the psychic from the spiritual, the matters of sensate responsiveness from those of intellectual consciousness, would be challenging, but simply having the two lenses of psyche and spirit and having a consistent epistemology to facilitate the analysis could make the enterprise rewarding. At the same time, such refinement in analysis could also bring more coherence to Buddhist teaching, eliminating the "paradox" (Helminiak, 1998, pp. 249–264; 5.8.3) and contributing to possible consensus on these subtle matters.

In a similar vein, Western dream analysis could provide another resource on psyche. To be sure, once again, insofar as they express meaning, dreams are the product also of spirit, which interpenetrates human psyche; but through and through, the medium of dreams is psychic: mental *images*, laden with *affect*, dependent on *memory*, often driven by *conations*, serve as symbols for "unconscious" psychodynamic materials. Dream images provide the paradigmatic example of how intelligence uses the psyche to creatively construe familiar patterns into provocative ones and then casts them up as data from which novel, explicated insight might emerge.

Gestalt psychology offers another clue. It has discerned the principles of figure-ground, closure, proximity, and similarity, which control perceptual experience. With an eye toward wholeness, integration, and intelligibility, these principles or perceptual laws govern the addition to sensation of perceived characteristics that depend on prior, and elicit further, insightful interpretation. These laws provide a powerful example of how the drive of consciousness toward meaning, coherence, unity, already guides and structures the function of perception in the psyche (4.14.3; 5.9.4). Similarly, perceptual psychology overall has discerned processes that are "*automatic, selective, contextual*, and *creative*" (Halonen & Santrock, 1996, p. 117). The neuroscience of vision, for example, discerns and explains mechanisms of completion, surface interpolation, contrast enhancement, temporal summation and the stability of images, color constancy, and blind sight, all of which entail real differences between what is perceived and what is physically presented (Pinel, 2014, pp. 129–159). These characteristics of perception provide possible beginnings for an account of psyche as a distinct facet of human mentality.

Finally, Carl Jung's specification of archetypes of the unconscious provides another account of structure within the psyche, namely, universal patterns of experience. Similarly, Stanislav Grof's realms of the unconscious suggest another possible universal patterning (Helminiak, 1996a, pp. 163–186). These considerations envision a whole new research paradigm regarding the mind (Henman, 2013) and brain: explicit focus on theoretically differentiated facets of the human mind. Whatever one's response to this proposal, Lonergan's theory does raise and focus far-reaching questions that could guide further research.

5.9.4. Research on the Integrative Effect of Transcendent Experiences

The possibility of integrating neuroscience and spiritualogy suggests another important research question. This question is truly proper to neuroscience: how does transcendent experience reorganize the functioning of the brain?

It is a commonplace in spiritual circles that transcendent experiences facilitate mental health and well-being overall (Greeley, 1975; Hay & Morisy, 1978). Research on the religious and therapeutic use of psychedelics offers evidence to this effect from one perspective (Grob, 1999; Grof, 1976, 1985, 1987; MacLean, Johnson, & Griffiths, 2011, with references; Griffiths et al., 2008; Richards, 2003, 2005). Similarly, research on the effect of meditation on emotions and the brain function associated with them (Lutz, Brefczynski-Lewis, Johnstone, & Davidson, 2008; Taylor et al., 2011) and on the density of gray matter over time (Hölzel et al., 2011) provides evidence from another perspective. Why or how does this positive outcome occur?

Psychologically, regular meditation and other transcendent experiences function, as does good psychotherapy, to release conflicted emotions, unearth sedimented trauma, diffuse self-defeating defense mechanisms, dissolve pettily self-serving and culturally conditioned categories, and, in general, as the bottom line, facilitate personal integration and open-ended growth. The result over time is an increasingly aware, sensitive, and responsive person who lives in habitual wonder, connectedness, gratitude, and good will: a highly "spiritual" person. Additionally, emergence theory would suggest that, via the top-down cycle of a feedback loop, the emergence of spirit and its intensification affect the underlying structures of psyche by eliciting a harmonization in sensate functions, and these, in turn, affect the neural substrate similarly and, thus, foster integration of the entire person. This process suggests a substantive meaning for the controversial "top-down causality" that bedevils consciousness studies (4.5; 4.14.3). The overall effect would be ongoing realignment of all facets of the human being—organism, psyche, and spirit—so that they more and more spontaneously and effectively move along the lines of the self-transcending dynamism of the human spirit—attentively, intelligently, reasonably, and responsibly—in its orientation toward embrace of the universe (Helminiak, 1996a, Part Four). Built on an understanding of the human spirit and its inherent transcendental precepts, the psychological proposal of this paragraph encapsulates a normative psychology of spirituality, and it entails norms for adjustments in the psyche and the in organism, the brain, as well. The neuroscientific question is this: How does such integration occur? What does it entail biologically?

This process of human integration appears to be McNamara's (2009) concern. He speaks in terms of "the divided Self" (p. 26) and the need to overcome it, and he notes that many facets of religion promote "the development of an executive Self by promoting development of character strengths" (p. 31). Although the terminology differs, the thrust of his analyses parallels mine. Moreover, McNamara has addressed that neuroscientific question head on. His theorizing suggests possible neurological bases and mechanisms of the spiritual integration I elaborate or of the "unified consciousness" or "unified sense of Self" (p. 254) he highlights.

On the other hand, McNamara's theory breaks down at a critical point. It is constrained by the superficiality of current psychological epistemology and methodology. McNamara cannot specify the virtues that would define genuinely positive human development because any enculturation, initiation, or brainwashing could conceivably qualify as McNamara's "strengthening an executive Self." McNamara struggles with this matter. He seems to cover this base by invoking God to specify the ideal Self. "The Self," he says, "can choose the true and the good by aiming at an ideal Self, ultimately God" (p. 43). However, he explicitly disavowed any metaphysical claims about God, so in "God," taken only as a symbol, he is left with an unspecified ideal. Religious history is replete with atrocities committed in the name of "God." Which God? Whose God? What religion is to reign? *God* does, indeed, function as a useful metaphor almost ubiquitously in contemporary psychology of religion (Helminiak, 2005a, 2006, 2008a, 2010,

2013a), but such appeal to God obfuscates the deepest questions facing psychology: What makes for a genuine, fully developed, integrated human being? Which values are life-giving, and why, and why does "giving life" itself matter? Alternatively and, again, in a way typical of most psychology of religion (Wulff, 2003), McNamara (2009) would solve the problematic lack of normativity in psychology by tacitly presupposing his own religious tradition in a way that most readers could comfortably accept. He recalls, "Love is the superordinate and ultimate goal of all other goals according to Aquinas" (p. 42). Yet again, he must apologize for so vague a criterion: *love*, "that much sullied but still necessary word" (p. 42). Indeed, some legitimation is needed here.

McNamara's appeal to Aquinas offers an important clue, for within the whole sweep of his thought, Aquinas could legitimate genuine love as the epitome of genuine humanity without needing to appeal to religion or God to do so. For Aquinas, genuine human love and love for God are continuous: human love is the natural component on which grace, the love of God, builds. Aquinas's analyses are grounded in attention to the self-transcending dimension of the human mind, consciousness or spirit itself—the *intellectus agens*, for example (Lonergan, 1967d). Following Aquinas, Lonergan has highlighted and refurbished that approach, and I have capitalized on it to propose a fully humanistic—that is, a non-theological—psychology of spirituality, complete with normativity, namely, Lonergan's transcendental precepts (2.6.3). Acknowledgment of self-transcending, dynamic consciousness as a self-regulating facet of humanity provides the missing prescriptive piece of the psychological puzzle of spirituality—and of human psychology overall (Helminiak, 2011, 2014). This piece explicates a principle of human integration or coherence that runs down to the level of neural function and provides a lens on that neuroscientific question: how and in what ways does genuine spirituality facilitate neuropsychological healing and reintegration? But beyond McNamara's suggestions, the question remains for neuroscience to answer.

David Hay (2006/2007) provides another very broad and laudably balanced discussion of such a thrust in research (pp. 177–180). Specifically, he offers the example of Michael C. Jackson's (Jackson & Fulford, 1997) research on the "schizotypal" personality and transcendent experiences. These experiences were discernibly useful for both normal and schizophrenic subjects' health and well-being. Long-standing research on temporal lobe epilepsy makes a similar suggestion (3.1.2). Additionally, recent research on meditation (3.1.3) and psychedelic drugs (3.3) is attempting to identify the neurological mechanisms—including the brain regions, their interconnections, and induced changes in them—of transcendent experiences apart from any reference to divine involvement.

Simply on the level of neuroscience, what realignments and shifts in functioning—changes in the brain due to learning—does transcendent experience effect? And how so? These questions are appropriate to a neuroscience focused on human mental phenomena. The results of such research are already grounding new technology for facilitating psycho-spiritual health. A new coherence of the physical and social sciences and religion could result. And gratefully welcome, such research is free from obfuscating speculation about "God in the brain."

5.10. Summary on Spiritualogy

This chapter has presented a fully psychological spiritualogy. Deploying Lonergan's epistemology, Chapter 4 suggested that the mind emerges from the brain as a reality truly distinct, but not separate, from it. Further consideration in this present chapter suggested that the mind itself is complex. It entails at least two realities: psyche and spirit, both of which are also real and distinct, but not separate, from the brain and from each other. All are properties or conjugates of one thing; all cohere to constitute a multifaceted human being. In contrast to current consciousness studies, this chapter also elaborated the very nature of the spiritual in terms of the non-reflecting presence "to" oneself that consciousness entails first and foremost, with a logical priority over any emphasis simply on intentionality. Granted, then, that a person is, in part, spiritual, in the first instance self-transcending spirituality appears to be nothing esoteric, theological, strictly religious, or supernatural, but, rather, the deliberate lived commitment to the natural enhancement of human spiritual capacity. The Buddhist tradition stands as admirable evidence to this effect. That enhancement results from attentive, intelligent, reasonable, and responsible everyday living and from specific practices designed to further human integration, including meditation, psychotherapy, and, increasingly, the clinical use of psychedelic drugs.

The differentiation of psyche and spirit within the human mind also suggested new angles on neuroscientific research on the brain. Geared to distinguishable aspects of human mental functioning, these angles—rather than older undifferentiated focus on altered states of consciousness, transcendent experience, and even "God in the brain"—are more appropriate to neuroscience as the biological science that it is.

All too easily, the differentiations and nuances highlighted here get muddled under a coverall of appeal to God and other supernatural explanations (e.g., Beauregard & O'Leary, 2007). But this book has already accounted for transcendent experience without yet broaching the question of God and human relationship with God. The implication is that, attentively, intelligently, and reasonably engaged, neuroscience and psychology have no need to indulge in such other-worldly speculation. Only a confounding of many subtle issues seems to excuse such indulgence because, from the perspective of the natural and human sciences, all the questions are already on the table and have nascent answers.

The existence of God and belief in it have nothing to do with such science, and the scientifically minded might even insist that the discussion should stop right here. Yet our topic, "God in the brain," came from scientific speculation itself (3.1.1). More important, to be honest, the exposition would not be complete until the valid contribution of theology is set off in illustrative contrast to that of neuroscience, psychology, and spiritualogy. Indeed, insofar as application of the very same epistemology and philosophy of science (2.3.5) must continue to guide the discussion, subsequent conclusions would seem to enjoy the same validity as those already proposed. Thus, the next chapter considers what God actually has to do with the brain, its functioning, and the experiences it supports.

Chapter 6

Theology and Theotics
Union of Creator and Creature

> "The world is charged with the grandeur of God.
> It will flame out, like shining from shook foil;
> It gathers to a greatness, like the ooze of oil
> Crushed. Why do men then now not reck his rod?"
> —Gerald Manley Hopkins

Finally, the question of God can receive its due. The ground has been cleared for the topic that prompted the writing of this book, yet it would now seem that discussion of God is unnecessary.

6.1. The Place of Theology in Scientific Explanation

Chapter 3 summarized putative neurological correlates and mechanisms of transcendent experience. Chapter 4 argued that those bases were insufficient to account for the experience because it is mental, not biological *per se*; and although dependent on the brain, the mind is not the brain, its functioning, or one of its properties. Mind and body are different realities, different kinds of being, distinct but not separate, and both are equally real, existing as conjugates of the polymorphous human being. Accordingly, transcendent experience must find its explanation in the distinctive capacities of the mind, not in the biological functions of the human organism.

So Chapter 5 distinguished two facets of the human mind: (a) psyche and (b) spirit, or consciousness. The characteristics of the human spirit do provide a credible basis for an explanation of transcendent experience. The open-ended dynamism of the human spirit, geared to the universe of being yet contentless in itself, is by its very nature, as conscious or spiritual, available to human experience. Indeed, the non-reflecting self-presence of consciousness is the essence of experience. Granted its peculiar nature, experience "of" consciousness or spirit would seem to account for the qualities that usually describe transcendent experience: unitive, unbounded, overwhelming, non-categorical, ineffable, gifted, and resulting in increasing personal integration, including reassured trust in the process of life, and goodwill toward all else and all others involved in this process. Ongoing commitment to spiritual practices is said to open people more and more to an abiding sense of such transcendence and, at times, to precipitate moments of total self-transcendence. When this process of increasing spiritual sensitivity is understood as identical to psychological integration, other facets of life—paradigmatically, psychotherapy—also emerge as potential spiritual "practices": intimate relationships, societal involvement, charitable works, art, science, and, in general, everyday living overall. All can provoke and foster personal integration and, perforce, spiritual growth.

Thus, I suggested that a psychology inclusive of attention to the spiritual dimension of the mind—not, of course, apart from the underpinnings of the psyche and organism—could already explain transcendent experience. Such explanation would be adequate to account for the phenomenon and would likewise exhaust the competence of the biological and human sciences. As a matter of natural science (including the human sciences), the explanation would be complete, and from this perspective implication of God would, indeed, be unnecessary.

Yet even neuroscientists and psychologists have implicated God in this discussion. Moreover, religious believers, who tend to be most invested in the topic of transcendent experience, are certainly interested in God's role in it. Thus, something does need to be said about God.

The theological contribution will not be vacuous. Indeed, it is important to recognize what the question of God legitimately adds to the exposition. Only oversight of this further input, only a watering down of talk of God to credulous piety, only a knowledge-gap of technical theology, allows the easy talk of "God in the brain" that prompted this entire discussion. Attention to God will demonstrate that, beyond the human experience of transcendence, Divinity entails other substantive issues. They cannot be reduced to the humanly spiritual, on the one hand; and on the other, their treatment is needed if the ultimate project of science itself, complete explanation, is not to be truncated.

Two questions will guide the explication of these further matters. First, what precision can be brought to the notion *God*, which gets invoked so indiscriminately in popular usage? Second, then, how could God credibly be said to be involved in transcendent experiences?

6.2. What Is God?

Talk of God in the brain usually fails to state what *God* is taken to mean (Delio, 2003). For this reason I have put quotations marks around the phrase "God in the Brain" throughout this book. The suggestion is that, although the word *God* is invoked, there is no telling what the word intends; and oftentimes its suggestive meaning is hardly what a theologically competent account would propose. I rely on the Western philosophical and theological tradition to propose some clarification (Armstrong, 1993; Cary, 1999; Hall, 2003; Helminiak, 1987b; Lonergan, 1957/1992, ch. 19; 1972, ch. 4).

6.2.1. Reasonable Hypotheses to Address Legitimate Questions

Virtually unanimous opinion holds that, ultimately, God is mystery and cannot be understood. At 6.2.3–6.2.4, I explain why. As Thomas Aquinas stated repeatedly in Part I of his *Summa Theologiae*, we can know *that* God is, but we cannot know *what* God is. We can know, we are constrained to affirm, that *Something* must be *There* (Hay, 2007), but whatever it is, we cannot understand it in itself. Attentive, intelligent, and reasonable thinking cannot avoid this conclusion.

Note a parallel with contemporary science. It affirms the existence of, say, invisible fields and particles on the basis of evidence that only makes sense in light of some such affirmation. To make sense of the evidence, scientists are constrained to draw their conclusions, the best available opinions of the day. On the basis of reasonable accounting for the evidence, only on this basis, they posit entities, and granted the entities they posit, science makes another productive step forward in coherent accounting for our universe.

Granted, too—as I have been urging from the beginning—that the real is what can be reasonably affirmed on the basis of the relevant evidence, the entities scientists posit are real. They exist, and their natures are as the accounts elaborate (cf. 2.2.4). These realities are what constitute our world and explain its functioning—as best we are able to know thus far. Like religion, science, too, affirms what cannot be seen, heard, or touched. Granted an intellectual epistemology, science and religion engage facets of the same enterprise—to understand and explain, to make sense of the world in which we find ourselves.

Every statement about God is a hypothesis, a reasonable account of what is likely to be so in light of the available evidence. In the case of God, the primary evidence is the fact of existence itself. "God" is the answer to the reasonable question as to why there is something, rather than nothing. Granted that things do exist and are there to be understood, in addition to explaining *what* (how and why) things are, which is the role of science, there also remains the equally legitimate need to explain the fact *that* things are, the fact that they exist at all. To meet this need is the role of philosophy and theology. Like the *x* that names the known unknown to be solved for in an algebraic equation, *God* is the name given to the expected answer to the question of existence. Anticipatorily and heuristically, *God* names the ultimate explanation of the existence of all things (Helminiak, 2008b, Ch. 5).

6.2.2. Accounting for Existence

However, the name *God*, the answer to the question, contains no more information than that which provoked the question in the first instance. We might name this Unknown, but we cannot solve this "equation" because we have only the barest of information on this *x*, namely, the fact of existence, and it is as much a puzzle to us as is God. The two are virtually synonymous. So supplying a name does not fill out our understanding of this Unknown in any substantive way. Nonetheless, as in all scientific explanation, from an empirical beginning point, namely, the existence of things, theologians hypothesize what God must likely be like to account for the datum, existence.

The beginning point is the realization that every existent in this world is contingent—that is, each just happens to be. Anything that exists in this world could well not be; nothing we know exists necessarily (2.3.6).

To recall the epistemology of Chapter 2 and to invoke Lonergan's terminology, we know the actuality of the world about us and affirm the "Yes" or "No" pertinent to this actuality only by a judgment of fact. A judgment is a *virtually* unconditioned (2.4.1)—something that is conditioned but whose conditions happen to be fulfilled. There is no necessity in human knowledge. Human knowledge enjoys no *absolute* necessity because everything we know just *happens to be* and to be as it is. The only necessity humans can approach is *de facto* necessity, factual necessity, the necessity inherent in what is actually so. According to the stock example, "While Socrates is standing, it is necessary that he be standing"—because in fact he is standing, so he could not but be standing . . . but only until he sits down. Factual necessity explains the status of *unconditioned* that pertains to the judgment of fact. Whatever actually exists must exist—insofar as, to the extent that, and as long as it actually does exist. To the extent that it actually exists, what actually is must be. Insofar as it does exist, its existence is unconditioned; that is, the conditions for its existence must have been, and remain, fulfilled—otherwise it would not exist. So at this point—"virtually"—its existence is without conditions; it is unconditional; it is a fact. Although we only know what happens to be, what we correctly know to be does truly exist, at least for as long as it continues to be. Human knowing and known human realities are all simply matters of fact; they do not exist by necessity. Their factuality is contingent, not absolute.

Given this realization—that the existence we know is real but is not necessary—it is only reasonable to inquire about the possibility of anything's existing at all. Why is there something rather than nothing? How can there be anything at all? If the existence we know could just as well not have been, what explains the fact of this existence? Facing this question and trusting human knowing as potentially valid, it is only reasonable to expect some plausible answer to the question about existence. A legitimate question expects a coherent answer.

One commonly accepted answer—and seemingly the only possible coherent answer—is to posit a Necessary Existent. We name it G-O-D and understand It to be the ultimate explanation of contingent existence. The buck must stop somewhere. If all this-worldly things could just as well be as not be, something that is free of such contingency must ultimately explain their existence. An infinite regress of contingent beings, each dependent on the one before but none ultimately self-explanatory, constitutes an illogical and impossible situation. One might imagine it—as in the now famous metaphor, supposedly borrowed from Hindu thought, about the support that holds up the world: it sits atop an elephant. What supports the elephant? It stands atop a turtle. Then what supports the turtle? It stands upon another turtle. Then what supports that turtle? Well, it's "turtles all the way down." Yes, imagination and sensate-modeled thinking can project an infinite regress, but one cannot coherently conceive it because it lacks intelligibility. It violates the principle of non-contradiction: what is inherently contingent cannot also be non-contingent. Nowhere in the regress, no matter how long it extends, is there an explanation of its existence because every part ever remains contingent. To suggest that, somewhere way back when, things just happened to come into existence is an intolerable affront to the rational mind. When one is seeking explanation, the response that "it just happened" is no explanation at all. Simply said, as in "Something Good" from the musical *The Sound of Music*, "Nothing comes from nothing, Nothing ever could, so. . . ." To account for the existence of what cannot explain its own existence, something else must be posited. To account for contingent being, there must be Necessary Being.

6.2.3. Derivation of Standard Attributes of God

Then the standard list of divine characteristics follows logically: eternal, omnipotent, omniscient, and all the rest. Lonergan (1957/1992, pp. 680–692) derives 26 of them. Consistent with transcendental method, this understanding of God results as a parallel to this-worldly scientific explanation, the best available opinion of the day. Although this supposed God is non-physical and invisible, science itself, in fact, also makes assertions about non-sensible and non-perceptible realities—such as quarks, leptons, mass, temperature, and infrared and ultraviolet electromagnetic waves. So, like scientific conclusions, which science never claims to prove but just proposes as the most coherent explanation thus far possible, this reasonable conclusion about God also invites, but could never coerce, acceptance.

It should be noted that even that list of characteristics tells us little about what God really is—because we do not understand the meaning of those terms. We might project, for example, what *omniscience* entails—namely, understanding everything about everything—but we really have no idea what this quality means. We have no possible experience of such knowledge, but human knowing depends on the data of experience. We cannot know that about which we have no data—zombies, for example (2.3.6). This same reservation pertains to all these other divine attributes: necessity, eternity, simplicity (no parts), perfection, immutability, omnipotence. The movie *Bruce Almighty* provided an entertaining picture of how the human and the divine minds differ. It playfully illustrated the inadequacy of popular notions of God.

At best, we predicate qualities of God only by analogy; and discussion, debate, and outright conflict about the meaning of analogy in the face of God fills the history of Western theology. This longstanding discussion even supplies technical terminology. On the negative pole, *apophatic* theology insists that we can only state what God is not, never what God actually is, and we must rest completely in unknowing. More positively, a *kataphatic* theology proposes to make valid statements about God, but even this theology imposes a three-part rule on the process: it affirms the quality (e.g., God is good); it then denies that the quality applies to God as it does to other beings; and finally, it clarifies the denial, suggesting that in God's case the quality must be expanded to an infinite degree—and, actually, we are back at unknowing.

In every case we are left to admit that we simply do not know what God is. Compared to the things we do know, God is of a whole other order of being, and even to call God "a Being" must leave us scratching our heads. We know only contingent beings, but God would be necessary being. Even while staunchly affirming the existence of God, unless we deceive ourselves, we, all of us, believers and unbelievers alike, live in mystery (Helminiak, 2005b). All ideas of God are inevitably too small. To make the point rhetorically: no one who speaks about God really knows what he or she is talking about! God ever remains the Great Unknown. With Aquinas we might be constrained by our innate rationality to affirm that God exists, but this same rationality requires us to admit that we cannot know what this Existent is.

6.2.4. Two Ways of Conceiving God: Fullness and Creator

Nonetheless, filling out our hypothesis, we do go on to speak about God. Two major and related concepts arise: God as Fullness and God as Creator.

The first emphasis appeals to divine perfection and speaks analogically. Thus, we see God as the Fullness of Beauty, Truth, Goodness, Love, Understanding, Knowledge, and so on. This extrapolation is valid. If God is to be the ultimate explanation of all things, God must somehow include all that could ever be in any and every realm of consideration. By definition, there could be nothing more perfect than God, so God can be conceived as the Fullness of all that is.

Yet even in this case, careful thinking must prevail. It would not make sense to say that God is material, the most perfect instance of physical matter, simply because physical matter does exist and God contains all perfections. God is not matter, nor is God any or all of the others things we know in our universe. To suggest as much would be to advocate pantheism, the belief that God is all things and all things together make up God—a self-contradictory suggestion that contingent being is necessary being. Even apart from the accusation of pantheism, God could not be material. We know matter. It is part of our world, and it is contingent. Therefore, it could not be an aspect of God. Yet the understanding of God as Creator can completely account for material reality. It is a contingent creation of God, dependent on God for its reality. Although in Godself God is not material, appeal to God can explain the existence of material realities. On this hurdle of rationality, the supposed embodied gods—of Greek and Roman religion and of contemporary Mormonism—trip and fall. Still, although none is God, some things in our universe, more than others, might be like God. The human being, for example, is said to be made in God's "image and likeness" (Genesis 1:26). Distinctive of humans, spiritual qualities could be projected onto God, and it makes coherent sense that they are.

Nonetheless, the three rules of analogy about God do apply, so this extrapolation runs a serious risk. It tends to portray too close an identity between God's characteristics and our own spiritual qualities. For example, we know, and God knows. If our knowing is true, what we know does not differ from God's truth. Yet we know bit by bit, piecing understanding together, correcting prior mistakes, accumulating and coalescing insights in a seemingly endless task, moving asymptotically toward an elusive goal. In contrast, God would know everything about everything in one intelligent act, in a single, infinite, comprehensive insight, identical with the divine being, wherein distinctions between experience, understanding, and judgment are meaningless. In God's knowing of everything about everything, knowing is all inclusive, absolutely coherent, infallibly self-confirming. Clearly, God's knowing and our knowing differ. However, they appear to be on a continuum. So we conceive God as the Fullness of Knowledge, and in some legitimate sense we think of our own knowledge as moving toward that Fullness.

The danger in such thinking is the persistent nemesis of this book, the perceptual model of knowing and its accompanying picture-thinking. "Fullness" can be readily imagined: a light becomes increasingly bright until it is blinding. Based on such an analogy, notions of divine fullness suggest a close similarity between the spiritual in us and the divine in itself. After all, our human spirits generate an unending flow of questions, and seeking answers to them, our understanding is open-ended, geared to the universe of being, *capax infiniti* (5.8.1). These similarities with God—unboundedness, infinity—make identification with God seem legitimate. So the human intellect is said to be the divine light within us. But is it Divinity itself within us? Is our spirit actually God within us? Or is our spirit, rather, merely something like God, sharing in some of the same characteristics—beyond space and time, geared to encompass all reality—but not actual Divinity? Is our spirit, as Genesis 1:26 phrases it, merely "made"—created!—"in the image and likeness" of God?

As the explanation of all existence, God is Creator. Now, if God is Creator and we are created, our spirits could not be divine. At best, they could be only similar to God—the "image and likeness" of Genesis 1:26. Nonetheless, similarity has regularly been turned into identity. Elsewhere I have summarized the historical accidents by which the divine and the spiritual came to be identified both in the West and in the East (Helminiak, 2006a, p. 212; 2008a, pp. 167–168; see Muesse, 2003). The identification is explicit in Eastern thought, as the Hindu maxims attest: "Atman is Brahman" (roughly, the human soul or spirit is the Absolute of the Universe), and "That art thou" (Zaehner, 1957, pp. 135–143). Likewise, since Plato, the identification regularly resurfaces in the West, as well (McGinn, 1995), for example, in Neo-Platonism, Gnosticism, New Age Religion, and numerous mystical and theosophical strains of thought. Meister Eckehart's condemnation in 1329 CE resulted from ambiguity on this very point (Colledge, 1981). Wilber (1980) boldly removes all ambiguity: "The core insight of the *psychologia perennis* is that man's 'innermost' consciousness is identical to the absolute and ultimate reality of the universe, known variously as Brahman, Tao, Dharmakaya, Allah, the Godhead" (p. 75–76). Even today an advocate for "theistic psychology" insists, "There is no evidence that [the human] spirit is human rather than godly" (Reber, 2006b, p. 199; see Helminiak, 2010, 2013a).

Presuming an image of growth toward fullness and employing picture-thinking, arguments accompany this misidentification. For example, supposedly, we are not fully divine but only somewhat so, a "spark of Divinity." Or again, our divinity is said to be real, but it is, supposedly, obscured by the grossness of our physical bodies, and anyone who has experienced deep meditation, supposedly, knows this claim to be true. The implication, however, is absurd. We have argued that, to reasonably and logically account for contingent existence, God must be infinite, eternal, simple, and perfect. In contrast, the implication here is that God could be divvied up into parts or exist in different venues in varying degrees of intensity. Or yet again, it is said that we are "expressions" of God—but with an ambiguity similar to that of epiphenomenalism (4.5; 4.7), it remains unclear whether this statement means that we are products of God (creatures) or extensions of God (Divinity). This very matter was at stake in the Christian Council of Nicaea (325 CE). It definitively clarified the identity of Jesus Christ as the Eternally Begotten of God—"God from God, light from light, true God from true God, begotten not made (or created), of one being with the Father"—by insisting on the logically inviolable distinction between the created and the Uncreated, between creature and Creator, between humanity and Divinity (see Lonergan, 1976). Such widespread mistaken thinking about God is surely behind current fuzzy talk about "God in the brain."

I say "mistaken." How can one be so sure? It is simply a matter of logic. Consider the following argument.

The second major concept of God is *Creator*. I have already been discussing it. Less imaginable than Fullness, free of the suggestiveness that characterizes images and metaphors, not obscured by picture-thinking, but expressed in propositions subject to logical consistency, the concept of Creator cannot be so easily fudged. *Creator* contrasts with *creature*. Said otherwise, there are the *Uncreated* and the *created*. They are defined in opposition to one another; the one is the negation of the other. By the principle of non-contradiction, they cannot be one and the same. Not speculation, dogma, or religious affiliation, but basic logic carries this argument.

6.2.5. The Misidentification of the Spiritual With the Divine

The thrust of this argument also pinpoints the mistake in identifying the spiritual and the divine. In many ways experience of the open-ended, trans-spatial, and trans-temporal dynamism of the human spirit might seem to be an experience of the infinity of God—the "infinity of God," as if we knew what that would be like! But on the one characteristic that determines the definitive difference between God and the human spirit, the two are unequivocally distinct. Unless the human spirit is Uncreated, it is not God. Even if the human spirit were timelessly preexistent, as some spiritual traditions imaginatively allow, it would not thereby necessarily be uncreated. If not, it is not God. The alternative notion, that the human spirit is, indeed, God but that it devolved into historical human beings, conflicts with everything reasonably affirmed about the nature of God. What is God is not dull, obscured, hidden, partial, scattered about, and somewhat divine. Such a notion can only be sustained on the basis of imagination—turtles all the way down: the picture of a "Great Chain of Being," ill-defined and fuzzily imagined "emanations," uncritical appeal to "the perennial philosophy" (Wilber, 1996). In each of these cases, some image of fullness serves to explicate Divinity. In contrast, the logic of attentively, intelligently, and reasonably conceived propositions about creation does not allow for such ambiguity.

6.3. Four Perspectives on the Possibility of Experiencing God

6.3.1. Building on the Hypothesis of God as Creator

The understanding of God as Creator has its validity. Of course, there is no suggestion that we actually understand what *Creator* means or how creation happens. Nonetheless, the term does indicate a reasonable answer to a legitimate question about the empirical existence of things and, thus, focuses and constrains our further thinking about God. From an overall perspective, this answer accords with the thrust of dynamic human consciousness because the answer is reasonable. *Creator* implies necessary being that would account for the universe of contingent being.

From a more specific perspective, this answer accords with the "leveled" structure of human intentional consciousness and its inherent propensities (2.6). Corresponding to the second level of consciousness, whose concern is to understand, the notion of Creator projects an understanding of everything about everything (2.3.1). Such comprehensive understanding is, in fact, an implicit presupposition in the endless human inclination to understand more and more. Some anticipation of that ultimate projection is built into us. Next, corresponding to the third level of consciousness, whose concern is to affirm or deny, the notion of Creator suggests an implicit human apprehension of an absolutely unconditioned. Only such an apprehension would give meaning to a notion of *unconditioned*, which specifies the meaning of the virtually unconditioned in the human judgment of fact (2.4.1). Some sense of unconditioned actuality is built into us. In sum, the notion of God as Creator can be grounded in the very dynamism and structure of human consciousness (Lonergan, 1972, pp. 101–103).

My point is that the theory of God as Creator is conceptually and methodologically robust. It provides a reliable basis—the best available opinion of the day—for addressing the second guiding question of this chapter: what is the possibility of one's actually experiencing God in transcendent experiences? This question has no one simple answer. Varying points of view introduce significant nuance. I will raise four considerations and answer the question in light of each.

6.3.2. Presence to God as Creator of All Things

A first consideration is that the possibility of experiencing God in transcendent experience is nothing unique or unusual. It is the same as the possibility of experiencing God at any other time, in any other place, and in any other experience.

The full meaning of God's being Creator has three facets, according to standard Western theology: creation, conservation, and concurrence (Thomas Aquinas, 1961 version, I, q. 104, a. 1 & 2, q. 105, a. 5). Affirmation of all three derives from coherent thinking about the contrasting natures of contingent and necessary being. That God creates means, first, that God sets things in existence. This is *creation*. But what is contingent in its initial existence continues ever to be contingent. Contingent being exists only as a matter of fact, and this fact carries no guarantee that existence should perdure. So God's creative work must also include *conservation*: God sustains things in being. Finally, because nothing new occurs or exists apart from God's creative work, because nothing *is* apart from God, every result that creatures effect must be under God's creative power. So God's creative work must also include *concurrence*: God acts to allow creatures to act and produce new, contingent effects proper to their respective natures and capacities.

This analysis suggests what it means to say that God is everywhere and in everything. Insofar as any creature exists, continues to exist, and functions, God must be present, sustaining that existence and functioning. So God is not separate from anything or anyone—hence, we speak of divine immanence. Yet, as Creator, God is inviolably distinct or different from all things, creatures all—hence, we speak of divine transcendence (1.2).

Popular misunderstanding of these terms sometimes pits divine immanence against divine transcendence. On one extreme, religion is faulted for making God too distant from us and our world. On the other extreme, panentheism holds that God is in all things or all things are in God. Neither emphasis corrects the other, and both are mistaken. The problem that bedeviled neuroscience and psychology, according to my analyses, is the same problem that bedevils theology. The problem is the application, intended or not, of a sensate-modeled epistemology and its accompanying picture-thinking—to this effect in theology: God is pictured as being distant, far away, from the world; or else God is pictured as being close to the world, either inside the world or the world, inside God. In either case, spatial distancing and perceptual picturing are at work, as if God could be here but not there, containing this or contained by that. Pictorial arguments—even in supposedly "high-end" theology: panentheism—attempt to address purely spiritual questions. Then popular religion's insistence on simplifying what is simply beyond us continues to propose science-fiction solutions and continues to allow so-called believers to avoid facing the utter mystery of life and the utter Unknown that is God.

The divine presence in question is not the physical instance of one thing's being next to another. The common, sensate metaphors of popular religion cannot accurately express this matter—as, for example, that God is the breath that breathes in all reality or that God pervades all things like salt dissolved in water. In a precisely parallel manner, popular metaphors cannot accurately express scientific understanding—for example, that electricity is like water flowing through a pipe or that mass is something like weight. Only a set of equations precisely expresses a scientific hypothesis. Similarly, only a set of logically coherent propositions can accurately express these non-spatial and non-temporal matters about the hypothesis, God: as Creator and by definition, God is wherever and whenever anything exists; and as Creator and by definition, God is of a different order and completely other than whatever else exists.

From this analysis it follows that, whether having a transcendent experience or not, every person, just as every creature, is present to God as the creating, sustaining, and enabling Creator. The extraordinariness of transcendent experiences gives no reason to suggest that they entail some extraordinary intervention of God. As I have argued throughout this book, although transcendent experiences are not routine, they are fully within the natural capacity of humans endowed with spirit. God's concurrence in these experiences is as routine as God's concurrence in any other functions that humans perform. When the conditions for any particular natural event are met—such as the appropriate neurological state of the brain and requisite harmonization of the psyche—the correlative experience occurs in accord with the natural functioning of the created universe. There is no reason to implicate any special intervention or special presence of God when a transcendent experience occurs (Helminiak, 2010, 2013a).

Of course, appealing to the omnipresence of God as Creator, one would be correct to say that God is, indeed, present in transcendent experiences. However, on this initial consideration, God is present there only in the same way that God is present everywhere and in any experience. On this understanding, the experience of God in transcendent experiences is nothing extraordinary at all. It is as routine as God's presence everywhere else.

6.3.3. Presence to God by Human Knowledge and Love

As a second consideration, humans are peculiar creatures. We are in part spiritual. As a result, we are capable of knowing and loving. Therefore, unlike other creatures, we might come to actually recognize and affirm the existence of God, to feel profound gratitude for the marvel of creation, and in an absolutely appropriate response, to engage in praising and loving God as best we know how. In this case, God would be present to us in a second way, namely, present as the known in the knower and the beloved in the lover (Helminiak, 1987b, pp. 197–199).

To gain some understanding of this matter, recall the axiom from 2.3.3: *intellectus in actu est intellectum in actu*: in the moment of actual understanding, the intellect is the understood. That is, human understanding entails an identity between the known and the knower. Insight actualizes the intelligibility of the understood even as the intelligibility of the understood "informs" the understanding to produce that particular insight. Far from involving confrontation—this against that—as in sensation, intelligence functions via identity with the understood. In this sense, knowledge entails a presence of the known to the knower.

In a similar way, love also entails such presence (Helminiak, 1987b, pp. 197–199). Simply said by way of illustration, we often hear the sentiment regarding a loved one that "you are in my heart; you are always with me." This sentiment is valid. We take into ourselves and become one with what we love. By affirming, prizing, appreciating something or someone of value, we take that value to ourselves, we affirm it, and it remains present to us. In this sense—not merely physically or emotionally, but spiritually, via acts of human consciousness on its fourth level—what we love of those we love is truly present in us by our loving and, then, in some way, they themselves are, as well.

In a similar way, we can say that God is present to us by knowledge and love. However, God as such (what God is) is not available to human experience. We have no immediate data on God. As a result, insight, knowledge, and love regarding God can only be expressed as acknowledgement of the existence of God (that God is); expressed as trusting surrender to living with the Unknown that God ever remains; as explicit prizing, valuing, praising, and thanking that Unknown, which ever sustains and eludes us; and as the longing for God that religion celebrates: "As a deer longs for flowing streams, so my soul longs for you, O God" (Psalm 42:1). Despite the unknowing in this sense of presence by knowledge and love, God is present to humans in a way that God is not present to non-spiritual creatures.

Then, again, however, this second kind of divine presence is the same whether people have transcendent experiences or not. Surely, belief in God and love of God are not restricted to those who have such experiences. Of course, it could be argued that those who do have such experiences are capable of deeper love for God. However, that "deeper love" is their own intensified experience, not an intensified presence of God. The depth of human love depends on the degree of integration within any individual person. Those who are more harmoniously whole than others are able to love more deeply. The realization of Chapter 5 emerges again: spiritual sensitivity is a function of psychological integration (5.2.3–5.2.4). Therefore, intensified spiritual experience is not a matter of some greater presence or extraordinary act on God's part.

Moreover, any deliberate attention to God's presence or deliberate attempt to love God during transcendent experience would be a distancing from the experience, a matter—during meditation, for example—of "distraction" or loss of mindfulness. If the presence "to" self of non-reflecting consciousness pertains on the first level of consciousness, any reflective observation, question, or thinking entails a distancing from the experience itself by engaging higher levels of consciousness.

Therefore, once again, there is no reason to suggest that, in comparison to ordinary religious commitment, God is more present—whatever that might mean—or operating in an extraordinary way in transcendent experiences. The extraordinariness of transcendent experience is only the extraordinariness that accrues to any natural experience that is not frequent or routine. To see a shooting star or a total solar eclipse is an extraordinary experience, but it is a fully natural one. Likewise, transcendent experience is extraordinary, but it is fully natural. Thus far, we have no reason to speak of transcendent experience as some privileged experience of God.

6.3.4. Presence to God by Spiritual Likeness

There is a third consideration. According to Genesis 1:26, humans are created in the image and likeness of God. To biblical scholars the inference is that Adam and Eve have dominion over the Earth, even as God has dominion. But with the theologians and philosophers, I take this teaching to ultimately refer to the root source of human dominion—human consciousness, the capacity to know and choose, the spiritual dimension of the human mind. Then, because God is also spirit, the human spirit must be the created reality most similar to God in all of creation. This similarity suggests another source of "closeness" to God.

Aquinas spoke of human intelligence as *quaedam participatio creata in luce increata*: some kind of created sharing in the uncreated light. The suggestion is that human spiritual functioning is a participation in the very nature—fullness, not uncreatedness—of God. On the same assumption, in his *De Trinitate* Augustine attempted to propose an analogy for the Trinity in God by seeking in the human spirit, the most subtle and godlike of all creations, some three-part process, function, or structure. Continuing this search through the centuries, Christian theologians, including Thomas Aquinas, Lonergan (1957/1992, 1967c), and the Lonerganian theologians (e.g., Crowe, 1959; Doran, 1997; for an overview, see Jacobs-Vandegeer, 2007; Helminiak, 2011), have meticulously attended to the human mind. As I hope to have suggested at 3.1.2 and 5.5.3, contemporary psychologists interested in the most subtle aspects of the mind could hardly go wrong by consulting their results.

Insofar as a transcendent experience is a pure experience of the human spirit, those who have such experiences could be said to have an experience that is the closest possible to the experience of God in this life. Believers through the centuries have certainly pursued transcendent experiences with this understanding in mind. On the correct supposition that all of creation is somehow an expression of God, even as the Psalmist proclaimed, "The heavens declare the glory of God" (19:1)—to the extent that believers enjoy such experiences, they could be said to have experienced "something of God." But this statement is generous, a bow to deserving piety. In fact, what mystics experience is first and foremost a wondrous aspect of their own being, the created human spirit. Who is to say that this experience is the same as, or similar to, the experience of God? If God is everywhere, God is ever available to our experience through every facet of creation. Are we, then, constantly experiencing God? Why do so few people recognize this experience? What, indeed, is the pure experience of God like? Who would ever know? Who could survive the occurrence? As the Lord says to Moses in Exodus 33:20, "No one shall see me and live."

Our working notion—our hypothesis—of God rests on an analogy of the human spirit, the projection of its ideal fulfillment. Thus, on less secure ground than talk of God as Creator, we say that God is the Fullness. God understands everything about everything; God is the actual epitome of intelligence toward which our questioning minds ultimately move; God is the actual epitome of love whose purity we seek in a lifelong quest; God is the explanation of all things, including the explanation of existence itself. If so, would not an experience of the human spirit indeed be at least an incipient experience of God, who is the fulfillment or fullness of the human spirit? Yes, indeed—but only if this hypothesis about God is correct! Yet like any scientific hypothesis, even the best available opinion of the day, this hypothesis about God might be wrong, and it certainly must be partial and imperfect. To claim that experiencing the human spirit is like experiencing God is to assume that we, in fact, know what God is like. We do not. We hypothesize. We merely suppose—attentively, intelligently, and reasonably, to be sure, but we merely suppose.

Therefore, again, even on the basis of this third consideration, there is no reason to affirm that in transcendent experiences a person has direct experience of God, and there is no reason to suppose that one experiences God more in transcendent experiences than in other experiences. Believers treasure transcendent experiences in their sincere desire to experience God, and in experiencing their own spiritual nature, they do experience something that is putatively like God, but we still have no reason to say that, actually and unequivocally, they have an extraordinary and immediate experience of God Godself.

6.3.5. Presence to God by Sanctifying Grace

A fourth and final consideration remains. It regards Christian belief about the indwelling of the Holy Spirit in the human heart (Romans 5:5) and the beatific vision in heaven. The *beatific vision* refers to the human possibility of seeing God "face to face" (1 Corinthians 13:12; also 2 Peter 1:4; 1 John 3:2). This possibility is a proposed instance of genuine immediate—i.e., non-mediated—experience of God; and according to Christian belief, it already begins in this life.

In question is the doctrine of sanctifying grace, strictly taken. It includes two correlative, chronologically simultaneous dimensions (Lonergan, 1971): logically prior uncreated (or operative) grace, the gift of God the Holy Spirit, Him-, Her-, or Itself; and logically subsequent created (cooperative) grace, the elevating transformation of the human spirit that makes it capable of receiving this humanly disproportionate divine gift and of responding in love for God. The term *disproportionate* expresses the precise technical meaning of the more familiar but now highly ambiguous term *supernatural* within Christian theology (Lonergan, 1972, pp. 309–310). The term regards a proposed dimension of redeemed humanity that exceeds the essentials of humanity as such: no creature ought to participate in the divine life itself, but grace transforms humanity by raising it to a new level, by effecting "a new creation" (2 Corinthians 5:17; Galatians 6:15), making this participation possible. This facet of redeemed humanity is disproportionate to human nature as such. Moreover, in contrast to the belief of some Christian denominations, with my Roman Catholic tradition and that of other mainline churches, I hold that such grace is universal, that every human being, knowingly or not, has been offered the disproportionate possibility of life in God. One need not be Christian to be "saved" (Helminiak, 1998, pp. 131–140). Thus, on the presupposition that God's sanctifying grace has been given, a person's transcendent experience is actually an experience of more than the naturally given human spirit. The experience also includes a direct experience of God, who is immediately present in the human spirit as the gift of the Holy Spirit. This experience would be an inchoate anticipation of the beatific vision in heaven, wherein the human spirit will attain its ideal fulfillment (Lonergan, 1967b), becoming like God in some respects, namely, knowing everything about everything and perfectly loving all beings. In this way, without becoming God—the created cannot become uncreated—the human spirit will share in qualities that are proper to God alone: unrestricted knowledge and unlimited love, qualities that are proportionate, but only in the ideal, to the dynamism of human consciousness, which reaches out to embrace all that is. That is, humans will attain deification, union with God, human participation in Divinity, some sharing in the very qualities of God—omniscience and infinite love—merited through the life, death, and resurrection of Christ and effected through the gift of the Holy Spirit (Helminiak, 1986b; 1987b, pp. 161–211; 1996a, pp. 123–142).

On the basis of these specifically Christian considerations, one could correctly say that one encounters God immediately in transcendent experiences. Of course, as I hope I suggested with the previous deliberately technical and perversely dense paragraph, this conclusion depends on a string of particularistic religious presuppositions and subtle theological arguments, which no neuroscientist or psychologist as such should be invoking. Accordingly, these considerations give the natural sciences no right to speak of God in the brain. On the other hand, precisely because of these considerations, in faith Christian mystics through the centuries have insisted on their direct experience of God. Likewise, for the sake of argument, presuming the objective truth and universal relevance of the Christian doctrines, Christians could say that others also encounter God immediately in their transcendent experiences. Whether the others would concur on these grounds is another question.

Still, claims of actual union with God—an academic or disciplinary concern that I have called *theotics*, in contrast to mere *theology*, from the ancient Greek Christian term for deification *theosis* (Helminiak, 1996a, 1998, 2011)—are not restricted to Christianity. However, apart from some such presuppositions as the subtle Christian doctrines summarized above, I see no way in which to warrant those claims. The Hindu belief that Atman is Brahman, for example, would verbally justify a claim of actual human union with God; but, as already indicated—if Brahman is taken to be God the Creator, as understood in Western theology, and this is a big "if"—this claimed identification of the human spirit and God is unsustainable (3.1.4; 6.2.4). It depends on an inadequate epistemology and, thus, inevitably incurs logical inconsistencies: the created is supposedly the uncreated, the historical is the eternal, the empirically verifiable is the illusory, the spiritual is the only reality, and the divine exists in separable parts and varying degrees of intensity in different people in different places at different times. Again, these criticisms come, not from religious commitment or personal belief, but from the need for logical coherence in scientific explanation.

The stark conclusion is that contemporary neuro-psycho-spiritual analyses—as in Chapters 3, 4, and 5—discredit the straightforward claim that transcendent experience is an experience of God. Through the centuries such experience has sustained the theist faith of many (Lonergan, 1973), yet critical analysis in light of current science cannot credit such a claim. It certainly does have its intuitive grounding—namely, the felt cosmic implications of the unrelenting human quest for understanding, truth, and goodness (pp. 52–54; see also Lonergan, 1972, pp. 101–103, and 6.3.1), that is, the experience of the open-ended dynamism of one's own consciousness fueling an unrequited longing. Moreover, in different subtle ways, the claim might well be correct. Nonetheless, so-called "religious experience" *per se* offers no evidence for the experience or the existence of God. As Lonergan carefully phrased the matter, such experience can open up the question of God—but then it must be answered on other grounds.

6.4. The Restricted Arena of Talk About God

This theological discussion suggests that, on the basis of a number of considerations, one could legitimately assert that in different senses transcendent experiences are the veritable experience of God. But only theological analysis sustains such assertion. In contrast, in their respective fields, neuroscientists and psychologists have no right—and, indeed, no need—to engage talk of God in the brain.

I am aware of the sensitive and even inflammatory nature of these assertions. Believers might be offended that I speak of "God" as a hypothesis (although I am engaging science here, not preaching); and non-believers might be offended that I mount a purportedly scientific argument for the existence of God. Perhaps in offending all sides, as they say, I have struck a genuine balance.

Be that as it may, I recall that these theological arguments, although plausible and reasonable, in no way command belief in God. As I hope to have suggested, an adequate epistemology and careful analysis can project a remarkable coherence of neuroscience, psychology, spiritualogy, and theology. Still, agnostics and atheists, free to reject belief in God, should find no reason in the theological discussion of this chapter to reject the conclusions of the earlier chapters of this book. Those conclusions rest on empirical evidence and standard scientific method more obviously than does this discussion of God—because we can propose a reasonable hypothesis about God, but we are unable to construct particular experiments that would confirm or disconfirm this hypothesis: God *per se* is beyond empirical testing. As "transcendent being," God does not fall within the realm of "proportionate being," namely, reality amenable to human understanding (Lonergan, 1957/1992, *q.v.*, Being, proportionate; Being, transcendent).

The hypothesis of God is peculiar: it names the necessary reasonable presupposition of any other enterprise whatsoever. Its disconfirmation would entail the affirmation of nothingness, a self-contradictory conclusion: if nothing exists (an oxymoron in itself), there is no one to make the affirmation. With David Hume, of course, one could insist that this "necessary presupposition" is not reasonable because it derives from a notion of causality within the natural order, whereas, in this case, it applies to what supposedly transcends the natural order. The response to Hume is to call for clarification of the meaning of "causality": is it perceptually conceived, push-pull, efficient causality, or is it the formal causality that expresses intelligently grasped relationships (4.6)? If the latter, then causality legitimately applies wherever there is being, and given being, argument about God is *ipso facto* implicated and legitimated. In any case, belief in God is a hypothesis of a peculiar kind.

Something similar also pertains to Lonergan's theory of consciousness: what it expresses is the presupposition of any argument. Perforce, any argument to disconfirm the theory would undermine the basis of the disconfirmation itself (2.7.2). A problem arises only if one accepts Karl Popper's (1985) negative emphasis on falsifiability as the criterion *sine qua non* of all credible knowledge claims. One could not construct a test that might falsify Lonergan's epistemology because the very construction of such a test presupposes the epistemology that the theory claims to articulate. An outright falsification would *ipso facto* discredit the falsification itself—and I recall Bertrand Russell's famous paradox: who shaves the barber in a town where the one male barber shaves everyone who does not shave himself? In these cases, mere logic breaks down (1.4; 1.7; 4.6.6). Of course, falsifiability is a useful working principle for distinguishing researchable hypotheses from fanciful speculation—but only regarding the material world. So one must wonder how much the criterion of falsifiability covertly imports a perceptual epistemology, which presumes that the real is material bodies interacting in the physical world out there. On the other hand, insistence on falsifiability is merely insistence that a reasonable hypothesis must entail some discernible difference, so falsifiability implies a positive criterion of knowing, after all. Indeed, no positive achievement can rest on sheer negativity. Bald insistence on falsifiability cannot be correct. However, the principle of falsifiability carries its own peculiarity and suggests its limitation: according to Popper, we could never be sure our scientific theory is correct even if it actually is. Irredeemably, insistence on falsifiability leads ultimately to agnosticism.

In contrast, Lonergan's positive criterion of credible knowledge is the judgment of fact, the realization that an idea or hypothesis does account for all the evidence and leaves no relevant questions outstanding (2.4.1). The judgment of fact constitutes the meaning of correct knowing and positively allows for correct knowing. Lonergan's theory even allows that, in the ideal, human judgment on the third level of consciousness could fully coincide with human understanding on the second level in an all-encompassing insight that understands everything about everything. At that point one would certainly know that one's understanding is correct. Indeed, at that point human understanding and divine knowledge would coincide; one would be sharing in a quality, omniscience, proper only to God (6.3.5). At the same time, however, without discrediting the unlimited human capacity to know, Lonergan's theory also explains why scientific hypotheses in this world do remain tentative even as ever self-correcting human knowing moves asymptotically toward comprehensive explanation (2.3.5). Lonergan's philosophy of science meets Popper's concern about the limitations of inductive method (2.3.5) and allows for correct knowing, as well.

Thus, although Lonergan's epistemology represents a peculiarly non-falsifiable theory, it is, nonetheless, credible. It is a fully self-consistent theory that accounts for the available evidence. After all, Lonergan's theory does rest on evidence, the data of consciousness (2.1.1), which can be understood and whose proposed explanation can be assessed against the evidence—just as in the case of any scientific proposal. Similarly, the scientifically peculiar affirmation of God also has its empirical base—the fact of the ever-contingent existence of things—and, again, as presented here, relies on the same methodological principles as does scientific method otherwise. Apart from the kinds of realities at stake in each case—physical, spiritual, divine—the seeming peculiarity of both Lonergan's epistemology and the God hypothesis turns out not to be very peculiar at all: it pertains to the one consistent intellectual theory of knowledge that applies across the board. Accordingly, this chapter's focus on God should not allow agnostics and atheists to defensively dismiss evidence for human spiritual reality, on the one hand; nor, on the other, should this theological treatment give theists and religionists license to make simplistic claims about religion, spirituality, or science. Biased excesses do occur at both extremes, and both depend on flawed thinking. Thoroughgoing commitment to the pure and unrestricted desire to know, to untrammeled authenticity, is ever challenging on every front.

Of all the chapters of this book, the present theological chapter is the least important from the perspective of biological and human science. This is a major point of the book. Indeed, on my understanding—apart from miracles, strictly taken, which I allow in theory but minimize to near negation in practice—whether God is in the presuppositional picture or not makes no difference for scientific explanation (Helminiak, 2010, 2011, 2013a). Hamer's scientific agnosticism regarding God, cited at 3.2, rightly insists on this point even as does Laplace's notorious response to Napoleon Bonaparte about God's role in planetary motion: "I have no need of that hypothesis." Concern about God, whether positive or negative, should play no part whatsoever in neuroscience, psychology, or even—as I have futilely argued for decades (see Engels, 2001; Helminiak, 2008c)—purely psychological spiritualogy. On the basis I have presented, talk of "God in the brain" is inane. Nonetheless, for those willing to pursue the further question and marvel at the very existence of the brain or of anything else, the inanity of neuroscientific talk of God does not invalidate a theological analysis and its conclusions.

Chapter 7

Conclusion

> We shall not cease from exploration
> And the end of all our exploring
> Will be to arrive where we started
> And know the place for the first time.
>
> —T. S. Eliot

> What we call a beginning is often the end.
> And to make an end is to make a beginning.
> The end is where we start from.
>
> —T. S. Eliot

7.1. A Brief Summary of the Argument

I have addressed the current debate over the capacity of the human brain to experience God. Crucial to this discussion is the resolution of the mind-body problem and the clarification of the nature of human consciousness. Indispensable for this achievement is an epistemology adequate to non-physical, as well as physical, reality. I believe that Bernard Lonergan has developed such an epistemology. Employing it, I considered in turn neuroscience, psychology, spiritualogy, and theology, and I suggested how each of these specializations makes its proper contribution and how these contributions coalesce in a coherent and comprehensive explanation of human mentality and its capacity for transcendent experiences.

- Neuroscience explains the biological structures and functions that at some level correlate with transcendent experiences.

- Psychology, in contrast to neuroscience, addresses the mind as a distinct reality and subject matter, governed by its own laws and capable of distinctive acts: self-aware imagery, emotions, memories, insight, choice.

- Spiritualogy distinguishes within the human mind a spiritual dimension—human consciousness—and a psychic dimension and explains transcendent experiences as the experience of the spiritual dimension. With repetition, such experience results ever more easily because of the ongoing accommodation of the personality structure of a person to the open-ended dynamism of the human spirit and, as well, because of the concomitant restructuring of the neurological base of the psyche and, then, of the human spirit.

- Finally, theology explains how God, conceived as Creator, accounts for, sustains, and facilitates the very existence and the ongoing functioning of the created human being: body, psyche, and spirit, including his or her capacity for transcendent experiences. But, while ontologically involved by definition in these and all created phenomena, the Creator-God provides no distinct object of direct experience. Only theist faith discerns an experience of God, placing the naturalistic explanation within a broader horizon of meaning.

In another exposition of the interrelationship of academic disciplines, I proposed a schema of four expanding, explanatory viewpoints on the human phenomenon: positivist, philosophic, theist, and theotic (Helminiak, 1984a, 1986a, 1987a, 1987b, 1996b, 1998, 2011). Never mentioned explicitly in this book, this system of higher viewpoints controls the presentation here and offers another illustrative perspective on the argument of this book.

7.2. The Contributions of the Various Disciplines

7.2.1. Neuroscience

Undoubtedly, neuroscience will eventually explain the organic underpinnings of transcendent experience. This endeavor is ongoing. Granted its validity, the availability of relevant research methods, and its restricted legitimacy, it is the least problematic aspect of discussion of "God" in the brain, the least shaped or distorted by differing philosophical commitments. Only the attempted leap from neuronal function directly to transcendent experience, ignoring the emergence of psyche as a mediating reality, seriously questions the current effort of neuroscientists to explain transcendent experience.

7.2.2. Psychology

The critical turning point requiring the longest chapter in this book regards the resolution of the mind–body problem. It is the stumbling block in studies of the brain, consciousness, and spirituality. Most argument about this problem deals with computer modeling of the brain and mind and attempts to explain mind as a version of, or synonym for, the computational capacities of a computer. Gödel's theorem conclusively discredits this enterprise. I argued that epistemology is all-telling in this matter, and I deployed Lonergan's intellectual—not sensate or perceptually modeled—epistemology. It determines realities on the basis of disparate intelligibilities, and their actuality on the basis of reasonable, that is, evidence-based, judgments; it specifies the real as what can be reasonably affirmed, not solely palpably experienced. Insisting that the mind's intelligibility—what there is to be understood about the mind on the basis of inner personal experience, the data of consciousness—is different from that of the brain, I mounted a consistent argument that the mind is a reality—that is, a particular kind of being—in itself. The mind emerges as a higher systematization of the sensate and perceptual functions of the organism and, as such, is different in kind from those functions and from the brain and its organic functioning. Perforce, the mind is distinct from the brain but emphatically not spatiotemporally separate from it.

Acceptance of the genuine existence of non-physical reality, I believe, presents the greatest challenge to contemporary thinking regarding resolution of the mind-body problem—because insistence on the reality of the mind endorses a dualism (indeed, a pluralism) of distinct realities in the natural world and calls up the ghost of Descartes's crassly articulated dualism of separate substances. Probably even more threateningly, insistence on the actuality of the mind is also often taken to support religious belief in ongoing life after death and even the existence of God—other-worldly commitments that seem unscientific and are sometimes distasteful and even destructive amidst the desperate uncertainty of the burgeoning, postmodern global society of the 3rd millennium. This challenge of the existence of non-physical reality is entangled with confounded epistemologies that uncritically mix sensate and intellectual ways of knowing.

Curiously, incoherently, irrationally, this epistemological confusion credits contemporary scientific accounts of completely imperceptible realities, on the one hand, while rejecting the possibility of non-physical realities, on the other. I argued that, if attentive, intelligent, and reasonable coherence were to prevail, assertions of the non-physical and even spiritual nature of the human mind could be accepted as easily—and with as much amazement—as are the assertions of contemporary physical science. Granted a coherent epistemology, these disparate assertions appear to be of one and the same vintage—the human need to understand.

Thus, with commonly accepted examples from the current scientific understanding of cosmogenesis and evolution, I appealed to emergence, an application of complexity and systems theory, specified by Lonergan's notion of emergent probability, to account for the relationship of the mind to the brain. As for the Cartesian problem: Lonergan's distinction between a thing and its conjugates (or properties), all determined by insight, not palpability or imaginability, secures the unity of the human being as one unity-identity-whole despite the multiplicity of the "facets" or different kinds of being in this polymorphous entity.

7.2.3. Spiritualogy

Acceptance of the actuality of mind as non-physical and distinct, but not separate, from the brain opens an easy approach to treating spirituality as a fully psychological phenomenon—humanistic, naturalistic, non-religious, non-theological, and non-other-worldly. The human mind is not monolithic but encompasses different kinds of realities, different conjugates. Following Lonergan, I specified two: psyche and spirit. *Psyche* encompasses imagery, emotions, conations, and memory, which cohere to form personality structures, patterns of interaction by which people engage the world and one another in their own ways. *Spirit* is but another word for intentional consciousness, and the term *spiritual*—despite its ambiguity by unnecessarily but oftentimes implicating God and other-worldly suppositions—offers our best commonplace descriptor for consciousness. It is the self-transcending dimension of the human mind geared to knowing and loving all that is.

Lonergan's analysis is the basis of my entire presentation. His account of the epistemology of intellectual knowing is one with his explanatory account of human consciousness in its three—and including human decision or choice, four—levels and two modes. The human spirit, or consciousness, grounds the naturalistic explanation of transcendent experiences.

Granted the spiritual nature of human consciousness, transcendent experiences are a person's increasing or even total non-reflecting experience "of" her or his own open-ended, self-transcending, dynamic, human spiritual capacity. Such experience would exhibit the characteristics typically attributed to religious or mystical experiences: "other-worldly," wondrous, ineffable, unitive, gifted. Accordingly, spiritualogy is first and foremost a psychological, not a theological, specialization. In no way does spiritualogy implicate God in the first instance although, like every other science, indeed, more so, its comprehensive treatment opens onto, and even begs for, theological elaboration.

7.2.4. Theology

Only a theological analysis allows legitimate talk of the supposed human experience of God in transcendent experiences. Moreover, dependent on specific religious beliefs, even this talk, if it is to be coherent, requires extensive nuance in the face of the Unknown that is the Creator-God. The understanding of God as Creator disqualifies the identity of the created human spirit with uncreated Divinity and allows the sciences to legitimately explain spiritual phenomena, as well as all others, on completely natural bases. Simultaneously, by affirming God, theology contributes to a comprehensive science by accounting for the initial, continued, and functional existence of these phenomena.

7.3. Summary About the Brain, Consciousness, and God

Neurological research shows that the structure and function of the human brain allows for transcendent experiences; but that these are *ipso facto* experiences of God is a credulous, rash, unwarranted, naïve, and misleading assertion, a veritable leap of pious blind faith. Psychologically speaking, the human mind includes two dimensions: psyche, the perceptual mentality found in various degrees also in other higher species, and a spiritual dimension, distinctively human consciousness. Understood as a reality *sui generis* and, thus, implicating, not just a dualism, but a pluralism of natural realities, consciousness is what explains transcendent experiences most fundamentally. But as a created reality, human spirit, or consciousness, could not be God in the brain. The theological relevance of neuropsychological findings should be left to theologians. It is not the place of neuroscientists or psychologists to talk about God, whether in the brain or anywhere else. Of course, in no way does this limitation of neuroscience and psychology disallow or discredit careful theological statements about God. Nor may theology impose itself on these other sciences. With its one, consistent intellectual epistemology, transcendental method operates in, and should govern, all human thinking; so conclusions about God may enjoy the same validity as the conclusions of physical, biological, and social science; and in individual autonomy and mutual interdependence, they should all cohere.

The challenge in this argument is substantial on many fronts. It outright counters many of the philosophical and methodological presuppositions that currently control the fields of neuroscience, psychology, consciousness, and even psychology of religion and spirtualogy. As in the famous case of the young David Hume's confronting Euclidean geometry, consistently attentive, intelligent, and reasonable thinking often forces upon us positions we might prefer not to have to take. Our own minds constrain us to affirm, "Yes, it is so," when, checked through collaboration with others, the pertinent available evidence confirms an explanation and leaves no further relevant questions. We are reminded that on every front, in every honest personal, academic, or scientific pursuit, we engage a wondrous, fascinating, multifaceted, and mysterious universe, still well beyond our ken. In a compounding spiral, it again and again calls forth the awe that drives intellectual pursuit from the first instance.

REFERENCES

Aaen-Stockdale, C. (2012). Neuroscience and the soul. *The Psychologist, 25*(7), 502–523.

Aanstoos, C. M. (1983). *A phenomenological study of thinking as it is exemplified during chess playing.* Ann Arbor, MI: University Microfilms International, 1984. (Doctoral dissertation, Duquesne University, 1982)

Adler, M. (1985). The intellect and the senses. In *Ten Philosophical Mistakes* (pp. 26–49). New York, NY: Touchstone Books/Simon & Schuster.

Albright, C. R., & Ashbrook, J. B. (2001). *Where God lives in the human brain.* Naperville, IL: Sourcebooks, Inc.

Alper, M. (2006). *The "God" part of the brain: A scientific investigation of human spirituality and God.* Naperville, IL: Sourcebooks, Inc. (Original work published 2001).

American Counseling Association (1995). *ACA code of ethics and standards of practice.* Alexandria, VA: Author.

American Psychological Association (1992). Ethical principles of psychologists and code of conduct. *American Psychologist, 47,* 1597–1611.

Anonymous. (1970, April 20). A great Christian mind. *Newsweek,* p. 75.

Armstrong, K. (2000). *The battle for God.* New York, NY: Knopf.

Armstrong, K. (1993). *A history of God: The 4000-year quest of Judaism, Christianity, and Islam.* New York, NY: Ballantine.

Ashbrook, J. B. (1984). Neurotheology: The working brain and the work of theology. *Zygon, 19,* 331–350.

Assagioli, R. (1976). *Psychosynthesis: A manual of principles and techniques.* New York, NY: Penguin Books. (Original work published 1965)

Baars, B. J., & Gage, N. M. (2007). *Cognition, brain, and consciousness: Introduction to cognitive neuroscience.* Boston, MA: Academic Press.

Barbour, I. G. (1974). *Myths, models, and paradigms: A comparative study in science and religion.* New York, NY: Harper & Row Publishers.

Bartz, Jeremy D. (2009). Theistic Existential Psychotherapy. *Psychology of Religion and Spirituality, 1,* 69–80.

Beauregard, M., & O'Leary, D. (2007). *The spiritual brain: A neuroscientist's case for the existence of the soul.* New York, NY: HarperOne.

Bekoff, M. (2002). *Minding animals: Awareness, emotions, and heart.* Oxford, UK: Oxford University Press.

Bekoff, M. (2007). *The emotional lives of animals: A leading scientist explores animal joy, sorrow, and empathy—and why they matter.* Novato, CA: New World Library.

Bekoff, M., Allen, C., & Burghardt, G. M. (Eds.). (2002). *The cognitive animal: Empirical and theoretical perspectives on animal cognition.* Cambridge, MA: The MIT Press.

Belzen, J. A., & Geels, A. (Eds.). (2003). *Mysticism: A variety of psychological perspectives.* New York, NY: Rodopi.

Bateson, G. (1972). *Steps to an ecology of mind.* San Francisco, CA: Chandler.

Begley, S. (2001, May 7). Your brain on religion: Mystic visions or brain circuits at work. *Newsweek.*

Berger, P. L., & Luckmann, T. (1967). *The social construction of reality: A treatise in the sociology of knowledge.* New York, NY: Doubleday & Co.

Bertalanffy, L. v. (1968). *General system theory: Foundations, development, application.* New York, NY: George Braziller.

Bertalanffy, L. v. (1981). *A systems view of man.* Boulder, CO: Westview Press.

Bickhard, M. H. (2012). A process ontology for persons and their development. *New Ideas in Psychology, 30,* 107–119.

Blackmore, S. (2012). *Consciousness: An introduction* (2nd ed.). Oxford/New York: Oxford University Press.

Blitz, D. (1992). *Emergent evolution: Qualitative novelty and the levels of reality.* Dordrecht, NL: Kluwer Academic Publishers.

Bloom, P. (Speaker) (2006). *Bodies and souls: The psychology of mind-body dualism* (The Teaching Company Research CD, Disk 1, # 553). Chantilly, VA: The Teaching Company.

Braman, B. J. (2008). *Meaning and authenticity: Bernard Lonergan and Charles Taylor on the drama of authentic human existence.* Toronto, CA: University of Toronto Press.

Brentano, F. (1973). *Psychology from an empirical standpoint* (O. Kraus, Ed.; A. C. Rancurello, D. B. Terrell, and L. L. McAlister, Trans.) London, UK: Routledge and Kegan Paul; New York, NY: Humanities Press. (Original work published 1874)

Brewer, J. A., & Garrison, K. A. (2014). The posterior cingulate cortex as a plausible mechanistic target of meditation: Findings from neuroimaging. *Annals of the New York Academy of Sciences, 1307,* 19–27.

Brewer, J. A., Worhunsky, P. D., Gray, J. R., Yi-Yuan, T., Weber, J., & Kober, H. (2011). Meditation experience is associated with differences in default mode network activity and connectivity. *Proceedings of the National Academy of Sciences of the United States of America, 108*(50), 20254–20259.

Broad, C. D. (1925). *The mind and its place in nature*. London, UK: Routledge & Kegan Paul.
Broadway, B. (2004, November 13). Is the capacity for spirituality determined by brain chemistry? *The Washington Post*, p. B9.
Brown, W. S. (2002). Nonreductive physicalism and soul: Finding resonance between theology and neuroscience. *American Behavioral Scientist, 45*, 1812–1821.
Buchler, J. (1991). *Metaphysics of natural complexes*. Albany, NY: State University of New York Press.
Cahoone, L. (2008). Reduction, emergence, and ordinal physicalism. *Transactions of the Charles S. Peirce Society: A Quarterly Journal in American Philosophy, 44*(1), 40–62.
Cahoone, L. (2009). Local naturalism. *Contemporary Pragmatism, 6*, 1–23.
Cahoone, L. (2010). *The modern intellectual tradition: From Descartes to Derrida* [CD Recordings and Course Guidebook]. Chantilly, VA: The Teaching Company.
Callaway, J. C. (1999). Phytochemistry and neuropharmacology of ayahuasca. In R. Metzner (Ed), *Ayahuasca: Human consciousness and the spirits of nature* (pp. 250–275). New York, NY: Thunder's Mouth Press.
Carew, T. J., Hawkins, R. D., & Kandel, E. R. (1983). Differential classical conditioning of a defensive withdrawal reflex in Aplysia californica. *Science, 219*, pp. 397–400.
Carhart-Harris, R. (2013). Psychedelic drugs, magical thinking and psychosis. *Journal of Neurological and Neurosurgical Psychiatry, 84*(e1). Retrieved at http://jnnp.bmj.com/content/84/9/e1.9
Carhart-Harris, R., Erritzoe, D., Williams, T., Stone, J. M., Reed, L. J., Colasanti, A., Tyacke, R. J., Leech, R., Malizia,, A. L., Murphy, K., Hobden, P., Evans, J., Feilding, A., Wise, R. G., & Nutt, D. J. (2012). Neural correlates of the psychedelic state as determined by fMRI studies with psilocybin. *Proceedings of the National Academy of Sciences, 109*(6), 2138–2143.
Carlson, N. R. (2010). *Physiology of behavior* (10th ed.). Boston, MA: Allyn & Bacon.
Carmody, D. L., & Carmody, J. T. (1996). *Mysticism: Holiness East and West*. New York, NY: Oxford University Press.
Carpenter, J. C. (2012). *First sight: ESP and parapsychology in everyday life*. Lanham, MD: Rowman & Littlefield Publishers, Inc.
Cary, P. (Speaker). (1999). *Philosophy and religion in the West* [Cassette Recordings]. Chantilly, VA: The Teaching Company.
Chalmers, D. J. (1996). *The conscious mind: In search of a fundamental theory*. New York/Oxford: Oxford University Press.
Chalmers, D. J. (1997a). Facing up to the problem of consciousness. In J. Shear (Ed.), *Explaining consciousness—the "hard problem"* (pp. 9–30). Cambridge, MA: The MIT Press. (Original work published 1995)
Chalmers, D. J. (1997b). Moving forward on the problem of consciousness. In J. Shear (Ed.), *Explaining consciousness—the "hard problem"* (pp. 379–422). Cambridge, MA: The MIT Press.

Chalmers, D. J. (2006). Strong and weak emergence. In P. Clayton & P. Davies (Eds.), *Re-emergence of emergence: The emergentist hypothesis from science to religion* (pp. 244–254). New York/Oxford: Oxford University Press.

Churchland, P. (1996). The hornswoggle problem. *Journal of Consciousness Studies, 3*, 400–408.

Clayton, P., & Davies, P. (Eds.). (2006) *The re-emergence of emergence: The emergentist hypothesis from science to religion*. Oxford/New York: Oxford University Press.

Cohn, W. (1962). Is religion universal? Problems of definition. *Journal for the Scientific Study of Religion, 2*, 25–35.

Colledge, E. (1981). Historical data. In E. Colledge & B. McGinn (Eds. & Trans.), *Meister Eckhart: The essential sermons, commentaries, treatises, and defense* (pp. 5–23). Mahwah, NJ: Paulist Press.

Colman, A. M. (2006). *A Dictionary of Psychology* (2nd ed.). Oxford: Oxford University Press.

Corning, P. A. (2002). The re-emergence of "emergence": A venerable concept in search of a theory. *Complexity, 7*, 18–30.

Corsini, R. J. (Ed.). (1984). *Encyclopedia of Psychology*. New York, NY: John Wiley & Sons.

Corsini, R. J. (1999). *The Dictionary of Psychology*. Philadelphia, PA: Brunner/Mazel, Taylor & Francis.

Craighead, W. E., & Nemeroff, C. B. (Eds.). (2004). *The Concise Corsini Encyclopedia of Psychology and Behavioral Science*. Hoboken, NJ: John Wiley & Sons.

Crowe, F. E. (1959). Complacency and concern in the thought of St. Thomas. *Theological Studies, 20*, 1–39, 198–230, 343–95.

Crutcher, K. (2003). Is there a God spot in the brain? *Advances in neuroscience: Social, moral philosophical, theological implications* (pp. 1–20): Proceedings of the ITEST workshop, September, 2002. St. Louis: ITEST Faith/Science Press.

Culligan, K. G. (Ed.). (1983). *Spiritual direction: Contemporary readings*. Locust Valley, NY: Living Flame Press.

d'Aquili, E. G., & Newberg, A. B. (1999). *The mystical mind: Probing the biology of religious experience*. Minneapolis, MN: Fortress Press.

Davidson, D. (2001). *Mental events, Essays on action and events* (2nd ed.) (pp. 207–224). New York, NY: Oxford University Press. (Original work published 1970)

Delio, I. (2003). Brain science and the biology of belief: A theological response. *Zygon, 38*, 573–585.

Dennett, D. C. (1991). *Consciousness explained*. Boston, MA: Little, Brown, & Co.

Doblin, R. (1991). Panke's "Good Friday Experiment": A long-term follow-up and methodological critique, *The Journal of Transpersonal Psychology, 23*, 1–28.

Donald, M. (2001). *A mind so rare: The evolution of human consciousness*. New York / London: W. W. Norton & Company.

Donceel, J. (1974). Transcendental Thomism. *The Monist, 58*, 67–85.

Doran, R. M. (1981). *Psychic conversion and theological foundations: Toward a reorientation of the human sciences*. Chico, CA: Scholars Press.

Doran, R. M. (1996). Response to Helminiak's "A scientific spirituality: The interface of psychology and theology." *The International Journal for the Psychology of Religion, 6,* 21–25.

Doran, R. M. (1997). "Complacency and concern" and a basic thesis on grace," *Lonergan Workshop, 13,* 57–78.

Drinan, R. (2006, April 31). A victory for religious freedom: Court decision introduces the writings of Chief Justice Roberts. *National Catholic Reporter,* p. 16.

Eckel, M. D. (speaker). (2001). Lecture thirteen: Buddhist philosophy. *Buddhism* (audio recoding). Chantilly, VA: The Teaching Company.

Eddington, A. S. (1928). *The nature of the physical world.* New York, NY: Macmillan.

Elkins, D. N. (1998). *Beyond religion: A personal program for building a spiritual life outside the walls of traditional religion.* Wheaton, IL: Theosophical Publishing House.

Ellens, J. H. (2009). *The spirituality of sex.* Westport, CT: Praeger.

Engels, D. W. (Ed.). (2001). Spirituality in counseling [Special issue]. *Counseling and Values, 45*(3).

Evans, J. R., & Abarbanel, A. (1999). *Introduction to quantitative EEF and neurofeedback.* San Diego, CA: Academic Press.

Fingelkurts, Andrew A., & Fingelkurts, Alexander A. (2009). Is our brain hardwired to produce God, or is our brain hardwired to perceive God? A systematic review of the role of the brain in mediating religious experience. *Cognitive Processing, 10,* 293–326.

Forte, R. (1997a). A conversation with R. Gordon Wasson. In R. Forte (Ed.), *Entheogens and the future of religion* (pp. 67–94). San Francisco, CA: Council on Spiritual Practices.

Forte, R. (1997b). *Entheogens and the future of religion.* San Francisco, CA: Council on Spiritual Practices.

Gallup, G. G. (1977). Self-recognition in primates: A comparative approach to the bidirectional properties of consciousness. *American Psychologist, 32,* 329–338.

Gallup, G. G. (1979). Self-awareness in primates. *American Scientist, 67,* 417–421.

Gallup, G. G. (1985). Do minds exist in species other than our own? *Neuroscience and Biobehavioral Review, 9,* 631–641.

Garrison, K. A., Santoyo, J. F., Davis, J. H., Thornhill, T. A. IV, Kerr, C. E., & Brewer, J. A. (2013). Effortless awareness: Using real time neurofeedback to investigate correlates of posterior cingulate cortex activity in meditators' self-report. *Frontiers in Human Neuroscience, 7* (article 440), 1–9. doi:10.3389/fnhum.2013.0040

Garrison, K. A., Scheinost, D., Worhunsky, P. D., Elwafi, H. M., Thornhill IV, T. A., Thompson, E., Saron, C., Desbordes, G., Kober, H., Hampson, M., Gray, J. R., Constable, R. T., Papademetris, X., & Brewer, J. A. (2013). Real-time fMRI links subjective experience with brain activity during focused attention. *NeuroImage, 81,* 110–118.

Gleick, J. (1988). *Chaos: Making a new science.* New York, NY: Penguin Books.

Goldman, S. L. (Speaker). (2007). Fields—The immaterial becomes real (Lecture 23). *Great scientific ideas that changed the world* [CD Recordings and Course Guidebook]. Chantilly, VA: The Teaching Company.

Goleman, D. (1995). *Emotional intelligence*. New York, NY: Bantam Books.

Goodenough, J., McGuire, B., & Jakob, E. (2010). Perspectives on animal behavior (3rd ed.). Hoboken, NJ: John Wiley & Sons.

Gorsuch, R. L. (2002). The pyramid of sciences and of humanities: Implications for the search for religious "truth." *American Behavioral Scientist, 45*, 1822–1838.

Granfield, D. (1991). *Heightened consciousness: The mystical difference*. New York/Mahwah, NJ: Paulist Press.

Greeley, A. (1975) *The sociology of the paranormal: A reconnaissance*. Beverly Hills, CA: Sage Publications.

Green, C. (1968). *Out-of-the-body experiences*. London, UK: Hamish Hamilton.

Griffin, D. R. (1991). What is consciousness and why is it so problematic? In K. R. Kao (Ed.), *Cultivating consciousness: Enhancing human potential, wellness, and healing* (pp. 51–70). Westport, CT: Praeger.

Griffin, D. R. (2001). *Animal minds: Beyond cognition to consciousness*. Chicago, IL: The University of Chicago Press.

Griffiths, R.R., Richards, W.A., Johnson, M.W., McCann, U. D., & Jesse, R. (2008). Mystical-type experiences occasioned by psilocybin mediate the attribution of personal meaning and spiritual significance 14 months later. *Journal of Psychopharmacology, 22*(6), 621–632.

Griffiths, R. R., Richards, W. A., McCann, U., & Jesse, R. (2006). Psilocybin can occasion mystical-type experiences having substantial and sustained personal meaning and spiritual significance. *Psychopharmacology, 187*, 268–283.

Grim, P. (2008). *Philosophy of mind: Brains, consciousness, and thinking machines* [CD Recordings and Course Guidebook]. Chantilly, VA: The Teaching Company.

Grob, C. S. (1999). The psychology of ayahuasca. In R. Forte (Ed.), *Entheogens and the future of religion* (pp. 214–249). San Francisco, CA: Council on Spiritual Practices.

Grof, S. (1976). *Realms of the human unconscious: Observations from LSD research*. New York, NY: E. P. Dutton.

Grof, S. (1985). *Beyond the brain: Birth, death, and transcendence in psychotherapy*. Albany, NY: State University of New York Press.

Grof, S. (1987). *The adventure of self-discovery: Dimensions of consciousness and new perspectives in psychotherapy and inner exploration*. Albany, NY: State University of New York Press.

Guignon, C. (2012). Becoming a person: Hermeneutic phenomenology's contribution. *New Ideas in Psychology, 30*, 97–106.

Hagerty, B. B. (2009). *Fingerprints of God: The search for the science of spirituality*. New York, NY: Riverhead Books.

Hall, J. H. (Speaker). (2003). *Philosophy of religion* [Cassette Recordings]. Chantilly, VA: The Teaching Company.

Halonen, J. S., & Santrock, J. W. (1996). *Psychology: Contexts of behavior* (2nd ed.). Madison, WI: Brown & Benchmark, Publishers.

Hamer, D. H. (2004). *The God gene: How faith is hardwired into our genes*. New York, NY: Doubleday.

Hameroff, S. (2007). The brain is both neurocomputer and quantum computer. *Cognitive Science, 31*, 1035–1045.

Hameroff, S. (2014, April). *Quantum vibrations in microtubules OrchOR—Twenty years on.* Paper presented at the international conference Toward a Science of Consciousness 2014, Tucson, AZ.

Hanna, F. J. (2000). Dissolving the center: Streamlining the mind and dismantling the self. In T. Hart, P. L. Nelson, & K. Puhakka (Eds.), *Transpersonal knowing: Exploring the horizon of consciousness* (pp. 113–146). Albany, NY: State University of New York Press.

Harrison, P. (2010). "Science" and "religion": Constructing the boundaries. In T. Dixon, G. Cantor, & St. Pumfrey (Eds.), *Science and religion: New historical perspectives* (pp. 23–49). Cambridge, MA: Cambridge University Press.

Hart, T., Nelson, P. L., & Puhakka, K. (Eds.). (2000). *Transpersonal knowing: Exploring the horizon of consciousness*. Albany, NY: State University of New York Press. (Original work published 1997 as *Spiritual knowing: Alternative epistemic perspectives*. State University of West Georgia Studies in the Social Sciences. Carrollton, GA: State University of West Georgia)

Hay, D. (2007). *Something there: The biology of the human spirit*. Philadelphia, PA: Templeton Foundation Press. (Original work published 2006)

Hay, D., & Morisy, A. (1978). Reports of ecstatic, paranormal or religious experience in Great Britain and the United States: A comparison of trends, *Journal for the Scientific Study of Religion, 17*, 255–268.

Hazen, R. M. (Speaker). (2003). *Origins of life* [Cassette Recordings]. Chantilly, VA: The Teaching Company.

Heidegger, M. (1962). *Being and time* (J. Macquarrie & E. S. Robinson, Trans.). New York, NY: Harper. (Original work published 1927)

Heffern, R. (2001, April 20). Exploring the biology of religious experience. *National Catholic Reporter*.

Helminiak, D. A. (1979). *One in Christ: An exercise in systematic theology*. Unpublished doctoral dissertation, Joint Doctoral Program, Andover Newton Theological School and Boston College.

Helminiak, D. A. (1984a). Consciousness as a subject matter. *Journal for the Theory of Social Behavior, 14*, 211–230.

Helminiak, D. A. (1984b). Neurology, psychology, and extraordinary religious experiences. *Journal of Religion and Health, 23*, 33–46. Accessible at http://www.visionsofdaniel.net/paperExtraRelExp1984.htm

Helminiak, D. A. (1986a). Four viewpoints on the human: A conceptual schema for interdisciplinary studies, I, *The Heythrop Journal, 28*, 420–437.

Helminiak, D. A. (1986b). *The same Jesus: A contemporary Christology*. Chicago, IL: Loyola University Press.

Helminiak, D. A. (1987a) Four viewpoints on the human: A conceptual schema for interdisciplinary studies, II, *The Heythrop Journal*, 29, 1–15.

Helminiak, D. A. (1987b). *Spiritual development: An interdisciplinary study*. Chicago, IL: Loyola University Press.

Helminiak, D. A. (1996a). *The human core of spirituality: Mind as psyche and spirit*. Albany, NY: State University of New York Press.

Helminiak, D. A. (1996b). A scientific spirituality: The interface of psychology and theology, *The International Journal for the Psychology of Religion*, 6, 1–19.

Helminiak, D. A. (1998). *Religion and the human sciences: An approach via spirituality*. Albany, NY: State University of New York Press.

Helminiak, D. A. (2001a). Rejoinder and clarifications on Helminiak's (2001) "Treating spiritual issues in secular psychotherapy." *Counseling and Values*, 45, 237–251.

Helminiak, D. A. (2001b). Treating spiritual issues in secular psychotherapy. *Counseling and Values*, 45, 163–189.

Helminiak, D. A. (2005a). A down-to-earth approach to the psychology of spirituality a century after James's Varieties. *The Humanistic Psychologist*, 33, 69–86.

Helminiak, D. A. (2005b). *Meditation without myth: What I wish they'd taught me in church about prayer, meditation, and the quest for peace*. New York, NY: Crossroad.

Helminiak, D. A. (2006a). The role of spirituality in formulating a theory of the psychology of religion. *Zygon*, 41, 197–224.

Helminiak, D. A. (2006b). Sex as a spiritual experience. *Reflections* (Yale Divinity School), 92(1), 4–11.

Helminiak, D. A. (2008a). Confounding the divine and the spiritual: Challenges to a psychology of spirituality. *Pastoral Psychology*, 57, 161–182

Helminiak, D. A. (2008b). *Spirituality for our global community: Beyond traditional religion to a world at peace*. Lanham, MD: Rowan & Littlefield Publishers, Inc.

Helminiak, D. A. (2008c). Whither the psychology of religion: A spirituality-focused discussion of Paloutzian and Park's (2005) *Handbook of the Psychology of Religion and Spirituality*. *Journal of Religion and Health*, 47, 525–540.

Helminiak, D. A. (2010). "Theistic psychology and psychotherapy": A theological and scientific critique. *Zygon*, 45, 47–75.

Helminiak, D. A. (2011). Spirituality as an explanatory and normative science: Applying Lonergan's analysis of intentional consciousness to relate psychology and theology. *The Heythrop Journal*, 52(4), 596–627.

Helminiak, D. A. (2013a). Religion versus science—the current dilemma: A reply to the "Reply to the Critics" of the "theistic psychologists." *Christian Psychology: A Transdisciplinary Journal*, 7(1), 40–57.

Helminiak, D. A. (2013b). *The transcended Christian: What do you do when you outgrow your religion?* (2nd ed.). Atlanta, GA: Author (via CreateSpace at amazon.com). (Original work published 2007)

Helminiak, D. A. (2014). *More than awareness: Bernard Lonergan's multi-faceted account of consciousness*. *Journal of Theoretical and Philosophical Psychology*, 34, 116–132

Helminiak, D. A., Hoffman, L., & Dodson, E. (2012). A critique of the "theistic psychology" movement as exemplified in Bartz's (2009) "Theistic existential psychotherapy." *The Humanist Psychologist, 40*, 179–196.

Henman, R. (2013). Can brain scanning and imaging techniques contribute to a theory of thinking? *Dialogues in Philosophy, Mental and Neuro Sciences, 6*(2), 49–56.

Henriques, G. R. (2003). The tree of knowledge system and the theoretical unification of psychology. *Review of General Psychology, 7*, 150–182.

Henriques, G. R. (2004). Psychology defined. *Journal of Clinical Psychology, 60*, 1207–1221.

Hilbert, D. (1971). *The foundations of geometry* (L. Unger, Trans.). LaSalle, IL: Open Court. (Original work published 1902)

Hill, P. C., Pargament, K. I., Hood, R. W., McCullough, M. E., Swyers, J. P., Larson, D. B., & Zinnbauer, B. J. (2000). Conceptualizing religion and spirituality: Point of commonality, point of departure. *Journal for the Theory of Social Behavior, 30*, 51–77.

Hofmann, A. (2000). The message of the Eleusinian Mysteries for today's world. In R. Forte (Ed.), *Entheogens and the future of religion* (pp. 31–39). San Francisco, CA: Council on Spiritual Practices.

Holland, J. H. (1998). *Emergence: From chaos to order*. New York, NY: Perseus Books

Holmes, B. (2001, April 21). In search of God. *New Scientist*.

Hong, G. (1995). Buddhism and religious experience. In R. W. Hood, Jr. (Ed.), *Handbook of religious experience* (pp. 87–121). Birmingham, AL: Religious Education Press.

Hood, R. W. (2003). Conceptual and empirical consequence of the unity thesis. In J. A. Belzen & A. Geels (Eds.), *Mysticism: A variety of psychological perspectives* (pp. 17–54). New York, NY: Rodopi.

Hood, R. W., Jr., Spilka, B., Hunsberger, B., & Gorsuch, R. (1996). *The psychology of religion: An empirical approach* (2nd ed.). New York, NY: The Guilford Press.

Hölzel, B. K., Lazar, W. S., Gard, t., Schuman-Olivier, Z., Vago, D. R., & Ott, U. (2011). How does mindfulness meditation work? Proposing mechanisms of action from a conceptual and neural perspective. *Perspectives on Psychological Science, 6*(6), 537–559. doi: 10.1177/1745691611419671

Hölzel, B. K., Carmody, C, J., Vangela, M., Congletona, C., Yerramsettia, S. M., Gardab, T., & Lazara, S. W. (2011). Mindfulness practice leads to increases in regional brain gray matter density. *Psychiatry Research: Neuroimaginng, 191*, 36–43.

Jackson, F. (1982). Epiphenomenal qualia. *Philosophical Quarterly, 32*, 127–136.

Jackson, M. C., & Fulford, K. W. M. (1997). Spiritual experience and psychopathology. *Philosophy, Psychiatry and Psychology, 4*, 41–90.

Jacobs-Vandegeer, C. (2007). Sanctifying grace in a "methodical theology," *Theological Studies, 68*, pp. 52–76.

James, W. (1950). *The principles of psychology* (vols. I–II). Mineola, NY: Dover Publications, Inc. (Original work published 1890).

James, W. (1961). *The varieties of religious experience: A study in human nature*. New York, NY: Macmillan Publishing Company. (Original work published 1902)

Jennings, H. S. (1906). *Behavior of the lower organisms*. New York, NY: Columbia University Press.

Jones, S. L. (1994). A constructive relationship for religion with the science and profession of psychology: Perhaps the boldest model yet. *American Psychologist, 49*, 184–199.

Joos, E. (2006). The emergence of classicality from quantum theory. In P. Clayton & P. Davies (Eds.), *Re-emergence of emergence: The emergentist hypothesis from science to religion* (pp. 53–78). New York/Oxford: Oxford University Press.

Joseph, R. (Ed.). (2003). *NeuroTheology: Brain, science, spirituality, religious experience*. San Jose, CA: University Press.

Kalapahana, D. J. (1992). *A history of Buddhist philosophy: Continuities and discontinuities*. Honolulu, HI: University of Hawaii Press.

Kaypayil, J. (2003). *Human as relational: A study in critical ontology*. Rome, Italy: Jeevalaya Institute of Philosophy.

Kaufman, M. (2005, January 3). Meditation gives brain a charge, study finds. *The Washington Post*, p. A5.

Kazdin, A. E. (Ed.). (2000). *Encyclopedia of Psychology*. Washington, DC: American Psychological Association / Oxford, UK: Oxford University Press.

Keirsey, D., & Bates, M. (1978). Please understand me: Character and temperament types. Del Mar, CA: Prometheus Nemesis Book Co.

Kelleman, R. W. (2004). *Spiritual friends: A methodology of soul care and spiritual direction*. Taneytown MD: RPM Books.

Kirk, K., Martin, N., & Eaves, L. (1999). Self-transcendence as a measure of spirituality in a sample of older Australian twins. *Twin Research, 2*, 81–87.

Kluger, J. (2004, October 25). Is God in our genes? A provocative study asks whether religion is a product of evolution. *Time*, 62–72.

Koch, S. (1971). Reflections on the state of psychology. *Social Research, 38*, 669–709.

Koch, S. (1981). The nature and limits of psychological knowledge: Lessons of a century qua 'science.'" *American Psychologist, 36*, 257–269.

Kosslyn, S. M., & Pomerantz, J. R. (1977). Imagery, propositions, and the form of internal representations. *Cognitive Psychology, 9*, 52–76.

Kounios, J., & Beeman, M. (2009). The *Aha!* moment: The cognitive neuroscience of insight. *Psychological Science, 18*(4), 210–216.

Kounios, J., & Beeman, M. (2014). The cognitive neuroscience of insight. *Annual Review of Psychology, 61*, 71–93.

Kuhn, T. S. (1970). The structure of scientific revolutions (2nd ed.). Chicago, IL: The University of Chicago Press. (Original work published 1962)

Lambert, P., & McShane, P. (2010). *Bernard Lonergan: His life and leading ideas*. www.axialpublishing.com: Axial Publishing, & Vancouver, BC, Canada: Grandview Printing Co., Ltd.

Larson, D. B., Swyers, J. P., & McCullough, M. E. (1998). *Scientific research on spirituality and health: A report based on the Scientific Progress in Spirituality Conferences*. Bethesda, MD: National Institute for Healthcare Research.

Lee, H-M., & Roth, B. L. (2012). Hallucinogen action on human brain revealed. *Proceedings of the National Academy of Sciences, 109*(6), 1820–1821.

Loevinger, J. (1976). *Ego development: Conceptions and theories.* San Francisco, CA: Jossey-Bass.

Lonergan, B. J. F. (1967a). Cognitional structure. In F. E. Crowe (Ed.), *Collection: Papers by Bernard Lonergan* (pp. 121–141). Montreal: Palm.

Lonergan, B. J. F. (1967b). The natural desire to see God. In F. E. Crowe (Ed.), *Collection: Papers by Bernard Lonergan* (pp. 84–95). Montreal: Palm.

Lonergan, B. J. F. (1967c). Theology and understanding. In F. E. Crowe (Ed.), *Collection: Papers by Bernard Lonergan* (pp. 221–239). Montreal: Palm.

Lonergan, B. J. F. (1967d). *Verbum: Word and idea in Aquinas* (D. B. Burrell, Ed.). Notre Dame, IN: Notre Dame University Press.

Lonergan, B. J. F. (1971). *Grace and freedom: Operative grace in the thought of St. Thomas Aquinas* (J. P. Burns, Ed.). New York, NY: Herder and Herder.

Lonergan, B. J. F. (1972). *Method in theology.* New York, NY: Herder and Herder.

Lonergan, B. J. F. (1973). *Philosophy of God, and theology.* Philadelphia, PA: Westminster Press.

Lonergan, B. J. F. (1976). *The way to Nicaea: The dialectical development of trinitarian theology* (trans. Conn O'Donovan). Philadelphia, PA: The Westminster Press.

Lonergan, B. J. F. (1985). Healing and creating in history. In F. E. Crowe (Ed.), *A third collection: Papers by Bernard J. F. Lonergan, S.J.* (pp. 100–108). Mahwah, NJ: Paulist Press.

Lonergan, B. J. F. (1990). Understanding and being: The Halifax lectures on insight (E. A. Morelli & M. D. Morelli, Eds.). *Collected Works of Bernard Lonergan* (vol. 5). Toronto: University of Toronto Press. (Original work published 1980)

Lonergan, B. J. F. (1992). *Insight: A study of human understanding. Collected works of Bernard Lonergan* (vol. 3). Toronto: Toronto University Press. (Original work published 1957)

Lonergan, B. J. F. (2001). *Phenomenology and logic: The Boston College lecture on mathematical logic and existentialism. Collected works of Bernard Lonergan* (vol. 18). Toronto: Toronto University Press. (Original lectures given 1957)

Lonergan, B. J. F. (2002). The ontological and psychological constitution of Christ (F. E. Crowe, & R. M Doran, Eds., & M. G. Shields, Trans.). *Collected Works of Bernard Lonergan* (vol. 7). Toronto: The University of Toronto Press. (Original work published 1956)

Lonergan, B. J. F. (Speaker). (2006). *Transcendental philosophy and the study of religion,* CD recording #481. Toronto: Lonergan Research Center. (Original lecture July 3, 1968)

Lonergan, B. J. F. (2009). *The Triune God: Systematics* (R. Doran & D. Monsour, Eds., & M. G. Shields, Trans.). Toronto: University of Toronto Press. (Original work published 1964)

Lutz, A., Brefczynski-Lewis, J., Johnstone, T., & Davidson, RJ. (2008, March 26). Regulation of the neural circuitry of emotion by compassion meditation: Effects of meditative expertise. *PLoS One, 3*(3), e1897.

MacLean, K. A., Johnson, M. W., & Griffiths, R. R. (2011). Mystical experiences occasioned by the hallucinogen psilocybin lead to increases in the personality domain of openness. *Journal of Psychopharmacology, 25*(11), 1453–1461.

MacLean, P. D. (1970). The triune brain, emotion, and scientific bias. In F. O. Schmitt (Ed.), *The neurosciences: Second study* (pp. 336–349). New York, NY: The Rockefeller University Press.

Margolis, J. (2010). *Pragmatism's advantage: American and European philosophy at the end of the twentieth century*. Stanford, CA: Stanford University Press.

Marquis, A., Holden, J. M., & Warren, E. S. (2001). An integral psychology response to Helminiak's (2001) "Treating spiritual issues in secular psychotherapy." *Counseling and Values, 45*, 219–236.

Martin, J. (2012). Coordinating with others: Outlining a pragmatic, perspectival psychology of personhood. *New Ideas in Psychology, 30*, 131–143.

Maslow, A. H. (1970). *Motivation and personality* (2nd ed.). New York, NY: Harper & Row. (Original publication 1954)

Maslow, A. H. (1970). *Religions, values, and peak-experiences*. New York, NY: Penguin Books. (Original publication 1964)

Maslow, A. H. (1999). *Toward a psychology of being* (3rd ed.). New York, NY: John Wiley & Sons, Inc. (Original work published 1968)

Matsumoto, D. (Ed.) (2009). *The Cambridge Dictionary of Psychology*. New York, NY: Cambridge University Press.

Mayr, E. (1965). Cause and effect in biology. In D. Lerner (Ed.), *Cause and effect* (pp. 33–50). New York, NY: Free Press.

McCarthy, M. (1997). Pluralism, invariance, and conflict. *The Review of Metaphysics, 51*, 3–23.

McCarthy, M. H. (1990). *The crisis of philosophy*. Albany, NY: State University of New York Press.

McGinn, B. (1995). *The presence of God: A history of mysticism: Vol. 1, Foundations of mysticism*. New York, NY: Crossroad.

McKenna, D. J. (1999). Ayahuasca: An ethnopharmacologic history. In R. Metzner (Ed.), *Ayahuasca: Human consciousness and the spirits of nature* (pp. 187–213). New York, NY: Thunder's Mouth Press.

McNamara, P. (2009). *The neuroscience of religious experience*. New York, NY: Cambridge University Press.

McShane, P. (1975). *Wealth of self and wealth of nations: Self-axis of the great ascent*. New York, NY: Exposition Press. Retrieved also at http://www.philipmcshane.ca/wealth.pdf

McShane, P. (2013a). *The everlasting joy of being human: A sequel to* Futurology Express. Vancouver, BC: Axial Publishing.

McShane, P. (2013b). Futurology express. Vancouver, BC: Axial Publishing.

Menzel, R. & Fischer, J. (Eds.). (2011). *Animal thinking: Contemporary issues in comparative cognition*. Cambridge, MA: The MIT Press.

Metzner, R. (Ed). (1999). *Ayahuasca: Human consciousness and the spirits of nature*. New York, NY: Thunder's Mouth Press.

Monroe, R. (1971). *Journeys out of the body*. New York, NY: Doubleday.

Muesse, M. W. (Speaker). (2003). Lecture 8: The way of wisdom [Cassette Recording]. *Great world religions: Hinduism*. Chantilly, VA: The Teaching Company.

Muesse, M. W. (Speaker). (2007). *Religions of the axial age: An approach to the world's religions* [CD Recording]. Chantilly, VA: The Teaching Company.

Murphy, N. C. (2006). *Bodies and souls, or spirited bodies?* New York, NY: Cambridge University Press.

Muthukumaraswamy, S. D., Carhard-Harris, R. L., Moran, R. J., Brookes, M. J., Williams, T. M., Errtizoe, D., Sessa, B., Papadopoulos, A., Bolstridge, M., Singh, K. D., Feilding, A., Friston, & K. J., Nutt, D. J. (2013). Broad band cortical desynchronization underlies the human psychedelic state. *The Journal of Neuroscience, 33*(38), 15171–15183,

Nadel, L. (Ed.). (2003). *Encyclopedia of Cognitive Science*. London/New York: Nature Pub. Group.

Nagel, T. (1974). What is it like to be a bat? *Philosophical Review*, 83, 435–450.

Natsoulas, T. (1978). Consciousness. *American Psychologist, 34*, 906–914.

Natsoulas, T. (1979). The unity of consciousness. *Behaviorism, 7*, 45–63.

Natsoulas, T. (1983). A selective review of conceptions of consciousness with special reference to behavioristic contributions. *Cognition and Brain Theory, 6*, 417–447.

Natsoulas, T. (1986). Consciousness: Consideration of a self-intimational hypothesis. *Journal for the Theory of Social behavior, 16*, 197–207.

Newberg, A. B., d'Aquili, E. G., & Rause, V. (2001). *Why God won't go away: Brain science and the biology of belief*. New York, NY: Ballantine.

Newberg, A. B., & Waldman, M. R. (2010). *How God Changes Your Brain: Breakthrough Findings from a Leading Neuroscientist*. New York, NY: Ballantine.

Nowicki, S. (Speaker) (2004). *Biology: The science of life* [Cassette Recordings]. Chantilly, VA: The Teaching Company.

Oliver H. H. (1981). *A relational metaphysic (Studies in philosophy and religion)*. Leiden, NL: Martinus Nijhoff.

Otto, S. L. (2012, November). America's Science Problem. *Scientific American*. Retrieved at http://www.scientificamerican.com/article/antiscience-beliefs-jeopardize-us-democracy

Pahnke, W. N. (1966). Drugs and mysticism. *International Journal of Parapsychology, 8*, 295–313.

Paloutzian, R. F. & Park, C. L. (Eds.) (2005). *Handbook of the psychology of religion and spirituality*. New York, NY: The Guilford Press

Park, C. L. (2005). Religion and meaning. In R. F. Paloutzian & C. L Park (Eds.), *Handbook of the psychology of religion and spirituality* (pp. 295–314), New York, NY: The Guilford Press.

Pargament, K. I. (1997). *The psychology of religion and coping: Theory, research, practice*. New York, NY: Guilford Press.

Pargament, K. I., & Maloney, A. (2002). Spirituality: Discovering and conserving the sacred. In C. R. Snyder & S. J. Lopez (Eds.), *Handbook of positive psychology* (pp. 646–659). New York, NY: Oxford University Press.

Pellerin, C. (1998). *Trips: How hallucinogens work in your brain*. New York, NY: Seven Stories Press.

Penrose, R. (1994a). Mechanisms, microtubules, and the mind. *Journal of Consciousness Studies, 1*, 241–249.

Penrose, R. (1994b). *Shadows of the mind: A search for the missing science of consciousness*. Oxford, UK: Oxford University Press.

Penrose, R., & Hameroff, S. (2011). Consciousness in the universe: Neuroscience, quantum space-time geometry and Orch OR Theory. *Journal of Cosmology, 14*. Retrieved at http://journalofcosmology.com/Consciousness160.html

Percy, W. (1990). The fateful rift: The San Andreas fault in the modern mind. *Arts Education Policy Review, 91*(3), 2–7, 51–53. (Original work published 1989)

Persinger, M. A. (1999). Near-death experiences and ecstasy: A product of the organization of the human brain? In S. Della Sala (Ed.), *Mind Myths: Exploring Popular Assumptions about the Mind and Brain* (pp. 85–99). New York, NY: John Wiley & Sons.

Persinger, M. A. (2001). The neuropsychiatry of paranormal experiences. *The Journal of Neuropsychiatry and Clinical Neurosciences, 13*, 515–524.

Persinger, M. A. (2002). Experimental facilitation of the sensed presence: Possible intercalation between the hemispheres induced by complex magnetic fields. *The Journal of Nervous and Mental Disease, 190*, 533–541.

Persinger, M. A. (2003). The sensed presence within experimental settings: Implications for the male and female concept of self. *The Journal of Psychology, 137*, 5–16.

Persinger, M. A. (n.d.). The God Helmet. Retrieved at http://www.youtube.com/watch?v=y02UlkYjSi0

Peters, R. S., & Mace, C. A. (1967). Psychology. In P. Edwards (Ed.), *The Encyclopedia of Philosophy: Vol. 7* (pp. 1–27). New York, NY: Macmillan.

Piaget, J. (1963). *The origins of intelligence in children*. New York, NY: Norton Library. (Original work published 1936).

Pinel, J. P. J. (2011). *Biopsychology* (8th ed.). Boston, MA: Pearson Education, Inc.

Pinel, J. P. J. (2014). *Biopsychology* (9th ed.). Boston, MA: Pearson Education, Inc.

Pittendrigh, C. A. (1958). Adaptation, natural selection, and behavior. In A. Roe & G. G. Simpson (Eds.), *Behavior and Evolution* (pp. 390–416). New Haven, CT: Yale University Press.

Polkinghorne, J. (Ed.). (2010) *The Trinity and an entangled world: Relationality in physical science and theology*. Grand Rapids, MI: Wm. B. Eerdmans.

Pope, A. (2006). *From child to elder: Personal transformation in becoming an orphan at midlife*. New York, NY: Peter Lang.

Popper, K. R. (1985). *Popper selections* (D. Miller, Ed.). Princeton, NJ: Princeton University Press.

Poston, T. (2014). Foundationalism. *Internet Encyclopedia of Philosophy*. Retrieved at http://www.iep.utm.edu/found-ep/=H4.

Premack, D. (1986). *Gavagai! or the future history of the animal language controversy*. Cambridge, MA: MIT Press.

Prigogine, I., & Stengers, I. (1984). *Order out of chaos: Man's new dialogue with nature.* New York, NY: Bantam Books.

Principe, W. (1983). Toward defining spirituality. *Sciences Religieuses / Studies in Religion, 12,* 127–141.

Principe, L. (2006). *Science and religion* [course guidebook and cassette recordings]. Chantilly, VA: The Teaching Company.

Proudfoot, W. (1985). *Religious Experience.* Berkeley, CA: University of California Press.

Pylyshyn, Z. W. (1973). What the mind's eye tells the mind's brain: A critique of mental imagery. *Psychological Review, 88,* 16–45.

Raichle, M. E., MacLeod, A. M., Snyder, A. Z., Powers, W. J., Gusnard, D. A., Shulman, G. L. (2001). A default mode of brain function. *Proceedings of the National Academy of Sciences of the United States of America, 98,* 676–682.

Rayburn, C. A., & Richard, L. J. (2002). Theobiology: Interfacing theology and science. *American Behavioral Scientist, 45,* 1793–1811.

Reber, J. S. (Speaker). (2002, August 23). Spiritual experience as relationship. In *Varieties of Religious Experience—An Update for the 21st Century,* chair J. S. Reber. Symposium conducted at the 109th annual meeting of the American Psychological Association in Chicago, IL.

Reber, J. S. (2006a). Response to Cooper and Browning's Commentary. *Journal of Psychology and Theology, 34,* 272–275.

Reber, J. S. (2006b). Secular psychology: What's the problem? *Journal of Psychology and Theology, 34,* 193–204.

Redgrove, P. (1987). *The black goddess and the unseen real.* New York, NY: Grove Press.

Ricardo, A., & Szostak, J. W. (2009, September). Origin of life on earth. *Scientific American, 301*(3), 54–61.

Richards, P. S., & Bergin, A. E. (2005). *A spiritual strategy for counseling and psychotherapy* (2nd ed.). Washington, DC: American Psychological Association.

Richards, W. A. (2003). Entheogens in the study of mystical and archetypal experiences. *Research in the Social Scientific Study of Religion, 13,* 143–155.

Richards, W. A. (2005). Entheogens in the study of religious experiences: Current status. *Journal of Religion and Health, 44,* 377–389.

Richardson, F. C. (2006). Psychology and religion: Hermeneutic reflections. *Journal of Psychology and Theology, 34,* 232–245.

Riedlinger, T. J. (1997). Sacred mushroom Pentecost. In R. Forte (Ed.), *Entheogens and the future of religion* (pp. 97–117). San Francisco, CA: Council on Spiritual Practices.

Robb, M. (2004, April 26). Imaging God? *Radiology Today, 5*(9), p. 17.

Robinson, D. N. (2012). Personhood: What's in a name? *New Ideas in Psychology, 30,* 89–96.

Roll, W. G. (2004). *The poltergeist.* New York, NY: Paraview. (Original work published 1972).

Roseman, L., Leech, R., Feilding, A., Nutt, D. J., & Carhart-Harris, R. L. (2014). The effects of psilocybin and MDMA on between-network resting state functional connectivity in healthy volunteers. *Frontiers in Human Neuroscience, 8*, article 204. doi: 10.3389/fnhum.2014.00204.

Rosenau, P. M. (1992). *Post-modernism and the social sciences: Insights, inroads, and intrusions.* Princeton, NJ: Princeton University Press.

Roy, L. (2003). *Mystical consciousness: Western perspectives and dialogue with Japanese thinkers.* Albany, NY: State University of New York Press.

Sacks, O. (2007). *Musicophilia: Tales of music and the brain.* New York, NY: Knopf.

Saylor, F. (2004, July 1). Searching for God amid the ganglia. *Science & Theology News.*

Schudel, M. (2006, March 1). Henry Morris; Intellectual father of "creation science." *The Washington Post,* p. B6.

Searle, J. R. (1980). Minds, brains, and programs. *Behavioral and Brain Sciences, 3,* 417–424.

Searle, J. R. (1997). *The mystery of consciousness.* New York, NY: The New York Review of Books.

Searle, J. R. (Speaker) (1998). *The philosophy of mind* [Cassette Recordings]. Springfield, VA: The Teaching Company.

Shafer, J. (1967). Mind-body problem. In P. Edwards (Ed.), *The Encyclopedia of Philosophy: Vol. 5* (pp. 336–346). New York, NY: Macmillan.

Shannon, C. E., & Weaver, W. (1998). *The mathematical theory of communication.* Urbana & Chicago, IL: University of Illinois Press. (Original work published 1948)

Shaw, R. A. (1984). Tabula rasa. In R. J.Corsini (Ed.), *Encyclopedia of psychology* (vol. 3, pp. 398–399). New York, NY: John Wiley & Sons.

Shepard, R. N. (1978). The mental image. *American Psychologist, 33,* 125–137.

Slife, B. D., & Melling, B. S. (2006). Psychological method and the activity of God: Clarifications and distinctions. *Journal of Psychology and Theology, 34,* 280–284.

Slife, B. D., & Whoolery, M. (2006). Are psychology's main theories and methods biased against its main consumers? *Journal of Psychology and Theology, 34,* 217–231.

Slife, B. D., & Richards, P. S. (2001). How separable are spirituality and theology in psychotherapy? *Counseling and Values, 45,* 190–206.

Smythe, W. E. (Ed.). (1998). *Toward a psychology of persons.* Mahwah, NJ: Lawrence Erlbaum Associates, Publishers.

Snell, B. (1960). *The discovery of the mind: The Greek origins of European thought* (T. G. Rosenmeyer, Trans.). New York, NY: Harper & Brothers.

Spilka, B., & Ladd, K. L. (2013). *The psychology of prayer: A scientific approach.* New York, NY: Guilford Press.

Stairs, J. (2000). *Listening for the soul: Pastoral care and spiritual direction.* Minneapolis, MN: Augsburg Fortress.

Stein, H. (1989, June). Yes, but . . . some skeptical remarks on realism and antirealism. *Dialectics 43*(1–2), 47–65.

Stengor, V. (2013, September 27). The rising antiscience. *The Huffington Post.* Retrieved at http://www.huffingtonpost.com/victor-stenger/rising-antiscience-faith_b_3991677.html

Sterling, E. E. (1997). Law enforcement against entheogens: Is it religious persecution? In R. Forte (Ed.), *Entheogens and the future of religion* (pp. 165–169). San Francisco, CA: Council on Spiritual Practices.

Stetsenko, A. (2012). Personhood: An activist project of historical becoming through collaborative pursuits of social transformation. *New Ideas in Psychology, 30,* 144–153.

Sternberg, R. (1986). A triangular theory of love. *Psychological Review, 92,* 119–135.

Strogatz, S. (2003). *Sync: The emerging science of spontaneous order.* New York, NY: Hyperion.

Summarizing the judgment on intelligent design. (2005, December 25). *The Washington Post,* p. B5.

Swanson, L. W. (2013). Basic plan of the nervous system. In L. R. Squire, D. Berg, F. E. Bloom, S. Du Lac, A. Ghosh, & N. C. Spitzer (Eds.), *Fundamental neuroscience* (4th ed.) (pp. 15–38). Oxford, UK: Academic Press/Elsevier.

Szalavitz, M. (2011). *"Magic mushroom" can improve psychological health long term.* Retrieved at http://healthland.time.com/2011/06/16/magic-mushrooms-can-improve-psychological-health-long-term

Tan, S.-Y. (2003). Integrating spiritual direction into psychotherapy: Ethical issues and guidelines. *Journal of Psychology and Theology, 31,* 14–23.

Tanquerey, A. (1930). *The spiritual life: A treatise on ascetical and mystical theology.* Tournai, BE: Desclee and Co.

Tarthang Tulku. (1979). A view of mind. In J. Welwood (Ed.), *The meeting of the ways: Explorations in East/West psychology* (pp. 40–44). New York, NY: Schocken.

Taylor, V. A., Daneault, V., Grant, J., Scavone, G., Breton, E., Roffe-Vidal, S., Courtemanche, J., Lavarenne, A. S., Marrelec, G., Benali, H., Beauregard, M. (2012). Impact of meditation training on the default mode network during a restful state. *Social Cognitive and Affective Neuroscience,* doi:10.1093/scan/nsr087. Retrieved at http://www.ncbi.nlm.nih.gov/pubmed/22446298

Taylor, V. A., Grant, J., Deneault, V., Scavone, G., Breton, E., Roffe-Vidal, S., Courtemanche, J., Lavarenne, A. S., & Beauregard, M. (2011). Impact of mindfulness on the neural response of emotional pictures in experienced and beginner meditators. *NeuroImage, 57,* 1524–1533.

Teske, J. A. (2006). Neuromythology: Brains and stories. *Zygon, 41,* 169–196.

Thomas Aquinas (1961). *Summa theologica.* Madrid, ES: Biblioteca de Autores Cristianos.

Thomas, A., Chess, S., & Birch, H. G. (1963). *Behavioral individuality in early childhood.* New York: New York University Press.

Tinbergen, N. (1951). *The study of instinct.* New York, NY: Oxford University Press.

Vago, D. R., & Silbersweig, D. A. (2012). Self-awareness, self-regulation, and self-transcendence (S-ART): A framework for understanding neurobiological mechanisms of mindfulness. *Frontiers in Human Neuroscience, 6,* article 296: doi: 10.3389/fnhum.2012.00296. Retrieved at http://journal.frontiersin.org/Journal/10.3389/fnhum.2012.00296/full

VandenBos, G. R. (Ed.). (2007). *APA dictionary of psychology.* Washington, DC: American Psychological Association.

Wade, C., & Tavris, C. (2008). *Psychology* (9th ed.). Upper Saddle River, NJ: Pearson Prentice Hall.

Waldrop, M. M. (1992). *Complexity: The emerging science at the edge of order and chaos.* New York, NY: Simon & Schuster.

Walsh, R. N., & F. Vaughan (Eds.). (1980). *Beyond Ego: Transpersonal dimensions in psychology.* Los Angeles, CA: Tarcher.

Watts, R. E. (2001). Addressing spiritual issues in secular counseling and psychotherapy: Response to Helminiak's (2001) views. *Counseling and Values, 45,* 207–217.

Webb, E. (1988). *Philosophers of consciousness: Polanyi, Lonergan, Voegelin, Ricoeur, Girard, Kierkegaard.* Seattle, WA: University of Washington Press.

Weiner, I. B. (Ed.). (2003). *Handbook of Psychology.* New York, NY: Wiley.

Weiten, W. (2007). *Psychology: Themes and variations* (7th ed.). Belmont, CA: Thompson Wadsworth.

Whitehead, A. N. (1978). *Process and reality: An essay in cosmology.* (D. R. Griffin & D. W. Sherburne, Eds.). New York, NY: Free Press. (Original work published 1929)

Whitehead, J. D., & Whitehead, E. E. (2009). *Holy eros: Recovering the passion of God.* Maryknoll, NY: Orbis Books.

Wilber, K. (1980). The nature of consciousness. In R. N. Walsh & F. Vaughan (Eds.), *Beyond Ego: Transpersonal dimensions in psychology* (pp. 74–86). Los Angeles, CA: Tarcher.

Wilber, K. (1996). *Eye to eye: The quest for the new paradigm* (3rd ed.). Boston, MA: Shambhala.

Willis, J. W. (2007). *Foundations of qualitative research: Interpretative and critical approaches.* Thousand Oaks, CA: Sage Publications, Inc.

Wulff, D. M. (2003). A field in crisis: Is it time for the psychology of religion to start over? In P. Roelofsma, J. Corveleyn, & J. van Saane (Eds.), *One hundred years of psychology and religion: Issues and trends in a century long quest* (pp. 155–167). Amsterdam, NL: VU University Press.

Wynne, C. D. L., & Udell, M. A. R. (2013). *Animal cognition: Evolution, behavior and cognition* (2nd ed.). New York, NY: Palgrave Macmillan.

Zaehner, R. C. (1961). *Mysticism: Sacred and profane.* London/New York: Oxford University Press. (Original work published 1957)

Zimmer, C. (2004, October). Faith-boosting genes: A search for the genetic basis of spirituality. *Scientific American, 219*(4), 110–111.

Name Index

Aaen-Stockdale, C., 1–2, 82, 90, 106
Aanstoos, C. M., 309
Abarbanel, A., 82
Adler, M. 327
Albright, C. M., 149, 333
Alexander, S., 173
Allen, C., 176, 327
Alper, M., 1, 7
Aquinas, T., 26, 50, 88, 130, 139, 164, 258, 262–264, 271, 298, 329, 339, 345, 354
Archimedes, 243
Aristotle, 26, 35, 50, 52–53, 60, 68, 70, 88, 120, 126, 130, 134, 156, 164, 174, 251, 264, 329, 332
Armstrong, K., 41, 345
Ashbrook, J. B., 1, 149, 333
Assagioli, R., 4
Augustine, 26, 258, 298

Baars, B. J., 335
Bacon, F., 24
Bartz, J. D., 69
Bates, M., 306
Bateson, G., 224
Beauregard, M., 2, 7, 85–86, 89, 129, 174, 332, 341
Beeman, M., 285, 302, 332
Begley, S., 82
Bekoff, M., 1, 176, 245, 305, 311, 327–328

Belzen, J. A., 2, 319
Bergin, A. E., 2, 29, 69, 78, 325
Berkeley, G., 19, 55
Berkeley, G., 23–24, 29
Bertalanffy, L., 174
Bickhard, M. H., 298
Birch, H. G., 306
Blackmore, S., 11, 58, 107, 187, 209, 315
Blitz, D., 174
Bloom, P., 121
Boodin, J., 173
Boyle, R., 40
Braman, B. J., 7
Brefczynski-Lewis, J., 337
Brentano, F., 272
Brewer, J. A. 91–93
Broad, C. D., 173, 193, 237
Broadway, B., 82, 100
Brodman, K., 95
Brown, W. S., 5, 111, 116, 137, 152, 175, 321
Buchler, J., 168
Buddha, 72, 98
Burghardt, G. M., 176, 327

Cahoone, L., 7, 40, 47, 48, 55, 89, 138, 158, 164, 168, 173–174, 178, 188, 212, 233, 277
Callaway, J. C., 103
Cameron, J., 151–152

389

Name Index

Carew, T. J., 246
Carhart-Harris, R., 102–104, 325, 329
Carlson, N. R., 335
Carmody, D. L., 2, 319
Carmody, J. T., 2, 319
Carpenter, J. C., 123, 129
Cary, P., 345
Chalmers, D., 20, 22–23, 31–35, 40, 43, 50, 58, 59–60, 80, 126–127, 137, 142, 152, 160, 164–166, 169, 175, 178, 185, 188, 192–197, 199–206, 210, 215, 222–235, 237, 256–257, 259, 265, 268–272, 280, 282–290, 292–300, 302, 309, 311
Chess, S., 306
Churchland, P., 11
Clayton, P., 173, 193
Cohn, W., 86
Colledge, E., 351
Colman, A. M., 298
Copernicus, N. 24
Corsini, R. J., 298
Craighead, W. F., 298
Crowe, F. E., 258
Crutcher, K., 1, 5
Culligan, K. G., 253

d'Aquili, E. G. 1, 7, 29, 65, 74, 82–86, 90–91, 177, 321, 328, 334
Dalai Lama, 97
Darwin, C., 74
Davidson, D., 201
Davidson, R. J., 337
Davies, P., 173, 193
de Saussure, F., 36
Delio, I., 5, 83, 321, 345
Dennett, D. C., 20, 23–24, 59, 125, 151–153, 192, 206–211, 213–215, 223, 227, 231–232, 259, 321
Derrida, J., 55
Descartes, R., 38, 68, 80, 98, 124, 137, 164, 247, 288, 367
Dilthey, W., 21
Doblin, R., 18, 325, 328

Dodson, E., 3, 57
Donald, M., 177, 213, 221, 223, 244, 278–280, 301, 304–305, 311, 329, 333–335
Donceel, J., 25
Doran, R. M., 66, 243, 249, 250, 258
Drinan, R., 101

Eaves, L., 99
Eckel, M. D., 323
Edding, D., 75
Eddington, A. S., 147
Einstein, A., 26, 32, 38, 78, 122, 167, 170, 184, 191, 195, 319
Eliot, T. S., 365
Elkins, D. N., 69
Ellens, J. H., 322
Emerson, R. W., 241
Engels, D. W., 2, 364
Euclid, 31, 68
Evans, J. R., 82

Fingelkurts, Alexander A., 18
Fingelkurts, Andrew A., 18
Fischer, J., 176, 327
Forte, R. 1, 101
Freud, S., 74, 109
Fulford, K. W. M., 339

Gage, N. M., 335
Galilei, G., 24, 32, 34, 39, 126, 170
Gallup, G. G., 304
Garrison, K. A., 30, 92–93
Geels, A., 2, 319
Gleick, J., 174
Godel, K., 26, 186–192, 195, 201, 210, 282, 367
Goldman, S. L., 168, 178, 212
Goleman, D., 335
Goodenough, J., 176
Gorsuch, R., 81
Gorsuch, R. L., 29, 69, 77, 81
Greeley, A., 307, 337
Green, C., 329

Name Index

Griffin, D. R., 28, 125, 126, 127, 142, 168, 176, 200, 210, 214–222, 223, 234, 235, 252, 282, 286, 327
Griffiths, R. R., 325, 328, 337
Grim, P., 208
Grob, C. S., 337
Grof, S., 328, 337
Guignon, C., 298

Hagerty, B. B., 1
Hall, J. H., 345
Halonen, J. S., 327, 328, 336
Hamer, D. H., 1, 100
Hameroff, S., 106–107, 223
Hanna, F. J., 2
Harrison, P., 24, 80
Hart, T., 29, 69, 123
Hawkins, R. D., 246
Hay, D., 152–153, 265, 307, 337, 339–340, 345
Hazen, R. M., 176
Heffern, R., 82
Hegel. G. W. F., 25–26, 41, 63, 164
Heidegger, M., 41, 308
Helminiak, D. A., 1–6, 10, 14, 30, 52, 57, 72, 79, 87, 89, 97, 111, 116, 123, 128, 131, 140, 149, 151, 177, 184, 239, 242–243, 249–250, 252–257, 272, 289, 300–301, 312, 323–326, 330–332, 337–339, 345–346, 349, 351, 355–356, 364, 366
Henman, R., 86
Henriques, G. R., 9
Herrmann, R., 78
Hilbert, D., 12, 26, 31, 131
Hill, P. C., 2, 69
Hoffman, L., 3
Hoffman, L., 57
Hofmann, A., 5, 101
Holden, J. M., 69
Holland, J. H., 174
Holmes, B., 82
Hölzel, B. K., 91, 95, 97–98, 337

Hong, G. 205
Hood, R. W., 30, 81
Hume, D., 34, 74, 114, 126–127, 133, 160, 236, 290, 299, 362
Hunsberger, B., 81
Husserl, E., 26, 41, 96
Huxley, A., 325
Huygens, C., 40

Jackson, F., 197
Jackson, M. C., 339
Jacobs-Vandegeer, C., 258
Jakob, E., 176
James, W., 47, 67, 177, 220, 226, 236, 257–266, 268, 271, 273–274, 280, 302
Jennings, H. S., 246
Jesse, R., 325, 328
Jesus, 72
Johnson, M. W., 325, 328, 337
Johnson, S., 29
Johnstone, T., 337
Jones, S. L., 69, 133
Joseph, R., 1
Jung, C., 337

Kalapahana, D. J., 97, 323
Kandel, E. R., 246
Kant, I., 26, 39–42, 56, 65, 72, 74, 113, 124, 164, 169, 281, 316
Kaufman, M., 82
Kaypayil, J., 132, 168
Kazdin, A. E., 298
Keirsey, D., 306
Kelleman, R. W., 253
Keller, H., 36
Kirk, K., 99
Kluger, J., 82, 100
Koch, S., 67
Kosslyn, S. M., 251
Kounios, J., 285, 302, 332
Kuhn, T. S., 325

Ladd, K. L., 86

Lambert, P., 262
Laplace, P-S., 179, 191, 201, 364
Larson, D. B., 2, 69
Lavoisier, A., 40
Lazarus, R., 327
Lee, H-M., 102
Leibniz, G., 176
Levi-Strauss, C., 36
Linnaeus, C., 40
Locke, 27, 39, 114, 170, 236
Loevinger, J., 88
Lonergan, B. J. F., 22, 25, 28, 36, 38, 41, 42, et passim; challenge of, 54, 69, 79–80, 115, 120, 153, 171, 237–238, 309, 367, 370; theologian, 80; and causality, 129–130, 132–134; and consciousness, bimodal, 254–257, and levels of, 27, 254–255; and emergence, 179–181, 183–186; and empirical method, 57–61; and epistemology, sensate and intellectual, 8, 37–38; and foundationalism, 7; and the human, tripartite model of, 243; and implicit definition, 131–132; and method, 8–10; and judgment, 62–63; and logic and intelligence, 12; and Kantian problem, 42–44; and Lonerganians, 10; and metaphysics, 26–27, 194; and mind-body problem, 171; and objectivity, 43–44; and philosophy of science, 57; and postmodernism, 44, 54–55; and reflexive consistency, 64–66; and scholasticism, decadent, 262; and self-appropriation, 7, 18–20, 69; and spirit, 3; and terminological contribution of, 197, 199, 346–347; and transcendental precepts, 71–73
Lutz, A., 337

Mace, C. A., 3
MacLean, K. A., 325, 328, 337
MacLean, P. D., 333

Madonna (entertainer), 306
Maloney, A., 2, 69
Margolis, J., 48
Marquis, A., 69
Martin, J., 298
Martin, N., 99
Maslow, A, 4, 253
Matsumoto, D., 298
Maxwell, J., 194
Mayr, E., 173, 331
McCann, U. D., 325, 328
McCarthy M. H., 7, 11, 40, 64, 66, 89
McCullough, M. E., 2, 69
McGinn, B., 351
McGuire, B., 176
McKenna, D. J., 103
McNamara, P., 7, 86–91, 93, 102, 128, 252, 338–339
McShane, P., 262
McShane, P., 5, 10
Melling, B. S., 69
Menzel, R., 176, 327
Metzner, R., 101
Mills, J. S., 236
Monroe, R., 329
Morgan, C. L., 173
Morisy, A., 337
Muesse, M. W., 4, 101, 351
Murphy, N. C., 7, 137, 139, 152
Muthukumaraswamy, S. D., 82, 102, 104

Nadel, L., 298
Nagel, T., 203, 198–200, 229, 283, 300, 302, 308, 310
Natsoulas, T., 52–53, 259, 271–281
Nelson, P. L., 29, 69, 123
Nemeroff, C. B., 298
Newberg, A. B., 1, 7, 29, 65, 74, 82–86, 90–91, 177, 321, 328, 334
Newman, J. H., 26
Newton, I., 34, 38, 39, 40 179, 184, 191, 195

Name Index

Nowicki, S., 176

O'Leary, D., 2, 7, 85–86, 89, 129, 174, 332, 341
Oliver, H. H., 132, 168
Otto, S. L., 70

Pahnke, W. N., 325, 328
Paloutzian, R. F., 10
Pargament, K. I., 2, 69
Park, C. L., 10
Peirce, C. S., 47, 216
Pellerin, C., 102
Penrose, R., 20–22, 106–107, 186–189, 223, 282
Percy, W., 8, 66
Persinger, M. A., 1, 5, 105–106
Peters, R. S., 3
Piaget, J., 120, 305
Pinel, J. P. J., 102, 335, 337
Pittendrigh, C. S., 173
Plato, 26, 56, 68, 70, 122, 156, 351
Polkinghorne, J., 132, 168
Pomerantz, J. R., 251
Pope, A., 309
Popper, K., 173, 362
Poston, T., 7
Premack, D., 277
Priestley, J., 40
Prigogine, I., 174
Principe, L., 80
Principe, W., 6
Proudfoot, W., 138
Puhakka, K., 29, 69, 123
Pylyshyn, Z. W., 251
Pythagoras, 32, 122, 130, 133, 161

Qoheleth, 174

Rause, V., 82, 85
Rayburn, C. A., 1, 69, 325
Reber, J. S., 2, 69, 325, 351
Redgrove, P., 123, 129
Ricardo, A., 192

Richard, L. J., 1, 69, 325
Richards, P. S., 2, 29, 69, 78, 325
Richards, W. A., 1, 325, 328, 337
Richardson, F. C., 3, 69
Riedlinger, T. J., 101
Robb, M., 82
Robinson, D. N., 298
Roll, W. G., 123, 129
Rorty, R., 41
Roseman, L., 104, 328–330
Roth, B. L., 102
Roy, L., 2, 15, 243, 272, 290
Ruck, C., 102
Rumbaugh, D., 278
Russell, B., 33, 363

Sacks, O., 335
Santrock, J. W., 327–328
Savage-Rumbaugh, S., 278
Saylor, F., 82
Schudel, M., 69
Searle, J. R., 4, 23, 31, 80, 109, 121, 125, 127, 137–138, 140, 142–152, 154, 161, 170–171, 179, 188–190, 192, 208, 321
Shafer, J., 4
Shannon, C. E., 224
Shaw, R. A., 27
Shepard, R. N., 251
Silbersweig, D. A., 30, 86, 91, 93–98
Skinner, B. F., 272, 280
Slife, B. D., 3, 29, 69
Smuts, J., 173
Smythe, W. E., 298
Snell, B., 19
Socrates, 7, 25, 26, 68, 347
Sperry, R., 219
Spilka B., 81, 86
Spinoza, B., 221, 241
Stairs, J., 253
Stein, H., 168
Stengers, I., 174
Stengor, V., 70
Sterling, E. E., 101, 325, 328

Sternberg, R., 327
Stetsenko, A., 132, 298
Strogatz, S., 174
Swanson, L. W., 95
Swyers, J. P., 2, 69
Szalavitz, M., 2
Szostak, J. W., 192

Tan, S.-Y., 69
Tanquerey, A., 6, 325
Taube, M., 126
Tavris, C., 328
Taylor, V. A., 91–92, 337
Templeton, J., 78
Teske, J. A., 111, 137, 150, 152, 321
Thomas, A., 306
Thompson, D. G., 264
Tinbergen, N., 246
Tulka, T., 289

Udell, M. A. R., 246, 249, 304, 327

Vago, D. R., 30, 86, 91, 93–98
van Leeuwenhoek, A., 40
VandenBos, G. R., 298, 327
Vaughan, F., 123

Wade, C., 328
Waldman, M. R., 82
Waldrop, M. M., 174
Walsh, R. N., 123
Warren, E. S., 69
Wasson, G., 102
Watts, R. E., 69
Weaver, W., 224
Webb, E., 11, 64
Weiner, I. B. 298
Weiten, W., 328
Whitehead, A. N., 28, 215, 219–222
Whitehead, E. E., 322
Whitehead, J. D., 322
Whoolery, M., 3, 69
Wilber, K., 29–30, 78, 205, 321, 351–352
Wilde, O., 75
Willis, J. W., 11, 55
Wittgenstein, L., 36
Wulff, D. M., 339
Wynne, C. D. L., 176, 246, 249, 304, 327

Zaehner, R. C., 324, 351
Zeno of Elea, 78
Zimmer, C., 100

Subject Index

abortion, 181
acquaintance, and consciousness as conscious, and Chalmers, 256, 271, 283, 284, 288
act, Aristotelian, 158
actuality, and question for judgment, 62
afterlife, 116, 329, 333
agent, unity of, and Fido, 176
agnosticism, intellectual, xii, 43, 44, 84; theological, 100, 364; and Popper's falsifiability, 363; and d'Aquili and Newberg, 85
algorithm, and misunderstanding of, 223–224
Allah, 351
already-out-there-now-real, 38, 54, 66, 77, 112, 217
American Counseling Association, 69
American Psychological Association, xi, 69
analogy, and consciousness, 238; and knowledge of God, 348–349, 350; and God as Fullness, 349; and Searle, 179
analysis, levels of, 113–114, 200, 326, and Searle, 144–147; linguistic, 7, 22 133, 164
angels, and souls, 263
animal psychology, 110, 129, 150, 159, 169, 175–177, 198–199, 201, 214, 220–221, 229–230; and bats and Nagel, 282; and cognition and emotion, 327–328; and red, the color, 291–294; and consciousness, 221, 310, 311, 315; and insight, 305; and "knowledge," 35, 291; and mentality, 244; and perceptual responsiveness, 247–248; and psyche, 44, 176, 250, and research on, 333, 335; and *qualia*, 296, 291–292, 300; and rationality, 249; and self-awareness, 304–305, 315; and body-recognition in a mirror, 304; and sense of self, 275, 315, and Kanzi, 278, 279–280; and something it is like to be, 302–305
anthropomorphism, and ambiguous terminology, 126, 220, 229, 301; and life, 181; and James, 259; and panpsychism, 218–220, 223
appropriation, James's, 259, 266, 271, 272
argument, conceivability or modal, 57
arithmetic, and algebra, consistency of, 183–184, 191; and Gödel's Theorem, 187
asceticism, Western, excessive, 330–331
Associationism, and James, 236, 258–259, 264, 266
Atman, 3, 4, 239, 351, 361. *See also* Brahman

attention, and consciousness, 290, 293; and James, 220, 226
attractors, 329
authenticity, human, xiii, 44, 254; challenge of, 364; criteria of, 72–73; and knowledge, 64; and meditation, 96
automobile, one thing, 112–113, 151–154, 161; and descriptive conjugates, 161
Avatar (the movie), 151
aware, versus *conscious*, specific usage, 15, 272, 290
awareness, always subjective, 19; as understanding, 188; spiritual, 152, 337; of insight, 51, 273, 309, 317; of the body, 91, 278; of self, 65, 93, 94, 95, 158, 217, 230, 273, 278, 303, 366; unconscious, 286; and awareness of, 15, 95, 267, 305, 306; and Chalmers's usage, 34, 225–230, 286, 290, 293–294; and/ versus consciousness, 14, 53, 55, 84, 93, 95, 107, 177, 266, 272, 293, 302, 310, 312, 317, 320; and first level of consciousness, 25, 314; and intentionality, 14, 28, 34, 61, 98, 158, 188, 220, 221, 242, 245, 246, 255–256, 267, 273, 281–283, 290, 312, 316, 334; and James, 258; and Natsoulas's behaviorism, 272–274
Ayahuasca, 101, 103

behavior, and brain function, 270
behaviorism, 272–280, 291; and functionalism, 208, 270, 291; and James, 259; and Chalmers, 270
Being, Chain of, 352
being, constituted by meaning, 43; contingent and necessary, 62–63, 354; inexplicable in itself, 265; kinds of, 265, 327; notion of, 55–56; structure of, 44, 178, 194, 204; unity of, and distinctions within, 323–324;

and bodies, *q.v.*; and doing, priority of, 166; and existentialism, 166; and knowing, 43, 64, 324, 330; and the mystery of mere givenness, 265, 290, 307–308, 319; and the one and the many, 320–324; and "something it is like," 302–308
beliefs, religious, 1, 9, 38, 56, 69, 117, 121, 149, 152, 254, 325, 332, 360, 369; and dualism, 124; and God, 2, 9, 80, 106, 332, 341, 350, 357, 359, 361, 362; and global community, 367; and judgment, 295; and logical coherence, 361; and science, 136, 241
bias, unavoidable 71; and authenticity, 96–98, 364; and enlightenment, 96–98, 330; and non-contradiction, 75; and value neutrality, 10; and subjectivity, 42, 63, 315
binaries, and judgment, 177
biology, 9, 113, 142, 158, 184, 201, 344, et passim; symbol for natural, 140, 149–153; and consciousness, 22–23, 59, 121, 125, 142, 232, 343–344; and the person, 118, 125, 159, 171, 189, 208, 302, 338, 366, et passim; and theology, 1, 18; and top-down causality, 59–60; and transcendent experience, 81–107
bodies, and beings, 34, 35, 41, 42–43, 47, 50, 54, 64, 79, 85, 130, 168, 171, 175, 310, 363
body-mind problem, 254. *See also* mind-body problem
body-recognition, and self-awareness, 278
Brahman, 3, 4, 78, 98, 239, 312, 351, 361; and the Creator-God, 361. *See also* Atman
brain, function, complexity of, 86, 89, 90, 93, 95, 107; in a vat, 159; restructuring of, 94, 97, 337–340, 366; triune, and MacLean, 333

Subject Index

brain, structures and systems of: amygdala, 83, 89, 91, 94; attention association area (AAA), 83; autonomic nervous system, sympathetic and parasympathetic, 83; cerebellum, 101, 334, lateral, 95; cortex, 101; cortex, cingulate, anterior, 91, 94, dorsal anterior, 95, posterior, 92, 103; cortex, insular, 91, anterior, 95; cortex, prefrontal, 83, 94, dorsal, 91, dorsolateral, 89, 95, dorsomedial, 89, 95, medial, 91, 92, 103, orbital, 89, rostral frontopolar, 95, ventromedial, 91, 94, ventromedial, right, 95; cortex, parietal, 92, anterior inferior, 95, medial, 94, posterior superior, OAA, 83; cortex, temporal, 5, 85, 86, 89–90, 105, 92, 334, 339; cortex, retrosplenial, 94; cortex, temporoparietal junction, 91, 105; cortex, occipital, 334; cortex, regions of, primary, secondary, and tertiary, 83, 333–334; default-mode network (DMN), 91–92, 93, 103; dopamine system, 89; hippocampus, 83, 89, 91, 94, 101, 334; hypothalamus, 83; papahippocampal gyri, 92; precuneus, 92; "religious circuit," 86, 89, 90, 102; serotonergic system, 89; thalamus, 94, 334

brain-imaging, 81, 92, 99, 104

bridge, problem of, 30, 40; solution to, 50, 52

Buddha Nature, 3, 97

Buddhism, 83, 89, 95–99, 252, 308; and "no self," 97–98, 273; and paradox of two truths, 323, 336; and psyche, 336; and spirituality, non-theist, 252, 325, 340; and term *kun-gzhi*, 289

categories of the mind, and Kant, 39, 42, 65; and Lonergan, 72

Catholicism, 83, 85, 360; and psilocybin, 101

causality, 13, 84, 110, 125–134; bottom-up and top-down, 60, 174, 175, 176, 191, 193, 215–216, 338; efficient, 35, 125–126, 128–129, 137, 165, "mechanistic," 129, and behaviorism, 282, and functionalism, 165, and human activity, 135, and sensate-modeled epistemology, 229, 279, and social causation of mind, 279–280; final, and biology, 173; formal, 35, 134, 129, 179, 183–184, 192, and Gödel's Theorem, 186–192, and implicit definition, 130–134; formal and efficient, 35, 129–134, 190, 362; meaning of, 194; and Aristotle, 35, 126; and consciousness, 126–127, and Chalmers, 34, 35, 127; and emergence, 178–186, 190, 192; and epiphenomenalism, 125–126, 137, 215; and explanation, 194; and Galileo, 126; and Hume 34, 126–127, 128, 160, 290, 299, and God, 362; and Kant's categories, 39, 72; and the mind, 134–135, 137; and neurological base of, 84; and nonreductive physicalism, 138; and sensate-modeled epistemology, 35, 126, 128–129, 133, 137, 165, 190, 279, 282; and systems, closed, 179, 199

certainty, cognitive, 38, 55, 56, 57, 68, 70–73

chaos theory. *See* complexity theory

chemistry, 156–157, 158, 167, 247–248, et passim; and biology, 116, 134–135, 173, 181–182, 192, 201, 205, 213, 216, et passim; neuro-, 101–107; and God, 100, 136; and the person, 9, 150, 158, 159, 201, 209–211, 248; and water, 58, 144–145, 154–156, et passim

Subject Index

Chinese Room argument, 147–148, 209
Christ, and redemption, 360
Christianity, and divinity of Jesus, 352;
   and immediate experience of God,
   359–361; and notion of *person*, 298;
   and resurrection of the body, 124,
   139; and ritual use of intoxicants,
   101; and the "psychological analogy"
   for the Trinity, 357–358
circle, hermeneutic, 13
climate change, 70
cognition, definition of, 327; and
   James's usage, 260, 271, 272;
   and Chalmers's usage, 227; and
   Lonergan's usage, 267–268, 282,
   298, 301, 327; and confounded
   psychological usage, 327; and animal
   psychology, 327–328
coherence, definition of, 132; logical,
   and idealism, 56, 57, 310, and
   emergence, 180–183, 190–191, and
   scientific explanation, 361; of all
   knowing, 55, 136, 192–195, 205,
   216, 324, 326, 336, 339–340, 362;
   of ontology and intelligence, 185;
   and accuracy of knowledge, 66; and
   actuality, 58; and insight, 45, 50,
   132, 332
collaboration, in knowing, xiii, 10,
   70–71, 370
common sense, defined, 46–47,
   146–147, 149; and description, 146;
   and theory, 34, 49, 144–147, 165;
   and sensate-modeled epistemology,
   32, 146, 157; and pragmatism,
   46–47, 49; and reality of the mind,
   121, 275; and the priority of theory
   over, 159–161, 166–168
communication, skills, 62
complexity, (or chaos) theory, 168,
   174, 368; of brain function, 1, 84,
   91, 95, 100, 104–105, 334
computer modeling, and complex
   molecules, 156; and the mind,
   20, 86, 147–148, 167, 186–188,
   208–210, 259, 313, 367, et passim
conceivability, argument, 57–61
concept, universal, 122, 319; and
   animals, 304, 305; and d'Aquili and
   Newberg, 84; and insight, 61, 122,
   132, 153, 262, 269, 271, 295, 297,
   304, 305, 313, 329
conceptualizations, varying across time
   and epistemologies, 265
concurrence, divine, 354, 355
conjugates, 115, 159, 368; defined,
   159–160, 181; descriptive and
   explanatory, 159–161; of the person,
   119, 161, 169, 170, 171, 179, 182,
   237, 340, 343, 368; and life, 182;
   and things, 172, 186, 213, 214, 298
conscious, versus aware. *See* aware
consciousness, altered, 83; aggregation
   of, 34, 215; conscious, 3, 14, 52,
   96, 271, 280, 281, 302, 308, 310,
   311, 312–314, 319, 320, 344, and
   Augustine, 260, and Chalmers, 271,
   272, 283, 284, and Griffin, 282, and
   James, 257–264, and meditation,
   96, 318, and priority of, 255, 259,
   312–313, 316–317, 340; defined
   restrictively in this book, 245–246,
   249; intentional, 96, 255, 271,
   302, 303, 308, 316, and Chalmers,
   282, and James, 266, 271, and
   Natsoulas, 281, and perceptual
   responsiveness, 247; bimodal, 96,
   255–257, 266–268, 276, 302, 308,
   309, 368; contentless, 96, 242, 307,
   318, 330, 344; contents of, 53, 93,
   96, 245–246, 257–260, 266–268,
   270–271, 281, 283–285, 287–288,
   307, 309, 310, varied, 315; data of/
   on, 26, 227, 231, 232, 237, 243,
   268, 309, 313–315, 363, 367;
   differentiations of, 335; denial of,
   206–207, 211, 236; emergence of,
   and psyche and brain, 250, 251;

Subject Index   399

extraverted, biological, sensate, 244; fourth level of, 49, 71, 314, 327, 356; heightening of, 317–318; human, uniqueness of, 110, 169, 310, 317, ever presupposed, 300, and divine, 322, and animal, 300, 303; centrality of, in this book, 13, 14–15; irrelevance of, 227, 231; level of, empirical, 27–45, intellectual, 45–61, rational, 61–66, and interaction of second and third, 118–119, and correlates of realities and things, 117–118; levels of, 27, 49, 50, 254, 368, implicitly defined, 12, 28, 309; invulnerability of, Lonergan's theory of, 25, 362; limited to intentionality, 244, 249, 275, 279, 281–284, 312; medieval contribution to understanding of, 88, 297–298, 358; metaphors for, 27, 85, 50–51, 53, 63, 176, 177, 238, 282, 288, 291, Griffin's *experience*, 218–221, Dennett's, 209, Chalmers's *information*, 223–224, James's 177, 257–260, 274, life, 151–153, sight, 29, 30, 33, 37, 39, 50, 85, 162, 321; modes of, concomitant, 229, 242, 254–255, 258, 266, 267, 269, 281, 300, 308, 313, 316, 320; naturalism of, 140, 149, 153; nonefficaciousness of, 215; "of" consciousness, 242, 256, 307–308, 318, 330; problem of, hard, 284, 287, 289, 309, really hard, 317; proto-, 107; reality of, and James, 262; reflecting and non-reflecting, 96, 256, 264, 271, 284, 290, 302, 315; science of (*see* science, of consciousness); stream of, 236, 257; studies, current, of, 6, 49, 57–61, 110, 167, 195, 196–235, 236, 248, 249, 267, 269, 284–285, 301, 308–309, 310–312, 314, 338, 340; sui generis reality, 24, 123, 188–189, 199–200, 266, 369; transcendent of space and time, 122, 123, 319; *Toward a Science of*, 2014, conference, 215; umbrella term, 244; "unified," of McNamara, 338; unity and structure of, 249–250; unattended to, 267, 317; and attention, 266, 290; and awareness, 14, 55, 293, 320; and the brain, 4, 97, 104; and causality, 126–127; and computers, 147–148, 291, 259, 275, 313 (*see also* computer modeling); and emergence, 171, 196, 204, 222, 233, 235; and evolution, 232, 234, 301, 315; and "feeling" of, 288, 290–292; and God, Brahman, 312; and immateriality, 98, 118, 139, 153, 169, 262, 264, 271; and life, 142; and mentality, (*see* mentality); and perception, 34, 96, 206, 232, 244, 245, 273; and perceptual responsiveness, 230–231; and problem of infinite regress, 274–275, 279; and *qualia*, 292 (see also *qualia*); and quantum physics, 106–107; and self-consciousness in Chalmers, 230–232; and spirit (*see* spirit, human); and subjectivity, 257, 266, 318; and terminology for, varied, 271–272

conservation, divine, 354
contingency, of the universe. *See* existence
consistency, and logic, 155, 157, 183–184; top-down, 184, 190–191
contemplation, ordinary moments of, 318, 320; and meditation, 30
construction, social, of reality. *See* reality
cosmogenesis, 137, 174, 331, 368; and the human spirit, 253–254
creation, three aspects of, 354
creativity, and inner experience, 278–279

Subject Index

Creator, 4–5, 136, 349–357, 366; and consciousness, 322–323; and cosmogenesis, 174; and entheogens, 102; and mental experiences, 325

Dasein, 308–309
data, notion of, 18, 28; different kinds of, 313–316; of consciousness, 24, 267, 272, 280–281, and James, 259, 260–261, 262, and transcendent experience, 322; of the senses, 19, 21, 245, limitation to, 314; of consciousness and of the senses, 18–20, 67, 269, 257, 315–316; "publicly accessible," 19, 23–24, 314, 315; requisite of knowledge, 43, 59; and understanding, 28, 42, 45, 50, 54, 55, 76, 112, et passim
decentering, and McNamara, 87
decision, 28, 157, 243, 255, 280, 285, 314, 368; and fourth level of consciousness, 327, 356
decoherence, quantum, 106–107, 186, 212–213
deconstructionism, 55, 133
deduction, bottom-up, 156–157, 193, 204–205 (*see also* causality); and emergence, 180, 183–185, criterion of, 206; and foundationalism, 7; and ideal of knowledge, 68, 70, 232; and intellectual consistency, 155, 157; and explanation, 187, 201, 204; and supervenience, 201
default-mode network, 91–92, 93, 103
definition, implicit, 12, 28, 110, 130, 169, 180; defined, 130–132
deification, 181, 360
description, explanation of, 131, 146, 159; and explanation, 162–164, 167; and personal meaningfulness, 46
desire, pure and unrestricted, to know, 26, 37, 61, 265, 307, 324, 364; and being, 64, 150, and knowledge of God, 364. *See also* eros, longing

devil, and evil, 72
Ding an sich, 40, 113, 124
disciplines, academic, divisions among, xii; multiplication of, 1, 6, 7–9; and emergent realities, 158, and the person, 118; and science, 10
disorders, mental, and meditation, 90–91
distinction, defined, 115–117; and separation, 322, 323
Divinity, spark of, 351–352
dopamine, 89, 100, 102
dream analysis, and research on psyche, 336
drugs, addictive (and dopamine), 102; and religious use of, 101
dualism, defined, 123–124; misconceived but controlling, 215, 367; naturalistic (Chalmers), 80, 152; property, 124, 140–141, 171; rejection of, 150, 169; substance and property, 140–141, 170; unavoidable, 171; and Descartes, 38, 111, 124, 137; and functionalism, 225; and pluralism, 78–80, 171, 367, 369; and sensate-modeled thinking, 215
dynamism, of universe, 222, 136; of consciousness and the universe, 331

Eastern philosophy, and enlightenment, 307; and the really real, 330; and sensate-modeled epistemology, 307
East/West, differences, 83, reconciliation of, 324; philosophy, and confounded neuroscience, 84, 99; and identity of spirit and God, 351; and non-dualism, 205, 321–322
education, current decline in, 37
ego, transcendental, 262; and self, 88
electroencephalograph (EEG), 81, computerized, 81
emanations, 125, 141–142, 352; and epiphenomenalism, 125

Subject Index

emergence, 171–206; criterion of, nondeducibility, 204, 206; history of, 173–175; notion of, 171–172, 196–197, 214; portrayals of, 175–178; probabilistic and wasteful, 185–186, 213; strong and weak, 196–206; and algebra and arithmetic, 183–184; and causality, 178–186; and insight and intelligence, 135–136, 180–181, 183, 185; and coherence within, 184, 186; and computability, 189; and consciousness, 222, 233, 242; and human uniqueness, 279, 329; and mind-body problem, 326, 368; and Newtonian and Einsteinian physics, 184; and reductionism, 173; and panpsychism, 215–216, 219, 235; and plurality of beings, 323; and quantum physics, 106–107, 186, 213; and unexpectedness, 196–197, 204–205; and water, 154–157
empirical residue, 33; and indexicality, 199
empiricism, canons of, 60, 213; sensate, 23; and causality, 126–127; and Berkeley's criticism, 19, 23–24, 29, 55; and Lonergan's theory, 19, 21, 25, 65–66, 67, 72–73, 74–75, 314, 363, and James, 261; and psychology, 18; and God, 346–348, 353, 362–364
energy, in Einstein's equation, 32
enlightenment, 2, 320–321, and mysticism as a way of life, 330
entheogens, 101–102
epilepsy, temporal lobe, and transcendent experiences, 5, 86, 89–90, 105, 339
epinephrine, 100
epiphenomenalism, 123, 124–125, 134–137; and causality, 125, 134, 137; and panpsychism, 215; and theism, 351

epiphenomenon, notion of, 20–21, 142
epistemology, adequate to the immaterial, 84, 143–144, 168; centrality of, xi, 99, 365, 367; confounded, 35, 162, 163, 166, 170, 171, 202, 203, 235, 367, and Chalmers, 34–35, 164–166, and Searle, 143, 144–147; consistency of, across disciplines, 368; crisis of, 38–41, 68–69; definition of, 6; history of, 38–42; empirically grounded, 19, 25, 66–67, 69; intellectual, and explanation of a person, 118–119; kinds of, two basic, 8, 9, 13, 32, 63–64, 98, 146, 148–149, 162, 298, *et passim*, and priority between, 164–169; Lonergan's, 18–80; sensate/perception-modeled, 8, 31, 112, 113, 195, 197, 206, 310, 350, et passim, and efficient causality, 126, and functionalism, 164–166, and mystical unity, 321; and Buddhism, 97, 99, 323, 325; and Eastern philosophies, 321–322; and non-material realities, 239; and theology, 341; and theoretical consistency of, 64–66, 74, 363
eros, desire to know, 64. *See also* desire, longing
essence, and explanation, 7, 32, 50, 130–133, 156, 282; and form, 130, 179, 190
essentialism, 298
ethics, 9, 10, 71, 186; cultural criteria of, 40
evidence, criterion of science, 68; procedural, 75. *See also* data
evil, 85, 186; meaning of, 72
evolution, 38, 68, 137, 174, 214, 315, 331, 368
executive suite, and Donald, 334–335

existence, contingent, 5, 58–60, 62, 346, 349, 350; explanation of, 369; necessary, 346–349, 353; and creation, 322–323; and *de facto* necessity, 62, 347

existentialism, 28, 166

experience, commonsensical and technical meanings of, 27–28, 219–220, 310; of God, 3, 353–361; patterns of, 307, 335, and the psyche, 104, 209, 337; immediate (non-mediated), perceptual, 29, 31, 36, 294, conscious, 220, 259–261, 265, 268, 270–272, spiritual, 29, 30; "religious," 2, 330–331, 357; transcendent (*see* transcendent experience); ubiquitous, 34, 215–216, 223, 229; unconscious, 219–221; unitive (*see* unitive experience); and animals, 292, 303, 315; and Chalmers's double usage, 272, 294–295; and first level of consciousness, 27–45; and Griffin, 215–222, 229, 248, 286, 311; and information theory, 228, 229; and knowledge, 29–31, 321; and Lonergan's usage, 219, 313–314; and understanding, mutually defining, 28, 316

explanation, bottom-up and top-down, 155, 190, 193; defined, 131, 133, 138, 146; scientific, always tentative, 14, 55–57, 68, 82, 133, 173, 327, 345–346, 359, 363; and current trends, 168–169; and deduction, 204; and formal causality, 129–134, 179, 190; and formulation, precise, 133; and matters of fact, 56; and models, 133; and understanding, 57, 62; and relationships, 170, 185. *See also* reductionism

fact, brute, 195; matters of, 55–57; and data, 197–200, 201; and explanation, 57; and percepts, 197; and third level of consciousness, 57; and truth, 63; and truths and laws, 197–200, 203

falsifiability, 362–363; and religious beliefs, 289; and Lonergan's theory, 363

features, and properties, 143

feelings, and "prehensions," 221–222; and *qualia*, 199, 288, 290, 296

finality, and cosmic process, 136, 331

fixed action patterns, 246

fMRI (functional magnetic resonance imaging), 92, 104

form(s), Aristotelian, 50–52, 120, 122, 129–131, 156, 158, 179, 356; conjugate, 181; and intelligibility, 130, 190 (*see also* explanation); Plato's World of, 56, 68, 70, 122, 188

formulation, precise, 133, 209. *See also* implicit definition

foundationalism, 7–8, 69, 164; and logical deduction, 7, 187; and pragmatism, 47

fraud, in science, 71

functionalism, dualistic version of, 225, 232; nonreductive, 137, 143–144; notion of, 125, 164, 207–208; and behaviorism, 208, 273, 291; and epiphenomenalism, 207; and epistemology, sensate-modeled, 167; and hard sciences, 167–168; and Chalmers, 22, 226–227, 231, 233, 270; James, 259; and perceptualism, 234; and pragmatism, 47, 49

fundamentalism, religious, 41

genes, 1, 209, 81, and transcendent experience, 99–101

geometry, non-Euclidean, 38; and the ideal of knowledge, 68

givens, of nature, 195; and *qualia*, 290–293, 299–300

Gnosticism, 351; and current idealism, 229

Subject Index

God, as Creator, 346–348, 349–354, 358, 366, 369; attributes of, 348–349; existence of, 100–101, 361, 362, 367, 370, and empirical basis for, 346–348, 363; experience of, direct, 101–102, 106, 325, 348, 366; as Fullness, 349, 358; Helmet, 106; human image and likeness of, 350, 351, 353–361, 365, 369; hypothesis of, 346, 359, 361, 364, and peculiarity of the, 362; identified with human spirit, 3–5, 75, 102, 106, 239, 322–323, 350–351, 352–353; in the brain, ambiguous notion, 345, inane, 364, and consciousness, 60, 99; knowledge of, 346–349, via pictures or propositions, 352–353, 354–355; mystery of, 345, 346, 348–349, 355, 356, 359, 362, 369; notion of, 345–348; omnipresence of, 3, 355; presence of, by creation, 354–355, by knowledge and love, 356–357, by spiritual likeness, 357–359, by grace, 359–361; question of, 361; and cosmogenesis, 136–137; and levels of consciousness, 353; and neuroscience, 83, 85–86, 361, 364; and spirituality, 252

Gödel's theorem, 20, 26, 186–192, 195, 201, 210, 282, 367; and computers, 187–188; and the mind, 188–189

good, the, notion of, 72; and evil, 85

grace, sanctifying, 359–361; universality of, 360

growth, personal 2, 93, 263, 337; spiritual, 6, 251–254, 263, 344; and self-transcendence, 2, 263

heat, functional and scientific accounts of, 165

Hinduism, 3, 239, 347, 351, 361; and afterlife, 124; and logical incoherence within, 361

hippocampus, 83, 89, 91, 94, 101; and tertiary cortex, 334

Holy Spirit, and indwelling, 359–360; and notion of person, 298

human, the, essence of, 25, 64, 72, 166, 236; models of, bi- and tripartite, 111, 171, 243–250, 329, 333, 338, 344 (*see also* dualism); and the divine, identity of, 4, 239 (*see also* God)

I, and me, 257, 259, 319

idealism, defined, 40, 55–56; halfway house between materialism and critical realism, 40–41, 316; and alternative universes, 212–213; and consciousness studies, 57; and judgment of fact, 169; and Kant, 40; and reality, 60; and spiritualism, 78

ideas, and facts, 57, 61–62

identity, personal, 306–307, and the self as "I," 257–258

imagination, creativity, 187, 209–210; internal imaging, 37, 115, 122, 164, 195, 217, 245, et passim, and Aristotle's causes, 129, 134, 179, and criterion of reality, 172, and dualism, 129, and infinite regress, 347, 352

immanence, divine, 354, 355

immateriality, and insight, 153; and the mind, 118, 169; and the soul, 139, 262, 264; and the spiritual, 264

immediacy, world of, 36. See also experience, immediate

immutability, and the soul, 262–263

implicit definition, 12, 28, 31–32, 110, 137, 163, 190, 191, 192, 209; explained, 130–133; and Chalmers and Russell, 33; and explanation, 131, 169; and formal causality, 132, 134; and Lonergan's theory of consciousness, 12, 28, 309

indexicality, 199; and empirical residue, 33
individual differences, 306
induction, and modern science, 56, 68; and Popper, 363
information, confounded definitions of, 225, 228, 234–235; metaphorically taken, 223, 224 234; technically defined, 224; and Chalmers's pure causal flux, 32, 33, 34, 37; and data, 224, 234; and ubiquitous consciousness, 210, 233, 286, 310; and "experience," 234; and sensate-modeled epistemology, 228, 233, 235
insight, dependent on data, 28; effect and nature of, 45–46, 88, 251, 252; experience of, 288–289; human and animal, 305; unitive, 49–54; and actualization of consciousness, 329; and catching oneself at, 51, 273, 309; and creativity, 278–279; and dream images, 336; and judgment, 61–62; and language learning, 277 (*see also* concept); and mysticism, 54; and phantasm, 251, 329, 332
inspiration, 29, 69; and the ancients, 19; and logical positivism, 163
instinct, 247
integration, human psychological, and spirituality, 253, 338, 340, 344, 357
intellect, 51–52, 329, 350, 356; agent, 88; and reality, *adequatio*, 85; and sense, 53
intellectus in actu, and the unitive moment of insight, 51, 225, 271, 313, 356; and McNamara's agent intellect, 88; and *sensus in actu*, 53
intelligence, and intelligibility, 49–54, 217–218; and ontology, 185
intelligibility, constitutive of being, 43; defined, 46–47, 113; different for mind and body, 118; potential and actual, 49; pure, and mature science, 122; and essence or nature, 50–52; and formal cause, 129; and implicit definition, 31; and insight, 45, 49–54, 76, 118, 185, 329, 356; and intelligence, 49–54, 217–218, 331; and judgment, 62; and meaning, 49
intentionality, defined, 244; equated with consciousness, 281–285, 301–302, 315–316; other than conscious, 248–249; self-conscious, 268; sensate and intellectual, 302, 312, 316; and behaviorism, 273
interiority, 200
intuition, uncertain usage, 22, 76; and consciousness, 24; and Dennett's pumps, 210, 214; and immediate experience, 29, 37, 43, 69; and insight, 49; and science, 69

Judaism, and body-soul unity, 124, 139
judgment, criteria of, 62–63 (*see also* unconditioned); of fact, and universal statements, 55–57; third level of consciousness, 26, 61–66; and Chalmers's usage, 272, "first order," 292, 293, 295, 296, 297, 300, "second order," 268, 272, 293, phenomenal, and paradox of, 268–272, and belief, 295–296; and falsifiability, 363; and insight, another kind of, 26, 61–62; and knowledge, criterion of 42–43, 61, 314

knowledge, Aristotelian ideal of, 68, 70, 174–175, 233, 232; commonsense and scientific, validity of both, 162–164; by confrontation and by identity, 29, 30, 41, 50–53, 54, 356, and phenomenology, 41, and the soul, 263 (*see also* intentionality); evidence-based, 24, 37, 40, 232, 270, 367; factual/

intellectual and sensate/perceptual, 30–31, 33–38, 44, 162–164, 197–199, 221, 291, 350; human, nature of, 63–64; of knowing, 25–27, 257; self-correcting, 71; observer dependent and independent, 161, and primary and secondary qualities, 170; sensate-modeled, and intentionality, 281, and metaphysics and James, 261, and pragmatism, 48; spiritual, 29, 69, and science, 69; and accuracy of, 70–75; and Chalmers's usage, 272; and data, dependence on, 57, 66; and "God's eye view," 63, 70, 161; and mysticism, 30; and science, 19, 21, 24, 37–38, 66, 315; and sight, the metaphor, 8, 30, 311–313, and causality, 126–127, and the color red, 289, and Kant, 39, 41, and Wilber, 29–30; and subjectivity, 42; and three-level process, 237–238, 317. *See also* desire, epistemology
kun-gzhi, 289

language, and meaning, 36; and reality, 58
laws, emergent, trans-ordinal, or fundamental psychophysical, 237; naturalistic, 193; and facts, 197–200, 203
learning, conditioned, 246; and sense of "I," 276–280; and generalization, 276, 279
levels of analysis, 113–115 (re thing and parts); and Searle, 146
levels, metaphor for aspects of consciousness, 27. *See also* consciousness
life, actuality of, 134–135, 182, 206; before life and after death, 116–117, 367; emergent reality, 172–173, 181–182, 192; mystery of, 176; reified, 181–182; and matter, 213;

and metaphor for the spiritual, 151–152
linguistic analysis, 7, 22, 133, 164, 174, 22, 316
logic, criterion of reality, only negative, 58–60; symbolic, 38; and intelligence, 7, 12–13, 183, 363, and Gödel's theorem, 186–188
longing, human unrequited, and consciousness, 361; and God, 356, 360, 361. *See also* desire, eros
LSD, 5, 101; and serotonin, 102

magnetic induction, and geomagnetic fluctuations, 105; and transcendent experiences, 81, 105–106
magnetoelectrograph, 81, 104
magnetoencephalography (MEG). *See* magnetoelectrograph
many, the, and the one, 320–324. *See also* being
mass, described and explained, 160–161; and Chalmers and "massiveness of," 33, 160, 167, 169; in Einstein's equation, 32
materialism, 77–78, 111, 316; presupposed as inviolable, 125; and critical realism, 169; and Dennett, 207; and meaning, 43, 129; and primitive category of matter, 122, 213
mathematics, and reality, 57–58, 221; and implicit definition, 12, 131, 132–133
Matrix, The (movie series), 210; and idealism, 19, 24, 40, 56, 79
matter, meaning-laden, 178; nature of, 77–78, 80; oversimplified notion of, 80, 178, 212–213; and form, 120, 129–130 (*see also* form); and sensate-modeled thinking, 212
MDMA, methylenedioxymethamphetamine, 104
me, and I, 257, 259, 319

meaning, carriers of, 36; constitutive of reality, 43; meaning of, 46–49; spiritual in nature, 77; and experience mediated via, 315; and matter, 77, 178; and meaning-making, 28, 46; and world mediated by, 36, 43, 261; and value, world of, 36, 46, 315

medieval sources, overlooked, 88, 297–299; and anti-intellectualism, 80. *See also* scholasticism

meditation, 19, 30, 291, 307, 351; three basic types of, 83, 93; mechanisms of, 91, 92–93, 321; and contemplation, 30; and first level of consciousness only, 318; and hallucinogens, 81; and heightened consciousness, 318; and neurophysiology of, 83–86, 90–99, 339–340; and self-presence, 331; and stages of unfolding of, 331; and unitive high-point of, 96, 321

mental health, and transcendent experience, 337

mentality, 244, 246, 247, 327, 337; human, 135, and brain, 136, 365; undifferentiated, 327; and psyche, 337, 369; and behaviorism, 291; and consciousness, 230, 244–248, 291, 365, 369. *See also* animal psychology; mind; mind-body problem; responsiveness, perceptual

mescaline, 101, 325

metaphysics, current bipolar disorder of, 178, 233; relational, 132–133, 168, 170; unavoidable in science, 79, 122, 194, 266; and Lonergan's project, 26, 194; and sensate-modeled epistemology, 261; and structure of being, 194

method, canons of empirical, 156; classical, statistical, and genetic, 180–181, 191–193; Chalmers's double-aspect, 229; definition of, 73; generalized empirical, 23, 60, 57, 60, 67, 117, 213, 265; interdisciplinary, xi, 8–10; misguided, and James, 236; neuroscientific, 14, 239; phenomenological, 41; scientific, 21, 66–70, early and 20th-century, 38, 162; statistical, 181, 183, 192; theological and social-scientific, 9–10, 80; transcendental (*see* transcendental method); and functional specialization, 9–10; and neuroscience, 82; and psyche, study of, 332–337; and science, notion of, 10, 21; and specialized methods, 158. *See also* induction

mind, both psyche and consciousness/spirit, 110, 254, 327–328, 332–333, 340; emergence of, and social interaction, 279–280; nature of, in contrast to body, 122; reality of, 109, 121–122; undifferentiated notion of, 252; and computer modeling, 186–188, 208, 209–211; and God, sensitivity to, 109. *See also* mentality

mind-body problem, 8, 13, 110, 112, 148, 216; 241, 284, 326; controlling concern, 4–5, 11, 110, 238, 284, 285, 365, 367; oversimplified leap, 178; resolution of, 161, 162, 169–171, 235–238, and d'Aquili and Newberg, 84, and Chalmers, 226; and causality, 125, 126–128; and confounded epistemology, 110–111, 127, 162, 209, 222, 235, 237; and emergence, 171–206, 326; and epiphenomenalism, 134, 137; and physicalism, nonreductive, 140–141; and properties of the brain, 143–148

mindfulness, defined, 93

Subject Index

miracles, 69, 364
mistakes, and correct knowing, 70–71
modernism, and certainty, 38, 54–55, 57, 156
monoamines, 100, 103
Mormonism, 350
muscimol, 101
mystery, cosmic, 123; unavoidable, 349, 355; and consciousness, 127, 285; and emergence, 176; and existence, 265; and God, 4, 345, 355
mysticism, definition of, 2; explanation of, 3, 97, 152, 254, 318–320, 330, 369; extraordinary experience or way of life, 2, 320, 330–331; "true," and "artificial," 324–326; and d'Aquili and Newberg, 82–86; and God, experience of, 102, 325, 358, 360; and knowledge, 30; and Maslow, 4; and neuroscience, 91, 95; and non-duality, 54; and theology and spirituality, 6
myth, 84

naturalism, biological, 150; of consciousness, 140, 149–153; of spirituality, 151–153, 251–254, 318–320, 368–369; and theology, 366
nature, human (*see* human); laws of, 130; and explanation, 5, 31–33, 133, 179, 190; and form, 130–131, 156, 179, 190; and the physical universe, 5, 20; and reality, kinds of, 117
necessity. *See* existence
neo-behaviorism, 259
neo-Platonism, 351
neuronal function, restructuring of, 329
neuroscience, 81–107, 366–367; competence of, xi; contribution of, 366; importance of, in this book, 14, 107; and epistemology, 354; and God, xi, 1, 5, 14, 254, 341, 344, 361, 369; and its methods, 239, 285, 326, 332, 333; and phenomenology of consciousness, 298, 327; and philosophy, xi, 18; and psyche, 327, 332, 335–37, 340, 367; and psychology, 8; and theology, 139, 360; and transcendent experience, effects of, 337–340
neurotransmitters, and genes, Hamer, 100; and transcendent experiences, 101. *See also individual neurotransmitters*
New Age Religion, 351
Nicaea, Council of, 352
nirvana, 83; and samsara, 97
no self, 73, 97–99, 307
non-contradiction, principle of, and creation, 352; and further facts, 202; and infinite regress, 348; and non-dualism, 321; and radical postmodernism, 75; and the thing, 114
non-dualism, 80, 98, 205, 321–323; and insight, 52, 329
nonreductive physicalism, 137–143
norepinephrine, 100
normativity, in psychology, 9–10, 87, 337–339; in science, 55; in spirituality, 339; and recourse to God, 338–339, 340
noumena, and phenomena, in Kant, 40, 54, 65
nous, 3

objectivity, despair of, 41; and being, 40; in the humanities, 48; and extraversion, 37, 43; and "God's eye view," 63–64, 70, 161; and judgment of fact, 63; and public observation, 19–20, 24; and sensation, 44–45; and subjectivity,

objectivity *(continued)*
43–44; and value-neutrality, 10.
See also bias; knowledge; subjective;
subjectivity
"of," 256, 310, 318; peculiar usage of,
explained, 255. *See also* "to"
omniscience, divine, 348, 363; human,
360, 363; and scientific explanation,
131
one, the, and the many, 320–324
ontology, first-person, 150; notion of,
266; process, 176–177; relational,
31–32, 132–133, 168, 170, 185;
subjective, 157; and intelligence,
180–181, 185; and nouns or verbs,
176–177, 182; and psychology,
97–98; and relationships, 133
organism, and brain and body, 178,
338; and human constitution,
118, 152, 154, 333; and mind, 4,
157–159, 170, 179, 237, 367; and
properties of, 145–146. *See also*
human, models of
oversight of intelligence (in theorists),
235

panentheism, 354–355
panexperientialism, 215
panpsychism, 107, 142, 245; defined,
215; and Chalmers, 272; and
C. S. Peirce, 216; and emergence,
215–216, 219, 222–223, 235, 246;
and epiphenomenalism, 215; and
epistemological confusion, 219, 221,
272; and quantum physics, 106–107
pantheism, 78, 349–350
parapsychology, 128, 129; and
consciousness, 123; and term *psychic*,
250
parts, of a thing, 13, 110, 112–115,
161, 172, 235, 236; and emergence,
190; and academic disciplines,
113–114; sum of, and the whole,
45, 175; and sensate-modeled
epistemology, 112–113, 115, 158,
210, 219
perception, explanation of, 162–164;
notion of, 250; subliminal, 220,
294; and animal mind, 35,
44–45, 64, 77, 129, 176, 221,
247–250, 301, 315; and being,
43, 64, 79, 99, 123, 185; and
causality, 126–128, 133, 362; and
consciousness, 104, 206, 225, 232,
245, 270, 284, confounded, 282,
304, 312; and data, 251, 257, 314;
and description, 159–160; and
emergence, 178, 183, 205–206, 248,
305, 329; and Gestalt psychology,
336–337; and knowledge, 35–37,
66, 85, 164, et passim, and the
soul, 262; and objectivity of, 19,
336–337; and psyche, 176, 329,
332; and qualities, primary and
secondary, 39, 147, 162–163; and
separations, 116, 323
percepts, and Associationism, 258; and
bridge, problem of, 50, 52, 96; and
brain function, 269–270; and data,
28, 45, 54, 76; and facts, 197–200,
202–203; and *qualia*, 271, 289,
296, 314
perceptualism, 238, 262, 281, 291,
314; criterion of reality, 29; and
functionalism, 225–230, 234,
259; and idealism, 41, 169;
and intelligence, 164–168; and
intentionality, 281, 315, 316;
and limitation of examples of
consciousness, 272, 276, 283–285,
301–302, 314, and red, the color,
268–269, 285–287, 289, 292, et
passim; and realism, naïve, 29–35
person, conjugates of, 161; essence
of, 119, 173, 243, 307; unity of,
119, 123, 128–129, 134–137, 171,
and epistemology, 159, and insight,
171, and life, analogy of, 134–135;

and constitutive realities, 118; and human agent, only one, 128, 170, 235, 340; and properties, 141; and psychology, contemporary, 298; and thing, 113; and third level of consciousness, 119

personality, schizotypal, and spirituality, 339; and psyche, 176, 243, 250, 313, 333, 368; and psychotherapy, 253

personhood, experience of, 307; and abortion, 181

personification, and polymorphous humanity, 170

perspective, first-person, 22, 150, 280; third-party/person, 22, 23, 25, 163

phantasm, and mental imagery, 251, 329, 332

phenomena, Kant's, 40, 54, 65

phenomenology, 7, 19, 28, 41, 164

philosophy, Aristotelian, 50, 251; Buddhist, 323; crisis of, 7, 67–68, 164, 166, 235, 325–326; Eastern/Vedantic, 4, 84, 98, 99, 321; existential, 28; history of Western, 38–44, 262, 316; medieval, 318, 327; perennial, the, 352; Scholastic, 51, 117, 124, 166, 262–264; and God, 346; and neuroscience, 82, 139; and other disciplines, 8, 114, 133, 167. *See also* epistemology; foundationalism

philosophy of science, 110; Lonergan's, 22, 56–57, 66, and Popper, 363; trends, recent, in, 47, 168–169; and psychology, xi, xii; and sensate-modeled epistemology, 40, 168; and theology, 341

physicalism, nonreductive, 137–143, 152; and the Bible, 139–140

physicalism/materialism, all controlling ideology, 138, 140, 142–143, 149–153

physics, 9, 22, 113, 158–159, 370, et passim; Newtonian and Einsteinian, 20, 34, 38–39, 48, 175, 179, 184, 191, 195, quantum, 21, 34, 38, and causality, 129, and consciousness, 106–107, and decoherence, 106–107, 186, 212–213, and reductionism, 173, and science, ideal of, 68; and biology, 173, 201–205, 247–248; and epistemology, 168, 233, 310; and experience, 216–220; and God, 136, 370; and implicit definition, 131; and paradigmatic science, 162, 167, 238, 248–249; and parapsychology, 129; and phenomenal reality, 32–35; and "physical" matter, 178, 212–213; and plausibility argument, 58; and psychology, 18, 239, 315, 316; and psychophysical laws, 193–194; and the "substantiality" of substances, 31–35, 40, 160, 169, 368

picture-thinking, and being, 324; and Chalmers, 271; and Dennett, 209, 210; and efficient causality, 126; and Griffin, 219; and popular religion, 136, 350, 352, 354; and sensate-modeled epistemology, 37, 111, 112, 163, 182, 235; and the soul, 124

pluralism, xiii, 7, 41. *See also* postmodernism

positivism, logical, 79, 163

postmodernism, moderate, and Lonergan, 44, 54–55; radical, and nihilism, 75; and agnosticism, 18, 43, 367; and constitution by meaning, 43, 44; and relativism, 9, 41, 43, 69, 75

poststructuralism, 36, 234. *See also* postmodernism

potency, Aristotelian, 52, 53, 158

potential, human, 186, 253

practices, spiritual, 83, 86, 87, 88, 253, 318, 344; psychology of, 252; and austerities, 330. *See also* meditation

pragmatism, 7, 22, 47–49, 121, 164
precepts, transcendental. *See* transcendental precepts
predictability, bottom-up, 156, 157, 193, 204–206
presence, by knowledge and love, 356; contentless, and Buddhism, 290–291, 299; non-reflecting, and consciousness, 256, 271, 272, 290, et passim; and God, 353–361
prescription, in science (*see* normativity)
probability, emergent, 174–175, 212, 368; and theoretical grounding, 38, 68
process theory, 168–169, 176–177, 214–215, 217, 218
properties, 114; emergent, 141–142; explanatory, 159; microphenomenal/protophenominal of Chalmers, 34, 43, 233; of the brain, 140, 150–151, 157, and consciousness, 158; perceptual, 33–34; and features, 143; and realities, 139, 177; and systems, 144, 146. See also conjugates
property pluralism, 171
psilocybin, mechanism of, 103–104
psyche, 96, 118, 154, 158, 159, et passim; definition of, Lonergan's, 250, 368; oversight of, 327–337; research on, 332–337, and Buddhism, 336; restructuring of, 252–253, 329, 366; and animal mind, 176, 250; and brain and consciousness, 327, 332; and consciousness, emergence of, 179, 251; and mind and consciousness, 110, 243–244, 254; and perceptual responsiveness, 249–251; and psychedelic experience, 328; and spirit, interaction between, 251–254; and the tripartite brain, 333. See also human, models of

psychedelics, 2, 86, 101–104; religious use of, 325, 337; therapeutic use of, 337; and entheogens, 101–102; and psyche, 329; and serotonin, 102
psychology, behaviorist, 67, 69, and consciousness, 272–280, 292, and functionalism, 208, 259, 292; cognitive, 69, 86; competence of, xi, 366; Gestalt, 336; humanistic, 8, 28, 69; normative, 72–73, 338 (*see also* precepts, transcendental); of religion, and coherence with science, 370, and normativity, 87, 238–239, and confounding spiritual and divine, 239; perceptual, 336–337; prescriptive (*see* psychology, normative); psychoanalytic, 69; of spirituality, 338, 339; "theistic," 1, 69, 351; theoretical and applied, 46, 162 (*see also* psychotherapy); transpersonal, 8, 123; and epistemology xi, 18; and God, 14; and ontology, 97–98; and theology, xi
psychotherapy, 340; task of, 252–253, 331; and consciousness, 19; and intentionality, 245, 255; and meaning, 46; and psyche, 252, 253, 331, 335; and psychedelic drugs, 328; and spiritual direction, 253; and spirituality, 128, 252, 337, 344; and theism, 69
Pythagorean theorem, 31, 32, 76, 122, 179, 190, and explanation, 130–132, 161, and formal operational thinking, 160, and implicit definition, 31–32, 133; triples, 130–131

qualia, 271, 295, 297, 309, 314; defined, 284; identified with consciousness, 284–285; unspecifiable, 285–287, 289–292, 293, 296; and animal mind, 291–

292, 300–302; and hard problem of consciousness, 284, 289; and human consciousness, 289, 299–300, 302, 310–312; and Penrose, 282; and percepts, 272, 288, 301, 314; and seeing red, 289–292, 296; and sensation, 301; and "something it is like to be," 302–303, 306

qualities, primary and secondary, 39, 170

quest, human, 70; spiritual, 128, 253, 361; for understanding, 10, 55, 64, 130, 204, 361; and meaning-making, 46; and path, 64

question, fundamental ontological, 176, and God, 346–347, 353; kinds of, and levels of consciousness, 40, 61–62, 71, 122, 261, 315, 318, 320, 357, 370, and terms *reality* and *thing*, 117–119; three major, in Lonergan's theory, 26–27; and animal mind, 292, 315; and *qualia*, 293, 294, 296; and self-appropriation, 25–26, 313; and self-transcendence, 2, 29, 51, 55, 64, 74, 131, 177, 235, 285, 319, 350 and God, 358; and specialized methodologies, 158; and transcendent experience, 321

reactivity, physical and chemical, 247–248

realism, commonsense (*see* realism, naïve); critical, 42, 291, 316, defined, 42, and history of Western philosophy, 38; critical and naïve, 29, 77, 237; naïve, 85, 111, 112, 146, 197, 321, defined, 29, in Chalmers, 31–35, 197, in d'Aquili and Newberg, 85, in Seale, 31, in Wilber, 29–30, and dualism, 124, and idealism, 40–42, 316; and materialism, 169, 316, and non-dualism, 321; sensate and intellectual, 38

reality, "already out there now real," and naïve realism, 38, 42, 54, 66, 77, 112; *de facto* status of, 57–61, 213; human, 43, 112, 122; many kinds of, 76, 99, 237; material and meaningful, 77, 112; mediated by meaning, 36, 42–43; non-palpable, 6, 18, 20, 18, 75, 76, 79, 110, 128, 144, 152, 153, 348, 365, 367, 368; socially constructed, 40, 44, 54, 79, restrictions on, 43, 44, 55, 60, 152, and consciousness, 280; spiritual, 43, 75–79, 265, 266; and intelligibility and perception, 76, 172; and judgment, criterion of, 64, 66, 76; and person, 169; and properties, 177; and things, 149–150, and terminological usage of, 117–119, 153–154

reduction, biological, 150–153, 269; eliminative and explanatory, ontological and causal, 137–138, 139, 190, 204, 326; materialist and spiritualist, 78; and behaviorism, 208; and Dennett, 24, 207, 213; and emergence, 172–174, 201–206, 248; and functionalism, 271; and epiphenomenalism, 149; and Murphy, 139

reentrance, neural, 329, 331

reflexivity, animate and sensate, 246, 247, 250, in primitive life, 246

Reformation, Protestant, 38

registrations, sensate, in Chalmers, 225, 290, 294, 296, 297; and states, 294–295, 300

regress, infinite, 210, 279; and God, 347–348, 352

reification, 217, 219, 258, 263; and dualism, 124; and James, 257, 263; and life, 181; and metaphors, 177; and the mind or soul, 111, 124, 262, 264; and verbals, 176–177, 182. *See also* epistemology, sensate/perception-modeled relationships, and explanation, 28, 49, 54, 126, 155, 169, 170, 179, 194, 319, and brain and mind, 134–135, 189, and causality, 33, 35, 132–134, 179, 183, 190, 194, 362; and implicit definition, 12, 31–32, 130–132, 158, 160–161; and insight, 45, 50, 171, 180–181, 185, 217–218; and metaphysics, 132, 168, 180, 185, 194, 204, 217, 324. *See also* epistemology, intellectual, and sensate/perceptual-modeled

relativism, postmodernism, 43, 55; and Kant, 42; and Lonergan, 44, 55

relativity theory, and intelligence-based epistemology, 34, 38–39, 68, 122; and pragmatism, 48; and top-down explanation, 184

religion, power of, 44, 80, 117, 121, 142; psychology of (*see* psychology, of religion); and conflicting opinions, xiii, 9, 30, 38, 40, 41, 44, 80, 332, 338; and drug use, 101–102, 103, 328, 330, 337; and God, 5, 356, 367; and science, coherence of, xi, 72, 93, 103, 340, 346, 369, conflict between, 364, 40, 69, 80, 111, 136, 149, 324–326, confounding of, 95, 99, 102, 239, 312, and Kant, 40, and priority of, over, 352, 361, and rejection of, 70, 355; and transcendent/ mystical experience, 2–3, 6, 89–90, 252, 254, 325–326, 340, 344, 357, 368–369; and theology, 3, 80, 106, 325, 355, 360; and truth, 38, 57, 69, 70, 117

religious circuit, McNamara's, 86, 89–90, 102, 338

religiosity, and neuroscience, 1, 6–7, 84, 86–87, 91

representation(s), body-, 85, 304; symbolic (Donald's), 177, 224, 304; and neuronal encoding, 198, 293–294; and perceptual images (Aristotle's), 251

residue, empirical, 33, 199

responsiveness, animate, 246–247 (*see also* reflexivity, animate); emotional, 154, 229; human, 249; perceptual, 229, 230, 231, 244, 246–248, 250–251, 275, 327, defined, 247, and intentional consciousness, 230, 246–249, 276, 281, 284, 300–303, 310–312, 315, 332, and mentality, 246, 247, and psyche, 250–251, 327, 335–336; different kinds of, 244, 247, 248

revelation, religious, 29, 37, 57, and science, 69–70

ritual, animal, 246; and drug use, 101–102; and meaning, 36; and neuroscience, 84, 87; and psyche, 253; and transcendent experience, 318, 325

Sacred, the, 2, 102
samsara, and nirvana, 97
S-ART (self-awareness, -regulation, and -transcendence), 93, 95
scholasticism, axioms of, 51, 166; decadent, 262, 264; and *substance*, 117, 124. *See also* medieval sources
science, comprehensive, 193–195, 205, 341, 343–345; early and 20th century, 31–32, 34, 38–39, 68; empirical, dependent on data, 20–27, 59, 60, naïve, 23–24, 316, 161–162 (*see also* materialism); ideals of, 26, 49, 66, 67–68, 80, 130, 162, 232, 324; notion of, 21–22, 315; perfected, 28, 179; philosophy of (*see* philosophy of science); unity of, 14, 55, 158, 193–195, 205, 319, 340, 370, and higher viewpoints, 366; and anti-

science, 70; and certainty, modern, 55–57, 68 (*see also* certainty, cognitive); and common sense, 146, 147, and priorities of, 159, 162–164, 165, 167; of consciousness, 20–27, 107, 215, Lonergan's, 21, 24–25, 57, and incoherence, methodological, 34, 60, 167, 233; and formal causality, 35, 126, 129–134, 137, and emergence, 179–183, 186–187, 190–192; and formal-operational thinking, 120–121, 160; and German *Wissenschaft*, 21; and normativity/prescription (*see* normativity); and pragmatism, 34, 48; and proof, 56, 68, 186–187, 348; and religion (*see* religion, and science); and ontology, 266

seeing, and knowing, 8, 30, 33, 39, et passim. *See also* consciousness, metaphors for, sight

self, 87–88, executive, 88; higher, 3, 4; sense of, 257, and neuronal process, 94, 105; and behaviorism, 274; and meditative effects, 103–104; and no-self of Buddhism, 97–99

self-actualization, 4

self-appropriation, 21, 51, 243, 336; explicated, 19, 65, 242, 280–281, 313; and personhood, 307; and phenomenology, 309

self-awareness, and animals, 230, 305, 315; and self-appropriation, 65; and S-ART, 93, 95; and experiences, 217, 303; and behaviorism, 273, 280; and self-recognition, 278. *See also* self-consciousness

self-consciousness, 14, 28, 177, 182, 230, 245, 281, 304, 311, 327; notion of, 249, 268, 281; and Beauregard, 86; and animal mentality, 301, 305; and/versus awareness, 220, 245, 257; and behaviorism, 273; and Chalmers, 230; and experience, 220, 245; and James, 266; and personhood, 169; and *qualia*, 292; and/versus self-awareness, 230, 305, 317; and self-recognition, 304; and somnambulation, 230

self-contradiction, procedural, 25; and Buddhism, 98, 307, 323; and mistaken epistemology, 65–66, 323; and nothingness, 362

self-intimation, and consciousness, and Natsoulas, 271

self-organization, and emergence, 174

self-presence, non-reflecting, 96; and consciousness, 14, 219–220, 302, 312, 313, 330; and material objects, 260; and the senses, 313; and subjectivity, 15, 330. *See also* self-consciousness

self-transcendence, defined, 2; quintessential human quality, 2–3, 64, 78, 122, 170, 242, 263, 279, 284, 320, 338, 339, 368–369; and consciousness, 317–320, 366, et passim; and genes, 99–100; and God, 5, 90, 110, 340, 353–361; and growth, personal/spiritual, 263; and insight, 76; and judgment, 63; and logic, 12; and meditation and neuronal function, 82–99, 329; and neurochemicals, 101–105; and parapsychology, 123; and spiritual practices, 344; and transcendent experience, 344

senses, *in actu*, 52–53 (see also *intellectus in actu*); and description versus explanation, 162–164. *See also* data

separation, definition of, 115–117; and distinction, 322, 323, 332–333; and perception-modeled epistemology, 324

serotonin, 89, 100, 102, 103, 104, 326
sexuality, and transcendent experience, 83
shamanism, 101
significance, personal, and meaning, 46–47, 49, 165–166; and transcendent experience, 320
single photon emission computed tomography (SPECT), 82
skepticism, 25, and postmodernism, 55
social interaction, and emergence of mind, 279–280
social science, status of, 8–9; and "hard" sciences, 162; and normativity, 9–10, 73
something it is like to be, notion of, 305–308; and animals, 302–305, 310–311 (*see also* experience, and Griffin)
somnambulation, 54, 128, 230, 249, 270; and animal psychology, 230, 292, 303
soul, 3, 111, 124, 139, notions of, 177, 262, 263; and bipartite model, 111, 250, 327; and Atman, 351; and existence before or after life, 115, 116–117, 124; and James, 262–266; and immutability of, 262–263; and mind, 111, 114, 124, 139, and distinctive meanings of, 116
space, Euclidean, 130, 132; and current physics, 24, 37, 39, 48, 167, 170, and reality, 32, 147; and human transcendence of, 122, 123, 170, 351, et passim; and information, 224–227; and Kant, 39, 72; and Newton, 34, 39; and primary qualities, 39; and Wilber, 78
speculation, neuroscientific and philosophical, excessive, 83, 86, 87, 105–106, 211–214, 229, 234, 239, 286, 310; other-worldly, 341; and conceivability argument, 57–61, 164, 175; and empirical science, 232; and mathematics, 56, 58
spirit, human, identical to consciousness, 3, 245, 254, 368; identified with God, 4–5, 323; release of, and psilocybin, 103–104; similar to God, 358–359; and naturalistic spirituality, 88; 241–341, 368; and psyche, interaction of, 251, 252. *See also* consciousness
spiritual, definition of, 75–76, 122, 266, 288–289, 308, 313, 368, and vital force, 322; growth, 263; and insight, 88, 170; reality of, 43, 76–79, 85; reductionism, 78, 124; the term, 241, 288–289, 308, and conscious, 54, 110, 169, 250, 266, 288, 308, 313; and the divine, 3, 4–5, 14, 106, 289, 322, 350–351, 352–353, 359; and James, 260–262
spiritual direction, 253
spiritualism, and James, 262–264; and perceptualism, 262
spirituality, definition of, 6, 252; mechanisms of, 251–254, 338, 366; naturalistic, 3, 4, 88, 151–153, 241–341, 252, 254, 340; relevance of, universal, 332; positive effects of, 337; practices (*see* ritual); and keys to, theoretical and practical, 253; and morality, 87; and theism, 3, 239, 254, 344–345
spiritualogy, 5, 8, 13, 241–341, 362, 364, 365, 366, 368–369; defined, 6; naturalistic, 368, 369; and neuroscience, 326–332, 337–340; and Wilber, 30
states, phenomenal, "first order," and Chalmers's, 294, 295, 296, 297, 300. *See also* judgment

statistical method, 38, 191, and emergence, 175, 183, 192–193; and classical method, 175, 180, 192, 194; and psychology, 8; and transcendental method, 193
structuralism, 36, 133; and oversight of intelligence, 234
studies, consciousness, current. *See* consciousness
stuff, 8, 35, 41, 42, 111, et passim; usage of term, 77. *See also* realism, naïve; reality, "already out there now real"
subject, existence of, 97–99; and James, 258–264; and self as object, 14–15, 273; the turn toward the, 41, 74, 281, 316; and Whitehead, 220; et passim
subjective, meanings of, 15, 42–44, 199–200, 242; and objective, 63–64, 73, 79, and the quality/feel of experience, 283–285, 302, 306–312
subjectivity, notion of, 14–15, 242, 257, 265, 311; objectification of, 74, 259, 313, 316; and animals, 304, 311; and behaviorism, 272–277; and bias 42; and consciousness, 74, 256, 264, 267, 280, 316–318; and James, 258; and judgment of fact, 63; and neuroscience, 96; and personhood, 268, 307; et passim
substance, confused term, 12, 111, 182; physical, 77; and Descartes, 124, 127, 367; and dualism, 140–141, 170; and Kant, 39, 72, 124; and mind, 169; and properties, 140–141; and soul, 124, and James, 262–264; and thing, 111, 113, 124 169
substantial, and Chalmers, 32–35, 40, 50, 233, 283
supernatural, popular usage of, 2, 4, 75, 80, 87, 111, 140, 151–152, 252, 312, 340, 341; technical meaning of, 359–360
supervenience, logical, 185, 201, 204; laws, 193
synergetics, 174
systems theory, 168, 174

Tao, 351
teleonomy, 331; and teleology, 173
temperament, 94, 306, 308
terminology, pervasively ambiguous, 5, 21, 110, 140, 179, 197–200, 203, 225, 244, 250, 271–272, 294–296, et passim; Whiteheadian, 220; and implicit definition, 12, 131, 133, 209; and Lonergan's, 26–27, 115–117, 170, 197, 199, 200, 203, 255, 269, 346–347; and responsiveness, kinds of, 246–249
theism, 1, 69, 351; and spirituality, 239, 254
theology, apophatic and kataphatic, 349; ascetic, 6; competence of, 366; mystical, 6; and science, 343–345, 345, 348, comprehensive, 341, 344–345; and autonomy of, 370
theory, cognitive, Lonergan's, 18, 25–27; instances of, many particular, 8, 10, 19, 22, 29, et passim; and common sense, 46–47; and description, 46, 159, 167. *See also* common sense; description; implicit definition
theotics, 343, 359–361, 366; defined, 360
thermostats, 229, 230, 246, 286, et passim. *See also* consciousness, and computers
thing(s), defined, 112–113, 114, 149–150, 153–154; in itself, 30, and Kant, 39–44, 65; within a thing, 114; and emergence, 214; and judgment of fact, 175; and

thing(s) *(continued)*
  parts, 112 (*see* parts, of a thing); and person, 118–119, 169, 298, 368; and substance, 113, 124; and realities, 117–119, 153–159
thinking, concrete and formal operations, 120–121, 160; sensate-modeled and intellectual, 13, 31, 40, 47, 63, et passim (*see also* epistemology, kinds of, two basic)
thought, stream of, and James, 177, 257–258, 260–266, 311
time. *See* space
"to," 53, 219, 246, 256, et passim; peculiar usage of, 242, 255
top-down causality, of consciousness on brain, 337–340, 338; of consciousness on psyche, 336, 338. *See also* causality, bottom-up and top-down
transcendence, divine, 354, 355; human, 123, capacity for, 2, 152, explanation of, 3; and God, 3, 5
transcendent experience, defined, 2; described, 320; kinds of, 325; and appeal to God, 2–3, 18, 320, 341; naturalistic explanation of, 4–5, 15, 110, 242–243, 317–320, 324, 369, neuroscientific versus phenomenological, 326; religious/theist, uniqueness of, 324–326; unity of, 320–324; and consciousness, first level of, 320–321; and genes, 99–101; and magnetic fields, 105–106; and meditation, 82–99; and mental health, 330, 337; and neurochemistry, 101–105; and neurophysiology, 82–99; and psychopharmacology, 101–105; and quantum physics, 106–107; and temporal lobe, 89–90. *See also* self-transcendence
transcendental, the term, 2, Chalmer's usage of, 123, 152

transcendental method, 67, 70, 73–75, 79, 80, 117, 158, 323, et passim; irrevisable, 74–75, 362–364; and its formulation, 73–74; and generalized empirical method, 67, 117; and scientific method, 66–70, 168; and unity of sciences, 158, 193–194, 319, 340, 370
transcendental precepts, 70–73, 150, 338, 339, et passim; cited (attentive, intelligent, reasonable, and responsible), 6, 70, 73, 76, 80, et passim
truth(s), crisis of, 38; criteria, varied, of, 40, 85; notion of, 63, 72–73; quest for, 361; two, of Buddhism, 323, 325; and facts, 197–200, 203; and God, 349, 350; and religion and science, 40; and postmodern "interest," 69
Turing test, 208
twin studies, and spiritual sensitivity, 99–100

unconditioned, absolutely, 353; virtually, 62–63, 64, 346–347, 353
unconscious, archetypes and realms of, and psyche, 337; awareness, 286; bias, 71, 73; data, 316; experience, 219–221
understanding, commonsensical and intellectual, 146, 148, 163–164; human and divine, 350, 353; notion of, 45, 49, 61, 314; quasi-, 210, 215; of everything about everything, 67, 324, 348, 350, 353, 363; of understanding, 218; and intellect, 51–52; and knowledge, 6, 8, 12, 25–26, 42, 49, 55, 63–64, 200, et passim; and levels of consciousness, 27, 45–61, 117–118; and logic, 12, 187–188, 190
unitive experience, 96–97, 242, 321, 344, 369; and affect-laden, 90,

96–97; and insight, 49–51, 54, 225, 313, 319–323
unity, of human being, 119, 123, 124, 125, 128, 134, 135–136, 137, 141, 153, 170–171, 368; and information theory, 226; and the soul, 262, 264
universal(s), categories, 122, 243, 319; statements, 55–57, 200; and classical ideal of science, 68, 70, 174
universe, alternate, 106, 212–213; dynamism of, 136–137; static and dynamic, 168, 174–175, 178, 181, 193, 207

Vedanta, 4, 101
verbal, and nominal usage, 176–177, 181–183; and James, 259
view, God's eye, 63, 70, 161

viewpoints, system of higher, on the human, 366
virtue, and knowledge, 73
vision, beatific, 359–360; neuroscience of, 284, 291

water, historical explanations of, 156; H_2O and XYZ, 58; unique reality, 154–157; and emergence, 181; and watery stuff, 165, 167
whole, greater than parts, 45
will, 83, 87, 88
World of Ideas or Forms, 56, 68, 70, 122, 188

zombies, and consciousness studies, 58–60, 165, 227, 231, 232, 259, 269–271, 310